John McDonnell

John McDonnell

The Most Successful Coach
in NCAA History

Andrew Maloney and John McDonnell

FAYETTEVILLE
THE UNIVERSITY OF ARKANSAS PRESS
2012

ISBN-10: 1-55728-992-1
ISBN-13: 978-1-55728-992-6
E-ISBN: 978-1-61075-520-7

17   16   15   14   13   5   4   3   2

Text design by Ellen Beeler

♾ The paper used in this publication meets the minimum requirements of the American National Standard for Permanence of Paper for Printed Library Materials Z39.48–1984.

Cataloging-in-Publication data on file at the Library of Congress.

To my wife, Ellen, who has been there for me night and day throughout the years. I love you with all my heart, and you are the voice of reason, comfort, and unending love.

To my son, Sean, who has been an instrument of peace, love, and companionship to me. You are my son of strength, talent, and success.

To my daughter, Heather. You are the apple of my eye, and you make the world a better place to be because of your love, personality, laughter, and encouragement.

Contents

Author's Acknowledgments

My first encounter with John McDonnell occurred in my first few weeks as a collegiate coach at a cross-country meet on a hot September day in Joplin, Missouri, in 2005. It was still early in the season, but Arkansas had put ten runners in the top fifteen at the first mile of the race at a pace that simply seemed unsustainable, yet they didn't seem to be slowing down. Over in the shade underneath the trees at the second mile, I observed John calmly but forcefully exhorting his eighth and ninth runners that they could do better. It was an interesting juxtaposition to say the least. The man whom I understood to be the most successful coach in American collegiate sports history hustling around the course harder than I was at a third of his age, seemingly dissatisfied with the perform- ance of a team that had just laid waste to the entire field, paying as much and possibly more attention to those at the back of his team than those at the front. This was the quiet intensity and underlying humility and decency that appealed to so many of us who have encountered him over the years.

This book is not merely about success in athletics, though it follows the life of a man singularly successful in that field over four decades. It is about an individual so specially attuned to the human condition that he was able to lead hundreds of student athletes in discovering something about themselves they didn't know was within them. It is also about his own journey as an athlete, coach, father, and mentor, and about the profound impact he has had on those around him.

In chronicling the life of John McDonnell, I relied upon the candor and assistance of many of those who had come across him throughout his life, including his family, for- mer athletes, fellow and opposing coaches, athletic directors, and friends. Where I have quoted individuals in this book without footnotes, such material comes from personal interviews conducted over the past year and a half and published with the interviewees' permission. I am also grateful to the University of Arkansas Athletics Media Relations for the archives, pictures, and materials supplied for this endeavor.

But most of all I am grateful to John and his wife, Ellen, and Larry Malley of the University of Arkansas Press for their guidance. It was a pleasure working with each of you throughout this process.

—Andrew Maloney

Foreword

One of the great joys that I had as president of the University of Arkansas System was the opportunity to become friends with arguably the most outstanding coach in the history of collegiate athletics. The winning record of John McDonnell as the track coach of the University of Arkansas is phenomenal. John's track and cross-country teams won forty NCAA championships and eighty-four conference titles in the Southeastern and the Southwest Conferences. His record is truly unbelievable.

I have been a university president for thirty-two years, and I have personally known many great leaders in education, business, politics, athletics, the military, and other fields. I can honestly say that John McDonnell is one of the most, if not the most, productive and successful leaders that I have ever known. He has a special God-given talent to encourage and inspire young men to achieve goals that they never dreamed were attainable. And those young men love and respect their coach like a father.

John's human qualities are very much a part of his tremendous leadership ability. He knows what it takes to be a great track athlete. He works extremely hard, is completely honest, and always treats others with dignity and respect. John created a winning environment by first believing that the Razorback men's track-and-field program could be the very best in the nation. But his confidence in himself and his team was coupled with a profound humility that led him to win the right way—with class and grace.

You simply cannot buy the kind of positive national publicity that John and his teams brought to the University of Arkansas and our state. While we are all proud of what was accomplished during his tenure, the real winners are the young men who had the privilege to run track under John McDonnell. They learned the valuable life lessons of hard work, self-discipline, and commitment.

John McDonnell represents the best of what coaching is all about. He is a great role model for young people, especially for aspiring coaches, and I encourage them to read this book about an exemplary human being.

Dr. Alan Sugg, President of the University of Arkansas Systems, 1990–2010

Foreword

Oifig an Taoisigh
Office of the Taoiseach (Prime Minister of Ireland)

Message from Taoiseach Enda Kenny

John McDonnell epitomises the Irish abroad at their very best. Having emigrated to the United States in the 1960s, he achieved extraordinary success both on and off the running track, winning numerous national honours, firstly as an athlete and later as a coach. The seeds of John McDonnell's passion for athletics were planted in his beloved Co Mayo. He was an accomplished athlete in his youth, winning six Irish National Championships and gaining a coveted place on the Irish team for the Rome Olympics in 1960. Sadly, the financial state of the country prevented some of the Irish team from travelling to Italy and John missed out on a glorious opportunity to win Olympic honours. But he was not to be deterred and went on to win the mile event at the 1966 British Selection Games, also defeating the legendary Jim Ryan in a two-mile race in Louisiana, USA.

After his emigration to the United States in the late 1960s John was quick to make his mark in the athletics arena, winning six All-American track and cross country honours. His success as a university coach has been nothing short of astonishing. During his 30-year tenure as head coach of the University of Arkansas athletics squad, a record 40 National Collegiate Athletics Association titles have been claimed.

I am delighted to have the opportunity to contribute to this book, which chronicles the life of one of Ireland's finest sons. The honours bestowed on John McDonnell to date have been many and include his induction as a member of the United States Track Coaches Hall of Fame. His legendary status in Arkansas is reflected in the fact that, in 1998, a multi-million dollar running track at the University of Arkansas was named in his honour. I am glad to say that he has also been recognised in his home country, having been inducted in the Western People Mayo Sports Stars Hall of Fame.

Yeats warned us not to "wait to strike till the iron is hot but make it hot by striking" and John McDonnell's life has been one built on hard work, dedication and a desire to help others. He is a man who has shared his talents generously and who, in doing so, has made an immeasurably valuable contribution to his adopted country as well as a significant and lasting impression on the very fabric of history.

Very best Wishes
Yours sincerely
Enda Kenny

1

Growing Up in Ireland (1938–1963)

"If he'd had the right horse and the right opportunity he would have ended up training horses. He always had that instinct of how to train."

—*Michael McDonnell*

It is one of life's ironies that the greatest of men often originate from the humblest of beginnings. Their later triumphs are rooted in their early struggles, their prodigious success a product of the environment in which they were born and raised. It was thus from a nation struggling in every way imaginable that a man who would become the most successful coach in American collegiate sports history would emerge. He learned his earliest and most important lessons there and gained a fundamental philosophy that would sustain him throughout his life.

To say things were not going well in Ireland in the early part of the twentieth century would be an understatement. In the nearly four hundred years since Henry VIII had conquered the island, Ireland had seen more than its share of bloodshed and famine. An uprising in 1641 was successful in establishing Irish rule until Oliver Cromwell reconquered the island eight years later in a bloody war that saw the loss of nearly a third of Ireland's population due to death or exile. Another uprising toward the end of the eighteenth century led to a brutal suppression and the Act of Union in 1801 that ended Irish self-government and the temporary disenfranchisement of Roman Catholics.

In the fields, the vagaries of absentee land ownership and poor harvests led to two major famines, the first of which in 1740 saw nearly a half-million either perish or emigrate. That suffering only served as a precursor for the Irish Potato Famine or Gorta Mor (Great Hunger) one century later. Starting in 1845, this second and more virulent famine was caused in part by a fungus infecting potatoes and resulted in the death of over one million and the emigration of one million more out of a population of eight million.[1] Some of the issues that contributed to this calamity were resolved through the various Irish Land Acts intended to redistribute ownership of farmland in Ireland from absentee English landlords to rural Irish farmers. The burning question of Irish independence was not resolved.

Two failed attempts to pass Home Rule at the end of the nineteenth century precipitated the bloody Easter Rising in 1916 and the Irish War of Independence immediately following World War I. Although the Irish Republican Army reached a truce with the English after two years of bloodshed, the Solomonic compromise reached in the Anglo-Irish Treaty of 1921 only further divided the country—both literally and figuratively. The twenty-six southern counties were separated into an independent dominion within the British Commonwealth, known as the Irish Free State, while the six northern counties remained part of the United Kingdom. The treaty split Irish nationalists into pro-treaty and antitreaty forces who fought a yearlong civil war that financially crippled the Irish Free State in its infancy.

Among the twenty-six counties that became Ireland in 1936, County Mayo was hit hardest. For one thing, the Potato Famine had been particularly felt there—90 percent of the population was dependent upon potatoes—and it is estimated that upwards of 100,000 died in County Mayo alone.[2] Because of high birthrates and scarce opportunities for employment, the cycle of hunger and emigration caused the population of County Mayo to dwindle from 388,000 in 1841 to 161,346 in 1936 and to a low of 133,052 in 1956.[3] Parents raised their children to send them away from the dreariness of home to a better life abroad.

At the end of the 1930s, Ireland, and much of the rest of the world, was recovering from the economic calamity of the Great Depression and was on the verge of a war that was ultimately to be waged on an unprecedented scale. Although Ireland was officially neutral, tens of thousands of its sons volunteered for the British and American armies, while those left at home were forced to eke out an existence made ever more meager by the food and coal rationing prevalent across Europe.

It was into this reality that John McDonnell was born at home and delivered by a midwife on July 2, 1938, to Michael and Bridget McDonnell on a dairy farm near Crossmolina, County Mayo—a mountainous region some 135 miles west of Dublin and less than 10 miles from Ireland's west coast.

John was the seventh child in a family of eight children, all of whom had been born at home: five older sisters, Mary, Annie, Philomena, Margaret, and Catherine, and two brothers, Patrick, the oldest boy of the family, and Michael, the youngest. The homestead was located in Woodville and had a kitchen, living room, dining room, outhouse, and three bedrooms with two beds, as well as a fireplace in each room for the boys and girls. John never knew any of his grandparents, all of whom had passed away before his first birthday.

On farmland settled by provision of the Irish Land Commission, the family raised cattle, sheep, dairy cows, and just about anything else that would help the burgeoning clan make ends meet. The coast, which was a mixture of sandy beaches and cliffs, was too cold for swimming.

His father, Michael, rose early each morning to work on the farm, instilling the values of hard work and physical fitness to John at a young age.

"He was the type of guy who could have been a good athlete because he used to do those jumping jacks and stretch every morning before a ten- to twelve-hour workday, but that was between the wars when people were more concerned with getting something to eat than running," said John. "He always said he could have been a runner, and

I believe him because he wasn't tall. My height came from my mother's side. My dad was five foot nine and slightly built and light on his feet."

With no electricity until the 1950s, the family extracted water from a well, used kerosene lamps, and laundered clothes outside. His father Michael toiled in the fields each day to provide a better life for his sons and daughters than he had had for himself.

"He would always tell me how much they made when he was younger, and I thought, 'How did they live in those days?' It was two shillings a week, which are twenty-four cents each," said John. "It didn't make sense to me and now as the pendulum has swung I can't understand how we lived when I was young either because the money had so little value. He had a team of horses and no tractors until later, so there were things that he handed down like hard work."

Joining the exodus of youth from Ireland's shores, both of his father's brothers immigrated to the United States and settled in Scranton, Pennsylvania. Each of them fought for the United States toward the end of the World War I, which they survived but not without being badly injured in the process.

John's mother, Bridget McDonnell (née Hopkins), ran the house while Michael worked in the fields, where John was occasionally dispatched at a very young age to bring tea and sandwiches to his father. Bridget was integral in the management of the farm and disciplining of the children.

"She was a very strong woman and a great lady," remembered John's older brother, Paddy McDonnell. "She taught us not to use any bad language—and a few times she gave it to me on the back side for that and I deserved it. She would look after us, and in those days she did everything. She would make clothes and made sure everyone was doing what they were supposed to be doing. Times were tough, and money wasn't plentiful, but we got through."

Given the dire circumstances, Bridget McDonnell also ensured what meager resources were available to the family were used as efficiently as possible and that each child did their share of chores.

"My mother was a fantastic cook," remembered John, "and back then everything was rationed so you could only get so much sugar or flour. You could grow things on the farm, but to bake bread she had to get yeast. They were tough times. You would go to the store with your coupons, and it didn't matter if you had money or not; they allotted it to you based on the size of your family."

One staple of the McDonnell household was a mixture imported from the United States called Indian Meal.

"It was basically ground corn," John's younger brother, Michael McDonnell, recalled. "I have no bad memories of it at all, and it was probably good for us, but I didn't realize it at the time."

"Gosh I hated that stuff," John lamented. "We used to make it for breakfast, and my mother would make bread out of it by mixing it with the flour to make it go further. That went on until 1948 because all of the countries in Europe were devastated, and it took them a long time to recover."

Although Ireland was largely spared from the horrors of World War II by virtue of its neutrality in the conflict, the rationing of food was a reality of life across Europe. While no armed conflict ever took place on Irish soil as it did in central and eastern

Europe, several Irish cities such as Dublin were bombed on multiple occasions, albeit not on the scale suffered by London.

"The only thing I remember," said John, "were the planes used to circle over Ireland, and that was in 1944. My mother would gather us, and we would always get down on our knees and pray. I must have only been six years old, but that's something I'll never forget."

Each Sunday the McDonnell family walked nearly three miles to the Catholic parish in Moygownagh for mass and gathered together each night before bed to say the rosary.

"I remember my mother saying that the family that prays together stays together," remembered John. "We'd pray every night as a family and say the rosary. Our parents taught us at a very early age what was right and what was wrong. At the time you thought you were being punished, but it was a way of bringing up kids."

Bridget McDonnell kept the children occupied with chores at home, starting with milking the cows early in the morning before school and picking potatoes or harvesting wheat after school.

"Our mother was a tough task master, so she always had us doing something," said Michael. "She was always saying that 'Idle hands makes for the Devil's work.' And we would always wake up early in the morning. I vividly remember we didn't have an alarm clock or anything, but it was my mother's fire tongs. She would start the fire about 5:30 a.m. We had to get up and get going."

Milking the cows was a laborious task in an era before electricity and milking machines.

"I hated it," recalled John, "because it was always before school and sometimes you had a cow that wasn't used to being milked, and she would kick the bucket, and it wasn't good if you lost milk. My mother would get mad because milk was important, and we used to sell it."

The children worked day and night on the farm, picking potatoes after school and burying them in dirt and grass to keep them through the winter. Bridget kept chickens, duck, geese, and turkeys and tended to a full vegetable garden and vineyard. Even hogs became a staple of the McDonnell household.

"The hogs were really good business because we used to breed them and sell them, and there was a lot of money in them," said John. "We butchered one for ourselves. We would hang it for a few days, and the neighbor would cut it into a few pieces, put it in a wood barrel and salt it to preserve it. After it was in there for a few weeks we'd take it out to hang it in a cool place. We used every part. Even the blood would be saved to make black pudding with rice and lots of other things, and it tasted really good."

When the future Razorback coach wasn't eating black pudding, he was sent out with his older brother Paddy to hunt badgers, foxes, pheasants, and rabbits. They would hunt rabbits on dark evenings with nothing but a carbide lamp and two greyhounds in an open field.

"The greyhound would catch the rabbit, and I'd put the legs together and hang them on my back, and boy, it would start getting tough after a while carrying fourteen or fifteen rabbits," recalled John. "Foxes were a kind of vermin that would kill chickens so when they got overpopulated the government would give ten shillings for the head of a fox. Foxes were smart, but if we caught two or three that was quite a bit of money so that's what we did. You wouldn't get anything for hunting badgers. They are tough animals. They would tear your dog's face off with those big old claws, so we tried to keep the dogs away from the badgers."

When there was no more work for the boys milking the cows, working the fields, or hunting in the bush, they were sent elsewhere to work. As it turned out, food wasn't the only resource rationed in those days. Coal became a scarce commodity, which made peat a necessity for heat in the winters. When John's aunt and uncle, who lived out in the mountains, needed help taking peat from the bog and stacking it, John's father was only too happy to volunteer him into service when he was twelve years old.

"It was like a week in prison," said John. "My sister Philomenia brought me back there on a bike and left me for a whole week, and when I saw her leaving, I almost had tears in my eyes because I hated that place. I had a donkey with a cart and I filled it up with turf. That old donkey was so slow a snail could have moved faster. I saw the turf I had to put out and it was a quarter mile long and I said 'I'll never get out of this place,' and I remember it was halfway through the week when I said 'I'm getting out of here.' So I started throwing the turf back into the brush and you couldn't see it because the brush was so high. I was getting rid of a whole lot of turf, but I wasn't helping my uncle's winter any."

Only a month after John escaped his week from hell, word got back to his father about what he had done with the peat.

"Oh my dad was mad and said, 'What in the world got into you?'" recalled John. "It was a terrible thing to do because that was their firewood and heat for the winter, and it was wasted because it was wet from the brush; but I was never asked back there again, so I fixed that one."

Still, in those days there was no end to the work. When there was nothing left to do on the farm, Bridget McDonnell would send John and his brother to do work for one of the local widows.

"In the history of the Irish, the Irish men married old," explained Michael. "Usually the eldest son inherited the land and waited until all the rest had gone before he could get married, and he'd be an older man. So he'd generally marry some young girl, and they'd have a large family. He'd die and she'd be a widow. So we used to do a lot of work for the widows."

When the work with the widows was completed, their neighbor Joe Birane hired John and his brother to plant potatoes every spring.

"You're supposed to plant them so far apart," said Michael, "but every now and then (Mr. Birane) would skip a few. He'd get the job done and was a very nice old guy. He'd pay you well. At the end of the evening you'd get half a crown, and you'd be happy as hell. In those days, half a crown would be like fifty cents maybe."

On other occasions, John and his brother did work for their Protestant neighbors, the McKinleys.

"There were four or five Protestant families, and they were all good people and there was no animosity at all," said John. "I used to go help them with their potatoes, and they wouldn't pay any money, but they'd come help us in return. I remember I came home from the McKinley's one Friday night and my mother asked me, 'What did you have to eat?' I said I had the best chicken and she said 'I knew that! Didn't you know it was Friday?' I had forgotten."

It was Catholic tradition to refrain from eating meat on Fridays to honor the Lord. The McDonnell family often ate mackerel fresh from the nearby sea on Fridays, which was brought by a door-to-door vendors.

Occasionally the tinkers, who were nomadic Irish traders, would swap dogs and other animals with the boys. Other days of the week a traveling shop owned by the Gough brothers, Bill and Edmond, brought by an assortment of luxury and consumer goods by automobile on the narrow dirt roads.

"They had everything you imagined in that travelling shop," said John. "And if they didn't have it they'd say they'd have it next week for you. They were in operation until the 1950s when the travelling shops died out."

Of course, the meals at the McKinley house were not always sumptuous.

"The McKinley's were great folk," said Michael. "Sonny's wife passed away, and he used to bake the bread, and he also made his own butter as most people in Ireland do. But butter, if you don't do it right has a terrible taste. It's got a tack to it. And the bread, he probably didn't get the right baking soda in the bread. It would be okay a half-inch down and okay a half-inch up but it would be real doughy in the middle. We'd come to lunch and Sonny would give you this butter and bread and John couldn't eat it. He'd just starve. He couldn't eat it because it tasted so horrible and the butter was so bad."

Apart from major planting and harvest seasons, the children spent most of their days at school. The national education system at the time still had a compulsory Gaelic component, although the mother tongue of Ireland had declined in use throughout the country. The children attended the Carn School, which was a three-room schoolhouse with seventy children and three teachers. Since neither John nor Michael owned a bicycle until late in their teenage years, the boys ran three miles to school each way.

"It took longer for us to get there than to get home," recalled John. "You had to be home to be at the table first. We used to cut across the fields. We wouldn't go on the road. And in the summer the weather was nice and the creeks weren't very high, and it was the shortest point from A to B."

Protestant children seamlessly mixed with Catholic children in that old schoolhouse. Although the Protestant-Catholic conflict was an affliction that had plagued Europe, and particularly Ireland, for centuries, John didn't recall any differences or tensions at the time.

"It wasn't a Catholic school; it was public, and all of the Protestants went there, and we didn't know any different," said John. "Of course in southern Ireland there weren't many Protestants. They were good people and we used to work closely with them. A lot of the conflict was in the six northern counties ruled by the British. When we were young, we tried definitely not to marry a Protestant. When one of the Protestants died, the Catholics weren't allowed by their own religion into the Protestant church, but stayed outside to show their respect. It was I think more respect for the dead, but it worked evenly both ways because the Protestants would come to a Catholic funeral and stand outside as well."

Although religious distinction was not prevalent, class distinction certainly was at the time.

"Class distinction was big in Ireland," said John. "As the old saying goes, a dime looked down upon a nickel. If you had money, you were treated better, and that was always one thing I felt wasn't good when affluent families got special treatment."

The knife of class distinction cut both ways as Michael found out when he saw the treatment Major Harmitage received after buying the Greenwood Mansion upon moving from England.

"The major provided an opportunity for local people that wanted to work," remembered Michael. "He was just a decent human being, but some of the local people didn't treat him well. He was an English transplant that came and bought this place. Eventually it was split up and sold, and he moved to Spain."

The McDonnell boys, however, were not ones to tolerate mistreatment of others, even if it meant fisticuffs in the schoolyard when they saw certain children being taken advantage of by bullies.

"If anything happened in the playground, the kids with less support would take the brunt. My parents brought me up to stand up for what was right," said John. "That's how my brother and I got into fights. We could use our hands, and we'd take up for a kid that was wronged and take on those bullies. We'd just give them a good hammering, and they'd stay away from us."

When the two boys changed to an elementary school closer to home in Rathnamagh in 1948, they had to assert themselves all over again.

"We were the new brats who showed up at the school, and we were challenged," remembered John, "but it soon settled down. I remember a few times the teacher made me pick my own switch from a tree and would hit me with it across the palms of my hand. Sometimes it was well deserved."

Although the boys did find themselves standing up for themselves and others and caught flak for it, not all of the mischief they caused was entirely for benevolent purposes.

One of the fields they cut across each day on their way to school was a magnificent apple orchard on the property of Major Harmitage, and the boys could not resist helping themselves.

"The major, he couldn't care less," recalled Michael, "but he had a garden, and the gardener was this pompous guy who always locked the gates. Everything was locked. They had about five acres and a stone wall that was fifteen feet high, but trees grew outside of it. So you could climb the trees and get on the top of the wall and climb down plum trees on the inside and fill your bag with apples."

When they weren't ransacking that orchard, the boys found others nearby.

"I remember coming home from school," said John, "and another guy did such a good job pruning the apples. They were top notch. He had these yellow ones and a hedge to keep us out, but it was no match. We could get in easily, but he'd always be watching when we came home from school especially when the apples were getting ripe. I remember one time getting behind a hedge and looking over, and he was looking right at me thirty feet away, and we took off. He had a bike and was gaining on us so we took to the field."

When they weren't raiding apple orchards, the boys were in the gooseberry patch owned by Sonny McKinley. John would talk to Sonny and distract him while the others went to take what they could.

"He had the finest gooseberries," remembered Michael. "They were big fine gooseberries, and the young kids liked them. They were a treat. He knew we were taking them. He'd give us enough time to get some, pick the ripe ones, and then he'd arrive and be screaming at us and we'd be climbing over that hedge. I'm sure he got a real kick out of us clambering and falling on the other side. If he wanted to catch us I think he easily could have done so."

It was on one of those trips over the hedge that John ripped the expensive new pants his mother had bought for him.

"We used to wear short pants, and that's what we wore going to school," said John. "I always wanted to have a pair of long pants, and I remember when I was twelve my mother bought me some. I'll never forget they were blue, and the first time I wore them I was jumping over a fence, and I caught them and ripped them. I never heard the end of that. Of course she ended up sewing them up."

Michael did not have such a similarly happy ending the following year.

"My brother had these new glasses, and in this field there were two donkeys and nobody ever rode them. Well one day I asked, 'Wouldn't it be fun to catch them?' So we tried to ride them but had no bridle or anything," recalled John. "We got them cornered and started riding them. The donkey is galloping, and all of a sudden stops. Michael goes flying over the donkey's head and lost his glasses. When we finally found them the glasses were broken right in the middle."

Needless to say, Bridget McDonnell was none too pleased when she found out.

"We got a few whacks from my mother when we got home because the glasses were new and expensive back then, and we didn't have much money," said John.

When the boys returned home late because they had been raiding apples or gooseberries, or when word got back to their mother that they had been involved in a scuffle at school, there was little doubt in either of their minds regarding how Bridget McDonnell would handle the situation.

"She used a switch," recalled John, "and most of the time we needed it, but a lot of times it was just the tone of her voice that was enough, and you knew you better get in line. She always preached doing the right thing and not being caught up in trouble. So when we got into those scuffles at school she'd get mad and ask, 'When are you going to grow up and stop with that nonsense and get back to being good?'"

While other parents might let things go, Bridget McDonnell was not one of them.

"She didn't forget much," said Michael. "She ran the household basically. She was always assigning duties. She was someone that kept everybody busy. She was a good foreman because she needed to be."

The discipline she instilled in her children was nowhere more in evidence than when it came to school and the importance she placed on education. Although John was not as fond of school as he was of the outdoors, he passed all of his subjects with comparative ease.

"She always had a saying that education is no load to carry, so get an education or you will be working like we are," said John. "My mother and father pushed education because I was going to have to leave the home. Most of the Irish families were big but only one person could stay on the farm."

At school John had both good and bad experiences with teachers. Although some of his teachers had favorites that seemed to be based on class, John later encountered a teacher named Mr. Lynch who influenced him in profound ways and confounded him in others.

"He was a brilliant man," said John, "never married, and he used to live in a boarding house. He'd visit the local pub three miles away for socializing and have a pint or two of Guinness each night. My brother and I would often think later about him and say, 'What a life.' He had this big old cane, and he'd slap you with if you got out of line, and you usually deserved it. I didn't mind because I would rather get that than the lashing of the tongue, which can leave a heavier scar. I learned a lot from him because he was a decent person and a good influence in my life. He'd always emphasize: 'Boys, you may not think it now but you need this education because there is nothing here for you, and you will go abroad and run up against kids that have an education.'"

It was the dismal reality of Ireland that the flower of each generation was raised and educated only to be sent abroad to England, the United States, Canada, Australia, or elsewhere once it had bloomed.

"It's kind of sad in a way," reflected John, "because I'd hate it if my kids said they were going to Australia or somewhere, but that's what the Irish had to do. They raise them and then export them."

Although few of his childhood friends left Ireland during the first fifteen years of his life, the exodus began shortly thereafter as neighbor after neighbor left for better opportunities elsewhere.

"All of a sudden they started to leave, and one time we all met with one of the guys, who was only twenty, the night before he left," remembered John. "He went to New York, and I remember a plane flew over, and we wondered if that was him. I never saw him again. A lot of Irish did that and never came back."

It was around this time when the arrival of electricity on the McDonnell farm and across Ireland in the early 1950s created a temporary opportunity to work for the utility company installing the poles across the countryside. John took this on for a year following his elementary education.

"He always took on a lot of the hard work," remembered Michael. "I always remember him being very dedicated to work and took on another job with the electricity company supply board when they went around putting in poles."

The coming of electricity benefited not only John but the entire McDonnell family and their farm. Milking machines meant the boys no longer needed to milk the cows manually, while tractors gradually replaced horses to also lighten the load considerably.

"When we got milking machines, boy that was a relief," said John. "We still had to attach them, but it was great because some of the cows were so hard to milk."

Running water and indoor toilets came to the homestead in the early 1950s with central heat and telephones installed ten years later. It was around 1950 when John got his first radio, which allowed him to listen to boxing matches in Dublin and, on some occasions, from the Polo Grounds or Madison Square Garden in New York City.

"I remember listening to Rocky Marciano and Joe Louis," remembered John. "One time there was an Irish fighter named Billy Kelly. He was from Northern Ireland, and he was fighting a Frenchman for the world featherweight title, and the fight was in Dublin. The commentator must have been pro-Irish because we thought Kelly killed the man, but the decision came up, and they gave it to the Frenchman. They tore that place up in a riot, pulling seats out."

As they grew older the boys kept themselves entertained through various games and sports with friends and neighbors. At Christmas time, there was a raffle at two shillings each for the opportunity to win a turkey. Other times they would gather at the local field to play Gaelic football, which is similar in some respects to rugby as the ball needed to be moved every so many steps. Then there were the horses.

"John always had an interest in horses," related Michael, "and he trained this horse and had a professional jockey that John talked into riding it at the Palmerston's Sports Race for two pounds. The winner got twelve pounds, which was good money back in those days. And John went there, and damned if he didn't win and enter him again and won the second year before he went off to Dublin. So I think John's interest in horses was such that he could have gone in a different direction. If he'd had the right horse and the right opportunity, he would have ended up training horses. He always had that instinct of how to train."

Amazingly, it was not until the eighteenth year of his life in 1956 when that instinct was to be applied toward the sport in which he would one day lead athletes to the very top of the world: running.

"My younger brother Michael was a runner, and I was out in the pasture kicking a football, and he had a 220-yard track set up, and he asked if I would help him run an 880-yard time trial," remembered John. "I asked him 'What do you want me to do?' And he said 'I'll give you a twenty-yard lead.' I said 'You'd better give me more than twenty yards,' so I got fifty yards. When he told me to go, I took off like a scalded dog. You know how brothers are. I didn't want him to beat me, and I sprinted as long as I could as far as I could until I saw stars. When I looked back, he never closed the gap and said 'Dang, you can run.'"

Two weeks later, John entered the local sports race in Moygownagh, a nearby village in County Mayo against two highly trained university athletes on a 220-yard track with pegs carrying red, green and blue colored tape flags.

"Among the runners in the race were two college runners," said Michael. "One was a national champion in the 880 yard, Liam McHale. He gave John a little handicap and came up to him and caught him. And I always remember him hanging on and, by golly, John realized 'I can beat him' and he did. After that I think his interest in running picked up immediately."

John remembers racing another experienced runner at the time named John Gardiner.

"We were pretty evenly matched, and that's where I got the idea that I could run," said John. "I still visit John (Gardiner) when I go home."

The McDonnell boys soon began training together around an old derelict building in the middle of the field and running up and down the country roads, but not for any significant amount of miles.

"We were beginning to get educated about running," admitted Michael. "Bannister had just run the first sub-four-minute mile and John Landy, the Australian, had come along. Those were names we were reading about because running was becoming a big thing back in those days."

The two of them would travel to local meets where they won prizes in just about every event from the sprints to the high jump and the distances.

"In those days you got good prizes. It was a great deal," said Michael. "If you did second or third, you'd get some sort of prize, and if you finished first, you'd get a good prize."

That summer of 1956, the great miler Ron Delany of Villanova University won a gold medal for Ireland in the 1,500 meter at the Olympics in Melbourne, Australia. It was a seminal moment in John's life.

"He was my idol even before he won the medal," said John. "I started to get interested because of him, but when he won that gold medal that's when I decided I had to go to America. [Ron Delany] roused up tremendous interest in athletics in Ireland."

Academically, athletically, and socially, it was becoming time for John to move on from County Mayo. His parents wanted him to finish his secondary-school (high-school) education so he could become a policeman. Suddenly there was nobody to challenge him in races, and few boys of his age in town to play Gaelic football, as many of them had moved on to greener pastures, either in Dublin or other countries. It was the inevitable fate of Irish youth and John would prove to be no exception to the rule.

"Our mother didn't want people going away," said Paddy McDonnell, "but she was a great person and organized an education for each of us the best she could."

In 1958, John's parents sent him to Dublin to stay with his older cousin Frank Lynn, who worked for the postal service during the night and ran his own car-rental business during the day.

"Frank was one of the greatest guys I've ever known," said Michael. "I learned a lot from him because nothing ever bothered him. He was always very generous and would take us to this hotel, where we'd go for lunch, called the Castle Hotel. And the one thing I remember was that the food was always good, but they had a trifle, a sherry trifle that you'd get, and it was fantastic. We used to always have the sherry trifle. And Frank would always pick up the tab. I never paid, ever."

When John arrived on a bus to Dublin for the first time, he waited and waited and waited.

"I was so homesick," admitted John. "If there was a bus home, I would have gotten on it. I was scared because I had never been away from the county."

Finally, his cousin Frank pulled up to the curb over an hour late.

"He was a great guy," said John, "but I found out later that he was always late."

"Oh, he was unbelievably late," laughed Michael, "but he was so personable that people liked him. He had a wonderful way with people."

"He was one of God's gentlemen," said Paddy McDonnell. "Just a great guy and always seemed to have cars going from one end of Ireland to the other."

Dublin toward the end of the 1950s was undergoing a transformation into a modern city. Although the issue of insurrections had not yet come to the fore as they would in the north and during the nearly thirty years of Troubles starting in the late 1960s, the winds of change were blowing. Many of the differences were brought on as much by the private development and planned government demolition of historic buildings to make way for modern ones as they were by the manifesto of the Irish Republican Army's to occasionally bomb or destroy statues and other vestiges of colonial rule.

The pace of life certainly quickened for John as he adjusted to living at his cousin's two-bedroom flat in the heart of the city. The two ate out often, usually indulging in fish and chips wrapped in greasy newspaper.

"It took me a while to really accept the type of life in the big city," said John. "I could have gone home in a heartbeat, but my pride wouldn't let me because people would have said, 'Oh he couldn't cut it.' It probably took me two years to get used to living in the big city and getting the hang of the entertainment of going into pubs and dance halls to meet girls."

John soon enrolled in school in Dublin to continue his secondary education. His cousin Frank not only encouraged John in his academic pursuits but let him live with him.

It was around this time when John first joined the Clonliffe Harriers Athletics Club and came under the tutelage of a coach who helped shape his athletic career and coaching philosophy, Don Appleby.

"I wanted to please him because he was really a good guy and would show up on cold nights and stand up timing me on workouts," said John. "I didn't want to let him down because that was time away from his family. In the summer we'd be on the track, but in the winter we'd be on the soccer pitch, and that took dedication because he'd be standing there freezing to death."

In his first Irish national junior cross-country championship, John remembers losing by over a half-mile and contemplating that perhaps running was not in his future.

"Don Appleby and Larry O'Byrne [another coach with the club] said to me, 'Hey John, you can win this race next year. You just have no training or conditioning whatsoever, and you're a novice. I thought they were making me feel good, but exactly one year to that day their predictions came true and I won by two hundred meters. That's when I started believing that if someone told you something and you trusted them, you could do it."

Larry worked for Guinness, which at the time gave its employees a free pint for lunch every day. Others in the club would often go for a few pints of beer after a workout, but John never drank with them.

"I remember going on a trip to then-Czechoslovakia when I got good in 1960," recalled John. "There were three people invited from each country to run a road race, but I didn't drink, and they had this famous beer called Pilsen beer. The interpreters thought they were going to make me drink, but our team manager kept saying 'No, no, he doesn't drink.' They couldn't understand because most people in Europe drink. My dad drank, but mother didn't. She didn't like alcohol and preached not to drink."

His decision was also based on his utter dedication to becoming the best athlete he could and the desire to not have any excuses for not succeeding.

"Don Appleby used to say you can't blame the coach, and the worst thing in the world is to make excuses," said John. "He said nobody cares about your excuses. The competition definitely doesn't. People look at you when you make excuses and think you're a loser. The more excuses you make the less competitive you look in the eyes of others. Your competition doesn't care. They'd love to see you fall flat on your face."

For someone who never participated in the sport at any level prior to turning eighteen in 1956, his improvement trajectory mirrored that of the Sputnik satellite launched into space the following year.

"I improved real quick," admitted John. "A lot of improvement in a year and a half. It was tremendous."

Within two years he went from a 4:40 miler when he left County Mayo to under 4:10 and won the Irish national championship a remarkable six times in the mile, three mile, and steeplechase, and represented Ireland twice at the International Cross Country Championships (which in 1973 became the World Cross Country Championships) in Manchester, England, and Saint Sebastian, Spain.

John went from running local county meets to competing against the finest athletes in the world. In 1961, he anchored a four-mile relay in Dublin against Olympic gold medalist Peter Snell of New Zealand and ran against Ethiopian marathoner Abebe Bikila, who had won the Olympic gold medal running barefoot, the year before at a road race in Czechoslovakia. Still, the greatest thrill was meeting and working out with his idol, Olympic gold medalist Ron Delany.

"Appleby asked Delany what he was doing [for a workout] and he said 400s and so Don asked, 'Do you mind if John goes with you?' And he said sure," remembered John. "Well, I'll tell you that was almost like competing in the Olympics because I was training with the Olympic champion. He was a nice quiet guy, and you wouldn't know he was the Olympic champion because he wouldn't talk much. I hung in as best I could, but he was pretty fast."

That spring of 1960, John's remarkable improvement continued as his three-mile time dropped from 14:30 to 13:54. At the national championships that same year, John emerged victorious and had an Olympic qualifying time in the three-mile and the expectation of being sent to Rome.

"I made the Olympic standard and won the nationals, but this university student was three years older and had more experience," said John. "I was the country boy. So they sent him even though both of us had the qualifying time because Ireland didn't have money back then to send more than one person. Everyone said, 'Oh, next time you'll make the team,' but the next Olympics I hurt my Achilles."

The experience taught John an important life lesson at an early age.

"Don't put off something you can do today," said John, "because tomorrow may never come."

The runner selected ahead of John ostensibly for his experience did not have a successful Olympiad, and in the years following, McDonnell beat him head-to-head on a few occasions. The experience also left John much in favor of the Olympic Trials format used in the United States, where the top three eligible finishers are selected to the team with no questions asked.

"I remember him being very disappointed," said Michael McDonnell. "He got shafted out of the Olympics."

With his graduation from secondary school, John's ambition and focus remained in the sport but was increasingly focused on a move to America. By the summer of 1963, he finally made the trip to the United States by flying over to visit his cousin Betty

Gallagher in New York. He was barely off the plane when she took him on a whirlwind tour of New York City in the ninety-eight-degree weather engulfing the city on an August day. If Dublin took some getting used to at first, the boy from County Mayo was in for a real shock this time.

"Oh it was an eye opener," recalled John. "I couldn't believe any place on earth was that hot. She was showing me around, and I missed a night's sleep. She looked at me and asked 'Are you getting tired?' And I said yes. So she said we could look at the Statue of Liberty the next day. I was never so happy."

John returned to Dublin for three months before flying back to live with his cousins, the O'Boyles, in New Jersey on November 24, 1963—only two days after President John F. Kennedy was assassinated. This time John was staying.

2

Early Experiences in America (1963–1972)

"They brought these things with tentacles and eyes staring at me and started breaking them up. I just sat there and they asked me 'Are you going to eat?' I said, 'No, I'm waiting for the fish.'

—*John McDonnell on eating his first crawfish*

America had emerged from World War II as the preeminent economic and military superpower of the world. Twice it had saved Europe from itself and assisted its western European allies in beating back the forces of autocracy and fascism that threatened the world order through the first five decades of the twentieth century. The world owed the United States a debt—both literally and figuratively—for its selfless defense of freedom during two major worldwide conflagrations and later for its protection from the creeping Iron Curtain of communism. Nowhere was this moral, political, and financial ascendancy more evident than New York City.

There stood the Statue of Liberty and the United Nations, both testaments to the goodwill and high esteem in which the world held the United States. New York's Ellis Island had long accepted the world's "tired . . . poor . . . huddled masses yearning to breathe free." The men in suspenders up on Wall Street increasingly bought, sold and leveraged much of the world's capital, equity, and stocks. New York was the ultimate proving ground for anyone trying to make their way in the world.

In the 1960s, the city nonetheless became a microcosm of some of the afflictions that had begun to plague the country as a whole: war protests, urban crime, race riots, and white flight. While criminal misdemeanors increased an incredible 25 percent between 1965 and 1968, it is estimated that approximately 1.7 million Caucasians left New York City in the decade prior while anti-war and civil rights fervor gripped the nation.[1] It was a time of transition for the city and the nation as a whole.

John McDonnell arrived in New York while the nation was deep in mourning. Camelot and the squelching of the great fire of hope embodied in President John F. Kennedy had ended two days earlier with his assassination. McDonnell had come to America for a better life and had left the Troubles at home just as the United States was entering one of the most challenging periods of its existence.

15

His cousin Betty Gallagher, who sponsored his immigration, lived in the Bronx, but John lived with his cousin Mike O'Boyle in Jersey City for several months.

Although John was not the first member of his immediate family to move to the United States, he was the first to stay permanently. His oldest sister, Mary, had moved to Chicago in 1957 for a few years before moving to England and working the rest of her life as a nurse in London. One of his other sisters, Catherine, also came to the United States to work as a nurse after he had arrived. John's younger brother, Michael, arrived in July 1965.

After obtaining a job that paid far above anything he could have earned in Ireland, Michael sought and obtained his green card and, shortly after that, an unwelcome piece of news.

"About six weeks later, I got my draft notice," said Michael. "The mentality at the time was different. It was kind of romantic to go off in the army or marines."

Although Michael was excused from serving in Vietnam due to poor vision in his left eye, two of his Irish schoolmates were not so fortunate.

"One of them didn't make it back and one did," said Michael. "The one who did ended up doing very well working for Shell Oil as a helicopter pilot."

In the meantime, John was encouraged by several athletes in the New York Athletics Club to enroll at Emporia State University in Kansas based on the success of a local Long Island boy, John Camien, who had run a 4:01 mile and captured the National Association of Intercollegiate Athletics (NAIA) Championships early in his career. McDonnell had not been promised anything from the university but took the advice and arrived in Emporia, Kansas, in January 1964 for the spring semester. The team was led by legendary coach Fran Welch, who for a time was coaching both football and track at the university, which later named its stadium after him.

"By gosh, he was a good coach," McDonnell said of Welch. "He really knew his stuff and was a tough hombre who made everyone toe the line. He really knew what he was doing training wise."

John had made the commitment to Emporia without considering whether his tuition and living expenses would be covered by an athletic scholarship, but he quickly learned that they would not be. Rather than pout about his circumstances, he found a job washing dishes to pay his way through his only semester in Kansas. Unfortunately that wasn't his only unpleasant experience.

That same season John received one of the scares of his life while on an airplane heading to Winnipeg, Manitoba, Canada, for an indoor track meet with teammates John Camien and Ireland Sloan. Upon entering the cold Canadian air, the plane lost contact with the tower and had a rather precarious descent before it finally landed safely.

"We could see the sweat just running down the pilot's face," remembered McDonnell. "I said to myself when we get close to the ground I'm opening the door and jumping into the snow, but about ten minutes later he re-established contact. Then a few years later I had an engine quit on the way to Dallas. After that I have had a real fear of flying small planes."

That spring went much better, as John competed on the distance medley relay team that won the Texas Relays, Kansas Relays, and Drake Relays. His placing second in the 1,500 meters and third in the steeplechase at the outdoor nationals helped Emporia win an NAIA Outdoor Championship.

Although an Achilles would derail his Olympic hopes that summer, John still had aspirations of competing at the European Championships the following year. When he returned to New York during that summer of 1964, he began training regularly with the New York Athletics Club (NYAC).

Dick Weis, who would later coach against John during his illustrious twenty-five year career at Oklahoma State, was coaching the Gaelic-American Athletic Club when he first met John at MacCombs Dam Park, adjacent to Yankee Stadium during John's first trip to the United States in 1963.

"We tried to get him on our team but didn't have any money," explained Weis. "The New York Athletics Club flew him back and forth from New York to school, so he ran for them. They were our big rivals in the AAU [Amateur Athletic Union]. He was a very good runner, and they would win the Metropolitan Championships all of the time."

During the winter, many of those meets took place at the legendary 168th Street Armory, which had been converted into an indoor track facility. Although it would later be considered one of the fastest banked 200-meter tracks in the world, racing at the Armory in those early days could be precarious.

"When I was running, it was flat board track that had to be shined," said John. "They polished that sucker and you had to run in flats. It was scary, and the first time I ran there for NYAC someone told me to be careful not to have my feet go [from] underneath me. I ran so tight my shoulders hurt. I thought my feet were going to slip under me."

It was at the NYAC where John met another young man making his way in the world, Roone Arledge. Although Arledge would later rise to become chairman of the television conglomerate, American Broadcasting Company (ABC), for a twenty-year span starting in 1977, he was just a young man who had originated what would become ABC's famous *Wide World of Sports* show.

At the time John worked for WOR-TV. Arledge later interviewed him for a position with the *Wide World of Sports,* but there were no vacancies. When Arledge did offer John a permanent job the following year, he had already decided to go back to university.

In the meantime, John's main responsibilities with the station were staying late at the station for *Million Dollar Movies* and working as a cameraman for the comedian Soupy Sales, whose zany television show made children laugh and parents cringe. During the spring and summer, the station asked him to help film the baseball telecasts for the upstart New York Mets baseball team.

The Mets were only in the third season of existence and had just moved into Shea Stadium from the Polo Grounds when John was assigned to film the catcher at all of their home games for WOR. Only three years after setting the Major League record for losses with 120 as an expansion club in 1962, the Mets had "improved" to 50-112 in 1965 when John began working the telecasts before mostly packed crowds who had come to watch the lovable losers stumble through the season.

"I didn't know much about baseball," said John. "But that was fine because the Mets didn't know much more about baseball than I did."[2]

The team was full of characters on the field and in the dugout. Long-time Yankees catcher Yogi Berra had been hired as a bench coach while legendary manager Casey Stengel, who had won nine World Series championships with the crosstown Yankees, was hired as the first Mets manager. Stengel became so frustrated with the Mets sloppiness on the field he once wondered aloud "Can anyone here play this game?" It was a valid question.

"They were the worst team in baseball," said John. "The thing I couldn't understand was they had a full house, and I wondered how people could come out and watch them get beat every single game, but I guess they were loyal fans."

Stengel and Berra kept the mood lighthearted amid the gloom of losing.

"You'd have these postgame meetings with Casey Stengel and Yogi Berra, and they were just characters," said John. "They had some players at the time like Ron Swoboda, who became a lot better later in his career."

At the time, Stengel sarcastically quipped that Swoboda had the strength and power to become a great player once he learned how to catch a routine fly ball. While that may not have been far from the truth in 1965, Swoboda would wind up playing a pivotal role in leading the Miracle Mets from oblivion to perhaps the most unexpected World Series triumph in baseball history in 1969.

The cameraman job paid $225 per week—a decent salary in 1965. John worked at it for nearly eighteen months and seriously considered doing it permanently, but fate intervened.

John met a person who would change his life forever. On Thanksgiving night, the Catholic War Vets held a cocktail dance at their local club with a band playing rock-and-roll music.

"I'll always remember another runner from the club suggested we go because there were always girls there," said John. "I don't remember if I was coming out and she was going in or the other way around, but we both turned around and it was love at first sight. I realized there was something special about her. She didn't drink or smoke and wasn't too bad looking at the time."

The young lady was Ellen Elias of Bayonne, New Jersey. Like John, she had been brought up a Catholic and shared his outlook on life and had many of the same values.

"We argue about, this but I thought it was kind of dull, so I was leaving and saw him coming in," remembered Ellen. "He said he was leaving and saw me, but either way it was a thing where we saw each other. I had the car, but my friends took it, and he asked me to dance and took me home that night."

Several dates later, including one at the Jersey Shore, and their relationship was in full bloom. However, it was not long afterwards that John was offered the opportunity to attend school 1,500 miles away in Lafayette, Louisiana.

While he waited for a permanent contract offer from the network , John was convinced by an English athlete, Malcolm Robinson, who at the time was studying and training at the University of Southwestern Louisiana (USL), (now the University of Louisiana at Lafayette) that it would be a great opportunity for him to attend college on a scholarship. He soon received a call from the USL head coach, Bob Cole.

"Cole called me the next night, and I told him the times I had run," said John. "I asked him if he had a scholarship, and he said 'Hell yeah, I have a scholarship!'"

Although he was becoming comfortable in New York, John and Ellen made the decision at that point that it would be best for him to accept the offer. John enrolled at USL in January 1966.

"When I told her I was going back to college, she advised me to do it," said John. "I would come back whenever I got the chance on Delta flights out of New Orleans."

While John was away in Louisiana, Ellen continued to work at AT&T during the day and attend Rutgers University at night.

Upon his arrival in Louisiana, the boy from County Mayo was in for his third culture shock in less than a decade when Coach Cole greeted him at the airport.

"When I got off the plane, there was this guy standing with cowboy boots and hat and jacket, and I said that couldn't be him, but it was," remembered John. "On our way home he said, 'Do you like fish?' I said yes and he said, 'Well, the track boys will take you to Breaux Bridge, Louisiana, the crawfish capital of the world.' I didn't know what a crawfish was. I remember they brought these things with tentacles and eyes staring at me and started breaking them up. I just sat there and they asked me, 'Are you going to eat?' And I said, 'No, I'm waiting for the fish.' I ended up eating a hamburger, and those guys still laugh about it."

It did not take long for him to realize a few other nuances of Cajun culture.

"In Ireland they called Americans, 'Yankees'" said John. "When I came to Louisiana, I found out that Yankee really means someone from up north."

No stranger to fishing, McDonnell agreed to accompany teammate Robert Gilbert on an expedition to nearby Lake Henderson. He had no idea what he was getting himself into.

"It had these big old stumps of trees and logs floating around with snakes resting on them," remembered McDonnell. "(Robert) told me he was taking me fishing, but I thought it was a real lake. He didn't tell me it was a swamp with snakes everywhere. He was going so fast with the boat in and around stumps that I had to tell him I couldn't swim. He kept saying, 'Oh, no problem.' He was a daredevil, and we got home very late that night, and I was never so happy to be back. Then he wanted me to get into a two seat-plane with him, but I knew better by that point. He had taken another kid up and flown the plane upside down, and the guy was sick for a week."

McDonnell thoroughly enjoyed the culture and hospitality of those he met in Louisiana.

"Some of the people took time to warm up to you," recalled McDonnell, "but once you became friends you were friends for life."

There were some less savory aspects of southern culture at the time. Just over one hundred years after the North had defeated the Confederate Army in the American Civil War, many of those wounds had not healed, nor had some of the old attitudes changed among some in the South. Racial segregation and discrimination remained prevalent even after the 1954 Supreme Court decision *Brown v. Board of Education* and the 1965 Voting Rights Act had outlawed segregation and the Jim Crow laws that unfairly prevented blacks from voting.

During his first semester at USL, John roomed on road-trips with an 800 meter runner named Curtis James, who was the first black track athlete to receive a scholarship to the university.

"He was a super nice guy, liked by everyone," said John. "He was always my roommate on trips and used to always call me, "Sir." I'd say 'Curtis, my name is John' but he'd still say 'Yes, sir.'"

Segregation was as ingrained in the culture as Creole and Cajun cuisine. When the team travelled back from meets, finding a restaurant that would serve them with Curtis as part of the team proved to be a challenge. On one particular trip to Mobile, Alabama, John remembers the scene descended into a messy confrontation.

"We stopped at a hamburger joint, and it was a girl that took our order, but at the back of the restaurant an older man walked out with a tray of hamburgers and all of a sudden I heard a loud bang," said John. "We had a discus thrower named Craig Mayes, who had taken the guy and threw him back against the deep freezer. All of a sudden Craig throws the burger tray onto the floor, and one of the guys on the team said, 'Let's get the hell out of here!' I still didn't know what happened when we sped over the Louisiana border. When we finally pulled over, I asked what happened, and they told me the man wanted to make Curtis eat outside, but Craig Mayes had said, 'Like hell, he's eating outside!'"

Nothing John had been exposed to in Ireland compared to some of the hatred he witnessed in the American south during that period.

"They'd use the N-word during races and would be saying stuff like 'Beat that nigger,'" remembered John. "That was the biggest culture shock I had coming to America, the black-white thing."

One experience that particularly sticks in his mind for more positive reasons occurred after he had already graduated from USL in 1970. John was invited to compete at the Pelican Relays to be held at Southern University, which was an all-black college in Baton Rouge, Louisiana.

"Southern had some great teams and had this black kid from California who had run 8:58 for two miles, and they invited me to run against him," said John. "So I did and when I went over there, that was the first time I really got a feeling of being alone. There was maybe one or two white people in the whole place. I sat behind him and took the lead with two laps to go. As I was coming into the straightaway on the finish, they just stood up and started screaming and hollering, and I thought their man was coming, but they were cheering for me. That was a great experience because they just loved sports and competition. I learned a lot of valuable lessons in those years."

Never one to let time drift idly by at any point in his life, John worked on a construction job during his first summer back in New York from Louisiana in 1966. During that same summer John proposed to Ellen at a restaurant in Jersey City. She did not hesitate.

Although Ellen remained in New York working for AT&T throughout the next year, the two of them were never apart for long. She went to visit him a few times, while on other occasions he was flown up to New York by the NYAC to compete for the club in various events at Madison Square Gardens or Randall's Island.

Down in Louisiana, his main training partner was the Englishman who had convinced him to come to USL in the first place, Malcolm Robinson. Although Coach Cole did not plan or manage their training, he was never far from the picture.

"Coach Cole was one of the best motivators I had met," remembered John. "I learned everything about motivation from him."

Though Cole was typically upbeat and positive, McDonnell remembers he could be stern when needed. Before the 1967 Gulf States Conference Cross Country Championships in Ruston, Louisiana, Cole delivered an ultimatum to Ronald Landry, who was sometimes prone to inconsistency.

"[Cole] said, 'Ronnie, if you don't get out there and run well and we lose this meet, you're going to be walking back to Lafayette,'" remembered McDonnell. "That poor kid said, 'Yes sir, yes sir' and he ended up finishing third. I was already at the finish line and looked back, and he was stumbling in that last eighty yards, but by gosh he finished."

Those USL teams tended to be very balanced with a few strong distance runners and a strong 4 x 440 yard relay, which captured the national title one season. In the field, the program also had talented jumpers, such as national high-jump champ Jackie Causey, and a bevy of throwers in the shot, discus and javelin, including Louis Lefant, the national javelin champion. Louisiana was one of the few states whose high schools contested the javelin at their state championships.

During his two seasons in Lafayette, John was named an All-American and helped lead USL to two Gulf States Conference Championships in 1967 and 1968. For those who followed USL at the time, however, his greatest legacy was the race that took place on a hot April afternoon in 1967—the day Jim Ryun came to run at the Southwestern Relays in Lafayette, Louisiana.

Ryun was a running phenomenon, lionized as much by those who had no knowledge or association with the sport as those that did. Only two years after he broke the national high-school record for the mile by running 3:55.3 as a senior in Wichita, Kansas, in 1964, Ryun shattered the world outdoor mile (3:51.3) and 880-yard (1:44.9) records in 1966. That year he was named by *Sports Illustrated* as its Sportsman of the Year and would later win a silver medal in the 1,500 meter at the 1968 Olympics in Mexico City.

The night before the race, McDonnell was eating dinner at a restaurant in Lafayette when some fraternity guys began mocking his chances.

"'Oh, you're going to beat Jim Ryun!'" McDonnell remembered them saying before he replied, "You're damn right!"[3]

Just over nine thousand spectators crammed into the USL track stadium on that day to watch Ryun. Outside the stadium, several local children, including a local Lafayette boy named Randy Melancon, skipped class to catch a glimpse of the world-record holder.

"We didn't have tickets, but they had a gate where you could look in, and there were a bunch of people doing that," remembered Melancon. "At that time a lot of people were in the stands with Ryun being the big draw."

The race was contested over two-miles, which Ryun would later win at the 1968 NCAA Indoor Championships. On that hot day in April 1967, however, Ryun was just a little off his game, and John McDonnell was as ready as ever. Ryun took the lead through six laps before John noticed something.

"I guess he was hurting," McDonnell remembered. "That's what you have to know—when an athlete is hurting. You can move up to him, see if his face is contorted or if his shoulders are getting tight. He's beginning to feel it. I saw that and went for it."[4]

McDonnell surged into the lead with one-half mile remaining and never looked back, finishing in a time of 8:48. Ryun dropped out 300 meters from the finish. The crowd erupted in hysteria.

"I remember this huge roar from the crowd when John beat Jim Ryun in the two-mile," said Melancon. "That was pretty amazing. He was a legend at USL after that."

Only two months after that triumph, John and Ellen McDonnell, were married in Bayonne, New Jersey, on June 17, 1967. Neither of John's parents could attend the wedding; that summer his father passed away and his oldest brother Paddy returned from England to take over the family farm. However, his younger brother Michael was the best man, and his sister Catherine was a bridesmaid. John and Ellen spent their honeymoon visiting Niagara Falls on the Canadian border.

During the fall of 1967, the newlyweds moved into a married dormitory on the USL campus. Although Ellen had tried to get a transfer from AT&T to Louisiana, none was forthcoming at the time, so instead she worked at the university in the library and School of Music. The culture change would be striking for the girl who had lived her entire life in New Jersey and spent time working in New York City.

"It was such a slow place," Ellen said of Louisiana. "Everybody went to bed early, and everything closed early compared to New York and New Jersey. It took me a year to really like it, but I'm the type of person who learns to like where they live. The pace was slower but I liked it."

Back at USL, John convinced Coach Cole to sign Tommy Hopkins, a talented distance runner from Ireland, to replace the graduating Malcolm Robinson. The two helped balance out a strong USL track team in the distance events, but the team lacked the depth to make an impact as a team in cross country.

"We were always a man short," remembered John. "We used to run against Houston, and they'd beat us because we didn't have a strong fifth man."

The following year, Coach Cole also signed another distance runner, Arthur Botterill, from Australia. Together, Arthur and John would lead USL to its final Gulf States championship of the decade in 1968. Although John continued to battle Achilles issues, the ailment did not prevent him from earning six All-American certificates throughout his career.

Upon John's graduation from USL in June 1970 with a degree in industrial education, he and Ellen immediately made plans to move back to the East Coast. John accepted a job teaching industrial technology and coaching track and soccer at the high school in New Providence, New Jersey, which was just a short twenty-minute drive from New York City. He continued to compete for the NYAC. Meanwhile, Ellen took a job with Bell Laboratories, which conducted a good deal of research for NASA.

It did not take the couple very long to discover the high cost of living in that part of the country. Given how prohibitively expensive property was in the area, buying a house was out of the question, so the couple rented a one-family house from a local landlady who only rented to teachers.

"When he graduated, we couldn't wait to get back [to New Jersey]," said Ellen, "but once we got there, we said this is a rat race and the property is expensive."

Although Ellen certainly didn't mind being close to her family, the two could never see themselves owning a home or getting ahead in New Jersey.

"So I called my old coach Bob Cole and asked if he could help me get a teaching job in Lafayette, and I would help with the distance runners and he said, 'You're damn right I will,'" remembered John. "He was such a great guy. He called me back, and the principal knew me from years back and hired me just like that."

After one year in New Jersey, the McDonnells packed up and departed for Louisiana following the end of the school year. They drove down in their Nash Rambler on a scorching hot summer day in 1971.

"We pulled a U-Haul, and it may have been too big," remembers John. "We had to stop in so many places."

When the radiator continued to overheat, John found out from a mechanic in Chattanooga, Tennessee, that the problem could be solved by turning the heater on, which would have been a reasonable enough thing to do if it were not as hot as Hades outside.

"So we rolled down the windows and drove with the heater on when it was 98 flipping degrees outside," lamented John. "That Rambler wasn't an old car. It just wasn't a good car."

John took a four-thousand-dollar pay cut with the move to the high school in Lafayette, while Ellen took a job with South Central Bell for three thousand dollars less than she had been making. Still, they were able to afford their first house in Lafayette—a brick home for which they paid an affordable twenty-one thousand dollars.

Once again John started teaching industrial technology and coaching track, but many of the old racial issues bubbling under the surface in Louisiana had come to the fore once the schools were integrated. John quickly found himself in the middle of it.

"Things had changed quickly in Lafayette because they had integrated the schools, and there were some problems," said John. "I had broken up some fights with knives, and one of the other teachers had to intervene in a gun incident, so it wasn't fun at all."

Toward the end of the school year, he interviewed with State Farm Insurance with the intention of remaining in Lafayette but getting out of high-school teaching entirely. Then fate intervened once more.

His brother Michael had been working in New York City in the Latin American Sales office of the American Potash Company when the company was bought out, and he was asked to transfer to Oklahoma City. Although Michael initially balked at moving to the Midwest, a visit from the chairman of the company, Dean McGee, convinced him otherwise.

"I guess he heard that I was not wanting to come to Oklahoma, so he came in and sat down in my office, which for me was a big deal," said Michael. "And he got talking to me. He heard I used to run and told me he used to throw the shot put at the University of Kansas. And then he got up and said, 'Why don't you come to Oklahoma City. I'd like to show it to you. It's a really nice place.' So I went down, and he basically made me an offer I couldn't refuse, and I've been here ever since."

While Michael settled in Edmond, Oklahoma, in 1970 and began raising a family, he joined a running club that used to meet on the University of Oklahoma campus underneath the football stadium. They called it "Pneumonia Downs" because of how cold and drafty it was, but at that club Michael met Larry Aduddell, who later helped found the Tulsa Run, and Gary Lower, who was the assistant track coach and head cross-country coach under J. D. Martin at the University of Oklahoma.

Around that time John spoke with his brother about coaching at the collegiate level.

"I introduced John to Gary and they invited him to OU," said Michael. "I think they offered him a deal where he would be coaching part-time with the university and teaching at the high school in Norman."

Simultaneously, John caught wind of the fact that the University of Arkansas was also looking for a cross-country coach. He made a trip to Fayetteville where he met with the head track coach Ed Renfrow, who at the time was the lone coach overseeing all of the events. Arkansas was also offering a part-time position that paid $2,500 a year and the opportunity to work at nearby Greenland High School.

"When I met Ed Renfrow, he was a real nice guy," said John. "He said I can't pay you that much, but you can have the cross-country team."

Ellen remembers the glow in John's eyes when they visited Fayetteville, and he saw the Arkansas countryside and Ozark Mountains for the first time.

"He really liked it here because he thought it reminded him of Ireland," said Ellen.

"Fayetteville was a place with a lot of hills and was very country compared to what it is now," said John, "and it was a great place for distance runners."

Without much hesitation, John accepted the offer from Arkansas.

"I could tell Oklahoma was just looking for a recruiter to bring athletes from Ireland and had a young distance coach at the time, so I didn't see what I was going to do," said John. "When I came to Arkansas the head coach, Ed Renfrow, had been a great high hurdler for the school. He flat told me, 'I don't know distance running, and I don't have time.' He gave me the chance to run the distance program and some scholarships. And they had some good kids at the time and were in the Southwest Conference, so I thought in a year or two we could beat those schools."

When he interviewed at Greenland High School, John remembered the superintendent warning him of discipline problems at the school that he would have to deal with on a daily basis.

"He was telling me they had some tough kids here," remembered John. "So I asked, 'Do they carry guns?' 'Oh no, he said.' 'Do they carry knives?' 'No.' So I wondered, who was he kidding? These kids are great."

The McDonnells sold their house in Lafayette for a tidy nine-thousand-dollar profit and packed up for the third time in three years. While the two would move several times throughout the next several decades as they upgraded one home after another, one thing would not change: they would never leave Fayetteville.

3

Starting Out at Arkansas (1972–1978)

"God help us all."

—*Texas miler Reed Fisher*

Arkansas was swept into the 1970s by the winds of change and progress making their way across the country. Civil disobedience and antiwar protests had erupted in cities as the young began challenging the assumptions of the established order. Winthrop Rockefeller, who had only recently been elected as the state's first Republican governor since Reconstruction, completed the integration of Arkansas schools that had been allowed to stagnate for over a decade. An upstart retail outlet based out of Rogers, Arkansas called Walmart, named after its founder Sam Walton, had only recently incorporated, opened its thirty-eighth store regionally, and become listed on the New York Stock Exchange. Down the road in Springdale, Tyson Foods was processing and marketing beef, chicken, and pork on a scale that would soon exceed all but one of the industry leaders in the world.

Economic development was certainly not a foreign concept to this region, but with its sweeping mountainous countryside and a population that stood a shade north of two million, the Natural State had certainly been preserved from some of the social developments of urbanization and secularism seen elsewhere. Its undisturbed scenic beauty and rolling hills resembled the Irish countryside. As the hold of Christianity on other parts of the country began its wax and wane, Arkansas remained a state of fervent believers with the Southern Baptist Convention predominating.

Tucked away in rustic Fayetteville, the University of Arkansas was founded in 1871 as the Arkansas Industrial University before adopting its present name in 1899. Although it soon emerged as the preeminent state-funded land-grant institution in the state, the University of Arkansas had hardly distinguished itself on the sporting field during the first half of the twentieth century. The tradition of "Calling the Hogs," which would later become a celebratory aspect of Razorback athletics after every touchdown, home-run, slam-dunk, or victory, in fact traces its roots to local farmers trying to inspire a listless football team mired for decades in the Southwest Conference cellar.

Eventually including Baylor University, the University of Houston, Rice University, Southern Methodist University, the University of Texas, Texas Tech University, Texas A&M University, and Texas Christian University, the Southwest Conference was largely composed of Texas schools who openly wondered whether the perennially weak Arkansas athletics programs even belonged in the league.[1] The facilities on campus, which were below average, could not make up for funding that was inadequate in football and virtually nonexistent in every other sport.

Much of that began to change in 1957 when athletics director John Barnhill hired a bright young coach named Frank Broyles to lead a moribund football program out of the bottom of the Southwest Conference. The returns were immediate and long lasting. It took Broyles only two seasons to capture the Southwest Conference championship in football and another six to bring the ultimate glory to Fayetteville—a football national championship.

Between the Arkansas players who went on to successful professional careers and the assistant coaches who eventually led teams that contended for Super Bowls or college national championships—Barry Switzer, Jimmy Johnson, Joe Gibbs, Raymond Berry, Johnny Majors, Hayden Fry, Doug Dickey foremost among them—Broyles impact was certainly felt on the field. By 1985 twenty of Frank Broyles's former players or assistant coaches led major collegiate football programs. Eventually, the Broyles Award for college football's assistant coach of the year was created in his honor.

"I believe to this day that he turned out more great head coaches than any coach in the history of the game," said Terry Don Phillips, a player, coach, and administrator under Broyles at Arkansas and later athletic director at the University of Louisiana at Lafayette, Oklahoma State, and Clemson. "What he did was bring in outstanding coaching talent, and he was a CEO in the sense that he was bringing good coaches but still setting the tone and the parameters for the program. He let his coaches coach. So from that perspective he didn't micromanage, but he would give his opinion. He didn't shy away from that. There wasn't any question who was in charge. And as an administrator you knew the tone and parameters, but he let you do your job."

Off the field, the positive notoriety and attention his program gained for the university could not be quantified. Even President Nixon thought it was worthwhile to make the pilgrimage to Fayetteville in 1969 to watch Arkansas play Texas. Only months before his death in 1973, Barnhill called the hiring of Frank Broyles the best decision of his life.[2]

"It was obvious to me when he came that our budget was going to go up," said Barnhill. "He was used to the finer things, and we were cutting corners. It has all paid off so well. You couldn't buy our reputation for a million dollars."[3]

By 1972 Broyles began contemplating a retirement from the sidelines and a move, which would begin the following year. Rather than relinquish the coaching reins immediately, Broyles and the university's board of trustees agreed that an orderly transition would occur once he had completed a badly needed upgrade of the football facilities, which would allow the program to remain competitive nationally in the long term.[4] During his final three seasons of coaching, Broyles took both roles and soon realized that major competitive deficiencies were prevalent throughout the athletics department.

As successful as his effort had been in putting the football program on a solid footing, other Razorback sports remained unsupported and unproductive. There had been intermittent triumphs such as Clyde Scott's Olympic silver in the 110-meter hurdles in 1948 and the basketball team's Final Four run that same decade, but such success was the exception rather than the rule. In Scott's case he had trained without a proper track or experienced coach, with football line coach Hobe Hoosier dutifully filling in as best he could.[5]

As Orville Henry and Jim Bailey wrote, public interest in Razorback athletics "used to die down from the day after the bowl game until the start of spring practice."[6] It was Frank Broyles's mission during his first few years as athletic director to change the mentality of Razorback athletics and create a broad-based athletics program beyond pigskin.

"Everywhere I went people would say to me, 'Why can't we have an all-sports program?'" said Broyles. "They would say, 'My son was a track athlete or baseball player and had to go to Tulane or LSU' because we didn't have scholarships at the time [in the other sports]. I was determined I was going to fulfill what Razorback fans wanted and that was a competitive all-sports program. So we increased our revenue to where we could finance and hire full-time coaches and give full scholarships and build the facilities to be nationally competitive in all sports."

Broyles certainly had his work cut out for him—few of the sports were competitive at the conference level, let alone nationally. The basketball team played its games in dusty old Barnhill Arena on a dirt floor—and for one particular five-year span starting in 1966 the program lost a grand total of eighty-five games.

The track-and-field team had similar issues. Although at one time it did have the use of cinder track in the football stadium, that was removed in 1973, and the team was forced to practice at Fayetteville High School with no facility of any kind on campus. Dr. Alan Sugg, who would later become president of the University of Arkansas system, remembers pole-vaulting for Ab Bidwell's Razorback track-and-field teams as an undergraduate in the late 1950s.

"We were lucky if we scored a few points at the Southwest Conference meet," said Sugg, who placed second individually in the Southwest Conference (SWC). "We were not a competitive track team in the conference."

The track team was so poorly funded and uncompetitive throughout most of the twentieth century that the 1939 April Fools edition of the *Arkansas Traveler* joked about the Razorbacks winning events at the prestigious Penn Relays—a ludicrous notion at the time.[7] By 1972 the head coach of the track program was Ed Renfrow, a decent man stretched thin coaching all of the events. A successful hurdler during his athletic career, Renfrow lacked the time, knowledge, or inclination to monitor the distance runners training on a consistent basis.

It came as little surprise then that Arkansas finished second to last at the 1971 Southwest Conference Cross Country Championships and scored a paltry one point at the 1972 Southwest Conference Outdoor Track Championships the following spring.

"The distance runners told me they used to go down to the playground during their runs and shoot baskets and get a good sweat before coming back," recalled McDonnell.

Although the track team had begun to receive meager scholarship funding as a result of the efforts of Frank Broyles and Wilson Matthews, who early on worked as the athletics department fundraiser, it was clear Renfrow was stretched thin, and the program needed an assistant coach to attain any level of respectability. Still, with only twenty-five hundred dollars to find a head cross-country/assistant track coach, it would be hard to attract quality candidates for what was essentially a part-time position. They settled for a man named John McDonnell.

When that modest group of Arkansas distance runners reported for cross-country camp on a hot August morning in 1972, few could have expected to be greeted by a fiery thirty-four-year old Irishman with a thick accent, quiet intensity, and the expectation of excellence every day of the week.

"Oh my gosh, I never saw people's eyes get so big because I was starting to tell them what we were going to do," remembered McDonnell of that first team meeting. "Back then we were doing 110–120 miles in a week, and those guys hadn't been doing anything more than 50 miles in a week. We were doing more in a day than some of them had been doing in a week."

Off in the corner of the room, two seniors on the team, Jim Smith of Searcy, Arkansas, and Terry Smith of Shawnee Mission, Kansas, listened and stared back at the new coach in disbelief.

"I remember those Smiths when I started talking 120-mile weeks, I thought their eyes were going to pop out of their heads," laughed McDonnell. "They probably hadn't run 20 miles a week. They accepted it and got their weight off though. They were talented guys."

McDonnell inherited a senior-laden team, which also included Terry Smith's teammate from Shawnee Mission, Kim Wisner, a 1:52 half-miler, and Ron Hendee, from Kansas City. Despite the limited time between his hiring and the start of cross-country season, he managed to land two other athletes for his first season in Fayetteville.

The first was Randy Melancon, who only a few years earlier as a young boy in Lafayette had watched through the fence in awe as John vanquished the once-invincible Jim Ryun at the Southwestern Relays. After a remarkable freshman year at Southwestern Louisiana, during which Melancon improved from 4.40 to 4:03 in the mile and qualified for the NCAA Championships, his immediate future at USL was murky when his only training partner, the Australian, Arthur Botterill, graduated from the university.

"I had no ideas about training," admitted Melancon. "I thought just making a college team was good, and then all of a sudden I was the best guy and had no idea what kind of training I was going to get, and there was pressure on me to do better. John was not only coaching himself at USL, but he was also coaching the Australian, who was now coaching me. So I thought, 'I want to go wherever John goes.'"

When Melancon broke the news to the head coach Bob Cole, he was informed that he would not be released and would have to sit out his first season at Arkansas.

"He wasn't too happy," said Melancon of Coach Cole. "In fact, he was pretty upset."

The other athlete McDonnell brought to Fayetteville that fall was an Irishman from Tipperary by the name of Desmond O'Connor.

"He was something else," remembered Tom Aspel, an Irish athlete who came to Arkansas the following year. "Dessie looked like Rod Stewart and he played the part. He could have easily been a con man because if it wasn't nailed down it became his."

Struggling to attract talent of any kind to Fayetteville in those days, McDonnell took a flyer on him.

"I will be honest that when I went over to Ireland, I was advised not to take him," admitted John. "Every coach I knew said they didn't think he would suit America."

McDonnell had little alternative at the time. Although he would later place an emphasis on recruiting kids with speed on the track and character off of it, recruiting distance talent of any kind to Arkansas at that time was a challenge. In many cases, even getting high-school athletes to speak with him was problematic.

"Some of them were almost rude to you," remembered John. "I remember talking to a kid from New Jersey who had run 9:10 for the two-mile. I would have loved to have given him a scholarship back then. When I told him I was from Arkansas, he said he had never heard of it. He was being a smartass. I felt like saying, 'Well, you don't know your geography,' but instead I said to him, 'We're not very good right now but we will be.' He ended up walking on at Oregon and never did anything."

Led by the indefatigable Steve Prefontaine, who had placed fourth in the Olympic 5,000-meter finals that very summer while he was still a collegian, the University of Oregon was the gold standard of track-and-field programs in American collegiate athletics and had a case full of NCAA championship trophies and capacity crowds at Hayward Field to prove it.

McDonnell's early training philosophy was formed from what he had been exposed to throughout his running career and the principles he had picked up from the legendary New Zealand coach Arthur Lydiard, whose revolutionary volume-based training approach had brought Kiwi athletes to the pinnacle of the sport during that period. Training literature was hard to come by in those days.

"I read a bunch of different coaches, but you didn't get much because they didn't always tell the truth," said McDonnell.

"You have to remember back then there was nothing written on this stuff," said Dick Weis, who was coaching at Albertus Mangus High School in Bardonia, New York, at the time. "I bought John Cannon's book in the 1960s and later found out the actual workouts were harder when I spoke to his athletes. People were doing more, but nobody published it because they didn't want to be called slave drivers. You couldn't get anything on training. You learned from experience—what works and what doesn't work—and you took whatever you could get. Everybody knows the basics of fast twitch and slow twitch fibers now, but people don't realize John [McDonnell] was at the forefront of a lot of this stuff."

While some coaches traditionally viewed slow-twitch fibers, which are used for longer endurance efforts, and fast-twitch fibers, which are used for shorter and more explosive efforts, as being trained on a one-dimensional and mutually exclusive basis during different periods of the year, McDonnell often trained for endurance and speed simultaneously. Although he took the fall cross-country season seriously, he always viewed it within the context of being a springboard for the track season.

"I always told my guys, there is no Olympics in cross country, so what we are getting ready for is the track," said McDonnell. "The best preparation for track is to run a good cross-country season."

John's cross-country training program didn't vary much from athlete to athlete at the time, but after encouraging his athletes to run at least 60 miles per week in the summer, his squad would run easy mileage of 110–120 each week for six weeks and only incorporate 200-meter strides and plyometric circuits after three weeks.

"I didn't change my philosophy for getting ready late in the year," said McDonnell.

"I remember there were teams that often beat us early but they wouldn't beat us at the end of the year."

The weekly mileage remained constant for six weeks, after which John would typically introduce twenty-four controlled 400-meter intervals on grass one day and six repeats of one mile on the hill at the Razorback Golf Course a few days later on workout days. On easier intensity days when they were not conducting a workout session, his athletes would run six miles in the morning and anywhere from ten to twelve miles in the afternoon with a long, slow run of eighteen miles on Sunday usually incorporating a hill somewhere along the way. On weeks when the team was not racing, they often ran a hard ten-mile run behind the golf course on Saturday.

"Looking back he had the training down perfect," said Aspel. "The only problem was if you were out carousing and didn't get enough sleep, it wore you down. That with races kind of wore us down."

In the days before practice regulations, McDonnell met with his charges every day and often twice. It was a tough training regimen to say the least.

"I was lucky I didn't kill those guys," admitted McDonnell, "but we didn't have a lot of injuries. It was an Arthur Lydiard type preparation, and we ran slow, but it was a lot of miles. The reason for the 400s was that even though they didn't have a place in cross country, they did have a place in track, and I kept that leg cadence there so the transition to track wasn't such a drastic move."

As a coach who placed a premium on team building throughout his career, John quickly decided that fartleks, which involved athletes speeding up on runs at an indefinite rate for a fixed period of time, could not be part of the equation.

"I love fartlek, but it's an individual thing," said John. "It's hard with a bunch of people because there are always egos that get in the way. I tried it for a bit but got rid of it because even though it was good for individual training, it didn't work as a team."

There was no place for egos on McDonnell's teams and never any question he was in charge.

"When we did quarters, he'd never tell you how fast you were going, he'd just say 'Too slow or right on the money,'" said Steve Baker, an English athlete who arrived in 1974. "You didn't ask questions, and he never volunteered it. It was just get the workout done. On the mile repeats he'd tell you to run a 4:50 repeat going up that hill. He wanted us in a close group and didn't want people breaking off."

Although John ran with the team on many of the easy days during the early part of his coaching career, his competitive career came to an end the previous year when he helped a friend complete a marathon in Galveston, a small island thirty miles southeast of Houston, Texas off the Gulf of Mexico.

"I ended up finishing, and I never would have if not for him," said John. "That wall . . . I hit it. At twenty-two miles, I thought the last four miles would never end!"

On the days he taught industrial arts education at Greenland High School— where he was voted the outstanding teacher of the year—he met the team at 3:30 p.m., but sometimes couldn't make it on time.

"It was never a problem," remembered Aspel. "John would say if he wasn't there by twenty to four to just get warmed up."

The 1972 cross-country season started modestly enough. After back-to-back losses to Oklahoma and Oklahoma State at the end of September, the team headed to the

Southwest Conference Championships in College Station. There, the University of Texas put on a clinic, as they had for years, scoring 29 points and placing five athletes in the top ten—led by the talented twins, Paul and John Craig, from Canada. The Longhorns continued their stranglehold and satisfied the team objective in cross country of scoring as few points as possible based on the individual finishes of their top five finishers.

Still, despite placing fourth at that conference meet, it was Arkansas, not Texas, that would be heading to the 1972 NCAA Cross Country Championships after winning the District VI regional meet. In a career that would see many of his teams peak at the right moment, this was the first of many remarkable turns of events for John. The team was composed of athletes he had, for the most part, not recruited. For those seniors who had lacked purpose and endured nothing but mediocrity until that point, it was the experience of a lifetime.

"When we won that district, I tell you they had tears in their eyes," remembered John. "They were hugging me and said we wish you would have been here sooner. They were kids who worked hard and realized it was the end of the road for them and were happy because they had finally done something and were going to a national championship."

For that first Razorback team, simply qualifying for the NCAA Championships was an accomplishment. Only twenty-eight teams and two-hundred and forty athletes in all of Division I qualified for the national meet in those days, and it was not something the Razorbacks were accustomed to doing. That soon became obvious once they arrived at Glenbrook Golf Course in Houston, Texas. As early as the first mile of the race it was apparent that they were out of their element.

Nick Rose of Western Kentucky took the field through the mile in 4:23 with Neil Cusack of East Tennessee eventually surging for the individual win on the six-mile course in 28:23. East Tennessee's largely Irish-born team was nipped for the national title by a mere fourteen points by their cross-state rivals from the University of Tennessee, who were coached by Stan Huntsman and led by Olympic steeplechaser, Doug Brown.

Arkansas finished twenty-sixth at the meet, beating only their Southwest Conference brethren, Rice and Houston. Desmond O'Connor was the final Arkansas finisher in 238th place—and fourth from last in the entire meet. An assortment of issues plagued the enigmatic O'Conner, and it soon became apparent that his time in Fayetteville would be short.

Discipline had always been an issue with the boy from Tipperary, and when John put his foot down by requiring him to cut his hair, O'Connor decided to transfer to Angelo State in Texas rather than comply. That solution seemed to make everyone happy.

"I think John was as happy to see Desmond go as we were," said Melancon. "He was bad news."

Pleased as they may have been at O'Connor's departure, the fact remained that his loss and the graduation of three seniors left a major void on a team lacking depth in the first place. Although Steve Houk and Ron Hendee would run 14:02 and 14:22 for the three-mile that spring, it was clear John had his work cut out in putting together a strong team for the next fall. With little success attracting American athletes and no recruiting budget to speak of at the time, John paid for a trip home to Ireland himself that summer to watch a few Irish athletes in action and meet with them in person.

"I knew a guy named Ronnie Long, and I was recruiting Mike O'Shea, who had run 3:47 [for 1,500 meters]," said John. "He said he'd come if I took Niall O'Shaughnessy, who had run 1:55 [for 800 meters]. I was taking Niall anyway but O'Shea didn't come. He went to Providence and never beat O'Shaughnessy."

Growing up in Adare, Niall had gone to the same high school as that year's NCAA cross-country champion, Neil Cusack of East Tennessee.

"I was hoping for a scholarship from a school where some of the Irish athletes had gone such as Villanova, Providence, or East Tennessee," said O'Shaughnessy. "I had never heard of Arkansas and didn't even know where it was."

On his way to visiting O'Shaughnessy, John confessed to his brother Paddy that the athlete he was more interested in was the highly touted O'Shea. Still, the visit went well. Given the fact O'Shaughnessy was only seventeen years of age at the time he was approached by Arkansas, his parents were reluctant to allow him to go to the United States before that visit from John convinced them otherwise.

"You have to put that in the perspective of 1973," said O'Shaughnessy. "Travel and communication weren't as easy, and they really wanted me to wait another year. John actually came to my house. My father was a veterinary surgeon and had dealt with farmers all his life. With John being an old farm boy, I think my parents saw the character John had, and he actually changed their mind. He didn't come in trying to change their mind, but they just saw he was a person of character, and his word was valid and they would trust him to take care of me."

Niall had never run the mile, but with only a modest 1:55.4 personal best 800-meter time to his name, John told him that the event was in his future.

"When he told me he was signing me as a miler, I didn't know what the hell he was talking about," admitted O'Shaughnessy. "The mile was nowhere on my horizon, and I was so indignant that I asked what would it take for me to continue being a half-miler. He said 1:52. Later that summer at the European Junior Championships, I ran 1:51.8 and told John, 'I'm coming over as a half-miler.' He laughed and said to come on over, but we'll see about that."

Standing six inches taller than Niall at 6 feet, 3, Tom Aspel was an equally raw athlete who had run 1:54 for 800 meters and 3:54 for 1,500 meters and finished eleventh at the Irish Cross Country Championships despite being a low-mileage athlete who also dabbled with the high jump. Originally from Waterford, Ireland, it was made clear to Aspel by other Irish athletes that unless he wanted to spend his life working in the crystal factory that had made his hometown famous, his high-jumping hobby ought to come to an end.

"[Future Providence coach] Ray Treacy told me after I ran that first 1,500 meter and beat some of those guys that I had better be giving up my high jumping because I might be getting a scholarship," remembered Aspel.

Completing John's recruiting class was Derek Reilly, a 4:14 miler from Dublin, Ireland, and Steve Barr, a supremely talented 13:54 three-miler from Essex, England.

The lone American recruit, Stuart Penn, was a 9:15 two-miler from New Jersey, who amazingly enough not only could find Arkansas on a map but decided to sign with John's fledgling program.

"He was tough as hell," remembered John of Penn. "A big guy, 170 pounds, no speed and [he] shuffled. He was like a badger. The race wasn't over until it was over. He did a lot of great things, not at the front but in the pack."

Given the fact that Randy Melancon would be eligible to compete for Arkansas for the first time that fall, John had managed to put together a team that could potentially knock Texas off its lofty perch at the Southwest Conference Cross Country Championships.

As much as that prospect came about through John's tireless efforts, Ed Renfrow, the head track coach, held the purse strings and supported him every step of the way.

"Ed would give me whatever scholarships I needed if I could get good kids," said John. "He was very fair. He wanted to win and didn't care what event."

The transition for those Irish boys during the fall of 1973 was not easy. It was not just the jump in training volume from doing, in Aspel's case, more mileage in one day than he had previously done in a week. The heat was more intense than anything he had ever experienced in Ireland.

"It wasn't easy, but I just kind of gritted my teeth and took to it," said O'Shaughnessy. "I came here in good track shape from the European Championships but hadn't done any distance work. The most difficult thing for me was the heat because I wasn't used to it and had to take a salt tablet. John was very big on that to avoid cramps."

Aspel remembers the shock from racing the first time in the sweltering one-hundred-degree heat.

"The first race was Oklahoma State, and it was four o'clock in the afternoon in September and I had never raced in those temperatures," said Aspel. "I thought my head was going to explode it was so hot."

Although Arkansas won the meet, John Halberstadt, the eventual NCAA champion from Oklahoma State, captured the individual crown, followed closely by Steve Houk and Randy Melancon. None of the Irish boys placed in the top ten.

It was easy for a young man away from home for the first time to be caught up by distractions but not something any of John's athletes could afford given how hard he was working them.

"When I came to Arkansas it was just go, go, go, go all of the time," said Aspel. "There was a lot of excitement and a lot of people, and it was hard to keep your mind on the task at hand. John told us not to burn the candle at both ends. I remember after those eighteen-mile runs going home and sleeping all day."

Another major adjustment, particularly for those from Ireland and England, where one might go a lifetime without traveling more than three or four hours by automobile, was the long, arduous van rides to meets—whether it was down to Houston during cross-country season, up to Champaign, Illinois, or Columbia, Missouri, during indoor season, or off to Des Moines, Iowa, during the outdoor season. It would not be out of the ordinary for the team to travel up to ten hours to a competition.

"We went to some strange places," remembered Steve Baker. "We ran at Jackson, Mississippi, once on an indoor track that was thirteen laps to the mile."

When the van wasn't heading southeast, it was pointed southwest.

"I remember having a race at Lubbock, and my God, it was a long way to drive out there," said O'Shaughnessy. "We'd always have someone up front talking to John to make sure he stayed awake. There was never a safety issue."

Well, almost never. As hard as the trips were on the athletes, they became even more grueling for the coach, who couldn't sleep through them because he was driving the entire way. On one occasion as they were making their way through Sallisaw, Oklahoma, on Interstate 40 on their way back to Fayetteville from a cross-country meet at the University of Oklahoma, John became very drowsy.

"I saw Niall looking at me anxiously from the passenger seat," remembered John. "And he said, 'Are you tired?' and I said 'Oh, I'm just resting my right eye.' And he said 'You're what?!'"

The frequent trips to the Dallas–Fort Worth area for the Southwest Conference Championships or other invitational competitions was no less taxing on the man driving the van.

"Driving with John, we never hit that exit," laughed Aspel of the trips to Fort Worth. "I always tried to be awake, but we would miss it."

During those years, the regional meet that qualified teams for the NCAA Cross Country Championships was held at the beginning of November, two weeks before the conference championship. Given how well his young team had run through the midpoint of the season, John had reason to expect his Razorback squad could dethrone Texas for the Southwest Conference cross-country championship and improve on its performance at the national meet.

Those expectations went out the window at the regional meet on a hot November afternoon at Glenbrooke Golf Course in Houston. The thermostat may have said eighty degrees, but with 95 percent humidity the toll on the athletes was immeasurable. Heading into the sixth and final mile, Arkansas controlled the race before Steve Houk and Randy Melancon, who were running first and third respectively, passed out with less than 800 meters to go and did not finish. With their sixth and seventh runners well back, Arkansas fell to fifth place in the meet. For both the first and final time, a cross-country team coached by John McDonnell would not qualify for the national championship.

"I swore after that meet I would never live in Houston," said O'Shaughnessy, who finished twenty-second at the regional. "It was the high humidity that got us and made some people on our team pass out."

Although he was hardly one to tolerate failure, as generations of Arkansas athletes would find out, McDonnell was stoic about the turn of events, which were largely out of everyone's control.

"He didn't blame anyone," said Aspel. "It was just Texas weather. He just told us we are going to train and come back here and not let this happen again."

Heading into the 1973 Southwest Conference cross-country meet at College Station two weeks later, John's strategy for his wounded team to finally topple Texas involved staying together in a strong pack to avoid another catastrophe late in the race. While disaster had not struck until the final 800 meters of the regional meet, it was clear to John by the first 800 meters of the conference championship that things could unravel. Freshman Steve Barr took a fifty-yard lead in spite of the prerace instructions to stay together.

"I didn't have the respect yet of the kids," admitted McDonnell. "I had a plan to stay near the front and keep a good pace going because we had enough guys. Well, Steve Barr took off like he was on fire, and it sort of broke all of the rhythm of the rest of the guys because that's not what we were supposed to do. He was good enough to finish in the top three but ended up sixteenth [because he had gone out too hard]."

By seeking individual glory, Barr had put himself and the team out of the race. Arkansas finished ten points behind Texas—second place overall—an improvement over the previous season's fourth place at the conference meet but a disappointment for McDonnell that he would not soon forget.

After the meet, as Reed Fisher, a 3:59 miler from Texas, cooled down with Tom Aspel, he casually asked how many freshman were on Arkansas's roster. Aspel told him seven.

"God help us all," Fisher said to Aspel, almost resigned to the inevitability of what was to come.

The Razorbacks would never lose another conference cross-country championship for the remainder of John McDonnell's thirty-six year coaching career.

"I remember John told me that the Texas cross-country coach [James Blackwood] came by and congratulated him on how well we had done and given them a scare," recalled Melancon. "Most coaches would have thought that was nice of him to give a pat on the back, but John actually came back and said, 'He thinks we're doing well now? We're going to come back and kick their ass.'"

As the season shifted to track, the Razorback athletes had the ignominy of training at Fayetteville High School when the cinder track on campus had been removed from the stadium the previous year.

"That was pretty tough," said McDonnell. "Barnhill Arena was there, and when you look now we've come a long way, but at the time it accommodated everybody. We threw shot in there and did starts. There was a lot of activity in there and the floor was dirt."

Often the distance runners worked out on the golf course, even in the winter. On days it snowed, John would shovel the snow off the inside lane of the outdoor track or have the athletes run easy on the roads.

"I remember days when they had a snow storm, and we were sharing the road with eighteen-wheelers, and we'd have to jump off the surface and get into the snow bank," said Steve Baker. "You just did it. We didn't have the facilities."

McDonnell let none of the handicaps be used as excuses, and the results were starting to show. O'Shaughnessy became McDonnell's first Southwest Conference individual champion by winning the 1974 SWC indoor 880-yard race with a strong kick in a slow tactical affair—as well as the first Arkansas track athlete to win any Southwest Conference event since 1967.

Less than a month later, O'Shaughnessy also became John's first All-American athlete—and the first Arkansas track athlete in twenty years to earn the honor—by placing sixth in the event as a true freshman at the 1974 NCAA Indoor Championships at Cobo Hall in Detroit, Michigan. Even the distance medley relay qualified for the first time for the national championships during a meet at the Astrodome in Houston.

"I liked that track," said Aspel, who at 6 feet, 3 could use the long curves. "It was four laps for the 1,500 meter. I loved running down there and led off in 2:58 so couldn't complain about that."

At the Southwest Conference Outdoor Championships that same year, Arkansas began its gradual ascent from the cellar of the conference to finish seventh overall with

24 points—the majority of which came from the distance athletes. As was becoming tradition, the dominant Texas Longhorns scored 182 points to outpace their closest rivals by over one hundred points. Unlike in cross country, which is scored based on place with the lowest cumulative score of five runners winning, track is scored with higher points associated with higher finishes and thus more points are desirable.

In those humble days, however, for every two steps forward John took with the upstart program, there was usually a reciprocal one or two steps backward. Steve Barr was heading home to England.

"He was a nice guy," said John, "but his girlfriend came out and didn't like [Arkansas] and took him home."

After rooming with O'Shaughnessy during their freshman year, Barr had become homesick and was not fitting into the team concept.

"Steve was a good athlete," said O'Shaughnessy, "but he was one who would want to race in training, and that caused some issues on the team."

Soon after Barr left the program, junior half-miler Larry Bauldree also walked into John's office.

"He came in one day and quit to go work the oil fields in southern Arkansas," remembered John. "No degree. I told him he was making a mistake. He was good, ran on his toes, good build; and I was desperate because I had nothing in those days. He was going to make twelve or fifteen dollars an hour, which was a lot back then."

Several decades later, Bauldree would walk back into Coach McDonnell's office with his wife and children with a fresh perspective on that decision.

"They seemed like they were doing well," said John. "When they were leaving, [Larry] said to his family that he would follow them out after he talked to me. And he closed the door and said 'Coach, why did you let me quit?' And I said, 'If I remember Larry, I was on my knees begging you to stay and nothing was going to stop you.' And he said, 'Yeah, I know.' And I said to him, 'Well, you're doing all right, aren't you?' And he said, 'Yeah, but nothing like I would have done if I had my degree.'"

Finding his team depleted, John once again tapped into his English and Irish connections, signing Steve Baker from Nottingham, England, and Derek Carroll, a 4:12 miler from Dublin, Ireland.

Baker had spent the two years since completing his GCSEs (General Certificate of Secondary Education) in England working in a factory and running in his spare time—eclipsing 8:55 in the 3,000-meter steeplechase in the process. Originally offered a scholarship by the University of Houston, Baker committed to McDonnell and Arkansas when the Houston head coach Johnny Morriss asked him to spend a year at Odessa Junior College to prove himself.

Expecting to meet John McDonnell for the first time when he arrived at Tulsa International Airport on a hot August day in 1974, Baker soon learned that John had broken his arm earlier in the week wrestling a cow on the ranch he and Ellen had recently bought out in the country. If Baker had not previously been aware how rugged of an individual his new coach could be, he was now.

"One of the cows had pink eye," remembered Ellen. "[John] tried to spray her, and it was muddy, and the cow turned and went after him, and he fell and broke his wrist."

The find of the year in that recruiting class was Richard Nance, a 4:13 miler from Sepulveda, California, a community that was later renamed North Hills.

"His father was a promoter for the Beach Boys," said John. "[Richard] was a real cool looking guy and liked to wear sunglasses. He played a lot of instruments and had music in his blood. And boy was he a talent. What a flipping talent. He ran so light on his feet."

On his visit to Fayetteville, the rapport Nance developed with Niall O'Shaughnessy was instrumental in convincing him to come to Arkansas.

"He really hit it off with Niall," said John. "A lot of the guys we got came here because of Niall O'Shaughnessy. They didn't come here because of me. Niall was such a classy guy, very sincere and very studious. He did it all. He was the whole ball of wax, and a lot of guys really liked him."

The cross-country team may have entered the 1974 season with only eight runners, but among those that remained there was a real camaraderie. One of the team leaders with that young group was the lone Louisianan on the team, Randy Melancon, the red-shirt junior who appreciated the opportunity after escaping what could have been a lonely four years in Lafayette.

"Randy was a top-notch guy and very much a team builder," said O'Shaughnessy. "We had a good bunch of guys who got along and did stuff away from the track."

There were bumps in the road. Aspel remembers one minor spat when Baker purported to teach him how to play gin rummy without telling him all of the rules.

"We could all be obnoxious at times, but were like brothers," said Aspel. "We took care of each other."

Still, as many good feelings as there may have been among the athletes, there were only eight of them. McDonnell knew how thin the line was between success and failure and was not going to accept the latter under any circumstances. After early victories against Oklahoma and Oklahoma State, the Razorbacks were upset by two points by Wichita State at the Southwest Missouri meet on October 19.

The day had not been a complete disaster. Randy Melancon and Niall O'Shaughnessy were the class of the field in 8-kilometer times of 23:58 and 24:03 respectively, a massive jump for Niall especially after struggling with the 8,000 meter race during his freshman season. Led by Randy Smith, Wichita State had a strong group that would place seventeenth as a team one month later at the NCAA Championships—but none of that was relevant to Coach McDonnell when he addressed the team after the meet. The loss did not sit well.

"We thought John was going to be mad, but at first he didn't show any anger," said Aspel, "and then he called us into the locker room and gave it to us up one side and down the other. We should have had pride and should have done this and should have done that, and then he looked at one of the guys and said, 'Geez, so and so, my grandma could have run faster than you, and she's in a wheelchair!'"

Even though Aspel thought John had told the team to run steady before the race, there was no confusion in Aspel's mind what that meant when he left the locker room that afternoon.

"When he says run easy, you'd better be jogging and winning," said Aspel. "If it's a Wichita State runner, you beat him."

It was with those early teams that John first developed the gravitas and coaching style that would eventually make him the most successful coach in American collegiate sports history. He could motivate, inspire, cajole, discipline, and hold athletes accountable to the point that each of them understood whatever pain they might have been experiencing during a particularly tough part of the race was only a small discomfort compared to the unpleasantness afterwards if they gave anything less than their best.

"John was unique before psychology was even in the sport on how to motivate people individually," observed O'Shaughnessy. "It was not one size fits all. When John would talk strategy and expectations, I didn't need the shouting or the pep talks other than just a good discussion about the tactics. Others needed focus, and John would pump them up and get their adrenaline going, and he knew not to try and fit everyone into one style. That was unique about John. He really looked to the athlete and tried to understand what motivated them."

John clearly understood what made an older and more mature athlete like Steve Baker tick. When it came to handling the younger and sometimes wilder Aspel, McDonnell didn't exactly treat the Waterford boy like crystal. After a poor performance at an indoor meet in Oklahoma City, the Irishman received a tongue-lashing he will never forget.

"He had me crying and someone said, 'I can't believe he called you all of those names,'" remembered Aspel. "That wasn't what bothered me. It was the pride. I had let him down. Getting chewed out didn't bother me. You learned from it and moved on."

When the carrot didn't work for others, John also had the stick for certain occasions.

"I'd hear stories from the year before that if he thought they hadn't run fast enough, he'd take them and run a time trial right after to show them they could run faster," said Baker. "He'd scare the shit out of them."

Melancon remembers one such occasion when John took the team to the track at Fayetteville High School after a disappointing performance at a meet earlier in the day.

"John wasn't happy with how we ran and had us run a time trial to show us we could run better than we did," remembered Melancon. "And we did run better, but boy that was hard. It was a miserable day. It probably didn't make much sense, but we did it."

In a time before the proliferation of sports psychology, it was John's way of showing an athlete that they had been physically, but not mentally, ready to race. What he also did was set a tone and convey a message passed down to future Razorbacks that he lacked tolerance for anything resembling mediocrity. Such outbursts of displeasure were not uncommon to those who ran for him and always had a purpose.

"I wouldn't call it a temper," said O'Shaughnessy. "He did get excited. If he saw that you were not engaged in a race, you heard about it. When we had disappointing losses, he would let you know if he didn't feel you had performed well. It wasn't that we didn't win but that we didn't perform to our capabilities, and the athletes felt if we didn't perform, we were letting him down. It wasn't a fear at all, but we felt like we owed it to him to perform for him."

Of all the emotions John inspired in his athletes over the decades, the predominant one was trust.

"I had the utmost respect and admiration for John," said O'Shaughnessy. "If John told me to do something, I had total trust in him and his judgment, and nothing told me otherwise. Before I even knew I was a miler, he had me pegged as a miler. He had a vision for me long before I had a vision for myself."

The trust McDonnell engendered in his athletes—which some had not placed in him the previous season when they did not heed his race strategy—came from sound decision making and firm leadership. When McDonnell scolded an athlete in the middle of a cross-country race at Oklahoma only to hear the athlete shout profanities to himself as he ran into the trails, John kicked him off the team despite being only left with seven cross-country runners on the roster as a result.

"It was only two or three days later when the guys came in and said, 'We were wondering when you were going to do that,'" remembered McDonnell. "That's when I learned early in my career that you don't let things slide because everyone on the team knows it, and they lose respect for you."

Heading into the 1974 Southwest Conference Cross Country Championships, which were held at Roman Forest Country Club in Houston, the University of Texas was once again favored. The Longhorns had two sub-four-minute milers, the Canadian twins, John and Paul Craig, as well an assortment of other talent. Though the Longhorns attracted top talent to Austin, many of them did not develop.

"Texas had great talent but not discipline," said John. "If you looked on paper, it scared you to death, but they would disintegrate."

McDonnell was determined that the opportunity would not be allowed to slip away as it had the previous season. Once he had convinced his own athletes of their destiny, he soon became intent on sending a message to the other teams in the conference and the region that Arkansas's impending hegemony in cross country was imminent, inevitable, and irreversible.

"We arrived the night before, and we got out of our van after twelve hours," remembered Baker. "John had us run six to eight miles around the course, and I think the other teams looked at us like 'What are they doing?' Then the next day we sprinted out the first mile and had maybe seven of the top ten or twelve places. We made other teams come get us. We made people run our race, and we hurt like crazy, but made other people hurt too. The difference was we hurt every day in training and were used to it."

McDonnell's knack for training, which he had first discovered with horses as a young boy in Ireland, was only getting better with age. John knew how to control his runners, instructing them to "check their instruments" which he would convey with a mellow intensity when he wanted them to relax.

The race played out exactly as he expected it would.

"I had a bunch of guys who listened, and I said what happened with Barr wasn't going to happen again," vowed McDonnell. "And we set a good pace and stayed together. I told them you wear red and white, but nobody cares about the red and white yet. Texas was the standard at the time. So I said if you don't pull together, you are going to be watching them on the podium."

Although Jeff Wells of Rice took individual honors over the four-mile course, Arkansas freshman Rich Nance finished in second and was followed by Melancon, O' Shaughnessy, Baker, and Aspel in the top ten. The Razorbacks blew out Texas to finally capture the Southwest Conference cross-country title.

"That was sweet to win your first one after it had slipped away from us the year before," said John of his first conference title. "The first one of many is very important and to eventually run a streak like we did with all of the things that happened or could have happened was amazing."

From that point forward, no Arkansas team coached by McDonnell lost a conference cross-country championship ever again—a mind-boggling streak of thirty-four that did not end until November 3, 2008, exactly five months after his retirement from the sport.

Nonetheless, the emphasis and intensity both John and the athletes had put into that first conference championship led to an emotional letdown seven days later at the NCAA Championships in Bloomington, Indiana. Never a fan of flying, John had the team drive up from Arkansas. They finished in twenty-seventh place overall—a mere fifteen points ahead of last-place Syracuse.[8]

"We put so much into winning the conference meet that the national meet was an afterthought," admitted John. "It takes a while for guys to believe in themselves that they're good at the national level."

O'Shaughnessy finished fifth from last as the Razorbacks had four of the bottom twenty-five individual finishers. Nick Rose of Western Kentucky held on for the individual win this time, his team barely edged by Oregon for the national championship.

"John put so much pressure on the early meets and the Southwest Conference that by the time we got to nationals we were tired," remembered Baker. "We'd run the one-hundred-mile-plus weeks, and all of the racing caught up to us."

The racing schedule for those early Razorbacks did not become any lighter during the track season.

Part of that busy schedule included what was once the holy trinity of Midwest relay meets—the Texas Relays in Austin, the Kansas Relays in Lawrence, and the Drake Relays in Des Moines. In an era when the Razorbacks dreamed of winning one national championship in a lifetime, let alone three in a single season, winning the triple crown meant capturing all three of those major relay trophies in a single season.

Even though that was exactly what the Arkansas distance runners would eventually accomplish over the next few years, the trifecta eluded them at first. A dropped baton at the 1975 Texas Relays put Arkansas out of the money in the four-mile relay, but a few weeks later they redeemed themselves by conquering the four-mile and distance medley relays at the Kansas Relays.

The relay order varied but it usually included Melancon or Aspel leading off, followed by either Baker or Reilly. What never changed was the person who received the baton for the final leg.

"O'Shaughnessy was always the anchor," Melancon said matter-of-factly. "Our job was just to keep him close."

To win the Kansas Relays for the first time in 1975, Arkansas had to beat a strong Kansas State team led by sub-four-minute miler Jeff Schemmel and coached by the legendary DeLoss Dodds, who would later become the long-time and highly influential athletic director at the University of Texas.

"They had a good team back then, but they were sore losers," remembered McDonnell. "Most of the kids were from Kansas, and when we beat them, they wouldn't even shake our hands and talk to us. I'll always remember that same year we went to Drake, and we didn't run the four-mile relay, but Western Kentucky was anchored by [Englishman] Nick Rose, and they beat Kansas State. Rose was a nice guy with long blond hair and went over to shake hands with the Kansas State guys, and one of them refused and turned him away. Rose followed him and boy he lit them up and said, Don't ever do that crap to me!'"

Foreign athletes had long been involved in American collegiate athletics but the proliferation of international athletes into prominent NCAA programs around the country at that time had engendered a xenophobic attitude towards them from some.

"Foreigners were not very well liked back then," said McDonnell. "There were certain schools constantly writing letters [to the NCAA] trying to find ways of preventing scholarships [being given] to foreign athletes. You had some schools that would only have Americans, and boy, they would let you know about it. It didn't make you feel very welcome."

Although there were programs that historically relied on foreign athletes to fill portions of their roster, some of the athletes that arrived either from north of the border or from overseas came with their own agendas and little idea that a team concept existed in a sport that for them always had an individual focus. It was John's first major challenge in coaching, especially considering the litany of coaches over the years who failed to control the egos and individualism that often accompanied the talent they had recruited.

His first lesson on the subject came from the contrast between Washington State under John Chaplin and the University of Texas-El Paso (UTEP) under Ted Banks. Both programs had an influx of talented African athletes but with dramatically different results.

"Washington State usually fell short, and they had the horses," said John. "I remember they had the world-record holder in the 5,000 meter, 10,000 meter, and 3,000 meter steeplechase—two guys with those three records and guys right behind them—and still couldn't win it."

Meanwhile, UTEP won seventeen NCAA championships under Banks, also with outrageous talent but with the discipline to match.

"Banks did a good job coaching them," said John. "They were good, but he kept them in line and ready on the day. People say he had older athletes, but they were available to everyone, and Washington State had them and didn't do anything with them. They'd drop out or find a way to lose. People can say whatever they want, but Ted Banks was a very good coach. He got good talent and they performed. Some people get good talent, and they do nothing because they are going in all different directions."

Ultimately, like Banks, McDonnell's success in handling foreign athletes and earning their loyalty and acceptance of his concept of the team set him apart from most others coaches early in his career.

"The problem I had with the foreign athletes was they didn't care about the team," said John. "It took me a while to get that really cranked up. I think I got better and slowly got them to buy into it. As we started to get better I would say, 'Everyone wants to see Arkansas go down, and you better remember that. You may have disagreements, but you leave that crap at home. When you come to a race, they don't care, they just want to beat you.' We got that string going in conference, and they bought into it, and as we got stronger and stronger as a team, I heard guys say, 'Boy, I didn't want to be on the team that lost.'"

Amazingly enough it was one of the first American recruits to McDonnell's team who decided he'd had enough of collegiate running after one year. After finishing second at the SWC Cross Country meet his freshman year, Rich Nance could not overcome his homesickness and moved back to California. The irony was not lost on those who had travelled from farther than Los Angeles County to arrive in Fayetteville.

"We had five foreigners and three Americans and it was one of the Americans who got homesick," commented Baker wryly.

Although O'Shaughnessy had developed a close relationship with the Californian and tried to change his mind, those efforts were in vain. Nance could not be swayed. For O'Shaughnessy the loss of Nance would be one of the few disappointments in a year when both he and the Arkansas team continued their ascent at the national and international level. The remainder of the team had developed at such a rate that for the first time, the Razorbacks were able to steamroll through their entire schedule heading into the 1975 NCAA Cross Country Championships.

Arkansas beat Oklahoma and Oklahoma State with ease in two early dual meets and followed that up with solid wins at the Oklahoma State Cowboy Jamboree and Southwest Missouri Invitational, where they dispatched the defending Division II national champions, Southwest Missouri State, and their nemesis from the previous season, Wichita State.

Most impressive was the half-miler Niall O'Shaughnessy, who was translating his success during the spring track season into the fall. After struggling to maintain any form during his freshman cross country and showing encouraging progress his sophomore year, O'Shaughnessy had continued to emerge as an elite distance runner during the fall of 1975. Other than a narrow loss at the Cowboy Jamboree, Niall won every cross-country race he entered heading into the conference championship.

After Arkansas once again halved Texas's score for its second consecutive conference championship, O'Shaughnessy would lead the Razorbacks to a school-record thirteenth-place team finish at the 1975 NCAA Cross Country Championships in State College, Pennsylvania.[9]

In a race won by Craig Virgin of the University of Illinois, the University of Texas-El Paso captured the first of many team championships to come during their decade of dominance in the sport.

For his part, O'Shaughnessy finished in thirty-eighth place—a full 206 spots ahead of and over four minutes faster than at the same meet exactly 365 days earlier. Suddenly, seven months out from the 1976 Montreal Olympics, with a 1:46 800 meter under his belt and now significant cross-country success, O'Shaughnessy's inclusion on the Irish Olympic team did not seem to be a question. The real issue was which event.

"He just kept improving," said John. "The one thing I told him when he was a junior was that he needed to move up to the 1,500 meters because he was a little guy, and he'd get pushed around in the 800 meter so he said, 'Okay.' The first mile race he ever ran was in Memphis, Tennessee, against Nick Rose so of course Niall followed him and beat him in 4:04 and wasn't even breathing. He said afterwards, 'I love this race because it felt really slow' compared to the 800 meter. So I knew then, and so did he, that from that point forward he would run the 1,500 meter and mile."

It was a philosophy McDonnell consistently applied throughout his career—preparing strong half-milers to become phenomenal milers, but waiting until they were almost pregnant with anticipation and aerobic strength before letting them even attempt the event.

"I tell them when I recruit them that I'll move you eventually," said John. "They'll usually ask, 'Can I try one to see if I like it?' And I'll say, 'No. When you run it, you'll like it,' and I've had really good success with guys that way.'"

The Arkansas distance program was not only cementing its hold on Southwest Conference cross-country supremacy but starting to make an impact on the national level. Apart from O'Shaughnessy's Southwest Conference individual titles and All-American certificates in the 880 and 1,000 yards in 1974 and 1975, Melancon captured the 1975 and 1976 SWC indoor two-mile and anchored the distance medley relay to a conference title in 1975. The Louisianan followed that up by earning All-American honors in the 5,000 meter at the 1976 NCAA Outdoor Championships. Although an injury would prevent Melancon from contesting the Olympic Trials, the 4:40 miler from Lafayette had come a long way in five years.

" [Being an All-American] was real special because that was really the goal my collegiate career," said Melancon. "Washington State had three Kenyans take off and leave the rest of us. I didn't have a great kick so John had me throw in a surge with two or three laps remaining to break away from people."

That summer, John accompanied Niall O'Shaughnessy to Montreal for the 1976 Olympics, where his young charge had been selected to represent Ireland in the 1,500 meters—competing against college rival Paul Craig of Texas, who represented Canada. Only four years after the hostage crisis in Munich, these Olympics would be the first occasion since the World War II when the Summer Games were being held in North America. While the Los Angeles Olympics, which would be held only eight years later, were generally regarded as a model for how to organize the Games effectively and profitably, the Montreal Olympics were plagued by cost overruns and worker strikes in the months and years leading up to them.

Upon receiving the bid from the International Olympic Committee, the mayor of Montreal, Jean Drapeau, famously declared the Games could no more turn a financial loss than a man could have a baby. When the Olympic Stadium, which was later named the Big O (for "Olympic" as well as "Owe"), was completed and refurbished, it was nearly 1,000 percent over budget from its originally estimated cost. The retractable roof itself didn't even arrive until a decade after the Games had ended and then would not retract properly—and it leaked. Approximately $1.5 billion dollars in government dollars would be put into the white elephant long after the Games had left town. Drapeau's medical miracle had happened.

None of that stood in the way of O'Shaughnessy, who was happy to be on the grand stage and primed for a golden summer after showing astonishing range—anchoring the Arkansas 4 x 400 meter relay in 47 seconds that spring after becoming an All-American in cross country the previous fall.

"He was a kid that worked well with some speed work," said John. "I did lots of short stuff with him, 150s, 200s, 400s, and I never went past that with him. It suited him because he had great leg cadence and fast twitch fibers."

Niall showed good form in the rounds of the 1,500 meters where he and three others —Richard Wohlhuter of the United States, Ivo van Damme of Belgium, and Paul-Heinz Wellman of West Germany—separated themselves from the field on a dramatic final lap.

"It came down to a big kick, and it was just a good big man beating a good small man," remembered McDonnell. "They were bigger and more powerful, and he was just trying to get by and couldn't."

"I remember getting boxed in," reflected O'Shaughnessy. "I have a slow motion of it and watch it every so often."

There was so little separating the four men, it was difficult in the immediate aftermath to even determine who had advanced—first was 3:39.86 and fourth was 3:40.12.

"You could have thrown a blanket over them," said McDonnell. "From where I was sitting, I thought he made it through but only the top three went through, and he was fourth."

O'Shaughnessy was nudged out from advancing by two one-hundredths of a second—a wound made all the more painful when two of those three runners captured medals in the final behind the eventual champion, John Walker of New Zealand.

"I was glad to know I was in one of the tougher heats, but it was not satisfying," said O'Shaughnessy. "I felt like I could have and should have gone through to the next round."

As disappointing as it was for Niall, he had still had a brilliant season. He had attained national success and international glory for himself and for the school—the first Olympian from the University of Arkansas on the track in over a quarter of a century. His success had also brought glory to a Razorback distance program that had been moribund only five years earlier.

Still, despite the cross-country team's success in the fall and the individual successes of the distance runners in the spring, the Arkansas track program was still languishing at the bottom of the Southwest Conference. The team was no longer practicing at Fayetteville High School after a modest track facility had been built for them on campus that fall, but other aspects of the program had not improved.

Apart from one individual SWC title in the 660 yards by Lionel Adams in 1975, there had been no other nondistance-event champions or All-Americans and few points scored at the SWC meet by Razorbacks other than those coached by McDonnell. While John was originally hired to help coach the distance runners for head track coach Ed Renfrow, a major difference was beginning to emerge in the style and results of the respective coaches' event groups.

"Ed was a very knowledgeable coach and very technical but also very nice, almost too nice to some of the ragtag suckers he had on the team," remembered McDonnell. "We got on real well, but he told me a couple of times he'd rather be back coaching high school."

On one particular occasion, John remembers the head coach's frustration when some of his sprint hurdlers refused to run a cool-down mile after a practice session .

"I followed [Ed] up into Barnhill Arena to his office and asked him what had happened," remembered McDonnell. "He said, 'I told them to cool down, and they refused.' I said, 'Hey, let's go down and make them run stadiums, and next time they don't want to cool down, they'll think twice about it.' And he said, 'No, if they don't want to cool down we can't make them.' It was his personality that he didn't want confrontation with them."

In stark contrast to John McDonnell, whose intolerance for mediocrity brought some athletes to tears, Renfrow sometimes coddled athletes who needed a kick in the rear. Aspel remembers hurdler Mark Scott receiving the award for most-improved runner two years in a row as a means of encouragement when another approach might have yielded better results.

"He just didn't have the heart to tell some people to get their ass going," said Aspel. "We were going to an indoor meet at Missouri my freshman year, and I remember Coach Renfrow telling me, 'Tom you're a freshman; if you finish between sixth and seventh that would be great.' I asked someone how many are in the race and they said eight. I couldn't believe it. I guess he figured a freshman couldn't win it, but I just looked at the others and said, 'I didn't come here to get sixth or seventh.'"

Instead, Aspel set a school record in the mile of 4:06, which would be unceremoniously broken by O'Shaughnessy in the years that followed.

"(Renfrow) was trying not to finish last," said Steve Baker. "John would tell us you are going to win and hammer this thing. Renfrow would say if Texas Tech and SMU don't do well, we can finish seventh or eighth."

Though many of the sprinters Renfrow coached were from the region, the head coach did recruit one African sprinter known only as Peter via the mail. It soon became apparent the sprinter had falsified his times in order to come to the United States and was rudely greeted by the January weather in Arkansas.

"I remember going to [Peter's] room to see if everything was okay when he got here," McDonnell remembered. "He had the heat to about 90 degrees and an overcoat on and was all bundled in blankets. All you could see were his eyes, and you could barely see them."[10]

By all accounts, Renfrow was a fair and decent man who distributed a limited budget as evenly as possible and gave John enough scholarship money to field a competitive distance program.

"He was a nice guy, but I don't think the guys respected him," said Melancon.

By the summer of 1976, McDonnell was beginning to itch with the ambition of either moving up or moving on. Other programs were noticing the success he had had in a short time at Arkansas, and while he and Ellen were happy in Fayetteville, John was beginning to grow weary of splitting time between teaching high school and coaching an upstart national-level distance program on a part-time basis. He also wanted to be a head coach. When he was approached that summer by Division II powerhouse Southwest Missouri after their coach, Chuck Hunsaker, left for a job with Army, John had some thinking to do.

Always of good counsel, the assistant athletic director, Dr. Lon Farrell, advised him to be patient.

"[Southwest Missouri] had asked if I wanted the job; and it didn't pay a lot, but it was paying better," remembered John. "So I talked to Dr. Farrell and he advised me not to do it. He said, 'You've already won the conference championship here. Don't make a move like that.' I was tired of waiting, but he convinced me to stay. And I'm glad I didn't move because [Southwest Missouri] didn't have the finances."

It was that kind of sage advice that Lon Farrell had provided to John and so many others during his career as a coach and administrator in the University of Arkansas athletics department. After coaching the Bishop Miege High School football team in Kansas City to a 54-7-2 record, Farrell had been hired by Frank Broyles to join his football coaching staff in 1961. He later moved into sports administration along with Broyles and continued to serve as his indispensible right-hand man—overseeing compliance and operations. One of Farrell's responsibilities was supervising track, which he continued to oversee until his death in 1986.

"Lon was a real gentle sort of guy," remembered John. "He'd be there from seven in the morning until seven in the evening, and he did a lot of Frank's work. He did everything. If there was a flood, he'd be down there with a squeegee and his pants rolled up to his knees. He was so loyal to Frank, and I can honestly say that he and Wilson Matthews were some of the best assistants he ever had."

The more brusque and rough Matthews was a different breed from the softer Farrell, but an equally effective lieutenant in Frank Broyles's athletic department. Matthews had been the most successful high-school football coach in Arkansas history—winning ten state titles at Little Rock Central High School before Broyles hired him in 1958. Matthews later moved into administration and became an important figure in the department until his retirement in 1992. Apart from handling parking, season-ticket priorities, and general operational matters, Matthews began the first major stand-alone fundraising effort for the University of Arkansas athletics department, which later became the Razorback Foundation.

"Now they probably have ten or fifteen people doing what he was doing," said John. "He was the type of guy that if he had something to say to you, he said it. I liked him. Him and Lon came from different ends of the spectrum but ended up in the same place. Wilson would get on you in a heartbeat, but the next time you saw him he was friendly."

Early in his tenure, John remembers conducting a workout on the Saturday morning of a home Razorback football game. As he tried to park in a designated parking lot near the stadium in order to avoid carrying a large Gatorade cooler several hundred yards, he was stopped by a boy guarding the parking lot on behalf of the athletic department. John urged the boy to let him pass through with the heavy cooler but the young man wouldn't budge on the issue due to strict orders from Wilson Matthews.

"He said, 'I'm not supposed to let anyone in,'" said John. "The next Monday, Wilson calls me up to his office and says, 'McDonnell, don't you realize that when someone says no they mean no!' Oh, he chewed me out and then sat back and said, 'I just wanted to get that off my chest.' I always liked that when he had something to say to you he actually said it to your face."

Future University of Oklahoma and Dallas Cowboys head coach Barry Switzer, who played for, worked with, and coached against Wilson Matthews, once endearingly called him "a truly unique old dinosaur."[11] Another major figure within collegiate athletics who remembers playing for Wilson Matthews during his own career at Arkansas was Terry Don Phillips.

"He was one of those coaches who could just eat you alive, but he would also find something to hug you about and make you feel good," said Phillips. "He would work your rear off and was a disciplinarian. Of all of the football coaches I've been around, Wilson Matthews was absolutely the best one. He was just a tremendous coach and a tremendous man."

A few years later, McDonnell was given a car by the athletics department through a dealer in Fort Smith, who was also a booster for the athletics department. When the dealer refused to give John a four-door car he needed for his family, Wilson Matthews got involved. In charge of setting ticket priorities, Matthews usually handled things requiring confrontation immediately.

"He had this black book," remembered John, "and flipped the pages and called the dealer down in Fort Smith and said 'This is Wilson, and I have the track coach here with me. What's this about the car?' And all I can hear is 'Uh huh, uh huh, yeah,' and then all of a sudden Wilson called him a blankety-blank and started yelling, 'If you don't get John a four-door, you can get your ass in the end zone [on the ticket priority list]!' And he hung up. That's the type of guy he was. He would stand up for you."

Down the hall in Barnhill Arena, the athletics media-relations department was ably manned by Orville (Butch) Henry III, a brilliant and devoted sports-information director who gave each sport its proper due until he left in 1979 for the athletic director's position at Louisiana Tech. He later moved on to a long and successful career at the University of Arizona.

"Butch was a real knowledgeable guy," remembered John. "He loved track and understood the sport. He gave every sport a fair play and really got it out. When he left it was never the same."

The mid-1970s were a period of tremendous transition within the Arkansas athletics department as Frank Broyles continued to strengthen other sports as part of his quest for a broad-based athletics department. In 1974 Broyles's first major basketball hire as athletics director was a young coach from Buslin, Kansas, named Eddie Sutton, who had led an overachieving Creighton squad deep into the NCAA Tournament the previous season.

It was not long before Sutton was replicating that success in Fayetteville. By the 1976–77 season, he led a once-hopeless Razorbacks basketball program to a Southwest Conference title and an NCAA Tournament appearance during only his third season. Despite the success of Sutton's teams on the hard court, McDonnell remembers how down to earth and caring the basketball coach could be regarding other sports.

"He was fantastic," said McDonnell. "Later on, he and his wife would come in to Frank [Broyles] to talk about getting more publicity for the track program. He was a real advocate of getting a coach credit, no matter what the sport was, if he wins at the national level."

On the baseball diamond, Norm DeBriyn was brought on-board and gradually given the resources to lead the Arkansas baseball program to a Southwest Conference title of its own in 1979—the same season the Razorbacks, led by future Major League star Kevin McReynolds, finished as runners-up at the College World Series.

Still, it was football that ruled the roost in Fayetteville, and Broyles never lost sight of that fact. Although it had long been ordained that the man who brought college football's national-championship trophy to Fayetteville would retire from coaching following the 1976 season, a heightened degree of concern surrounded the open question of who might replace him on the sidelines.

As he had done for much of his career, Broyles kept his own counsel before ending the suspense on a cold, misty, thirty-two-degree day on December 11, 1976, when he introduced Lou Holtz as the next head football coach at the University of Arkansas.[12] Broyles had exceeded all expectations once more—convincing Holtz to resign his job as the head coach of the New York Jets in the National Football League. It was a stroke of brilliance that paid off enormously, at least in the short term.

"Lou was great for the visibility of the school, which was important," said McDonnell. "Frank used to say that Niall O'Shaughnessy was a walking billboard for the University of Arkansas. When Frank made decisions, he didn't check with anybody. He was a smart guy and thought now that he wasn't the football coach, 'How can I be important?' Most ADs were football coaches who moved up to AD, and they just took care of football and eventually the new football coach became bigger than them. Frank was different. He stayed in control by taking care of the entire athletics department."

As Frank Broyles transitioned from football coach to athletic director, he surprisingly spent most of the next several years off-campus during Razorback football games while he provided color commentary for Saturday-afternoon college football telecasts on ABC. Still, Broyles retained tremendous control over the department's operations and continued to focus on raising money for the Olympic sports.

Entering his fifth season in Fayetteville, McDonnell was still working part-time. As his team's stranglehold on Southwest Conference cross country became stronger, the Razorbacks would make another major breakthrough on the national level during the fall of 1976, led by newly minted Olympian Niall O'Shaughnessy, who was ready for great things entering his senior season.

John soon became a victim of his own success. As he weighed other coaching opportunities away from Arkansas, word had spread of his uncertainty and coaches attempted to use it against him in recruiting. The situation surrounding his future in Fayetteville led some recruits such as Greg Lautenslauger to consider other options such as Texas Tech.

"Someone told me [McDonnell] was applying for another job, and when I told him, he denied it, but those were some of the doubts," said Lautenslauger. "Looking back at the time who would have ever known he would be the best college coach of all time."

Despite missing out on Lautenslauger, John's recruiting did not miss a beat, signing two talented athletes: Mike Clark, a junior-college transfer from Allegheny College in Pennsylvania with a 4:02 mile best, and Malcolm East, an 8:07 3,000-meter high-school athlete from England with limitless athletic potential and talent . . . and ego.

"He was a talented kid but you talk about cocky. He thought he was an Olympian," remembered John. "We were up at Missouri indoors, and he was running the two-mile, and he started waving to the crowd . . . and ended up getting beat. He was a real slender blond-headed kid, but he was one of those guys who was sheltered at home and came to America and found out there were girls."

As John would discover throughout his career, when his athletes embraced all-consuming social lives in college, either their academics or athletics suffered. It was often the cause of the athlete's downfall.

Other than a shellacking at the hands of the seemingly invincible Kenyans from UTEP at a meet in Denton, Texas, in October, the Razorbacks sailed through the calendar with easy wins over Oklahoma, Oklahoma State, and Southwest Missouri in successive dual meets in September followed by a convincing win over Kansas and Wichita State at the Cowboy Jamboree in Stillwater.

"That was our breakthrough year," said John. "I think we could have run even better, but the thing that did help was we ran against El Paso early, and they kicked our ass and taught us we weren't that good."

O'Shaughnessy was on fire that fall, winning all but the meet against UTEP, and taking the 1976 Southwest Conference cross-country title in Lubbock, as Arkansas again outpaced Texas 29–71.[13]

At the regional meet, which by that point had been moved two weeks after the conference meet, McDonnell used a strategy that would lead to success at the national championships for years by resting his top runners. Neither O'Shaughnessy nor Baker competed at the regional in Georgetown, Texas, a luxury afforded by a squad deep enough to comfortably outpace Southern Methodist for the win.

The strategy paid off when O'Shaughnessy took seventh at the 1976 NCAA Cross Country Championships in Denton, Texas, a once almost unthinkable accomplishment for the boy who arrived in Fayetteville intent on being a half-miler. On a day when UTEP outpaced Oregon for the national championship, while Washington State's Henry Rono became the first freshman to capture individual cross-country title, the Razorbacks finished in tenth place, the program's best result as a team at the national meet.

"That was probably the best year of my career," said O'Shaughnessy. "I came off the Olympics in really good shape and into cross-country season with no off time. I kind of surprised myself at nationals because I never anticipated being that far up there in cross country. It was surprising and very enjoyable."

O'Shaughnessy was a runaway train. With his natural speed that John had refined and now the strength from a phenomenal cross-country season behind him, his coach understood it was only a matter of time until he uncorked one on the track.

On January 21, 1977, John invited the sports information director Butch Henry to join the team for an indoor meet at the Hearnes Center in Columbia, Missouri, in order to witness a world record attempt at 1,000 yards. O'Shaughnessy only missed the world record by 0.4 second, running the event in 2:05.5. It was only a warm-up act for the performance of a lifetime seven days later.

With few alternatives to running indoors other than way up in Champaign, Illinois, at the time, John asked the head coach of University of Missouri, Bob Teel, to make an exception to his rule of allowing teams only one meet per season at the indoor facility by allowing Arkansas to come to more than one meet at what was then one of the best collegiate indoor facilities in the United States.

"He said 'Yeah, I can fit you in,' and boy that was a relief because we were driving vans in wintertime, and there was ice on the roads," remembered McDonnell. "That was the closest indoor track (five or six hours drive) we went to and the only one really."

Upon their second trip to Columbia on January 28, 1977, O'Shaughnessy once more shattered the collegiate record books by running the second-fastest indoor mile in world history in a time of 3:55.4 on the flat 200-meter track. Of all of the NCAA champions and Olympians in the mile coached by McDonnell over the next thirty-two years, none would ever run faster while in college.

As surprised as O'Shaughnessy was to see the school record still intact years later, he appreciated the contribution of Tom Aspel and other teammates who took out the pace in 1:57.

"We were a pretty tight team, and the one thing I will say about my teammates is we all helped each other, and they went out and helped maintain and set the pace," said O'Shaughnessy. "I felt really good that night, and it was a big track and we went to do what we did."

At the Southwest Conference Indoor Championships, O'Shaughnessy once more dominated the 1,000-yard race in a conference-record time and was joined on the winner's podium by Steve Baker, who was victorious in the two-mile. Held before 9,583 fans at the Tarrant County Convention Center in Fort Worth, Texas, the meet had an electric atmosphere.[14]

"I remember that place would be full," said John. "Texas had a sprinter called Johnny Lam Jones, who was later a great pro football player, and he ran 9.9. When we flew down there with Niall earlier in the week for a press conference everybody in Texas wanted to see Lam Jones. They had six inches of snow in Dallas that weekend, and the place was still packed."

Heading into the 1977 NCAA Indoor Championships in Cobo Hall in Detroit, O'Shaughnessy appeared to have a strong opportunity to become the first Arkansas athlete to capture an individual national title in the mile. He had already won the Wannamaker Mile at the Millrose Games earlier in the year and dominated the SWC meet like few others had. Yet as he and Ray Flynn of East Tennessee battled to outsprint each other in the final lap of the race, it was Wilson Waigwa of UTEP who passed them on the inside for the win.

"Niall went to pass [Flynn] on the final lap, and Ray just elbowed him and put him right on the outside with one turn left," remembered John. "Niall came back and closed, but Waigwa from El Paso saw the two Irish guys fighting on the outside lanes and snuck up the inside lane and won it."

Niall was second in 4:01.1—ahead of Flynn—but unable to capture the individual NCAA crown that had eluded him throughout his college career.

"There were always elbows indoors but it was just a stupid move on my part," reflected O'Shaughnessy. "Going into the back straight, Ray and I got into it, and we kept going higher and higher on the boards and Wilson Waigwa ended up coming on the inside and beating us both."

After being eliminated in the preliminaries of the 800 meters, Aspel remembers seeing McDonnell get upset with both milers after the race, only one of them a Razorback but both of them Irish.

"He said you've got two Irish guys fighting it out at the end and you let a Kenyan sneak up the middle on you," remembered Aspel.

Despite the setback that afternoon, McDonnell has fond memories of those NCAA Indoor Championships held in Detroit at the Cobo Hall.

"They used to get close to 15,000 in [Cobo Hall], and it was packed," remembered John. "The AD at Michigan, Don Cannon, was a tough guy and some people hated him, but he looked at things from the point of putting butts in the seats. He dropped the 5,000 meter [which was twenty-five laps on a 200-meter indoor track] one year and put in a 3,000 meter, and people put up such a fuss. He would say 'Why have a 5,000 meter? People will just go have a coke.' That was the right thing to do because nobody wanted to watch the 5,000 meter."

As he did each year, John stepped back on the intensity after indoors to reload his athletes for the long outdoor season. The focus remained on the ultimate goal of winning the triple crown at Texas Relays, Kansas Relays, and Drake Relays that had eluded the Razorbacks to that point.

"That was a big deal back then," said McDonnell. "Those three meets were considered important when people spoke about the triple crown. The weather was never super, but that was one of the things that gave us notoriety and people started to look at us as a track power. Winning the relays and beating Kansas, Kansas State, and Stanford was special."

It was the distance medley relay featuring Tom Aspel on the 880 yard, Kerwin Washington on the 440 yard, Mike Clark on the 1,320 yard, and Niall O'Shaughnessy anchoring the mile that proved unbeatable at all three meets that spring.

The Razorbacks blasted off to a fast start at Austin, Texas, on April 1, 1977, by winning the Texas Relays distance medley relay in 9:31.81—with help from a blazing 3:55 mile split from O'Shaughnessy.

Three weeks later in Lawrence, Kansas, O'Shaughnessy once more outkicked Paul Craig of Texas and Steve Plascencia of Minnesota with a 4:01 mile to capture the distance medley relay at Kansas Relays in 9:41.6. Later, Niall outkicked Craig again along with Craig Virgin of Illinois in the four-mile relay in a meet record time of 16:19.39, which stood as a Kansas Relays record throughout McDonnell's career.

That left only Drake Relays, where a familiar script was playing out. Niall O'Shaughnessy's predatory come-from-behind act was getting old for his victims.

"A lot of the relays it would come down to O'Shaughnessy against one of the Craig brothers from Texas," said Baker. "They were so sick of getting outkicked that one time one of the Craig brothers started walking. He was actually walking, and O'Shaughnessy walked right behind him. They didn't want him to sit and outkick them but Niall wouldn't go around him. The rest of the field eventually caught up, and they had to get going again."

One week later, the Hogs won the distance medley at Drake Relays in Des Moines, Iowa, in 9:39.46 to complete the trifecta. The triple crown was finally theirs.

"Those were always enjoyable because we operated as a team, and John was such a great motivator," remembered O'Shaughnessy. "I loved the relays because of the team camaraderie."

In his final collegiate outdoor season, O'Shaughnessy entered the 1977 NCAA Outdoor Championships seeking an individual crown in the 1,500 meter. All looked well until a cold felled him in the days leading into the big race held at Champaign, Illinois.

"We stayed in a flipping lousy dormitory back then, and there was no sheet or blanket on the bed, and the air conditioner was turned on high," remembered John. "He got a sore throat and ran the first round, and the doctor told him he shouldn't run the final, but he said 'I'm running' and he did, but Steve Scott of Cal Irvine beat him."

Losing to Scott, who would later capture the silver medal in the event at the 1983 World Championships in Helsinki, was nothing to be ashamed of under any circumstances. Doing so in a time of 3:41.5 with an illness was even more remarkable. Still, it was of little solace that an incredible collegiate career for O'Shaughnessy would end with another medal—he would finish second place at the following year's NCAA indoor meet—but no individual national titles to his name.

Although the decision to forego a hotel for a dormitory, ostensibly to save money, was not John's to make since he was not the head track coach at the time, that soon changed. No sooner did the season end when after seven years as the head track coach,

Ed Renfrow resigned to finish his PhD in order to teach at the university level. Although Renfrow agreed to oversee the women's team for the following year, he ultimately opted out of college coaching entirely and moved to John Brown University in Siloam Springs.

"Deep down I think it was his idea from what he said to me because when I asked him, he said he was just tired of it," remembered John. "He was really nice to me and we had a good relationship. I think he did what he wanted, and I could see he was not enjoying it. Those were the years when everything started with the long hair, and there was a real rebellion going on with young people, and he did not want to fight it."

Although some within the Arkansas high-school coaching community favored Guy Kochel of Arkansas State for the job, Frank Broyles kept his own counsel on most decisions, including this one.

"It's hard to remember that far back but best I can remember I was still coaching, and he was coaching the cross-country team," recollected Broyles. "I was on the practice field, and the track team dressed in the visiting team locker room; and while we were practicing, I would see the cross-country team come out, and John McDonnell would be running with them, and they'd be gone for over an hour, and at the end of practice I'd see them coming back down the hill just east of the stadium, and John would still be leading them. I thought, 'Well, he ought to have the head job if he's that devoted and that committed and can get performances like that.' So we hired him, and everything he has done since will never be equaled."

Nearly a decade later, Terry Don Phillips, who by that time was the athletics director at the University of Southwestern Louisiana, went looking for a coach to replace the retiring Bob Cole. Phillips called over to Fayetteville to ask Lon Farrell what sort of exhaustive search process they went through to find a track coach as successful as John McDonnell. The response floored him.

"They had started two-a-days and Coach Farrell said [he and Broyles] were getting undressed and in the dressing room," said Phillips. "So Coach Broyles asked 'Lon what are we going to do about a track coach?' And Lon said, 'I think we need to hire John McDonnell.' And Coach Broyles thought on it and said, 'Well . . . who's he?' And Lon said, 'He is that big tall fellow we see running with the cross-country team and, keep in mind Frank, we won the Southwest Conference Cross Country Championships.' And Frank said, 'We did?' So Frank asks, 'Well, how much does he make?' And Lon said, '$2,500 a year.' So Frank asks, 'Well, how can he live on that?' Lon said, 'He teaches industrial arts at Greenland.' So Frank says, 'Lon, I think you need to try and hire him. You won't have to pay moving expenses.' You're talking about the greatest coach in the history of NCAA track and field, and that's how he was hired."

Although he was not a chief decision maker in the hiring, Butch Henry remembers an air of inevitability to McDonnell's ascension to the head coaching position.

"I remember it being a very easy and obvious decision as to him being the next head coach," said Henry. "Almost like why hadn't we done this sooner?"

McDonnell's salary increased to sixteen thousand dollars during that summer of 1977, but it would be another year before he was provided the budget to hire another full-time assistant for his program. It was a situation that Frank Broyles was adamant about changing.

"We were determined to have an all-sports program like other big schools, and we didn't have the money for a long time, but I was determined we would get the money," said Broyles. "We started our scholarship program, and that money was used to fund our spring sports. We didn't have to raise ticket prices and developed a way to do it without penalizing our longtime fans."

Never one for small talk, Broyles was succinct with John when he explained his expectations.

"You went in there only to talk business, but Frank was always fair to me," remembered John. "He said to be conservative and spend just what you need to get the program going. I asked him what he expected from me as a head coach, and he said if you finish in the top-half of the conference, he'd be happy, and if we won a national championship every fifteen years he would be happy. So I'm sure he's happy."

Using these figures, John had accumulated six hundred years of job security by the time of his retirement.

"I told Broyles we would spend money to get to the meets we needed," said John. "I wasn't going to spend money just to spend it. That's the kind of budget we had, and it went like that right until I retired."

Entering the fall of 1977, McDonnell had some holes to fill on a squad that lacked depth. Stuart Penn and Tom Aspel had graduated, while Niall O'Shaughnessy was returning with only indoor eligibility and was therefore not eligible for cross country. The talented Malcolm East was another story. John sent East to Allegheny Junior College in Pennsylvania after his academics continued to deteriorate.

"I remember John going to Malcolm's room and finding him there when he was supposed to be in class," remembered Butch Henry. "He told him he couldn't run for him if he wasn't going to take care of his academics."

Despite the losses, John signed another promising class that included Mark Anderson, a 4:10-mile, 9:00 two-mile athlete from San Antonio, Texas; Tony Conroy, a six miler and strong cross-country runner from Mountmellick, Ireland; Michael Lawther, a 3:54 1,500-meter runner from Northern Ireland (and brother of 3:56 miler Paul Lawther); Tom Camien, a 4:10 miler, 9:00 two miler from Long Island, New York; and Pat Vaughn, a 9:13 two-miler from Tulsa, Oklahoma.

Camien was the brother of John's teammate at Emporia State, John Camien. While the younger Camien possessed many of the physical attributes of his elder sibling, the self-discipline was not the same.

"The worst thing that happened to him was he ran 4:06 for the mile as a freshman and then his father died and left him the house," remembered McDonnell. "He sold the house and had a girlfriend, and you know the rest of the story. He was eating out breakfast, lunch, and dinner and spent every dime and flunked out. That romance came to an end when the money came to an end."

Camien played a prominent role on several SWC Conference championship relay teams, but is perhaps best known for making national headlines for more inglorious reasons.

"Our first national newspaper picture was at the Drake Relays," McDonnell once told Nate Allen. "Tom Camien was running the steeplechase and fell into the water jump head first. I think it made every paper."[15]

Though others such as Pat Vaughn eventually had successful Razorback careers, it was Mark Anderson who was one of the first major American recruits to commit to McDonnell and his program.

"In my wildest dreams I didn't imagine I was going to Arkansas," said Anderson. "All I knew about it was what my neighbor told me Mark Twain had said about Arkansans. Twain was not kind to them. So I got this letter, and then John called me right before the Millrose Games where O'Shaughnessy was competing. He kind of described the program and what they were doing, and it was kind of fascinating. He was a pretty interesting and convincing guy. So I walked in to tell my parents how impressed I was with him. I never told John but he had me on the first phone call."

McDonnell would need all the help he could get that season. While the team was set up for a strong indoor campaign—which O'Shaughnessy was eligible for—cross country would be a major battle. With so many freshmen on the roster, the SWC winning streak was in serious peril with a rebuilding team.

"Rice is very strong and is the team to beat," John commented to the media at the start of the 1977 cross-country season. "A lot depends on Mike Clark and Steve Baker and their leadership. If they demonstrate the leadership they are capable of, we will have a good team."[16]

Clark and Baker were the top seniors on the team, but did not share the same lifestyle habits and were very competitive with one another. McDonnell implored them to put their differences aside.

"Mike and I were pretty competitive, and John could see that he and I had it pretty bad with each other," said Baker. "It was all about he wanted to win and I wanted to win. John got onto me about not being a good teammate with Mike."

Although the freshman Mark Anderson occasionally stuck with them, Baker and Clark were the veteran mainstays of a team that won all of its early season meets. Heading into the 1977 Southwest Conference Cross Country Championships on November 7 at Connally Golf Course in Waco, Texas, McDonnell's squad had its hands full and little room for error facing an older and more mature Rice team.

After four runners from each team had even crossed the finish line, Rice held a one-point advantage, as its first runner, Mike Novelli, ran away from the field:

ARKANSAS		RICE	
2.	Mike Clark 30:13	1.	Mike Novelli 29:34
5.	Steve Baker 30:24	8.	Bert Warren 30:32
13.	Anthony Conroy 31:19	9.	Marty Froelick 30:36
17.	Pat Vaughn 31:54	18.	Larry Nettlee 31:55
———		———	
37 points		36 points	

By the time Rice's fifth runner, Mike Bonen, had crossed the finish line in twenty-seventh place, Camien and Lawther had already finished fifteen seconds earlier.

22.	Tom Camien 32:21	27.	Mike Bonen 32:36
———		———	
59 points		63 points	

It was a close call. With only a four-point edge, the Razorbacks had pulled out a squeaker. Never again would they score higher than forty points at any of the following thirty conference championships, and only once more would the margin be within ten points in John McDonnell's career. While some of John's future squads had the luxury of resting certain runners to prepare for nationals, that season the Razorbacks had thrown everything but the kitchen sink and barely come out ahead.

At the NCAA Championships in Olympia, Washington, Arkansas finished twenty-first as a team. Still, the season was gratifying from the perspective of keeping the conference-championship streak alive, despite fielding a young and vulnerable team with so many new faces.

"I was so busy that first year [as head coach] just trying to get bodies in there," remembered John.

For Steve Baker, who became the very first of many future Razorbacks to win four Southwest Conference cross-country rings, he recognized that a tradition was slowly being built that would withstand everything fate could throw at it.

"Over the years Arkansas was Arkansas because of the aura that was built up and that was all started with the 1970s group," said Baker. "By the time we brought in Frank O'Mara and Gary Taylor, they saw what being a Razorback was all about, and it was an aura."

Never a fan of redshirting athletes that are ready to compete—which involves training but not competing athletes with the intention of having them eligible for a fifth season when they are older and stronger—John began to accumulate the depth through recruiting that allowed him to avoid such a drastic rebuilding season ever again. The Razorbacks would never fail to crack the top ten at an NCAA Cross Country Championships for another thirty years—a streak as remarkable as the conference championship run itself, given how slippery the slope can be at the top of the national mountain.

Although heavy in the middle-distance events and lacking much field-event depth, John led his first track team as head coach to a third-place showing at the 1978 Southwest Conference Indoor Championships. O'Shaughnessy helped score thirty of those points by himself—winning the 1,000 yards before anchoring the 4 x 800 meter and distance medley relays to victories.[17] Unable to stop him on the track, some of the Southwest Conference coaches resorted to absurdities to disqualify him off of it.

"In the distance medley relay, the guy from Baylor was well out ahead by the time I got the baton," remembered O'Shaughnessy, who would pass the runner. "Clyde Hart [the Baylor coach] actually filed a protest because the announcer kept saying I was coming up on him and his guy kept taking off. Well, I was upset that he was telling him where I was! But old Clyde objected because the announcer should not have been doing that."

Although Hart's protest was not upheld, it was one of many accusations the longtime Baylor coach leveled against O'Shaughnessy over the years.

"He also accused me of being overage and having a false passport," said O'Shaughnessy. "He did not like me."

There was only one athlete O'Shaughnessy would not be able to outrun that season—James Munyala of UTEP—who would finish just a step ahead of him at the NCAA Indoor Championships. Between O'Shaughnessy's second-place finish in the mile and the fourth-place finish of the distance medley relay, the Hogs had finished seventeenth as a team at the NCAA Indoor Championships—also a school record.

Yet John understood that the progress had been one-dimensional in the distance events—a phenomenon explained by the fact that his duties had been confined to coaching cross-country and distance runners during his first five years in Fayetteville. Now that he was the head track coach, McDonnell looked at successful programs around the country to understand their formula for success—Ted Banks at UTEP, Bill Bowerman at Oregon, Jumbo Elliott at Villanova, and Bob Timmons at Kansas.

"They had the same types of athletes, same types of jumpers, throwers, and distance athletes," observed John. "And that's what I patterned myself after because if it was good enough for them it was good enough for me."

Although the actual training of Timmons's teams was not one he necessarily emulated, John was impressed with how the Kansas program was constructed across a variety of event areas.

"His teams had good middle-distance runners and distance runners and good field-event people and a couple of good hurdlers," observed John.

Originally McDonnell operated under more scholarships for the entire team before the NCAA limitations reduced that to 14 and, shortly thereafter, 12.6. Given that over twenty events have traditionally been contested at the NCAA Outdoor Championships and only a few less events indoors, McDonnell needed to construct his program in a manner that would also allow for success in cross country as well as track and field. Each season John would spend days poring over information and studying other programs as he decided where to allot scholarship dollars for the year ahead.

"I knew I'd always have the distance guys, but I started to think about good field-event guys," said McDonnell. "So I looked at jumpers and hurdlers. If you got a good one, they weren't like sprinters. For some reason a hurdler could always get a job done because it wasn't flat out speed, it was technique. We always had a good quarter miler, but just one so we could have a good distance medley."

The plan was sound but the only missing ingredient was a field-event coach and the funds to hire one. When the Arkansas athletic department stepped up with the budget for a full-time assistant, John went looking for the best one he could find with the limited salary he had to offer.

In a fortuitous turn of events, John received a call that spring from Mark Sutherland, a 69-foot shot putter and 210-foot discus thrower from Overland Park, Kansas, whose family owned the chain of Sutherland hardware and lumber stores in the region. After competing during his freshman season at Colorado, Sutherland opted to transfer to Arkansas because his parents owned property in the state.

"He called me and asked if I knew who he was," remembered John. "I said 'I know who you are.' He was a great athlete, about 230 pounds but solid as a rock."

After he arrived in Fayetteville, Sutherland learned that McDonnell was in the market for a field-event coach and suggested John speak with his high-school coach from Shawnee Mission South. That coach's name was Dick Booth, a native of Blue Mound, Kansas, who had sprinted during his own college career at Ottawa University (Kansas). Once in coaching, Booth quickly learned the fundamentals of throwing and jumping events and tutored several Kansas state high-school champions.

"I didn't know Dick, but I knew they had one heck of a program," remembered John.

When Sutherland prodded his high-school coach about his thoughts on Arkansas, Booth was equally unclear. The prospect of coaching in college was not on his mind.

"One evening Mark called me and asked 'Coach, what do you think about the University of Arkansas?'" said Booth. "And I told him, 'Mark, I haven't thought about it at all.'"

Although neither McDonnell nor Booth can recall who called whom first, they are in agreement that the first conversation went very well.

"We were real compatible and were talking about philosophy and expecting to win," said Booth. "I told him I coach hard and try to learn my event, and I will put any time and effort to win because that's why you compete. We found we were very philosophically compatible."

John remembers being immediately taken with the smooth-talking Kansan.

"Oh, he was a talker!" recalled John. "I couldn't get a word in edgewise. He really knew his event and told me everything they did in workouts. I thought, 'This guy is going to be one heck of a recruiter.' His record was fantastic and not just with one thrower."

After an ensuing visit to Fayetteville went well, Booth noticed a subtle change in the tone of his conversations with John.

"I noticed he started using the word 'we,' and I picked up on that like he meant me and him," said Booth. "He was real down to earth and easy to talk to on the phone. I had to struggle a bit with his accent at first, but the thing I was real comfortable with right from the start was I grew up as a coach believing you can do what you say you are going to do. We were on the same page philosophically. When I talked to him, I could sense his belief level, and he wasn't thinking we were going to win but knowing we were going to win."

As excited as Booth was about the prospects for what the two could accomplish, the position came with a four-thousand-dollar cut in pay from what he had been earning teaching and coaching at the high school.

After praying on the decision and speaking with his wife at length about the move, Dick Booth agreed to be John McDonnell's assistant coach at the University of Arkansas for the start of the 1978–79 season. The most successful coaching tandem in American collegiate sports history was thus formed and the march to a national championship began.

Climbing the Mountain (1978–1981)

"Anyone can get things done the right way, but the winners get the right things done. That's exactly what John McDonnell did."

—*Frank Broyles*

The latter part of the 1970s was a heady time for the University of Arkansas and for the state in general. Somber though the national mood may have been in the aftermath of the Vietnam War and the Iranian hostage crisis, the prospects for the state were looking up. Local retailer Walmart had become a national colossus of unprecedented size, scope, and profitability, while a young law professor at the university named William Jefferson Clinton was chosen as the state's attorney general in 1976, only two years before he was elected as the country's youngest governor at only thirty-two years of age.

In the Razorback athletics department, Frank Broyles efforts in raising the profile of the all-sports program were bearing fruit. The selection of Lou Holtz as his successor had paid early dividends as the football team won thirty of its first thirty-five football games under Holtz and captured the 1979 Southwest Conference Championships. With Eddie Sutton's and Norm DeBriyn's success with the basketball and baseball programs, the department was achieving broad-based success at the conference and national level.

For John McDonnell, life was equally sanguine. After building a house in the summer for him and Ellen to reside, John built another one across the street that they moved into in 1979. As someone who had grown up in an environment where manual labor was almost as essential to life as breathing, fixing up and improving houses during the summers had been a hobby for John up until he became a head coach.

Although Ellen worked for years with AT&T, Bell Labs, and Southwestern Bell as a secretary and service representative, she now had other responsibilities as the couple also bought a three-hundred-acre ranch in Elkins, and their first child, Heather, was born. While John continued laying the foundation for what would become the greatest dynasty in collegiate sports history, it was his loving and supportive wife who made that possible through her own sacrifices and understanding. She took care of all of the details and paperwork of the ranch and looked after the children during whatever dual meet, conference championship or recruiting trip John found himself.

"I was lucky to have a great wife," admitted John. "Ellen was great. She raised the kids and took care of everything."

Whether he was at the ranch or on the track, John would always understand the importance of having a bell cow. The bell cow led the others and set the standard for others to follow. For years, Niall O'Shaughnessy had been the bell cow of the Razorback track and cross-country program. While Niall remained in Fayetteville training professionally under John as he pursued his masters in environmental engineering, he could no longer play that role for the collegiate team.

In the spring, John recruited two young men from opposite sides of the world with the expectation they each could potentially become the new bell cows of the Arkansas track-and-field/cross-country program: Frank O'Mara from Limerick, Ireland, and Randy Stephens from Birmingham, Alabama. While the bells would ring louder for Stephens than O'Mara for a few years, eventually each of them took the standard of excellence O'Shaughnessy had set and raised it to an entirely new level.

Given the initial difficulties he had faced in attracting American talent to Arkansas, McDonnell certainly never shied away from providing opportunities for aspiring Irishmen as a means not only of helping his program but also jumpstarting the careers of young men from the junior (under nineteen years of age) to senior levels (over nineteen).

"Most of the athletes who did well on the junior level came to the United States," said John. "The weather was against them in Ireland, and they didn't support them financially enough. The kid was getting a free education and it bridged the gap between junior and international levels [of athletics] so by the time they finish college they are ready to run in an international field [at the Olympics or Worlds]."

O'Mara had won the Irish junior national championship with a personal-best time of 3:53 for 1,500 meters and had attended the same high school in Limerick as Niall O'Shaughnessy.

"Niall was a model student in all ways. So I came to Arkansas and studied engineering, which was the same thing he did," said O'Mara. "I was recruited by a bunch of schools. The only one I remember for certain was Providence. I would have preferred Villanova (because of Eamonn Coghlan), but I didn't get recruited by them. John came to my home and convinced me. He had been to speak to me before the summer and really connected with my mother. She thought she was putting her son in safe hands."

Stephens's father had been in the military and moved all over the country before settling in Birmingham, Alabama. It was there that Randy ran 1:52 for the 880 yard and 4:10 for the mile in high school. Heavily recruited all over the country from schools as far flung as Villanova and Southern California, Stephens's observations and personal connection with John sold him on Arkansas.

"The thing that stuck out was that John did everything with the kids," said Stephens. "There was so much hands-on coaching. I had an individual coach in high school, so I had gotten used to having someone there. A lot of schools I visited, the coach would hand the workouts to a graduate assistant, and they would supervise the workouts. I would talk to the guys, and they would say the coach is not really there. With John he set every workout and timed everything. Sometimes he'd even get the watches mixed up and shout a 400-meter time for the 800 meter and vice versa, but he was there every single minute of every single workout for the guys. I thought, 'This is the way I'm going.'"

John roomed the two boys from different worlds together during their freshman year. It was a combination of personalities that never led to a dull moment.

"I heard more stories about those two," laughed John. "Most of it had to do with girlfriends."

Frank still remembers Randy's disbelief when they met during the first day of cross-country camp.

"When Randy arrived at the dorm to find out he was rooming with a foreigner, he went to the track office to say he wasn't sharing with a damn foreigner," remembered O'Mara. "Coach told him to be a broad enough thinker to share with me so he came back over."

When Stephens re-entered the room, O'Mara was unpacking his meager belongings, which included a record collection with Lynyrd Skynyrd's "One More for the Road."

"With him being from Alabama, he thought I must be all right, and we got on famously from there," said O'Mara.

Stephens's belongings certainly took up a bigger portion of the room.

"He was the first non-American I had ever met," said Stephens. "He had come over with a little suitcase, whereas I brought a U-Haul with everything: televisions, stereo, and golf clubs, which for some strange reason I thought I would have time to play with but never did my whole time."

Along with freshman David Taylor, another of John's incoming freshman class, the three went everywhere together.

"We were known as the three amigos," said Stephens. "We were basically three freshman who bonded together, and we stuck that way through four years at college. We lived together for four years. We fought a little but never any huge fights. Guys had a fight, and the next day it was over with. If we were girls, we probably would have killed each other."

It did not take long for his older teammates to call the burly Alabaman by another name.

"My freshman year, in the 'Blazing Saddles' movie, a guy named Alex Karras was playing 'Mongo,' and when he walks out of the bar, his horse rides into him, and he hits the horse and knocks it out," said Stephens. "We got into a lot of altercations my freshman year just because we were so crazy. We got into a fight somewhere one night, and I got the name after that. It had nothing to do with track and not anything I'm really proud of, but John kind of adopted it to track and that's what he called me."

The signing of David Taylor was almost an accident. When John flew to Ireland that summer to watch O'Mara race the 1,500 meter at the 1978 Irish Junior Track and Field Championships, he saw a boy from Dublin outkick him. Considering Taylor had placed twenty-sixth at the junior World Cross Country Championships, only nine months after Eddie McDonagh of Dundrum Athletics Club had convinced him to begin seriously training for the sport, John thought it wise to introduce himself.

"I said 'Have you ever thought about coming to America?' And he said, 'Not really,'" remembered McDonnell. "He asked me if I would be at the senior meet in Dublin next week, which I was, so he asked me to let him think about it, and he would talk to me the next week. The next week [David] runs even better and says he'd give it a try. It was that simple."

After the meet, a group of coaches, athletes, and officials went into a nearby pub.

"In Ireland you have to go into a pub after the meet even though not everyone drank," said McDonnell. "There was a big shot-putter named Gerry McEvoy. Dave introduced me, and I asked him, 'Gerry, you wouldn't mind going to America, would you?' He thought about it and said, 'Yeah.' They were all good students. You talk about how simple recruiting was back then."

To go with the throwers who had already fallen into his lap that spring, John had corralled himself the Irish national champion in the shot put. As it turned out, McEvoy was not an individual to be messed around with and did not take guff from anyone—including a few players on the football team he verbally admonished on one occasion when they were messing around in the weight room.[1]

McEvoy roomed during his freshman year with distance runner Dave Taylor, who remembers feeling secure with the biggest man on campus as his roommate. Despite McEvoy's lack of inhibition with some, Dick Booth remembered the three-hundred pound Irish policeman being overcome with nerves and pushing his throws during his first collegiate competition.

"That first meet he is white as a ghost," remembered Booth. "I couldn't go out on the track because the ushers wouldn't let me, so I'm on the edge of the stands and say, 'Gerry, come here!' I take both hands and hit him right on the chest and say, 'What the hell is wrong with you? You look scared to death!' The red came right back into his face, and he got mad at me. He says, 'I'm not afraid of anybody!' I go back up into the stands, the guy I had been sitting beside said, 'What happened?' And I said, 'It wasn't planned but I just hit Gerry in the chest.' And he said, 'You hit Gerry in the chest?!' When the meet was over, Gerry comes over and I'm thinking, 'Uh-oh.' He says, 'I really needed that.' He's still one of our program's great fans and lives in Fort Smith.'"[2]

The field event puzzle was starting to come together in other areas as well. The missing piece was a 7 foot high-jumper from Blue Mound, Kansas, named Tony Kastl, who was being coached by Dick Booth's father but proving ever more difficult to convince to leave the state.

"He was a homebody and wanted to stay close," remembered John. "Dick was blue in the face talking to him so he said you better try. [Tony's] dad owned the gas station in [Blue Mound], and it was a hot day in Kansas when I visited. I guess the dad liked me and had the connection with Dick so [Tony] changed his mind and came to Arkansas."

If McDonnell's program was still in the embryonic stages of becoming a multidimensional national powerhouse, the foundations of that dynasty and the mentality that pervaded all event groups was starting to form. The distance runners pounding hard ten milers behind the golf course could always rest assured the field events and sprinters were lifting, jumping boxes, and running stadiums with the same intensity. Although the event groups were separated by virtue of the fact that the field-event athletes did their work in the north end zone of the Broyles Building, Randy Stephens remembers always being able to hear Coach McDonnell's voice at one end of the track during races and Coach Booth's at the other.

The training regimen had not slackened any since John's first year. Although incoming junior transfer Mark Muggleton, a 3:44 1,500-meter runner and 8:51 two-miler from Edinboro College in Pennsylvania, had already adapted to collegiate training, neither O'Mara nor Stephens had ventured much beyond thirty miles per week during their high-school days.

"There was no transition," said O'Mara. "It was immediate and precipitous. It took a few years before I finally reached a threshold in my career where I could run well in cross country and double well at the conference meet."

Those days would be well into the future. At 5 feet, 10 and 135 pounds, the transition was hard enough for O'Mara. At 6 feet, 170 pounds, Randy Stephens was simply not made of a dimension McDonnell was accustomed to dealing with in his runners.

After McDonnell had Stephens wear a wetsuit on some short runs, as much for the weight loss as the embarrassment, he also had Randy examined by a sports doctor who discovered that his body fat percentage was only 6.2. It was then that the wetsuit he had been wearing on runs was cast aside as all parties came to the realization that he was just going to be big. Although thoughts of leaving Arkansas did cross his mind when McDonnell was hard on him, there was a certain decency and caring in Coach McDonnell that made Stephens realize he always had his best interests at heart.

"He could tell me to do the most absurd things, but during my four years there I never thought he didn't love me," said Stephens. "We all thought he cared about us first as a parent and an athlete second. There was never a time when I felt he would have me do anything that wasn't for my benefit."

It was a school of hard knocks and Stephens was Coach McDonnell's prized pupil. During the first indoor race of his career at Columbia, Missouri, in January 1979, Randy Stephens remembers being on the receiving end of a lesson he would not soon forget.

"That first indoor race was interesting," remembered Stephens. "I was in the mile with about four or five Arkansas guys. I was a kicker, that's all I ever did in high school. So I sat in the top four with a couple of laps to go and Pat Vaughn was leading. With about 250 meters to go, I flew around him and ran a personal record of 4:08, which was the winning time."

Stephens headed into the change room at the Hearnes Center with his head held high.

"I was taking a shower, and all I remember was a guy coming into the shower room and screaming," said Stephens. "I was shampooing, and I was thinking some poor guy is getting yelled at. But I looked around and I was the only guy left in the room. So there's John at the door screaming, and when he was really mad, his Irish accent would come out, and you couldn't understand what he was saying. I was thinking, 'What in the world is he yelling at me for? I just ran the best race of my life!'"

After Stephens got dressed, McDonnell returned to the change room to explain his disappointment in his star freshman.

"He comes back in and sits down and has calmed down some, and the basic gist was that if I ever sit behind another guy from this school and kick him down, I'll be on my way home," said Stephens. "I'm crying. Here I am, a freshman, hundreds of miles away from home, I've just won my first race, and I'm being told I screwed up."

As the team bus pulled into a restaurant during the trip back to Fayetteville, Stephens walked towards the door only to be told by McDonnell to remain seated.

"He said, 'No, I'll get somebody to bring you something out. If you can't be part of the team, you can't eat with the team,'" remembered Stephens.

Back in the dorm room that evening, Stephens was resolved to leave Arkansas and return home until he was called into McDonnell's office the next morning.

"John explained his philosophy. We're here as a team," said Stephens. "You're not here to showboat or win individually. If you want to win, you push the pace, but you don't kick your own teammate down. It was something that stuck with me throughout college and my whole life. You're going to win with your teammates, not kick them down. It stuck with a lot of other guys too as we were all pretty impressionable. I understood where he was coming from when he explained that to me."

It was a message John was intent on conveying by whatever means necessary.

"Some guys just needed to be taught," said McDonnell. "I told them all when you put on the red and white that you are teammates, so act as teammates. If you are in a race with two Arkansas runners, don't just piggyback and win it, help out. If you are in a race with a runner from another school, run as a team against him and try to beat him."

That strong team dynamic was one of the many attributes that separated John's team of champions from the other programs filled with individual superstars running in different directions.

"The thing about John that made his teams great was he kept the team concept in an individual sport," said Terry Don Phillips, who was the assistant athletic director at Arkansas from 1988 to 1994 before moving on to become the athletic director at Oklahoma State and Clemson. "Sometimes that gets lost in track and field because you have such outstanding athletes, and they worry more about themselves. He was able to maintain and promote the team concept and mold teams together. He was so unpretentious and humble that if you were to meet him you would have no idea you were talking to the greatest coach in the history of NCAA track and field."

John's humility and team-centered philosophy was grounded in the belief that serving the team would become a means to eventually improving the individual as a person and athlete.

"I've always maintained that if you become a good team man, it makes you a good individual because you are responsible for others," said John. "That's one of the reasons you see people run good relay legs because they don't want to let the others down. I say to them that the day may come when you will run for an individual NCAA title and you won't have all of the support, but you will say, 'I'm nervous now but I will do it.' You have to translate it from a state of mind where everything is positive, and you get that from having a team and other people depending on you. Even if you are nervous, but people are depending on you to do something, you will do it and afterwards think, 'That was all right.'"

As McDonnell's training and psychological philosophy led to success with his earliest runners, he gradually attracted more and more talented runners interested in Arkansas—with more and more swollen heads accompanying them. Fundamentally, his success at managing expansive egos within the confines of a team concept had less to do with any powers of manipulation or persuasion and nearly everything to do with the athletes' belief that their personal investment in the "team" was not simply for John's own personal aggrandizement as a coach, but for their own collective benefit.

"How did he get that out of us?" O'Mara often has wondered to himself over the years. "It was because he so clearly cared. He managed as all good leaders do—to find a way to make you feel as if you were running for him and not the school. He spent so much time with us. He almost put us ahead of his family, and when someone invests that much time, you want to give them something in return."

Those athletes who arrived in Fayetteville unable or unwilling to check their individualism and personal baggage at the door rarely lasted.

"If they didn't fit in, they didn't stay very long," said Stephens. "Most of the Irish guys bonded with us, but we had one come over who did not get the team concept. The sad thing was some of them were great athletes and had great workouts but would not adapt to our way of thinking. They were going to do what was best for them and not the team. Any other program, it would have worked out, but it didn't work out with John's philosophy."

After rolling through an early season schedule, which included victories at home and at Oklahoma State, the Razorbacks once again put on a strong performance before the home crowd and media at the Razorback Golf Course for the 1978 Southwest Conference Cross Country Championships. By now a national-level program, John's harriers attracted coverage from nine daily newspapers, five television stations, and nine radio stations for the only show in town that day.[3]

On a clear, sixty-eight-degree Monday morning at the end of October, the team arrived at Razorback Golf Course set to defend their title—but not before some potentially damaging news. Mark Anderson was suffering from the effects of food poisoning and told McDonnell immediately before the start of the race that he did not know if he could go that morning. The coach calmly considered the options.

"He said, 'Okay' but asked me to take the line so the other teams wouldn't have any idea about it," said Anderson. "I ran a couple of steps and felt horrible but then somehow my stomach cleared up. It turned out to be a memorable race."

Running up Razorback Hill four times, the course physically taxed those unused to it.

"One time up that hill it takes something out of you, the second time it had your attention, the third time it really hurt, and the fourth time it killed some people," said Anderson. "I was way behind the leader with a half-mile to go and people started screaming that the leader Mike Novelli (of Rice) was dying. John actually got in my ear and said, 'If you sprint down this hill, you will beat him!' I did and I won."

Thirty minutes after he nearly didn't even start the race, Mark Anderson broke the tape and helped Arkansas halve second-place Rice's score, 29–62, for their fifth consecutive conference championship. If ever there was an example of mind over matter and McDonnell's ability to extract greatness, this was it.

At the 1978 NCAA Cross Country Championships at Yahara Hills Golf Course in Madison, Wisconsin, which was won individually by Alberto Salazar of Oregon (whose Ducks were nipped by UTEP by sixteen points for the national title), the Razorbacks finished tenth. It tied their best finish two years earlier at the national meet and was impressively accomplished on a snowy and windy, nineteen-degree day, when things had not gone well for Mark Anderson, Anthony Conroy, or Pat Vaughn. In a manner that would become characteristic of many of John's teams over the years, other Razorbacks stepped up when needed—Mark Muggleton finished fourteenth overall to earn All-American honors, while freshman David Taylor ran an impressive forty-third at his first national meet.

All of this boded well for the 1979 indoor track season, when John would lead the strongest group of distance runners he had ever had, along with a handful of throwers and jumpers, into the Tarrant County Convention Center to accomplish the once unthinkable task of winning a Southwest Conference Indoor Track and Field Championships.

"John had convinced us we could win, and we just started feeding off each other," said Stephens. "You had guys running much better than they were capable of just because they thought they could win a championship."

Although middle-distance star Todd Harbour of Baylor would prove to be unbeatable over 1,000 yards, Arkansas won every other event from the 400 meter to 3 mile.[4] Fifth-year senior Mike Clark was especially impressive in winning the mile before anchoring the distance medley and 2-mile relays to wins in meet-record times. With a few throwing points sprinkled into the mix, it was left to Tony Kastl to put the final nail into the coffin in the high jump late that afternoon. Momentum was on Arkansas's side.

"I remember standing on the curve at Fort Worth, and we were banging on the track while he was jumping," said Stephens. "I think that one event probably symbolized our whole season. There were a lot of good jumpers in that conference, so when he won, I remember us jumping on the mat going absolutely crazy. It was big for the whole team to be there watching and be a part of that."

The winning performance by the muscular freshman from Blue Mound, Kansas was all the more remarkable for the fact that he increased his personal best by two inches (7 feet, 2 inches) and had beaten NCAA champion and future Olympian Jimmy Howard of Texas A&M. It was a remarkable individual and collective breakthrough.

With only the relays remaining, McDonnell sat back and counted the points to his satisfaction. Arkansas had scored 91 points—20 more than second-place Houston—and the 1979 Southwest Conference Indoor Championship was in the bag.

"That was the first time where we were becoming a complete team," said McDonnell. "The nucleus had formed, and all of the pieces were starting to fall into place."

Upon the team's return to campus, sports-information director Butch Henry had the honor of carrying that first Southwest Conference track-and-field trophy into Barnhill Arena only to be greeted by an astonished Frank Broyles.

"We came back and Frank asked me, 'Is that a real Southwest Conference Championships trophy?'" remembered Henry. "I told him, 'Yes Coach, it's just like the football one except it has a person running instead of kicking a football.' He was really pleased by that."

Despite the good feelings from the team championship, all was not right in the Razorback track world. O'Mara was floundering. The miles and the races were overwhelming him. As one listless performance followed another on the track, it was the freshman's failure to place in the top-six of the 880-yard run at the Southwest Conference meet—and 2:06 time—that prompted John to deliver a message to O'Mara before the finals of the 4 x 800 meter relay that he would never forget.

"I was struggling getting used to the training and all of the racing all of the time," said O'Mara. "I had run poorly, and he clearly expected more from me after he had given me a full scholarship. So he came up to me before the 4 x 800 meter relay and looked around to see if anyone else could overhear what he was about to say. There were loads of people milling around as he leaned in and said quietly, 'O'Mara, if you don't hand that stick off in first place, you can row your butt home to Ireland.'"

Running as the second leg, O'Mara received the baton 15 meters out of first place and handed it off with a 50-meter lead.

"It scared the life out of me," remembered O'Mara. "That was exactly what I needed to hear. That was what was so good about John. He knew what pressure points to push on. He didn't have one way of doing things. He could be gentle and encouraging or he could be rough and intimidating if required."

Frank split 1:52 on the tiny indoor track—a full fourteen seconds faster than earlier in the day.

"That was the same day, so his conditioning really improved," commented John wryly.

On many occasions, John's effectiveness in eliciting responses from his athletes were not necessarily derived from the message itself, but the calm, credible manner in which it was delivered.

"John could make it sound believable too," said Stephens. "Looking back it seems ridiculous, but he made it sound believable."

Notwithstanding the fire lit under him that afternoon by Coach McDonnell, O'Mara's struggles would continue for another full year as he gradually adapted to the increased training and racing and learned how to translate some of his fantastic workouts into race performances. Although Niall O'Shaughnessy helped him on the academic end of things, that was about all that was going well. After that first season, Frank wondered whether there would ever be a light at the end of the tunnel.

"We didn't think Frank was coming back after his freshman year," admitted Stephens. "He had a hard time adjusting to American life and being away from home that long. We knew he had talent from what he had run in high school and workouts. He never had a problem with workouts, just with racing."

After an unimpressive outdoor season, O'Mara returned to Limerick for some rest, relaxation, and home cooking and ran 3:45 for 1,500 meter—a seven-second personal best.

"I would take a little break and not race as much [at home]," said O'Mara. "I got home and had two or three weeks off. Then I only raced once every few weeks and didn't double and got my legs back under me. I'd done a lot of good training in the States, which eventually paid dividends."

Although the triumph at the indoor conference meet on a cold February afternoon in Fort Worth would prove to be the high point of the season for the team, Mark Muggleton became the first 2-mile All-American in Razorback history at the NCAA Indoor Championships and won the 3 mile at the outdoor conference championship in 13:58.

Starting with Niall O'Shaughnessy, John was starting to put together a group of former Arkansas athletes intent on challenging the world's best. One year before the 1980 Moscow Olympics, O'Shaughnessy remained among the elite milers on the circuit—losing to mile world-record-holder Filbert Bayi of Tanzania on the tiny 160-meter track at Madison Square Garden in New York only after some questionable race tactics.

"He would have beaten him," insisted John. "Niall took the lead with one lap to go and Bayi reacted to him and tried to pass him on the backstretch and couldn't. So heading into the final turn Niall was on the inside and Bayi grabbed him and almost turned Niall around and used him to catapult past. I was so pissed I went down to protest. The meet director was Ray Lump who I knew from the New York Athletics Club. I said to him, 'Christ, aren't you going to disqualify him?' And he whispered to me, 'John, we never disqualify anyone here.' And I thought to myself, 'Well, that's nice to know now.'"

It was during that season when O'Shaughnessy developed the beginnings of a dry-heaving condition that would prove increasing difficult to shake the following year.

McDonnell soon realized that although his team had won the indoor conference championship largely on the backs of a two-headed monster in the distance and field events, the glaring lack of depth in the sprint events would hold them back outdoors until it was addressed. Although the sprints rarely become point of emphasis for the Razorbacks, especially since the 12.6 scholarship cap imposed by the NCAA on all Division I programs made it difficult to invest everywhere, John knew the area could use improvement.

That spring he visited a talented high-school quarter-miler named Stanley Redwine at his home in Richardson, Texas, just outside of Dallas. With Redwine's 48.1 400-meter, McDonnell hoped to convince him and his mother that track offered a better future than football.

"He came down and sat with my mother and explained to us his expectations," remembered Redwine. "I was sold, and my mother was sold about going there. She wanted to make sure it was a good place, but also she wanted to feel comfortable about who I was going to be around. John was a great leader and the team showed potential."

The signing of Redwine dramatically changed the Razorbacks' relay options. While McDonnell continued to recruit the best athletes available and studied which athletes were graduating from other teams so he could focus his efforts on the athletes that could score the most points, it would be a long time before McDonnell would invest heavily in short sprinters.

That didn't stop him from trying to find them where he could on campus. When McDonnell learned that running back Gary Anderson had signed with the Razorback football team, he approached football coach Lou Holtz about letting the future NFL Pro Bowl running back sprint during the spring.

"I went in to talk with him," said John. "[Lou] would let him out only if I could guarantee that he wouldn't pull a hamstring. I said, 'Lou, I'm not God.' So he said, 'Okay,' and let him out anyway."

Entering the 1979 cross-country season, John brought in three distance athletes, Brian McDonald, a 1:52 half-miler from Dublin, Ireland, as well as Steve Delano, a 9:15 two-miler from Winfield, Kansas, and Greg Avery, a 9:03 two-miler from Ponca City, Oklahoma, whose careers at Arkansas would never get on track for various reasons. With most of the team returning, McDonnell looked to his senior All-American, Mark Muggleton, to provide much of the leadership.

"Muggs is a super leader," John told the media on October 3, 1979. "He is our team captain. For a guy that has won All-America in cross country and track, I just can't say enough about him. He has a good head and helps everyone stay together as a team. I'm real pleased with the work he has done."[5]

That discipline to keep his athletes singing from the same hymn book would be needed at the Southwest Conference Cross Country Championships at Texas National Golf Course in Willis, Texas. The conditions were as miserable as they had been six years earlier—84 degree heat, 99 percent humidity—and McDonnell wisely advised his athletes to lay back and run as a pack. This time they listened and Arkansas cruised to its sixth consecutive conference championship ahead of second-place Rice.

Nonetheless, the race had taken its toll. Mark Anderson was felled by kidney infection and would not return to form for the remainder of the cross-country season. After the Hogs impressed at the regional meet by running aggressively and setting a school record with a low of 26 points, they entered the national championship ranked fifth in the country by *Harrier Magazine*. For the first time in his career, McDonnell had each of them in the frame of mind to challenge for the crown.

"We'll get out fast and hope to hang on," McDonnell told the media on November 7, 1979. "That's the way we ran last week, so it will be nothing new to them. All the runners at the NCAA meet are qualified, and everything is close and packed so that if you fall back you've had it."[6]

On a cool November afternoon at Lehigh University in Bethlehem, Pennsylvania, the Razorbacks may have flown too close to the sun and were burnt by the brightest lights of collegiate distance running, UTEP and Oregon, who once again battled to within ten points of each other. As they had the previous season, the Kenyans from El Paso emerged victorious.

The Razorbacks had not completely melted down. They again placed tenth as a team. Sophomore Dave Taylor moved up from the previous season to place thirty-first but not much else had gone to plan.[7]

Never one to take the shortcut to success, McDonnell's path to the pinnacle of the sport would not happen overnight as he slowly and systematically improved the Razorbacks depth of talent and learned from every small mistake and setback he faced. While a national championship was likely not in the offing that afternoon no matter how well things had gone, it did mark the first time the Razorbacks entered a national championship contemplating the possibility of trying to win it all.

As the clock ticked into 1980, McDonnell was hard at work examining what had gone well and what could be done better. He began to understand that less racing could lead to better racing.

"He used to have you run four events at the indoor conference as a test to see if you were up for it," said O'Mara. "One year I ran heats of the mile in the morning, 4 x 800 meter relay in the afternoon, and the mile final and distance medley relay in the evening. Four races in one day. Niall O'Shaughnessy did it. They all did. John got wiser. Bob Timmons seemed to have one method that he stuck with over the years. It worked for some but not for others. John was always adapting. He used to ask kids when they came back from the summer what they had done, and he'd modify things. He was very smart in that regard."

While his athletes would continue to make legendary sacrifices for the team at conference track championships until the day he retired, McDonnell became more and more adept at picking his spots. During cross country, he continued to race Oklahoma State and Oklahoma early in the cross-country season but instead of racing hard week after week, he began spacing out the schedule.

"We had an agreement we would run three weeks in a row," remembered Dick Weis, who coached twenty-five years at Oklahoma State. "After a while we got smart and separated it a week between. So we would do an 8k at Jamboree and then a few weeks later do a 10k at the old Razorback Golf Course."

The other evolution in McDonnell's thinking was the gradual trimming down of volume and subsequent increase of intensity from how his earliest teams had trained in the early 1970s.

"It changed all over," said John. "I felt like some of the miles we were doing were junk miles, so I decided to cut back the miles and increase the quality. For the most part we maxed out at eighty-five miles per week but picked up the tempo and did quality miles rather than quantity. We also stayed off the roads where the impact on their bodies was greater and ran on the cross-country course, the trails, and the golf course."

Although some Razorbacks would continue over the years to maintain one-hundred-plus-mile weeks, John lowered the mileage norm for his team with the purpose of training optimization. He also became more adept at managing talented personalities and the diverse ideas they brought with them to training.

"Each person is an individual, and you've got to find out what makes him tick and the best way to do that is to talk and ask him," said McDonnell. "Once he spills his guts to you, give him feedback where 90 percent of what you are telling him is what he already thinks and make him think the rest of it is his idea. I never ran down a high-school coach. I would always say to a kid, 'Look, you had a great coach and did fantastic things, and we're going to take it right from there and tweak it and do this and do that.' So they are still riding on the confidence of their high-school coach. If you tell them to cut that person off because they're in college now, a lot of times you lose that kid."

His program never encouraged shortcuts—McDonnell always preached the road to success was paved with hard work—an idea that came from the environment he was raised in. Eight years into his coaching career however, John McDonnell had begun to understand that his athletes could arrive at a better destination by training smarter rather than longer and gradually became more adept than anyone at handling the nuances of sports psychology.

Nonetheless, even he realized he was far from a professional psychologist. Eighteen months after Frank O'Mara arrived in Fayetteville, the future world champion had not yet found a consistent racing form. Neither John nor Frank's teammates could understand why. His workouts were at an Olympic level, but his races were barely competitive in the Southwest Conference. While O'Mara did run a leg on the distance medley relay that finished fourth at the 1980 NCAA Indoor Championships, something was holding him back from racing well with any semblance of consistency or predictability.

His roommate Randy Stephens, who captured three individual conference titles on the track during his first twenty months at Arkansas, grew especially frustrated with O'Mara. One spring afternoon in windy Norman, Oklahoma, during the 1,500 meter, Stephens literally willed Frank O'Mara to perform better.

"Randy was an extraordinary personality and a big character. He was roundly determined that I was to become a good athlete," said O'Mara. "My sophomore year when I still wasn't running well, he was in the infield running up and down shouting at me, running as quick as I was on the grass."

From the other side of the track, McDonnell watched the spectacle in astonishment.

"Randy was running along sideways screaming at him, and I think Frank was saying something back to shut up," remembered McDonnell.

When Stephens approached a steeplechase barrier lying in the infield, he leapt it sideways with ease as he continued to berate his roommate.

"I yelled at Randy to watch for that steeple barrier," said McDonnell. "He paid no attention to it and leapt over it and never even looked at it. He was that coordinated. He stayed with Frank all of the way into the top of the turn, which you couldn't do today without being disqualified. Frank finished second, and I was going over there to talk with him but Randy was already there chewing his head off and Frank was telling him to get away. They ended up being very good friends."

McDonnell tried everything with O'Mara. Stephens certainly couldn't be expected to shadow him every race. It would have had a diminishing effect in any case—just as there was not enough wood in the world to construct all the rowboats McDonnell would have needed to send O'Mara back home in if he tried to cajole him in the same manner week after week. O'Mara's body was adapting to the mileage and racing, yet there was something else standing in the way of O'Mara's ability to compete well on a consistent basis.

For a man who would become more successful than any collegiate coach at controlling and understanding the factors affecting athletic success, it suddenly dawned on John McDonnell that spring that no amount of hollering, motivation, or alterations to training would change a psychological trait in Frank O'Mara that was beyond his control or understanding.

"It was unlocking it," said John. "Frank was one of those guys in fantastic shape who always found a way to screw it up. He had some great races, but then he'd run a bad one. Either it was a tactical mistake or he felt bad. Everything that could go wrong did."

Eventually McDonnell suggested O'Mara see Dr. John Childers, a sports psychologist in Springdale. O'Mara unhesitatingly agreed.

"Something between the ears wasn't getting through," said John. "I was worried he might take it the wrong way, but he said it would be a good idea. He wanted to be a really good athlete. If a guy wants to explore every avenue, you can correct things like that. If you have psychological problems, it's like a cramp, you treat it. If you have a hamstring problem, wouldn't you go to a trainer? It's the same thing. If there is a problem whether it is psychological or physical, take care of it. Once Frank got his head straight and nothing changed in training, he really started popping off some times."

The process was gradual—Frank anchored the four-mile relay to a Drake Relays record 16:14 that spring—but would slowly improve over the years. Although John would experience success using sports psychologists for athletes throughout his career, rarely was the transformation as dramatic as it would be for Frank O'Mara, and sometimes it wasn't effective at all with other athletes.

"It really helped with particular kids, but not everyone bought into it," said John. "The doctor told me with a couple of them, 'Coach, you're wasting your money. He's locked tighter than Fort Knox.'"

At the 1980 Southwest Conference Outdoor Championships, it was a foregone conclusion Todd Harbour of Baylor, who would eventually run 3:50 for the mile, was going to win the 1,500 meter convincingly. Ever the opportunist, John seized on a chance to boost O'Mara's confidence and score more points for the team by entering him in the 3,000-meter steeplechase. It was not an idea O'Mara was enthralled with at first.

"I wasn't going to beat Harbour, but John thought I could win the steeplechase because of my leg speed, even though I'd never run one," said O'Mara. "Of course I whined and moaned about it. I came over here to be as fast as possible, so we agreed I wouldn't practice for it. I didn't want to waste valuable mile-training time running 70 second laps over barriers when I could be running 55s on the flat."

O'Mara won his steeplechase debut with ease against a weak field. His time of 8:53 was accomplished without a water jump—one small detail the Southwest Conference coaches had overlooked when they grudgingly voted to introduce the event into the meet.

"Frank got in there and high-jumped every barrier," remembered John. "I said don't fall or hit your knee. He won but of course nobody else was any good."

The steeplechase gambit was not the only success story. Mark Anderson won the 10,000 meter at the conference meet only a month after beating the Kenyans from UTEP in a school and Texas Relays meet record time of 13:41.28 over 5,000 meters in the crushing Austin heat. The distance wins, combined with a rare Southwest Conference victory by the 4 x 400 meter relay catapulted the Razorbacks to fourth at the Southwest Conference Outdoor Championship—their highest finish at the meet in nearly forty years.

McDonnell had been nothing if not methodical in improving the Arkansas program across the board. He started by winning the Southwest Conference Cross Country Championships in 1974 and capturing it six years in a row. After bringing Dick Booth on board, the combination of field-event athletes and distance runners led to an indoor conference crown in 1979. Now, in order to capture the outdoor conference championship, John understood the Razorbacks had to diversify into other areas.

Frank Broyles continued to provide increased support for John's program, giving him the ability to travel to better meets and hire more assistant coaches. That summer John brought in Doug Williamson as a graduate-assistant coach. A half-miler from Lockport, Illinois, and graduate of Northwestern University, Williamson would assist John for a few years before taking over the sprinters on a full-time basis from Daryl (Doc) King in 1983. Williamson's presence in recruiting would be felt immediately.

The other major factor in building a national-championship program occurred in the fall of 1980 when the athletic department built an indoor tennis and track facility. Although the original blueprint envisioned a tennis-only facility, John approached the tennis coach, Tom Pucci, who had raised a majority of the funds, to ask whether track and field was welcome to be included in the final design of the project.

"I owe that to Tom Pucci," admitted McDonnell. "He was instrumental in building that facility, so I asked him if we could put a track around it and he said 'Sure, we can probably get more money.'"

When McDonnell approached the assistant athletic director overseeing his sport, Dr. Lon Farrell, for that very purpose, he was pointed towards the door of Frank Broyles. The athletic director was only too happy to oblige. Despite his natural preoccupation with ensuring the viability of the prominent football and basketball programs, Broyles had been paying close attention to what McDonnell was beginning to accomplish with his track and cross-country program and liked what he was seeing.

"In analyzing coaches you look at their ability to motivate and improve," said Broyles. "Anyone can get the fundamentals right. There's an old saying that anyone can get things done the right way, but the winners get the right things done. That's exactly what John McDonnell did."

No longer would the tennis team need to travel to the tennis club at some unearthly hour to hit balls. Likewise, the days when John McDonnell would shovel snow off the track before a workout or Dick Booth would compete for time and space in Barnhill Arena or the Broyles Center were over.

"John's success obviously had a big influence on that, but he convinced me that we needed an indoor facility," remembered Broyles. "We had profits, so we built the indoor facility for tennis and track."

There was certainly nothing elaborate about the facility—to call it barebones would be an understatement. It barely had enough room for a flat 200-meter track and John would often have his runners practice on it using lane six because of the tight radius. The metal building came with holes for ventilation and Arabian heat lamps at the ceiling. Since it was generally used in the winter, the ventilation holes had to be shut, while the ceiling heat lamps were not as effective as they could be given the fact that heat travels upwards.

Lacking space to put spectator seating around the track, the bleachers were placed on the tennis courts during track meets, partially blocking the spectator's view of the track's curve. Although the building was not suitable for hosting a conference championship or even a major invitational meet, it nonetheless served a valuable purpose for the Razorback track team during those early years.

Freed from the vagaries of weather and facility limitations, McDonnell finally had a facility to build a top-flight multidimensional track program. With a plywood runway for the pole vault, a high-jump pit in one corner and a shot put ring in the other, the field-event athletes were protected from the elements and never had to miss a day of training. Likewise the sprint and distance runners could now train at a higher intensity during the early winter, which would allow them to catch teams unprepared at the indoor conference and national championships. Beyond the practical elements related to training, the indoor facility also helped recruiting in the Southwest Conference, where all the Texas schools enjoyed warmer weather.

With confidence regarding the future of the program and a bottomless reservoir of energy, each of the coaches on McDonnell's staff hit the recruiting trail hard. It was not out of the ordinary for McDonnell to make phone calls until as late as ten or eleven at night—depending on the time zone he was trying to call. No longer having to plea with prospective student athletes to consider his program, McDonnell became increasingly selective as he sought distance athletes not necessarily with the most mileage underneath them but with the leg speed and work ethic needed to compete for a national championship.

"I tried to check with the coaches," said John. "What was his character like? Would he be a dependable person or a hell-raiser? Then not so much was he a winner but was he tough? Was he somebody who could be counted on to consistently run well? I didn't want a guy who would win once and blow up other times. I made a living with guys who were consistently second or third because they knew how to lose. The kids who won all of the time came in and thought they owned the world. Then the world came out from under them when they lost, and you couldn't get through to them."

For years Niall O'Shaughnessy was John McDonnell's best recruiter, either as an athlete on the team or as an assistant coach training and competing professionally while he pursued his master's degree. There was a certain dignity and likeability to Niall as a person that accentuated the obvious athletic and academic success he had experienced throughout his career at the University of Arkansas.

That career was winding down. Geopolitics had not helped matters—in reaction to the Soviet invasion of Afghanistan the United States and other Western countries boycotted the 1980 Moscow Olympics—but was not a deciding factor since Ireland was still sending a team. Although he was selected to compete for Ireland, Niall increasingly experienced dry-heaving episodes during and after workouts and races that made sustained success at the international level problematic.

"He had just married a girl and came in one morning and said, 'I made a decision, and I know you're very persuasive, but you're not going to change my mind,'" remembered John. "The next thing he said was, 'I'm not going to the Olympics.' I asked him why. He said now that he was living and working in America, he was going to go along with the boycott. I said to him, 'I'm not going to change your mind, but I think it's a mistake because you don't mix politics and sport.' The whole boycott was a mistake. Still, he had been having problems at the end of races from dry heaving, and I think it was probably a good idea that he retired. Niall had always been very practical. When I first recruited him (as a seventeen-year-old), he told me that school was his first priority, and then when he graduated, his job would be most important."

The practical side of John also saw that Niall O'Shaughnessy's magnificent career as one of the finest milers in the world had run its course.

"John was supportive of whatever decision I made," said O'Shaughnessy. "We all knew I was winding down anyway, so he supported it. Had I not been to the 1976 Olympics, I don't know if I would have made that decision [to retire in 1980]."

Frank O'Mara, always close to O'Shaughnessy over the years, remembers his decision to retire from the sport in light of the limited opportunities for postcollegiate runners at the time.

"He was a very pragmatic individual, and there were more options for him in the business world where he has been very successful," said O'Mara. "My postcollegiate career came along during the last few years of amateurism. I remember in the early days of my professional career when I waited for our fee outside the meet director's door at one in the morning to my last few years when it was outright start fees. I was there from pure amateurism to pure professionalism. I don't think for Niall's era, unless you were totally into your running, that it was a difficult decision with regards to your career."

The other things that had changed from O'Shaughnessy's era were John McDonnell's constantly shifting goals for his athletes and his team. Arkansas once aspired to win the triple crown of relay events at Texas, Kansas, and Drake Relays and accomplished that in short order. McDonnell had now set a new goal—to become the first Southwest Conference program in history to win cross-country, indoor, and outdoor track conference championships during the same academic year.

"That was one of the really good jobs that John did was getting people to believe that we were capable of doing great things," said O'Mara. "At one point if John had said that we were going to win the NCAA title, we would have laughed at him. His own athletes would have thought it was preposterous. What he was really good at was setting goals. He'd set original goals and then stretch them again. So the thing he really wanted us to do as a team first was win the Southwest Conference Triple Crown."

That effort got off to a solid start in the fall of 1980. While Muggleton had graduated, others such as Mark Anderson, Dave Taylor, Frank O'Mara, and Pat Vaughn had developed significantly from the previous fall. At an early dual meet with Oklahoma State, Arkansas athletes and alumni took up fourteen of the top fifteen spots in the race.

Compounding the misery Arkansas was about to inflict on other teams was the recruiting class John brought in that fall—starting with Dave Barney, a 14:03, 5,000-meter junior-college transfer from Arizona; Randy Reina, a 14:34, 5,000-meter transfer from Texas A&I-Kingsville; and Scott Jones, a 9:12 2-miler from Houston who would break 14:00 for 5,000 meters within eighteen months.

Across the pond, McDonnell's touch was only becoming more adept. He landed Tommy Moloney, a 1:48 half-miler from Thurles, Ireland, and an Irish transfer from East Tennessee State named Ronnie Carroll, who had grown up only miles from Dave Taylor in Dublin. Carroll would sit out that first season in Fayetteville after transferring, but the team was loaded without him. As McDonnell's athletes continued to develop rapidly, and he consistently attracted increasingly talented distance athletes from across America and overseas, Arkansas's cross-country lineup had become breathtaking in its depth and breadth.

The only thing that needed upgrading was the schedule. The dual meets with Oklahoma and Oklahoma State were becoming lopsided, and the Razorbacks weren't being tested prior to the national championships. Their cross-country record heading into the NCAA Championships over the previous seven seasons was 48-1, with the one humbling loss coming in 1976 to eventual NCAA champions, UTEP.

Rather than cruise through another season before a rude awakening at nationals, John opted to head to Madison, Wisconsin, on October 18, 1980, for a triangular meet at Odana Hills Golf Course. The meet wasn't lacking competition and featured number-two ranked Penn State, coached by Harry Groves, number-eleven ranked Wisconsin, coached by Dan McClimon, and perennial powerhouse Iowa State, led by Bill Bergan. Although Alan Shcarsu of Penn State won in 23:33, and Penn State led at three miles, the Hogs pulled out the win on the backs of late surges by Mark Anderson, Dave Barney, and Pat Vaughn.

"The victory at Madison showed our guys that they can run with anybody in the country," McDonnell told the media after the meet. "They didn't get over excited, they were just ready to run. This will really help us at nationals. We know now that we can run with the top teams in the country."[8]

After cruising to their seventh consecutive Southwest Conference cross-country championship at Los Rios Country Club in Plano, Texas, where Mark Anderson out-sprinted Geoffrey Koech of Texas to capture the individual title, John rested Anderson at the regional meet where the Hogs easily qualified. The victory did not come without cost—Pat Vaughn injured his lower back and Dave Barney strained a hamstring—taking wind out of their sails heading into the 1980 NCAA Championships in Wichita, Kansas.

"If we can finish in the top three I'll be very pleased," John told the media on November 17, 1980. "We can't fold up camp because of a few injuries. I hope Barney and Vaughn can be ready. With this one big race left, Pat may try to go it. He wants to run awfully bad."[9]

Any suspense about the outcome of the team championship was ended when Suleiman Nyambui, Mathews Motshwarateu, and James Rotich of UTEP appeared as three of the first four finishers across the finish line and the Miners scored 58 points to outdistance their competition by nearly one hundred.

"No team was going to beat UTEP," said Anderson. "That was probably the best team ever."

For a Razorback team that had every reason to fold, they put forth their most gutsy effort yet. Both injured runners gutted it out and competed, while Mark Anderson and Dave Taylor finished sixth and eighth individually.[10] The battle for second was much closer—Arkansas edged Penn State by one point, 152–153. It was a breakthrough of epic proportions.

"This is the biggest moment of my career at Arkansas," John told the media moments after the meet ended. "We had a good team last year but got blown away. These guys never doubted they could get in the top three this year."[11]

For the senior Mark Anderson, one of the earliest elite American athletes to show faith in John McDonnell's program, he deflected all of the success to the coach.

"John is a hard worker and a fantastic motivator," Anderson said to the media. "He's not set in his ways. He knows when he makes mistakes and he corrects them. That's the sign of a great coach."[12]

As generations of Razorback runners would learn, only those actually competing were able to cover as much ground during a cross-country race as John McDonnell—and the margin wasn't very much.

"If it was a six mile race he would run four or five of it," remembers Dave Taylor. "He used to get from one end of the course to the other. You definitely picked it up when you saw him."

McDonnell elicited a response from his athletes based on their trust and confidence in him.

"There was something about him," said Mark Anderson. "He was a great motivator, and there was an air of confidence that you believed in this guy. He was very much a father figure and was intense to put it mildly. I think he was able to better focus that intensity later in his career, but you always believed he had your best interests at heart. At the track he was all business, but away from the track he taught you family values and how to live a good life. He could relate very well to his athletes and recruited well."

The results in cross country spoke for themselves. With the indoor season around the corner the Razorbacks recruited more strong jumpers and the program was coming together. Although the coaching staff possessed similar energy and corresponding training philosophies, there were a few occasions when McDonnell had to control the enthusiasm of his staff and advise his assistant coaches that sometimes less was more.

"Dick (Booth) sometimes thought if they were still standing at the end of a workout, that they could have done more," said McDonnell. "So there were times he kept pushing and pushing, and I had to tell him to ease up or some of these guys were going to get hurt."

Since they now had the ability to compete in smaller meets at home, McDonnell was able to add higher-profile meets to the indoor schedule to qualify more individuals for the national championships.

Heading into the 1981 Southwest Conference Indoor Track Championships, John realized that his team would not be able to run away from the conference as they had during cross country. Every point would matter. In what would become an Arkansas tradition, he went through every event before the meet, explaining his expectations for how many points each individual should be expected to score.

The level of talent in the Southwest Conference was staggering. Todd Harbour of Baylor ran the mile and distance medley relay—winning each in meet-record times. In the 880-yard run, even a school record by Randy Stephens was no match for Sammy Koskei of Southern Methodist, who had run 1:42 over 800 meters. The University of Houston was led by the legendary Carl Lewis, who won the long jump in a staggering 27 feet, 10 inches and doubled back to win the 60-yard dash in a meet record time of 6.06.

The Razorbacks won fewer events than they had in 1979, but still scored more points, 96, against arguably better competition and came out with their second SWC Indoor Conference trophy.[13] What McDonnell had done in the meantime was to widen the depth of talent in each of the event areas. It was a winning formula for fifteen consecutive indoor track conference championships starting in 1981.

At the NCAA meet, the Razorbacks continued to progress. Stanley Redwine placed second in the 600 yards while Pat Vaughn placed third in the 3 mile at the NCAAs. For the good of the team, Randy Stephens left his comfort zone in the 1,000 yards by anchoring as the mile leg on the distance medley relay—a decision driven by his 3:59 mile at a Last Chance Meet in Illinois two weeks earlier.

"We probably should have finished first or second but John decided I should run the anchor leg rather than the 800 or 1,200," remembered Stephens. "I was probably a better miler but didn't realize it."

Stephens was handed the baton at the 1981 NCAA indoor meet with a lead, but unable to hang onto it when Sydney Maree of Villanova, the future 1,500-meter world-record holder, went flying by him.

Stephens faded to fifth, good enough for the Razorbacks to end the meet with six All-American certificates and a school record eleventh-place NCAA finish, but the Alabaman wasn't satisfied by any of it.

"That was probably one of the lowest moments," recalled Stephens of losing the lead. "We all got around and talked about making sure that never happened again."

When Stephens returned to the NCAA Indoor Championships the following year, he would be determined not to let anybody beat him. In the meantime, the Hogs had little time to regroup over spring break before facing another stiff challenge at the 1981 Texas Relays.

McDonnell had long been preparing Stanley Redwine for the 800 meter but his debut was a matter of timing. Needing an anchor for the 4 x 800 meter relay he finally seized the moment by running Redwine in the first 800 meter of his career head-to-head against the defending NCAA champion from Southern Methodist, Sammy Koskei. It was an audacious decision but one both coach and athlete faced with utmost confidence.

"Coach McDonnell said we could win it, and I was naïve to believe everything he said," remembered Redwine. "If he said I could do something, I went out there to do it. It was a situation where those other guys were going to give me a lead and that was kind of the goal because Koskei ended up running 1:46 that day. I had a lead but I knew I wouldn't give that lead up. (Koskei) came and caught me and ran on me and attempted to pass me but I said 'No way,' and we ended up winning the relay. That was probably the beginning of my 800-meter career. Coach McDonnell had said prior to that I could be a good 400-meter runner or a great 800-meter runner. So he boosted my ego, and I thought I could do anything."

That same season, McDonnell made the decision to switch from attending Drake Relays in favor of attending the prestigious Penn Relays in Philadelphia.

"There was no dissatisfaction with Drake," said McDonnell. "It's just that I had always wanted to go to Penn, and they had been calling for the previous few years. Then they offered airfare and rooms, and that was a pretty good deal. We had bused to Drake."

While Arkansas had climbed its way to the top of the ladder at Drake, Penn was a different matter. Villanova was the alpha dog of the meet, winners of fifteen consecutive distance medley relays. If the Razorbacks were still sick from the Wildcats' victory at NCAAs, they would be even more nauseous from the humble pie Sydney Maree was dishing out at Penn. They definitely weren't in Des Moines anymore.

"The next year we ran 7:13 for the 4 x 800 meter relay and got fourth," remembered Stephens. "It was unbelievable. Stanley ran 1:46, I ran 1:46, and we had a 1:48 from Tom Moloney, and Paul Jones ran a 1:50 leg. Other teams were just going 7:12 every time."

On the first trip to Philadelphia, John shuffled the lineup by anchoring Frank O'Mara on the end of a 4 x 1,500 meter relay, but the order made no difference so long as Villanova had Sydney Maree anchoring.

"The guys were all saying how we were going to beat Villanova," remembered O'Mara. "I was a bit more nervous about it. Being from Europe I was aware of Maree and how good he was from having watched him on the circuit. Randy Stephens said he was going to go out there and do a number on them, so he committed the absolutely mortal sin of kicking their third leg down to give me, his teammate and roommate, a one-meter lead. Sydney Maree sat on me for four laps and tried to pass me with 450 meters to go. We ran a 51.2 final lap, and he got me by about two hundredths of a second. The picture of Sydney made *Sports Illustrated*. He was a complete rock star."

O'Mara won the steeplechase at the Southwest Conference Championships again—this time with a water jump—and qualified for the 1981 NCAA Outdoor Track Championships at Baton Rouge, Louisiana, in the 1,500 meter. Once there, he ran a lifetime best of 3:39 but finished ninth in a loaded field.

"The winning time was 3:35 and there were eight guys in front of me," remembered O'Mara. "It was an absolute who's who of superstar runners there, but I felt like I was on the verge."

The entire program was on the verge of something special. At those very same national championships, Randy Stephens finished third in the 800 meter and Scott Lofquist placed fifth in the discus, only weeks after breaking the Southwest Conference record. Collectively, the contributions allowed the Razorbacks to crack the top-twenty-five for the first time at the NCAA Outdoor Championships.

It was another successful year and step in the right direction for the team. While they had fallen short of McDonnell's goal of winning an unprecedented triple crown of the Southwest Conference Championships, that too was on the horizon. Arkansas had become an elite program in the Southwest Conference and was now arguably among the strongest across the three seasons—cross country, indoor and, outdoor—at the national level. To make another leap forward, the coaching staff realized they needed someone who could leap forward better than just about anyone else. They needed a Mike Conley.

John as a toddler with his older sisters in County Mayo, 1940. *Photo courtesy of John McDonnell.*

The entire McDonnell family in mid-1940s. John is sitting on his father's knee. *Photo courtesy of John McDonnell.*

The family homestead in
Woodville, Crossmolina,
County Mayo, Ireland. *Photo
courtesy of John McDonnell.*

John after a race in
Crossmolina in 1958. *Photo
courtesy of John McDonnell.*

Within a few years, he and Michael *(right)* had won more than their share of trophies from athletics. *Photo courtesy of John McDonnell.*

Paddy and John working in the hay, 1969. *Photo courtesy of John McDonnell.*

John and Ellen in
New Jersey, 1966.
*Photo courtesy of
John McDonnell.*

Off the west coast of Ireland in
1969—"It was love at first sight."
Photo courtesy of John McDonnell.

John with his teammates on the University of Southwestern Louisiana 1967 Gulf States Cross Country Conference Championship—*(from left)* John, Ronald Landry, Tom Hopkins, Robert Gilbert, Richard Henderson, James Romero, and head coach Bob Cole. *Photo courtesy of John McDonnell.*

John accepting an award as the outstanding athlete of the 1967 Southwestern Relays after beating Jim Ryun in the two-mile. *Photo courtesy of John McDonnell.*

John beat mile world-record holder Jim Ryun in the two-mile at Southwestern Relays in April 1967—"He was pretty much a legend at USL after that." *Photo courtesy of John McDonnell*

84

Frank Broyles brought long-lasting changes to the Arkansas athletics department after his hire as head football coach in 1957. *Photo courtesy of University of Arkansas Athletics Media Relations.*

Niall O'Shaughnessy signed with Arkansas in 1973 as a 1:55 800-meter runner with no intentions of ever competing in the mile—three years later he was running in the Olympics for Ireland in the 1500 meter. *Photo courtesy of University of Arkansas Athletics Media Relations.*

The 1974 Southwest Conference cross-country champions after their first title at Roman Forest Golf Course in Houston—the start of a thirty-four-year conference winning streak that was the longest in Division I history: *(from back left)* Tom Aspel, Derek Carroll, John, Steve Baker, Stu Penn and *(from front left)* Rich Nance, Niall O'Shaughnessy, Randy Melacon, Derek O'Reilly. *Photo by Steve Baker.*

The winners of the first Southwest Conference 4 x 400 meter relay title, in 1980: *(from left)* John, Stanley Redwine, Pat Mitchell, Kerwin Washington, Charles Freeman, and assistant coach Doc King. *Photo courtesy of University of Arkansas Athletics Media Relations.*

5

Reaching the Pinnacle (1981–1984)

"Coach, Bui is gone. Arkansas will win now."

—Suleiman Nyambui of UTEP

When Doug Williamson was dispatched to watch a high-school track meet in Chicago during the spring of 1981, he could hardly have expected what he was about to find. The Razorbacks were already heavily recruiting one of the hottest high-school sprinters in the country, Wallace Spearmon, who was competing that day. It was not until the triple jump when destiny hit the rookie assistant right over the head.

"Williamson called me around twelve at night," remembered McDonnell, "and said 'Coach, I found myself a steal! A kid here broke the national record in the triple jump and went over 24 feet in the long jump, and he's dating Wallace Spearmon's sister!' So I said bring him for a visit immediately."

The kid's name was Mike Conley, a 6 feet, 1 inch, 173-pound jumper and sprinter from Luther South High School in Chicago, Illinois. He was as talented physically as he was magnetic personally, possessing a natural ability but lacking technique. His fouls were as breathtaking as his marks and his unorthodox form belied the speed he had over the short sprints. Both his demeanor and attitude transcended any athlete in Arkansas track and field history before or since.

"He was to Arkansas what Michael Jordan was to the Chicago Bulls," said John unequivocally. "He was so absolutely special. He was a great athlete but an even better person. He was talented, smart, and could do exactly what he wanted to do when he wanted to do it."

Doug Williamson had already been working hard on Spearmon but wasted no time following up on Conley and did not hesitate playing the two off each other in an effort to land both. It was not until Conley's visit to Fayetteville that he first met John McDonnell. He remembers being impressed by John but also struggling to understand him.

"I remember I could barely understand what he was saying," laughed Conley. "It was the first time I had been around someone with an accent. When I spoke to the athletes they really trusted John and knew that he had their best interests at heart. John was able to motivate them in his own way."

Not only did the Arkansas coaching staff need to fend off other track programs, who did not take long to notice Conley's national triple-jump record, but also other sports given his prowess in basketball. On Conley's official visit, McDonnell arranged a meeting with Arkansas basketball coach, Eddie Sutton. One of Conley's good friends and future NBA star, Darrell Walker, was playing for the Razorbacks at the time.

"We had him in to speak with Eddie Sutton," remembered McDonnell.

Sutton would give Conley an opportunity to play basketball in the winter and jump in the spring—the only caveat being that he would have to walk-on. So that's exactly what the future Olympic champion did during his first semester in Arkansas. He paid his own way.

"After my first semester Coach Sutton called me into his office and told me I probably wouldn't play for him for a couple of years," remembered Conley. "He heard I had a chance to be really special in track and make the Olympic team. So he encouraged me to go that route and pursue my dreams in track. After that first semester I left basketball."

The connection with Wallace Spearmon, whose sister Conley took to the prom, only made things easier. Although Spearmon would be plagued with injuries during his first two seasons in Fayetteville, his addition made an impact for its own reasons. At 10.38 (100 meters) and 20.89 (200 meters), he was the first legitimate, national-level short sprinter signed by John McDonnell. In a Razorback track and field program that would often be tilted towards distance and jumps, John now had as complete a team as possible with potential All-Americans in every event area.

"People were saying Arkansas doesn't have sprinters because we were traditionally known for distance runners," said Stanley Redwine, who was still an athlete at the time. "Wallace Spearmon brought totally different expectations in the sprint area, and now Arkansas was good at everything."

The coaching staff was hardly finished in its recruiting binge. Against great odds, both the football and track programs landed Marty Kobza, a 6 foot, 4, 222-pound thrower from Schuyler, Nebraska, who had thrown 66 feet, 11 inches in the shot put and did just about everything else very well, including football. Not only did the football coaches have to navigate the tremendous pressure on Kobza to stay in state and play ball for the Cornhuskers—the governor of Nebraska wrote Kobza a personal letter—but also had to agree to allow the talented multisport athlete to compete in track each spring.

After a year and a half, when the football coaches attempted to renege on their commitment of allowing Kobza to compete in both sports, Kobza quit football for track. It was at that point when Frank Broyles made the football program honor its original commitment and maintain the All-American thrower on a football scholarship for the remainder of his career.

McDonnell was also busy augmenting a distance group that appeared to be only a few athletes away from winning a national championship. Aside from gaining Ronnie Carroll's eligibility and signing Randy Reina's brother, Roland, who was a 9:00 2-miler from San Antonio, John once again worked his connections back home. In a major coup, he landed Paul Donovan and Anthony Leonard, who had run 8:07 and 8:09 respectively for 3,000 meters as secondary-school athletes in Ireland.

A former rugby and soccer player, Donovan was a tough but lightly trained runner from Galway, Ireland, whose phone was literally ringing off the hook during the spring of 1981.

"I had bloody well everyone calling the house," remembered Donovan. "I went through a phase when every evening a coach was ringing and I started zoning out. I had no idea who they were, and I had no interest. It helped that John was from Ireland, but more than that it helped that Frank O'Mara was there. I had Eammon Coghlan calling me from Villanova and John Treacy from Providence. So Frank called me from Arkansas and mainly because we were close in age, and I would run against him and just the type of athlete he was, I was more interested."

Since McDonnell did not personally visit Donovan, the factor that ultimately tipped the scales in Arkansas's favor was their track and field focus—and its media guide.

"All of the propaganda started coming through the mail," remembered Donovan. "Maybe other people liked getting this stuff, but I couldn't give a damn. My whole thing with Providence was they were this little cross-country school, and I wasn't as interested in cross country. I remember when the propaganda rolled in there was lovely picture of Providence, Rhode Island, in the wintertime and then the Arkansas magazine had bright sunshine and a cheerleader on the front. That was the one! I was going to go to a track school with nice, warm weather and good-looking girls! I made up my mind right there, but really it was down to Frank [O'Mara] and the track emphasis."

With such an array of talent coming to Fayetteville in the throws, sprints, jumps, and distance events, the foundation for sustained across-the-board excellence had been laid in that recruiting class.

"Boy, that was a good class," said John. "The thing about it is they were all successful. Sometimes you have a class, and they all turn good or they all turn bad like the plague. That was an awesome class."

Still, as talented and tough Donovan may have been, he hardly came over as a finished product. When he had trained, it was only thirty miles per week. The summer before he arrived in Fayetteville, he didn't run much and arrived at camp badly out of shape.

"Paul had ice water in his veins when it came to racing, but was a little laid back in training, so I had to keep after him so he would do what he needed," said John. "I don't know if he liked it or not."

"I thought I had died and gone to hell," admitted Donovan. "First off it was so hot, over 100 degrees every day. On that Razorback golf course, we'd run a mile and a half loop and I'd stop on every loop to rehydrate. I was terribly unfit going over there and did 64 miles that first week, then 75 miles the second and mid-80s by the third; and by that point, I was legless and said I'd never survive. I will never survive."

After opening up with a respectable performance at Southwest Missouri State on September 19, Donovan would not race the remainder of the 1981 season.

"I was so heavy legged that I didn't do well and was the tenth or eleventh man on the team. I know John must have been disappointed," said Donovan. "I remember doing mile repeats on Razorback Golf Course and pulling myself up that hill by my arms. John was being a real sport; and in fairness, concessions were being made, but my first year as a Razorback was kind of a washout."

There were some strong personalities on that 1981 cross-country team, not the least of which was the transfer from East Tennessee State, Ronnie Carroll, whose presence was not for everyone.

"He was a good runner, but always a handful," said McDonnell.

Originally from Dublin, Carroll's Irish passport was about all he had in common with some of his teammates from the Emerald Isle.

"He was from Dublin and the rest of us were country boys, and there was a big difference in personalities," said Donovan. "The Dubliners looked down upon the rest of us. They had a different outlook. I had my ups and downs with Ronnie as everyone would. Good, bad or indifferent, he just wasn't of the same mold or same kind of character as the rest of us."

It wasn't that Carroll didn't hit it off with others on the team—he and Taylor had grown up nearby one another and became good friends. He was simply a large personality on a team filled with them.

"Ronnie was a guy who told it like it is," said Dave Taylor, "but was a fun guy to banter with."

Harold Smith, a 9:30 2-mile runner from Connecticut, who didn't believe he was good enough to run at Arkansas, also remembers another side to Carroll he came to know during their calculus class.

"Ronnie was not exactly God's gift to mathematics and was having a hard time grabbing a hold of some of the concepts," said Smith. "I would go over to the dorm and help him with the exercises and getting ready for tests. I was doing it because I liked the guy and he was a fellow runner, but I was not on the team at the time. One day he asked me about my running. I told him I was doing eighty miles a week and ran a 15:30 5k on the roads. He said 'Harold, you need to be running with us,' and said he'd talk to John."

Smith appreciated Carroll for who he was and what he did for him.

"He was raised on the streets and had to fight for everything he had," said Smith. "He was a rough customer and rubbed a lot of people the wrong way. He was brash, he was grandioso and was definitely an alpha male, which some of the guys didn't like. I loved him. He was a powerful personality. When he walked into the room, it was something else."

The cross-country team became a melting pot not only of talent and personalities working together for a common goal, but also one with different accents and cultures mixed together.

"Some of the Irish lingo got incorporated into our vocabulary," remembered Smith. "Ronnie Carroll was always 'Bleeding this,' and Bleeding that.' The other guys were more plain. It was hard back in those days not to adapt an Irish tint to your speaking. You'd be at the grocery store checking out and the girl beside you would be like, 'Are you from Ireland?' I'd have to say, 'No, sorry, Connecticut.' We spoke everyday with those guys so it was like being in little Ireland."

As the season got underway, O'Mara was fitter than ever before. Just as Niall O'Shaughnessy's initial cross-country success forecast virtuoso track performances,

Frank O'Mara had turned a corner, winning the first two meets at Southwest Missouri and Oklahoma State by breaking 24:00 for 8 kilometers.

"That was when I was finally getting to where I was strong," said O'Mara. "When I was in Ireland, I had done such little mileage. I would go to the track and do speed-work and no long runs, so it took me a while to get strong and that was the first confirmation of it."

O'Mara was gaining confidence in the sport and demonstrating ever more moxie outside of it. When he and his teammates cut through the Broyles Complex after a run, football coach Lou Holtz became irate as he was preparing his team to face Texas that weekend.[1]

"Hey! Hey!" Holtz yelled at the runners. "Don't you know this is Texas week?"

"What's the blooming fuss about?" O'Mara replied. "Texas never gives us any trouble."

The Razorbacks were not just winning meets, but throttling opponents with a race plan that often saw them run aggressively in the early miles. After a perfect score at Southwest Missouri, they set a meet record for low points at Oklahoma State two weeks later. Even a case of indigestion at the Southwest Conference Cross Country Championships did not stand in the way of their eighth consecutive title.

"We went down to College Station on Saturday for a Monday meet, which was probably a mistake, but you learn as you go along," said John. "So we had Sunday to sit around and watch football and eat. They had this breakfast buffet, and I remember Tommy Moloney and those guys who were really good just ate and ate and ate. I should have stopped them, but they went back for seconds and thirds. The next day their bodies were so tired from digesting all of that food."

The race was a disaster—salvaged only by the incredible depth of the team at the time. Although Arkansas halved Texas 32–67 to win, the score was closer than John had expected with Moloney, Carroll, O'Mara, and Leonard almost all finishing outside of the top-ten. The only Razorback runner who had a stellar day was Dave Barney, who unexpectedly won the individual SWC title in 29:58.

"Barney was a vegetarian," said John. "All of those guys were dying, but he kept coming through."

Heading into the 1981 NCAA Cross Country Championships, with their eating indiscretions behind them, John had reason to be confident of his team's chance to dethrone UTEP, winners of five of the previous six NCAA cross-country championships, and the previous three in a row. Arkansas was deeper, fitter, and more mature than the previous year's second-place team. Meanwhile, the rumor making the rounds was that UTEP's captain and fifteen-time NCAA champion, Suleiman Nyambui, was banged up.

"We thought we had a shot going in because Nyambui was hurt and hadn't run," said McDonnell. "Well, we went down there and, Lord Almighty, they scored 17 points. We ran well with Taylor in the top ten but scored over a hundred points. They scored 17. That was the greatest cross-country team I've ever seen. They were out of this world."

Incredibly, UTEP was only two points from a perfect score on a day when the two-mile world record holder, Nyambui, was injured and crossed the finish line in seventh place as their fourth man. It was a remarkable performance—not only for the obvious talent of El Paso's Kenyans, but also the discipline instilled in them by their coach, Ted Banks, and the utter selflessness of Nyambui, the ultimate team man. While Kenyan athletes had long competed in the NCAA, never before had a collegiate cross-country team done so with that level of depth, discipline, pedigree, and maturity.

"That was before the age limit went in for eligibility," remembered O'Mara. "They had one of the best track and cross-country teams ever with a bunch of names you would look out for on the circuit. To us they were almost unreachable. It was a little intimidating because there were so many good athletes."

If the 1981 NCAA Cross Country Championships represented the zenith for UTEP's domination of collegiate running, it also marked the beginning of the end. While assistant coach Ted McLaughlin had already departed for Southern Methodist, an even greater blow was delivered only weeks after the season ended. Longtime head coach Ted Banks, winning coach of seventeen NCAA championship teams, resigned.

"Banks called me and asked if I would be interested," remembered John. "They had a downtown track club supporting it really well, which was legal then, but it would have been a lateral move."

John and Ellen were comfortable in Fayetteville with a two-year old daughter and another house under construction. Plus, it made little sense to follow Banks at El Paso when Arkansas was on the cusp of greatness. While UTEP's run of national championships had not yet ended, the dynasty Banks had built would slowly crumble as each of his athletes eventually graduated and the culture he instilled went away.

The Razorbacks were only getting better as each season passed. As autumn turned to winter, the time was nigh for John's milers to unleash all of their newfound strength on the track.

"We didn't have a lot of pure cross-country runners," said O'Mara. "We just wanted a good base, which was what John had always preached. Get a good base and you'll run fast in the track season."

Things could not have been going better for the field-event athletes. While the throwers fed off each other, the burgeoning jumps group was developing just the dynamic needed to reach the next level. It soon became apparent that Conley's natural talent was matched by his confidence, positivity, and prodigious work ethic. He would need every bit of it as he often found himself a test subject in the laboratory that was Dick Booth's practice.

"Dick did a great job to make me the kind of athlete I became regardless of what kind of crazy stuff he thought of that day," said Conley. "And believe me, he thought of some crazy stuff."

It did not take long for Conley to pick up on the technical changes he needed to make.

"I went to a small high school with a cinder track and had never really been coached, so I didn't have a technique to speak of when I came to Arkansas," said Conley. "We did a lot of plyos and things that sprinters do now. We were doing it for jumping, but it also made me more explosive for sprinting, so I had an advantage when sprinters weren't doing those exercises."

It was during those early days when Mike Conley became more than just a great jumper.

"I remember we were doing 100s, and that day I drank a ton of chocolate milk and I wasn't feeling too good," said Conley. "There I am throwing up on the fence after I think the workout is over, and Dick comes up to me, after I had run faster than anyone else and says, 'So and so didn't make it in time, and I need the guys to run another one, and they can't do it unless everyone does it.' I learned very early on that being an example is important."

Conley certainly was not lacking for work ethic, but was also pushed every day by a walk-on triple jumper from Neosho, Missouri, named Terry Osborne. Although not blessed with Conley's athleticism, speed, or explosiveness, Osborne developed into a fifty-foot triple jumper, one of many foot soldiers in the Arkansas program over the years. He also had a burning desire and work ethic that set a standard his more talented teammate needed to meet every day at practice. Although the two were different in many ways, Conley and Osborne complemented one another.

"It was interesting because we were from opposite worlds, and I think that attracted us together," said Conley. "He was a great influence on me. He worked so hard in practice, and it rubbed off."

It was during the indoor season when another walk-on emerged from the woodwork. Harold Smith, who had been permitted by McDonnell to train with the Razorbacks, ran 9:08 for the 2-mile as an unattached runner at the University of Oklahoma—a mere two seconds behind Paul Donovan.

"The next weekend I had an Arkansas uniform, and it was like my dream come true," said Smith. "I had an immense amount of pride wearing that uniform. One of the things John came to realize was that these walk-ons are worth looking at because sometimes you'll run into someone who wants to improve and is more motivated than some of the scholarship athletes."

After opening up the 1982 indoor season at Columbia, Missouri, John took Randy Stephens and Stanley Redwine up to the Millrose Games two weeks later at Madison Square Gardens in New York, where he knew the meet director, Howard Schmirtz, from his New York days.

"He was a really nice guy but tough," remembered John. "He didn't mind telling you your kid couldn't get into the race. If you crossed him and didn't show up, it didn't matter who it was, they never ran there again. I'd always bring our good kids starting with O'Shaughnessy."

Although Stephens distinguished himself in the 800 meter to place fourth, it was Stanley Redwine who won the 500 yard in a spectacular time of 56.2.

Heading into the Southwest Conference Indoor Track Championships in Fort Worth, the question was no longer whether Arkansas would win but by how much. Mike Conley became the first Arkansas jumper to win a conference title in the long jump. In the triple jump he finished second to the indoor world record holder from Southern Methodist, Keith Connor, who set a meet record in the process. The Razorbacks ran away with the meet to outpace Texas, 129–87.

It was but a warm-up for the 1982 NCAA Indoor Championships two weeks later in Detroit where they had qualified a record thirteen athletes. Never before had an Arkansas team placed in the top ten at an indoor national championship, nor had John ever coached an individual national champion.

UTEP ran away with the national title once more. Nyambui won two events by himself—the mile and two-mile—and the Miners won the meet with 67 points—more than double that of the next team.

Still, Arkansas had scored well across the board in a variety of events[2]—including a fourth place from the distance medley relay of Paul Jones, Paul Donovan, Tom Moloney, and "Special" Ed Williams—the latter of whom claimed a warm spot of his own in Razorback lore by once famously launching into his kick during an indoor 800 meter when the final lap gun was mistakenly fired with two laps remaining.[3]

Heading into the 1,000-yard run, Arkansas could have left the facility right then with a top-ten finish and plenty of reason to hold their heads high—but there was unfinished business.

"John wanted an NCAA champion. Even though Niall ran faster than all of us, he was up against all of the good Kenyans," said Stephens. "I happened to get into a year when there were good runners but not great runners."

Before the race, John told Randy not to allow the race to dawdle and to make the decisive move.

"It went out slow, so when I told Randy to go, he just took it," remembered John. "He just blew them away and won by ten steps or more."

There was no doubt in Randy's mind when he went that nobody would catch him.

"I was third until two laps to go, and when I took off, I knew nobody would kick me down," said Stephens. "John had run us in so many indoor meets that I was confident if I got the lead with a lap to go."

Not only had McDonnell now coached his first national champion, but the Razorbacks had placed second as a team at nationals. John could not have been more ecstatic after the meet was over.

"I am so proud of our guys," John told the media after the meet. "Finishing second behind a great team like UTEP is like winning the championship. We faced a lot of adversity and still ran a great meet."[4]

Stephens remembered enjoying a well-deserved week off at spring break in California.

"David [Taylor], Frank [O'Mara], and I went out to Santa Monica for a week, so it left a good taste in our mouths," said Stephens. "Saint Paddy's day was on the Tuesday, and we had one big glass of rum before coming back to Arkansas ready for outdoors."

It was back to business. From the very beginning of the outdoor season, McDonnell had the team focused on the unprecedented "Quest for the Triple Crown"—the goal of becoming the first Southwest Conference team to win cross-country, indoor, and outdoor conference championships the same season.

Things got off to a good start at Texas Relays a few weeks later when the 4 x 800 meter relay team successfully defended its title, and the sprint medley relay of Conley, Spearmon, Redwine, and Stephens—a high-powered combination if ever there was one—also won with ease.

There was however a thin line between success and failure as the team would find out that very season at the Southwest Conference and NCAA Championships. On the final exchange of the sprint medley, Stephens and Redwine attempted a blind exchange and botched it. They were disqualified, raising Coach McDonnell's blood pressure a few levels that afternoon.

"Randy and I felt bad because we were leaders and had let the team down," said Redwine. "Coach McDonnell was really disappointed and told us never to attempt the blind exchange again."

At Penn Relays, the Razorback emergence continued. Mike Conley won the long jump and triple jump—setting a school record in 53 feet, 7 inches—and Scott Lofquist won the battle of the shot put underneath the stadium. Still, they had some lessons to learn. Not even consecutive 1:46 splits from Stephens and Redwine could secure a win, or even a podium finish, in the ever-elusive 4 x 800 meter relay. The Hogs were fourth in 7:13.47, with Villanova continuing its domination of the event and the meet.

"It was a fantastic performance for Mike Conley to come in and win both the triple and long jump," McDonnell told the Philadelphia media on April 24, 1982. "We ran against some great teams in the 3,200 meter relay. It had the four best times ever run in collegiate competition, and we were fourth. It was the best overall team performance we've ever had."[5]

The stage was thus set for the Razorbacks to accomplish what had never been done before in the history of the Southwest Conference—the triple crown of conference championships. By early May, there were enough major injuries to key athletes to cast real doubt on whether winning the outdoor championship would be attainable in 1982.

Stanley Redwine had hurt himself badly enough that he was unable to compete, while Frank O'Mara and Mark Anderson had both seen their seasons come to an end due to iliotibial (IT) band syndrome. The University of Houston looked like the team to beat and would be running at their home track at Robertson Stadium and in their element in the punishing Texas heat. Somebody on Arkansas needed to step up, and everybody in the locker room knew it.

"John used to sit us down before each meet and tell us what points we needed," said Stephens. "He hammered into us that if we did this we would achieve something that no one else could ever duplicate. We may win triple crowns every year, but nobody could duplicate this. We wanted to be the first team to do it."

Although his practice of going through each event and stating points he expected from each athlete and event was habit, John could sense when the team needed a moment of levity to break the tension.

"Javelin, 10 points," John deadpanned.

Within a few moments, the mood lightened considerably when the Arkansas athletes realized nobody on their team threw the javelin.

In the first event of the meet, Mike Conley got things off on the right foot by winning the long jump in 26 feet, 7 inches. He certainly didn't make things easy for himself, fouling all but one of his attempts.

"I was real nervous," admitted Conley to the media afterwards. "I have never been this nervous before. The pressure was on me for the first time. Coach told me I had to score 10 points."[6]

Although Conley would not face the same pressure in the triple jump, where nobody was expecting him to beat Keith Connor of SMU, the seemingly overmatched and inexperienced Conley would give the world record holder from England all he could handle.

"I wanted to beat him so bad," said Conley. "I know he was a lot older and more seasoned in the triple jump. The thing that made it worse was he ended up being a really good friend and nice guy, but boy I wanted to beat him so bad."

Connor put nearly four feet on Conley that day, but it would not stop the younger Conley from continuing to go after him every year, and eventually surpass the one-time world-record holder.

The surprise of the meet happened the following night when walk-on Harold Smith, only months after putting on an Arkansas singlet for the first time, ran out of his skull to finish second in the 3,000-meter steeplechase in a time of 8:55.

"I couldn't wait for that gun to go off," remembered Smith. "The next thing I know there are three laps to go, and I'm passing people left and right, and all I can see in front of me is the Kenyan from Texas. Suddenly the race is over and I'm second."

Smith's own teammates were as flabbergasted as anyone. Back at the hotel, Smith's old calculus partner, Ronnie Carroll, was stunned to hear the news.

"Ronnie was resting up before his 5,000 meter," said Smith, "when Dave Taylor shouted, 'Ronnie, Ronnie, get down, Harold finished second in the steeplechase!' I wasn't expected to get anything, so John had an extra eight points on the second event of the night."

They would need every one of them. Despite Randy Stephens's win in the 1,500 meter in 3:44.1, Arkansas found itself in a ten-point hole to Houston with only five events remaining in the meet.

"So it fell on the shoulders of Randy Stephens. John still knew it would be close, but Randy stepped up and did what he had to do, the 800-meter/1,500-meter double," said Smith. "It was a monumental effort and unbelievable display. It still gives me goose bumps to see what that guy did that day. What an animal."

Only forty-five minutes after winning the 1,500 meter against great competition in ninety-six-degree heat, Stephens dragged himself to the line and made the ultimate sacrifice in the 800 meter.

"I felt horrible," remembered Stephens. "It was the only race I can remember where John didn't come up to me beforehand and tell me anything. He never spoke to me. Maybe he was worried by what I would tell him. I came through in 55 seconds, which is pretty pathetic. I was at the back and didn't think I was going to be able to run any faster. Then I saw Tommy Moloney in front of me and thought maybe if I can get to Tommy we could move up and finish fourth or fifth and get some points out of it."

It was on the backstretch when Randy caught his second wind.

"I got to Tommy on the backstretch and started feeling good, and I could see the second group, and we made it coming off the curve to the second group," said Stephens. "Then I could see the Rice guy dying [in the lead]. Coming from behind it's always easier, so I just started running faster and faster. Inside of me I knew we needed the points. I don't remember running the last fifty or sixty meters other than just running as fast as I can and passing the guys in front of me."

Stephens blew by the entire field and Jerry Fuqua of Rice to win in 1:48.06—a staggering double.

"What an animal!" McDonnell exclaimed in the stands. "Pure animal!"[7]

Years later, McDonnell's admiration for the sacrifice remained undiminished.

"It was the most unbelievable performance by someone that had never done that," said McDonnell. "Randy had a good head and never got scared of competition. He was a great team man."

His selfless effort put Arkansas in a position to bury Houston. In what would become a common theme for the Razorbacks, it was the 5,000 meter that put the final nail in the coffin. Arkansas scored twenty-five points, led by Ronnie Carroll's first-place performance, to pull ten points ahead. After Houston was disqualified in the mile relay, the meet was a foregone conclusion—Arkansas had won 134–115.[8]

The unprecedented Southwest Conference triple crown was finally a reality. Every single Razorback particularly savored "Calling the Hogs" for that special occasion, which a Fayetteville television station was on hand to witness for their documentary *Quest for the Triple Crown*. It was a great moment in the history of the program.

The hangover would be just as great. Just as when Arkansas poured everything into its first conference cross-country championship eight years earlier, it was hard for the Razorbacks to replicate the emotion and effort that went into that first outdoor conference championship. At the 1982 NCAA Outdoors in Provo, Utah two weeks later, there was a noticeable letdown.[9] It was the denouement after the climax and high drama of the first SWC outdoor conference championship and triple crown.

Senior Randy Stephens, NCAA indoor champion in the 1,000 yards, and hero of the Southwest Conference Outdoor Championships only days earlier, did not make it out of the preliminaries of the 800 meter. In his case, the letdown was not merely an emotional one.

"We had a barbecue at my place," said John. "Everything Randy did, he had to win. He'd beat you at tiddlywinks he was so competitive. So they were playing badminton, and Randy kept winning, so he kept playing and the next week that sucker was so stiff he could hardly walk. He was the favorite to win (NCAAs) but got knocked out in the first round. I look back on it, and I was there watching the whole thing and didn't do anything about it. You learn as you go along sometimes."

Stephens blames nobody but himself.

"Looking back if I had to go back and do it all over again I'd use some common sense," admitted Stephens. "When we got out to Provo my legs were so jacked from the starting and stopping and cutting and all of this stuff. We should have known better."

UTEP dominated its way to another national championship in Sulieman Nyambui's last race as a collegiate athlete. Still, the sun was clearly setting on El Paso, and a new day was beginning in Arkansas.

"They had beaten us in everything and [Nyambui] was always such a friendly guy," remembered John. "He came by to shake hands and reached up into the first row and grabbed me around the neck and said, 'Coach, Bui is gone. Arkansas will win now.'"

Six months previously, head coach Ted Banks had resigned and now Sulieman Nyambui was graduating. Although talented athletes remained behind in El Paso, the mind, heart and soul of the program had evaporated. Bui was gone. The dynasty was over.

"Nyambui was like a coach," said John. "I remember him at the NCAA meets in the 10,000 meter at LSU running all of the way to the back to get his teammate and running all the way back to the front. He was that good, and he was a great team man. Of course, Banks was a great coach. When Banks left UTEP, that group sort of caved in, and that was the end of that."

The meet also ended a terrific career for Randy Stephens—a four-time All-American and John McDonnell's first NCAA champion. Although Stephens would run professionally for two years for the Bud-Lite Track Club in Alabama, he never replicated what he achieved at Arkansas.

"It was never the same," said Stephens, who would later coach state champions of his own at Mountain Brook High School in Alabama. "The team aspect, the camaraderie, it was so much harder to run for myself. The biggest thing John drilled into me was that in every way the individual comes second. I learned that the hard way, but I learned it the entire time I was there. The other thing was the amount of love he had for all of us. He would treat walk-ons the same as he treated me. You got that feeling that deep down inside he loved you and cared for you, whether it was on the track or off the track."

McDonnell's eyes would be opened that season to other things as well. Before Mark Anderson and Frank O'Mara injured their IT bands he had never seen nor experienced the stark difference and consequences between qualified and unqualified sports-medicine personnel. Both athletes missed the entire 1982 track season with the same IT band ailment, but while Frank O'Mara would recover and go on to a successful career, Mark Anderson's collegiate career came to an end completely.

"Mark was one of the first that had it, and he told me there was a doctor in San Antonio who knew all about it," remembered John. "He asked if we would pay for surgery, so I went to our trainer Dean Weber and he said sure. Well, needless to say we would find out later the doctor did the wrong procedure. The IT band needed to be stretched but he took a piece out and shortened it."

With Frank O'Mara felled by the same ailment for nine months, John spoke with renowned local orthopedist Dr. James Arnold. Although Arnold admitted to not understanding how to treat the ailment, he was about to attend a physiology conference in New Zealand with doctors from all over the world.

"So he calls me from New Zealand and says, 'Coach, I have the name of a doctor and his phone number,'" remembered John. "It turned out that the best doctor for dealing with this was in Cincinnati. He was a former eighteen-foot pole-vaulter. I told Frank we would call the doctor, and so we started talking to him and he said, 'I know exactly what he's got.' He asked to speak to Frank so I handed him the phone. Back then you had that big long cord on the phone, and the next thing I know Frank is on the ground doing these stretches and was back running within three weeks."

John remains grateful to Arnold for pointing him the right way and saving Frank O'Mara's career.

"That's why I always say there are doctors and then there are doctors," said John. "He didn't try and do what that San Antonio guy did and ruined a guy's career. Dr. Arnold didn't know what to do but found the person who did. It was refreshing to get people like that because none of us knows everything. There are people who think they know everything, and that's dangerous."

Entering the summer of 1982, McDonnell could certainly have been forgiven for basking in some of his early success, but that was not his style. He and his assistants were hard at work trying to get better, and the momentum of their earlier efforts was now starting to propel them further. There would be no letup—ever. After bringing the program to historic heights, McDonnell had reached a level of success that left him increasingly insatiable and unsatisfied. UTEP had set the standard he wanted to achieve— winning the triple crown at the NCAAs in cross country, indoor track, and outdoor track.

"I remember being up at the Cobo Hall in Detroit watching Texas-El Paso put on a clinic," remembered McDonnell. "I was leaning with my back against the wall in the stands and my arms folded watching them go crazy and I said, 'If I could just win one [national title.]'"[10]

McDonnell never took his foot off the pedal, recruiting another stellar class of athletes to Fayetteville to replace those who had graduated. The program attracted two more field-event athletes who would ultimately make a tremendous impact at the national level: 7 feet, 3 inch high jumper Bill Jasinksi, and 15 feet, 6 inch high-school pole-vaulter Jeff Pascoe, who McDonnell had recruited from within Arkansas.

If there was a maxim McDonnell was putting into practice, it was that success was hardly a reason to rest on one's laurels. The hundreds of hours spent studying opposing programs and potential recruits to assess their potential impact for Arkansas at the Southwest Conference and NCAA Championships was something he made into an art form. It was a machine meticulously assembled and steadfastly maintained.

"His best skill was in man management," said O'Mara. "In terms of using resources, getting good guys in who could do multiple events, he was superb."

To augment an already potent cross-country lineup, John signed a class including two English athletes with impressive credentials: David Swain, a mature 1:50 (800 meter), 3:44 (1,500 meter) athlete from Surrey, as well as Gary Taylor, a 1:49 (800 meter), 3:40 (1,500 meter) runner from Middlesex. Not to be overlooked was Ian Cherry from Nevada and Carlton Efurd from nearby Greenwood, Arkansas, both of whom would develop well.

Although he had graduated from secondary school some years prior, Swain's family did not have the money for him to attend university in England, so he had spent the previous few years working at a butcher shop. Often he would run at four o'clock in the morning before going to work.

"It wasn't until later on that John explained that was a positive thing and an attribute he liked to have on his team," said Swain. "That's the way he recruited. He looked into things. He never went for the stud but knew exactly what he was looking for. He was pretty canny."

After also corresponding with Iowa State and Southern Illinois during the recruiting process, Swain still remembers receiving an Arkansas media guide in the mail with Frank O'Mara's arms raised in the air after winning the Drake Relays. The image made a profound impact on him. He was sold on Arkansas when he spoke to Anthony Leonard and learned that Gary Taylor was planning to be a Razorback that fall.

"Gary is like my brother, my closest friend in the world," said Swain. "We booked flights and sat beside each other on the plane."

Of course, the addition of Swain, while Ronnie Carroll was still on the team, only meant there was one more rooster in the hen house—a phenomenon McDonnell would face several times in his career.

"They called Swain, 'Spanky,'" said Harold Smith. "He was very talented and personable, just like Gary Taylor. Those two guys were like Rhodes scholars, intelligent and eloquent in the way they talk."

Given his maturity, Swain had an easier transition to Arkansas than most athletes who began attending university at a younger age. Although he had come from a structured program in England, it did not take long for him to embrace becoming a Razorback.

"I went from probably running 60 to 70 miles per week when I came over to running twice a day, five days of the week," said Swain. "I was lucky not to get hurt."

Gary Taylor didn't make it as easily. He hurt his knee in his apartment and missed the entire semester. The training at Arkansas required mind-numbing consistency and the discipline to avoid activities and situations that would prevent the body from recovering.

"John's a very uncomplicated person, and I mean that in the best possible way," said Swain. "Our training was very simple. It was just good, solid, hard work. John was about hard work and reaching out to each one of the athletes to see what made them tick. He knew he'd lose a few to injury, but if he kept up the numbers he'd do well."

As one who has observed John for years in various capacities as a collegiate athlete, professional athlete, coach, and later as an executive, Frank O'Mara felt the same way.

"He never did anything fancy in training," said O'Mara. "There was always one long strong workout and one speed session per week on the track. The rest was a lot of long runs. It was very steady, consistent, and timed very well but wasn't extraordinary in terms of content."

It was not uncommon for those entering Arkansas as freshmen to struggle at first.

"I used to tell guys it will take you eighteen months to get used to my program, and I won't expect anything from you as freshmen or your second cross-country season," said John. "After that we are going to hit it. We aren't going to sacrifice anything during the first year. It used to work out because the guys relaxed a little bit, and we would do slower work to build up and try not to get them hurt."

Paul Donovan was one person emerging into the sunshine of his career after a year in the darkness.

"I remember coming back with a chip on my shoulder," said Donovan. "I wasn't going to go through what I went through the previous year. I had lost some of the weight I needed to lose and was well able to cope with the training this time so I could get up to ninety miles per week."

With a history of patella tendon injuries dating back to Ireland, Donovan often did his easy runs alone on the golf course because it was a softer surface. While he remembers John being open-minded to individualizing aspects of his training, Donovan also remembers his coach quickly getting on his case when necessary.

"I remember times we used to do a long run on the golf course and it was me, Tommy Moloney, and Harold Smith," remembered Donovan. "We agreed to go really easy one day and there was a little pond down the way; and Harold, who is a surgeon now, got some cottonmouth snake and wrapped it around his hand and was giving us a biology lesson. We didn't want to know about it, but anyways it took us ages to run that lap. We are heading to the top of the hill, and the next thing you know John pops out from behind the trees. And we're thinking, 'Oh we're fucked!'"

McDonnell walked directly towards Donovan.

"We were lucky if we were going 10:00 pace. It was a half walk," remembered Donovan. "So John said, 'Paul, I'm taking your heart rate right now.' It was probably only eighty beats [per minute]. I know we didn't break a hundred. And then he looks at me and said, 'G'damn, I had to look at the trees just to see if you were moving! You'd have a higher heart rate if you were sitting at home watching football!' So the rest of the run we ran hard and I mean extra hard."

John's sudden appearance out of trees, bushes, and other inanimate objects was most prevalent during cross-country races.

"Gary Taylor gave the best description of John during a cross country race when he said it was like he was herding chickens," laughed Donovan. "He'd pop out of everywhere you were on the course. I mean you'd be running, and he'd pop out of some tree out of nowhere, and he'd be half running beside you, half bent over, half whispering in your ear saying, 'You gotta go get that sucker.' And you'd think to yourself, 'Why are you whispering?' Next thing you know you round the corner and he is at the other side. And you'd talk with your teammates after the race and everybody would say the same thing, 'He's bloody well everywhere!' You never had a chance to go easy. It wasn't until I finished competing and was helping out that I was worn out running beside him. With the amount of mileage he put in a race, he'd have won the bloody race! He was at every single point on that course, and he certainly had a presence in cross country. It meant so much to him, and it came across to everyone that, Jesus, there are no half-hearted efforts to be accepted here."

That message became crystal clear to everyone after the Oklahoma State Cowboy Jamboree on October 2, 1982. Despite scoring twenty-six points and throttling Big Eight schools Oklahoma State, Oklahoma, and Kansas by one hundred points each, John was livid when one of the Arkansas athletes was outkicked.

"We're thinking [John] is going to say, 'Good job!'" remembered David Swain. "But he just starts winding himself up getting more and more upset. 'You all ran like dogs! By God, if we have a man up front, we ought to win the race! We ought to dominate!' We were all confused."[11]

In the middle of the tirade, assistant coach Doug Williamson jokingly staggered into the middle of the group and fell down, completely unaware of the tongue-lashing the team was receiving after the win.

"Doug is lying on his back, and he hears John giving us all kinds of hell and he realizes, 'This is not a good thing while we are getting chewed out.'" remembered Swain. "He just kind of crawled out from underneath it. And John never missed a beat. He just kept chewing us out.'"[12]

Swain remembers not understanding the message until a few years later.

"It wasn't until about my junior year that I realized John's speech was all planned," said Swain. "We were getting a little cocky, and that was John's way of centering us, not letting us get the big head. He does it every year. He'll pick some event somewhere two or three weeks into the cross-country season and lay down the law for the freshmen and sophomores who haven't figured it out yet. That's a key part of what makes John good. He wants guys to be quietly confident, but if hears bragging and talking trash, he'll cut it out pretty damn quickly."[13]

Wearing the Arkansas jersey now came with higher standards and expectations than ever before.

"A lot of it was instilling the belief that when you wear that shirt, everyone is expecting you to be a great runner so don't disappoint them," said Paul Donovan. "And guys were buying into it that there was an acceptable level of performance, and you don't fall below that. You don't quit in a race, there's no out, and you give it what you have because there's plenty of time to rest afterwards. When you are wearing that shirt there are standards to uphold, and if you didn't meet those standards, he was quick to remind you. You knew you couldn't chuck it in at any point because it just wouldn't be worth the grief you'd get afterwards."

The long runs became a weekly rite of passage for his runners no matter the circumstances.

"We'd drive back from Dallas or Fort Worth and get in at two o'clock on a Sunday afternoon and go straight to the locker room," remembered O'Mara. "John would have us all put on our running gear, and then we'd get back in the vans, and he'd drive us fifteen miles out into the countryside and drop us off. There was no reprieve with the man, but it wasn't punishment like we thought at first. It was just his way of making sure nobody skipped a workout."[14]

Those who made it back to the truck in the time John wanted usually stopped at fourteen or fifteen miles and were driven back to campus. The others got to run an entire eighteen miles.

"Later we had Doug Consiglio and Espen Borge, who were buddies," remembered John. "One day on a long run they were running so damn slow, I said I'd teach them a lesson. I was supposed to pick them up in the van after fourteen miles, but I left them and they ran eighteen. The next day Espen said, 'Coach did you know you left us? That wasn't very nice.' And I said, 'Yes I did. If you guys weren't up drinking beer last night you would have been able to handle it.'"

Paul Donovan frequently joined the eighteen-mile club on Sundays.

"My first eighteen-mile run was the result of John just taking off on me and not waiting any longer," said Donovan. "If you ran with me, you ran the risk that he'd be gone."

After winning a close home meet against highly ranked Colorado on October 16, the Razorbacks scored an all-time low of 21 points to win their ninth consecutive Southwest Conference Cross Country Championship. Still, it wasn't good enough for John—especially when Sam Sitonik of Texas broke the tape before any Razorback crossed the finish line. He let them know it.

"We were fortunate a lot of times we won with subpar performances, and I'd go over it and say we won but we should have lost; and if you think this is going to continue, we have to change our attitude because it's not," said John. "So I'd point out all of things they did wrong after winning, and the guys would say, 'G'damn, that guy's never satisfied. We won. Forget about the mistakes.' And I'd say, 'No, you have to realize you made the mistakes because when the next competition comes they may be better and the mistake might cost you.'"

The Hogs blew away Sitonik at the regional meet—scoring a perfect fifteen points while running as a pack—with Anthony Leonard taking the win.

"At the time we didn't have the depth, so I thought running as a pack would be easier for us to do then to leave two or three out and have to run hard," said John.

Only Paul Donovan rested the regional meet. The decision would turn out to be a wise one—he placed twenty-fourth at the 1982 NCAA Cross Country Championships on a muddy course in Bloomington, Indiana.

"I sat back and came through the field," said Donovan. "Normally we went out hard, but I think the conditions mattered that day. That's what I was used to back in Ireland."

While Donovan may have worked his way back through the field, the rest of his teammates did not. Wisconsin, who placed all five runners in the top twenty, and put four before Arkansas's first, scored 58 points. It would turn out to be both the first and final national championship for head coach Dan McClimon, who died in a plane crash the following year. With Arkansas in third place behind Providence, it was another solid performance for McDonnell's team but once again just short of the pinnacle.

An equally impressive indoor season saw the Razorbacks rack up 164 points at the 1983 Southwest Conference indoor meet and outscore second-place Houston by a mind-boggling 83 points.[15] Heading into the 1983 NCAA Indoor Championships before a meet-record crowd of 15,060 at the Pontiac Silverdome in Detroit, McDonnell had every reason to believe Arkansas's time had finally arrived.

It was not to be. Only weeks after finishing seventh at the conference meet with thirty-six points, Southern Methodist had inexplicably scored forty points to win the national championship on wins by Robert Weir in the weight throw, Michael Carter in the shot put, and runner-up places in the 4 x 400 meter relay and by Keith Connor in the triple jump. Southern Methodist head coach Ted McLaughlin had never put much emphasis on conference meets, but this was something else. It was the kind of elevated performance on the national stage that Arkansas teams would become famous for over the following decades.

The meet had gone well in some respects for the Razorbacks. Mike Conley became the first triple-jump national champion in school history with an upset victory over Keith Connor. After being in third place going into his sixth and final jump, Conley leapt a staggering 56 feet, 6½ inches to finally overcome his nemesis. All of the hard work and courageous attempts were paying off.

Other things had not gone according to plan. Despite the triple-jump victory, Mike Conley long jumped over a foot below what had won him the Southwest Conference two weeks earlier, while Frank O'Mara faded to eighth in the mile finals and failed to score. The 4 x 800 meter relay of Donovan, Moloney, Swain, and Ed Williams got behind early and was never a factor in the race.

"John's expectations had not settled down," remembered Swain. "My freshman year he thought we could win [the national title] indoors. He thought our two-mile relay could win but we got fourth. I screwed up, running 1:53 or something ridiculous like that."

Arkansas finished third overall at the NCAA meet with 28 points.[16] It was telling that during a time when he had consistently elevated Arkansas to among the national elite, John McDonnell was beside himself. If some of his athletes thought he was hard on them and never satisfied with what they did, what those closest to John McDonnell would soon realize was that he was hardest on himself.

"We definitely had a letdown at that meet," remembered John. "It was the coaches not having them ready. They were ready physically but not mentally."

After the indoor season, Frank O'Mara and Mike Conley paid John a visit in his office to discuss what went wrong and how they were dealing with the pressure he put on them.

"You can learn from your athletes and the mistakes you make as a coach," said John. "In 1983, we should have beaten SMU indoors. They came and talked to me and Frank said, 'When you said ten points for O'Mara my legs just bent under me.' Conley said the same thing. That time I used to name the athlete and how many points I expected before the meet. So I said I appreciate you guys telling me because if you had your usual meet in the mile and long jump, we would have won. So I changed and before championship meets I would say how many points for the event, if there was more than one person competing in an event, rather than for each individual. Instead of saying ten points for Frank I might say twelve points in the 1,500 meter. I always told my athletes if you have an idea, I want to hear it. In that particular case I changed my approach to championships."

Others thrived off the pressure built up by John allotting points expectations before the meet.

"I kind of relished in the pressure," said Swain. "I think generally it worked."

Still, John's nuanced understanding of the fine line between getting some athletes prepared and pushing others over the edge was typical of his growth as a coach and the small adjustments he made every step of the way on his journey to the top of the sport.

"I remember he changed it, but by that point I was expected to win both events so it didn't matter," said Conley. "I didn't know any better. You take someone who doesn't know any better who believes everything his coaches tell him—when they told me I will accomplish something, I didn't think any different. So when John comes before the team and says, 'Mike, I need you to do X, Y, and Z.' You think, 'Boy, I better do X, Y, and Z.'"

Conley was not the only Razorback whose trust for John was absolute. He was alternatively loved, feared, and respected by almost all of his athletes. Trust was the common denominator.

"I don't know why sometimes, but he'd put the fear of God into you but still the next day you could go into the office and have a chat or whatever," said Donovan. "He was clearly the boss. He would call me all kinds of names after races and say things like, 'G'damn, you were like a tourist out there today,' but there was never a falling out."

While he would continue to have such an effect on athletes for the remainder of his career, John was also beginning to understand the limitations of negativity and the power of positivity.

"Fear is not a good motivator," said John. "It has to be positive. A few years later I had a jumper come into my office, and I asked him what the problem was and he said, 'I've had it. I'm working too hard and Coach said I have to do this and do that, and I'm always compared to Mike Conley.' I said to him, 'That's kind of funny because Coach was just in here and said that by the time you leave here you will have broken all of Mike Conley's records because you're that good.' He looked at me and said, 'He said that about me?' And I said, 'Yes, you have more speed, more strength, and can run a forty-five second 400 meter.' After I was done talking to him he walked out of the room on a cloud. So that was positive. The negative stuff you cannot use too much."

John's inability to be satisfied with anything other than resounding success and intellectual curiosity with regards to having each athlete meet their potential also led him to a few conclusions about the need for individualized training suited to the physiology and psychology of the athlete.

"I learned that early in my career from Pat Vaughn," said John. "He was a 10,000-meter guy, and every time he was doing well, he'd want to do speed work and his last lap would get worse. So I did some checking around, and a coach I knew in Europe said Americans spend too much time working on the weak point rather than the strong point."

Exploiting the strengths of his runners was a lesson John would apply that very spring with Frank O'Mara who after years of struggle and injury was primed for one of the most special outdoor seasons in Razorback history. Once Frank became aware of his immense physical fitness, he gained a mental confidence that made him unbeatable.

"The best thing that ever happened to Frank was getting injured my senior year, taking that time off, and coming back the year after that," said Randy Stephens. "I told him you're going to be the leader. He stepped up and took it and never looked back. He did some insane workouts. It's not like he wasn't in shape. He just needed encouraging."

The ball really got rolling at the 1983 Penn Relays, where O'Mara was determined to avenge the humbling loss to Villanova two years earlier.

"I was looking for revenge after 1981," said Frank. "I anchored the distance medley relay, and we won it. Then I anchored the 4 x 1,500 meter, and we won that too. I ran 1:50 on the 4 x 800 meter relay, and we didn't win, but Stanley anchored the sprint medley to a win. We'd never won at Penn before and won three relays that year. I got most valuable performer of the meet."

After O'Mara's impressive 1,500-meter (3:42.81) and 5,000-meter (14:12.38) victories at the Southwest Conference led Arkansas to its second consecutive outdoor championship and triple crown, there would be no emotional letdown this time for any of the Razorbacks. Frank entered the 1,500-meter final at the 1983 NCAA Outdoor Championships in Houston both physically and mentally prepared to win.

It was a loaded field—including the likes of Marcus O'Sullivan of Villanova, as well as Joaquim Cruz of Oregon and Earl Jones of Eastern Michigan. The latter two would win medals at the Los Angeles Olympics the following year. Jones, who had run 1:42.9 over 800 meters, entered the race as the favorite.

"We weren't so sure because Earl hadn't run many 1,500s," said John. "Frank had really good top-end speed. I just told him to try and be behind him if you could, but it didn't happen that way. So I told Frank if he is behind you with 350 meters left to start really cranking it up. He did that, and Jones tried to come back on the final straightaway, but Frank had taken quite a bit of the steam out of his legs."

Boxed in heading into the last lap, O'Mara had no doubts in his mind about what he needed to do.

"I was locked in and apparently barged my way out with elbows and other appendages," said O'Mara. "I was just determined to win. I got out and headed for home. Jones came charging after me and with the slow pace in the 1,500 meter he was obviously dangerous, but I held him off at the line."

All of the toils and struggles in the trails, at the track, and over the hills at Razorback Golf Course had finally and monumentally paid off.

"I remember that the one thing I told him is that when you beat that hill at Razorback Golf Course nobody on the track can beat you," said John. "Frank said, 'I thought of that hill and nobody was going to beat me.' Nobody thought he could beat Earl Jones but him."

For an athlete who failed to score at a Southwest Conference meet three years prior, it was a staggering turn of events that would see him win a national title, qualify for the Olympics, and win a World Championship in the space of four years. After everything they had overcome together, Frank O'Mara's faith in John McDonnell was unshakable.

"My father had died when I was a freshman, so I was clearly looking for someone to respect and admire," said O'Mara. "Coming from a similar Irish background where great value is placed on work ethic, John McDonnell's was beyond extraordinary. He seemed to put our success ahead of him or his family."

O'Mara would no longer compete collegiately, but he never thought about training anywhere else.

"I thought I needed to come back," said O'Mara. "It was working, so why change it? Plus it was very apparent to anyone who was paying attention that John had a great group of athletes there. Those were the golden years. It was just a Camelot period in Arkansas track and field."

McDonnell retained both O'Mara and Redwine, who had placed third in the final 800 meter of his NCAA championship career, as graduate assistants while they continued to pursue their graduate-school education. Both of them had opportunities to run elsewhere but chose to stay with McDonnell, whose stable of professional running talent continued to multiply.

Not everybody stuck around. Anthony Leonard headed home after only two years when his girlfriend, Sharon, came over from England to run during his second year and became disenchanted.

"He did well here and loved it but hated leaving," said John. "I remember we were coming back from the Southwest Conference outdoor meet and dropped him off at Dallas–Fort Worth Airport. He was hugging and crying, and it was really sad. I heard they got married and did well. He was a classy kid."

The sentiment was not the same when Ronnie Carroll graduated. The three-time SWC champion rubbed enough people the wrong way even before he accepted a coaching position with rival Texas.

"We were glad to be rid of him," said Swain. "He was just a bad egg. He was all about Ronnie Carroll, not about the team."

Although McDonnell managed Carroll, as he would the multitude of other personalities that would make their way through Fayetteville, he was hoodwinked by the Dubliner on one occasion.

"He always had an angle on everything," said John. "The meet before conference he comes in and had hurt his instep in the steeplechase and kept using that as an excuse. So he came in and asked, 'Would it be okay if I stayed off this meet because you know how important the conference meet is and my foot is in bits, it's just in bits. If I run now, I won't be able to run the conference meet.' I let him miss that meet. Vaughn and Barney were rooming with him, and he went back to them and said, 'I just talked to McDonnell and told him I'm not running. If he makes me run, I'm on the next plane.' Twelve years later at Pat Vaughn's father's funeral we were talking and Pat said, 'Do you remember Ronnie didn't want to go to the meet before conference? I always wanted to run that by you.' He told me what Ronnie said to them. I said, 'That's not true.' It had upset Pat. He said, 'All of these years I thought you favored Ronnie.'"

Years later, once he had returned to Dublin and opened up a successful printing service with his wife, Ronnie Carroll sent a letter to McDonnell.

"I got a nice letter from him thanking me for what I did and straightening him out," said John.

While the Dubliner's departure was not lamented by some, it was by others.

"Ronnie Carroll was a loyal friend, and I stuck up for him when he needed help and he stuck up for me," said Smith. "He's still a good guy no matter what anybody says about him. Ronnie was out for Ronnie. After he graduated from Arkansas, he got a deal where he could help coach at the University of Texas, and he went there for a while. He had no allegiance to anyone at Arkansas. He was doing the best he could for Ronnie, and I totally understand that."

While the football program was looking for a new head coach following the departure of Lou Holtz for Minnesota, McDonnell's program had become a pillar of stability that was being reinforced each year by increasingly strong recruiting classes. That same year, McDonnell was paid a visit by future All-American Mike Davis, a 23 feet, 8 inch long jumper and 6 feet, 8 inch high jumper from Hawaii who asked if he could walk onto the team. While his development alongside Conley would become a sight to behold over the years to come, attracting other athletes with strong pedigrees was hardly a problem.

Texas was becoming fertile recruiting ground, where John was able to convince Matt Taylor, a 1:52 half-miler from Kerrville, Texas, as well as Michael Byrd, a 3:48 1,500-meter runner from Longview, Texas, who had been training under Chris Schrader and was convinced to skip the Marines, to sign with the Razorbacks.

From north of the border, McDonnell signed Doug Consiglio, a wiry 6 foot, 5, 141-pound provincial champion from Cambridge, Ontario, Canada, who had run 3:48 for 1,500 meters and 5:41 for the 2,000-meter steeplechase. Recruited by Kentucky, Florida, and Tennessee, Consiglio had not been invited to visit until he beat top American prep two-miler, Bryan Yeager, at Florida Relays that spring. The young Canuck was sold on Arkansas after a conversation with Frank O'Mara and Stanley Redwine.

"It was going to be an Olympic year so I asked them where they were going to be training," said Consiglio. "They were staying, so I said to myself, 'They must like it here, otherwise why would they stay?'"

After signing half-miler Liam Looney from Limerick, Ireland, John's focus began to shift from finding athletes to turning them away. He was being bombarded with talented athletes but couldn't possibly sign all of them. One such athlete, Arturo Barrios of Mexico, who eventually signed with Texas A&M, went on to break the world record for 10,000 meters.

"His coach called, and he was dying to come here, but I didn't have a full scholarship," said John.

After a year in which *Track And Field News* had proclaimed Arkansas the track and field program of the year[17]—they were third in cross country, third in indoor track, and seventh in outdoor track at the NCAA Championships—it wasn't hard to understand that a buzz was surrounding the program. Still, with all of the accolades, Olympians, conference championships, and All-Americans, John McDonnell still had not accomplished his ultimate goal—to lead Arkansas to an NCAA championship.

Although the Razorbacks would capture their tenth straight Southwest Conference cross-country championship during the fall of 1983 against a resurgent Texas squad by a slim 29–42 margin, the NCAA championship was another matter. The graduation of Dave Taylor had not helped matters, but many of the young milers brought in that fall were simply not yet ready to contribute meaningfully in cross country. On many of the mile repeats at Razorback Hill, some of the freshmen distance runners ran the same volume as graduate assistant Stanley Redwine, who was doing strength work for an 800 meter on the track.

When Arkansas finished fifth as a team at the NCAA Cross Country Championships with 206 points, John did not hesitate to share his frustrations publicly.

"We're a little disappointed," John told the media on November 21, 1983. "Before the season we just wanted to win the Southwest Conference, but by the time we reached the NCAA meet, we thought we had a pretty good shot to win. It was just one of those days."[18]

Paul Donovan improved into the top ten, but sophomore David Swain regressed to seventieth.

"I was desperately disappointed," said Swain. "I still hadn't made that step. I cracked. You get to nationals and you slip, and people start streaming by you. Honestly, I quit in the middle of the race."

After the close calls and disappointments at the previous few NCAA Championships, McDonnell began wondering whether his team would ever capture a national championship. He had painstakingly brought the program so far up the mountain, but reaching the pinnacle was proving to be impossible.

"You hear those things about people who can't win the big one, and I thought I was one of those guys," said John. "Five times we were second or third, and we couldn't win. I thought we were jinxed, and I was getting paranoid. Then all of a sudden we win one, and it's like this is our world. I have always believed winning is a habit and losing is habit."

The Razorbacks entered the 1984 indoor season firing on all cylinders. The field-event group alone had a staggering four national qualifiers at the first home meet on January 20, 1984—Marty Kobza in the shot put (63 feet, 8 inches), Bill Jasinski in the high jump (7-5), Mike Davis in the long jump (25-3), and Mark Klee in the pole vault (17-7). McDonnell held out Conley from any of the jumps until February so he could be fresh later in the season, but that didn't stop the Chicago native from nonetheless blazing a school-record 300 meters in 30.24 on the flat 200-meter track in Fayetteville.

"This is probably the best opening night we've ever had," John told the media that evening. "It kind of scares you really. Especially with those field-event guys jumping so high and throwing so far."[19]

Despite some of the early successes, John sensed that something was amiss with David Swain. After the Englishman lost by five seconds in the 1,000-yard run to Gareth Brown of Iowa State and struggled through other aspects of training, McDonnell called him into his office and closed the door.

"John looks at three aspects of life in a college runner: academics, social, and running," said Swain. "He knows you cannot do all three. If you had an active social life or a girlfriend, which he didn't like, something had to give, either your school or your running. I had a girlfriend at the time. I was hanging in there at school, but my running was suffering. So I got the closed-door speech, straightened it out, and realized there were expectations of me."

Upon capturing their fourth consecutive Southwest Conference indoor championship, the Razorbacks were focused on the task at hand. With Southern Illinois, Washington State, and Iowa State all expected to be in the mix for the national championship, Arkansas brought its biggest and most experienced group yet to the 1984 NCAA Indoor Championships—which were being held for the first time at the Carrier Dome in Syracuse, New York.

Things had already begun to go wrong before the meet even began for Arkansas when pole-vaulter Mark Klee was admitted to the hospital with pneumonia during the week of the championship. High jumper Bill Jasinski failed to advance to the final on Friday afternoon, and the distance medley relay was put into a massive hole by Liam Looney's pedestrian 1:55 800-meter split—which ultimately may not have mattered on a day when Earl Jones of Eastern Michigan blew by the entire field to win the event.

It was not until the second day when senior Tom Moloney turned the tide for the Razorbacks by placing second in the 1,500 meter behind Bob Verbeck of Iowa State. The rest of the afternoon went well from there—Marty Kobza scored in the shot and Mike Conley cemented his Razorback legend by capturing the long-jump title and followed that up three hours later with a victory in the triple jump. It was a Herculean effort made to look easy by the junior's abundant athleticism and composure under pressure.[20]

There was a sense that destiny might finally be upon them. With one event to go, Arkansas led Iowa State by six points. The national championship depended on the outcome of the 4 x 400 meter relay, which John McDonnell, the team, and fans watched helplessly from the stands without a team qualified in the event. Iowa State finished second-from-last in the relay but after the disqualification of Southern Illinois, Alabama, and Mississippi, an air of uncertainty regarding the overall result pervaded the stadium.

"Oh my gosh, that thing must have gone on for an hour," remembered John. "If they had disqualified another team, Iowa State would have tied us. So we are standing there waiting to find out if we won our first national title and finally they showed the results from the mile relay on the screen. We had won our national title."

The Razorback athletes jubilantly lifted John onto their shoulders to celebrate the victory, which was only the second national championship in school history in any sport after the 1965 football title.

"This is our biggest thrill ever," an elated John McDonnell told the media. "You just can't explain how excited everyone was for us at the meet. We've come so close at this meet so often, everyone was pulling for us to win it. This is a great honor for the school and for the team."[21]

Ever the family man, John's first call that night at the hotel was to Ellen McDonnell.

"He always called me after meets," said Ellen. "He was so excited about winning the first NCAA title because it was his dream come true. He worked so hard."

Ever the competitive workaholic, John's second call that night was to recruit high-school senior Chris Zinn, the Missouri state cross-country champion.

"He called me from the hotel when the ink wasn't even dry on the presses!" laughed Zinn.

When the team arrived back in Fayetteville, a huge reception was held in Barnhill Arena.

John McDonnell had worked so hard to reach the pinnacle of the sport. Now that he was on top of the world, he would work twice as hard to stay there. The effort, emotion, and endurance that went into that first national championship would pale in comparison to what it took to win it over and over and over again.

6

John McDonnell on Physiological and Psychological Preparation

"It's important to not just physically prepare athletes, but have them in the right psychological state of mind as well."

—*John McDonnell*

My philosophy has always been that strength is speed. If you do not develop the body physically, it will never develop mentally. I learned that from the early stages of my own running career. A lot of things I did as a coach were things I did myself. I always thought more was better, but I learned that more was not necessarily better. Part of the reason I thought that more was better was because I always felt when I was in great shape, I was confident and everything went well, but if you weren't in great shape, it was like you were walking on thin ice waiting for it to break. A lot of that relates to Arthur Lydiard. I read his book, and his philosophy was that with more strength the faster you are going to get and the more confident you are going to get.

People would ask me, "How do you get someone to concentrate and go out there and push themselves to the limit?" It starts by being aerobically prepared for a race. I always say if a kid comes to me and is an 800-meter runner but asks to try the 1,500 meter, I usually already had in the back of my mind they were going to do it eventually. If they ask about trying it in the first meet this year, I'd say no, but we'll try it in the first meet next year. That's the thing. If you are in great physical shape with great strength and not even much speed and can go three-quarters of the way without hurting, it really helps your concentration.

Early in my coaching career we did 120 miles per week. People just did more mileage at that time. Dave Bedford and Gerry Lingdren did over 200 miles per week, and so there was vast experimental volumes back then and you had to find your own because nobody agreed on anything in those days. I remember myself when I was down in Louisiana with an English guy named Malcolm Robinson. We worked out, and when I think about what we did, it was asinine. I ran twenty-four 400s on a cinder track and I was wearing 9.9 sprint shoes. All it had was a little bitty pad on the heel and lateral movement, and the heel was rocking. My Achilles hurt so bad the next day. That was the year I beat Jim Ryun, and I was going to do it all but that derailed me. That was just a lack of direction. My gosh, I wish I had someone to tell me to run in flats. Shoes were terrible back then.

Lydiard was one of the first to come out with literature that was complete, and it was kind of simple. People say I had simple training, well, so did Arthur Lydiard. He had more Olympic champions than anyone, and most of those athletes were from his own neighborhood. I thought he had a lot of the answers, and he was very down to Earth. At the same time, Herb Elliott's coach had some ideas about training on sand dunes that we didn't have. People would try to do that and hurt their Achilles. He also had great ideas, but I felt like he exaggerated and didn't give you the whole story.

I believe Arthur Lydiard got as close to it as possible because he took his own training methods as a marathon runner, and that's what he did. I also initially learned from mistakes from my own personal training such as running in the heat. I'd get cramps in my calves and nobody knew what you were supposed to take. They'd give you these salt pills and that was it. Now we take an array of minerals like potassium and calcium. So we learned the hard way, much like Lydiard.

I have tremendous belief in his method of training because it worked—and for different types of people. It wasn't just Peter Snell and those who won gold medals. He had others run really well for him. It goes back to strength and development and the things I learned. When O'Shaughnessy was here, I was smart enough to have him run big miles, but we also did a lot of speed work because he had the speed—150s, 200s, 300s—and he got really fast. I tried to train athletes individually and get them in groups for certain workouts. Cross country was not individualized as much, because it was just conditioning, but getting them into groups on the track was important.

In the summertime I'd tell our guys to run 50–55 miles per week and take it nice and easy. All I wanted them to do was to be in shape to start working out when they came back. They didn't need to be in shape to race, but their legs and tendons and joints needed to be used to taking some work before we moved into the season. At the beginning of my coaching career, we may have done 120 miles per week, but I later cut that back to 100 miles and then to 85 miles per week. The philosophy stayed the same: six weeks of aerobic preparation for strength then gradually during the second three weeks [of the six-week period] we'd start doing some leg play as I call it, or leg cadence, where we'd do 150s or 300s three times a week, and I felt like that kept their leg speed constantly there, even during cross-country season. It didn't help cross country because you don't need to run fast 200s to run cross country, but it did help when you made the transition to indoor track.

I think we could have won more cross-country titles if we had done things a little differently. I'd sacrifice cross country even though I loved it. I loved the idea of eight or nine guys and you knew where they all were, and you ran one race and then packed up and went home. You just have to make choices, and to me cross country was a preparation for track, and that's why I think our 1,500-meter guys ran well during cross country because I told them we are going to run faster and get stronger. I'd tell them if you can run with these 5,000-meter guys during the fall, can you imagine what you are going to do on the track with that 5,000-meter strength and 1,500-meter speed? It's very hard to *get some of them to understand. You have to be able to sell something to get them to buy into it.*

Not everyone had that kind of foot speed. I had a guy named Pat Vaughn, who didn't have great foot speed at all. Every time we did speed work it seemed like his last lap would get worse. So I talked to a gentleman in Europe who told me to develop his strength, and that paid big dividends. I used that on everyone because if it suited Pat Vaughn, it would also suit a guy with speed and make him superb. It is easier to develop the 90 percent strength than focusing on the 10 percent weakness. Sometimes by trying to improve the 10 percent, they go backwards. If a kid doesn't have fast twitch fibers, doing speed work is not going to help. So when you work on a strong point of a kid and get 10 percent improvement of 90 percent that is a lot more than 10 percent of 10 percent, which is virtually nothing. So if you have a kid who is strong but doesn't have a kick in races, have him go from 1,200 meters out with a fast 400 meters, then back off for 200 meters and then relax and hit another one. Run the race his way, and you can break your competition.

It worked with Falcon. I never intended him to run 10,000 meters in college, but he asked to do it. He was trained on many of the same preparations as Pat Vaughn with the strength; but of course Joe had so much more foot speed and that was why he could win any event from the 1,500 meter to 10,000 meter. Even though I loved Pat Vaughn to death and he was a great runner, there is no way he'd beat Joe Falcon in a 10,000-meter race no matter what he did, because Joe had so much more foot speed. When Joe ran the 10,000 meter he would just sit on guys, and they couldn't do anything about it. The guy could run a 4:02 mile and Joe would be right there with him. There are certain things that just aren't fair. That's why those Moroccans and Kenyans are running 1:44 and 27:00. I mean it's not fair when you have someone who can do both.

If I thought someone like Pat Vaughn was in a race with guys who are equal to him or maybe even a little better than him, you had to handle things a certain way. The biggest thing is having a guy buy into it because everyone thinks the reason they don't win races is because they haven't done enough speed work. They'd say, "Coach, if I had more speed work, I know I'm just as fast as that guy." You hate to say, "'No, you aren't,' and you really can't tell him that because psychologically it would be real damaging. So instead you have to say, "Yeah, he has that top-end speed you can't handle, but there is a way of handling it." So with Pat Vaughn he had a lot of success during his last two years, and I'd have him take it 600 meters or 1,200 meters out. My favorite was taking it 1,200 meters out and hitting a really fast lap then relaxing for a lap.

When it came to racing, I always felt like if you were prepared that it was important to lead a race or take control of it. Don't run a race and try to win it cheap. That's how you get beat. Have a plan if you cannot outkick a guy over 600 meters or 800 meters to take it far enough out to finish them off. Always save your best weapon for a big meet. Never show your hand so you can surprise your competition.

We used to do oxygen-debt runs during cross country-season where we'd go out in the first mile in 4:25 to 4:30 and then back off to 4:45 and then back to 5:10. That was the kind of workout where if you can handle that fast pace in a workout, then you will be able to handle it in a race. Do something that will reassure them they can handle the fast pace because a lot of kids think, "Oh my gosh, I'm a 1,500-meter guy and this race *is 10,000 meters, so I need to go out steady.' I have a saying that nothing good happens at the back of a race. Nothing. From a psychological standpoint, it's a disaster. If you are a little bit weak between the ears, looking back and only seeing a few guys behind you is only going to make it worse. You start thinking about home, and your mind wanders. You start feeling sorry for yourself and start thinking about dropping out. When that happens, you will just throw in the towel. I've always said to stick your nose in it, and if you are up in the race at the front and you can get halfway, the adrenaline takes over. Now you're thinking, "Damn, I'm up at the front. I'm doing fantastic." Suddenly there is something to run for now, there is something to hurt for; and your concentration is so much better because now you're competing with the leaders. There is something positive, and you are going to hurt for something that is worth getting.*

The 10,000 meter was a race where some guys didn't always want to listen. It's tough when someone is telling you to do something, and you still have half a race left. There were many times I'd have two Arkansas guys in the same race like I did once with Jason Bunston and Godfrey Siamusiye in the 10,000 meter at Eugene [in 1996]. When that happened, I would say to each of them, "I love both of you, but I'm going to tell each of you how to beat the other guy after you've beaten everyone else in the race, and the best athlete will win." Nobody complained to me about that because it's only fair.

Teddy Mitchell's 10,000-meter win [in 1994] was a little different. It was at altitude, and I told him we didn't know what the Kenyans were going to do, but I said more than likely they are going to try to work together and take it hard because they are from the same team. So I said to sit back and wait for what happens. As the race went along, I saw they were moving pretty good and alternating every 200 meters, and I knew that wasn't going to work for them. They'd sprint for a while and the other would hang back. There was old Teddy chugging along 40–50 meters back and I said, "You got them Teddy, just stay right there! They're not going to maintain this. They are doing fartlek and are at altitude. They aren't going to maintain this, Teddy!" Well one started coming back. Once he broke from his teammate, and Teddy passed him that was like a shot of adrenaline to Teddy. He was up on his toes. He smelt blood. And he did exactly what I told him. He listened and he ended up winning that national championship that day.

You had to handle everyone differently. Paul Donovan was a tough cookie and a great competitor. I remember at NCAAs in Oklahoma City in 1986, he won the 3,000 meter and came back and anchored the 2-mile relay on the same day. So he was a winner, but he was one of those guys who had injuries that played a part. He had an old soccer injury that plagued him his entire career. The patella tendon in his right knee was rolled up on one side, and they didn't want to operate on it, but they said if he stayed on soft surfaces—grass, wood chips or trails—he would manage. We used to go on gravel roads and wood chipped trails, and we'd run there. He eventually got second to Frank O'Mara at the World Championships. When he went over to London and Europe, he had nowhere to train but on hard surfaces, so he got hurt and they had to operate on it. He was finished, but went four more years, and we had to baby it. So the moral of the story is to stay off the pavement.

We had a guy that went to school here named Gerard Hartmann. When he graduated from here, he went to Florida and trained under a fantastic physical therapist who was renowned for his work with athletes. He was eighth in the Hawaii triathlon and then got in with the agent Kim McDonald. Kim hired him full-time to work on the Kenyans he had. Gerard was great when he was living in Florida. I'd call him up whenever we had a problem and he'd say, "Send them down." Every kid saw him. Graham Hood went down there. Ryan Wilson saw him. They were guys that had problems that our people here didn't know what was wrong. Gerard would keep them for three days. I don't know what he did but he obviously had gifted hands and put them to good use. He spent some time in Florida and then when Kim McDonald hired him he spent his time in Europe. When Kim passed away, he opened up a clinic in Limerick and now works with soccer, football, and track and field athletes.

You couldn't always avoid injuries, so sometimes you needed to cross-train. That G-Trainer is a great machine, but it is nothing compared to the swimming pool. I could tell you stories about that swimming pool. Gary Taylor hurt his knee in his apartment fooling around during one cross-country season. He had swum in high school, so we had him in the pool twice per day. He would do intervals in the pool, and he was back jogging three weeks before he had his first indoor meet. He said, "Do you think I should run? I'm feeling great." I'd say, "Let's do two sessions of 200s," and he did and lined up for the first indoor meet and ran 3:58 for the mile and that was a personal best. He had done nothing but swimming cardiovascular-wise.

Different guys would go in the pool. [Daniel] Lincoln was in there. Alistair [Cragg] was in there. [Joe] Falcon was in there. Frank O'Mara did it. They'd be crawling out of that place. The problem is it's so time consuming because you have to go to the pool, get changed, get in the pool, and have someone supervise you. Some of the workouts, we'd go in and do 40 x 30 seconds with 30 seconds recovery and 40 x 1 minute or 20 x 2 minutes. I never had a guy in better shape cardiovascularwise than coming out of a pool. If they were swimming it would be twice a week. The only thing you are missing is the surface contact, but you can solve that by two or three weeks of just jogging. You don't have to line up for the pool like you do for the G-Trainer—you can put four or more guys in it at once.

After a few years I began to lower the mileage we did and then again at the beginning of the 1990s when I had Godfrey Siamusiye. Boy, he loved to run fast, but he started getting sore legs and aches and pains and I said, "Godfrey, you can't keep doing this," because I could see what he was doing was what I was doing when I was an athlete—faster and more. He wanted to run huge distance, and he was big on running fast. So I talked to him and said, "Godfrey, you are just going to get hurt. There is a trend developing here. You are missing workouts because you are just flogging yourself." He was running away from guys because we had such a young team, and he was head and shoulders above them. Some of our guys I'd tell them to stay with him for eight miles instead of ten and, boy, that team won NCAAs despite being so young. I'm thinking maybe less miles is better, so it was all experimental.

Upper-body strength is important. I feel that when you build up lactic acid and your arms slow down, so do your legs. I'm a firm believer in upper-body strength. We would do weights followed by an eight-mile run. You don't need to do anything extraordinary, just chin-ups, dips, things like that. I did nothing for the legs. If you are a distance runner with skinny, skinny legs, and you try to push that iron, you end up with joint problems from the weights. So that's why I stopped it from the hips down. If you are running eighty-five miles per week, that is a lot of weight training for your legs. Bounding and all of that stuff has its place, but it has to be controlled. The problem when you have a team is that it's not going to be controlled.

If we would run a hard workout and they were supposed to have their easy day, weights and eight [miles], you always had some ego guys. Sometimes I'd go up on the trails to see who was flying and who was walking. That was a hard thing to constantly keep on because you didn't know which way they were going on the trail. The trail was great because it was so easy on their legs and shaded in the summer. I used to go up there to keep an eye on them, but some guys would try to trick me. They would run the opposite way on a figure eight. We had a certain way to run it, and they'd run opposite and you'd find out a year later. You never knew if guys pulled that stunt on you.

You need to have easy days and hard days. I always said to the guys, "If your legs are trashed, tell me. We can do the workout tomorrow." Reuben Reina was good at that. He'd tell me, "Oh coach, my legs are trashed," and I'd say, 'Okay, we'll do it tomorrow but you may be on your own." He'd go the next day and have a great workout. You are dependent on the guys being honest. People would ask me why I trust the kid and I'd say, 'If you're telling me your legs are trashed and they're not, you aren't hurting me. Who are you kidding?"

I found it interesting to read about Marty Liquori. He said when he finished college if he had nagging injuries, he would skip a race and rest. It took him a long time to realize that he always had nagging injuries in college too, but he ran because Jumbo Elliott of Villanova would say you run the anchor leg or you run the third leg, and it just wasn't an option. It sunk in for me because that's exactly what happens to people. I tell guys that when they are in Europe and have a bad race and are thinking of calling it a season. I'd say, "Hold on, you called it quits last season too." I'd tell them to finish the season and a lot of times they'd end up having another great race. I'd say one day all of those years will be gone. I tell that story because Marty Liquori said he skipped this race and skipped that race and all of a sudden before he knew it his career was over.

Of course, any good coach needs to listen to what the athletes have to say whether they have been with you for years or not. The worst thing to do, no matter how good a coach you are, if you have an new athlete who believes in his high-school or club coach, you cannot pull the rug from underneath that kid. If you do, you are making a big mistake, and he'll resent you and fight you every inch of the way if he really believes in his high-school coach. And he should believe in that person if he had any success with them.

So I'd sit down a new kid and ask, "Can you write out three weeks of cross country, three weeks of indoor track and three weeks of outdoor track, because you and your coach did some fantastic things," even if I really didn't believe in the coach's background. And the kid would say, "Oh yeah, I'll do that," and we'd go over it. So I'd pick out the good workouts and say, "Wow, there are some good workouts in there." And then I'd say, "Johnny, I'm just suggesting this, but I think we should keep what made you great and the state champion or national champion or whatever. We're going to keep it. We're going to keep it . . . but if we could just work in this and this and that, I think those would just be the finishing touches." The kid would smile and say, "Sounds good to me, Coach." Then all of a sudden that kid is eating out of your hand.

On the other hand, if you tell that kid, "This is Arkansas. What you did in high school, forget about it. It's my way or the highway!" Well, you have just built a barbed-wire fence between you and that kid. Believe it or not, coaches do that. It's common sense to me that you would talk to a kid and ask him because if he has run a good time in high school under a coach, then he is going to like that coach. It doesn't matter if the college coach is good, that kid is going to say that their high-school coach was good too. So if you are a smart coach, you will recognize that. Communication is the most important thing. Everybody knows the X's and O's, but to be able to communicate and learn how that kid thinks is the most important thing a coach can learn. Don't become a dictator. You can have discipline without pushing things down a kid's throat. I think egos a lot of time interfere with good judgment. I don't mind giving a kid credit. He's the one out there sweating on the track, not me.

The other thing I tried to use a lot when I talked to them was the team concept. Joe Falcon was just super, super confident when he was in college and had a hell of an ego, which I didn't want to take away because that's what made him great. So before a workout I'd say, "Joe, when we are out on the golf course, old Jay and John are going through a rough spell. Maybe on a couple of the intervals you can give them a pat on the back there." I'd do that with a lot of good athletes and unless they are real jerks, and you do get the odd one, they are fine with it. Godfrey was fantastic at that stuff. He just loved helping other people.

It is important to know when to control workouts. There is a pecking order on any team, but if you let it get out of hand, your team gets out of hand. People say, "Why are you keeping the good guys back?" I'd always say, "No, the good guys career starts after they leave Arkansas. If they're going to be great, it starts after they leave." There would be no team if you let one guy run rampant over everybody else and screw up the workouts. You have to draw the line in the sand. I would tell Matt Taylor sometimes if you want to keep your pace, you can do extra intervals. Once he found out he had to do more, suddenly the pace the others were doing seemed all right. A lot of times it is ego and people thinking they had to make the team in workouts. I'd counteract that by saying, "You pick the team, not me, and it happens in races."

It was hard managing all of the egos sometimes but you talk to a guy with a big ego and tell him 'You are better than that guy," even though he may not be. Joe Falcon said he came to Arkansas to run with Frank O'Mara and within two years he beat him. I know Frank didn't like it. He'd say, "That sucker thinks he's hot stuff. And you know . . . he is!" A lot of it was politicking. If you have a guy with an ego, you can make him feel really important and think that he is helping the team by asking him to help this kid. Telling him, "This kid came here because of you so give him a pat on the back." He would and then all of a sudden he's feeling better and that kid is feeling better. You can't take the ego away because that's what made him good.

Sometimes guys would wonder why I wasn't happy after a win. I remember one kid said to me, "Jesus, you're never happy." So I said back to him, "Oh, I'm happy. What scares me is you're happy, and you shouldn't be because you are better than that." And they think, "I am?" I'd say, "You're happy with that? That's a crumb, baby. I want the whole loaf." So I was always trying to get guys to realize their potential, and you can also turn it around and try to build up their ego. I'd tell a guy, even if he won, that you *made enough mistakes to get beat—you got away, but don't think that's going to happen again. Some of the guys thought I was hard. I think it's good to be that way because later in life they respect you because that's true in life in general. You get lucky once in a while.*

When it came to energy systems in training and workouts I mixed them. People would ask me, "You have anaerobic and aerobic, but how do you fix it? Do you do more aerobic or what is the sequence?" I said, "I don't know how I am supposed to fix it. There is no sequence." I had a training system, and I started it way back, that used both energy systems. The one thing with workouts that I started myself, and I think they were the most beneficial ones which I would save for track season, were step-downs. I loved step-downs. We'd start with the 5,000-meter guys at 2 kilometers, then 1,600 meters all the way down to 200s or 150s. That's where I mixed anaerobic and aerobic all together. That was the best workout, and even guys like Alistair and others said that was the greatest workout. I loved that workout.

So I mixed the energy systems and saved that workout for track. During cross country, we ran distance—interval miles, or interval two miles, or interval mile-and-a-halves. The step-downs might be great, but I wanted to have something different for them to look forward to on the track. We didn't do the fast pace indoors that we'd do outdoors. So I'd say, "This is cross country, it's a preparation for indoors, and indoors is a preparation for outdoors." That's why we have the three seasons. We did distance preparation, started mixing in a little bit of pace indoors, and then speed work outdoors.

I've heard people say high volume and fast-paced work interfere with each other. I don't think they do, and the reason I don't believe they interfere is because you can get into a 5,000-meter race, and all of this is thrown at you, and you better be able to handle it. It doesn't matter what you are planning when you get into a race. You can have ten different plans, and it'll be the eleventh one that will work. So you have to be ready for anything. That's why I felt like you had to mix these different systems so that if someone makes a move you need to be able to cover it and to be able to handle it. If you have done the right work, there is no reason why you cannot handle it.

I don't believe in peaking. I always thought you need to keep yourself in great shape at all times of the year. You look at the Moroccans and Ethiopians that run well whenever they step on the track at all times of the year. Are they peaking all of the time? No. You have to keep the platform high at all times. I've always said with my cross-country guys that if you have run a 3:55 mile, I want to be able to go to the track after cross-country season is over and run 4:00 for the mile. I want to maintain. You never go back where you started. I always used a ladder as an example—you go up three steps and come back one, go up four steps and come back one. However, if you go back to the same table top you started, which a lot of coaches and athletes do, it takes you half the darn season to get to where you were before.

Its common sense to keep the platform high, and I believe Lydiard did the same thing. You should not regress greatly from the jumping-off point where you finished the season. You have to say, "I love where I was last season. That was a great year. In my off season I am only going to come back so far, and then next year I'm going to go an even higher jumping-off point and that platform is going to keep coming up after me." When there is too much work usually injuries and illness set in because you are demand-

ing too much of your body. You have to keep your body at a high threshold of fitness at all times, not competing, just physical. Not even psychological because your mind needs a break.

The mind does need a break sometimes even if the body doesn't. We would get on the grass for a few weeks after indoors. That was as much psychological as it was physical because they'd be on the grass and just relaxing. It may have hurt our outdoor season some years. We had some guys trying to run in Europe in the summers. I sometimes kept the outdoor season too low-key. All of a sudden the conference meet and national meet were here. If the kid ran well though, I didn't care where he did it.

No matter the time of the year I always believed you needed one long run per week. For some that would be as short as twelve miles and others that would be fourteen miles. We used to do a seventeen mile run but cut that back to fourteen. That was one of my tough workouts because it was the same one all of the time, and we'd run it fast—usually under 6:00 pace but sometimes as fast as 5:30 pace. There was no substitute for that kind of work. It was a workout. We'd do two pace or interval/speed workouts during the week and then the long run. That long run was the toughest and most beneficial in my books because that was the catalyst and the base work that was never going to let you down.

The most important thing was weight. I have seen our guys beating guys they have no business beating because the other guys were overweight. I'd watch the other guy lose and say to myself, "I hope nobody tells him to lose ten pounds." They were that much overweight. There is a thin line, and you have to know it because there is nothing scientific about it. You can't tell a guy, "This is it." When you are feeling good and training well and getting your weight down, sometimes a guy gets to where their weight is just right, and then all of a sudden they lose three or four more pounds and are underweight just like that. When that happens you lose your strength and don't feel good. So you need to recognize that maybe your ideal weight is three or four pounds heavier, and that is where you need to go.

A 6 foot, 5 guy like Doug Consiglio, considering how tall he was, appeared to be underweight. I thought we'd put a little weight on him, and he'd get stronger. So he got up to 147 and ran like a dog, so we had to get him back down to 142, and the reason was his skeleton was very small. He had little arms and legs, and he was carrying extra weight, and the extra five pounds was detrimental.

With Joe Falcon I used the analogy of horse racing. There has been more money spent on research in thoroughbred racing than any other sport because it's the sport of kings. It's a multibillion-dollar business. I was raised close to a racing stable, and I noticed the jockeys were always 110–115 pounds. Those guys were riding an animal that weighed 1,200 or 1,300 pounds bred for one thing and one thing only, to run as fast as possible from point A to point B. That's their only purpose on this Earth. I watched the San Anita and the Breeders' Cup in Canada, and there was this American horse that was undefeated and had been winning all of its races by five or six lengths. Well, they handicapped him five pounds one race. It would have been better if the jockey was five pounds heavier because at least he would move with the horse. Anyways, the horse had to carry five more pounds than the other horses and lost it in a photo finish. So I would tell the guys, if five pounds does that much harm to an animal that weighs 1,200 pounds, what is it going to do to your little 130-pound body? When I explained it that way, the kids would understand and get to the weight they needed.

I only coached guys and most of them, when you explain it, understood what you were talking about. Every kid is looking for a way to get better. There is the odd one that fought me on it. They would agree in person but tell the other guys, "I'm not overweight. I'm fine." But they never ran fine. So the kids have to buy into it, and if they do, it will work with 99 percent of them. There will always be one or two kids that you will knock heads with over it, but most kids deep down want to be good, and most of them will go along.

Some guys are just born bigger, and there really isn't much you can do about it. Track and Field News did a study and determined that Eric Henry was the heaviest man ever to run a sub-four-minute mile. He ran like a Joe Falcon. He had a very tidy stride for a guy who was 6 feet, 4 and weighed 185 pounds. He was just a nice looking runner, real tidy. He wasn't a lumbering guy at all. He was a big guy, but had a great head and was real special.

There were some things that just weren't physical with some people. Our use of sports psychologists started with Frank O'Mara. I felt like it was very hard to bring up the topic of seeing a sports psychologist because when you mention that to a guy their first reaction is, "You think I'm a head case?" That wasn't what I was trying to say. If you need your appendix removed, you get a doctor to have surgery. If you want to have your tooth pulled, you go to a dentist. If you have problems handling certain pressures in your life, shouldn't you go to a person trained to handle those issues? There are doctors in that too. It's a stereotype in that runners would think they are a head case if they were seeing the psychologist.

Frank O'Mara would tell you the sports psychologist he went to turned him into a new man. He could always do the workouts but had problems handling pressure. The media in Ireland loves tearing guys down that went to America because they didn't want them to stay here. So if they had a bad race it was, "Blah blah blah." I always stood behind them. We were lucky to have this Dr. Childers in Rogers. Frank went to see him, and all of a sudden he was a different person. Sports psychology plays a big role if a kid buys into it. People get nervous, and nerves are good if you can channel them in the right way, but if your knees are bending and all of your nervous energy is expended psychologically, there is nothing left for the physical demands of a race. You have to find a good doctor. It's like going to a dietician. There are good ones and bad ones. We've sent guys to dieticians, and they've gained weight. The important thing is finding the right doctor.

A lot of it was handling the athletes and managing expectations. I remember we took Ryan Wilson out to Mt. SAC his sophomore year and he went from 13:54 to 13:28 for 5,000 meters. He even beat Reuben Reina. I asked him after the race how he felt, and he relived the whole thing. I told him you are not going to beat Reuben every time. You are running in front of your family and friends and told him he would not repeat that performance for at least another two years. And sure enough it was two years later when he ran 13:19 for 5,000 meters. It was important to manage expectations, especially if the improvement was so much.

There would be many years we would enter the season ranked first in the country. So sometimes I used reverse psychology. It's agreeing with what's real. I would tell the guys, "They've put you number one, and we deserve to be number one. The whole country says you are the best. So now we have to just go about our business. It's going to be tough but nothing exceptional. We just have to be ourselves. You cannot hide from it. Accept it. I've been telling you all along, and now the rest of the country is saying you are going to win it."

It depends on the group. After all of the hype was over and they forgot about the ranking, I'd sometimes get on them after a race, "That was the most pathetic performance. You wouldn't beat a junior-high school team," or some comment like that. If you're after winning, you cannot pat them on the back for mediocrity and say "That's great." They're smart kids; a lot smarter than their coach probably. These are guys studying engineering, pre-med, whatever. So if you're telling them something that isn't the truth, they are going to say to themselves, "Is this guy for real?"

That being said, there is no place for negative motivation because you cannot enforce it. More than likely negativity will work one time, but you can only threaten to throw the kid out the window one time, and if you don't throw him out, it's tough. Positive reinforcement is the only way, and that's where it comes to individualization with a kid and talking to them to get them motivated. Tell them "This is what so-and-so did, and here is what you did," and "Do you realize how close you are to that guy?" It's all right here. So you have to sit down and talk to them individually and convince them they are as close as that guy.

When we were getting ready for an NCAA race, I'd pick out guys and say "You are going to get fourth and you are going to get twelfth and you are going to get twentieth." I'd say run ten or fifteen places back, and I want you to run with three or four guys that you feel like you could beat and can get five places if you need to get five places. There might even be a guy favored to win it, who is fading in the latter part of a race, but you're feeling good and go flying by him. Then if you go into a race with that type of goal, you don't have to worry about your other teammates because if you don't do your job, it doesn't matter what they do.

Sometimes you can put too much pressure on kids. At the beginning of my career, Mike Conley and Frank O'Mara came in to talk to me because they felt I was putting too much pressure on guys by naming them individually before races. From that day forward when we had a team meeting, I would have figured out how many points we needed—ten points in the mile, twenty points in the jumps—and I'd go down and figure out who was in each event, and I'd say, "If we get these points, we are going to be conference champions." And then we'd go to the meet, and the only other meeting we'd have is before the finals.

I didn't want to have too many meetings because they make kids nervous. I'd stay away from them and tell them to each take care of their business individually and not worry about that other guy. If they were finished competing, then go watch the others, but if they were not finished, then do what you need to do. I know schools that met for breakfast, lunch, and dinner, and they would rehash what happened earlier, and they were basket cases. My philosophy was that each kid should know exactly what he is there to do. He isn't a moron. You don't need to keep reminding him, "Hey, do you know you have that 10,000 meter tomorrow?" Of course he does.

A lot of kids that come into your office are lacking self-confidence and want reassurance to talk about their event. I'd say to them, "I appreciate you coming in, but we're going to relax until then, and right before you go out to compete, we'll talk about it.

Until then don't even worry about it." Otherwise this kid would be analyzing it over and over if you started worrying about it that early. Can you imagine how wound up tight that kid would be heading into a competition? Sometimes I'd just tell him to enjoy the trip and do something to get your mind off of it. If I saw some kid get too wound up at NCAAs or conference, I'd tell him to go out to the mall or the arcade, and sometimes that helped. It took their mind off competing and rehashing their strategy several times until they were a basket case.

I was a hands-on type of person, maybe too much, but I knew what was going on at all times, or at least I think I did. Of course there were things later that kids told me that I'm glad I didn't know, but you have to be hands-on and develop a personal relationship with each kid. That kid shouldn't be afraid to come into your office. If he is afraid, then he probably did something wrong. Sometimes they did do something wrong. When that happened, I would have them write a letter (describing their misbehavior) and sign it and put it in my drawer, and I'd say you have one more time. You always had guys on the team that were instigators, and that letter worked pretty well with them. When I retired I opened up that file, and I remembered all of the characters we had on the team. They turned out to be great people but were hell-raisers in their youth and were into anything and everything that was wrong.

I had standards off and on the track. I would tell the guys when you are a senior at Arkansas, and you don't run 3:35 for 1,500 meters, then you are not ready to step up to the international level. We are the steppingstone from juniors to the international level. If I think you can get under 3:35, I will tell you. That's the one thing some guys would get upset about if I didn't think they could do that. Some of them did fantastic, but had unrealistic ideas, and I'd tell them. I had a kid from Louisiana named Ryan Travis who ran 4:06 for the mile in high school and then 3:59 in his first college race, but he had no speed. I mean that guy flat out would have a hard time breaking 21 seconds for 200 meters, but he was real efficient and had good feet under him, almost like a machine. After he graduated, he asked me if I thought he had potential to make the Olympics in the 1,500 meter and I said, "No, if you want the truth." I barely had the words "5,000 meter" out of my mouth when he said, "I don't want to run the 5,000 meter." He had run one of them in 13:50 or something, just at the conference meet, but didn't want to do them. So just like that he shut it down, and said "I'm going to work a job." You know that was a good decision because there was nothing I could say to turn his mind. He didn't even think about it. He just immediately said "I don't want to run the 5,000 meter." If you looked at him you'd think to yourself he could have been a great 5,000-meter guy, but he didn't have the interest.

Alistair Cragg was a modest type of guy, and when he came to Arkansas, he was just recovering from the loss of his brother and was kind of fragile. It shocked me when I asked him what his goals were and he said, "Coach, if it's okay with you, I'm going to leave that up to you. I'm not trying to not give you an answer, but I don't want to think about it. If you tell me to do, something I'll do it." I smiled and said, "Boy you are going to regret that!" But that's how he was.

You had to know how to handle people after a bad race just as much as a good one. Sean Kaley was a pretty intelligent guy. He was a deep thinker. When you were looking at him, it was like he was just looking right back at you trying to read your mind. So my *favorite thing with him after a bad race was to talk to him and say, "Sean, this was a disaster. It was so bad, let's not even think about it. It was just a disaster, and we never worry about disasters. Now if it was close, you and I would be having a talk, a real talk." That seemed to work with him.*

Others needed another approach. Running them on the track immediately after a bad race was something I did sparingly later in my career because I started using a sports psychologist more. The reason they didn't run well in the race was usually not because they weren't physically ready, but because they weren't mentally ready. They wasted their energy through nervousness. So sometimes I'd bring them back on Monday, and if it was a cross-country race, we'd do a four-mile time trial, and they'd be high-fiving afterwards. I tell you, it's a good idea when kids just had a terrible race and not feeling good about themselves to spring something like that on them. The other guys would be clapping for them as they go by, and it seemed to work at getting them back on track and realizing how good they actually were. One thing I came to understand is that it's important to not just physically prepare athletes, but have them in the right psychological state of mind as well.

7

On Top of the World (1984–1986)

"You're sub-4:00 but that's nothing, kid."

—*John McDonnell*

It is a peculiarity known only to collegiate track and field that the rest and relaxation following most seasons lasts less than the time one takes to exhale. Cross country begets indoors, indoors begets outdoors; and only those who choose to forego a summer season of competition can truly call any part of the year an off season. John McDonnell understood this somewhat dismal phenomenon better than anyone.

"John built his program on middle distance and jumpers," said David Swain. "For those of us who did cross country, it is very difficult to run a full cross-country season, a full indoor season, and a full outdoor season. Most of us would be getting pretty tired by the end of it. I think the reason he was so successful indoors was that he had many frustrated track runners who were coming off cross country and couldn't wait to run on a track."

Many Razorbacks stayed in Fayetteville over Christmas to get a head start on their competition by training on the indoor track.

"We were in a much better position than a lot of other people who may have come back out of shape," said Reuben Reina, who joined Arkansas in 1986. "We were ready to get national qualifiers our first two meets rather than trying to just get back into shape. The rest of the indoor season we could just concentrate on training so our mentality was different."

While McDonnell had the sense not to train his teams at the pace nor the intensity during the indoor season that they typically did towards the latter part of the outdoor season, the sacrifices required of winning an indoor national championship nonetheless required a level of intensity and sharpness that was difficult to sustain throughout an entire year.

True to form, the Razorbacks trained on the grass and did not race for over four weeks following the 1984 NCAA indoor meet until Texas Relays. Despite attending smaller meets at Oklahoma and a windy and rainy invitational at home—where Mike

Conley set Olympic qualifying marks in the long and triple jump—it was not until 1984 Penn Relays when the intensity truly got dialed up.

Villanova still was not yet willing to cede its perch as the dominant power of the meet—capturing the 4 x 800 meter and 4 x 1,500 meter titles—but the tide was turning. Arkansas defended its distance medley relay title in 9:26.57 thanks in no small part to a 3:56.7 split from Paul Donovan. Freshman Doug Consiglio captured the steeplechase in 8:43.5, followed only a second later by Harold Smith.

Weeks later the Hogs won their third consecutive Southwest Conference triple crown following a 50-point victory over second place Texas at the outdoor meet before finishing a program-best third at the 1984 NCAA Outdoor Championships in Eugene, Oregon.[1] It was a total team effort accomplished through two more NCAA titles by Conley in the long and triple, as well as his contribution to a sterling 4 x 100 meter relay. In what would become a trend, that relay team nearly saw itself disqualified when two of its members opted to wear tights in the cool Oregon air.

"One of the other teams turned Arkansas in for wearing tights on the 4 x 100 meter relay," remembered Doug Consiglio. "John told us, 'If I ever turn someone in for something like that, let me know because it's probably time for me to retire. That's just hurting the kids.'"

"[Someone] filed a protest saying Arkansas should be disqualified for running out of uniform," McDonnell recalled years later. "The appeals judge looked at me and said, 'Can you believe this shit?'"[2]

Suddenly in John McDonnell's incubator of expectations, the aspirations of the program had grown from capturing the triple crown in relay meets and conference championships to the oncoming reality of accomplishing the once-unthinkable goal of winning three NCAA Championships in one season. The momentum was becoming hard to stop, and if the present was going well, the future was even brighter.

After years of struggling to attract elite American distance talent, Arkansas's success and McDonnell's developing gravitas suddenly had the Hogs in the running for two high-school seniors from Missouri—Chris Zinn and Joe Falcon—considered among the best prep distance runners in the country.

Zinn, who was coached by longtime West Plains High School coach Joe Bill Dixon, had captured three Missouri high-school cross-country titles and run 9:05 for two miles on the track during an All-American senior year that left him deciding between Arkansas, Wisconsin, and Missouri State.

"I had spoken to Martin Smith [of Wisconsin] and was good friends with Richard Clarke at Missouri State," said Zinn. "I just really liked John. He met Joe and I at the Missouri state cross-country meet and talked to us separately afterwards. He came to my house and met my folks."

As the number-one prep miler in the country with a 4:07 mile to his name, Falcon had been even more bombarded by coaches from across the country, who openly drooled about his upside given his relatively low mileage and the fact that he had only recently given up playing tennis.

"You'd have coaches from well-established universities calling and saying come to my university and you'll be the man and you'll do this," said Falcon. "The entire opposite occurred with Coach McDonnell. He said 'You're pretty good, kid. You've done some good things, but I've been working the last twelve years on a system that will win national championships, and I feel like I'm one or two runners away from that. I am confident if you come to Arkansas you can be part of a national championship team before you graduate.' That was very profound to me."

Before Falcon agreed to visit, he asked John if there was any good fishing and hunting nearby.

"He said 'It's real good,'" remembered Falcon.

Falcon's visit led to an inevitable clash of cultures. Eyebrows were certainly raised by some of the Europeans on the team when the boy from Belton, Missouri, arrived on campus.

"We got to know Joe a bit on that trip," said Swain. "We met him in the hotel with his cowboy hat on and his fishing pole in the corner and thought to ourselves, 'Wow, what have we got here?'"

Nobody was more openly astonished by Falcon's garb than Frank O'Mara. Less than six years after his first roommate in college Randy Stephens had been caught off-guard by the concept of rooming with a foreigner, the shoe was now decidedly on the other foot.

"Frank had never been around a redneck before until I came to the University of Arkansas," said Falcon. "So the first time he saw me I'm wearing jeans, cowboy boots, and a big old cowboy hat, and I'm all of 5 foot nothing, 120 pounds. He literally went to Coach and said, 'You have to send this guy home. He's one of those rednecks I've heard about.'"

If Falcon was impressed with John on the phone, it was during that visit when his trust and confidence in Coach McDonnell only grew.

"Sitting across from him and listening to the passion he had in his voice and for him to clearly tell me what my strengths and weaknesses were and how I needed to improve and how he was going to help me do that as a coach, I was like, gosh, he is not only confident but also humble and very, very methodical in how he was building a team," said Falcon.

The decision was not an easy one. Despite a visit from legendary Kansas coach Bob Timmons, Falcon left his encounter with John McDonnell spellbound by the man he would soon call coach.

"One of my heroes growing up was Jim Ryun, and we were lucky to have Coach Timmons in our house," said Falcon. "That was a tough decision, but when it came down to it, Kansas had such a historic track-and-field program and was still doing great things, but there was just that spark in Coach McDonnell's eye and in his voice. He had a real humble but sincere and fierce confidence that I had never been around and that ultimately was what I decided upon. He told me I was going to be part of a national championship. That was what I wanted, and who would have known I'd be a part of eight of them."

Once he had decided where he was going in the weeks leading into the April signing period, Falcon turned his attention to ensuring his high-school rival would soon become his college teammate.

"We had gotten pretty close during our senior year as we had both gone to nationals, raced for the Mid-West and were roommates at the meet," said Zinn. "I still have a letter from Joe on hotel stationary about staying in touch and hopefully seeing each other down the line. Later, Joe and I spoke on the phone, and he told me he was going to Arkansas. He told me he hoped to see me there too, but if not he'd kick my butt if I was a Badger!"

It was not a hard sell. Only days later, Zinn committed to McDonnell, who in turn drove to Kansas City to sign Falcon before signing Zinn at his home in Pottersville on the way back to Fayetteville.

"Missouri had a pretty good group back then and Roger Grooters was the coach," said McDonnell, "but when they found out Joe was signing with Arkansas, they called him and said, 'What do you mean you are signing with Arkansas? We haven't even started recruiting you yet!' I was thinking, 'Gosh almighty.'"

Signing the duo was a major coup and, as it turned out, the foundation for several national championships in cross-country that had so far eluded the Razorbacks.

"Once John got those state champions things really started to move," said Dick Weis, who had been hired at Oklahoma State the previous fall. "The big one was Falcon. That's when everything changed. He just had an attitude about winning and went right after it."

It was a time of comings and goings both in the McDonnell household and the Razorback program as John and Ellen welcomed their son, Sean McDonnell, into the family on May 22, 1984, only weeks before it became apparent that Dick Booth's time in Fayetteville was winding down.

Following the retirement of longtime Southwestern Louisiana head coach Bob Cole that spring, USL athletics director Terry Don Phillips was looking for a replacement and called his former coach at Arkansas, Lon Farrell, to discuss the exhaustive search they must have gone through to find John McDonnell. After being astonished at how simple that process had actually been, it was mentioned to Phillips that Dick Booth was exactly the person to lead the program at USL.

"Dick had done a great job and wanted to be a head coach," remembered Phillips. "John was very supportive and thought it would be a good opportunity for him."

With a booming oil economy and an energetic president named Ray Authement leading an effort to rebrand USL into a national-level university by renaming it the University of Louisiana (which was eventually successfully challenged by Louisiana State), it was heady times in Lafayette. Still, as intrigued as he was about the prospect of running his own program, Booth was unsure about making the move and preoccupied with the task of preparing one of the best triple jumpers in the world for the 1984 Olympic Trials.

"John said 'You really ought to look at it. You'll be surprised they have better facilities than us, and it's a good situation,'" remembered Booth. "So I flew out there and really liked it and when I got back I told my wife, 'I think we are moving.' Bless her heart because she has always been a great coach's wife and was very encouraging."

After providing him with his first collegiate coaching opportunity six years earlier, McDonnell had selflessly assisted Booth in advancing his career once again.

Despite the boycott from several Eastern bloc countries such as the Soviet Union, the Los Angeles Olympics soon became one of the great financial and organizational success stories in Olympic history. With three athletes qualified for the meet—Conley in the triple jump for the United States, as well as Donovan and O'Mara for Ireland in the 1,500 meter—Arkansas was well represented on the world's biggest sporting stage. It was Mike Conley who was touted by some as a potential Olympic champion in the triple jump. Those hopes unfortunately began to unravel when he bruised his heel before the games and twisted his ankle in the qualifying rounds.

Overcoming such adversity and the fact that his flight was the only one with a headwind, Conley sat in second place (17.18 meters) heading into his final jump, only centimeters behind countryman Al Joyner (17.26 meters), who had jumped phenomenally well.

"I struggled and struggled," remembered Conley, "and finally on my last attempt I said forget about it and made a jump that would have broken the Olympic record but it was a foul."

Despite the pain from coming so close to the pinnacle, Conley would leave Los Angeles with an Olympic silver medal in the triple jump, while Donovan and O'Mara both followed in the footsteps of O'Shaughnessy and barely missed qualifying for the 1500 meter final.

"It was unfortunate but that's how it goes," said Donovan. "I remember coming back to Fayetteville that fall and college athletics seemed so small and petty."

Along with the additions of Falcon and Zinn, John signed a tall, blonde Norwegian transfer from Wyoming named Espen Borge who had qualified nationally in the 800 meter. The most overlooked signing of all however was that of a young man from a small school in Lindale, Texas, named Richard Cooper.

"We were running the regional meet in Georgetown, Texas, and the Texas state cross-country championship was right after us, so we waited around and watched the high school race," said John. "He was in the class B race and was a smooth runner and won it by 200 or 300 meters. So I talked to him for a minute and sent him a questionnaire. He wasn't super fast because he was in class B but had run around 9:20 (2-mile)."

Cooper took much less scholarship to go to Arkansas than he could have received elsewhere. Although he redshirted that fall and would not develop into a national-level presence for many years, the Razorbacks had more depth and talent heading into the 1984 cross-country season than ever before.

Not only were upperclassmen David Swain, Paul Donovan, Gary Taylor, Ian Cherry, and Roland Reina returning in great shape, but the newcomers were not giving them an inch. Freshman Chris Zinn, who was dubbed "Baby Swain," won an early season time trial well ahead of anyone on the team.

"It took a while to get up to speed," said Zinn. "I was used to training at seven minutes per mile, then I stepped into college, and these guys were doing ten miles under six-minute pace. This was guys just stepping out the door to go for a run. Luckily I had older guys there, and Roland Reina really took me under his wing. I usually did eighteen miles on the weekends with Richard Cooper, and we generally averaged about one hundred miles per week. John quickly figured out the more miles I ran the better I got. He had an uncanny knack for figuring out individuals and what they needed to contribute."

Although he had trained at low mileage in high school, Joe Falcon seemed impervious to the vagaries faced by most aspiring freshmen who attempt to simultaneously double their weekly mileage while hammering every run.

"The freshmen wanted to smash all the runs trying to impress everyone," remembered Swain. "So we'd pick a day and show them who was boss. What we soon learned with Joe was we couldn't do it. I'd say to Paul [Donovan], "It's your turn today, you go get him." Paul would go after him and catch him but he wouldn't die. The next day Joe would do the same thing, and I'd have to catch him. He never got injured his entire career. He was an enigma."

"We used to tell him there is a long way to go in the season," said Donovan of Falcon. "You always had guys look impressive at the start and then fade away. Well, Joe certainly improved and was able to take the training and move on."

The team hammered away its "easy" days up in shaded trails off West Markham Road above University Heights owned by Jane and Julian Archer. The couple graciously allowed the Razorback harriers to train on the property for four decades. Amidst the forested swath of land with a wood-chipped trail, the soft and shaded surface allowed Arkansas runners to train hard and avoid injuries throughout the year. For opposing runners visiting Fayetteville it became almost a pilgrimage site, a place where others could soak in some of the Hog magic. It was there that John attempted to keep his finger on the pulse of his team.

"I had to monitor that because it could get out of hand," said McDonnell. "The egos were the biggest problem. When you had a bunch of good guys, it was keeping the egos down without hurting the guy who has the ego and helping the guy you want to come up a little bit."

There were also times when he chose not to interfere with the organics of the training dynamic.

"We pretty much hammered every day unless John told us not to," said Falcon. "When you have all of those college athletes along with the post-collegiate guys like Frank O'Mara, it was pretty darn competitive. That was one of the hardest things John had to do was keep the reins on the guys, but he really loved not keeping the reins on us sometimes. He liked you going out as a freshman and getting your butt handed to you and saying, 'I want to be as good as those guys.'"

McDonnell took every opportunity to reinforce the impressionable freshman.

"He'd pull you in and say those guys are great because of things they are doing, and you can be great too if you do this and do that," said Falcon. "That was such an encourager for a young athlete. I got to see the guys doing great things, and then Coach McDonnell would show me what they were doing as freshmen and would say you can be just as good or better than them if you are willing to put in the work."

The dynamic and chemistry between coach and athlete was apparent right from the start.

"Joe was the kind of guy John could build the program on," said Swain. "He was a head case, but if you could get into his head, he was unbeatable. John could get inside and reach him and build him up. He was amazing."

It was not only John who would make a profound impact on Falcon; Frank O'Mara did as well, being one of many reasons Falcon had attended Arkansas in the first place. Apart from demonstrating the fundamentals of being an elite international athlete, O'Mara never hesitated to share tidbits of wisdom on matters other than running.

"He was extra hard on me about wearing jeans and cowboy hats and boots," remembered Falcon. "He told me I need to show you some style and help you learn how to dress. He took me under his wing in a lot of ways and was unbelievable."

For the first time, McDonnell scheduled Arkansas's first competition during the 1984 cross-country season late, into the third week of September, giving the talented and experienced squad all the more time to train and prepare for the battle they were inevitably prepared to fight at NCAAs in late November.

"We had tons of confidence as a team," said Donovan. "There was confidence and talent that we didn't have to put our A team out there every day."

Heading into the Oklahoma Triangular on September 21, 1984, the Razorbacks had been undefeated at every cross-country race other than NCAAs since 1976. Despite not doing any interval training or sharpening work to that point of the season, there appeared to be no reason to believe the long regular-season streak was in any danger of being broken. That misconception would soon be rectified.

Things had changed in Stillwater since the last time the Razorbacks sauntered in and blew out the Cowboys by one hundred points on their own course two years earlier. After being offered the Arkansas women's track head-coach job, which eventually went to Bev Lewis, Dick Weis had turned around a moribund Oklahoma State distance program in a manner that caught the Razorbacks unprepared that afternoon.

Already resting Paul Donovan and forced to red-shirt Chris Zinn after the freshman ended his season blowing out his knee in a gopher hole, John decided to pull the redshirt off Joe Falcon after seeing some new faces on Oklahoma State, such as future national champion Paul Larkins.

"I didn't even know I was going to race," remembered Falcon. "John had said he wanted to take me just to watch a college race, but came out of the coach's meeting and threw a singlet at me. I said, 'What's that?' He laughed and said, 'If I have to tell you what that is, I don't think you are even ready to race today.' I smiled and said, 'So you mean I get to run?' I found out an hour before I am running, it's Oklahoma, it's three in the afternoon, 100 degrees outside, and he sits us down before the race and tells us what we are supposed to do individually. He told David [Swain] to go to the front, Gary [Taylor] to go with their second guy and for me just to finish, have some fun, settle into the pack, and as the race goes on move up."

With a slow pace and large cluster of athletes in the front pack, a change of pace on a wooded downhill approximately 6,000 meters into the race led to one of the leaders tripping, followed by a pileup of bodies at the bottom of the hill.

"It was just comical," said Falcon. "So the dust clears, and I sprinted between them into the lead. I may not be the best athlete, but I'm an opportunist, so I took off sprinting as hard as I can and am about 60 meters ahead when we came around the corner with a kilometer to go. Coach McDonnell is absolutely flabbergasted because he didn't see what happened. He had this saying 'Check your instruments,' which meant to keep going but relax. Well he's saying that, and I don't know what the heck he was talking about, so I took off harder. I got about ten meters from the line and was about to pass out because I had never run that hard for so long, and I knew they weren't going to catch me. So I walked across the line and fell over."

When the dust settled, Oklahoma State edged Arkansas by five points, ending the Razorbacks' long regular-season undefeated streak. The loss did not sit well.

"John was really upset and told us how we didn't compete as Arkansas athletes," remembered Falcon. "Me being a freshman, I'm sitting there thinking I ran a race I wasn't supposed to run and won my first Arkansas race. Not only is he not going to say bad things about me, but he is going to congratulate me. Well, he looks at me and takes his hat and throws it on the ground and says, 'If you ever walk across the line wearing an Arkansas singlet ever again, you will never wear it again.' I was scared to death."

If the message that losing was not to be tolerated had not sunk in during the talk, John took the team to McDonald's to reinforce the fact. At Arkansas, mediocrity was never followed by a proper meal.

"It was one of those things where OSU was better than we thought, and we just didn't run well," said John. "I thought we could still win not being in top shape, and we went into it too relaxed. So I always had to shake them up when they did something like that, and I had a rule that started way back that if we lost we ate at McDonald's and if we won we ate somewhere nice."

Although a more prepared and complete Arkansas turned the tables on Oklahoma State at a newly revamped Cowboy Jamboree course the following week, the early loss marked a turning point in the season.

"That was a huge wake-up call," said Swain. "We were resting Paul [Donovan] and had done no intervals by then, but we all had a heart-to-heart and said that was our only loss for the year. Done. John did not take the loss well. He worked himself up into a frenzy about expectations and kept us centered. He never let us get arrogant. He let it rip and used this as the time to dress us down. I had fallen down, Gary was a bit hurt, Espen was a little overweight, and we had others who hadn't run well."

After steamrolling the competition at the home meet in October, another piece of bad news befell the Razorbacks when Paul Donovan had a tooth infection two days before the 1984 Southwest Conference Cross Country Championships. Only hours after completing the arduous Tulsa Run on Saturday, junior Ian Cherry returned to Fayetteville that evening only to receive a phone call from John informing him he would be needed to run the conference meet on Monday.

"Donovan got a tooth infection and turned up to practice looking like Richard Nixon so John had to get Ian Cherry to step in," said Swain. "He was knackered [after running a fifteen-kilometer race]."

Despite early season concerns about a Texas squad recently bolstered by Kenyan and Irish athletes of their own, the Razorbacks followed a convincing win at Mae Simmons Park in Lubbock, Texas, for their eleventh straight SWC cross-country championship and an equally easy victory at the regional meet. As it had been all year long, the team's focus was on the NCAA Cross Country Championships, set to take place on November 19 in State College, Pennsylvania. It would turn out to be a battle right to the finish.

After being given individual instructions from McDonnell the night before the race, Arkansas found itself holding onto a tenuous lead over Arizona and Tennessee with one mile remaining.

"That was directly attributable to John because he put each person in place to be successful," said Falcon. "The thing that separated John from other coaches was he clearly knew what each of his athletes was capable of and put them in place with a strategy to be successful. He told David and Paul to get out with the leaders but told me the race is going to go out hard so not to be in the top fifty but to work my way up because there are going to be guys who won't be able to finish."

Following his top-ten finish the previous season, Donovan found himself in tenth place late in the race before a stitch in his side slowed him to twenty-third in the final mile.

"I never found out what that was, but all of a sudden I had some almighty pain in my side," said Donovan. "I remember Swain coming by me, and I thought I had lost it for us."

Although their fourth man, Espen Borge, was comfortably in the thirties, fifth man Gary Taylor was twenty seconds back and starting to fall apart as the field made its way up a hill with a mile to go.

"I said to Gary, 'Nobody can pass you! Nobody! Just hold what you've got!" remembered John. "There were about fifty guys right on his ass and I said to myself, 'Boy, if they go by him, we're done.'"

Not only did Taylor hold on for fifty-sixth, but freshman Joe Falcon passed dozens of runners to catch all the way up to Donovan and placed twenty-fourth. In what would become an Arkansas tradition of teammates stepping up when others faltered, Swain made a conscious decision to move up unlike the previous year.

"I was dying, and I can't understand why but I finally said, 'I'm not going to let this team down,'" remembered Swain. "I passed about twenty people to finish fourteenth."

After the official score took some time to be announced, Arkansas had narrowly edged Arizona 100–111 for its first NCAA cross-country championship in school history.

"It was just fantastic and a great experience," said Swain. "John loved cross country. It was his baby, and it was the harder one to win. That set the tone to win everything in 1984-85."

As much emotion and energy had gone into the national championship victory that afternoon, little did many of the Razorbacks know that the drama in State College, Pennsylvania, was only just beginning as the sun went down and the snow started falling on that cold November evening.

"After the meet was over there was an Irish pub in State College where the owner was either from the hometown of Donovan or O'Mara," remembered Falcon. "So we went down there, and I had never really drunk before in my life and was just enjoying things after the national championship. We got out of there and were walking back to the hotel when the guys started "Calling the Hogs." Then Swain took off and was running up and down cars."

Only when the Englishman climbed to the top of a lamppost and began ripping down municipal Christmas decorations—he stuffed one of the wreaths into his jean jacket[3]—did he attract the attention of State College's finest.

"They had their Christmas decorations up the Monday before Thanksgiving and I just thought that was wrong," said Swain. "So I climbed up the damn lamppost, and some woman saw me do it and called the cops. They identified me by my footprints believe it or not. I was wearing white Nike tennis shoes and they matched the footprints on the top of the car I used to get up."

Although Falcon and Roland Reina were able to make it back to the hotel unscathed, others were unwilling to allow Swain to be taken away in the police car without a fight.

"Half that evening was a blur," said Donovan, "I remember Spanky getting arrested and then I found myself pulling Espen Borge back because he was about to start a fight with the cop. He was getting in people's faces. I mean anybody."

The man David Swain once referred to as "the quintessential Norse madman,"[4] would not let his teammate be taken quietly into the night.

"I'm sitting in the back of the squad car driving off when I hear on the radio that Espen Borge is about to be arrested too," said Swain. "Apparently he had shoved some kid off his bicycle and was chasing after the police car saying, 'You can't take my friend! You can't take my friend!' The police were deciding whether or not they should arrest the blonde guy, but they just left him."

Upon informing the police they had to leave at 6:00 a.m. for an early morning flight out of Pittsburgh, graduate assistant Frank O'Mara took the responsibility of rounding up the money for Swain's release.

"We were back in bed when Frank came in and asked whether we had any of our meal money left," said Falcon. "I said, 'Yeah, I've been saving it. Why?' He said, 'We need it. They arrested Swain, and we told them we just won a national championship and the judge gave him a bond and said if we pay the bond they will let everyone go home.' So we put all our money together."

After paying the bond at a judge's house in the middle of the evening and grabbing a cup of coffee at an all-night diner, the boys walked back into the hotel at 5:45 a.m., where they were greeted in the lobby by a bright-eyed and bushy-tailed John McDonnell.

"John sees us in the lobby, and he was still buzzing and I mean really buzzing and he said, 'Great lads. You're up and ready to go!'" remembered Donovan. "And we still had to go up and get our bloody bags out of the room. I don't think he had even slept after winning. I told Doug Williamson, there is no bloody way I'm going in John's car because we were so wrecked and he was going to talk the entire way."

As they packed into the cars heading to Pittsburgh for their flight back to Tulsa, McDonnell was of such high spirits that some of the athletes wondered whether he was even aware of what had happened.

"We thought we pulled one over on him," said Swain, "but a few years later he found out what happened. He just let it go. That was why he was so good. He knew when to push and when not to push."

After a connecting flight and another drive from Tulsa—along with some motion sickness along the way—the team faced the Fayetteville media upon their return.

"When we got back to campus, there were media and cameras waiting for us," remembered Donovan. "For someone who was almost not there at all, Spanky carried us through the interviews when the rest of us weren't ready to talk."

After a close call with the Arizona cross-country team and even closer call with the State College police, the cross-country national championship was but an opening act for what would become one of the most special track-and-field seasons in American collegiate sports history. The Razorbacks harriers were oozing with confidence to stand their ground with any team in the country.

On a Sunday morning in early December 1984 after a long run, the distance runners entered the training room for ice baths. With the football team preparing for a Liberty Bowl matchup against Bo Jackson and the Auburn Tigers, head football coach Ken Hatfield was a little more wound up than usual.

"[Hatfield] was surprised to see a bunch of skinny runners in the training room, and he wanted us all out immediately and told [head trainer] Dean Weber so," remembered Consiglio. "Dean tried to argue, but Ken told him to tell us to come back later when football was done."

A highly regarded trainer, Weber had served on the U.S. Olympic staff in Los Angeles in 1984. Along with his expertise, Weber was also known for a sharp, biting wit and a marvelous sense of timing. With no choice but to comply with Hatfield, Weber managed to turn around what could have been an awkward situation.

"Since it was just football and cross-country guys, Dean called out, 'All athletes that have been on a national-championship–winning team need to leave and come back later!'" remembered Consiglio. "Gary Taylor and I took our time and made sure as we were leaving to clarify, 'So all national champs must leave, right?' As we were saying this we were moving our gaze to the football players on the tables."

Long before the indoor season got underway, McDonnell did not waste any time hiring an assistant coach for field events. Although there was no shortage of interest in the position, he had his eye on Ted King, an Englishman who had trained at Loughborough University and had a background coaching elite athletes at Wolverhampton and Bolston athletic clubs in the United Kingdom before joining Ted McLaughlin's Southern Methodist coaching staff that won the indoor NCAA championship in 1983.

"Ted and I got on really good, and he was as sound a technical coach as I have ever been around," said John. "He had that great English jumper [Keith Connor], and that's how I had gotten to know him."

For the ever-affable Mike Conley, who had come so far under Dick Booth's tutelage, the opportunity for a fresh perspective was one he embraced rather than resented heading into his senior year.

"Ted came into my life at a good time," said Conley. "He was Keith Connor's coach, and he was different from Dick in the sense that he was more of a technician. He had his own philosophies on biomechanics and a different way of looking at the event. I didn't understand half of the stuff he was saying at first [because of his accent], but I began to understand him better. It was a good learning process for me."

Heading into such an historic season that was set to reap the full harvest from seniors of the 1981 recruiting class, the addition of more world-class jumpers and sprinters to the mix only made the collection of talent in Fayetteville all the more awe-inspiring.

To augment an already potent jumps group, Joey Wells, a long jumper who placed sixth in the Olympics for the Bahamas the previous summer, transferred from UTEP. Future All-American John Register, a prolific jumper/hurdler from Oak Park in Chicago, also followed in the footsteps of Conley.

"When I was recruited by Coach Williamson I couldn't even put Arkansas on a map," remembered Register. "Once I did some research I found out that the folks I really admired such as Wallace Spearmon and Mike Conley were both from down there. I was awestruck by Conley."

Though a different style of jumper, it did not take long for things to rub off on the newcomer.

"When you surround yourself in the center of excellence, you can only do well because you are held to that standard," said Register, who later developed into an All-American jumper. "I think for me the whole program just elevated my track-and-field

IQ for one. Everything was becoming more effortless. I wasn't fighting my body anymore but working in concert with it."

The crown jewel of that 1984 recruiting class was from nearby Texarkana, Texas. His name was Roddie Haley, the top prep sprinter in the country with a 45.5 time in the 400 meter to his name.

"Roddie was probably the best athlete I have ever seen," said Stanley Redwine, who was a graduate-assistant coach at the time. "If he told you he was ready to do something, he would just go out there and do it. He was proof of the old example of getting a guy in shape and letting him do his thing."

When McDonnell and Redwine drove down to Texarkana to visit with Haley at his home, the high-school senior kept them waiting for almost an hour as they sat in his living room.

"We were sitting in the house waiting and this other kid came in and made himself a sandwich," remembered McDonnell. "Finally Roddie showed up, and we got to talk to him. He was a laid-back kid and kind of cool. Very nice guy and one of the fiercest competitors I have ever seen in the 400 meter."

While John McDonnell's team had already become multidimensional at the conference level four years earlier with strong national-level athletes in certain events, there was now not one single event on the team that did not boast a potential conference champion or All-American, while several of those events now had one or more potential NCAA Champions and future Olympians. It was a team absolutely staggering both in its depth and breadth of mature, seasoned talent across the board.

That became apparent enough at a home meet on January 18, 1985, when the Razorbacks blew out the previous year's second-place national team, Iowa State, in a four-way scored meet. Before the rest of the country had even worked off its Christmas eggnog, Arkansas had six automatic qualifiers in its first meet of the season: Bill Jasinski (high jump), Paul Donovan (mile), Gary Taylor (mile), Doug Consiglio (1,000 meter), David Swain (2-mile), and Mark Klee (pole vault), who also broke his own school record in the process.

Following a uniquely formatted meet that Arkansas was invited to at the Universite de Sherbrooke in the Canadian province of Quebec on February 2, 1985, the Razorbacks had small tune-ups at the Dallas Times Herald Meet and Daily Oklahoma Track Classic before making their yearly pilgrimage to the Tarrant County Convention Center in Fort Worth, Texas, for the SWC Indoor Championships.

It was another breathtaking performance. Arkansas captured eight individual or relay titles and scored a remarkably high 156 points to second-place Baylor's 60. Not only did Roddie Haley and Paul Donovan break SWC records in the 440-yard dash and the mile respectively, but Arkansas smashed two SWC records for the highest indoor point total and largest margin of victory.[5] It could not have been just talent that produced such a juggernaut—it was the entire equation of coaching, chemistry, and utter selflessness of its superstars.

"It was the type of personalities and the character of the guys on that team," said John. "It was like a piece of cake working with those athletes. There was no trouble; they were all self-motivated, and wanted to win. It was a pleasure going to workouts. They had that burning desire they were going to win the triple crown no matter what."

Nobody exemplified this better than Mike Conley.

"He was the reason we won the triple crown," said Consiglio. "My freshman year at the conference meet, he asked me how I did. After I told him my time, he said it was my new indoor PR [personal record]. I couldn't believe it. Here I was a freshman, and he knew all of our PRs."

Conley could hardly have been blamed for focusing on his own event given the pressure on him to perform, but he was always concerned about more than just himself.

"I was always like that," said Conley. "I was always involved in thinking about how we are going to win championships. It took all of the events, and I've always been involved in cheering them all on and being involved in all events of the sport."

If the previous season's NCAA Indoor Championships had been a nail-biting affair, the second and final installment of the meet at the Carrier Dome in Syracuse was anything but close. Arkansas athletes brought home fourteen All-American certificates and racked up 70 points to Tennessee's 29. Donovan's 1,500-meter win was trumped only by Conley's double wins in the long and triple jump.

The Razorbacks nearly won both relays too. Roddie Haley's 45.5 anchor split nearly rocketed Arkansas into the win in the 4 x 400 meter , while a weak 800-meter leg by Liam Looney prevented victory for the second-place distance medley relay.

"[Liam] was a stylish, classy looking kind of guy," remembered McDonnell. "Kind of a ladies' man. He was talented, but that was as far as it went. He didn't have that killer instinct. If he was feeling good, he ran good. If he was feeling bad, he would run bad. I told him you have to run well no matter how you feel."

Such miscues would not factor into the outcome of an NCAA championship that was won in such lopsided fashion. In a tradition other teams would start getting used to after national championship meets, the Razorbacks lifted John onto their shoulders once more and screnaded a disappointingly small Syracuse crowd by "Calling the Hogs" for the second year in a row.

Ever the steady hand at the wheel, John reloaded for an outdoor season and the quest for what had so far eluded Arkansas, and the only possible outcome upon which the season could be judged a success: an NCAA outdoor championship and the triple crown that came with it. It was telling that only seven years following the capture of the Arkansas's first triple crown of relay wins at Texas, Kansas, and Drake, the Razorbacks no longer even attended the latter two events. Expectations had shifted upwards in a hurry.

If one thing was for certain, winning the outdoor national championship with outdoor events brought into the equation would certainly not be a cakewalk. While it was difficult to imagine any team in the Southwest Conference standing in the way of the Razorbacks, the outdoor preseason rankings by *Trackwire* had John Chaplin's Washington State team ranked first in the country ahead of Arkansas.

For nearly a month following the indoor season, McDonnell reloaded the distance runners on the grass and kept things low-key before heading to Texas Relays on April 5 and paying his old friend Dick Booth a visit at the Cajun Invitational in Lafayette, Louisiana, the following week.

Earning one's spot on the relays became a feat in itself. At the home Tyson Invitational, which took place only a week before the Hogs geared up to battle with the East Coast powers at the Penn Relays in Philadelphia, the underrated Keith Iovine beat out several teammates for the final spot on the 4 x 1,500 meter team. At Penn, Swain, Donovan, Gary Taylor, and the plucky Iovine, won the relay in a meet record of 14:50.2—with Taylor's 3:38.6 split putting it out of reach, despite a charge by Abdi Bile of George Mason.

"We loved it, the carnival atmosphere and running in front of all of those people," said Swain. "We used to always call Gary Taylor 'Mr. Penn Relays.' He was faster than anybody at that meet."

At the 1985 Southwest Conference Outdoor Championships, which was being held in Fayetteville for the first time since 1972—when the Razorbacks had scored only one solitary point a few months before hiring McDonnell—Arkansas racked up 167 points (a feat made all the more impressive by the fact there were only six scorers in each event) and outscored second-place Texas by a meet-record 87 points.

In such a complete victory, there was not a weak event on the Arkansas team. Even in the sprint events, traditionally a limited area for the Razorbacks, Arkansas athletes were rewriting the SWC record books. The 4 x 100 meter relay of Fred Cleary, Roddie Haley, Wallace Spearmon, and Mike Conley broke the conference record (38.81), while Haley and Conley both came back to break the 400 meter (44.67) and triple-jump (56'3.75) conference records respectively.

As McDonnell soaked in such a decisive and complete conference championship win at the home track in front of home fans on a warm May afternoon in 1985, everything appeared to be coming so easily to the Razorbacks. In reality, the fruits of years of labor had ripened. The level of Arkansas dominance was so profound and the chasm between Arkansas and the rest of the conference was growing so great every year that it was certainly not unreasonable for one to wonder whether any team in the Southwest Conference would ever be able to challenge Arkansas at a conference meet ever again.

McDonnell remained as humble and self-effacing as ever. After the meet was over, John headed over to George Cole Field to support the Razorback baseball team in its own SWC tournament game.

"Spontaneous applause started rippling then mushroomed to a crescendo during a lull in the baseball game," wrote Nate Allen in *More Tales From Hog Heaven*. "The subject of the applause kept looking around to see what the fuss was about until realizing it was about him. For all of the accolades he would receive John McDonnell never had a more spontaneous tribute."[6]

Heading into the 1985 NCAA Outdoor Championships that was expected to be a dogfight, John McDonnell did not have the luxury of fanciful thoughts as Arkansas sought its first outdoor national title and triple crown at Memorial Stadium in Austin, Texas.

With Mike Conley offering to compete in every event possible, the challenge facing McDonnell was keeping his frenetic jumper from running, jumping, and cheering himself into the ground.

"He was like having another coach and would always come up with points for each event," said John. "He came in one time and said how many points do you predict? I said a certain number, and he had come up with two more points. So we went down event by event to find the discrepancy and finally got to the 4 x 400 meter relay, and that's where we differed because I didn't have us scoring any points. He said 'I'm going to anchor it.' And I said 'Like hell you're going to anchor it. You're already doing the 4 x 100 meter, the 200 meter, the long jump, and the triple jump. You're not doing the 4 x 400-meter relay.' That was the kind of team man he was. He wanted to do everything."

The burden would weigh heavily on Conley's shoulders after Wallace Spearmon injured his hamstring at the SWC meet. Not only was Conley expected to score big in the jumps, but in the sprint events as well. Although the shorthanded 4 x 100 meter relay was unable to place higher than seventh, Conley had already exceeded expectations earlier on that boiling hot Friday afternoon in the 200 meter.

"When Spearmon pulled his hamstring we thought, 'There goes our national championship,'" said Swain. "Then Mike came second in the 200 meter to Kirk Baptiste in 20.15, his feet flapping everywhere. He was the ugliest runner."

Conley may not have been the most graceful looking sprinter on the track, but he certainly had no problems finding the finish line before most others.

"I think when you look at Mike from the waist down, he was doing everything else that world-class sprinters were doing," said Redwine. "Maybe it was a little unorthodox, and he was a little longer legged, but everyone else was taking tiny steps to keep their ratios higher. He got it done. I've never seen anyone run a curve the way he could run it."

In the 400 meter, Roddie Haley ran 44.71 in the finals to beat Gabriel Tiacoh of Washington State and break the stadium record Tiacoh set in the heats. It was an important head-to-head battle that put the Razorbacks ten points ahead of WSU—and a staggering victory by a college freshman in a field of several Olympic finalists.

In the 1,500 meter, the indoor NCAA mile champ, Paul Donovan, entered the outdoor final as a decided underdog against the emergent Somalian from George Mason, Abdi Bile, whose coach, John Cook, opted not to enter him in the 800 meter despite the possibility of winning both events. A fresh Bile beat the field by over a second in a tactical time of 3:41.62 ahead of Donovan, who was third.

"Abdi probably could have won the 800 meter as well, but he was not permitted to eat anything until the sun went down since it was Ramadan," said Cook. "It never seemed to get dark in Texas and I wasn't about to get involved in that mess. I'm not going to compete against Allah. I really felt bad for him because he was getting dehydrated from spitting all day long. He couldn't even swallow his own saliva."

The only man who seemed to make doubling at a national championship look easy was the one who had done it with such ease three times before, Mike Conley. In the long jump, Conley tied a stadium and meet record with a 27 feet, 2 inch long jump. He then found himself leading the triple jump before John Tillman of Tennessee unleashed a 55-7 mark on his second-to-last jump of the day to take the lead.

With the scorching heat elevating close to 115 degrees at noon down by the track in Austin, Conley had been shielding himself from the heat by lying underneath a tent made out of a pole vault cover draped over two hurdles. It was at that point Conley jumped up after hoping he had the victory in hand.

"Ted [King] and I were sitting together and told Mike we're going to win the meet anyway," remembered McDonnell. "His calf was cramping but he absolutely wouldn't give in. He said, 'No I'm going to win it.' He was amazing."

Conley didn't just win the event—he jumped 58-1.75, which was not only a personal record, but an Arkansas record, collegiate record, American record, and the third-best triple jump in the world of all time. That was hardly the only amazing thing about the accomplishment.

"Ten minutes before the final of the triple jump, Conley jogged over to Ted and me and said that he forgot his triple-jump shoes at the hotel," remembered McDonnell. "He asked if there was anyone on the team that had running shoes that would fit him. I said David Swain had a pair of distance spikes a half-size smaller. So he said that would be okay and on his last jump he burst the shoes."

"I was notorious for [forgetting] that stuff," said Conley. "There were times I brought one shoe or left two shoes behind."

Arkansas extended its lead significantly. With Washington State's discus and javelin throwers unable to make up for the difference, it was left to Bill Jasinski in the high jump and Marty Kobza in the shot put to put the cherry on top of the championship cake with All-American performances of their own. Only thirteen years removed from scoring one point at the SWC championship, Arkansas outdistanced Washington State 61–46 to capture its first NCAA outdoor track championship and triple crown.[7]

As Razorback athletes were "Calling the Hogs" once more at Memorial Stadium in Austin, educated observers of the sport began putting their accomplishments into proper perspective.

"*Track and Field News* without even contacting me said at the time they believed it was the greatest collegiate track and field team ever," remembered McDonnell.

Although future Arkansas teams would also capture triple crowns by runaway margins at the NCAA Championships, rarely would it be done with such balance across nearly every event and such significant points in the sprints, distance, jumps, and throwing events.

"I think the 1985 team was the best," said Conley. "It was really special. I just think across the board it was special, and you think that it was done when Wallace [Spearmon] was even hurt. If he didn't get hurt, it would have been even more special."

When one considers that future All-Americans Joe Falcon and Richard Cooper were redshirted for the entire track season, the feat becomes even more mind-boggling.

Such success had certainly not come without deserved attention paid to John McDonnell by athletic directors around the country. Legendary track-and-field coach Deloss Dodds, who had been hired away from Kansas State to be the Texas athletic director starting in 1981, certainly was not unaware of what was happening. With the retirement of Cleburne Price at the University of Texas, many in the local media began to focus on the coach up in Fayetteville, who had upset the applecart in the powerful Southwest Conference by stepping on Texas year after year.

"At the NCAAs in Austin they kept putting the camera on John every time Arkansas did something," said Dick Weis of Oklahoma State. "I think he was interested in Texas, but Cleburne was the outgoing guy and vetoed him. Arkansas would go to Texas Relays every year and kick their butt, and Texas was losing kids to them. There was a bad rivalry there."

Given the tremendous potential of a program that had under-produced for years, there was no shortage of qualified coaches interested in the Texas position. Despite winning two

NCAA Championships at the University of Tennessee, head coach Stan Huntsman had become unhappy with the resources being invested into the program and facilities in Knoxville.

"I had been offered the job at Southern California the year before, and I turned it down," said Huntsman. "The [Tennessee] AD made some promises that he reneged on, so I was kind of upset and fortunately for me Texas came along, and he made some of the same offers to keep me. I knew Deloss Dodds first from watching him run at Kansas State, then knew him as a coach there."

Dodds hired Huntsman that summer, which turned around the Longhorn fortunes quite sooner than perhaps anyone anticipated. In the game of musical chairs that followed, it was Huntsman's former star athlete and Olympian on those two NCAA championship teams, Doug Brown, who was selected to succeed him at Tennessee at only thirty-three years of age and with no collegiate coaching experience.

"I didn't know my ass from a hole in the ground," admitted Brown, "but fortunately Stan left me a good program behind, and I managed to stumble my way through it and win an SEC Triple Crown [in his first season]."

The summer brought a well-deserved opportunity to rest for John McDonnell. With a six-year-old and one-year-old to raise in a new home he had constructed out in the countryside, John spent the summer following his greatest triumph relaxing at what he always did best: working. Whether it was at his ranch or in the track office, John never stopped.

"That summer was when it all started and went right until 2000," said John. "I did nothing but walked, talked, and breathed track. I never took a holiday, and that turned out to be a mistake. We won cross country, then I had to win indoors, and then I had to win outdoors; and when that's over July comes around; and I'm recruiting for next year until the guys come back in August. It was like I got into a wind tunnel and couldn't get out. I got possessed by recruiting."

Following a trip home for his mother's funeral in 1986, it would be nearly fifteen years before John again flew across the ocean to visit his family.

"He wouldn't go to Ireland," said Ellen. "I used to encourage him to go home and see his family, but he wouldn't. He didn't like to fly, and his mother passed away, so some of the family started coming over here."

Just as it had been growing up in County Mayo, whenever John was finished with the hard work there always seemed to be more left to do. What little time he did have available for leisure was spent during the summers working at the ranch in Oklahoma. It was his outlet for deep thinking.

The demands of raising the young children were often shouldered alone by Ellen McDonnell.

"She was great at taking care of the kids and ran the financial end of the ranch," said John. "We all had fun at the ranch together. Heather and Sean loved to ride horses and fish. We repaired fences, fed cattle, and rode four-wheelers. The one thing I really regretted was that I should have spent more time with my family. There always seemed to be a meet. The kids turned out great in spite of me."

When August rolled around in Fayetteville, the Razorback athletic department had taken on a much different complexion. Although he lost his first bowl game to Auburn, football coach Ken Hatfield was off to a great start despite the misgivings of some who might have preferred Jimmy Johnson.[8] Not only was Hatfield winning but the devout fundamentalist and former punt returner on the 1964 national-championship football team was recruiting locally and refraining from putting his foot in his mouth quite as often as his predecessor.[9]

After nearly a decade of guiding Razorbacks hoops to among the nation's elite, Eddie Sutton had been unable to refuse an overture from Kentucky to take over their renowned basketball program. In one of a long series of sound decisions as athletics director, Frank Broyles simultaneously managed to turn that loss into Arkansas's gain by luring Nolan Richardson from the University of Tulsa, where he had guided the Golden Hurricane to the NIT Championship and second round of the NCAA tournament.

For the second year in a row, the success of the Arkansas track-and-field program meant John had staffing decisions to make of his own. After Doug Williamson was hired as the head coach at the University of Virginia, John decided to create two part-time positions out of the previous full-time assistant position.

"I took his salary and split it between Mike Conley and Stanley Redwine, which you could do back then," said John. "That was a good move because Stanley was great with the sprints and hurdles, and Conley was a great coach and recruiter. He could get an Eskimo to come here. His mere presence was enough. The guys just wanted to be on the same track with Mike because he was so talented and mild mannered."

While Mike Conley's graduation from college hurt the Razorbacks, the fact that someone of his talent and personality remained closely associated with the program paid dividends for years to come. Even Paul Donovan, who won many national championships as a Razorback, also chose to continue training in Fayetteville following his lone remaining indoor season.

There were also other examples that the program was continuing its upward trajectory into rarified heights that few collegiate programs ever ventured. Far from the days when athletes were thumbing their nose at McDonnell's offers in order to walk on at places such as Oregon, the tables had in fact turned. Despite thinking about his decision until early June, Canadian prep prodigy John Castellano ultimately opted for Arkansas despite being personally recruited by Bill Dellinger at Oregon.

The Toronto native had run a phenomenal 13:51 for 5,000 meters on the track and finished third at the World Cross Country Championships with less than forty miles per week of training. With John McDonnell having guided lesser talents to the pinnacle of the sport, it was almost surreal to think about the possibilities of what someone of Castellano's pedigree could accomplish at Arkansas. Surely once he became a Razorback, only greatness could follow. It was almost too good to be true—and as it turned out, it was.

"The coaches up there told me he was different," said McDonnell. "One of them told me he had dropped out of a race with ten yards to go because he was getting beaten. He was a great talent, but they told me he won't stay. The kid will not stay. Of course I just thought they were trying to keep him up there."

Despite whatever misgivings he may have had based on those conversations, McDonnell offered the scholarship to Castellano but did not push the decision prematurely.

"He signed really late, and I didn't try to rush the situation," said McDonnell. "I told him I did not want him to come down unless he was sure. It was between us and Oregon. So one day he called me up and said, 'I'm going to be a Razorback.' So I said, 'Great! Is it all settled in your mind?' And he said, 'Yep, I've decided Arkansas is the spot for me.' So I told him, 'John, don't come down here just to get the correct time.' He said to me, 'No, if I go down, I'm staying.'"

After driving down from southern Ontario in Doug Consiglio's Volkswagen Rabbit, it did not take long for the heat, miles, intensity, and competitiveness of the training program to weigh on the newcomer.

"I did sixty-five miles my first week, which was way more than I had done, and it was just brutal weather," remembered Castellano. "It was way hotter than anything I had experienced in Toronto."

Along with redshirt freshman Chris Zinn, who was now recovered from knee surgery, and Richard Cooper, the Razorbacks would be relying on youth after the loss of cross-country eligibility for Paul Donovan, Roland Reina, and an NCAA decision that David Swain had exhausted his eligibility as well.

"You have to be worried about being so young," McDonnell told the media. "You don't know how they will react to the pressure of being national champions. Wisconsin will be tough. They finished fourth a year ago and lost only their third man, but had another injured athlete out who they will get back."[10]

Opting for five weeks of uninterrupted training, McDonnell opened the cross-country season on September 27, 1985, in a home meet against Oklahoma on a clear, seventy-two-degree day. Any concerns the Razorbacks might have had about being too young were quickly dispensed once they put up a perfect score against the Sooners. The meet had gone as well as it could for the team but Castellano was extra hard on himself.

"He didn't know how good Joe Falcon was," remembered McDonnell. "So he ran well at Oklahoma, but Joe beat him that first meet and so did a few others. I told him when I recruited him that we had a bunch of guys he hadn't heard of who weren't great in high school that are very good now."

While Castellano moved up to the second spot on the team at Oklahoma State the following week—this time only thirty seconds behind Falcon and fifteen seconds behind future national champion Paul Larkins of Oklahoma State— he was undergoing an adjustment similar to the one that O'Shaughnessy, O'Mara, and Donovan had all undergone and many Razorbacks would experience as freshmen in the future.

"I never felt rested the whole time I was there," said Castellano. "I ended up getting sick, and on one of the days they were doing an eight-mile time trial, I stopped at four miles. I couldn't do it. I just didn't have it."

The workouts were one thing, but it was also becoming apparent that Fayetteville was not big enough for both John Castellano and Joe Falcon. There was certainly never a paucity of competitiveness and ego on the forty national-championship teams McDonnell ultimately coached, but never was the dynamic of personalities so doomed to failure as it was during the fall of 1985.

"I hated the guy," admitted Castellano. "[Falcon] would tell us about these amazing workouts he did. He was all show. He had just barely beaten me at the Keebler [high-school] meet in Chicago. I think if I had stayed I would have beaten him by NCAAs."

Rather than stabilize, the situation degenerated as September gave way to October. Not only were some of the other athletes on the team questioning whether the bally-hooed Canadian was for real in private conversations with Doug Consiglio, who assured them that he most definitely was, but his teammates did not appreciate his unwillingness to buy into McDonnell's training philosophy.

Castellano soon became uninterested in his academic program, which led to poor mid-semester grades. His relationship with his teammates continued to deteriorate from there. Many nights were spent on the phone as he called long distance to his girlfriend to weigh his options until finally in mid-October he asked McDonnell if he could attend a wedding in Toronto during the Canadian Thanksgiving weekend.

"Frank O'Mara called me Sunday night and said, 'Castellano is leaving,'" remembered McDonnell. "And I said, 'No, he just got back today.' 'No,' Frank said, 'he's leaving. Period.' I said, 'What?' 'He's back from Canada,' said Frank, 'but he's packing his bags to leave, and he'll see you in the morning.'"

Although Consiglio and Donovan tried to speak with him before he departed, Castellano's mind was made up. He had bought a one-way ticket to Canada. That next morning there was nothing McDonnell could say to convince him not to board the plane back to Toronto in the middle of the semester.

"The funny thing is I almost knew it was going to happen," said McDonnell. "I should have listened to some of the Canadian coaches who told me he wouldn't stay. Doug had said he'd be okay after he settled in down here, but Doug was a different kind of person. Doug could live anywhere, and it wouldn't bother him. John was more or less a home person and didn't want to get out of Canada."

After refusing McDonnell's request that he finish the semester of classes, Castellano also balked at the idea of sticking around to help the team defend its NCAA cross-country title.

"It didn't matter to me," said Castellano. "I just wanted to get out of there and go home. I didn't feel bad at all about leaving. I felt bad about leaving Consiglio, but half those guys on that team were competitive buggers. They were like sharks."

As damaging a departure as that may have been, coming as it did in the middle of the semester, introspection was a luxury neither John McDonnell nor any of the Razorbacks had at that point of the year.

"We'll have to manage without him," McDonnell told the media on October 21, 1985. "We've got people here now that want to be here and want to win."[11]

The Southwest Conference Cross Country Championships had the potential to be close with a new head coach at the University of Texas breathing life into the program, but the young Razorbacks were a runaway train now free from the baggage of earlier in the season.

It was not uncommon for Falcon to break 4:20 on the mile repeats up Razorback Hill. Long after his days as Razorback ended, he still remembers the confidence he gained from the physical strength it took to get through those workouts and the reinforcement from McDonnell that followed.

"Coach would sit us down after one of those workouts if he saw you were on the verge of something special," said Falcon. "He would sit you down and say there's nobody in the country that can do that, and by the time you got to the national championship you were saying, 'I don't know who I am running against, but I'm ready.' You never went into a big race not knowing if you were ready. When you could accomplish going up that hill, there was nothing you couldn't do."

The Southwest Conference Cross Country meet certainly was not an obstacle they had to be concerned about in 1985. Following a solid 28–60 victory over Texas, where Falcon sacrificed the individual win so his teammates could pack it together, the Razorbacks entered the 1985 NCAA Cross Country Championships in Milwaukee, Wisconsin, looking to repeat as national champions.

They could have hardly expected the conditions that would greet them.

"I remember how cold it was and the snow and ice all over the course," said McDonnell. "It had to have snowed two feet, so they cleared off a path for the race. Then the day before the sun came out and melted some of it, and it rolled down the hill and formed ice, and they couldn't get it off. It was really tough because you'd slip, but of course if you wore long spikes, it tore your calves up."

Already lightly favored heading into what was expected to be a tight race, the Wisconsin Badgers, who were now coached by Martin Smith, had the advantage of not only being acclimatized to the weather but also understanding the terrain. With the course impassible for the most part until race day, few teams had an opportunity to even run a preview of it.

"The second half of that race was much tougher, and it definitely would have helped to know that," said Consiglio. "At three miles, I was our seventh man and Wisconsin's fourth man was behind me. We were all running over our heads. I went back like a rock. They just ate us up during the second half of the race. We hated to lose, but we lost to a classy team, and they beat the crap out of us."

Classy as the Badgers may have been, that group of seniors from Madison, who had won the national championship three years earlier, were not going to let anything, or anyone, stand in their way.

"Joe and I took off and were running down that first hill in the snow when Tim Hacker of Wisconsin and Yobes Ondieki of Iowa State come running down behind us and full shoulder shoved me and Joe to the side," remembered Chris Zinn. "I go off to the left side and Joe goes off to the right through the flags. We got back on the course and we're like, 'What the hell was that?'"

Wisconsin flipped Arkansas with a strong final two miles to win the meet by a margin of 67–104.[12] With some of his athletes fading during the second half of the race, John reflected on his fateful decision to instruct his runners not to wear tights in the blizzard conditions.

"It was a mistake not to run in the half tights like Wisconsin did," said McDonnell, "but I tell you cross country shouldn't even be run in a place like that."

Second place at a national championship was hardly reason for despair, but there were innumerable what-ifs for the Razorbacks that season, not the least of which was whether an Arkansas team with John Castellano could have beaten Wisconsin that day.

"If John had stayed there is no telling how fast he would have run," said Consiglio. "Look how much he improved in two weeks. He might have even beaten Joe at NCAAs."

It is a question that will never be answered.

Never one to dwell on things, McDonnell focused on an indoor season that was shaping up to be sensational. Although Mike Conley was no longer a Razorback, Ted King attempted to replace him with triple jumper Femi Abejedi, a 54 feet, 8 inch Nigerian triple jumper from England. On the track, Wayne Moncriefe of Central Tech in Toronto brought some much needed 800-meter depth. The ripest fruits of all were in the mile, however, with the maturation of Doug Consiglio, Gary Taylor, and Paul Donovan, in his last season of eligibility.

At the Razorback Pentangular on January 17, 1986, Consiglio set a facility, school and, collegiate record in the 1,000 meter in 2:19.64, while Gary Taylor ran 3:58.26 in the mile only weeks after he stopped cross training in the pool. Among six other national qualifiers that day was Roddie Haley, who set a world record in the 500-meter dash in 1:01.18. It was an athletic blitzkrieg if ever there was one.

"We've never had that many qualifiers in a first meet before," McDonnell beamed before the media. "Haley's world record was amazing considering he had some back problems over Christmas and is only 90 to 95 percent healthy. When he gets in shape, there's no telling what he can do. I think before this year is over he could be the first man to break 60 seconds in the 500 meter."[13]

While Haley indeed had more left in the tank, the home meet served merely as the opening act for what was to come the following weekend. Frank O'Mara was intent on breaking Eamonn Coghlan's indoor-mile world record of 3:49.78 and was going to bring as many current Razorbacks with him as possible. The fact that the attempt was being made on the flat 200-meter track in Fayetteville did not faze any of them.

"It was a metal building, colder than hell with heaters hanging on the ceilings and only two bathrooms that would freeze up because they had no heaters," remembered Swain. "There were bleachers on the back stretch looking at the home stretch and when you were running down the back stretch it was like you were running down a damn tunnel, which was kind of cool because you had people on the bleachers hanging over shouting at you. We loved it and there were some quick performances in there."

With Joe Falcon and Gary Taylor rabbiting, Frank went through 800 meters on world-record pace.

"We went out really hard," said Consiglio. "I was at 1:55 for 800 meters and in dead last. Frank went through the 1,200 meters in 2:53 and was still within world-record range somewhat before we all started dying."

O'Mara closed in 3:52.3, followed by Consiglio in 3:55.91 and Donovan in 3:56.39. Even short of a world record, it was a spectacular performance that left the 2,560 spectators who crammed into the tiny track facility in a state of frenzied exhilaration.

"We gave the crowd a good show," McDonnell told the media. "They gave us some good support and it really helped. I'm sure there are a lot of people who haven't seen a mile run that fast. We're going to put Arkansas track on the map."[14]

As much attention as was paid to O'Mara's performance in the Irish media, Doug Consiglio was also attracting attention north of the border as the new Canadian record holder in the mile. After the meet was completed, John told Doug to come to his office on Monday. If Consiglio expected high fives and congratulations that morning, he was to be sorely disappointed.

"He only gave me one day to think I was good," said Consiglio. "When I got there he said, 'You're good kid, you're world class, you broke 4:00 for the mile, but let's see who else has broken 4:00 for the mile,' and he names off about forty people. Then he says, 'Frank beat the crap out of you. At 800 meters, he was pulling away from you. If you wanted to call him at the finish line it would have been a long-distance call. I don't want to take anything away from you. You're sub-4:00, but that's nothing, kid. You have the wheels, we'll get you strong, and you can run even faster.' So suddenly my perspective on things changed. On Saturday I run a sub-4:00, and everyone in Canada is saying you're so fast, and Monday you leave John's office, and you're just dying to train to get better. That's where John was a real good motivator."

It was a psychological technique John used throughout his career.

"That was something I always did," admitted John. "I'd say, 'That's great, Doug. You got your ass beat. Why should Frank beat you? Frank O'Mara is good, but he's not unbeatable. You've got talent and can beat him.' I'd always try and reassure guys that I thought they were better than they thought they were. I always wanted to make them think, 'You're only as good as that? Just that? You're way better than that!' And they'd think to themselves, 'He's right. Next time I run against that sucker I'm going to go for him.'"

Of course, not everybody in Canada had reserved their skepticism for Consiglio's performances.

"We used to laugh because every one of his Canadian records was done in Fayetteville," said Paul Poce, who was the head coach for the Toronto Olympic Club and Athletics Canada at the time. "We thought they had a short track. I'm only kidding of course, but there was always some smartass who brought that into the picture."

Following a competition at the Dallas Times-Herald Invitational before 12,162 fans at Reunion Arena crammed in to see Carl Lewis, Joe Deloach, and a pro-football sixty-yard showdown between Herschel Walker and Darrell Green, Arkansas returned to Fort Worth a few weeks later to capture the Southwest Conference Indoor Championships for the sixth year in a row.[15] Then it was off to the 1986 NCAA Indoor Track and Field Championships, which had been moved to Oklahoma City after two disastrous years in Syracuse.

"It was a good ten-lap-to-the-mile track," said McDonnell, "J. D. Martin was the coach at Oklahoma at the time, and Oklahoma City did a pretty good job because they had a warm-up track in the other building, and it was the same size track. It was almost like an Olympic setup."

The Razorbacks once again entered the meet as the presumptive favorites. Rather than feeling the pressure of being ranked number one, John used reverse psychology to put his athletes at ease.

"A lot of times they'd rank us number one and put us up there so everyone could have a shot at us," said McDonnell. "I'd say to the guys, 'Well they're doing my job. I don't have to tell you you're number one. Everyone else believes it. I believe it, and your competition believes it, but it won't happen unless we keep doing exactly what we're doing. Nothing else. We can win this championship and don't have to do anything we haven't done before.'"

Before nearly 7,614 spectators at the Myriad Convention Center, Roddie Haley nonetheless did something nobody had ever done before.

"He would relate everything to a race car," said assistant coach Stanley Redwine. "So he would tell me, 'I am going to go out there for the first 400 meters and then drop it and shift it and take off.' And exactly as he said, he took off in the race and set another world record."

Haley's mind-boggling time of 59.82 not only broke his own world record in 500 meters set at the home meet in mid-January, but fulfilled McDonnell's prophecy that he would break sixty seconds once he was in shape. The win would stand forever, but the record, along with others that day, would eventually be nullified because the track did not have a rail on the inside lane.

"What a farce," said Oklahoma State coach Dick Weis of the ruling. "If you ran inside on that track you would have fallen off about a foot."

The Razorbacks picked up several more points across the board before Doug Consiglio finished second in the 1,000 meter behind the great Freddie Williams of Abilene Christian, who was permitted to compete in the Division I national championship that year.

While the Razorbacks were never in serious jeopardy of losing the meet, the performance of the weekend clearly belonged to Paul Donovan, who anchored the 4 x 800 meter relay to victory in a time of 7:20.22.

"That was what was so good about the team . . . guys would raise their game," remembered Donovan. "There was an example of a team rising to win an NCAA title."

The following day Donovan came back to contest a 3,000 meter with no shortage of talent in the field.

"There was a guy named Gerry O'Reilly from Villanova and good steeplechaser from Auburn named Brian Abshire, " said Donovan. "They all knew I was anchoring the 4 x 800 meter, so they made me run quicker in the heats to take it out of me. I much preferred a flat track, but I had to run on this shitty little board track. I had a long stride, and it definitely didn't suit me."

Tight track or not, Paul Donovan refused to be beat by anyone that day, winning the 3,000 meter in 7:54.60. Arkansas won its third NCAA indoor championship with 49 points to Villanova's 22.

It was at that meet when a freshman jumper from Montreal, Canada, named Edrick Floreal, who was competing for Nebraska, noticed the power of a strong team dynamic at the national championships.

"I remember being at the NCAA meet and the announcer telling the team from Arkansas to be quiet because they were going crazy cheering for each other," said Floreal. "I had jumped well at Nebraska, but I didn't have the team dynamic of twenty guys at nationals cheering for each other, and I wanted to be a part of that and move on to a different environment with team bonding."

Those who had always experienced track and field as an individual sport were continuously amazed by McDonnell's ability to harness the disparate event groups into a collective unit.

"Usually a track team is a bunch of individuals," observed All-American jumper John Register. "It is [a society in miniature]. You have your distance crew, your sprinters, your jumpers, and your weight men. All of those individuals are in their own little silos working out, but John brought us together by having us work on a lot of projects together.

So during one summer we poured foundation for the outdoor track. We also had land donated for the trails and went up there with backhoes and tractors to widen it. At first I thought, 'This is for the distance guys. What good is this for me?' But what happened was we all got up there and were laughing, and they made fun of the city guys like me because it was the first time I had seen a snake. I reflected on it later when we were at the NCAA Championships, and our distance guys were on the track. Our whole team was still there cheering while other teams were not. That was the difference."

The title was one of many celebratory moments to come for Arkansas track and field. During the spring of 1986 however, the euphoria from that victory would be short-lived for McDonnell and many others in the Razorback athletics department. The assistant athletic director overseeing track and field, Dr. Lon Farrell, was not doing well.

"It was sad because during his last few years he was depressed," remembered John. "He had a lot of Irish in him, and I tried to get him to go back to Ireland and look up his ancestors and he said, 'Oh no.' I kept saying, 'Believe me when you get over there someone will claim you,' but he would never do it. I think if he took some time off and got away, he would have felt better. The job got to him. He did everything."

Ten years after convincing John to stay in Fayetteville and after a lifetime of devoted service to young athletes, Lon Farrell took his own life on April 19, 1986. The loss hit John hard and left a major void within the Razorback athletic department. A departmental academic award was named in his honor.

"He was such a great person," remembered Terry Don Phillips, who played for Farrell on Frank Broyles's Arkansas teams in the 1960s. "All through the years and of all of the coaches I was around at Arkansas, as a player and coach I would check in with Coach Farrell all of the time."

Following the funeral, John managed to keep the pain inside of him as he took his team to Penn Relays for what would turn out to be another record-setting weekend in Philadelphia.

After wins by Bill Jasinski in the high jump and a meet record by Jeff Pascoe in the pole vault, the Hogs took two more victories in the 4 x 1,500 meter and distance medley relay largely on the backs of superb performances by Gary Taylor and Roddie Haley.

Finding themselves in an eight-second deficit to Auburn in the 4 x 1,500 meter, Taylor not only took the lead but put another five seconds on Auburn with an astounding 3:36.2 leg that was the fastest in the history of the Penn Relays.

"Gary Taylor was Mr. Penn Relays," said Consiglio. "Nobody ever ran a faster 1,500 meter at Penn Relays than him."

Roddie Haley was no less spectacular in teaming up with Taylor, Espen Borge, and Doug Consiglio for a distance medley relay victory for the ages.

"[Roddie] would get us so fired up before the relay, and you knew he was going to run so hard," said Consiglio. "You knew he gave everything."

After a 2:51.2 split by Gary Taylor put Arkansas just behind Villanova, Haley blew it wide open.

"I remember the announcer at Penn was from Arizona, Jack O'Reilly, and he said, 'And here comes Roddie Haley!'" said McDonnell. "Villanova had a great quarter miler, too but Haley made up a few yards and put about fifteen on him. The crowd was absolutely going crazy. That was the greatest race I ever saw him run and first time I had ever seen a 400-meter guy win a distance medley relay. He put it out of reach."

Haley's 400-meter split of 43.5 was also the fastest in the history of the Penn Relays.

"I always remember his favorite saying was, 'I never got out of fourth gear,' said McDonnell. "He'd say, 'I had one left. I never got into fifth.' He had all of these sayings related to a car."

Despite Consiglio mistakenly stopping ten feet short of the line to saunter past it in 3:59.0, Arkansas set a world record in 9:22.6—taking the record from a 1980 Villanova team that had every member of its team split faster except in the 400 meter.

Just over five years since they first began attending a meet once dominated by Villanova, the Penn Relays was increasingly becoming Arkansas's world. Even their postcollegiate group was getting into the act with Frank O'Mara taking the Olympic Development 5,000-meter win in 13:28.8.

Sometimes pride goeth before the fall. Among many things John McDonnell had been consistent about communicating over the years was to never underestimate an opponent, never give your competition an extra reason to dislike you, and always correct your mistakes. If generations of Arkansas athletes would wonder why he focused on the mistakes they had made in victory, it was because he understood how thin the line could be between success and failure.

If the 1986 Penn Relays had shown the astute observer anything about the upcoming Southwest Conference Outdoor Championships at Rice University, it was that unlike in previous seasons the Texas Longhorns did not appear willing to roll over and play dead. With the distance runners running well combined with the outdoor throwing events that the Longhorns always seemed to be proficient, first year Texas coach Stan Huntsman's crew appeared ready to challenge Arkansas. The meet was shaping up to be anything but the cakewalk of the previous season.

After scoring big points in the javelin and discus, the Longhorns unexpectedly extended their lead 44–20 over Arkansas after Joseph Chelelgo and Harry Green swept the 10,000 meter.

"I think when we went 1-2 in that 10,000 meter that really shocked them," said Huntsman. "They had won by almost double the year before, and I think John was a little shocked when we did that."

Arkansas never seemed able to catch up. Despite a win from Mike Davis in the long jump, a second place from Bill Jasinksi in the high jump, and Marty Kobza valiantly scoring sixteen points in the shot and discus with a pulled hamstring, Texas wins in the high jump by James Lott (7 feet, 5 inches) and in the steeplechase by Patrick Sang (8:38.56) only made the margin wider after seven events, 75–50.[16]

For the duration of the meet, Arkansas seemed to be climbing a spinning wheel and unable to reach the top of it. Another SWC 400-meter record by Roddie Haley (44.48) was followed up with twenty-two points in the 1,500 meter led by Gary Taylor's win. The Razorbacks pulled within a point of Texas.

Then disaster truly struck. In the pole vault, Jeff Pascoe, who was expected to win the event, passed until 17 feet and then missed all of his attempts. The triple jump was no less of a disaster—Femi Abejide jumped nearly three feet below what he had done the week before and failed to score at all. Rather than going up ten points, Arkansas's miscues and a thrilling win by Pablo Sequella of Texas over Derwin Graham of Baylor in the 800 meter put the Razorbacks down seventeen points heading into the 5,000 meter.

With a fresh Joe Falcon joined by Chris Zinn and Ian Cherry after their 10,000 meter the night before, as well as Gary Taylor following his 1,500 meter win only hours earlier, McDonnell laid it all out on the table for each of them. They had to take the top three spots or the meet was essentially over.

After sitting on Patrick Sang of Texas for the majority of the race, Gary Taylor and Joe Falcon listened to McDonnell's instructions and kicked hard with a mile to go. That's when all hell broke loose. Falcon closed for the win and Sang faded to fifth, but Jon Warren of Rice flipped Taylor, who finished fourth. Nobody was more disappointed than Falcon despite his individual win.

"I tried to wear Sang out but it just didn't work out," Falcon told the media after the race. "I would rather place third and our team to win the meet than win this race. I came to Arkansas because of the program. I don't know of a man in track that works harder with his athletes than John McDonnell does. More than anything, I wanted us to win the championship for him."[17]

That was not to be. Although Huntsman was forced to scramble to find a 4 x 400 meter leg, the 1986 Southwest Conference Outdoor Championships was over. Texas had won in a stunning upset, 115–110.

"The best team won today," McDonnell told the media dejectedly. "Texas whipped us and scrapped for points anywhere they could. We've won many times and know how it feels, but the sun will come up tomorrow, and a hundred years from now and there won't be a word said about this meet."[18]

Years later, John remembers the upset well.

"The fire didn't go out but the flame was dull," said John. "We were a little lax going into that meet, and it was my fault because I thought we were so good, we were going to just walk through it. They had a good meet and we definitely had a subpar meet."

Ironically enough it was Southern Methodist, third behind both teams at the SWC meet, which captured the national championship two weeks later by a single point ahead of Washington State. It was a telling statement of the strength of the Southwest Conference at the time.

In perhaps an even more ironic twist of fate, Jeff Pascoe went on to win the pole vault for Arkansas at the NCAA Championships that same season, but not before McDonnell had gotten himself into a small brouhaha with a powerful figure in Little Rock.

In his initial reaction at learning of the Pascoe no-height in the pole vault at the Southwest Conference meet, McDonnell did not choose his words carefully.

"I said, 'Boy if that isn't putting yourself above the team,'" remembered John. "Well there was a reporter standing right behind me, and the next day the *Arkansas Democrat-Gazette* out of Little Rock put out a headline 'Pascoe puts himself above the team.' That day Frank Broyles calls me up and said, 'John, did you see the newspaper this morning?' I said, 'No.' 'Well you should read it,' Frank told me, 'the Pascoe boy on the team, his uncle is a state senator and called and said that was one helluva comment to make.' So I said to myself, 'Holy shit.' I went and bought the newspaper and read it and called Broyles back and told him, 'I said it all right, but I sure didn't know the g'damn reporter was right behind me.' So he said, 'Just give his dad a call.' I called his dad up, who was a really nice person, and told him the way it came out in the newspaper was exactly how

I said it, but it was just an emotional reaction, and I sure didn't know there was a newspaper guy there. So he thanked me for being honest."

Time has given John a great deal of perspective on the subject.

"It was the coach's fault," said John. "It's like an 800 meter where you need a 1:52 to qualify and you blow up trying to run 1:45. I really felt bad about that because you hate to place the blame on one guy, especially when he turns around and wins the NCAA championship."

8

Fayettenam (1986–1988)

"I always hated to go there. We knew we were in for a tough show whenever we went into Fayettenam."

—*Texas head coach Stan Huntsman*

It was not often that the head coach of a college track and field program personally knew the governor of the state and had the head basketball coach of the same college picking his brain for advice, but after five national championships that was the sort of relationship John McDonnell had with Bill Clinton, and Nolan Richardson.

Six years after becoming the youngest governor in the country, the former University of Arkansas law professor Clinton was a rising star in the Democratic Party, which selected him to provide the response to President Ronald Reagan's State of the Union Address in 1985.

"I knew him before and after he got into politics," said John. "He was as average a type of guy as you could meet and had no airs about him at all."

Nolan Richardson was an equally rising star in the collegiate basketball world, who had brought his patented "Forty Minutes of Hell," developed on the court at El Paso Community College and the University of Tulsa, with him to Fayetteville.

"His office was next to mine, and he was a class guy all the way," said John.

With burning ambition and endless energy of his own, it did not take Richardson long to realize he had many things in common with McDonnell.

"When I got here in 1985, John had been winning championships like it was going out of style," said Richardson. "I had graduated from a great track school at UTEP, which was Texas Western at the time, and high jumped, so I had a little understanding of what track was all about. Here I had a chance to pick the brain of someone who I thought was the best track coach in America at the time. I used to call him 'super-coach' and he would laugh at that, and from time to time we sat around and talked about distance runners and jumpers and how he was able to maintain things like he did from the standpoint of winning championship after championship."

There was a quiet dignity and humility that endeared John to those who knew him and even to those who did not. The athletes who ran for him craved his respect, and in turn he gave them his full attention. He not only gave many of them the opportunity they might not otherwise have had but tried to guide them towards excellence and away from their own worst human instincts and weaknesses.

"He opened a door in my life that I really needed to have opened and gave me the opportunity to do something with my life," said David Swain, who medaled at the World University Games in 1987. "He never kept his eyes off of me. He was always there helping me be the best and showed me some very basic things—like if you focus on something and work hard at it, it will come to you. He really showed me the benefits of hard work. He was like a father to me and has done a lot for me as well as a lot of other people."

John spent hours with his athletes, understanding what made them tick and motivating them to achieve their potential. He was often calm and coolheaded but could also be emotional and tough.

"I think he genuinely cared about us and worked with us individually and as a team," said Chris Zinn. "He was an athlete in his own right and knows running backwards and forwards and could be very inspirational and passionate about it. He could be funny and laugh at himself. When he'd get mad sometimes, he'd stump around and cuss in Gaelic so nobody understood him apart from the Irish guys, who'd be like 'Oh jeez.' When he got really pissed off, you didn't always know what he was saying."

His common decency extended even to his competition.

"He was always a gentleman and didn't ever complain about anything," said Corky Oglesby, the head coach at Texas Tech from 1977 to 1996. "I thought he was always fair and minded his own business. A lot of guys in the league seemed always to be concerned about the other schools and what they were doing, but John just took care of his own business, and I always admired him for it."

Nobody gave more attention to young coaches making their way in the profession, and certainly not anyone near his stature in the sport. Years before he won a national championship of his own at South Carolina, Curtis Frye often recalled the kindness John showed to him when Frye was a young assistant coach at North Carolina State.

"He gave me advice on different parts of track, including making athletes be accountable," Frye later told the media after McDonnell's retirement. "I could ask him for advice, and he would always give me good advice as a coach who turned young people into champions, not as someone trying to beat me."[1]

Considering how aloof and arrogant some elite-level coaches can be, even those who had only accomplished a fraction of what McDonnell had in the sport, those who came in contact with John were usually doubly impressed. Steve Silvey remembers how gracious and caring John was when Silvey was a young assistant coach at Southwest Conference rival, Texas A&M, in 1984.

"What I remember about John was that even with his success and stature he always took the time to talk to us nobodies, and I took a special interest in him because of that," said Silvey. "He didn't know me from Adam but would still take the time to talk and communicate with me at the coaches' meetings."

Of course neither McDonnell nor his staff were pushovers when it came to competing on the track or in the recruiting wars, a lesson that Silvey painfully learned early in his career.

"Mike Conley was coaching here and jumping professionally, so he had met this kid in Europe named Tyrus Jefferson from Tyler, Texas, who was going to a community college in El Paso," remembered McDonnell. "Tyrus was a really talented 26 feet, 8 inch long jumper and told Mike he was coming in at second semester so everything seemed like it was going well."

Unfortunately, Arkansas was not the only school Tyrus committed to for that spring.

"We had his cousin on the team here at A&M," said Silvey, who was an assistant coach for the Aggies at the time. "UTEP had gone on probation, so I thought this would be pretty easy to get. Back then they signed at 8:00 a.m. on a certain morning, so I flew out to El Paso to meet with Tyrus and went to the dorm the night before to speak with him and Norbert Elliot, who was his roommate. So I'm there, and Mike Conley calls the room at 10:00 p.m that night. I am in the room right then, and Mike is still in Fayetteville, Arkansas. I know how the connections work, so I'm sure there is no way in hell Mike can get there by 8:00 a.m. in the morning. So I go to the hotel and have some beers and am feeling pretty good thinking I'm going to land this twenty-seven footer."

To Silvey's astonishment, when he showed up at the apartment a few minutes before eight the next morning, he was greeted by none other than the Olympic silver medalist, Mike Conley, in the flesh.

"I said to myself, 'Shit! How the hell did he get here!'" said Silvey. "To this day I don't know how he made it."

When Conley and Silvey knocked on Tyrus Jefferson's door promptly at 8:00 a.m., the bleary-eyed junior-college sophomore seemed shocked and confused to see them both standing there.

"Tyrus didn't know if he was coming or going during that time," laughed Conley. "I was calling Tyrus, and he was telling me he was ready to sign and I'm sure he was telling the same thing to Coach Silvey. Obviously he told us both to come down and still didn't know what to do."

It was during those awkward few minutes when Silvey graciously invited Conley to join him for breakfast at the Denny's just around the corner and suggested the two give young Tyrus some more time to think about his decision before returning a few hours later. Conley agreed but told Silvey he would meet him at breakfast after he used a payphone to let Coach McDonnell know what was going on.

"So all Mike does is circle the block in his car and comes back up the stairs to Tyrus's apartment and says, 'Tyrus, what the hell are you doing?'" laughed McDonnell. "Tyrus says, 'I'm so glad you came back' and signed the paper right there. Mike put it in his bag and then went right back to have breakfast with Steve. When it came time to go back, Mike said 'Why don't you go back first.' So Steve went back to the apartment and Mike went to the airport."

By the time Silvey arrived back at the apartment, he realized he had been had.

"When Steve got back there I was already on the plane to Fayetteville," laughed Conley.

"They pulled a fast one on me that day," admitted Silvey. "You learn your lessons the hard way."

Jefferson was not the only elite jumper Arkansas signed that year. After a year spent in Nebraska, Edrick Floreal was looking for a change of scenery and was taken by the team spirit of the Razorbacks at the indoor national meet and even more drawn by the fact Mike Conley was on the coaching staff.

"I visited that summer, and Mike was the guy that hosted me," remembered Floreal. "Being nineteen years old and spending two days with Mike Conley was pretty cool."

When Floreal met with McDonnell the next morning he was equally impressed.

"He was a man of great vision," said Floreal. "It was invigorating to meet an old guy who was so passionate about winning and not just one way but with multiple events and having a successful team. It was quite a change."

Although Floreal was forced to sit out the 1986–87 season as a transfer, he roomed with his training partner Tyrus Jefferson during that first year in Fayetteville.

"Tyrus was a different cat," said Floreal, "but he was one of my good buddies, and we would go down to Tyler, Texas, together for Thanksgiving."

Though Ted King was still coaching the jumpers, it was becoming clear that Conley was the attraction. Not only had King become somewhat detached from the recruiting process, which was developing into a source of tension between him and McDonnell, but was very particular when it came to technique. In many cases his ideas led to improvements, but not everyone responded. After arriving on campus a 54 foot, 8 inch triple jumper, Femi Abejedi and King never connected. Abejedi went backwards.

"Ted tried to change him completely, and he ended up doing nothing," said McDonnell. "Just because you believe in a certain technique or philosophy doesn't mean it fits everyone. You cannot change people for the sake of changing them. If a kid jumps 54-8, he has to be doing something right, but you can't pull the whole chair from underneath him and expect him to get up without any hands or feet to help him."

After Abejedi ran into issues on campus multiple times, he was dismissed from the program.

"He was a nice guy," remembered John, "but he got into all kinds of mischief."

Free from the distractions of the previous fall, John brought the same distance crew back for the 1986 cross-country season that had been beaten by Wisconsin. Not only were the Razorbacks a year older and more physically mature, but had been augmented by the addition of Alex Hallock, John Holmes, and Reuben Reina. Hallock was a Kansas state champion who would later earn All-American honors, while Holmes was a 1:50 800m runner and 4:07 miler from Houston, Texas.

"He was a stud," remembered McDonnell about Holmes. "He was only here for two years and did well but started playing in a band and that's what he's still doing today."

The prize of the recruiting class was Reuben Reina from San Antonio, Texas. The younger brother of Roland and Randy Reina, Reuben won three Texas high-school cross-country championships and captured the Kinney National Cross Country Championships in record time during a decorated prep career.

Although Reina was recruited all over the country, he quickly narrowed down his choice to Arkansas and Wisconsin before making his first trip to Madison, Wisconsin.

"I left San Antonio and it was 85 degrees," said Reina. "I got up to Wisconsin and I was wearing a coat I had bought specifically for this trip, the biggest one I owned ever, and [Wisconsin coach] Martin Smith met me at the airport and asked, 'Do you have a bigger jacket?' I said no, but one of the guys let me borrow one. It was completely snowed over. We ran across the lakes there, which I wasn't aware of until someone told me we were running on one."

It was not long after that eye-opening visit when Reina's list got narrowed to one school.

"I had two brothers at Arkansas and so I was very familiar with the program," said Reina. "I saw it rise from the bottom up. I saw them win their first national title. I saw them come down to Texas every year to run district and conference meets there. So when John started to recruit me it was a very easy decision."

Although McDonnell remembered that the older Reina brother, Roland, could be temperamental at times, Rueben was the opposite.

"He was probably as level headed as you can get," said John. "He was just a real nice guy to coach. He was a class act, and as he got older he got better and better."

Coming from the low-mileage background he did in high school, Reina noticed the change in John's training approach even from the days when his older brothers ran at Arkansas.

"I had heard the stories in the early days of Arkansas when they did a lot more miles and a lot more volume, which was very typical of that time," said Reina. "I had read Jim Ryun's book when it came out, so I was familiar with Bob Timmons and the volume that Ryun did in high school. I just didn't come from that sort of background. I was very low mileage and hit most weeks during the high-school season in twenty to thirty mile range so my legs never really held up to that much volume. When I tried to run up to a hundred miles per week after college, my legs just didn't hold up to it well. I would feel dead legged and kind of flat. I'm glad that John changed. He started to conform more to the athletes that were coming in. We were from a different era and a different mentality. He had to change to keep guys healthy and was smart enough to do this to keep guys on track."

Although some of the volume changed for many individuals, the fundamentals of how John setup his training program throughout the season did not.

"We did a lot of steady work," said Reina. "We didn't do a whole lot of repeats or intervals really through October. It was all about building volume; then we started to get into weights and had a lot of steady states [faster tempo runs] in there obviously. The team atmosphere, a lot of time, created the steady state even if it wasn't scheduled. Everybody was feeling each other out. Long runs on the weekend were a pretty staple thing. Back in those days, we didn't have the NCAA rules where we had to have one day off, so we ran seven days a week, and John was there every day. You'd expect to see him there. There was still a lot of volume and a lot of running; getting guys back into the feel of things, getting the mileage in. Once October hit we started long intervals and hill repeats on the golf course. The 400-meter repeats started around then too with the hill running. That's the staple of cross-country right there. We didn't do anything quicker than 400s. With that and steady states, that was pretty much our fall."

The day-in, day-out grind and intensity of the program could certainly have led to internal friction, but John had a knack for managing diverse personalities and egos on the team with aplomb.

"By the time the 1986 cross-country season came around, Joe Falcon was already pretty successful," remembered Chris Zinn. "John sat me down and said 'Chris, you need to understand, you're my number two guy, Joe's number one. If you can beat Joe, beat him, but you're the number two and this is your role.' I was cool with that. There were some seriously talented athletes on that team. The thing is with John, it was never "Chris, you're the second guy, you're going to have to deal with it.' It was never like that. He just told you your responsibility for yourself and for the team. He wasn't trying to make me feel better or worse than anyone else, but was realistic with us about what our skill set could do and how far we could push it."

McDonnell had little tolerance for competition among teammates.

"One of the great lessons he said to us was, 'I don't want you guys to ever compete with each other until everyone else is beaten.' He was adamant about that," said Zinn. "If John ever saw guys being combatant or competitive with each other, he had quite a bit to say about it to them privately and in team meetings. He'd call them out. He did not tolerate disruptive influences in his machine. It was a well-oiled machine, and you were not going to come in and throw gravel in it. He was the boss, but he was a good man. You knew when you screwed up. If you knew you had screwed up and were remorseful about it, he wasn't going to sit and chew your ass because he knew that you were going to be harder on yourself than him. Nobody wanted to let him down. You wanted his respect, and you did everything to earn it and keep it."

It certainly helped having a post-collegiate group around with the collective wisdom older Razorbacks brought to the training group. Beyond O'Mara, Donovan, and Swain, Tom Moloney also stuck around Fayetteville to run a 3:54 mile following his graduation.

"I made time for postcollegiate kids," said McDonnell. "I told them, 'Once a Razorback, always a Razorback.' You are always welcome to stay here if you choose, and there will be no charge, and you can use all of the facilities. Many of them stayed but a few chose to go elsewhere, and that was no problem. I said you are always welcome back here."

Not only was John doing a good thing for those who had competed for Arkansas, but also understood their continued presence was generally a positive influence on current Razorbacks. A tradition that started with Niall O'Shaughnessy taking Frank O'Mara under his wing, and Frank O'Mara in turn taking Joe Falcon under his wing was being established with each generation.

"I likewise did that for Reuben because I saw the greatness in him," said Falcon. "I tried to nurture him, and he in turn did that for the next guy that came through. That's what made Arkansas special because you had the opportunities for older guys to encourage you and bring you along and you did the same."

With all of the talent and ego, it was never going to be possible or even desirable to completely remove the competitive element from the equation, but the team was closely knit in just about every way.

"We partied together and would go down to Doug's [Consiglio] before a big meet and cook a huge spaghetti dinner," said Zinn. "Everybody had everybody's back. We were brothers. That's how we rolled, and it was a huge part of our success. There wasn't any room for any kind of that crap with John. You either get on, or he was going to figure out another way for you. That was a testament to John. He was an excellent judge of character and still is."

Falcon and Reina were inseparable during the early meets as the freshman tried to stick with the upperclassman in training and races—including a particularly treacherous race in ankle-deep mud and water at Oklahoma State that left them both with sore

Achilles the following week. The weather from that day aside, the reconstructed cross-country course Oklahoma State coach Dick Weis designed in 1983 for the Cowboy Jamboree pleased McDonnell enough that he continued to return every year until he retired.

"We loved going there because it was such a challenging course," said John. "If someone thinks they can play around on that one, they are kidding themselves. It is a tough course and prepares you for anything out there."

Seeking their thirteenth consecutive Southwest Conference cross-country title at the Lake Oaks Country Club in Waco, Texas, Arkansas faced the prospect of a glorified dual meet with Texas. They were not let down. The two teams placed the first nine finishers with the Razorbacks coming out on top, 21–47.

"Our guys ran awesome," John told the media that morning. "That's the only word to describe them: *awesome*. I told the guys to set a hard pace, and between the mile-and-a-half mark and two-and-a-half-mile mark, Texas really cracked. It was a great team effort today. Chris Zinn took the early lead and set a hard pace to the two-and-a-half-mile mark, and then Falcon took over after that. Rueben Reina simply ran a great race for a freshman. Hey, what do you say about him; he ran like a veteran!"[2]

Considering Texas would place ninth at the NCAA Championships that season after tying a partial Arkansas team at the regional meet, the win was all the more impressive. With Wisconsin having graduated most of their team and Arkansas firing on all cylinders heading into the 1986 NCAA Cross Country Championships at Canada Hills Country Club in Tucson, Arizona, there was less suspense about the team championship and more focus as to who would emerge as the individual winner.

"John had never coached an individual NCAA cross-country champion to that point," said Oklahoma State coach Dick Weis. "Joe Falcon loved John and wanted to give that to him in the worst way."

With the heavy gravel sand on parts of the course slowing down the field, Arkansas was in total command entering the final mile. Richard Cooper was in the top twenty while Reuben Reina, Ian Cherry, Chris Zinn, and Gary Taylor all remained in the top forty. Up in the front pack, Joe Falcon bided his time.

"Coach and I put together a plan to sit on whoever was doing the majority of the leading and then wait until the last half-mile to go," said Falcon. "There was somewhat of an uphill before a turn and then a downhill to the finish. As soon as I got to the base of the hill I took off and opened up a big lead."

Up at the top of the hill, McDonnell was so confident Falcon was going to win he stopped paying attention to him and focused on his remaining runners. Falcon certainly appeared to be in complete control of the race as he continued to pull away. Then disaster struck with twenty-five meters to go in the race. Turning to see how much distance he had put on Aaron Ramirez of Arizona, Falcon tripped on a sprinkler head. With the wind knocked out of him and discombobulated from the fall, it took Falcon some time before he got up to make his way to the finish line. By that point, Ramirez had already crossed it.

"You know the old saying about Lot's wife," said McDonnell. "She was told not to look back and turned into a pillar of salt. I told him to wait to put the hammer down and to not look back. So when I came down the hill other coaches said, 'That was tough

Joe losing the meet.' I said to them, 'He got beat? How?' I was shocked. They said Joe tripped on a sprinkler head and rolled. When he got up he was in a daze and didn't know which way to go."

Following the meet, both runners had an opportunity to speak with the media.

"The Arizona boy decided to tell everyone that he was just sitting on me and was going to out-sprint me anyway," said Falcon. "Here was a 10,000-meter guy telling the media he was going to out-sprint a miler. John really didn't like that. One of the things he emphasized at Arkansas was that we were never to run our mouths. He believed you should conduct yourself in a professional manner whether you won or lost. I never let a peep out, shook the young man's hand, and stood on the podium with my teammates and smiled as national champions."

After John headed back to the hotel with the team, who had scored a school-record 67 points to win their second NCAA cross-country championship in three years, he pulled Falcon aside.

"It was at that point when I had one of the finest moments I ever had with Coach," said Falcon. "He said, 'I know you are disappointed. I'm proud of the way you handled yourself, but that young man had no right to act the way he did afterwards and you will get the chance to race him again.'"

Although no team came within eighty points of Arkansas, the school that did manage to secure second place was as much of a shock as anything else that happened that day.

"We had a javelin thrower as our captain and a 10:00 high-school two-miler as our sixth man," said Vin Lananna, who was the head coach of Dartmouth College at the time. "That was a tough course in Arizona, and we had no expectations. It was just a good group of kids who worked hard and formed a great team. All of a sudden we scored 140, Arkansas scored low, and we got second."

It would not be the last time Arkansas would have to deal with Dartmouth or Lananna at the national championships and only the first of many races between Falcon and Ramirez.

On the track, a Razorbacks field-event group hit hard by graduation and the one-year ineligibility of transfers Edrick Floreal and Tyrus Jefferson would heavily rely on contributions from freshmen such as 7-foot high jumper Kyle White and 59-6 shot putter Doug Koch. Although it was enough to win indoors, with Arkansas's dominance in the middle distance and relays more pronounced than ever, the field event holes would become apparent at the outdoor conference and national championships in the spring of 1987.

Part of the reason for the indoor success was the absolute embarrassment of riches from the 400 meter to the mile. It was telling that after running a phenomenal 3:45 for 1,500 meters as a freshman, sophomore Doug Keen of Toronto, Canada, found himself wondering whether he even belonged.

"He came back and got hurt, and it was tough," said Consiglio. "You're a 3:45 guy, and you have ten guys faster than you."

After certain voices outside of the program told Keen he would never make Arkansas's team, he transferred to the University of Alabama, which had recently hired Doug Williamson as their head coach.

"I think he was a little bit insecure, and they did a good number on him to coax him over there," said John. "He ended up getting his PhD and is a professor at the University of Arizona and helped me get several kids from California. He'd say, 'John I made a bad mistake,' but it's all behind us now."

It was during the winter of 1987 when another large figure in Arkansas middle-distance running, both literally and figuratively, arrived on campus after a six-year stint in the marines and two years at a junior college. After breaking Johnny Gray's California junior-college championship record with a blistering 1:46.9 800 meter (while also splitting sub-46 on the 4 x 400 meter relay), Lorenzo Brown was a force to be reckoned with who would play a crucial part of Arkansas's success that season.

"He was a big strong guy with speed to burn," said John, "but he had a big old butt on him, and if he tied up, he really locked up."

With sprints coach Stanley Redwine, who was still the school record holder over 800 meters at that point, continuing to train and compete at the international level, Brown had a natural training partner.

"He was competitive and didn't want to let the team down," said Redwine. "I remember at one of our team meetings, Coach McDonnell told him what he expected and all of a sudden Lorenzo blurted out, 'I won't let you down!' That was just his attitude. He was a great team guy and just wanted to do well."

Following their seventh consecutive Southwest Conference Indoor title on a day when Roddie Haley broke another SWC indoor record in the 600 yard and the middle distance runners scored 69 of the team's 91 points in the 1,000 meter, mile, and 3,000 meter, Arkansas headed to the national championship in Oklahoma City with their confidence riding high. Nobody exemplified that more than Joe Falcon, who was starting to become almost unbeatable.

"Coach gave me a real specific strategy," recalled Falcon. "Paul Donovan had won the 3,000 meter the year before in sprint finish with Gerry O'Reilly of Villanova. O'Reilly was back and was the best guy in the field but wasn't real fast on the boards, which John had picked up on the year before. So John told me to be prepared because O'Reilly will make a huge move with distance left in the race, and if I would just cover that move, John would tell me to go with two laps or one lap. Sure enough Gerry made that move, and I'm sitting on him and sitting on him and sitting on him. I look up and John either gives you the hands moving or the stop sign, and he had the stop sign. Finally with a lap to go, he told me to hit him and that's what I did."

Falcon won the 3,000 meter in 7:56.79, just a quarter of a second ahead of O'Reilly.

"It came back to a great coach knowing the strengths of his runner and the perceived weaknesses of a competitor and giving me the perfect strategy to be successful," said Falcon. "The great thing about John was that neither I nor any of my teammates had to be nervous about what to do because he would tell you what you needed to do and what he expected you to do. If you did that and you finished second or third, he was absolutely fine. It was when you tried to get outside of what he asked you to do and you didn't do well, those were some bad days. You had some conversations that were pretty one-sided where he pointed out what he asked you to do, and you assured him you would listen next time."

Not many Razorbacks were having those sorts of conversations with John that weekend. Liam Looney and the Arkansas 4 x 800 meter relay of Matt Taylor, Lorenzo

Brown, and Wayne Moncreife put it together for an NCAA victory in an incredible 7:18.67—both a collegiate and American indoor record. It was a personal triumph for Looney and the program after setbacks in that event over previous years.

Not to be outdone, Roddie Haley won the 500 meter in a blazing 59.90—this time with the trim on the inside of the lane—in a collegiate, American, and world record.

Following freshman Reuben Reina's fifth-place finish in the mile, the Razorbacks found themselves with a ten-point lead over Southern Methodist when the 4 x 400 meter anchored by Roddie Haley sealed it with a second-place finish. It was a national title that came through an absolutely breathtaking display of dominance on the track. Yet if anything demonstrated the heights the Arkansas program had elevated itself into, that same week three of its most successful alumni still training with the program managed to overshadow them at the 1987 World Indoor Championships.

Up at the Hoosier Dome in Indianapolis, Mike Conley won the gold medal in the triple jump. Frank O'Mara joined him in the pantheon of Razorback world champions by winning the 3,000 meter just ahead of fellow Irishman and Razorback Paul Donovan, who won the silver medal. Both runners had once struggled mightily handling the training had become the ultimate advertisement for the success of Arkansas program and an example to future Razorbacks suffering from their own troubled transitions to be patient and stick with it. It was, as O'Mara called it, a "Camelot period in Arkansas track and field."

Everything John touched turned to gold—or at least it seemed that way. Even the home meet away from home at Hot Springs, Arkansas, had elite teams from around the country clamoring to attend.

"That was a great meet," said Dick Weis. "He had some great teams show up, and you'd run really fast. After a few years everyone wanted to go to that meet, but he'd only take certain teams."

Heading into the 1987 Penn Relays, which was shaping up to be as competitive as ever, McDonnell gave Falcon the opportunity to avenge his cross-country loss six months earlier in Arizona.

"I had never run a 10,000 meter before in my life, but John came to me and said the Ramirez boy is in the 10,000 meter and would I like to run him again?" recalled Falcon. "I said, 'Absolutely, what do I have to do?' He said, 'Just sit on him and outsprint him' and that's what I did. I absolutely cleaned his clock during the last 400 meters and, Coach was really fired up about it and said I didn't have to run the 10,000 meter again."

After Falcon's time in the event put him ahead of the presumptive favorite Aaron Ramirez on the descending order list for the NCAA Outdoor Championships, McDonnell reconsidered his options.

"Coach, being the opportunist that he was, started thinking about it," said Falcon. "Ramirez was the favorite to win outdoors in the 10,000 meter, and I had just whupped him. So he came back to me a few weeks later and said, 'Hey kid, I think I'm going to have you run the 10k.' I said, 'Seriously?' And he said, 'Yeah, that's the best thing for the team.' So I said if that's the best thing for the team, then I'm all for it."

At the 1987 NCAA Outdoor Championships in Baton Rouge, Louisiana, Falcon outkicked Chris Brewster of Michigan to win in 29:10, well ahead of Ramirez, who had faded to seventh this time.

"Coach knew that was an opportunity and built upon it," said Falcon. "After the race he said, 'Joe, I will have you ready to win the NCAA cross-country next year.'"

While he was still in Baton Rouge, McDonnell also interviewed with the Louisiana State athletic director for the vacant head coaching position at LSU, but withdrew his name in order to remain in Fayetteville. Ultimately John's happiness at Arkansas and a pay raise convinced him to stay put. The Tigers position went instead to Pat Henry, who had won the junior-college national championship at Blinn College.

"We had a swim coach named Sam Freas who had gone there and told me about the job," said McDonnell. "We were there for NCAAs anyway so I agreed to speak, with their athletics director."

Although it may have seemed that way at the time, not everything McDonnell did turned up smelling like roses that spring. In a year when the Arkansas field events were already down, adding the outdoor throws suited Texas even more. Stan Huntsman's crew won the Southwest Conference outdoor meet for the second year in a row but this time by over thirty points. At the national meet, Arkansas was third. No team came within fifty points of Bob Larsen's dominant UCLA squad.

Even when the Razorbacks ran into bad luck, such as when an ill Doug Consiglio coughed up a lead in the Penn Relays distance medley relay or tripped in the NCAA 1,500-meter finals, there were athletes from other schools who had performed in a manner that made whatever misfortune befell the Razorbacks that day almost irrelevant. It was hard to imagine many people outkicking Georgetown's Mike Stahr on a day when he ran one of the fastest miles in Penn Relays history (3:54.9) and his Hoyas teammates set a world record in the distance medley (9:20.96). Even in the NCAA 1,500 meter final, nobody was going to beat Abdi Bile of George Mason. They certainly didn't at the World Championships that summer.

For someone who won as often as he did, John could accept losing. Although he always prepared to win, the victory or defeat in itself was not as meaningful as the achievement of one's potential. It's what gratified him when it was met and what infuriated him most when it was not. It would be many years before Arkansas would ever win the elusive 4 x 800 meter at Penn Relays, yet in a year when they had set an American indoor record in the event, his biggest disappointment of 1987 was when they fell short in Philadelphia.

Sometimes lacking enough pure half-milers and unable to run fresh milers after the distance medley and 4 x mile relay, John finally believed Arkansas had the team to get the job done in the 4 x 800 meter at Penn Relays. He gave anchor leg Lorenzo Brown explicit instructions on how to beat Penn State.

"I told him to stay behind and wait until you get into the final straightaway before you move," said John. "It was a short straightaway at Penn to the finish, and he had the speed. Well, he takes the lead from Penn State with 300 meters to go, and the crowd was going crazy. He started flogging it even more, and his legs ran out from under him up the straightaway. Penn State won it in 7:14 with us right behind them. I was never so pissed off in my life. They had some great 4 x 800 meter relays, and that was our one chance to beat them."

Just because John was willing to accept that losing was a part of life did not mean he was happy with it. Always a proponent of building as complete a team as possible, the dearth of field-event recruiting during Ted King's first three seasons, other than those attracted to Arkansas through the sheer force of Mike Conley's personality, was becoming a growing concern to him.

"Ted could coach but he just wouldn't recruit," remembers McDonnell. "He told me he had remarried, and his previous wife had left him because he had spent all of his time recruiting, and he wasn't going to mess this one up."

There was also a philosophical difference beginning to emerge between McDonnell, who believed in the need for developing the marginally talented athletes as much as those at the highest level, and King, who focused the majority of his attention on the elites.

"Ted at first was more in tune with the higher athletes that were winning national titles," said John Register, an All-American in the jumps and relays. "I was kind of like a junkyard dog. I could score a few points at nationals but wasn't going to win or be a national champ. I understood there were a lot of other things going on with the program, but I needed that support. So I talked to John, and when we had that meeting with Ted, there was an understanding. Once Ted started working with me more, I had some of the best hurdles times of my life. Ted understood biomechanics very well, and that was the only time I ran under 13.5 (in the 110-meter high hurdles). He was a great jumps coach and also understood the hurdles very well."

It was that same year when McDonnell signed a tall, powerful athlete from McCullough High School out of The Woodlands, Texas to run the mile. At 6 feet, 4, 188 pounds, Eric Henry was a bruising athlete whose frame belied the sub-4:00 mile he would eventually run at Arkansas.

"*Track and Field News* told me once they thought he was the biggest man to run a sub-4:00 mile," said McDonnell. "They looked into it and couldn't find anyone else. He was so tough and ran like a kid who was 130 pounds because he was tidy and light on his feet."

Bigger even than Randy Stephens, Henry's body type made it very easy for him to put on weight very quickly. His younger teammate from The Woodlands and later at Arkansas, Danny Green, whose father, Danny Green Sr., coached both athletes, remembers Henry's battles with weight very well.

"They had to work really hard to keep him under 190 pounds because he would gain weight so quick," said Green, who competed and was later an administrative assistant at Arkansas for several decades starting in 1988. "He would gain ten pounds just over Christmas. We weighed in every two weeks on this massive freight scale with a dial on it, and I remember John would say, 'Eric, just because we are the Hogs doesn't mean we have to eat like them.' It was a constant battle. John really harped on weight. He even made some of us run in these old football rubber suits for morning runs, which you probably couldn't do these days, but that was 1988 when you could still do stuff like that. It wasn't even that you sweated that much in them, you just didn't want to be the guy wearing the rubber suit."

Although Reuben Reina admittedly arrived into camp five pounds above what he considered to be his normal racing weight, the Razorbacks were favored for another national championship in cross country during the fall of 1987. There were plenty of reasons for optimism, not the least of which was the burning desire of Joe Falcon not to be denied an individual national title. The most impressive improvement of all was from Richard Cooper, the 9:20 high-school two-miler from Lindale, Texas, who was running so well that he was starting to be mistaken for an East African.

"People would ask me, 'Where did you get the African?' I'd say, 'East Texas,'" laughed John. "Everyone thought he was a Kenyan, so the guys started calling him 'Kip Cooper.'"

After steamrolling through early season victories at Illinois, Southwest Missouri, Oklahoma State, and at home, Arkansas hosted the Southwest Conference Championships for the first time since 1978. It was a trip others in the conference dreaded to make.

"We called it Fayettenam," said Texas coach Stan Huntsman. "I always hated to go there. We knew we were in for a tough show whenever we went into Fayettenam."

Doug Clark, an administrative assistant with the program, made sure the Razorbacks had as much of a home-course advantage as possible.

"He was great at promoting cross-country meets," remembered John. "He went downtown and talked to people and said we needed to set the meet back a few hours to promote it and by gosh the conference agreed. It was supposed to start at 10 a.m. but started at noon so we could get all of those people out to watch. McDonald's brought a tent out there and a place to eat. Doug invited the whole city and even the mayor gave people an extended lunch. There were about five thousand people. Doug was the mastermind behind it. He did all the footwork and all on a shoestring budget."

Although Harry Green of Texas took the win on a day Falcon was felled by a virus, it didn't stop Arkansas from beating Rice and Texas with relative ease for their fourteenth consecutive SWC cross-country title. The day also became notable when the women's team coached by Bev Lewis won their first SWC championship as well.

"We ran with a lot of pride and showed a lot of character when our top runner is ill," McDonnell told the media after the race. "It was a great race and the fans got their money's worth. We never get tired of winning championships. Winning never gets old."[3]

After an easy win at the regional meet, Arkansas entered the 1987 NCAA Cross Country Championships at Virginia facing a mature Dartmouth team led by Robert Kempainen and a collection of seniors who knew this was their final shot at glory. Winning would be anything but easy.

"They gave us fits I'll tell you," said McDonnell. "I figured Dartmouth would be tough because they had been there the year before and were pretty consistent. They had one star but were really a bunch of hard workers. Vin [Lananna] did a great job with the talent he had there."

Early in the race Arkansas set a hard pace, led by Joe Falcon, Chris Zinn, and Reuben Reina. With Dartmouth right with them at two miles, Lananna looked at his stopwatch to his chagrin.

"We wanted to run the way we had all season, which was aggressive without redlining," said Lananna. "I knew that if Arkansas and Dartmouth both redlined, Arkansas would win. Our only possibility was to come in the back door. We both went out aggressively. I looked at my watch (at two miles) and it was 9:20 and for three of our guys that was their PR. That's when I knew we were in trouble."

Not only did Arkansas athletes have the leg speed to handle the crushing pace but McDonnell had prepared them specifically to bury other teams early by getting out hard.

"He would ask us to sprint the first two miles and just dare any other team to go with us," remembered Falcon. "He felt we would be the toughest mentally because of how he trained us."

"John's approach was always to take the bull by the horns," said Reina. "You can't win cheap, and you have to lead from the start and take control. We prepared for it and that's how we ran our workouts and steady runs. We would always get out hard and be prepared to do that during races."

Towards the midway point of the race, Falcon and the lead pack began to separate themselves from Zinn and Reina. Then at five miles, Falcon attempted to separate himself from the lead pack.

"We decided to take it with 1,200 meters to go because there was a turn in it," said McDonnell. "They were all waiting for him to sprint, so at this turn you go up a hill. We were used to running hills, so he surprised them by going so hard up the hill. It seemed like in fifty meters he put about forty on them. I told Joe we want to make sure you can trip and get up and still win."

"He said, 'This year I need to make sure you are so far ahead that you'll have time to get up and they still won't catch you,'" laughed Falcon. "He put together a plan that anyone else would have thought was crazy by sprinting up this huge hill at five miles as hard as I could until the top and then hard for another quarter mile. That's what I did, and I got such a huge lead that by that last half mile I could really enjoy it."

When he crossed the line first, Falcon was overcome with emotion.

"It was the accumulation of everything Coach and I tried to do," said Falcon. "That was one of the greatest honors I had in being able to present Coach with his first individual NCAA cross-country champion. That meant a lot to me because he was really fired up about it."

About ninety seconds behind him, another drama was unfolding as Arkansas appeared to be in significant trouble holding off a late charge from Dartmouth. Although Zinn and Reina crossed the line in the top twenty followed by a surprising forty-seventh place from Alex Hallock, both Matt Taylor and Richard Cooper had faded badly and were not even in the top one hundred. Trucking along in the sixties was Doug Consiglio, who had run 3:38 for 1,500 meters that summer in Europe but never seemed to be in great shape during the fall.

"I used to make Doug run cross country for strength because he didn't like that stuff," said McDonnell. "We had an 8:32 steepler and 3:57 miler run like dogs, so even though Doug was our seventh man coming into the day, he was our fifth man when I saw him with 1,000 meters left in the race. I said to him, 'Doug you have to get ten guys from here in! You are the collegiate record holder in the 1,000 meter! Go after it! Now!'"

With Dartmouth's fifth man surging away from a tiring Consiglio heading up the big hill, McDonnell frantically sprinted over to the final straightaway to see the finish.

"After the hill it turned into a downhill and I have a long stride, so I said I'm going to catch this guy," said Consiglio. "I went to catch him and was going by him when I said to myself I'm gonna go by him hard. I opened it up and went flying by him and was hurting, but then I saw [Dartmouth's] fourth man, and then I flew by him so we had it sewed up. I turned the corner at 100 meters and was totally dead but held my position. I think I took out five years of frustration in cross country in 600 meters of running."

Consiglio ran so fast during the last kilometer that by the time McDonnell made it to the corner leading into the final straightaway he had already passed.

"I was out of wind after I ran across there," said McDonnell. "He ran so g'damn fast that I missed him."

"John looked up, and he saw Dartmouth's fourth guy go by and then their fifth man; and he didn't see me, and he's waiting and waiting until Cooper and Taylor came in 100th," said Consiglio. "He thought I dropped out. We would have definitely lost the race. So behind the finish chute I'm happier than a pig in shit because I had this little stick that said fifty-first on it but John looked like he was ready to tear my head off."

"I thought we were done for," said John. "Doug seemed pretty happy though and he gave me the stick and asked, 'Is that good enough?' I looked at him almost dumbfounded and said, 'How does a big tall guy like you go by me, and I don't see you?' He said, 'I saw you but you were delirious!'"

Arkansas had won its second consecutive NCAA cross-country championship over Dartmouth by a margin of 87–119 on a day when Falcon had won the first individual NCAA cross-country title in school history. Still, many other things had not gone according to plan. In what would become a tradition on McDonnell's teams, two Razorbacks stepped up when their teammates faltered.

"That was typical of John's teams that when one person shit the bed, someone else picked up the slack," said Consiglio. "Yes, he had the superstars, but he also had guys you wouldn't expect who would step up and run out of their minds. Alex Hallock and I definitely pulled one out of our asses that day."

Once the heat of the moment had worn off, John was able to laugh about the confusion.

"The next day he said, 'Jesus, Consiglio, I really thought you dropped out. You son of a bitch, you outkicked me,'" said Consiglio. "He was already pissed at me because some girl I had met before came to the hotel asking for me. If I had dropped out, I think I would have had to walk home."

By the time the Christmas holidays passed, the Razorbacks had put in another solid block of training and were once again off to their customary flying start. Junior-college transfer Troy Smith cleared 17 feet, 7 inches in the pole vault right away, Lorenzo Brown broke a school record over 800 meters and won the Millrose Games a few weeks later, while Doug Consiglio flew up to the Winnipeg Indoor Games to win the 1,500 meter—where he was fortunately spared from the flying scare McDonnell experienced twenty-four years earlier on the same trip. Most promising of all was Joe Falcon, who was at the top of his game—recording automatic qualifiers in the 3,000 meter and mile before the month of January had even ended.

Still, with Reuben Reina and jumper Edrick Floreal battling injuries throughout the indoor season, the chances of a fifth straight indoor national championship for Arkansas were looking bleak.

"We had some significant injuries that year, and Coach came to me and said he would need me to run the mile and 3,000 meter at the national championships because we were going to be pretty short on people," said Falcon. "He said we would train to run the mile and 3,000-meter double without being worn out because I would only have about thirty minutes between them. So we trained that way after cross country and again that comes down to a great coach thinking things through."

McDonnell was as prescient as ever. The first day of the 1988 NCAA Indoor Championships were a disaster for the Razorbacks. Although Tyrus Jefferson finished second in the long jump, it had largely been a day from hell—Doug Consiglio (mile), Wayne Moncriefe (800 meter), Eric Tatum (200 meter), Troy Smith (pole vault) and Mike Chism (shot) all failed to qualify for finals, while those that did such as John

Register (55-meter hurdles) and Lorenzo Brown (800 meter) finished out of the scoring in the finals the following day.

With the opportunity to win their fifth consecutive indoor national championship hanging in the balance, Arkansas was nearly mathematically eliminated from winning the meet. They needed big points in the mile and 3,000 meter to catch Illinois, but McDonnell only had two athletes remaining: Matt Taylor and Joe Falcon. Taylor had never scored an individual point at a national championship, period. While Falcon had won national championships on the track and in cross country, never had he done so twice in the span of an hour. It was a gargantuan task that John was asking of them but he gave them a plan to pull it off.

"John felt like I could dictate the pace [in the mile] so he asked me to go really slow through 600 meters and then really hard for 400 meters and then back off again," said Falcon. "By doing that it was going to allow my teammate Matt Taylor, who knew the strategy, to run an even pace while everyone else was running an up-and-down pace, and gain a tactical advantage to sprint at the end. So after being the last to qualify, Matt sat back like Coach said and sprinted like the dickens at the end. I won but he got third which was huge."

Falcon beat Robin Vanhelden of Louisiana State in 3:59.78 with Taylor not far behind in 4:00.56. The first part of the plan had been executed flawlessly but would be for naught unless Falcon came through again less than an hour later.

"In the 3,000 meter , John put together a plan, and it was to let them lead and go as fast as they wanted, but for me to go to the back of the pack and rest the first mile," said Falcon. "Then once I got my legs underneath me, start to move up. I was in dead last when [Jacinto Naverette] from Washington State bolted. So I went with him and was fortunate enough to be able to outsprint the field."

Falcon won the 3,000 meter in 7:55.80 over James Farmer of North Carolina. It was a gutsy double, attributable to the physical strength and mental toughness of the boy from Belton, Missouri.

"Those guys played right into his hands," said McDonnell. "Instead of taking the 3,000 meter out they sat around and, boy, that was the wrong thing to do with Joe."

In an incredible turn of events, Arkansas beat Illinois by a mere five points to win the 1988 NCAA Indoor Championships with only three scoring athletes. It was as much a testament to the resolve of Falcon as the guile of a coach who was better than anyone at pulling chestnuts out of the fire.

"We won that meet by only a few points, and it was directly attributable to Coach's strategy," admitted Falcon.

Even with the meet going to hell in a hand basket after the first day, John always conveyed a sense of calm amidst the storm.

"John was remarkable because of the incredible pressure he had on him," said Kyle White, a jumper at the time who would later return to coach the sprinters twenty years later. "He never let that radiate to us. I've never met a better motivator and never met somebody more concerned with the athletes on his team no matter what event. John seemed to know when to push the right buttons or pat an athlete, which was remarkable considering all of the talent and egos he had on those teams."

When a young sprinter, who had finished sixth at the Southwest Conference 200 meter and qualified for the NCAA Championships, boldly entered John's office that spring to complain about the lack of recognition he was receiving, John did not entertain it.

"He said to me, 'The only thing you care about here are the distance runners.' The discussion ended right there," remembered McDonnell. "I said, 'Get the hell out of my office. I'll give you a release in the morning.' That pissed me off because I was never the type to favor one event over another and treated everyone fair. I oversaw and made decisions for all of the events and always preached camaraderie so we were close as a team. And I bent over backwards to make sure they all got a degree. That kid went to TCU and never did anything for them but later became a policeman in Dallas."

There were a bevy of athletes in other events who always felt they had an opportunity to communicate with John when they needed.

"I would talk to John as much as my event coach," said Edrick Floreal. "I would go into his office and shoot the crap. If I had a problem with something, he would shake his head and always seemed to find a way to fix it."

At the first outdoor meet in Hot Springs, Floreal made a spectacular return from injury by winning the triple jump, a small start in what would be a fantastic outdoor season for him.

Arkansas typically reloaded in time for Penn Relays and with Falcon anchoring both the 4 x 1,500 meter and the distance medley, the dynamics had certainly changed from the year before. The Razorbacks took back the title (though not the world record) in a relatively easy distance medley relay victory before exacting their revenge on Mike Stahr and the Georgetown Hoyas in the 4 x 1,500 meter. After Falcon received the baton behind the leaders, he split 3:38.9 to outkick Georgetown's Stahr by less than a second.

"It was the best race I've seen in years," McDonnell told the Philadelphia media. "That last mile was a humdinger."[4]

Simultaneous to Villanova's slow descent following the death of Jumbo Elliott in 1981, the Georgetown Hoyas had emerged as a force to be reckoned with after the hiring of Frank Gagliano from Manhattan College. The rivalry that ensued would only intensify with each passing year. It became a Penn tradition for Georgetown supporters to pull out American flags after victories, since their athletes were all American at the time.

That season the Arkansas 4 x 1,500 meter relay also happened to have all Americans on it and set an American record. Considering that three more Americans, Reuben Reina (5,000 meter), Chris Zinn (10,000 meter), and Richard Cooper (3,000-meter steeplechase) had all set personal bests and automatically qualified for nationals (and in Cooper's case the Olympic Trials), a trend was developing. As he became more and more successful and scholarship limitations became more stringent, McDonnell's team went a few seasons with no foreign distance runners at all.

"I was finally able to get American kids to come to Arkansas, and you could get them to come for cheaper," said McDonnell. "Most foreign kids needed a scholarship, and you only have 12.6 of them."

The Razorbacks unfortunately did not have the luxury of getting too high on themselves. After two consecutive SWC outdoor team titles, Texas was even deeper in more events than ever before and was hosting the meet on their home track in Austin, Texas.

It was going to take a massive effort to beat the Longhorns, and John once again let his athletes know exactly what was needed to pull it off.

"I was not one of those crybaby types," said Edrick Floreal. "If I need to score twenty points, don't whisper it in my ear. Tell me I need twenty points. My first conference championship, John told me he might need me to high jump. My knee was bad, but I scored in the long and won the triple, and then we scored big on the 4 x 100 meter relay. So John told me I got my points and didn't high jump me because he didn't want my knee to continue to be a problem. I was just ticked off John didn't let me high jump."

The mentality of doing whatever it took to win the outdoor conference championship took hold of nearly every member of that team. After Floreal put up a personal best to win the triple jump in 56 feet, 3 inches, he and Tyrus Jefferson finished 1-2 in the long jump ahead of future Olympian Leroy Burrell of Houston.

The meet was going well. Even the 10,000 meter had gone much better than it had in 1986, with Falcon and Cooper beating out Harry Green of Texas in a kick finish that was not lacking any banter along the way. The rivalry between the schools was both real and palpable.

"I got a bit pissed off at Harry Green's girlfriend, who was just off the track, and I used some colorful language," said Zinn, who finished fifth in the event. "I apologized to Coach for embarrassing him and embarrassing myself and was determined to make up for it in the steeplechase."

Even with Texas scoring big in the discus and javelin, a steeplechase win by Richard Cooper (followed by Zinn) put the Razorbacks up by eighteen points after nine events, 92–74. Given the breathtaking array of talent in the Southwest Conference at the time though, no lead was safe.

On their home track, the Longhorns refused to go away. Even after a 1–2 performance in the 1,500 meter by Matt Taylor and Reuben Reina, Texas responded with spectacular wins by Pablo Sequella in the 800 meter (1:47.84), Rusty Hunter in the decathlon (7845 points) and Winthrop Graham in the 400-meter hurdles (48.87) in a meet record time to pull within three points of Arkansas after seventeen events, 125–122.

As was often the case, Arkansas ended the meet in the 5,000 meter, with a win from Falcon.[5]

"I was pleased with the way the race went," Falcon told the media. "We picked some good points that should really help us. John told me to sit on Tim Gargiulo of SMU until the last curve and then move. We were trying to slow it for the other guys since they had just run the 1,500 meter. If we win the team title, it will make the individual titles that much sweeter."[6]

In conference championship as epic as the cliffhanger two years earlier, Falcon was the high point scorer as Arkansas edged Texas, 155–149. Several Razorback athletes came through in more than one event. It was a memorable win especially for the Arkansas athletes from Texas who had the pleasure of "Calling the Hogs" in the cathedral of Longhorn nation. As hard as Huntsman took the loss, he always appreciated the level of competition from Arkansas.

"The thing I always admired about John was that his athletes competed across the board as hard as any coach's I have ever known," said Texas coach Stan Huntsman.

"When you went up against Arkansas, you always knew you were in for a battle that he usually won. He had such a tremendous rapport with his athletes, expecting them to do well, and they did do well."

If the Longhorns lost the battle on the track that weekend, they did win the battle for the heart of Heather McDonnell, the eight-year-old daughter of John and Ellen, who accompanied her mother to Austin that weekend and became a lifelong Texas fan thereafter. Austin captivated her young imagination. Even trips to Indianapolis, Indiana, or Eugene, Oregon, for the national championships could not compare.

"I was obsessed by Texas as a little girl," said Heather McDonnell. "I just loved Texas. I loved going to Texas Relays, and by the time I was nine, I told my parents I'm going to college there."

Two weeks later at the 1988 NCAA Outdoor Championships, which were held in Eugene, Oregon, the 1,500-meter showdown between Joe Falcon and Georgetown's Mike Stahr was shaping up to be titanic. Although each runner had speed and endurance others could have only dreamed about, it was still a match of contrasts—a man who had run 28:34 over 10,000 meters (Falcon) against another who had run 1:44 for the 800 meter (Stahr).

"John said you're good but not where you can let a guy with that kind of speed sit on you," said Falcon. "For that meet we prepared to run a really hard 300 meter midway through to separate from the rest of the field, and that's exactly what happened. People would watch Arkansas athletes and say, 'Wow, that guy is phenomenal.' Well, it's easy to be phenomenal when you have a coach tell you exactly what you need to do to win. Pretty soon you become confident that whatever he tells you to do you're going to be able to do it."

Following Falcon's win, Floreal won the triple jump with a leap of 56 feet, 4 inches and the Razorbacks placed third at the meet behind UCLA, who captured the NCAA outdoor title for the second year in a row.[7]

For many current and past Razorbacks though, the season was just beginning. Although Paul Donovan had ruptured his patella tendon and would miss three seasons with the injury, Frank O'Mara qualified for the 1988 Olympics, where he would represent Ireland in the 5,000 meter after running 13:13.02 the year before. North of the border, both Doug Consiglio (1,500 meter) and Edrick Floreal (triple jump) were selected to represent Canada at the 1988 Olympics in Seoul, Korea.

"A lot of people gave me a hard time because all of my fast times were at Arkansas, and I didn't run as well at Canadian nationals, so they said the track was short," said Consiglio. "When I showed up at Burnaby, British Columbia, that year and ran 3:35, I told the press the tracks in Burnaby must be short!"

Consiglio was felled by mononucleosis in his preparation for the Games that ended with him being knocked out after a poor showing in the heats, while Floreal also did not make it past the flights. Ultimately, the entire Canadian team had to endure the fallout from the Ben Johnson steroid scandal after the disgraced Canadian's gold medal in the 100 meter was given to Carl Lewis of the United States.

The qualifying process just to get to the Games was not as easy for others. Espen Borge ran an 8:25 3,000-meter steeplechase, but the Norwegian federation declined to send him.

The U.S. Trials had not gone much better. Roddie Haley was beat out for a spot by the three men who swept the Olympic medals in the 400 meter (Butch Reynolds, Danny Everett, and Steve Lewis), while Kevin Robinzine of Southern Methodist was also selected for the relay ahead of him. Although McDonnell had fought to keep Haley in school, he had become ineligible over a technicality and decided to drop out. It was the start of a downward spiral for the boy from Texarkana.

"I've thought about it many days," said John. "He was a really nice kid and not a bad student, but he didn't get many breaks in life. He got caught in a power play within the academic department not excusing him for days missed for track so he decided to quit school. I was trying to get him a degree, so I gave him an ultimatum that he couldn't train here unless he kept going to class, and he quit altogether. Maybe I shouldn't have given the ultimatum, but it's hard to second guess yourself over everything."

The star that burned so brightly soon disappeared, leaving many to wonder what might have been.

"He was the best pure quarter miler I've ever seen in my life," stated John Register. "I liken him to Tommie Smith. He was such a powerful runner and so fierce. Roddie just didn't get tired until he crossed the finish line. I think success came too early and too easy for him. He came in as a freshman in 1985 and beat four guys who made the Olympic finals the year before. He was amazing. I really believe if he would have buckled down like he did that first year, we might not even know who Michael Johnson is. If he would have continued on that path, I think he could have been the first to break 43 seconds [in the 400 meter]."

After making the final in the 1,500 meter at the same Trials, Joe Falcon also missed qualifying.

"Joe looked great in the first round," said John, "but in the finals, he went right to the back."

Even more disappointing was the failure of 1984 Olympic triple-jump silver medalist and world record holder Mike Conley to make the American team at all.

"Nike came out with these shorts, and my wife asked me why I was going to wear these shorts for the first time at the Trials," said Conley. "Every time I jumped they kept marking about eighteen inches behind where I jumped [because his new shorts were hitting the sand behind where his torso actually landed]. Finally on my last one I realized what was going on and missed making the Olympic team by a centimeter."

Apart from attending to those competing in the Olympics that summer, McDonnell was busy making personnel changes. Four years after he had gone looking for a field-event coach during the 1984 Olympic Trials, it was becoming clear that another change might be needed. Although Ted King had done a good job with several athletes throughout his four years in Fayetteville, most notably Edrick Floreal, and had gotten along well with McDonnell, the two men were having major philosophical differences in a few important areas.

"He was a great coach, real technical but not as good at motivating them," said McDonnell. "He just hadn't gotten away from coaching Olympic-type athletes. Conference meets weren't important to him so I said, 'Ted, the last time I checked, the University of Arkansas pays me, and they also pay you. The USATF [USA Track and Field] or UK Athletics don't pay us a dime.'"

Although King had never taken to recruiting, one particular situation the previous summer made John seriously begin contemplating making a change at the position.

"I asked him to call a kid from California," said John. "His brother was in the military and had visited here in the summer and came into my office and said, 'I have a brother, Percy Knox, who would love to come to Arkansas and has gone 26 feet, 6 inches in the long jump.' I almost went crazy and asked him to give me his information and told him we're on it. I gave his information for Ted to call and kept asking him whether he had called, and he kept saying he couldn't reach him. So after about four or five weeks of this I said, 'Ted, what about Percy Knox?' And he was still saying he couldn't get in touch with him. So I said, 'Give me the number.' It was a Monday morning around 8:00 a.m., and his father answered and said, 'Coach, you have to be kidding me. You're calling now? He just signed with Arizona.'"

When it became clear his field-event coach would never change, John decided it was time for one.

"So I hated doing it because we got along great, but I finally talked to him and said this isn't going to work," said John. "He ended up coaching the field-event guys in Canada for some time and then ended up back in England. He just decided that he liked to coach and none of the other stuff that went with it, which we would all like to do."

In the chain of events that followed, Dick Booth was also looking to get out of Lafayette, Louisiana, around that same time. Although things seemed to be going well from the outside—Booth coached Hollis Conway to an NCAA title and Olympic silver medal in the high jump that year—the University of Southwestern Louisiana was imploding as a result of the dramatic fall in oil prices in the mid-1980s that devastated the Gulf region economically.

"It was a difficult situation financially because you are trying to compete at a level where your resources are limited," said Terry Don Phillips, who would also leave the athletics director's role at USL to return as an assistant AD at Arkansas that same year. "The university was great and the president was great, but the oil economy at the time was just so bad that rigs were shut down and a lot of people were out of work. So we lost a lot of support we would have had otherwise."

It was perhaps fortuitous that McDonnell was also openly looking for an assistant coach.

"After Ted King's departure, John asked me to come talk with him, and I had an inkling he was going to ask me to come back," said Booth. "When he did, I made the decision I was going to come back."

Having won eight NCAA championships in cross country, indoors, and outdoors since Booth's departure for Lafayette four years earlier, McDonnell was looking for someone to help continue the program's success, and he had both the knowledge and confidence that Booth was the right man. His judgment would once again be well rewarded.

Frank O'Mara anchored Arkansas to a school and meet record in the 4 x mile relay at Drake Relays in 1980—the last of many triumphs at the iconic Des Moines event. The Razorbacks competed in the Penn Relays each year thereafter. *Photo courtesy of University of Arkansas Athletics Media Relations.*

Randy Stephens was the first individual NCAA champion under John McDonnell after winning the 1000 yard at the 1982 NCAA Indoor Championship at Cobo Hall in Detroit. *Photo courtesy of University of Arkansas Athletics Media Relations.*

The quest for the triple crown: Paul Donovan, Tom Moloney, John, and Frank O'Mara after winning the 1982 SWC indoor title in Fort Worth. *Photo courtesy of John McDonnell.*

Dave Taylor, Randy Stephens, and Frank O'Mara at the 1982 Southwest Conference Outdoor Championships in Houston after clinching the first triple crown in Southwest Conference history. *Photo courtesy of John McDonnell.*

The neverending van rides were an annual rite of passage for McDonnell's earliest teams— including *(left)* Frank O'Mara and *(right)* Paul Donovan. *Photo courtesy of John McDonnell.*

Heather with a baby calf. *Photo courtesy of John McDonnell.*

It did not take Sean and Heather long to share their father's affinity for baby calves at the ranch. *Photo courtesy of John McDonnell.*

John showing Heather and Sean how to handle a horse. *Photo courtesy of John McDonnell.*

Sean with a baby calf at the ranch. *Photo courtesy of John McDonnell.*

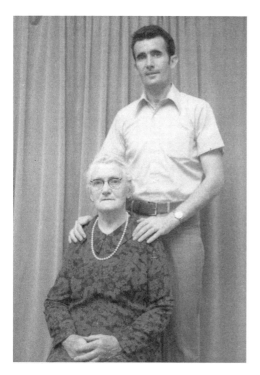

John and his mother, Bridget, in 1982.
Photo courtesy of John McDonnell.

John in a portrait with his
young family—Ellen carried
most of the load raising the
kids when John was out of
town for meets or recruiting.
*Photo courtesy of John
McDonnell.*

Mike Conley's national titles in the long jump and triple jump helped Arkansas win the first of twelve consecutive NCAA Indoor Championships starting in 1984. *Photo courtesy of University of Arkansas Athletics Media Relations.*

John being lifted into the air by his athletes after winning the NCAA Indoor Championships for the third time in 1986. It would soon become a habit for both John and the program as they reeled off an NCAA-record twelve indoor national championships in a row. *Photo courtesy of University of Arkansas Athletics Media Relations.*

The 1984 NCAA cross-country championship team had few dull moments—*(from left)* Espen Borge, Keith Iovine, Roland Reina, David Swain, Maurice Conley, Matt Taylor, Joe Falcon, Richard Cooper, Gary Taylor, Doug Consiglio, Michael Byrd, Paul Donovan, Ian Cherry, and Liam Looney. *Photo courtesy of University of Arkansas Athletics Media Relations.*

The Razorback track team is greeted by Arkansas governor Bill Clinton outside the state capitol building in Little Rock after winning their first national title in 1984. *Photo courtesy of University of Arkansas Athletics Media Relations.*

The Arkansas 4 x 1500 meter relay team won the Penn Relays in 1985 in a record time that still stands— *(from left)* Paul Donovan, David Swain, "Mr. Penn Relays" Gary Taylor, and Keith Iovine. *Photo courtesy of University of Arkansas Athletics Media Relations.*

Frank O'Mara, Mike Conley, and Paul Donovan wore their Olympic suits prior to the 1984 Olympics in front of a massive billboard celebrating the program's first indoor national championship that winter. *Photo courtesy of John McDonnell.*

Frank O'Mara leading Paul Donovan and Gary Taylor through another sub-4:00 mile effort on the indoor track in 1986. *Photo courtesy of John McDonnell.*

John travelled to Ireland for his mother's funeral in 1986 in his last visit to the island for fifteen years. He is pictured here with his siblings: *(front row from left)* Mary, Philomena, Carmel, Anne, and Margaret; *(back row from left)* Michael, Paddy, and John. *Photo courtesy of John McDonnell.*

"And here comes Roddy Haley!" The Texarkana native set a SWC record in the 400 meter, a world record in the 500 meter, and ran the fastest 400 meter in the history of the Penn Relays (43.5). *Photo courtesy of University of Arkansas Athletics Media Relations.*

Jeff Pascoe developed into the NCAA champion in the pole vault outdoors in 1986. *Courtesy of University of Arkansas Athletics Media Relations.*

The Razorbacks became a tight-knit group with an unshakeable faith their head coach. Spaghetti dinners prepared by Doug Consiglio *(top middle)* became a premeet ritual for the Razorback harriers in the mid-1980s. *Photo courtesy of John McDonnell.*

The 1986 national championship cross-country team sports homemade "Mac Attack" shirts. *Photo courtesy of John McDonnell.*

John outside his ranch in Fairland, Oklahoma, in 1987. *Photo courtesy of John McDonnell.*

Pete Squires of Adidas awards John the Golden Shoe award—the first non-soccer player to receive the award. *Photo courtesy of John McDonnell.*

"Calling the Hogs" in Oklahoma City. Coaches Ted King and John *(far left)* and Stanley Redwine *(far right)* celebrate with the 1987 NCAA indoor championship team after their fourth consecutive national title. *Photo courtesy of John McDonnell.*

Edrick Floreal *(pictured)* and Erick Walder won a combined fifteen NCAA individual titles in the long or triple jump between 1988 and 1995. *Photo courtesy of University of Arkansas Athletics Media Relations.*

Erick Walder overcame struggles and inconsistency his first season to become one of the most successful jumpers in NCAA history. *Photo courtesy of University of Arkansas Athletics Media Relations.*

Joe Falcon locked in prior to the Cowboy Jamboree at Oklahoma State in 1987. Nothing was going to stand in the way of an individual title that season; McDonnell gave him a plan to be so far ahead that "you can trip and get up and still win." *Photo courtesy of John McDonnell.*

Arkansas convincingly won back their title at the 1986 NCAA Cross Country Championships in Arizona. *(From left)* Richard Cooper, Reuben Reina, Ian Cherry, and Chris Zinn. *Photo courtesy of University of Arkansas Athletics Media Relations.*

Joe Falcon split a 3:53.8 mile to win the 1989 Penn Relays distance medley relay. *Photo courtesy of University of Arkansas Athletics Media Relations.*

Arkansas set a world record against a Mount St. Mary's team with Olympic gold medalist Peter Rono. John said to the team beforehand: "There isn't a Kenyan ever born who is going to beat Joe Falcon today." (From left) Reuben Reina, Joe Falcon, Charles Williams, and Robert Bradley. *Photo courtesy of University of Arkansas Media Relations.*

Roger Bannister *(second from left)* presents the Penn Relays wheel to John *(far right)* and the winning 4 x1500 meter relay team of *(from left)* Reuben Reina, Johan Boakes, Eric Henry, and Gilbert Contreras in 1990. *Photo courtesy of John McDonnell.*

9

Closing Out the Decade (1988–1991)

"This will go down as one of the greatest victories in Arkansas history."
—*John McDonnell at the 1989 Penn Relays.*

As the decade drew to a close, the ultracompetitive Southwest Conference suddenly found itself in a state of self-immolation. Several of the major football programs were on some form of NCAA probation, most notably Southern Methodist, which faced the ignominy of its football program being shut down completely for two years through the NCAA's Death Penalty. Even head-track coach Ted McLaughlin, two years removed from his third national championship, departed the Dallas-based school and was replaced by Dave Wollman of Stanford that same year.

Once the doormat of the conference in just about every way imaginable, Arkansas was now challenging Texas for all-sports supremacy due to the efforts of Frank Broyles, which had borne fruit most notably in football, basketball, baseball, and track and field. Arkansas had even led the national all-sports standings on several occasions. In 1988 alone, the Razorbacks athletics department captured the SWC championship in eight of the nine possible men's sports.

"The Southwest Conference was beginning to disintegrate from a competitive standpoint," said Terry Don Phillips, who returned to Arkansas as an assistant athletic director in 1988. "You'd go down and play Rice and you might get fifteen thousand people. SMU was in trouble, and TCU was really struggling. So other than ourselves, you had Texas, Texas A&M, and Texas Tech; and Baylor was somewhat okay, but the rest of the conference was hurting pretty bad."

On most statistical levels, Arkansas football coach Ken Hatfield had been nothing short of an unqualified success. Not only did he have the highest winning percentage (55-17-1, .760) of any Razorback football coach, including Frank Broyles, but won two Southwest Conference championships and earned two trips to the Cotton Bowl. What he was not winning was the hearts and minds of Razorback fans, who had lost interest in hearing biblical quotations on his radio show or watching his team play, if falling ratings or slumping season ticket sales were any indication.[1] Most damning of all for

Hatfield's prospects of remaining the Arkansas football coach for any length of time was his failure to win more than one out of seven Bowl games. When he refused Frank Broyles's advice to relieve certain assistant coaches of their duties following the conclusion of the 1987 season, their relationship began to sour.[2]

Simultaneously, John McDonnell's relationship with Broyles remained steadfast. Not only had the athletic director supported him through periodic facility upgrades and salary increases, sometimes in response to interest from other programs, such as LSU's in 1987, but he had provided the resources to feed the growing monster of championships that McDonnell proved ever adept at winning.

"The athletics department saw his success and supported it with resources that would give him a chance to continue to be successful," said Arkansas athletics director Frank Broyles. "We paid him a top salary and gave him good facilities and made it a prominent sport in the state. That's what every athletics director is supposed to do for their coaches. That's what you try to do if you can pull it off, and our fans allowed us to pull it off."

The signing of David Welsh in the following fall along with that of top prep athletes such as Gilbert Contreras from El Paso, and Paul Thomas and Ian Alsen from California, began a wave of American distance talent to Fayetteville that would not stop. Far from having to coax reluctant athletes who claimed to not have even heard of Arkansas, the challenge had now become simply making contact with people and then deciding who to let within the pearly gates.

"I never wanted too many distance runners, usually around fourteen to fifteen," said McDonnell. "I always felt if you had athletes on the team they should have a purpose otherwise you have dissension and discontent. I always had enough for every event from the 800 meter through the 10,000 meter so I could accommodate and travel them all during track season. I learned this from watching some early Texas teams. They would sign every good kid in Texas, and back then there were a lot more scholarships, so these kids would be tripping over themselves. I remember they had ten guys under 4:05 at one point, and you wonder where these guys went, but they were discontented and quit. So I always felt it was unwise to have too many of them. They get turned off, and it gives you a bad name because you may want those second-tier kids later and their high-school coach will remember an athlete that went there and you only worked with studs."

With the growing recognition of McDonnell's success at Arkansas, several athletes became interested in becoming walk-ons. While John always kept a door open to such athletes, he also held them strictly accountable to the standards of other Razorback athletes if they wanted to remain.

"John didn't want dead weight on the team," said Danny Green. "If they were behind on an eight-mile run, sometimes you'd have a talented guy lacking motivation who might run behind with them, when he would otherwise have had to keep up with the group. John was always very selective and it was like, 'Hey, on Sunday we have a fourteen-mile run, and if you can make it, you can stay.'"

Those that stayed earned not only McDonnell's respect and recognition, but also attention equal to that of the stars on the team. In a handful of cases, those walk-ons became stars under McDonnell's tutelage—earning All-Conference or All-American honors and in some cases, Olympic selection or an American record. Often, they were the difference at conference championships.

"It didn't matter if you were first or sixth in the 10,000 meter, I'd say 'Awesome job,'" said McDonnell. "It's easy to be a team man when you're winning. The newspaper didn't know their names, but I had several of them back there in seventh running for a couple of points. They thought that was the greatest thing, and they set the tone for the meet because we'd score thirty points where we might have only scored twenty-five without them. I'd say, 'That's what our team is about, guys,' and it fired them up to get that respect."

Despite the graduation of Doug Consiglio, Matt Taylor, and the exhaustion of Joe Falcon's cross-county eligibility, Arkansas entered the 1988 cross-country season with the first exclusively American-born roster of John McDonnell's career and the expectations of another national championship.

"We have four runners with NCAA experience," McDonnell told the media. "It's very important to have been there before. Our better runners will have to improve, and at the same time we're looking for our younger guys to contribute more."[3]

The Razorbacks certainly lived up to their preseason favorite status throughout the first two months of the season, beating Oklahoma State by 50 points at the Cowboy Jamboree and blowing away Oklahoma and Southern Methodist by 100. With redshirt freshmen John Myers and Eric Henry emerging that fall and upperclassmen Reuben Reina and Chris Zinn winning every meet between them entering the national championships—including a tie that was broken in Reina's favor at the SWC meet—the Razorbacks looked to be in good shape entering the 1988 NCAA Cross Country Championships in Des Moines, Iowa. That's when everything began to go wrong.

While Bev Lewis and the women's team departed Fayetteville with no problems on the Friday before Monday's national championship, by the time the men's team was scheduled to fly out of Fayetteville the following afternoon the entire region had been blanketed with snow in an early season blizzard.

"We ended up staying in an airport all day and then drove to the Tulsa airport and waited there again before arriving in Iowa the (Sunday) night before the meet," said Reina. "We had to run the course in the dark, which was not great preparation, and it kind of threw us for a loop."

Although McDonnell had learned his lesson regarding wearing tights from the national championship held in Wisconsin in 1985, there were other hard lessons to be taught on that frigid day. If Reina thought his last trip to a northern climate was uncomfortable, it paled in comparison to what he was set to face on that cold morning in Iowa.

"I talked to some of the guys who went to the meet in Wisconsin and heard they put Vaseline on their legs to keep warm so that's what I did," said Reina. "I ended up putting it on my legs and then I thought to put some on my face too since it was exposed to the air. In the end, it ended up suffocating me. I overheated and remember not being able to breathe. The race bottlenecked at the start, and we all failed to get out. By the 5k mark I had reached the leaders, but I was done."

One of the prerace favorites to win the meet, Reina finished 143rd that day. His teammates didn't fare much better, other than Chris Zinn, who battled Bob Kennedy of Indiana for the individual win.

"When I came by John he said, 'Reuben's out of it, we're out of it, you've got to go for it,'" remembered Zinn. "The next time I saw John he was saying something in Gaelic. I ended up getting fifth, which was the best I had ever done, but at the same time you want your team to win. It was a bad day."

As a team, the Razorbacks finished an unremarkable tenth place on the day.

"I thought we'd never finish," remembered McDonnell. "We stunk the place up. We didn't do it often, but we did it that day. Some of that stuff was unforeseen. Reuben took some advice from people he shouldn't have taken advice from. Even though he had set the Foot Locker championship record, he sometimes got stunned in cross country. Once you got him on the track he had no problem at all."

If McDonnell hadn't gotten the best out of his own team that day, the aura around his program was nonetheless being used by other coaches to motivate their own teams. Wisconsin won its third national championship in cross country, and second under head coach Martin Smith, but not before the Badger coach had used the fear of Arkansas earlier in the season to cajole his own athletes. Future Wisconsin coach Jerry Schumacher was on the Wisconsin team at the time and remembers those speeches very well.

"We'd hear about [Arkansas] when we were working out hard," recalled Schumacher, who was a redshirted freshman on that team. "Martin [Smith] would talk to us about winning a national title and he'd say, 'Do you think John McDonnell and the Hogs are fucking around right now? I guarantee you they are lining up and their toes are in the dirt doing five times a mile!' It created this image [of John] as a taskmaster and fiery competitive human being who wasn't going to accept anything less than your best.'"

Despite not competing that fall in cross country, Joe Falcon had still kept busy. The fifth-year senior married his fiancée over the Christmas holidays, six months before he was to graduate. It was a turning point both in Falcon's career and his relationship with John McDonnell, which for so long had been in perfect and synchronous harmony. It was the beginning of the end.

"It kind of put a wedge between me and him because his parents asked me to try and talk to him about not getting married until he was finished school, which I agreed with," said McDonnell. "I talked to both Joe and Karen that summer and explained that it would be better for Joe to graduate, go to Europe, make a name for himself, get a contract, and then come back and get married.' I don't think they liked it, and all of a sudden they got married at Christmas."

Now married, Joe had moved off-campus with his wife, Karen, but the disconnect was greater than a mere change of apartments. Throughout his career, McDonnell had seen a litany of athletes fail to attain their potential because of relationships that consumed their time and energy, both physical and emotional.

"It was like I was living the same bad dream over and over," said McDonnell. "Different guys and different women, and you would talk to them, and they'd say 'I'm different,' but they really weren't. I used to ask them, 'Do you want to be world-class?' They'd say, 'Yes, of course.' Well, I'd say, 'To be world-class you have to be selfish, self-centered, and care about nobody other than yourself. Because if you have a relationship with a girl, she deserves some of your time—time that you do not have—and that's where you have to make a decision. She demands your time, and quite frankly she deserves it. If you want to be world-class, you have to make the decision not to be distracted by women until your career is over.' There have been a couple of relationships that were great, such as Reuben and his high-school sweetheart, but a lot of them were nightmares and rarely lasted. They lose focus, stop recovering, and start complaining that the training is suddenly too hard. Then it all begins to fall apart."

For those observing from outside, nothing seemed at all to be amiss during the spring of 1989. As was becoming customary in Fayetteville, both Falcon and Reina qualified for the indoor national championship at the late-January home meet with automatic qualifying marks in the mile and 5,000 meter respectively.

Only one week later, Falcon put together one of the most virtuouso collegiate distance performances of all time, winning the 3,000 meter at the Meadowlands Invitational in New Jersey in a school and collegiate record time of 7:46.42, breaking a record previously held by Sulieman Nyambui of UTEP.

"Joe was like a superhero to the younger guys on the team," remembered Danny Green. "He ran 3:35 (1,500 meter) at the home meet all by himself. He even had this Razorback tattoo and had to go to the bad side of [Kansas City] to get it."

In the field events, Edrick Floreal was no less impressive coming off an Olympic appearance and made a smooth transition to Dick Booth following his initial disenchantment at the departure of Ted King.

"There were some issues with Ted leaving," admitted Floreal, "but John promised me Mike was going to be the one who oversaw my training and that made me feel better. I didn't want a third coach and to start back over since I had no idea at that time who the new coach was going to be."

Once Booth arrived back on campus, Conley continued to be highly involved with Floreal's training, but the focus for both men had clearly shifted once again with a new coach at the reins.

"When I got to Arkansas I realized that I didn't know as much about the triple jump as I thought I did," said Floreal. "Ted was a technician and went into the finer details, and I made my biggest adjustments with him. Dick was also a technician but he would really chisel the jumpers, and we'd work hard."

Hard work would be a guiding principle throughout Booth's career and one that he had learned from his father, who had coached his high-school football team in Blue Mound, Kansas. When he arrived in Fayetteville for the second time, Booth recognized how polished Floreal was as an athlete thanks to King's tutelage and due to his own abundant talent, but also that the young jumper was prepared to do whatever was necessary to be the best.

"He was a hard working guy with a lot of personal pride and a lot of talent," said Booth. "The problem you run into sometimes is that the gifted kid is sometimes lazier because he has gotten there without working. Where you get a champion is someone with the natural talent and the personal pride."

Joining Floreal that winter was Gary Johnson, a jumper from Morgan City, Louisiana, who opened up his Razorback career with an automatic qualifying mark in the triple jump at the late January home meet.

"Dick tried to get him at Louisiana and was disappointed we got him but then happy we did after he got here," said McDonnell. "He was a cheerleader in high school and very agile because he did a lot with a little. He had no speed on the runway but was consistently an All-American."

Although some things had changed in four years—Booth now had the benefit of Mike Conley's hands-on experience as a coach at practice—many things had not. Dick resumed coaching Conley and brought the same affable, outgoing personality to the track every day. It felt like he had never left.

More importantly, John once again had an assistant who brought the same aggressiveness to recruiting, and possessed a philosophy of coaching that corresponded to his own. While other coaches were sometimes considered to be more technical, both McDonnell and Booth shared a common bond based on the values they had been raised with and a shared outlook to training—the principle of outworking everyone else both for the physiological and the psychological benefits.

On days when many of the distance runners were pounding out fast miles up Razorback hill, the jumpers were doing quarter squats at mind-boggling weights several times greater than their own. On other occasions when the distance runners might be hitting ten miles as hard as possible behind the golf course on a dirt road that seemingly extended as far as the eye could see, the jumpers would be hopping as far as they could across the field on the same hot afternoon. The effect was the same—physical strength and mental toughness. If the Razorback distance runners felt like they could beat anyone after conquering Razorback Hill, the jumpers felt no less confident leaving the weight room or completing any other seemingly impossible task Booth had planned for them that afternoon.

Quarter squats became a staple in Booth's training gauntlet.

"The flexion in a jumper's knee is minimal," said Booth "You are taking your weight and catching it a high level and exploding off the ground with it. So why squat with your butt touching your heel? We'd do progressive squats starting at parallel with ten reps and then move it up a set and do six and then move it up again and do four and the last one would be a quarter squat, and it was crazy heavy. Those kids would walk out of there saying my little 160 pound body is nothing compared to that. The same goes for bounding and hopping in sand. We'd start at one end, and I'd count how many times they hit the sand, and if it was thirty-five times at the beginning of the semester and twenty-seven at the end of the semester, I'd ask them how far could they triple jump when you could only do thirty-five? Now what can you do? Are you the same person? And they'd say, 'No coach, I'm not.' To me it all ties together. You cannot expect someone to be truly confident unless they have tangible proof. Kids are smart, so you can't do it with smoke and mirrors."

Arkansas would need every bit of confidence heading into a national championship where they once again found themselves short on numbers. After capturing their ninth consecutive SWC indoor championship by seventy points at a meet where both Falcon and Reina had broken the SWC mile record by nearly four seconds, the Razorbacks were in for another battle at nationals. This time they were facing a cocky Florida team that was favored entering the meet in Indianapolis.

"They had Earl Diamond in the hurdles and Dennis Mitchell in the 200 meter and were just loaded," remembered McDonnell. "I didn't see it myself, but the story was they showed up at the airport and got black limos to take them to the hotel and were all dressed up in tuxedos and bowties. We sure turned the tables on them. It was like Murphy's Law. Everything that could go wrong did go wrong for them. To me that was a typical bunch of hot dogs."

Considering the Razorbacks brought only five athletes to the 1989 NCAA Indoor Championships, which would be contested for the first time at the Hoosier Dome in Indiana, the task was a tall one. Just as it had the year before, the outcome of the meet was down to two men coming through on the final day—this time it was Edrick Floreal and Joe Falcon.

In the long jump on the first day, Floreal placed second only to Leroy Burrell of Houston, whose individual performances in the 55 meter, 200 meter and long jump outscored all but eight of the teams at the national championship. In the mile, Falcon closed in 58 seconds for the win in 3:58.06, but faded badly later in the 3,000 meter. Heading into the triple jump, the reality was stark. Floreal had to come through or the Hogs were cooked. He did not disappoint—out-jumping the field by over a foot in 56 feet, 2 inches.

"My left knee was bothering me from the long jump," Floreal told the media afterwards, "but when Joe didn't win the 3,000 meter, I knew I'd have to win the triple jump if we were going to win the team title. That kind of pushed and motivated me. I went all out."[4]

Although Arkansas had only three scoring athletes again, McDonnell wasn't in a complaining mood after winning their sixth consecutive NCAA indoor championship by a slim 34–31 margin over Florida.

"We weren't a deep team, and not everything went right," said John, "but a win is a win. You never look a gift horse in the mouth."

The greatest challenge Arkansas would face that spring was still to come. After a month of lower intensity training on the grass, the Razorbacks opened up at Texas Relays and their home meet at Hot Springs before flying up to Philadelphia for Penn Relays. McDonnell often planned his training in such a way that the Razorbacks were ready to begin competing at their best at Penn Relays in late April. In 1989, their best did not look like it was going to be good enough. They needed to do the impossible.

Mount St. Mary's College, which was tucked away in the hills of Emmitsburg, Maryland, had assembled what many observers of the sport considered to be the greatest collection of talent ever on one team in the distance medley relay. They planned to run all of them at Penn Relays.

The twin brothers from Kenya—Charles and Sammy Cheruiyot—had both made the Kenyan Olympic team—Charles placed sixth in the 5,000 meter run at the 1984 Olympics while Sammy had finished seventh in the 1,500 meter finals at the 1988 Olympics. The quarter-miler, Dave Lishebo, was hardly a slouch either, having represented Zambia in the 400 meter at the 1984 Olympics. Such a team would have been hard to beat under any circumstances, but the mere idea that they could even be challenged became almost unimaginable once the 1988 Olympic 1,500 meter champion, Peter Rono, was added to the mix. For just about every informed member of the media covering the event, the result was a foregone conclusion.

With the talk in Philadelphia centering on how Mount St. Mary's was going to crush the entire field, at six o'clock in the morning on Friday April 28, 1989, John McDonnell picked up a copy of the *Philadelphia Daily News* and read something that made his blood pressure rise through the roof.

"Mount St. Mary's could break 9:20 and cruise to a world's best in this event, even if conditions are poor," said the *Daily News*. "Arkansas, with Falcon, should finish second in under 9:25."[5]

Returning to the hotel, John summoned the members of the relay to his room early that morning.

"I remember I got a phone call at 6:30 in the morning, and it was John and he said get to my hotel room," said Falcon, who was joined by the other members of the team, Reuben Reina, Charles Williams, and Robert Bradley. "I said, 'Oh gosh, I've been in bed so I can't be in trouble.' We got up there, and John gave us the finest motivational speech I have ever heard. He very calmly brought everyone in and said, 'You guys are probably wondering why I brought you up here and I want to show you why.'"

McDonnell unraveled the *Daily News* article marginalizing Arkansas's chances that afternoon.

"I said, 'Guys, this is bullshit,'" remembered McDonnell. "We have won this thing many times, and this is the respect we are given? We are going to go out there and kick their g'damn ass from one end of the track to another. And if we hold Joe Falcon close, we are going to win because there isn't a Kenyan ever born who is going to beat Joe Falcon today."

It was an emotional appeal straight from John McDonnell's heart, a speech that became so legendary it would be talked about by generations of Razorbacks. Like many legends, the story became exaggerated to such a degree that some versions had McDonnell ripping up the newspaper and smashing a chair against the wall. Nothing of the sort took place. For those in the room that morning, the reality was surreal enough. It was a compelling message from a man with the immense gravitas to deliver it.

"He unraveled this newspaper and his hands were shaking he was so mad," said Falcon. "He said, 'This is going to be a day that is going to go down in the history of Arkansas track and field as one of the greatest days ever and will be talked about for years and years. You guys are going to win today and let me tell you why. Those boys from Mount St. Mary's are running for themselves. There is no tradition there. You wear the red and white of Arkansas and have been privileged to run for this university. A torch has been handed down to you by all of the great athletes before you, and you will hand this torch off to all of the great athletes that will come after you. This will go down as one of the greatest victories in Arkansas history.' And he went through and told each and every one of us exactly what we needed to do to be successful. When he was finished, he said 'Let's go out there and win, and don't you ever think about anything other than winning.'"

All four members of the relay immediately jumped up with a shot of adrenaline.

"When we were done, they were all fired up and said, 'Let's go get 'em!'" said McDonnell. "I tell you they ran inspired. That Williams kid couldn't believe his eyes when he saw how many people were in the stands."

As Falcon looked outside later, he was astonished to see that his new wife, Karen, and parents, Lou and Pat, had flown up from Kansas City to make a surprise appearance in Philadelphia.[6]

Before the race had even begun, both McDonnell and the Mt. St. Mary's coach, Jim Deegan, each made fateful decisions that may have affected the outcome. Rather than anchoring the reigning Olympic champion Peter Rono in the mile, Deegan led him off on the 1,200 meter leg. McDonnell subsequently opted to run an untested sophomore in the 800 meter from Crossett, Arkansas, named Robert Bradley, whose personal best entering that season had been 1:51.7. It was an audacious gamble.

In front of a frenzied throng of fifty thousand at Franklin Field, the gun was finally fired on Friday afternoon. Reina led off the 1,200 meter for Arkansas and handed off a half-second behind Rono in 2:53.9. With Leshebo putting another second on Charles Williams during his 46.4 split over 400 meters, the Razorbacks were falling behind and looked to be in trouble even before the inexperienced Bradley was asked to matchup against the Olympian, Charles Cheruiyot. If ever there was a moment Arkansas could have been buried this was it.

Not only did Bradley not give up any distance to the Kenyan, but gained over three seconds on him during a remarkable 1:46.0 split over 800 meters to hand the baton to Joe Falcon with a slight lead. Despite running aggressively, Falcon was soon caught by Sammy Cheruiyot, who ran stride for stride with him over the next three laps. Neither man gave the other an inch as the crowd came to its feet.

"The crowd is going crazy and is so loud I can't hear my split or anything," remembered Falcon. "John told me before the race that when we get to the final 200-meter mark, 'I'm going to tell you either to hit it or wait, and when I tell you to hit it, you have to hit it hard.' So the next time I came around, John tells me to hit it, and I went by Cheruiyot as hard as I could and I looked at [Cheruiyot], and he looked back at me and smiled and I'm thinking, 'Gosh, this isn't good.'"

Up in the stands, McDonnell watched the thrilling climax to one of the greatest races in Penn Relays history along with distance runners Danny Green and Chris Zinn, who had run the long-distance races the previous evening.

"They were both hammering down the backstretch" said McDonnell, "and when they entered the final straightaway, you could see how jacked both of them were coming up. Fair play to Joe, he had intestinal fortitude, and the moment he got by Cheruiyot, he pulled away from him."

As his vision began to fade and his legs slowed due to the overwhelming buildup of lactic acid, Joe Falcon's burning desire and fiery determination was not going to be denied.

"I'll remember to the day I die, I came around the curve, and I looked up and saw my three Arkansas teammates holding hands behind the finish line," said Falcon. "I remembered what Coach said, 'It's not about you. It's about the great athletes that came before you and the great athletes that will come after you.' I shut my eyes and sprinted as hard as I could and leaned at the tape."

Arkansas had done the impossible—beating the seemingly invincible Mount St. Mary's team by a step and shattering both the American and world record in a time of 9:20.10. Four kids from Arkansas, Missouri, and Texas had beaten some of the best that the world had to offer. Falcon was awarded the outstanding performance of the meet following his 3:53.8 mile split.

"I told them we should pull out our American flags," said McDonnell. "It was a classic. What an upset. Four local kids put on a show. Those are the moments that are so great about this sport and you remember. It was awesome."

Following the Razorbacks was not exactly for the faint of heart. The intensity was not about to go down at the Southwest Conference Outdoor Championships in Waco, Texas, two weeks later. This time it was not only Texas but also Texas A&M with whom Arkansas needed to be concerned. As had been the case for three of the past four outdoor conference championships, the meet would not be short on drama.

Only a year after Richard Cooper outkicked Chris Zinn and Longhorn Harry Green in the 10,000 meter, the three men once again found themselves entangled when McDonnell told Cooper to take it with 600 meters remaining.

Despite another win by Cooper in the steeplechase in 8:39.9, Texas A&M found itself ahead of Arkansas by a fifteen-point margin, 148–133, following a 27-point Aggie barrage in the 200 meter after Michael Johnson of Baylor withdrew from the event. A dropped baton by A&M in the 4 x 100 meter relay (in a year when the Aggies finished second at nationals in the event), and that all came unraveled. As they often did, Arkansas took advantage with Falcon, Reina, and Eric Henry following up their sweep in the 1,500 meter with 23 more points in the 5,000 meter. The Hogs barely came out ahead in a thrilling finale, 163–156.

"They had the better team," admitted McDonnell, "but that dropped baton completely took the wind out of their sails."

Although Arkansas did not have the numbers to pull off a win at the 1989 NCAA Outdoor Championships, which were won by Pat Henry's Louisiana Tigers, the meet was similar in some respects to the last time the national championships has been held in Provo, Utah, seven years earlier. Floreal won the triple jump going away, but the rest of the meet was a series of close calls and disappointments.

After a wonderful five-year career in Fayetteville, the once unknown Richard Cooper had come a long way. He was a straightaway from capturing the NCAA championship in the 3,000-meter steeplechase before Tom Nohilly of Florida caught him after the final water jump to win by less than a tenth of a second. It was a heartbreaking end to Cooper's collegiate career.

In the 1,500 meter final, Falcon was once again matched up against Sammy Cheruiyot and Peter Rono of Mount St. Mary's, also the final race of one of the most glorious and accomplished careers in Arkansas athletics history. It was one race Falcon never finished—tripping in the middle of a tightly packed group halfway through the slowly paced affair.

"Someone came from behind and tripped me," Falcon dejectedly told the media after the race. "I stumbled, and then someone pushed me down. I'm not hurt, just maybe my ego. I got back up to run, but my coach told me to stop. It's not how you want your career to end."[7]

It was a bitter ending to a magnificent career—and the tragedy of it all was that the bitterness was only just beginning.

"After we left Provo, I did not hear from Joe Falcon for two years," said John. "He never said goodbye, hello, I'm leaving, give me a call. His wife came around for an award he had won and picked it up from my office. Then off they went to Springfield, Missouri."

Falcon began training with his high-school coach and focused on the mile. It was a shocking turn of events for two men who had been so close and in such sync with each another for so long.

"I saw superstar written on that guy," said McDonnell. "I wanted him to run the 5,000 meter and 10,000 meter because I thought he could have been America's greatest distance runner ever. He could handle the distance and had 1:47 speed. He had been so easy to coach."

Although Falcon had great things ahead of him—his 3:49 mile was the fastest time in the world in 1990—and his relationship with McDonnell would later be repaired and be stronger than ever. When he eventually did return to Fayetteville, it was not with the same physical or mental strength that he left with in 1989.

"It was the stupidest thing ever," said Oklahoma State coach Dick Weis, who watched it all unfold like a car accident in slow motion, "but you had two strong personalities, and they fell out."

John's way of relaxing during the summers was to spend time with his family at the ranch on Grand Lake in Oklahoma. The 1,400-acre ranch in Fairland, Oklahoma, which was owned by John and his brother Michael, had become quite a going concern. It was doing so well that it attracted the eyes of an Australian investor who would not take no for an answer.

"It wasn't for sale, but he kept coming back," said John. "Two weeks went by, and he came back and kept asking if I was interested in selling. I told him I wasn't. Then a couple of months went by, and he came back again. So he made me an offer I couldn't refuse and offered to buy all of the cattle. So I asked for a couple of days and found a place in Muskogee [Oklahoma] that my brother and I ended up buying with 2240 acres. Then we came back and sold the Fairland ranch to the guy."

With Michael McDonnell still only a few hours away in Edmond, Oklahoma, the two families and their children spent many summers on the boat at Grand Lake in Oklahoma. Still his older brother's greatest fan, Michael often made the trips to Fayetteville to watch home meets or travelled to Oklahoma City or Indianapolis to cheer on the Razorbacks at the indoor national championships.

It was around that time when Michael suddenly had more than one reason to make the trip. Proving that the apple doesn't fall far from the tree, Michael's daughter, Genie McDonnell, earned a scholarship to run at Georgetown University, where she eventually won the Big East title and earned All-American honors in the 3,000 meter in 1991. As it turns out her uncle's impact was most felt off of the track: "He was always so interesting to talk to about so many things outside of running," said Genie, "and full of good advice whenever I needed it."

Entering the fall of 1989, John's harriers were not lacking talent but, aside from Reuben Reina, were short on upperclassman experience. That would become painfully obvious as early as September 23, 1989, when Doug Williamson and his cross-country team from Alabama surprised a depleted Arkansas with a two point win, 37–39, at the Razorback Invitational in Little Rock.

"We didn't deserve to win," McDonnell bluntly told the media after the race. "I'm not panicking. It's a long a season and we're real young. I do know a few of our freshmen will no longer redshirt. We will be a better team by conference."[8]

The following week in Springfield, McDonnell did exactly that, racing true freshmen Brian Baker, David Welsh, and Frank Hanley, each of whom would become catalysts of another Arkansas distance renaissance. Baker was one of the greatest local talents to ever come out of Arkansas, with a 4:11 mile and 9:09 two-mile to his name, while Welsh, from Meadow Vista, California, had run 8:58 for the two mile. Although Welsh's roommate and longtime training partner, Hanley, came from the same high school in Limerick, Ireland, as Niall O'Shaughnessy and Frank O'Mara, his specialty ultimately lay in the longer distances and cross country.

Still, the incoming athlete who would make the most immediate impact that season was a transfer from the University of North Carolina at Chapel Hill named Johan Boakes—a worldly Englishman from the southern coastal city of Brighton with Swedish heritage and parents living in Sarasota, Florida.

"He had trained with Steve Ovett and was supposed to be coming here originally but all of a sudden went to North Carolina at the last minute," said McDonnell. "Well, he wasn't there long before he wanted to transfer, and he turned out to be a great guy. That sucker ran great for us in cross country and had 3:40 speed for 1,500 meter. He just loved the team concept."

Having run 2:20 for 1,000 meters as a junior in England, Boakes was heavily recruited by American universities and certainly could have expected to be wined and dined when he eventually visited Arkansas.

"The first stop on my official visit was to the Waffle House," laughed Boakes. "That's John. There are no frills. He doesn't have to prove anything. By that time he had a very successful winning formula, and I wanted to be a part of it."

Although Arkansas won an unprecedented sixteenth consecutive SWC cross-country championship that fall at Crow Lake Park in Dallas, McDonnell rested several members of his young squad at the regional and was beaten for the first time in a decade by a Texas team led by Steve Sisson.

"We just wanted to qualify," said John. "Second is as good as first at a regional, so we wanted to save it for the national meet. Some years we didn't have as much depth, and when we didn't run all out or run our best guys, we could be beaten."

The decision paid dividends at the 1989 NCAA Cross Country Championships, which were held at the Naval Academy in Annapolis, Maryland, when John's young squad placed fifth overall in what could only qualify as a success during a rebuilding season.

Seeking their seventh consecutive NCAA indoor championship that winter, Arkansas would be counting on the big Texan, Eric Henry, who was fresh off earning All-American honors in cross country that fall. Looking uncharacteristically trim, Henry took McDonnell's advice to remain in Fayetteville for most of the Christmas holidays. While John may have won that battle, it was a war that could never be won.

"He'd gain six or seven pounds just over the weekend," said John. "Our trainer weighed him every day. He was 6 feet, 4 and when you got him under 180 pounds he was dynamite. That one Christmas he stayed here he looked awesome, I mean absolutely awesome. Swain came in and asked me who the new guy was at the track and I said, 'Henry.' He couldn't believe it. I said to myself, 'This kid is going to run awesome this year.' Then he asked if he could go home to his mother for New Years. She loved to feed him whenever he went home. So I said, 'Stay away from the food.' Well, that sucker gained ten pounds in five days."

Henry's performance didn't suffer too badly—he nearly broke the four-minute barrier in his first race of the season at home. With the middle-distance talent McDonnell had accumulated and developed—Henry, Reuben Reina, Johan Boakes, Gilbert Contreras, and Mike Skinner went 1–5 in the mile at the 1990 Southwest Conference Indoor Championships—the Razorbacks could have done without double wins by Reina (mile, 3,000 meter) and Edrick Floreal (long and triple jump) and still won the conference championship by twenty-five points.[9]

"Never in my imagination did I think we could win ten straight indoor championships," McDonnell told the media. "I figured Baylor would be a little closer but our guys did an outstanding job yesterday and today. Charles Williams hurt his back earlier today, then busted his leg in the hurdles and couldn't even bend over to tie his shoe before the 400 meter but still gutted it out and placed third. Today's championship is just as sweet as our first one. To do it in the best track and field conference in the country is even better."[10]

Although it was Floreal and Reina who led the way to a seventh consecutive NCAA indoor championship at Indianapolis with individual titles in the triple jump and 3,000 meter two weeks later, Eric Henry's contributions were no less meaningful. Henry anchored the 4 x 800 meter relay team to a second-place finish and then nearly won the mile. One small fraction of a second proved fateful.

"Henry got beat by the Kentucky kid (Bob Whelan)," remembered McDonnell. "I told him with 500 meters to go to put the hammer down but [Whelan] was ahead and had the same flipping idea. So just as Henry moved out, [Whelan] got in front and that was exactly how it finished. They were both big powerful guys, and it went to whoever got the jump. They were one step apart the whole way."

The pleasant surprise of the meet was Johan Boakes. The Englishman, who had languished in Chapel Hill, finished fifth in the mile and was blossoming just in time for the outdoor season.

"Johan was starting to become a leader for us," said McDonnell. "He was a real outgoing kid, and his parents were fantastic people. His father was English, and his mother was Swedish, and they moved to America shortly after he did. His mother came to a lot of the meets and was a lot of fun. He was a delightful guy, and it was good to have someone who kept everyone loose."

Judging by Boakes's results on the track and happiness off of it, the feeling appeared to be mutual.

"As you go through the program you develop a very good friendship with John," said Boakes. "It was a challenging training regime in that I was doing over one hundred miles, which was much higher than I had ever done. It wasn't unusual for an easy day to be quicker than six-minute pace. You went how you felt, but it was a very competitive atmosphere and invariably somebody felt good and pushed the pace. The program got you very, very fit. John had a very successful training formula, but that's not enough.

You have to have someone who keeps all the personalities in check, and he was the best at it."

Following fantastic relay legs at Penn Relays, Boakes won the SWC Outdoor 1,500 meter in a kick off after a dawdling pace on a hot, windy day in College Station.

"The times don't matter but the points do," Boakes told the media after the race. "I thought the Rice guys would take it out like they had said, but they were walking out there. All of their talk in the newspaper gave us extra motivation. If you're gonna talk it, you need to walk it."[11]

Boakes backed up his own bravado by setting another personal best at the 1990 NCAA Outdoor Championships at Duke University and placing third. No less of a surprise was senior javelin thrower Ed Kaminski, whose 241 feet, 11 inch school-record toss earned him seventh place and an All-American certificate.

"It was an event we never put any scholarship money into because it was only outdoors," said McDonnell. "[Ed] walked on and had a great career here."

That spring Edrick Floreal closed out a fantastic Razorback career by remaining undefeated in the triple jump at every national championship he had competed in. If not for the misfortune of competing against Leroy Burrell in the long jump, the Canadian Olympian might have had several long-jump championships to go with them. It was a collegiate career that rivaled Mike Conley's, who was instrumental in ensuring that it turned out as spectacularly as it did.

"Mike Conley really helped him as far as a good influence to be around," said McDonnell. "At the beginning Edrick was kind of an individual, but he became a great leader and tremendous team man."

With few expecting Arkansas to prevent Louisiana State from capturing their second consecutive outdoor national championship, the highlight of the spring occurred within the confines of Franklin Field in Philadelphia. Only a year after the distance medley relay drama against Mount St. Mary's, the Georgetown Hoyas provided the most significant challenge to Arkansas hegemony at the Penn Relays in 1990.

"We're on a mission to win the DMR, 4 x 1,500 meter and 4 x 800 meter relays," Georgetown coach Frank Gagliano gushed to the media. "We've dedicated our season to the Penn Relays."[12]

After receiving the baton with a fifteen-meter lead on John Trautman of Georgetown, Reuben Reina inexplicably allowed Trautman back into the race before the Georgetown runner outkicked Reina with a 4:01.5 anchor leg. As a legion of American flags waved that Friday afternoon to celebrate the Georgetown victory, McDonnell could only shake his head when he spoke to the media.

"To say the least I am disappointed," John said afterwards. "This is the worst DMR performance by an Arkansas team that I have ever seen. We should have won that race and instead gave it away."[13]

Reina redeemed himself the next day in the 4 x 1,500 meter when he inherited another 15-meter lead on Trautman following a strong leg from Boakes. This time instead of blowing the lead, he blew it wide open with a 57-second first lap and 1:57 half mile that brought home the win for Arkansas in 14:54.84.

"It wasn't a smart performance by me yesterday," Reina told the media afterwards. "I didn't want to play any games today. Coach McDonnell was definitely mad. We had a meeting last night, and we never do that after the meet has started. He told us, 'We're gonna run tomorrow. We're not gonna wait around and let the whole field be in the race. We're going to go out hard and make the other teams beat us.' Yesterday's race definitely inspired us. Today we were out for blood."[14]

Reina and Trautman were not finished tangling. In the 5,000-meter final at the NCAA Championships five weeks later, ten athletes found themselves in the lead pack late in the race before Reina scattered the field with a sprint from 600 meters out. John Nuttall of Iowa State passed Reina with 200 meters remaining, and then Trautman passed Nuttall with 100 meters remaining to win by ten meters in a thrilling sprint finish.

Back in Fayetteville, athletic director Frank Broyles was busy plotting the future of Arkansas Razorback athletics. While many reasonably believed at that point in time his most important decision of the year had been the hiring of Jack Crowe as head football coach after Ken Hatfield left for Clemson, few were aware of the tectonic shift that the major-conference power structure was about to undergo and its seismic effect on college athletics in general and the University of Arkansas in particular.

"I never knew what Frank Broyles was thinking," said McDonnell. "He was a pretty sharp cookie and kept things close to the vest. All of a sudden he called us for a meeting, and that's when we found out."

What they found out was that the University of Arkansas, nearly seventy-six years after signing on as a founding member of the Southwest Conference, was bolting for the Southeastern Conference. As jaws hit the floor, Broyles explained to the room the rationale behind his decision, which was based in large part on the years he had spent in the television industry covering college football as an analyst for ABC.

"He knew that television was the big breadwinner, and that the gates were nothing compared to it," said McDonnell. "He started talking about television markets and how there was more population between Florida and Tennessee as well as Atlanta, New Orleans, and all of the big cities."

Along with South Carolina, the University of Arkansas was set to join the Southeastern Conference for the start of the 1991–92 season. The SEC was a loaded league that included Florida, Tennessee, Louisiana State, Georgia, Alabama, Auburn, Kentucky, Mississippi State, Mississippi, and Vanderbilt.

The departure of Arkansas was the first of many dominoes to fall in what would eventually lead to the complete demise of the Southwest Conference and the formation of the Big 12 four years later. Knowing he had to prepare his athletic department to be as competitive as possible in the new conference, Broyles launched another $50 million facility fundraising campaign. Not for the first time in his career, Frank Broyles was ahead of the curve.

"Coach Broyles was such a visionary and he understood what was happening before the rest of us," said Terry Don Phillips, who was an assistant athletic director at the time. "He understood what was happening in the Southwest Conference and that this was an opportunity to move to a very strong league with more financial opportunities than we had. He saw things the rest of us didn't see at the time."

As a new decade began, McDonnell had strategic decisions to make of his own. There was no need to diverge from the focus on distance running and field events given the success he had since his arrival eighteen years earlier. Although his program had won three NCAA cross-country championships and seven NCAA indoor championships on the backs of superb mid-distance/long-distance running and jumping, it was only when they had scored across the board with sprinters, pole-vaulters, and throwers that they captured their first NCAA outdoor title and triple crown in 1985. Entering the final decade of the twentieth century, the question became where to focus resources for another run at the triple crown.

Each year, McDonnell continued to spend days studying his competition to determine their strengths and weaknesses and what would complete his own roster at Arkansas. The actual events did not matter as much to him as much as how they would help the program win championships at the conference and national level. With the NCAA limiting schools to 12.6 scholarships, and as many as sixty athletes on the Razorback roster at the start of the season, difficult decisions had to be made each year.

While Arkansas was rarely considered to be a sprint power, the success of Roddie Haley and later Calvin Davis, Wallace Spearmon Jr., and Tyson Gay in either setting world records or winning Olympic medals hardly speaks to a complete abandonment of the sprint events. Nonetheless, McDonnell preferred to invest in distance runners and jumpers due to what he believed was a greater reliability from those areas.

"It sure didn't hurt to have Mike Conley," said McDonnell. "He was to jumping what Niall O'Shaughnessy was to middle-distance running. Not only was he a super jumper but a super nice guy and if anyone came to visit, and we had scholarship, we got them because of Mike."

There were a few misses along the way. Just as McDonnell regretted missing out on distance star Arturo Barrios seven years earlier after running out of scholarships, the strategic decision to not invest heavily in throwers also caused him to not offer a scholarship to a future Olympic champion.

"I remember John Godina came here to visit," said McDonnell. "He was a 206-foot high-school discus thrower but only threw about 57 feet with the high-school shot up in Wyoming. I said we can't put a scholarship in a discus thrower because it is an outdoor-only event. Well, he ended up going to UCLA and threw 71 feet [in the shot put]."

Despite missing out on Godina, the recruiting class that arrived in the fall of 1991 was as strong as ever, featuring future All-Americans, NCAA champions, and Olympians in the mid-distance, sprints, and jumps. Brian Wellman was a 54 feet, 5 inch triple jumper from Bermuda, who had spent two years at Taft Junior College in California, when he decided to attend Arkansas. Joining Wellman in Fayetteville that fall was Erick Walder, a 53-4 triple jumper from Alabama, who like Wellman could also long jump very well.

"Arkansas came into the picture late in the game," said Walder. "At the time I was looking at Tennessee, Florida, Kansas, and Houston. So I got a call from Coach Booth and he said, "I know you haven't made a decision, but I'd like to give us a chance and come visit and decide whether you like what you see." So he sent me a media guide with a bunch of rings on the cover, and I was like, 'Man, you have to be kidding me.' I took a visit over spring break, and once I saw the facilities and the championship rings with the triple-jump tradition they had, I knew this was what I wanted to do."

Part of the attraction was the opportunity to train with one of the best triple jumpers in the world.

"Mike Conley was such a nice guy and the whole nine yards," said McDonnell. "You'd think this guy couldn't be this nice but he was. Houston had sent Carl Lewis down there to visit so the high-school coach called and said, 'He's wavering. You better send Mike Conley down if you want to sign him.'"

As it often turned out, a visit by the personable Conley had exactly the desired effect.

Not wanting to overlook the sprint events, McDonnell attended the Arkansas high-school state meet that spring to watch another raw athlete from Crossett, Arkansas, named Chris Phillips, who had run the 110-meter hurdles in 13.82 and the 300 meter hurdles in 36.92.

"He won the highs and then in the 300-meter hurdles he hit the fourth hurdle and flipped upside down on the track and then got up and still ran 38.5," said McDonnell. "I said, 'We've got ourselves the right guy!'"

Along with Jimmy French, who had run 20.8 for 200 meters at the same Texarkana high school as Roddie Haley and had turned down an offer at sprint power Texas Christian University in order to win a national championship at Arkansas, the Razorbacks had reloaded with more firepower in the sprints.

John did equally well with regional distance runners by signing Louisiana state champion Mike Morin, along with two 4:10 milers from Missouri—Dan Munz and Dewayne Miner. As a high-school runner from Bolivar, Missouri, Miner had been transfixed watching Arkansas dominate the Southern Stampede at Missouri Southern and decided to become a Razorback himself.

To complete the remainder of the class, John ventured much further away. Along with Nigel Brunton from Bray, Ireland, who had run 3:45.9 for 1,500 meters, John signed two supreme talents that fall.

Graham Hood and Niall Bruton were two athletes with different attitudes from different parts of the world, both of whom nonetheless had the God-given talent of finding the finish line faster than just about anyone else. Each of them in their own way would become the new bell cows of the Arkansas program over the mile, a designation they shared grudgingly.

A graduate of St. Aidans College in Dublin, Ireland, Bruton showed range from the 400 meter (48.8) to the two-mile (8:42) and even led Ireland at the World Junior Cross Country Championships.

"Oh, he was like O'Mara with the leg speed and, boy, could he accelerate," said John. "He liked to sit and kick. To outkick Niall you had to be awfully good."

Graham Hood had graduated from Nelson High School in Burlington, Ontario, Canada, and showed similar range to Bruton's, having run 1:48.50 for 800 meters while also competing at the World Junior Cross Country Championships. The difference was that he had significantly fewer miles on his legs when he arrived in Fayetteville. After being heavily recruited by several schools, Hood nearly signed with Southern Methodist—who had hired Canadian steeplechase record holder Greg Duhaime to coach the distance events—before speaking with Doug Consiglio and sending a letter to Arkansas.

"Coach McDonnell started recruiting me and just took so much time getting to know me and genuinely caring about the kind of athletes he was going to get," said Hood. "I knew right away this was the place, and it was mostly a comfort level with

Coach McDonnell. Yes, the school had had a lot of success, but my parents and I were really comfortable with him from the start."

The possibilities of bringing Bruton and Hood together on one team and in one training group were endless. The need for a strong hand to manage their very different personalities and control the raging competitiveness within each of them was also paramount.

"I'd tell each of them how to win so it was very simple," said McDonnell. "Niall had the advantage over Graham because he had more leg speed and a better kick over the last 150 meters but Graham could maintain a long drive from 350 meters out. They both won their share of battles."

From top to bottom, it was a recruiting class that established another unprecedented period of success in Razorback athletics.

"We were so lucky to get guys like that," said McDonnell. "They brought character and leadership with them."

Still, the success each of them would achieve individually and for the program did not happen overnight. McDonnell took his time breaking in the low-mileage half-miler Hood, while Bruton did not compete during the 1990 cross-country season until the home meet at Razorback Golf Course on October 13. He did not even make the trip to Stanford, where Arkansas and two other teams embarrassed the downtrodden Stanford Cardinal on their own course.

The conference championship held at the Texas A&M Golf Course would be the last cross-country meet for Arkansas in the Southwest Conference.

"We would like to go out with a bang," John told the media in the week before the meet. "But I'm sure they would like to send us out with our tail between our legs."[15]

By the time Steve Sisson crossed the finish line for the University of Texas as their first runner, five other Razorbacks had preceded him. The Razorbacks put up a perfect score and looked ready to take back the cross-country national title.

"Iowa State is a great team but we'll be ready for them," McDonnell confidently told the media after capturing his seventeenth consecutive and final SWC cross-country championship. "We've won three national cross-country championships and would like to win another."[16]

After holding their top four runners out of the regional meet, the rested Hogs headed to the 1990 NCAA Cross Country Championships in Knoxville, Tennessee, where they faced the tall task of upending the defending champions from Iowa State. Although Bill Bergan's squad no longer had the previous year's champion, John Nuttall, they still had two of the individual favorites, Jon Brown and Jonah Koech, and would not be easy to beat.

On a tough course with long gradual hills interspersed throughout, McDonnell let his young team know exactly what sort of sacrifice would be needed to take home the trophy.

"To be honest I didn't think we could win it," remembered McDonnell, "but I told our guys it will be thirty minutes of hell for three-hundred and sixty-five days of glory. You make up your mind, but it will be hell because this course is tough and you need to concentrate every step of the way. They did exactly what I asked them to do and we turned the tables on [Iowa State]."

Though Koech took the individual win for Iowa State followed by Brown twenty seconds later in fourth, Arkansas won the meet by twenty-eight points, 68–96, led by Eric Henry in fifth, and followed by Johan Boakes, Brian Baker, and Frank Hanley in the top twenty-five. Had it not been for the true freshman Niall Bruton, hanging on in forty-fourth place, Arkansas would have gone home empty-handed.[17]

For Boakes, who had languished before transferring to Arkansas, the win was especially sweet.

"This is the highlight of my career," Boakes told the media after the race. "I went out with the top group and tried to stay with them the whole way. I felt good as the race went on, and when we got over the last hill, I knew I was home."[18]

It was certainly foreshadowing that Arkansas's cross-country success had been achieved with milers. During the indoor season they would finish a mindboggling first to sixth in the mile and first to seventh in the 3,000 meter at the 1991 SWC Indoor Championships. Their depth was even more daunting considering Reuben Reina only had indoor eligibility remaining and freshman Graham Hood was ready for a spectacular freshman indoor campaign after redshirting the fall to get some much needed mileage under his legs.

"My first run down there they said they were going for an 'easy eight' by the Mexican Original Tortilla loop and I'm thinking, 'Whoa. Eight miles?'" remembered Hood. "It was over one hundred degrees and humid, and about five miles into it I was thinking, 'What have I gotten myself into here?'"

McDonnell often modified Hood's workouts during the fall, having the young half-miler do 1,200s when the group did 5 x miles, or cutting the volume down to 10 sets when the rest of the team did 16 x 400s.

"John was really patient with me, and there was no talk of me running cross country that fall," said Hood. "I think I may have run fifty miles a week once in high school, and he let me really build up to sixty miles per week, which wasn't a lot but took me some time to get there in volume. He was waiting to see how things would pan out indoors."

With Hood rooming with Reina on the away trips, the fifth-year senior took the true freshman under his wing just as Falcon had done for him years earlier. If Hood wondered what he had gotten himself into by coming to Arkansas, it did not take him long to find out.

"That first indoor meet guys are showing up and want to get their tickets punched to the NCAAs," said Hood. "You go around the locker room, and the culture is you are going to the NCAA meet, and if you aren't, then you aren't successful."

That culture did not take long to rub off. Only a week before Reina beat an elite field at the Millrose Games in New York over 3,000 meters, Hood set a Canadian indoor 800-meter record in his college debut.

"That was a culture John created and made us successful throughout the years," said Reina. "That's what Graham came into. He had a great freshman year but was down the pecking order, and the mentality was that you are going to take this over. We never heard about anything other than winning come from John. You'd never hear him say, 'We're shooting for second.' It just wasn't considered."

With all of the talk centering on Notre Dame football sensation Raghib "Rocket" Ismail's participation in the 55-meter dash at the 1991 NCAA Indoor Championships at Indianapolis, it was Reina who put on a dominating performance in the 3,000 meter. His victory in a meet record time of 7:50.99—during which he closed in 56 seconds—set the bar high for his younger roommate and just about everyone else wearing red and white that Saturday afternoon.

"I remember after watching [Reuben] killing everyone in the 3,000 meter," said Hood. "For me to make a final and get fourth in my race didn't seem like such a big deal. It's what all of the guys were doing and was just padding on the cushion of our win."

Hood's 800-meter run of 1:48.33 in the final pushed the Razorbacks over the top.

"Graham was a great competitor," said John. "He wasn't afraid of anything and had a great race head. You could tell him exactly what to do, and he would carry it out to a tee."

Even with subpar races from Henry and Boakes in a mile that was won by Bob Kennedy of Indiana,[19] Arkansas clinched its unprecedented eighth consecutive NCAA indoor championship.

"We had a few bad breaks but came back," John told the media afterwards. "The mile was a setback, but then we had a freshman come back for us in the next event. I've got to really hand it to Graham Hood. On a national level, to win with so many groups of guys, it's tough. You've got to hand it to them."[20]

Not everything was going as well. Erick Walder was having a hard time making the transition to college training. Blessed with a plethora of natural talent and fortunate to have Dick Booth overseeing his training while Mike Conley provided him with daily feedback at practice, Walder was nonetheless struggling to adjust to the volume, technical changes, and being so far away from home.

"I had never worked so hard in my life," said Walder. "I was jumping off natural talent in high school. When I got to Arkansas, they worked me harder than I had ever worked before and totally changed the way I jumped and tried to get me to go faster and faster and faster."

Although his long jump improved with his improved speed, Walder's furthest triple jump during the 1991 season was 52 feet, 8 inches—nearly a foot behind his high-school best—while he failed to make either of the NCAA finals indoors or outdoors during his freshman campaign.

"Coming in there was a lot of pressure because of the strong triple-jump tradition," said Walder. "I had never experienced failure on that level. I just completely bombed out at the [national] meet."

With the pressure of following in the footsteps of Olympians Mike Conley and Edrick Floreal weighing on the young freshman, McDonnell called Walder into his office at the end of the season.

"John told me he believed in me, and that when I was done, I would leave even bigger footprints than Mike Conley," said Walder. "I looked at him and said, 'You think I can be better than Mike Conley?' He said, 'I think you can be the greatest.' When he told me that I went back to my dorm room and thought about it and said, 'I can,' and ten championships later, I was. He saw that in me even when I didn't."

As the winter turned to spring, the Razorbacks, as always, had significant challenges to face on the track. Having only beaten Georgetown by seven points at the indoor national meet, the Hoyas were chomping at the bit to face the Razorbacks again. All eyes were once again on Philadelphia at the end of April and a ballyhooed showdown at Penn Relays in the distance medley relay. It seemed each year provided another tale for the ages.

After Graham Hood handed the baton off to Eric Henry with a slight lead on John Trautman of Georgetown, who was expected to win the event, the two men would not give an inch to one another before a rapt crown of fifty-two thousand on a Friday afternoon in Philadelphia.

"[Georgetown] used to pull out the American flags when they won because at that time they didn't have any foreign athletes," remembered John. "I told Henry if you have the lead he is going to try and sit on you so keep the pressure on him. Coming out of the last straightaway, Trautman was moving around him and this kid on Georgetown started pulling an American flag out of his bag. Well, just as Trautman tried to inch by, Henry dug in and won a thrilling race."

The American flag never got unfurled as Trautman fell across the line face first in a dramatic finish. Eric Henry recorded one of the fastest miles in Penn Relays history, 3:55.00, as Arkansas held on for an exciting win in a time of 9:22.24.

"I thought it was over with after he went ahead of me," Henry admitted to the *Philadelphia Daily News*. "But when he didn't open up any ground and stayed even, I felt like I could still pull it off. It wasn't by much, but it was clean."[21]

At the 1991 Southwest Conference Outdoor Championships, which were held at the University of Houston, there were definite mixed feelings heading into the final SWC competition in Arkansas history.

"It was the beginning of the end of the Southwest Conference," said McDonnell. "I remember at the coaches' meeting, Stan Huntsman (of Texas) stood up once it was over and said, 'I think we should all wish John and Arkansas good luck in the SEC because we are going to miss him and miss the competition. He made our conference better.'"

After a brief applause to Huntsman's gracious remarks, a short silence pervaded the room before Clyde Hart from Baylor deadpanned from the other side of the table, "Miss him? I'm damn glad that sucker's leaving."

"Everyone cracked up, and it was kind of funny, but he probably meant it." John said.

Hart, who would coach Michael Johnson to an Olympic gold medal the following year and every four years thereafter throughout the decade, had coached numerous teams that finished second to Arkansas at the conference meet.

Arkansas dominated the Southwest Conference like they, nor any team in SWC history, had ever done before, scoring 218 points for the highest point total of all time. The feat was all the more remarkable considering they did not field athletes at all in the 100 meter, 400 meter, shot, discus, hammer, javelin, or decathlon. Four Razorbacks scored 77 points between them—Eric Henry, Johan Boakes, Chris Phillips, and Brian Baker—to help lead Arkansas to another conference triple crown at the site where it had all first happened so miraculously nine years earlier.[22]

"It started here in 1982 when we won our first outdoor title and fittingly it ended here," John told media after the meet. "This stadium has been good to us over the years. I've been around a lot of great teams, but this one has no equal. We got super performance after super performance, and this is the place to do it. The kids were just awesome. I keep using that word but it fits."[23]

As the season came to a close, McDonnell learned that one of his recruits from the past fall would not be returning to Fayetteville the next fall. Irishman Nigel Brunton was feeling pressure to perform at the same level of Niall Bruton, but natural selection was never going to allow that to happen.

"Nigel felt when he wasn't beating Niall, that he wasn't running well," said John. "I kept telling him, 'You're doing fine. Just get adjusted, we'll give you a program for the summer, and you will come back stronger than ever.' Well, two weeks before the conference meet, he comes in and says, 'I'm not coming back.' He was getting pressure from home and was a nervous guy, so I hated to see him go back. So he ran 3:51 [1,500 meter] and placed at the conference meet and said to me, 'I'd like to come back.' And I said, 'Nigel, I already gave your scholarship away.' He had been dead set on not coming back. So I said maybe I can give you something after a year or after a semester, but he went home and ran 3:43 in Ireland."

At the 1991 NCAA Outdoor Championships, held at Hayward Field in Eugene, Oregon, the University of Tennessee won the national championship while Arkansas did not factor into contention.[24]

On the drive back to Fayetteville from Tulsa International Airport near the end of the season, freshman Graham Hood sat next to John McDonnell in the passenger seat as some of the distance runners in the back of the van began openly discussing the projected lineup for the cross-country team that upcoming fall. Ten minutes of conversation passed without Hood's name being brought up even once.

"All of a sudden Graham said, 'I didn't hear my name being mentioned,'" remembered John. "They dismissed him and said, 'Oh, you're just a half-miler.' So he said, 'Who wants to bet? Not only am I going to be on this team, but I am going to be in the top ten nationally.'"

After some guffaws, the athletes made a gentleman's bet that wouldn't be settled until the NCAA Cross Country Championships five months later.

"I was motivated that entire summer just to make that team," said Hood. "There was a lot of that at Arkansas. Guys who were All-Americans on the track, who wouldn't have to worry about that stuff if they were on any other team, were motivated just to make the team. It didn't happen anywhere else."

Hood returned to Canada to win the Canadian National Championships in the 1,500 meter over Olympian Doug Consiglio before capturing the gold medal at the Pan American Junior Championships in Jamaica. Once that was over, he began preparing for the cross-country season like never before.

"You tell Graham Hood he can't do anything," said administrative assistant Doug Clark, "and he'll want to do it five times as bad just because you told him he couldn't."

Those who doubted Graham Hood would soon learn to never do so again.

10

The Triple Crown of Triple Crowns (1991–1994)

"You knew the way he looked at you what he expected. He expected the best out of you and had a way of explaining things to you that was down to earth. He made you want to win for him. He could say 'Twenty points,' and I'd say 'Got it, Coach.' I just wanted to do it for him."

—Ten-time NCAA Champion Erick Walder

Doug Brown can certainly be forgiven for wishing that neither John McDonnell nor the Arkansas Razorbacks had ever stepped foot in the Southeastern Conference. Entering his seventh season as the head track and field/cross country coach of the University of Tennessee Volunteers, Brown was king of the roost. He had followed up a successful running career that saw him qualify for two Olympics in the steeplechase and lead Tennessee to two NCAA championships before returning to Knoxville in 1985 as the head coach following Stan Huntsman's departure for Texas.

Though Brown had begun accumulating accolades from the start, 1990 had been especially kind to him and the Volunteers. Tennessee followed up its SEC cross-country championship with two more conference titles during the indoor and outdoor seasons to capture the SEC triple crown, a feat topped only by its thrilling victory over Washington State to win the 1991 NCAA Outdoor Track Championships. That the national championship was made possible through across the board contributions in the javelin, high jump, decathlon, pole vault, 800 meter, as well as the distance running heroics of Todd Williams. all of which promised a bright future for the program and its young coach. Little did Doug Brown or anyone know it would be the last time he ever coached a team to a conference or national championship.

"We had a great team the next year and nearly scored as many points as we had the year we won it, but Arkansas was that good," remembered Brown. "John took a lot of titles away from us when he came into the conference."

Thirteen to be exact—which was the number of times Brown coached teams to second place in the SEC before the decade was over. In retrospect, it should have seemed obvious enough that Arkansas would continue to be as dominant in the Southeastern Conference as it had been in the Southwest Conference. Yet, not everyone felt that the thirteen-time NCAA champions and thirty-eight time SWC champion Razorbacks belonged after coming from what one SEC coach mockingly referred to as a "Mickey Mouse" conference.

By November 4, 1991, on a warm day in Athens, Georgia, it was the Razorbacks who must have felt like they were the ones on a trip to Disneyland. With Frank Broyles and University of Arkansas president Dr. Alan Sugg on hand to watch the first Southeastern Conference Championships in school history, the dignitaries watched in awe as not one, not two . . . but six Arkansas Razorbacks were the first to appear over the final hill of the University of Georgia golf course leading into the finish chute.

Arkansas scored a perfect fifteen points led by Brian Baker, with Graham Hood, Niall Bruton, Eric Henry, Frank Hanley, and David Welsh occupying the next five spots.

"What a performance!" Broyles gushed to the media afterwards. "This is a great day in the history of Razorback athletics."[1]

The athletic director was certainly in a better mood following the cross country championship than he had been eight weeks earlier when he canned football coach Jack Crowe one game into the season following an embarrassing loss to The Citadel. If the football team was destined to stumble in the new conference, at least the Razorback harriers could be counted upon to dominate as they always had.

Even McDonnell was caught by surprise at the totality of the victory in a conference where some had arrogantly claimed Arkansas did not belong—a preposterous claim, given the strength of the Southwest Conference they had just dominated and Arkansas's record of national championships.

"This was just outstanding," John told the media. "We knew we had a chance to win, but never in our wildest dreams did we think we could turn in a perfect score. What a way to win our first SEC championship."[2]

Having outscored second-place Tennessee by a staggering seventy-three points, 15–88, Arkansas set the tone early. If other coaches in the conference had mistakenly discounted the newcomers, Doug Brown was not one of them.

"It was true the SEC was strong, but Arkansas was dominant regardless of what conference they were in, and I knew that," said Brown. "Those coaches hadn't paid attention as I had because I was trying to win it, and when you are trying to win it you are paying attention to the other guys trying to win it, which Arkansas was doing year in and year out."

With just about everyone returning from the previous year's national championship team other than Johan Boakes, who had graduated, McDonnell had an embarrassment of riches that cross-country season. Combined with the additions of David Gurry, an 8:56 high-school two-miler from Seattle, as well as Alex Dressell, an 8:14 3,000-meter transfer from the University of Texas, and John Schiefer, a 4:05 mile transfer from the University of Utah, it was hard to see anyone matching the Razorbacks depth of talent from top to bottom.

When *The Harrier* magazine had tabbed Arkansas as its preseason number-one ranked team in August, McDonnell embraced the pressure rather than shying away from it. It was becoming old hat.

"Oh, it's terrible," McDonnell joked with the media. "No really, it's an honor. It puts a little pressure on us but also just reinforces what I've been telling the team. We can win the national championship. Now the rest of the coaches across the nation are telling us so. We will try to be as low-key as possible and continue as we always have."[3]

Being low-key during the cross-country season would be difficult after Arkansas showed up to Missouri Southern in Joplin on September 9, 1991 and placed the first thirteen runners in a field of 150—led by Brian Baker in 23:41 and All-American Eric Henry bringing up the rear in 24:30 for 8,000 meters.

The real surprise of the year was Graham Hood—to everyone but himself. After a great summer of training, Hood arrived in Fayetteville determined to win his bet and prove his doubters wrong. After opening the season with a personal-best time, the Canadian gained momentum as the season progressed.

"I planned on making the team in cross country that fall," said Hood. "I don't think Coach McDonnell did because I didn't make the travel squad going to Stanford, and there definitely wouldn't have been any guys going to bat for me to travel to Stanford based on what I had done the fall before."

After a strong meet at Oklahoma State, Hood continued his astonishing rise by finishing sixth overall at the Chile Pepper Invitational on October 19.

"I still remember the look on Coach McDonnell's face when I went by the 5k mark," laughed Hood. "He was pretty shocked. After the race, he was like 'Yeah, kid, you're on your way on this team.'"

Amazingly enough, in a year where they went largely unchallenged at the SEC and NCAA meets, the Hogs greatest challenge of the season came on that same hot October afternoon in Fayetteville against defending NAIA national champions from Lubbock Christian. The pace was even hotter—the leaders hit 4:35 through the first mile and 9:22 through the second mile of the 10k race.

James Bungei of Lubbock Christian broke the course record in 29:10, less than two seconds ahead of Brian Baker, who ran toe-to-toe with the African throughout the entire race. Fourteen seconds behind the pair was Arkansas alumni Paul Donovan, who had recovered from three years of injuries and was primed to make another Olympic run the following summer.

For Graham Hood, it all came together at the 1991 NCAA Cross Country Championships, which was being held at El Conquistador Country Club in Tucson, Arizona. Not only did the redshirt freshman half-miler make the top seven of the Arkansas team, but he finished seventh overall in a race in which Arkansas easily outpaced Iowa State, 52–114, for its fifth NCAA cross-country championship and second in a row. It was an astonishing and eye-opening feat leading into an Olympic year.

"Some of the guys thought he'd never make the cross-country team, but Graham was tough, tough mentally," said John. "That was a big weapon because he had no fears of anything. It was a shocker to me too because he ran heavy on his feet, and I thought cross country would kill him but by gosh he got seventh."

Finishing third overall that day was Brian Baker, the local Arkansas talent who John had first seen run at the high-school Meet of Champions. After arriving in Fayetteville with a 4:11 mile to his name, Baker quickly developed into one of the best distance runners in the country.

"Brian was a smooth guy and had a great career here," recalled McDonnell. "He was one of those guys who would always shake his head and say he felt tired before a race, and I had to tell him to not worry about it. Well, in Arizona that year for the national championship, he came up to me beforehand and said he was feeling good. I said, 'Oh no, that's a bad omen.' But he ran great."

Even more impressive was Niall Bruton, who had finished second. Though John cared deeply about the cross-country season, he had always preached that the fall was only a preparation for the track. In some ways it was a means of coaxing otherwise reluctant middle-distance runners into taking cross-country seriously, while it also reflected the reality that only track and field was an Olympic sport.

Having two runners with 1:48 800-meter speed and the strength to finish top-ten at the NCAA Cross Country Championships presented tantalizing possibilities not only for the collegiate track season but also for the Olympics eight months down the road. It also presented the possibility for conflict as the competitive fire of each supremely talented athlete had to be controlled from raging within the locker room.

"We were definitely competitive and wanted to beat each other," remembered Hood. "There was a lot of that on the team, but my relationship with Niall was always good. We wanted to beat the heck out of each other on the track. Off the track we were room-mates and friends."

With the emergence of Mike Morin of Louisiana during a season when he would run 3:39.87 for 1,500 meters, the equation became even more complicated.

"Morin surprised Graham and Niall because they were way better in high school, and he was this skinny beanpole and real Louisiana Cajun kind of guy," said McDonnell. "He redshirted the first year, and all of a sudden some of the workouts he was starting to do were unbelievable."

Each athlete came with their own strengths and weaknesses, both mental and physical.

"Niall was more fragile mentally unless you told him he was the best thing since sliced bread," remembered Ryan Wilson, who joined the team two years later. "He had to be pumped up all of the time. They were different personalities. Graham would want to kick your ass, while Niall would make jokes. John knew how to work with those per-sonalities. They got along, but there was tension. I would be lying if I said there wasn't. They were both competitive and wanted to win."

McDonnell had to do a lot more than simply planning workouts for the talented trio. He had to manage expectations, egos, and personalities.

"It was not always easy, let me tell you, but you have to manage it," said John. "The thing I always said was once we are here working out, you can help each other. It was great because we had Niall from Ireland, Graham from Canada, and Mike [Morin] was from the United States. I said you can help push each other, and it helped that in 1992 they all had a chance to make the Olympics from different nations rather than compet-ing for the same spot on a national team. If their egos came into it, I'd remind them that everybody in the race was out to beat them, so there was no sense in feuding amongst each other about pace and other things. When we go to the track we are wearing the Arkansas uniform. You work together to beat the competition, and once you have done that, the best man will win."

While the athletes invariably battled for supremacy among themselves at various local and national meets over the next few years, there was never any confusion over who was in charge.

"John would not hesitate to put any of us in our place," said Hood. "I think a lot of times he let guys sort it out themselves, but if he needed to smooth things over, he would do that. He understood what needed to be done for the dynamic. He knew when to step in to light a fire under guys. He always knew what was going on interpersonally and training-wise and how to manage that."

Like moths attracted to a bright light, several athletes on the team aspired to train with the three Olympic hopefuls, but not everyone could handle the speed or the intensity.

"David Gurry was a good little runner, but the problem was he wanted to train with Graham and Niall, and he didn't have the foot speed," remembered John. "He was a good 5,000-meter guy but always wanted to train with the milers, and a couple of times I put him in there to teach him a lesson, but he never learned. He'd have to stop and say his hamstring was bothering him, but he just couldn't stay with them."

Over in the field, the same issues were faced with the jumpers. Coming off a summer when Mike Conley had won a bronze medal in the triple jump at the World Championships in Tokyo with Brian Wellman close behind in sixth, Arkansas signed two more phenomenal talents in the vertical jumps.

Ray Doakes was a senior at McCullough High School in The Woodlands, Texas, the same institution that had produced Eric Henry and Danny Green only a few years earlier. Although Doakes had jumped 7 feet in high school, it was his potential with a 6 feet, 9 inch frame and impressive vertical jump off nothing but natural talent that ultimately convinced McDonnell to offer him a scholarship.

"The magic of Coach McDonnell was that if you look at his athletes over the years, you'd hardly find a guy who was ranked number one coming out of high school," said Doakes. "He always gets the number fourteen or number fifteen. I was ranked fifteenth coming out of high school. I couldn't squat my own body weight, and I wasn't very fast, but I could jump. So he said, you can't teach somebody to be 6-9. That has to just be given to you."

Around the same time Doakes visited campus, McDonnell received a telephone call from former distance runner, Pat Vaughn, who was working in Denver at the time.

"He told me he saw a kid named Matt Hemmingway jump 7-5 and said get on this guy right away; he's really good," remembered McDonnell. "I called him that night and invited him. So the next day I said, 'Dick we have a 7-5 guy visiting,' and he said, 'When?' We got him just like that."

Although the two freshmen high jumpers would eventually become great training partners and friends, they were also competitive with one another.

"I regret the relationship I had with Matt in college," said Doakes. "We're much better friends now. I came in and was getting a big scholarship and tried to show that in practice, in sprints, in everything. I couldn't initially. Matt was a lot stronger and developed than me. I was really mouthy about things, being from Houston and from the streets. We're always talking about it; I'm better than you in this and in that. After the first year, it calmed down a little bit. Coach Booth let the tension feed off each other.

He'd always tell me what Matt did to see if I could do more and eventually we kept doing it and everyone got better."

The most important development for the jumps group was the metamorphosis of Erick Walder.

"He had gone through some nagging issues in his shins," said Booth. "He would say, 'I don't understand why we go into the weight room because when I get out my legs are so tired I cannot run and jump, I am sore, my shoulders hurt, my back hurts, and the next day something else hurts.' I kept saying, 'It's a process. You do it to the point where it doesn't hurt anymore. You get stronger.' That first year the combination of injuries and him not buying into everything meant he basically relived his senior year of high school. He was a good freshman but nothing like what he became."

After not scoring at the national championships during his freshman season, Walder arrived in Fayetteville his sophomore year ready to light the world on fire.

"I was a totally different person," said Walder. "I was ten pounds bigger and so much faster and physically in so much better shape than my freshman year. I had finally pieced together what Dick had told me. It was a gradual process of doing things in practice and integrating it into the meet."

Not only was Walder physically prepared but his mentality had also undergone a change.

"He came into me on the first day and said, 'Coach, I don't know why you put up with me,'" remembered Booth. "Essentially the light bulb had gone on and he said, 'I know I have to do what you say to go to the next level, and I won't question it anymore. I'm ready to go.' That was the beginning of everything for him because he was very gifted and much less aggravated by injuries and had great commitment and winning attitude. When you put his physical gifts with a great work ethic and strong belief level, he became unbeatable. Guys were intimidated by him."

Just as with the distance runners, there were few easy days with that group. A physically prepared and mentally focused Erick Walder hardly needed motivation, but on the rare occasions when he might have arrived at practice not feeling his best on a particular day, Brian Wellman's mere presence would not have let him get away with anything other than a supreme effort.

"Brian wasn't as fast, but his gift was he was very strong and his work ethic was off the charts," said Booth. "I cannot recall him ever having one a pity party. If he said he couldn't go, I was looking for a bone sticking out of his skin. He was never going to cheat himself because he would say, 'I'm already fighting an uphill battle against the Walders and Conleys of the world.' He made them dig down and do more because they knew the effort he was going to give. He was always challenging me to throw something else in—we did stadium drills with medicine balls, pulling sleds, all kinds of stuff, and when they were done, they were shot."

Considering the athleticism and dedication of every member of the group, a case could be made that it rivaled any jumps group in the world at the time.

"Whenever people started talking about him winning a world championship," Booth recalled, "Brian would say, 'Heck, I'm not even the best at my own practice.'"

After losing to Jerome Romain of Blinn Junior College on January 17, 1992, at the first home meet, Erick Walder went undefeated the rest of the indoor season in the triple jump. Wellman, who had won the NCAA triple jump the previous season, was never far behind. Even in the dead of winter, national qualifiers were growing like weeds in Fayetteville—from the 200 meter (Jimmy French) on up to the mile (Graham Hood) and the 3,000 meter (Niall Bruton and Frank Hanley). Even the 4 x 800 meter relay had put up the number-one time in the country, a spectacular 7:19.27, thanks to a 1:47.17 split from Hood. With potential All-Americans in just about every event, Arkansas would need them in the ultracompetitive Southeastern Conference.

"You used to be able to scrap points, but now you could no longer score in that conference with developmental athletes," said Doug Brown of Tennessee. "That ended and the cheap points went by the wayside. Now if you scored in the SEC you were a potential All-American."

While the move to the SEC had come with its advantages—it was a deeper conference with greater revenue streams—the downside was the geography. The Razorbacks could no longer hop on a bus (or a van as in the early days) and head down to the indoor conference championships at the Tarrant County Convention Center in Fort Worth as they had for decades. With the closest school at Mississippi, the Razorbacks flew to Gainesville, Florida, for the 1992 Southeastern Conference Indoor Championships.

Despite being ranked number-one in the country, Arkansas had its hands full facing five top-twenty ranked teams in the country, including the number-two ranked Florida Gators, whom the Razorbacks edged, 146–123.[4] It was enough to win the conference trophy but not enough for McDonnell to be voted SEC Coach of the Year by a peer group that had not yet fully accepted him.

"I remember [Florida coach John] Webb had something to say in the papers about how Arkansas won cross country and indoors but we'll see about outdoors," remembered John. "Then he said outdoors is what it's all about and that we came from a Mickey Mouse conference."

While some of the comments were meant in the spirit of jocularity, there were was also an air of sour grapes from those who incredibly enough believed—or perhaps wanted to believe despite all evidence to the contrary—that Arkansas would be exposed in the new league.

"I don't know why they didn't think we were good because we had won many national titles," said McDonnell. "We went in at the best possible time because we had a great team going in there."

At the 1992 NCAA Indoor Championships, Arkansas would prove that once again—overcoming disappointment and adversity on the first day when all could easily have been lost. Though Hood anchored the 4 x 800 meter relay to third, Clemson led the meet after Bruton finished a disappointing fifth in the 3,000 meter.

"Lord Almighty, I always thought Niall could run an awesome 3,000 meter," said John, "but he just didn't have the mental capacity to handle it."

Even more damaging was the 200 meter, where the previous year's national runner-up, Jimmy French, placed a disappointing sixth. With Erick Walder simultaneously languishing in seventh place early in the long jump, Arkansas's national-title aspirations were disappearing before their very eyes. It was at that point when the sophomore looked over to McDonnell, whose calm, collected intensity conveyed exactly what was needed.

"You knew the way he looked at you what he expected," said Walder. "He expected the best out of you and had a way of explaining things to you that was down to earth. He made you want to win for him. He could say "Twenty points," and I'd say, 'Got it coach.' I just wanted to do it for him."

Walder slapped his hands before his next attempt and uncorked a leap of 26 feet, 3½ inches for the win.

"I congratulated him afterwards and said, 'Boy that was a really good performance,'" remembered John. "He said to me, 'Coach, you always had a saying that when someone goes down, somebody stands up. I was the only one standing.' You don't think kids remember that stuff but they do."

Being the final event of the first day, it was exactly what was needed to keep the Razorbacks in the national-title hunt. Such heroics became the cornerstone of a program whose athletes always seemed to find a way to get the job done at championship meets. Less than twenty-four hours later, Walder won the triple jump with Brian Wellman and Gary Johnson joining him on the podium in an incredible moment.

"I know without these guys pushing me every day in practice, this wouldn't have happened," Walder told the media. "Every day in practice is a national meet for us."[5]

Walder was the first Razorback to pull off two national titles in the jumping events at the same meet since Mike Conley, whose continued presence in Fayetteville as a coach and professional athlete helped nurture the young sophomore through his growing pains.

"My main focus was to double," Walder said to the media after the meet. "Everybody thinks of me as a triple jumper, but I wanted to show I can long jump too . . . like Mike Conley. We practice a lot together, and that helps motivate me."[6]

Comebacks were becoming a common theme in Arkansas that week. Only days prior, Arkansas governor Bill Clinton swept the Super Tuesday primaries to cap one of the great political resurrection stories in modern American history. Though he still faced an uphill battle to unseat a popular wartime president, George H. W. Bush, there was growing hope that the man from Hope, Arkansas, could reach the White House the following November.

As with many things in the ebbs and flows of life, the string of positive news and good feelings did not carry on unabated. On the morning of March 29, 1992, it came to an abrupt and tragic end as sprinter Jimmy French was making his way north on Highway 71 coming back from Texarkana at 7:00 a.m. in the morning. French's Mercury Topaz drifted into the oncoming lane of a narrow two-lane highway while crossing a bridge, hit the guardrail and then flew sixty feet above the ground, then another thirty feet into the air after slamming into the pavement.[7]

French was unconscious for three days. His two-year-old and five-year-old children in the car were seriously injured. His three-year-old, Karen, was killed. It would be four weeks before French was discharged from the hospital, and two years before he ever competed again, which itself was a miracle. The entire team attended the funeral for his daughter with French still recovering from head injuries in the hospital. When he was discharged, he had a noticeable limp, and though he was eventually granted an additional season of eligibility by the NCAA to compete, French would never be the same athlete nor would the scars of that fateful morning ever go away.

"He came back his senior year, which was amazing," said McDonnell, "but he was never the same. All the agents had been calling him trying to get him out of school like parasites, but after the accident nobody called him. He lost it all. It was a tragedy because he was such a great kid and great athlete."

Although he had been blessed with abundant speed, not everything in life had come easy to Jimmy French, who raised a family with his wife while running and studying at Arkansas. Through it all, the Texarkana native always maintained a positive outlook. McDonnell remembers walking into his office in Barnhill Arena during the Christmas holidays just as French passed by the door outside.

"I was just in there to grab a piece of paper, and he walked by outside and saw me in there and knocked," remembered McDonnell. "I said, 'Jimmy, did you have a good Christmas?' And he said, 'Coach, all of my kids got great gifts, and I passed all of my classes! What more could you want?'"

Though French was no longer an Olympic hopeful, Arkansas still had several others with aspirations of competing in Barcelona that summer. First they had to accomplish something they hadn't done since 1985: win the NCAA Outdoor Track and Field Championships and triple crown.

Things got off to a roaring start in Hot Springs, Arkansas, on April 11, when the Razorbacks hosted Villanova, Iowa State, Southern Illinois, Alabama, Georgia, and Ole Miss, at the resort town. It was there that Graham Hood began his meteoric rise in the 1,500 meter. Though he finished eighth in the event behind teammates Bruton, Schiefer, as well as Jon Brown of Iowa State and Louie Quintana of Villanova, Hood's outdoor opener of 3:43.15 was a massive personal best and the beginning of great things to come.

"The Olympics were on my radar as something I wanted to do one day, but it wasn't a given," said Hood. "Until that season started to roll and I really started to get fit, I thought it would be in the 800 meter."

At Penn Relays, Hood ran the 800-meter leg on a distance medley relay anchored by Niall Bruton to victory. Bruton sat on Louie Quintana of Villanova and outkicked him, after the freshman Wildcat set a blistering 55-second first lap in front of the Philadelphia crowd.

"Louie is ready to become America's next great miler," said long-time Villanova women's coach Marty Stern, who had been named the men's coach that season. "To put an 18-year-old in a field like that, at a meet as great as this one, and have him perform so courageously is incredible. It just wasn't in the cards this year but our future looks very bright."[8]

What few at Villanova realized at the time was that the future was never going to arrive. The days when the Wildcats dominated the distance medley relay at Penn Relays were over. Villanova became the latest victim, perennially waiting for next year to avenge whatever bitter defeat Arkansas handed them.

"This is the meet we wait for all year," Villanova miler Louie Quintana told the *Philadelphia Daily News* after again being outkicked by Niall Bruton in the distance medley relay the following year. "It used to be Villanova. Now it always seems like we're running to give Arkansas the glory."[9]

It was a lesson Tennessee coach Doug Brown was also learning the hard way. Following the SEC indoor meet, Brown had made a lighthearted comment to McDonnell that the outdoor meet would be a different outcome once the javelin was included.

"So we won outdoors too, and John Scheifer jokingly followed him around saying 'Doug, where are all of your spear throwers?'" remembered McDonnell.

At the SEC Outdoor Championships in Starkville, Mississippi, Doug Brown's spear thrower had indeed shown up. Lars Sumberg won the javelin with a throw of 239 feet, 7 inches, while Tennessee's Tony Parilla blasted by Graham Hood on the final straight-away to win an epic 800 meter by a half-second in 1:45.37. With three events left, Arkansas was deadlocked with Tennessee and LSU before sticking the dagger in the same spot as always—the 5,000 meter. Arkansas ended the meet by scoring 29 points in the event.

The performance of the meet belonged to Erick Walder, whose long jump of 28-1 was only two inches short of Carl Lewis's collegiate record and four feet longer than what he had jumped in high school.

Arkansas edged their conference foes from Knoxville once again at the 1992 NCAA Outdoor Championships in Austin, Texas, by a margin of 60–46. At a meet where Tennessee performed almost as well as it had in victory the year before, the Razorbacks won its second NCAA outdoor championship and triple crown, but the first since 1985, with across-the-board contributions in a variety of events.[10] As enjoyable as it was for the Razorbacks to "Call the Hogs" on the same track in Austin, Texas where they had celebrated their first NCAA Triple Crown seven years earlier, the season was just starting to get interesting.

Mike Morin's emergence in the 1,500 meter qualified him for the U.S. Olympic Trials, where he ultimately placed sixth. In the 800 meter, Graham Hood already had the Olympic qualifying time in the 800 meter of 1:45.99 from the SEC championship where McDonnell also clocked him at 46.9 on the 4 x 400 meter relay.

While it appeared that Hood was set for a strong Olympic appearance in the 800 meter, the plan began to change. He won an invitational up in Indiana in late June to meet the Canadian Olympic 'B' standard for qualifying in the 1,500 meter. Then after winning the Canadian Olympic Trials in the event, Hood suddenly had the option of competing at the Olympics in either event.

"The 1,500 meter was at the end of the Games, and you had to run the 800 meter first, so Coach Mac and I thought my best chance to do something special was the 1,500 meter," remembered Hood.

Only a week after the Trials, Hood headed to Europe and ran 3:35.27 over 1,500 meters, a full ten seconds faster than his personal best at the start of the season and a new Canadian outdoor record. As remarkable as his rise in the event was, it was only about to become even more remarkable.

"The funny thing was I'm cooling down after the race with Reuben Reina and Paul Donovan, and all they are talking about is where I rank on the Arkansas 1,500-meter list and how it's a school record," recalled Hood, "and I'm thinking, 'Hey, guys, it's also a Canadian record.'"

At the Olympics, Hood made it through the first round in 3:44.44 before outkicking Marcus O'Sullivan of Ireland in 3:36.12 to grab the last spot in the final. It was as mete-oric a rise as anyone could have possibly imagined. After each round, Hood called McDonnell, who did not make the trip to Barcelona, to update him and get feedback for what to expect next.

"It was amazing that a college sophomore made the Olympic final," said McDonnell. "He came in here as an 800-meter guy, and we talked about moving up, but it happened quicker than I thought. Once we did the 1,500 meter, he liked it because his kick was really dynamite. He was a Steve Ovett–type of runner who could take it from 300 meters out and really hurt you."

In the Olympic 1,500-meter final won by Fermin Cacho Ruiz of Spain, Hood placed ninth, which was only a spot behind Jim Spivey of the United States. It was the culmination of a remarkable season for Hood and promised a long and bright future in the sport.

In the 5,000 meter, Arkansas had three alumni qualified in the event, including Frank O'Mara of Ireland, who was geared up for one final run at an Olympic medal. Just as he had in 1987, O'Mara won the 3,000 meter at the 1991 World Indoor Championships in Seville, Spain, only two years after going toe-to-toe with Olympic champion Said Aouita of Morocco at the 1989 World Indoors in Budapest, Hungary.

"He was right there with [Aouita], and I thought Frank was going to win it before he faded to fifth," said McDonnell. "He had come such a long way because he didn't do anything in college until his fifth year. He was real weak when he got here and took a long time to develop."

O'Mara was not weak anymore, mentally or physically, and now had the experience to legitimately challenge in Barcelona. Drawing a tough heat that featured three of the top six finishers, O'Mara ran 13:38.79 and was the fastest athlete to miss the final. Only a second behind him was Reuben Reina running for the United States. In another heat, Paul Donovan of Ireland placed tenth to cap off a remarkable comeback from three missed seasons following surgery on a ruptured patella tendon.

Though he left the sport soon thereafter and returned to Ireland, Donovan maintained a lifelong friendship with McDonnell.

"He was always a father figure for us," said Donovan. "It was the genuine interest he had in both the sport and us as individuals. Beyond the track he had a genuine interest in people for who they were. He gave my wife away at our wedding when we got married, and it seemed right for him to fill that role because he was like a father away from home. I don't think most coaches have those relationships, but it seemed natural for him because that's the man he was. I'm not the only one who has that relationship with him."

Another Arkansas legend also saw his career begin to wind down after 1992. Only a year after reconciling with McDonnell and returning to train under him in Fayetteville, Joe Falcon was beginning to consider retirement from the sport.

"He had run really well that first year out of college and then started to slide," said McDonnell. "So he came back and we sat down and talked and straightened out a lot of things. He started working out and ran his first race in 28:20 (10,000 meter) and then he ran 13:20 (5,000 meter) so it was looking good."

Despite performing as well as he had in years, Falcon's shoe contract was later voided when he was photographed wearing another shoe company's clothing after a meet.

"That was the straw that broke the camel's back for him," remembered John. "He hadn't run well for a while and was on a big contract, so they took a picture of him and Reuben at some meet, and Joe had nothing on from that shoe company, and they canned him. He came in with that letter and was just devastated."

His edge was gone. While Falcon had been so mentally strong in college, he was suddenly struggling to race anywhere near what his workouts demonstrated and in some cases to finish races at all.

"We ran in a workout with O'Mara, and they did three intervals miles in under 4:04 with three minutes recovery," remembered John. "Then Joe went to a race the next week and ran 4:08 (for the mile). That was the end of him. He was a nice guy, and it was tragic to see him self-destruct. He would have done anything I asked him in training or racing. Alistair Cragg was a lot like him. What may have ended [Falcon's] career prematurely was he didn't know how to lose. He couldn't accept losing, and you have to learn how to lose just like you have to learn how to win."

Though he had good races left in him, Falcon left the sport a few years later having accomplished more than just about anybody before or since. He was a seven-time NCAA individual champion with eleven All-American certificates, nine NCAA team championships and the fastest mile in the world in 1990.

"It was bad timing because his two big years were in between the Olympics," said Doug Clark, who was an administrative assistant with the program. "It's easy to say he should have done this or done that, but look what he did do. He was amazing. I think a lot of athletes get to a point where they run to meet the expectations of other people, and I think Joe got to that point. Instead of clicking his fingers, and just saying he was going to stop, it was a long, drawn out process."

When he did finally announce he was retiring from the sport, Falcon never looked back.

"I accomplished every goal except making the Olympics," said Falcon. "I had a family and kids, and I didn't want to be the guy who kept running and didn't end up on top, so I sat down with Coach and told him I wanted to retire and go into law enforcement. He said absolutely let's not leave with any regret. We accomplished what we wanted other than making the Olympic team."

In the long jump, Edrick Floreal competed for Canada while Brian Wellman made the triple-jump final for the Bahamas. Missing the Games was Erick Walder, who pulled his hamstring on the first jump of the U.S. Olympic Trials and was out for the remainder of the season, in what would be the first of many Olympic Trials heartaches for the Alabaman.

Mike Conley could certainly relate to all of the possible things that could go wrong at the Olympic Trials after his experience four years earlier. Though Conley had already won a silver medal in the triple jump at the 1984 Olympics, his window of opportunity to win the gold medal was rapidly closing. Now older and wiser, he was doubly determined to not let anything stand in his way.

"Heading into Barcelona when people had anything to say to me I was all ears," said Conley.

Early in the preliminaries of the triple jump, Conley broke the world and Olympic record with a leap of 57 feet, 8 inches before Charles Simpkins of the United States nearly passed him in the finals. Still leading going into his final jump, Conley put the competition completely out of reach with a mind-boggling wind-aided leap of 59-7. The Olympic gold medal was coming back to Arkansas.

"It was a great reaction in Fayetteville," said Conley. "They had an event for me in the square and gave me the keys to the city and had a Mike Conley Day. The thing I remember most about it and to this day people come up to me and remember when we took the medal and passed it around to the crowd. I had a lot of police give me a hard time about how they were trying to follow the medal around, and it seemed like that was the most memorable thing about it. People ask if I was scared that someone might run off with the medal, and I'm like, 'No, I'm an Olympic athlete. I can catch anyone.'"

During a season that was remarkable for what Arkansas athletes accomplished at both the collegiate and international level, Canadian distance runner Jason Bunston began to longingly wish he had joined his high-school training partner from Canada, Graham Hood, two years earlier when he first had the opportunity. Having run everything from the 1,500 meter (3:44) all the way up to the 5,000 meter (14:07) in high school, Bunston opted to remain with his high-school coach, Jeff Gaynor, who had guided his and Hood's training in high school, and focus solely on qualifying for Canada at the 1992 Olympics.

With Hood at Arkansas, Bunston soon began to realize how hard it was to train at such a consistently high level on his own. The two boys had run hills, stairs, and workouts together an intensity that Bunston found increasingly difficult to match apart. After missing significant time with a lower spinal injury suffered in the fall of 1991, Bunston began to realize that he was not only missing out on the next Olympics but also a potential opportunity to attend Arkansas (or any university) on an athletic scholarship.

"I think a big part of the reason he came down was he saw my success," said Hood. "We had the same coach in high school, and that coach discouraged either of us from going down. Jason saw the breakthrough I had, and I think a big part of his decision was based on that."

The other part was the success of just about everyone else in the program as well.

"I went on a visit and saw all of these guys running fast," remembered Bunston. "I knew right then I could jump in and start competing with them."

On the final hour of his visit, Bunston had a long talk with McDonnell in his pickup truck.

"It was very low pressure," said Bunston. "He asked me if I liked what I saw and then said, 'We don't need you, but we'd love to have you.' That was perfect for me."

Though he made his mind up to attend Arkansas in the fall of 1992 on that recruiting visit, Bunston had voices other than just his high-school coach counseling him of the perils of the American collegiate athletics system in general and the Arkansas program in particular. His teammate on the Canadian team at the 1991 Pan-American Games in Havana, Cuba, was none other than John Castellano.

"I took his opinion about the school with a grain of salt," said Bunston.

Though it took Bunston some time to adjust, he was suddenly a very potent ingredient within the mix of a cross-country team seeking its third consecutive NCAA cross-country championship.

"My biggest adjustment was running seven days a week instead of six," remembered Bunston. "The volume wasn't an issue. I loved being around competitive runners and was asked to hold back, if anything, because in long runs the group was internally conscious with Falcon back in the group of people pushing the pace. So to run faster would be setting yourself apart from the group."

Not that there weren't plenty of days when the Razorbacks ran hard. That was often what ended up happening whether John unleashed them for eight miles in the trails or dropped them off eighteen miles down the road only to be picked up in his pickup truck four miles from campus—if they hit their pace.

"Some guys still did the entire eighteen, but most of us did fourteen," said Green. "He had a big farm truck, and he would pick us up and give us our times at twelve and fourteen miles. He may have told you twelve, but if you weren't there in time he would just leave you. So you were coming around the bridge at twelve miles just praying to see his truck still there because if it wasn't, you would go to fourteen miles, and if it wasn't at fourteen, you were doing eighteen back to the school because he wasn't coming back. It was good motivation to stay with the pack."

In the grind of a long cross-country season on a team as talented and competitive as that one, everyone was looking for an edge. For Dan Munz, the junior from St. Louis who had run 29:50 for 10,000 meters on the track, that meant training harder and more intensely during the summer than his teammates. At the Jayhawk Cross Country Invitational on September 12, 1992 at Rim Rock Farms, Munz set an 8k course record of 24:04 ahead of Baker, Morin, Hanley, and everybody else.

"A lot of people like Jim Ryun had run that course, and Munz came in and set the course record on the first flipping meet of the year," remembered McDonnell. "He had a good career here and was always in fantastic shape in the summer, but after that meet I said to myself, 'This sucker didn't do what I told him.' I used to say to do fifty miles (per week) in the summer and just be ready to workout. That very same year he didn't make our top seven at NCAAs."

Graham Hood likewise came into the fall riding on the momentum of his Olympic finals finish before his cross-country season ended scarcely before it began. After finishing ninth at the Chile Pepper Festival on October 15, Hood woke up the next morning with a throbbing pain in his knee.

"I came back and tried to get into things too quick," said Hood. "After the home meet my IT band was shot, and I didn't run another step for four months. A lot of that was probably on me wanting to get back quick when maybe the right thing to do was hold back. There was no shortage of good cross-country runners around so the team didn't exactly need me."

On a national-championship team that returned virtually everyone and added Jason Bunston, that was the case. In his first collegiate cross-country race, Bunston was fifth at the SEC Cross Country Championships on a wet, slick day at the Kentucky Horse Park as Arkansas beat Tennessee, 23–96.

"Bunston had a hell of a race," beamed McDonnell to the media afterwards. "Our SEC individual champion [Brian Baker] and Graham Hood are both at home because they are hurt. So I was pleased to say the least the way it turned out. Our kids did an outstanding job in a terrific field."[11]

At the 1992 NCAA Cross Country Championships in Bloomington, Indiana two weeks later, the weather was worse in the days leading into the meet and the travel experience more of a nightmare than anything the team had ever experienced before. Though

John drove with Ellen up to Indiana, as he often did following his own harrowing flight experience, his athletes finally had a firsthand understanding of the terror of being in a distressed airplane at thirty thousand feet.

"There was a tornado and horrible weather in Indiana," remembered John. "Everywhere flights were cancelled. Then when they tried to land the plane in Chicago, the landing gear wouldn't release, so they had to prepare for a crash landing after they circled for an hour. They were trying to get the landing gear to drop down. Finally a guy opened up a trap door and the landing gear released."

The shock of the experience really shook the team up.

"Niall said several rosaries," recalled John. "He said, 'I knew I was going to die.' He was so scared."

When the team finally regrouped to preview the course, Mother Nature had other ideas.

"The tornado was still on us, and the siren was on," said McDonnell. "So all of a sudden there was an announcement, 'Everyone off the course.' You're thinking what else is going to go wrong?"

Once the meet finally got underway, Arkansas had a nearly flawless performance. The Razorbacks ran aggressively from the gun. They were briefly challenged by Wisconsin midway through the race before surging over the final kilometers to win with a school-record forty-six points.[12]

"This is the proudest I've ever been of a group of guys after what happened with our plane almost crashing and not having two of our top runners in Baker and Hood," McDonnell told the media afterwards. "Very few teams in any sport could have left two of their best athletes at home and still won a national championship. We ran into trouble midway through the race, but our guys really sucked it up and showed a lot of character at the end."[13]

Another record was set on that Monday afternoon. Only eight years and eight months after coaching the University of Arkansas to its first NCAA indoor championship in Syracuse, the win marked Arkansas's seventeenth national championship in the sport, tying McDonnell with Ted Banks for the most championships ever won by a single coach in any sport at the Division I level.

"I owe it all to the athletes I have been lucky enough to coach," John told the media. "I've just been a watchdog for them. This team will be remembered for what they've achieved for a long time."[14]

A few weeks later at the United States Track and Field convention in Louisville, Kentucky, McDonnell bumped into Vin Lananna, who had been recently hired to revive a moribund track-and-field/cross country program at Stanford. After taking the Ivy League school Dartmouth to NCAA cross-country runner-up finishes in 1986 and 1987 from the sometimes dreary trenches of cold New Hampshire, it was only natural to wonder what Lananna was capable of once he had the reins in sunny Palo Alto of a program that had so badly underperformed for so long.

"We were checking in when John came up to me and said, 'Congratulations on getting the job,'" remembered Lananna. "I said it's going to be a lot of work because we were really terrible. John said, 'You are going to be a pain in my neck.'"

Apart from John McDonnell, there seemed to be no shortage of examples of Arkansas alumni finding fame and fortune all over the country. Only a few days after Bill Clinton's inauguration as the forty-second president of the United States and the first ever Arkansan to hold presidential office, former Razorback football player Jerry Jones and Razorback assistant coach Jimmy Johnson led the Dallas Cowboys to their first Super Bowl title as owner and coach respectively.

"I talked with [Jones] a few times," said John. "He was a very down to earth guy and invited me to come down to a [Cowboys] game anytime."

During the summers, former Razorback baseball star Kevin McReynolds would leave tickets for McDonnell to take his family to see the Kansas City Royals just a few hours up the road, where young Sean McDonnell was far from shy about running around Kaufmann Stadium trying to shag fly balls.

Even at the home meet on January 22, 1993, there were nearly as many alumni competing as student athletes. Razorback Olympians Paul Donovan, Reuben Reina, and Doug Consiglio all competed in a mile won by Joe Falcon in 3:57.54, while two-time world champion Frank O'Mara finished in 8:06.68 ahead of six current Razorbacks, demonstrating that the hierarchy hadn't changed over time.

It was also at that home meet—and a few weeks later at Iowa State—when Arkansas ran into Blinn College, which was coached by Steve Silvey. Having driven twenty-two hours to Ames from Brenham, Texas, the junior-college national championship team was loaded with talent, including Jerome Romain in the triple jump and Savieri Ngidhi in the 800 meter. Blinn more than held their own against the Division I national champions, even beating a 4 x 800 meter relay anchored by Niall Bruton.

It would be one of the few setbacks in an otherwise magical season. Even with Hood and Baker out of action, Arkansas nearly doubled second-place Tennessee 156–81 at the SEC Indoor Championships on the backs of several sterling performances, including a startling win by junior-college transfer Calvin Davis, who captured the 400 meter in 47.07 on the tight indoor track at LSU in Baton Rouge, Louisiana.[15]

"Oh, he was a good one," remembered McDonnell. "We got Calvin from a junior college in Alabama, and he ended up winning three NCAA titles for us."

Davis finished as a runner-up in the 400 meter at the 1993 NCAA Indoor Championships two weeks later as the Razorbacks easily outpaced second place Clemson, 66–30, on the backs of another two individual national titles by Erick Walder in the long jump and triple jump. In the mile, Niall Bruton outkicked Andy Keith of Providence to win in 4:00.05—with teammate Mike Morin third in 4:00.71.

"I'm so happy because this is my first NCAA title," Bruton told the media. "I wanted this so bad. I thought Andy was gone. I tried to get him in the backstretch, but I couldn't. I was hurting really bad and Andy was strong. I am a good kicker, and I guess the will to win is what got me past him at the tape."[16]

The indoor national championship was impressive not only for how it was accomplished—with wins in the jumps and distance, as well as points in the sprint events, but for what it represented in the grander scheme of things. As the tenth consecutive NCAA championship in indoor track and field, the win broke the all-time record for consecutive NCAA titles in any sport in the history of Division I athletics. No less of a luminary than United States president Bill Clinton noticed and personally invited the Razorbacks to the White House for a special ceremony to celebrate the occasion.

"I know this coach and his values and the way things are done," President Clinton told the media of John McDonnell. "He is a friend who this year became the most successful coach in the history of intercollegiate athletics. You don't have that kind of success that many times over that many years without caring for the well-being of your athletes."[17]

After the team presented the president of the United States with a Razorback warm-up suit, McDonnell took the microphone.

"I've always admired this man," John told the media. "I think he and our track team have a lot in common. When I came to the University of Arkansas we had scored one point at the conference meet the year before. I think [Clinton] is like a walk-on on our track team who became an Olympic champion, which is what Mike Conley did. [Clinton] was a walk-on in politics, starting from the ground up, paid his own way and he made it to the top, the number one man in America."[18]

Though Clinton would experience a challenging first two years in office before finding his political footing two years later, he was able to lighten the mood significantly that afternoon with several jokes. The president began by making fun of the negative Republican advertisements run against him months earlier in a bitter presidential election campaign that pegged him as a failed governor from a failed state.

"Just think of it, John," the President deadpanned. "If you would have come here last year they might have called you a failed coach from a small, southern state."[19]

Before the Razorbacks left the White House, Clinton and several Arkansas senators and congressman on hand for the ceremony joined the team in "Calling the Hogs."

With each passing year, it was becoming hard to ignore the accomplishments of such prominent Arkansans who had risen to the pinnacle of their professions, along with the companies such as Tyson Foods and Walmart that had gained national and global prominence. It was telling of the stratosphere McDonnell had raised his own program that the extraordinary was now becoming ordinary.

Arkansas easily won the outdoor Southeastern Conference and NCAA outdoor titles against an LSU team that finished runner-up at both. Both were complete team victories. Not only had Erick Walder come through on his final long jump to beat Florida's Deon Bentley at the SECs before winning the NCAAs two weeks later, but Jimmy French had made a miraculous return to help the 4 x 100 meter relay finish seventh in the NCAA finals.[20]

The success continued all the way up to the 5,000 meter and 10,000 meter. After running 13:58.35 along with David Welsh at a Last Chance Meet paced by none other than Frank O'Mara, Danny Green captured his only All-American certificate in the 5,000 meter, while teammates David Welsh and Frank Hanley soldiered for twenty-three points between them in the 5,000 meter and 10,000 meter. The latter was a staggering double in the New Orleans heat, made possible by the toughness of both athletes and the ingenuity of Arkansas trainer Scott Unruh, who did everything to help prepare Razorback athletes for the brutal heat.

"Scott was an outstanding trainer, and he had our guys ready," said McDonnell. "That's when I found out about Pedialyte. Everyone was wondering how our guys handled the heat so well. Guys were passing out in the 5,000 meter, but we had Hanley and Welsh run heats of the 5,000 meter, finals of the 10,000 meter and then finals of the

5,000 meter. They were taking Pedialyte two days beforehand, and what it did was retained water in your body, so you didn't pee it out, and it kept electrolytes in your body whereas if you just drink water you flush out your body. We were properly hydrated and did great because of it."

Arkansas had won its second straight NCAA Triple Crown—a testament to the talent, and physical and mental fortitude of the Razorback athletes—as well as the guidance from a coach becoming almost flawlessly adept at navigating the long cross-country, indoor, and outdoor seasons while keeping his athletes healthy and motivated.

"I always had a philosophy that the only important meets were conference and nationals, so if you feel your training isn't where you want, talk to me and we will get ready for the big dance," said John. "I think the kids respected that. If a kid tells me they are tired and I put off their workout to the next day, people would sometimes ask me what I would do if that person was pretending and pulling the same stunt. I'd say I have the wrong guy, and they are going to weed themselves out pretty quickly and he won't be around long. So you have to trust guys because they aren't kids, they are men. They know right from wrong, and if you treat them decent, they will respect that. I always gave them a say, but I had a line in the sand, and if they crossed it, I let them know."

When several athletes arrived back in Fayetteville three days late from spring break, McDonnell suspended all of them for Texas Relays.

"They said, 'But coach, we've won the sprint medley three years in a row,'" remembered John. "I said, 'Well, we aren't going to win a fourth.' Then they looked at me and said, 'You mean you're going to give it up?' I said, 'You've already given it up, not me.' That resonated for years because we left them home and left some jumpers home, and boy oh boy, we never had problems with guys getting back on time again. Sometimes you have to make tough decisions with guys to send the right vibes to the team."

In the days before extensive academic support within the athletics department, McDonnell often took it upon himself to ensure athletes went to class.

"I stressed academics first, then track," said John. "There were no rules back then on missing classes, but I was dealing with it to make sure they passed. It builds character because it lets them know that it won't be tolerated and that they are here to get a degree. I have guys come up to me years later saying I'm glad you pushed the education and getting a degree because the only thing I thought was important was track. I'd contact the parents sometimes if I thought it would do any good. After a while it became rare because the O'Shaughnessys, O'Maras, Floreals, and Hemmingways would tell guys that stuff isn't tolerated. That's what made our team close. There was accountability."

For someone whose team was among the most disciplined in the country, it was no surprise that the McDonnell household was an equally tightly run operation. Though Ellen looked after the children, especially on the extended weekends John found himself out of town, he was never far from the picture.

"Mom was at home with us all of the time and was always there for us," remembered Heather McDonnell. "She brought us up and took us everywhere. Dad was always there during the week. I never felt an absence from him ever. He was only away for extended weekends for track, but when he was at home, he was there for us. I just knew what he expected of me and knew he had confidence in me. He was very down to earth and logical about things."

Whenever Heather needed a helping hand her father was there to offer it, including on a particularly rainy and treacherous occasion visiting her cousins in Ireland years earlier as a six-year-old.

"I was prancing around the farm in my bright red Wellington rubber boots when we happened to come across a very muddy cattle crossing," said Heather. "We were confident all five of us would make it across, but I had my doubts, of course. The others all crossed it in one sweep each, and it was now my turn. Dad was not far behind walking with his walking stick observing cattle, and I turned around to spot him. I felt myself running across but realized I was sinking in the mud! I tried to lug my legs out, but instead my feet came out of the Wellies only to land full-fledged in the mud with my socks on. Dad quickly discovered his daughter's flailing arms and cries for help and quickly came to my rescue. He was able to pull me and his slowly sinking self out of the mud pile. I had never been so happy in my life to be out of there and safe in my dad's arms. If he wasn't there, I don't know what I would have done, but Dad was there just like he has always been throughout the years."

For Sean McDonnell, his father's presence was no less impactful throughout his childhood.

"Growing up, Dad and I had a lot of fun at the ranch riding horses, rounding up and working cattle, and learning to drive tractors and ATVs," remembered Sean. "I caught my first fish, and Dad brought it to the taxidermist and had it mounted. We used to go boating and water skiing with Mom at the ranch at Grand Lake [in Oklahoma]. Dad didn't like the water as much though because he had almost drowned as a child. He'd come to the boat sometimes but was happier working on the ranch. At night we would get together with Uncle Mike and his family and have a BBQ or go out on the town."

Though rarely in need of John's assistance to manage the affairs of the house, Ellen knew she could rely on John if needed.

"I was the disciplinarian," admitted Ellen, "but I could always threaten them with Dad. They were great kids so we never had any problems."

"My mother brought us to school and was always attending to us," said Sean McDonnell. "My father was the one who drove the stake into the ground. If it couldn't be handled by the time he got home, it must have been pretty bad. He was stern but never pushed me into anything. I ran track in junior high, but he never pushed it. He used to say he knew a great guy who could show me a few things if I wanted."

After attending St. Joseph's Catholic School in Fayetteville, Sean moved onto Woodland Junior High. It was there he became teammates on the junior-high track team with another aspiring young athlete named Wallace Spearmon Jr., the son of former Razorback All-American sprinter Wallace Spearmon.

"Sean used to beat me in races all of the time when we were little," remembered Spearmon Jr., who would become one of the fastest men in the world.

Though it was still a few years before Sean got heavily involved with dirt bike racing, it seemed that Heather was involved with everything at the elementary and junior-high level—dancing, gymnastics, flag football, soccer, cheerleading, cross country, equestrian events, and tennis. John and Ellen did not push Heather in one specific direction, but they did impart in high school the wisdom of choosing one activity to excel in.

"I was sad about giving up cheerleading, but I picked tennis and would go home at night and hit balls against the garage for an hour," said Heather. "I had a knack for it, and it just kind of happened. I was ranked fourth in the state in singles, and then we had a foreign-exchange student come to school from Mexico, and we won the state championship in doubles. Then I won the next year with a different partner."

Ellen took the children to most of the NCAA Indoor Championships at Indianapolis and elsewhere, but John would publicly admit in his retirement speech how many of Heather's tennis matches he missed over the years due to coaching. His daughter remembers him being there for the important ones.

"He didn't get to see a lot of it," said Heather, "but he came to the ones nearby, and he was always at the big ones."

When Heather ran cross country her junior year to get herself in shape for tennis, she suddenly found herself as the fifth runner on a team that won the state title. It was there at the Arkansas high-school state championship where Heather got a firsthand experience of her father's immense presence on a cross-country course.

"He was there at the state meet running beside me," said Heather. "I was hurting pretty bad and hated it, but he was shouting at me the whole way down. I collapsed afterwards. I didn't love running like my dad, but that was a good experience."

Whether it was in his own family or his extended family on the Arkansas track team, John had a way of bringing out the best in people.

"He was a real people person," said administrative assistant Doug Clark. "It was not a conscious effort; that's just the way he was. He could get people to run through a brick wall. He was an extremely hard worker and got people to buy into what he was doing and to work hard at it. He inspired loyalty and absolutely did not tolerate people who didn't work hard and try their best. There was no way around it. You had to give your best."

Though some athletes admittedly didn't come to Arkansas because they were intimidated by the training group or were leery of the intensity of training they might have to undergo, often based on exaggerated characterizations by opposing coaches, many others were attracted by the prospect of training with the best and aspiring to be one of them.

"Between John's personality and the strong brand he created at Arkansas, he was getting these blue-chip guys to come from all around America for very little," said Clark. "It was nuts how many good people he had there. It was just a matter of getting out there and beating the bushes. Some still tried to tag the team as a bunch of foreigners, but there were foreigners at other schools that didn't win. At one NCAA meet we figured out that if we had only scored the Americans or only the foreigners on our team, either group would have won nationals by themselves. People were willing to go there for free."

Amid an upheaval engulfing the Villanova program at the time, star miler Louie Quintana wanted out and contacted McDonnell.

"I remember he was very unhappy at Villanova, and I had a half scholarship left, but he had to have a full scholarship. So I said, 'Will you wait until January, and it will be a full?' He said, 'No, I better stay in school,' so he ended up transferring to Arizona State," remembered McDonnell. "The funny thing was six weeks later, school started and one of my kids, Dewayne Miner, comes in and says he's following his girlfriend to Southwest Baptist in Bolivar, and I'm like, 'You have to be kidding me?' This was my 8:02 [3,000 meter] stud. I had just turned down a sub-four-minute miler, so I called [Quintana] back but he had already signed."

Starting out as a 9:17 high school two-miler from Bolivar, Missouri, Miner's abbreviated career in Fayetteville had been an unqualified success in every way imaginable—including an All-American certificate and Penn Relays title in the 5,000 meter.

"He had met a girl," said John wryly, "and they wanted to transfer back home. We got on great too, and he was a nice kid. So he went there for a semester before she decided to transfer to Ole Miss, and he followed her there, and by gosh, didn't she leave there too and comes back to SMS [Southwest Missouri State] in Springfield. So he came back to Arkansas, but had stopped running by that time. He gave it all up but ended up marrying her and working for the Fellowship of Christian Athletes."

As disappointed as he was by Miner's departure and missing out on Quintana, McDonnell had no shortage of top-flight high-school talent joining the program that fall.

After running 4:12.5 for the mile, which was the fastest at the time in Oklahoma high-school history, and winning indoor nationals, Phil Price turned down a full scholarship offer from former Razorback Steve Baker at the University of Oklahoma, to run at Arkansas. Though Price had dreamed of running for the Sooners and had even staged a mock signing in the Catoosa newspaper after verbally committing to them, a phone call and home visit from John McDonnell changed his outlook on things.

"He started calling me, and I was kind of surprised, it was actually him," remembered Price. "When he first called, my mother said, 'Someone from Arkansas is calling,' so I answered, and when I found out it was him, I was just speechless. Basically he was like 'Hey kid, I've heard great things about you, and I'd love to have you come to Arkansas.' I was still dead set on going to Oklahoma, but then John came over and met with my family for an hour. That was important to me because here was a guy who was an icon of the sport and took a few hours of his time to drive over and speak with us. The next week when I said I'm coming [to Arkansas], he said 'Kid, I think you made a great choice.'"

Another American distance runner, Ryan Wilson of Westlake, California, who had won the California state cross-country meet and qualified for the Kinney National Championships, also signed for next to nothing despite offers from all over the country.

"Frank Gagliano [of Georgetown] said he could give me a half scholarship, and Marty Stern at Villanova said he had a full scholarship contingent on someone else not accepting," recalled Wilson. "Then John offered me books, which was really just a token. For me it came down to John's personality and his similar strength-based training philosophy as my high-school coach."

Coming from the same high school in California as Deena (Drossin) Kastor, who was running for the University of Arkansas at the start of a career that would eventually catapult her to the Olympic podium in the marathon, another factor that attracted Wilson to Arkansas was the warmer weather.

"He asked me if it ever snowed here, and I said, 'Very seldom,'" remembered John. "So the day he comes we had twelve inches, and he looked at me and said, 'I thought you told me it never snowed here.'"

Since Fayetteville had been so rarely exposed to winter elements of that magnitude and had no snow removal equipment to manage it, the town and the university were shut down during the visit.

"Luckily Deena had a 4x4 Jeep, and that was the only reason I got to see any of Fayetteville," said Wilson. "Me, Deena, and Doug Clark were slipping and sliding our way around the place. We made the best of it, and I got some sort of feeling for it. The guys worked out in the old indoor facility. Everyone was closed in, so I got to see everyone work out and the camaraderie with the team that maybe I wouldn't have had if they had been working outside."

Despite the unfortunate circumstances of his visit, Wilson shared the same strength-based training philosophy as McDonnell and saw the lofty expectations of the program as an opportunity rather than a detriment.

"I went out to Tucson to see them run cross country and was like, 'Wow, they really put a beating down," remembered Wilson. "I wanted to get into that environment, even if it meant I was redshirting my first year. I wanted the best people around me, and Arkansas was the best at the time."

A football player and sprint/hurdler early in his high-school career, the change to distance running was hardly the only conversion Wilson underwent before arriving in Fayetteville.

"His junior year he wore dreadlocks, and he told [women's coach] Lance [Harter] at a track meet in California that he wanted to come to Arkansas," remembered John. "Lance said, 'Not with that hairdo.' So [Ryan] said he would get rid of it, and he did get rid of it. I said, 'I bet he's a pretty good guy because he's sacrificing.' It's easy to come if someone is giving you a full scholarship and no strings attached, and after they get here, you tell them the rules. Well, I told them the rules before they came, and some of them I lost because of that, but I never missed them. I always said to recruits, 'if there is a surprise after you come here, it will be a pleasant one.' Ryan was a super nice guy with a great personality and a great team man."

Another runner prepared to do anything to crack the Arkansas lineup that same fall was Teddy Mitchell, who walked on after two years at the University of Tennessee. Having never broken 14:20 for 5,000 meters or finishing higher than 120 at the NCAA Cross Country Championships, Mitchell sought a change in scenery after an underwhelming start to his career in Knoxville.

"At Tennessee guys would run less than they were supposed to," recalled Mitchell, "but at Arkansas, everyone's respect for John meant they did the right things. John's word was as good as God's. His ideas were unchallenged, and people respected him. Doug Brown was a good guy, but the guys ragged on him because he only knew what he did as an athlete. John was a steeplechaser too but was a remarkable coach because he could adjust training to meet the needs of different people."

Not only did Mitchell benefit from the change in scenery but also had an added motivation. Though the Razorback distance runners had long been an eclectic group of personalities brought together from all over the country and the world, the addition of Mitchell created waves of its own.

"He didn't fit in to put it bluntly," said John. "I got along with him, but some of his teammates didn't. He came from a tough upbringing, and I always tried to help kids that came from bad situations, but his teammates didn't know or didn't care. He was a bit short of speed, and he'd come into the locker room and say to someone, 'If I had your leg speed I'd be kicking everyone's ass. What the hell are you doing?' That kid would say something back, and I'd have to tell Teddy to quiet down. It was almost good though because sometimes those kids needed to be told by someone other than me. Hanley and Welsh didn't like him because he showed them up sometimes. Nobody wants to be beaten by someone with no speed."

Whether some thought Mitchell's presence was a positive or negative depended on the person. What everyone agrees upon was that he definitely made an impact.

"Teddy was an interesting character, but the thing about him was that as often as he altered the team dynamic for the worse, he also altered it for the better," remembered Graham Hood. "He could be an engaging guy to be around and fun for guys to give stick to, and he'd give it right back. He contributed in his own way and ultimately was a positive influence and big personality in the locker room."

Though Mitchell had trained at volumes as high as 120 to 130 miles per week in Tennessee, McDonnell immediately cut back his mileage and incorporated more speed into his training.

"I cut it back to 85 or 90 and picked up the tempo," said John. "He'd be hanging on for dear life in some of the runs, but after doing it for a while he was feeling good about himself. Every once in a while he'd come in and ask to do twenty miles for a long run, and I'd say, 'Do you want to go back to Tennessee?' I wasn't cutting him any slack. I explained to him it was junk mileage. He was easy to coach because I improved his speed so much. He had been a plodder, but had more speed than he thought he had."

Respect from his teammates did not come immediately for Mitchell, who had a Razorback tattoo drawn on his arm even before arriving in Fayetteville.

"We asked him where he got the tattoo, and he said Tennessee," said Jason Bunston. "We laughed and told him you haven't even made the team yet."

After finishing as the second man on the team over 8,000 meters at the Oklahoma State Cowboy Jamboree on October 2, 1993, making the team didn't seem to be much of an issue. Commanding their respect, however, was going to be a gradual process.

"We showed up at the SEC meet that fall, and while the Arkansas kids were doing their strides, one of them came up to me and said, 'Coach, you can have Teddy Mitchell back,'" remembered Tennessee coach Doug Brown. "Usually kids are pretty nervous before the race, but this kid came over and found me on the sidelines to tell me that."

Like most things that season, the 1993 SEC Cross Country Championships at Highland Road Park in Baton Rouge, Louisiana, was a cakewalk. Arkansas scored 18 points to Tennessee's 75, led by an individual win from Michael Morin in his Louisiana homecoming. Not only did the win mark Arkansas's twentieth consecutive conference cross-country championship—and third consecutive in the Southeastern Conference—but it also reassured McDonnell that his team was ready for the national championship following a surprising home loss two weeks earlier.

The Chile Pepper Festival had featured a stellar field that included the defending NAIA national champions from Lubbock Christian, the defending Division II national champions from Adams State, the junior-college national champions from Blinn College, as well as the distance-running powerhouse from Oklahoma State. Though schools from these other levels did not face the same scholarship and age limitations of Division I schools, neither McDonnell nor Oklahoma State coach Dick Weis shied away from competing against any of them at their respective home meets.

"His philosophy and my philosophy was to go after the best," said Oklahoma State coach Dick Weis. "I remember teams wouldn't come because of that. Wisconsin wouldn't come. I remember one coach who had won national coach of the year saying he couldn't imagine getting beat by a junior college. I said, 'Hell, you're going to get beat by two junior colleges!' There were a lot of coaches who felt that way."

Though they may have been facing a team with some over-age athletes, Arkansas had not lost at home since 1970. Yet, when Jason Bunston went down with a cramp halfway through the race, it was Lubbock Christian and James Bungei that came out on top by a margin of 64–73.

"When someone has a bad day, you have to have someone step up and get it done, and we didn't," McDonnell told the media. "We haven't lost here in a long time, but it will do us some good."[21]

Though Brian Baker was expected to return from injury, it was that weekend when McDonnell decided to pull the redshirt off Niall Bruton.

"There is a very good possibility we will run Niall," McDonnell said afterwards. "I can see we are not an NCAA championship team without him. We just don't have the backup."[22]

At the regional meet, John sent only a partial team to qualify. For those who remained in Fayetteville, however, the ten-mile tempo they did could hardly qualify as rest.

"It got to the point where it was more restful to go to the regional than to stay and do the aerobic threshold run," said Clark. "In fact, running the regional was probably easier."

With his entire lineup finally together for the 1993 NCAA Cross Country Championships at a fast course at Lehigh in Bethlehem, Pennsylvania, McDonnell followed up his team meeting by speaking to each runner individually in their hotel room the night before the race.

"John should get a PhD in psychology because he already has one," said Teddy Mitchell. "He would sit down with each individual person throughout the year and learn who you were and learn what motivated you. He came into my room that night and told me that fortieth place would still be All-American. He knew he was basically insulting me. I was an ambitious person, and he knew that would make me motivated to show him I was better than that. Then he would go into Niall Bruton or Jason Bunston's room and tell them they could win the whole thing because he knew that would fire them up."

Midway through the race, Arkansas was in such control that they led by over one hundred points. It was at that point where McDonnell did something he regretted afterwards.

"[Niall] Bruton and [Jason] Bunston were sitting in second and third behind [Josphat Kapkory] of Washington State," remembered McDonnell. "There were a couple of miles to go, and they were well clear of the field and were about to go by [Kapkory] when I said to stay there. He was a good distance runner, and I was worried they might blow up, but it was [Kapkory] who ended up blowing up and almost came back to them. By the time I found out we were in great shape as a team, it was too late to tell them to go for it. If I would have just left them alone, they would have beaten that Kenyan. I always regretted that. I should have just kept my mouth shut because they were eating him up at the end."

Though the margin could certainly have been greater had Bunston or Bruton gone for the individual win, it was sizeable enough. Arkansas outpaced second place Brigham Young, 31–153.[23]

It was one of the more dominating performances in collegiate cross-country history and matched UTEP's record of four consecutive NCAA cross-country titles. Coming as it did with contributions from six All-Americans specializing in track events from the 1,500 meter to 10,000 meter, the win boded well for a track season that would rival the 1984–85 campaign as the greatest in collegiate history.

Though the jumps group was forced to deal with the graduation of Brian Wellman and Gary Johnson, the addition of Jerome Romain, a 55 feet, 7 inch triple jumper from the tiny Caribbean island of Dominica, went a long way towards filling the void. A junior-college national champion at Blinn College, Romain blossomed into one of the best triple jumpers in the world once he adjusted to training at Arkansas.

"He was just a special young man with the cheeriest outlook and the most grateful," recalled Booth. "He worked hard and was a good student. They ended up making a stamp of him in Dominica when he made the Olympic team."

In the sprints, the latest addition to Stanley Redwine's sprint crew was Shannon Sidney, a football defensive back from Russellville, Arkansas, who had run 13.6 for the 110-meter hurdles and 37.4 for 300-meter hurdles. Still, Sidney was told by new Arkansas football coach Danny Ford that his participation in track would not be viewed favorably when they penciled in the starting lineup.

"Him and Danny didn't hit it off too well," remembered McDonnell. "He told Shannon, 'If you go track, you'll be number four on the depth chart.' Shannon knew after the starter screwed up on the first play that he'd be right back in there. He didn't care if he started or not, he just wanted to play and run."

Entering a season where *College Sports Magazine* picked four SEC schools to finish in the top five at the 1994 NCAA Indoor Championships—Arkansas, Tennessee, Louisiana State, and Florida—the Razorbacks hardly had an easy path to either the conference or national championship. Still, nothing was capable of standing in their way that season. Two weeks after winning the SEC indoor title in Gainesville by 70 points over Tennessee, the Arkansas juggernaut came to Indianapolis to put on one of the most dominating national championship performances in track and field history.

Six national champions—Calvin Davis (400 meter), Niall Bruton (mile), Jason Bunston (5,000 meter), distance medley relay (Brian Baker, Calvin Davis, Niall Bruton, Graham Hood), and Erick Walder (long jump, triple jump)—plus six additional All-Americans scored an unprecedented 94 points over second-place Tennessee's 40 for the Razorbacks' eleventh consecutive NCAA indoor championship.[24]

The total could have easily been over a hundred. Coming off an injury, Graham Hood anchored the distance medley exclusively in order to break the collegiate indoor distance medley relay record, a luxury made possible with Niall Bruton poised to defend his indoor national mile title following an impressive win at Millrose Games that same winter.

"I always wanted the best kicker on the end in case it got tactical, and Graham was someone if you gave him a job and needed him to run 1:47, he would run 1:47," said McDonnell. "He was one of those true grit guys who didn't take any crap from anyone. He wasn't afraid to give someone an elbow if he needed."

With a 3:56.3 anchor leg for the Razorbacks, Hood crossed the finish line in an indoor collegiate-record time of 9:30.07. It also didn't hurt the team chemistry to avoid having Hood race Bruton straight-up in the mile. That was especially so with Bruton already upsetting Providence's Andy Keith by celebrating up the final straightaway and waving to his teammates before almost walking across the line.[25]

"I'm not pleased with the way Niall came down the final straight," said fellow Irishman Andy Keith after the race. "I don't like being shown up like that. I could look at it as a compliment that he's so pleased to beat me that he had to celebrate down the entire straight! It's a little bit like Steve Ovett isn't it? It's just not necessary."[26]

"I just wanted to stay with him," said Bruton after the victory. "He's a 3:56 miler, and I wanted to key off him and it worked. He's a good runner. My post race celebration was because I really wanted to win. I'm a quiet person by nature and am not usually that expressive."[27]

Though McDonnell abhorred such hotdogging or unsportsmanlike behavior, he had told the Arkansas athletes after the first day that the meet was essentially won and that individual pursuits could take priority. In the long jump, Erick Walder again attempted to break Carl Lewis's meet record of 27 feet, 10 inches. Walder fell short of the record by only two inches, but still won the event.

Back on campus, the Arkansas basketball team was playing as well as anyone in the country during a season that saw it regularly draw twenty thousand to the brand new Bud Walton Arena, which had been dubbed the "Basketball Palace of Mid-America" for its plush amenities. A far cry from the days of playing on a dirt floor in Barnhill Arena, Arkansas now boasted some of the best facilities in the country.

With McDonnell having moved into a new office in the new arena just down the hall from basketball coach Nolan Richardson, the two men continued to have long conversations about their respective cattle ranches and philosophies on coaching and training at the highest level.

"John got on a roll and it never stopped," said Richardson. "I don't know of a human being or coach who would have been able to do what he did. He was a very unique coach because he was gifted with something that nobody else had. That's why when I had a chance, I'd rub up against him, touch him, do every damn thing I could to get some of what he had. I know he thought I was crazy. I said, 'I just need a little bit John! I don't need a whole lot!' Super-coach was something else."

There was a mutual admiration between the coaches as well as an understanding of the challenges the other faced. Assistant coach Mike Conley remembers on many occasions sitting in the coaching offices while the two of them discussed domestic or global affairs—always managing to solve the world's problems by lunchtime.

Richardson was not the only person associated with the basketball program making frequent pilgrimages to John's office that winter. After winning the 1994 SEC championship, the team was deep in the throes of March Madness. As they sought their first national championship, it was not uncommon for members of the basketball team to stop by McDonnell's office to soak in the championship aura.

"The thing I really liked about that team was the kids used to come by my office and say, 'Do you have one of those championship rings?'" said John. "I remember Corliss Williamson would come in to just look at it. They were really just kids and wanted that national title more than anything. I'd say to them, 'You guys are going to get it this year.' They had a better team a few years earlier with Todd Day and the Big O [Oliver Miller], but they were all individuals. There was a big difference between them and championship guys. Corliss was just a super team guy. That team didn't have many pro players on it, but they wanted that national championship and were primed to do it."

Though Richardson never hesitated to pick McDonnell's brain when the occasion arose, he had a successful style to call his own based on many of the same fundamentals.

"We talked times about training and how hard we trained," remembered John. "I remember he ran those kids up that hill coming up from the west to the university on Cleveland Street in the mornings. Even that Big O had to run up the hill. That sucker was over seven feet tall and three hundred pounds. Nolan had that 'Forty Minutes of Hell,' and he would work them into such fantastic shape and would substitute guys in and just wear teams down. There were a lot of similarities between us. I'd say if the race doesn't suit you to take control of it. That's what Nolan's teams did. They forced their style of play on the other team. They didn't always match up well individually but they would win because they had a plan."

On April 4, 1994, the Arkansas basketball team won its first national championship in a thrilling 76–72 win over Duke in Charlotte, North Carolina. Having joined Frank Broyles and John McDonnell in the pantheon of national championship coaches at Arkansas, Nolan Richardson and his Razorback basketball team brought the championship trophy home to a rapturous celebration in Fayetteville and parade in Little Rock. It was a moment captured in time for Nolan Richardson—the pinnacle of his career at Arkansas.

Though John would win nearly twenty more national championships himself, a case could be made that the spring of 1994 represented the pinnacle of John McDonnell's coaching career as well. Never again would the Razorbacks score as many as 83 points at the NCAA Outdoor Track and Field Championships or 223 points at the Southeastern Conference Outdoor Championships.

If ever there was a telling example of McDonnell's absolute compulsion to win, it became ever apparent to Frank O'Mara as he ran by John's office at Bud Walton Arena at 6:30 a.m. on May 16, 1994—the day after the SEC Championships—and noticed the light was still on inside. He soon discovered, the light was not "still" on, but it had been turned on that very morning. Less than twelve hours after decimating the most powerful track conference in the country by nearly eighty points on their home track, John's anger at frequent appeals and protests by Tennessee during the meet propelled him out of bed to make early-morning East Coast recruiting calls in order to beat the Volunteers by an even greater margin next time.[28]

"People wonder why we were good," said McDonnell. "We were good because we worked our ass off. I worked sixteen-hour days for years. It was just ridiculous when I look back at it. We contacted everyone and shook every tree and got the people in that we wanted."

Unlike some who become complacent after winning a national championship, John became ever more motivated to stay on top. Ten years and twenty national championships after his first, he remained suffocated within a wind tunnel of his own making, increasingly obsessed with achieving excellence year after year, and ever more determined to continue feeding the insatiable championship monster he had spawned. All-American walk-ons, such as John Schiefer, could easily have ended up in Oregon or other elite distance programs had someone on those coaching staffs put the effort to return their calls and show an interest, a source of fermenting frustration for Oregon fans, boosters, and alumni alike.[29]

Just as in County Mayo decades prior, there was a direct correlation between the unimaginable hours of thought and work John McDonnell put in and the success that followed. As Doug Brown's trophy case slowly accumulated dust, it began to dawn on the Tennessee coach that there was no end in sight.

"John is put together differently than the rest of us," admitted Brown. "His ability to grind it out every year and be as tough as he is year in and year out is remarkable. He was just a tough, old farm boy and had a perseverance with which I'm not familiar. I kept waiting for that son of a bitch to retire."

At the 1994 NCAA Outdoor Championships in Boise, Idaho, a resurgent UTEP squad under coach Bob Kitchens, sprinter Obadele Thompson, and steeplechaser Jim Svenoy was capable of scoring fifty points even without the outdoor eligibility of NCAA hammer-throw champion Mika Laaksonen. Yet, Arkansas was so far above its competition that season that the team championship was a given.

After breaking the collegiate record in the long jump with a mind-boggling leap of 28 feet, 8 inches at altitude at the Springtime Invitational in El Paso in early April, Erick Walder once again captured two NCAA titles in the long and triple jump with training partner Jerome Romain right behind him in the triple.

Another deluge of points came in the 1,500 meter, 5,000 meter and 10,000 meter.[30] Incredibly enough, four Razorbacks drew the same heat of the 5,000 meter—Brian Baker, Jason Bunston, David Welsh, and Teddy Mitchell—and made it through to the finals despite contending with highly ranked Jason Stewart of Army.

"Mitchell kept pushing the pace," remembered Jason Bunston. "So Brian said, 'Jason, take the lead.' Well, Jason Stewart thinks he's talking to him and says, 'Okay, Brian.' I'm thinking this is convenient. Where else would a competitor and a better runner, quite frankly at that point, have responded, 'Yes, sir,' like that? That is what Arkansas did to people."

In the 10,000 meter, Teddy Mitchell certainly wasn't given much of a chance against NCAA cross-country champion Josphat Kapkory by his teammates nor anyone else. Even after a stellar triple in the 3,000 meter steeplechase, 5,000 meter, and 10,000 meter at the 1994 SEC Outdoor Championships, Mitchell remembers Graham Hood posting the odds against Mitchell winning nationals on the locker room bulletin board. There would have been few willing to place that bet. Still, Teddy Mitchell had at least one believer.

"Coach McDonnell teaches you things about life," said Mitchell. "It's okay to screw things up in life, but don't screw up things when it's on the line. When it's championship time, it's championship time."

As he always did, McDonnell gave his athlete a plan for victory amidst the thin Idaho air.

"I told him to stay back and let the two [Washington State] guys mix it up with each other," said John. "Even I didn't think they would do what they did which was to run themselves into the ground. Teddy was about thirty-five meters back, and each time I saw him I'd say, 'Keep the steady pace, Teddy! They're going to burn themselves out!' And by gosh, they did. One started coming back and the altitude got him just like that. I said, 'You got the first one, Teddy, and the other one is coming back soon!' [Kapkory] had about a seventy-meter lead but started coming back with five laps to go. I said, 'He's yours Teddy!' It was like blood in the water, and Teddy caught him with 500 meters to go. [Kapkory] tried to pass Teddy back, but by 200 meters he was out of it."

If there were those on the team unwilling to accept the transfer from Tennessee prior to that day, such sentiments were a thing of the past. Even Doug Brown congratulated Mitchell on his national title.

"You had to at least win nationals to feel like you belonged at Arkansas," said Mitchell. "If you were competitive at nationals in track, people accepted you and knew you belonged. There was never an exception to the rule."

Though hardly struggling for acceptance themselves, teammates Brian Baker and Graham Hood watched from the stands in Bronco Stadium and understood what they needed to accomplish for their own legacies at Arkansas as much as anything.

The next day Brian Baker kicked hard off a slow pace to win the 5,000 meter in 14:22.09 with teammate Jason Bunston right behind him. It was a sweet victory for the native Arkansan.

"It was ridiculously slow out there, and that played right into my hands because I'm a big kicker," Baker told the media. "I've waited for this national championship for a long time. This is my fifth year. I've had a lot of ups and downs, but my time came."[31]

In the 1,500 meter final, Graham Hood also kicked hard off a slow pace to beat a talented field that included Kevin Sullivan of Michigan, Paul McMullen of Eastern Michigan, Corey Ihmels of Iowa State, as well as teammate Niall Bruton, to win in 3:42.10.

"The race went out slow, but I was ready to run it any way it went," said Hood. "I'm very confident of my speed and felt comfortable at the back of the pack. With 200 meters to go I got up on [Providence runner] Andy Keith's shoulder and decided to take off and go for it. It feels great. It was a long time coming and lifts some weight off my shoulder."[32]

Though it hardly mattered in a national-championship meet they had won by thirty-seven points, Arkansas unbelievably could have scored over one hundred points had they not experienced some unfortunate circumstances. Not only was David Welsh disqualified in the 5,000 meter for contact with a Penn State runner but the sprint events had been a disaster. All-American Derrick Thompson false-started in the 200 meter, while NCAA indoor 400-meter champion Calvin Davis misjudged his pace and missed the final.

"Calvin was in lane two and followed a UCLA guy who was really good," remembered McDonnell. "Well that sucker must have been hurt because he was way back, and the other guys were flying. I kept asking, 'Is [Calvin] watching up front?' It was like he was brain dead until the final straightaway, and by that point he didn't have enough time to make the final."

McDonnell declined to play favorites when asked which team was his best, but *Track and Field News* went ahead and dubbed the 1993–94 team the greatest in collegiate history less than ten years after saying the same thing about the 1984–85 team. Whether that was true or not is a debate for posterity. What was becoming apparent was that after winning an unprecedented triple crown of triple crowns at the NCAA Championships, perhaps even John McDonnell might have a hard time outdoing himself this time.

Tale of the Tape

1984–1985	1993–1994
Olympians	**Olympians**
Mike Conley 1984, 1992 and 1996 Triple Jump (Gold Medal in 1992 and Silver Medal in 1984))	Calvin Davis 1996 400m hurdles (Bronze medal)
Joey Wells 1984 Long Jump	Matt Hemmingway 2004 High Jump (Silver medal)
Paul Donovan 1984 and 1992 5,000m	Graham Hood 1992 and 1996 1,500m
Doug Consiglio 1988 1,500m	Niall Bruton 1996 1,500m
	Jerome Romain 1996 Triple Jump

All-Americans (Collegiate personal bests)

1984–1985	1993–1994
Wallace Spearmon Sr. 10.23 (100m), 20.36 (200m)	Derrick Thompson. 10.20 (100m), 20.31 (200m)
Roddie Haley 44.48 (400m)	Jimmy French 20.20 (200m)
Bill DuPont 1:11.1 (600 yard)	Vincent Henderson 20.50 (200m)
Espen Borge 1:47.41 (800m)	Calvin Davis 45.04 (400m)
Liam Looney 1:49.1 (800m)	Graham Hood 1:45.70 (800m), 3:35.27 (1,500m)
Joe Falcon 3:35.42 (1,500m), 13:45 (5,000m), 28:34 (10,000m)	Niall Bruton 3:37.16 (1,500m)
Doug Consiglio 3:35.82 (1,500m), 8:43.21 (3,000m SC)	Mike Morin 3:39.8 (1,500m)
Paul Donovan 3:38.31 (1,500m), 13:24.46 (5,000m)	John Schiefer 3:41.1 (1,500m), 8:56 (3,000m SC)
Gary Taylor 3:39.88 (1,500m)	Phil Price 3:41.03 (1,500m)
Matt Taylor 3:41.67 (1,500m)	Matt Mitchell 3:41.9 (1,500m)
Richard Cooper 8:35.35 (3,000m SC)	Jason Bunston 13:22.08 (5,000m), 28:56.50 (10,000m)
Roland Reina 8:43.26 (3,000m SC)	Ryan Wilson 13:28.60 (5,000m)
David Swain 7:54 (3,000m), 13:54 (5,000m)	Frank Hanley 13:48.08 (5,000m), 28:56.20 (10,000m)
Ian Cherry 28:43 (10,000m)	Brian Baker 13:56 (5,000m)
Chris Zinn 29:02 (10,000m)	David Welsh 13:57.03 (5,000m), 29:01 (10,000m)
John Register 13.57 (110m HH)	Teddy Mitchell 13:56.69 (5,000m), 28:53.95 (10,000m)
Fred Cleary 13.71 (110m HH), 50.28 (400m H)	David Gurry 14:14.92 (5,000m)
Charley Moss 50.28 (400m H)	Chris Phillips 13.58 (110m HH), 50.83 (400m H)
4x100m Cleary, Haley, Conley, Spearmon Sr. (38.81)	Shannon Sidney 50.97 (400m H)
4 x 400m Dupont, Cleary, Moss, Haley (3:04.90)	4x100m Phillips, French, Thompson, Henderson (39.18)
Mike Conley 27'6 (Long Jump), 58'1 (Triple Jump)	4 x 400m Henderson, Phillips, Hughes, Davis (3:05.04)
Mike Davis 26'8 (Long Jump)	Erick Walder 28'8 (Long Jump), 56'2 (Triple Jump)
Joey Wells 26'1 (Long Jump)	Jerome Romain 26'7 (Long Jump), 56'6 (Triple Jump)
Mark Klee 18'0 (Pole Vault)	Ray Doakes 7'6 (High Jump)
Jeff Pascoe 18'0 (Pole Vault)	Matt Hemmingway 7'6 (High Jump)
Marty Kobza 66'9 (Shot Put), 196'9 (Discus)	

NCAA Championships Results
Cross Country 101 points (2nd place, Arizona, 111 points)
Indoor Track- 70 points (2nd place, Tennessee, 29 points)
Outdoor Track- 61 points (2nd place, Washington St., 46 points)

NCAA Championships Results
Cross Country 31 points (2nd place, Brigham Young, 153 points)
Indoor Track- 94 points (2nd place, Tennessee, 40 points)
Outdoor Track- 83 points (2nd place, Texas-El Paso, 45 points)

Southwest Conference Championships Results
Cross Country 35 points (2nd place, Texas, 88 points)
Indoor Track 156 points (2nd place, Baylor, 60 points)
Outdoor Track 167 points (2nd place, Texas, 80 points)

Southeastern Conference Championships Results
Cross Country- 18 points (2nd place, Tennessee, 75 points)
Indoor Track- 143 points (2nd place, Tennessee, 87.5 points)
Outdoor Track- 223 points (2nd place, Tennessee, 145 points)

** Note: Conference and NCAA track scored first to sixth place

** Note: Conference and NCAA track scored first to eighth place

Penn Relays Wins (Time/Mark)
Distance Medley Relay 9:28.20
4 x 1,500m Relay 14:50.20
4 x 100m Relay 39.90
4 x 200m Relay 1:20.90
Pole Vault Mark Klee (17'0)
Shot Put Marty Kobza (62'7.90)
Discus Marty Kobza (192'3)

Penn Relays Wins (Time/Mark)
Distance Medley Relay 9:28.07
4 x 1,500m Relay 14:52.81

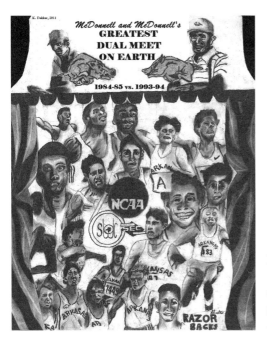

It is a debate for posterity whether the 1984–85 or 1993–94 Arkansas cross-country/track-and field-teams was the greatest college team of all time. *Illustration by Kyle Dekker.*

11

A New Generation (1994–1997)

"What Arkansas had in John was special and it will never happen again."
—George Mason head coach John Cook

One of the consequences of prodigious success is that it is frequently followed by turnover. Important cogs in the machine are lured elsewhere by the opportunity to lead programs looking for someone to replicate that success at their institution. Arkansas faced that exact issue during the summer of 1994.

Only six years after returning to Fayetteville following his tenure as athletic director at Southwestern Louisiana, Terry Don Philips tremendous work and leadership with the Razorback Foundation made it only a matter of time before he became an athletic director again somewhere.

"It was thought he would be the successor to Frank Broyles," said McDonnell. "He was here six or seven years, and Frank had no intentions of retiring, so [Phillips] went to Oklahoma State. He was a great guy to work for, real laid-back, appreciated what you did, and always had time to talk to you."

On John's own coaching staff, administrative assistant Doug Clark was hired away to coach the distance runners at UTEP in the spring of 1994. After he was replaced by Jim VanHootegem, Clark moved again to join Stanley Redwine during the fall of 1994 at the University of Tulsa, where the long-time Razorback assistant coach had been hired as the head coach. Still an elite 800-meter runner on the international circuit well into his thirties, Redwine slowly began to wind down his prolific running career.

"Towards the end doing both was hard for him," said McDonnell. "It wasn't good for his career as a coach, and I told him about a year or two before he gave it up completely to move on."

Redwine's replacement at Arkansas was Steve Silvey of Blinn College. While several junior-college coaches had ascended to Division I after success at the junior-college ranks, few had his credentials—fifteen JUCO national championships and coaching the Zambian Olympic team. Silvey was a tireless workaholic joining a coaching staff filled with them.

"Dick Booth was instrumental in hiring him, and Steve turned out to be a great success," remembered McDonnell. "He was just a recruiting fool, a hell of a coach, and one heck of a worker. He'd do anything for you and took no nonsense from anyone. He treated all of the athletes the same, and they all met the same standard. There are always people who think you can take a shortcut, but there was a reason the sprinters ran well when he was here. He worked them hard, and he had some great ones come in for nothing, and he turned them into something."

Though he had an entirely different personality than Redwine, who had achieved success through a more laid-back approach, Silvey took an already strong sprints group left by his predecessor and worked with minimal scholarship dollars to make them even better.

"Stanley didn't exactly leave the cupboard bare," said Silvey. "I was working hard behind the scenes, looking for anything. When Nevada dropped its program, I took advantage and recruited Brandon Rock pretty hard. There weren't many scholarships to work with [for the sprint events] but I'm kind of like a chameleon. You work within the limitations and do the best that you can."

McDonnell now had assistant coaches recruiting as aggressively as any in the country. In Silvey's case, John practically had to contain him from jumping on the next plane to make a home visit with whomever the team was recruiting.

"That sucker was absolutely tireless," said McDonnell. "If athletes grew on trees, he would shake every tree. You would have to tell him to take a week off because he was on the road like he was possessed. He had a lot of plusses. Steve was a great recruiter and a great coach."

It was that same fall when Katie Hill moved from the ticket office to replace Terry Don Phillips as the assistant athletic director overseeing track and field and basketball, among other sports and responsibilities.

As delicate as John could be handling certain situations, he was not averse to being tough, if and when the situation called for it.

"One day [head football coach] Danny Ford closed the football field where we used to run in the morning," said McDonnell. "So I went to the AD and said, 'What's this?' He said the women were out there, and [Coach Ford] was upset they were practicing on the field."

As it became clear that departmental politicking was not going to remove the locked gate blocking the Razorback track athletes from their own locker room, McDonnell solved the problem for everybody by using a lock-cutter to cut the lock preventing them from opening the gate.

"I did that because our locker room was up there, and we weren't going to be crawling over some fence," said McDonnell. "I talked to Danny and said, 'What's the story with the locked gate? If you don't want us to jog there, that's fine, but we need to get to the locker room.' He ended up saying it was fine, and we got along. He used to come with me to buy breeding stock cattle for his ranch in South Carolina."

One frustrating battle it appeared John was not going to win was over the location of the NCAA Cross Country Championships. Though Arkansas had won the bid to host the national championships that fall and had run home cross-country meets at Razorback Golf Course for as long as he had been in Fayetteville, women's athletic director Bev Lewis and others favored a location at the battleground in Prairie Grove. All of this chagrined the new proprietor of Razorback Golf Course, who had continued former UA golf coach Dean Solomon's generous use of the course for cross-country meets and workouts.

"It caused problems," remembered John. "The women ended up being kicked off and never let back on [at Razorback Golf Course], and we had to move the home cross-country meet. It was a nine-hole course but there was plenty of land at the side. The new owner of the course knew I had nothing to do with moving it because I was out there walking around trying to plan it with him, but Bev and others wanted to run it at the battlefield because they thought it was prettier. It didn't suit our athletes because it was dangerous and uneven underfoot and hilly."

With a newly renovated track that fall, which would eventually be renamed John McDonnell Field in 1998, the man himself faced an unprecedented exodus of talent with Brian Baker, Niall Bruton, David Welsh, Frank Hanley, Calvin Davis, and Erick Walder all graduating at the same time. Some of those athletes had rarely tasted defeat—winning eleven of twelve possible NCAA team titles in their careers.

Though Mike Morin had not yet graduated and was to earn All-American honors in cross country that fall, it gradually became evident to John that the Louisianan's best days were behind him.

"He came back to school and met this girl," said John wryly. "He ran 3:40s but never got back to what he was running before the Olympic Trials. He started looking for excuses. I remember one cross-country workout his junior year he said, 'Who is getting the medal for running fast this time?' He was getting dropped. So I called him over and said, 'Mike, cut the bullshit. They are running what I asked them to run. You are the one slowing down.'"

Over twenty-two years of collegiate coaching experience had taught McDonnell of the impossibility of successfully pursuing a heavy academic load, training at a high level, and living a heavily active social life simultaneously. Though never failing to preach this message to those who lost their way, one thing John rarely did was leave his athletes feeling stifled.

"He did a great job of allowing college kids to be college kids," said Ryan Wilson. "We needed to blow off steam, and we certainly had a good time and went out. He knew who could take care of their business and who couldn't and needed to be more focused on running and school. He usually knew what people were up to, and he chose to rein them in or not."

The same concept applied to training. Though John had held back Graham Hood and others on occasions when he felt individual circumstances dictated it, he was not afraid to expose other talented freshmen to the cutting edge of collegiate training right away.

Ryan Wilson and Phil Price had both redshirted the previous fall as part of the pattern of McDonnell sacrificing nothing from a training perspective during the first year of an athlete's college career with the expectations of national-level performances by their junior season.

"It's the first day of practice, and Coach is like, 'All right guys, behind the golf course today,'" remembered Price. "It wasn't like warming into it. It was just, 'Go!' Ten miles behind the golf course, and they're just flying. By three miles I can't see anyone and got lost and ended up running twelve miles. By the time I got back to the locker room everyone was showered. You weren't going to come into his program and work into shape. You had to be ready to go from day one."

It soon became clear that touted freshman Sean Kaley was not going to be ready to contribute immediately. Though he had run 8:12 for 3,000 meters and represented Canada internationally in cross country, the boy from Ottawa had never experienced anything resembling the volume, intensity, and competiveness he faced in Fayetteville during August of 1994. The heat had been turned up both literally and figuratively.

"My first year was a disaster, but I never got discouraged or thought about leaving," said Kaley. "John was a great motivator. It was what he did best. Whenever I left his office I felt better. He'd say, 'Kid, this isn't even a bad event. This was a disaster. And you know what you do with a disaster? You forget about it and move on.' And I'm like, 'All right!'"

Such a trial was exactly what Kaley had agreed to when he had signed with Arkansas the previous spring. Recruited by top programs all over the country and hearing no shortage of voices buzzing in his ear about the perils of training at Arkansas, Kaley became spellbound on his official visit by what McDonnell had done with others and what he could possibly do with him.

"He showed me these articles and gigantic trophies from Penn Relays, and he said 'If you come here people will know your name,'" recalled Kaley. "He said people from this program go to the Olympics and asked me, 'Do you want to go to the Olympics, kid?' And I'm like, 'Of course I want to go to the freaking Olympics!' And in this non-bragging kind of way he matter-of-factly began naming off people that went to the last few Olympics. Then he busted out this jeweled case of all the NCAA rings and said, 'If you go to another school and run really well, you might get one of these, and it will be a great honor. If you come to Arkansas, I guarantee you will get one of these, and you will probably get more than one.' I got back on the plane to Canada and was thinking there isn't a single reason not to come here."

The cross-country season started out promisingly enough with Arkansas ranked first in the preseason *College Sports* poll ahead of Iowa State.[1] Coming off a season that at least arguably rivaled the greatest in the history of the program and the sport, it was hard not to have high expectations, yet it soon became apparent with a young rebuilding team that Arkansas was vulnerable in cross country.

Though augmented by older transfers such as Brandon McGuire from Miami (Ohio), Carlos Paradello from Michigan, and Chris Wilson from Florida, the Razorbacks were largely reliant on three runners scoring as low as possible: Jason Bunston, Mike Morin, and Graham Hood.

"We are a good team if we stay healthy," McDonnell told the media prior to the season. "I think we are ranked based on what we have done in the past and our top three runners. We will get a true reading on how good this team is in about five or six weeks."[2]

As disappointing as an early-season loss to Kansas at the Jayhawk Invitational was for the team, the reality was it could at least be explained away by the fact that neither Bunston nor Hood competed. Running the Chile Pepper Festival for the first time at the

Prairie Grove Battleground National Park on October 10, 1994, Arkansas lost again, this time to Georgetown by seven points. Though they had still held out Hood after the Canadian eased back following the World Championships, the losses were a bad omen.

The worst omen of all came nineteen days later when the unthinkable nearly happened at the 1994 SEC Cross Country Championships on the same course in Prairie Grove. With a twenty-year conference championship winning streak on the line, Arkansas very unexpectedly found itself a few points behind Tennessee with less than 800 meters remaining in the race.

"Oh, we had them," remembered Tennessee coach Doug Brown, whose team was ranked number twelve nationally headed into the meet. "We had five or six good runners and nailed it that day. I have to give Arkansas credit. Everyone was hurting coming up that last hill and we had them beat, but they dug down and found a way."

ARKANSAS		TENNESSEE	
1.	Jason Bunston 23:49	3.	Toney Cosey 24:02
4.	Ryan Wilson 24:30	6.	Chris Brown 24:51
5.	Graham Hood 24:38	8.	Stuart Ellington 24:56
13.	Carlos Paradello 25:10	11.	Ben Goba 25:05
15.	Geoffrey Sidari 25:15	14.	Bob Dickie 25:12
38 points		42 points	

With substantial portions of the course having uneven footing and several Razorbacks ankles already taped up due to earlier sprains from that very course, it was a recipe for a poor performance.

"Tennessee had a great performance today," John told the media afterwards. "Our defending champion [Mike Morin] didn't have a good day [seventeenth], but those things happen. I don't care if we win by one, so long as we win."[3]

After running their most complete meet of the year at the regional championship to hold off a plucky Baylor squad, John had reason for optimism as his fourth-ranked team sought an unprecedented fifth consecutive cross-country national championship at home for the first time in school history.

"Any of the top ten teams could win the race," John said at a press conference. "It will be a real dogfight tomorrow."[4]

That prediction turned out to be correct, though not at all in the way John had intended.

"That was one of the darkest days because we had always wanted to host it, but when the gun went off everyone said the same thing. We felt like a ton of bricks," remembered Phil Price, who finished 118th out of the nearly 250 runners in the field.

With Colorado and Iowa State mixing it up front, only Bunston and Morin finished in the top fifty as Arkansas saw one thing after another go wrong on a day they fell to tenth place—their statistically worst finish since 1979.

"I was overpeaked and a lot of the team was overpumped because it was at home," remembered Bunston. "John didn't even get angry with us afterwards, which made us think he was really angry. He said he would take full blame."

If misery loves company, perhaps the only solace that could be taken from the debacle was the fact that sloppy conditions and a challenging course had treated other highly ranked squads as badly or worse. Wisconsin fell to fifth after entering the meet lightly favored to win, while second-ranked Georgetown tumbled all the way to fifteenth.[5] Emerging from the fray was Iowa State, who scored 66 points led by Corey Ihmels, and emerged victorious for its second national championship in five years.

"We were fortunate because we expected it to be much closer," said Iowa State coach Bill Bergan. "We thought Arkansas would run better at home."[6]

The Razorbacks never looked comfortable running at Prairie Grove that season, but ultimately it was youth, lack of depth, and nagging injuries that doomed their national championship hopes.

"It was a disaster all round," remembered John. "Our guys hated the course, and I didn't like running on uneven ground, but that didn't alter the result. Graham had an ankle problem and we had too many injuries; it didn't matter where the heck we ran it."

Though many of the underclassmen on the Arkansas roster would mature and develop significantly during the following year, the addition of Godfrey Siamusiye from Blinn College in January 1995 dramatically changed Razorback fortunes. Siamusiye had won everything there was to win in junior college, and though he was recruited all over the country, ultimately it was Godfrey's deep and abiding comfort level with McDonnell that made him decide to move to Fayetteville.

"I was supposed to go to Lehigh, but after a while I didn't hear anything from them, so I thought they weren't interested," remembered Siamusiye. "John congratulated me after Chile Pepper, and asked if I was interested to look at Arkansas. He wasn't very pushy about it and I said, 'Sure.' Other coaches were ringing me every day, breaking NCAA rules, but John was easy about it. There were quite a few things I liked about him, but it felt very easy talking to him. It was like talking to your dad, and his track record suggested he knew quite a few things as well."

When he arrived in Fayetteville, the native Zambian had one training gear: fast. For someone like Jason Bunston, who recalls being politely admonished by Niall Bruton and others on occasions he separated from the group by attempting to hammer runs harder than anyone else, the addition of Siamusiye to the group was like manna from heaven.

"I loved it because he cooked everything, and I finally had someone trying to drop me the first mile of fourteen mile run," said Bunston. "I had been pining for someone who liked to train hard all of the time, and when Godfrey got there, I finally had someone who wanted to burn it every day."

The two of them regularly ran the twelve-mile airport loop in 1:02 or under. Though they managed to survive hammering day after day, Siamusiye's training began to be periodically interrupted by minor injuries brought on by the blinding intensity and increase in volume.

"I told him, 'I want you to be the best guy you can be, but if you want to be the best, you can't get hurt. If you keep flogging yourself, you're going to get hurt,'" remembered McDonnell. "I had to be careful with both of them. The one thing Africans do all of the time is all-out running. There is no jogging, so I learned something about the hard running and cutting back on the distance. Both [Siamusiye and Bunston] were great examples of what it took to be great. They weren't bitching about somebody setting the pace. They took it. You have to have leaders like that."

Aside from controlling the volume Godfrey blasted on his easy runs, McDonnell also adapted the weight-room routine he had developed six years earlier, which consisted of him blowing a whistle every thirty seconds as his athletes worked their way through a weight circuit ranging from upper-body exercises to light leg and hamstring curls. Since it was immediately followed by an eight-mile easy run, the Tuesday and Thursday morning workout began to be referred to as "weights and eight."

"When Godfrey first came from Blinn, his legs were so skinny," remembered Danny Green, who rejoined the staff in 1997. "It looked like a baby deer standing up; they were that thin. So one day Godfrey was on the hamstring machine, and I think the lowest weight was twenty pounds and he was struggling to lift it. So John came over and said, 'Godfrey, you don't need these weights. You are only going to get hurt.'"

Though Godfrey's impact would be as profound as any current or former Razorback, he was hardly the only impact athlete entering the program that fall. Following the cutting of the men's program at University of Nevada, Las Vegas, Silvey managed to coax Brandon Rock to Arkansas for his final season. An 800-meter runner with 46.46 400-meter speed, Rock was a perfect fit in Fayetteville.

"What a find he was," said McDonnell. "He was a great kid and would do anything you told him. After he turned professional and went to Europe, [the agent] Kim McDonald told me we finally have an American not afraid of the Kenyans. He would take the lead in forty-nine seconds if he had to."

In the jumps group, the transition of Erick Walder from collegiate to professional athlete could certainly have been devastating to the Razorbacks title hopes if they had not managed to find the ultimate competitor to replace him in the unlikeliest of places. Hailing from Pawtucket, Rhode Island, Robert Howard had jumped 24 feet, 8 inches for the long jump and 51-5 for the triple jump, but brought a competitive streak in practice and during meets that would hardly dissipate during his prolific Razorback career.

Continuing what was fast becoming a Razorback tradition, most of the team trained hard over the Christmas holidays to gain whatever edge they could on their competition. Graham Hood was no different. He came back to Fayetteville a week early along with many of his teammates and did not back off at all during his brief time in Canada visiting family.

"I called John and told him I tried to pull off an indoor workout but it didn't happen," remembered Hood. "It was 8 x 800 meters with two minutes' rest. I had mistakenly read 2:03 on the sheet, so I went 2:03, 2:03, 2:03, 2:03, 2:03, and then by the sixth one, I started falling off, and the seventh one I completely fell off and had to stop. I called him up thinking he might not be happy and he just laughed. He said he had written 2:08."

As they often did, the Hogs set a high standard at their home meet on January 20, 1995, with automatic marks before most teams had even put their pants on to start the season. Graham Hood opened up with a massive personal best of 7:56.57 in the 3,000 meter, while Jerome Romain triple-jumped 54 feet, 1 inch and Ray Doakes high-jumped 7-4. Seven days later Hood popped a 3:56.79 mile on the same track. Amazingly, all of it before the month of January had even ended.

"My philosophy on peaking was to use every meet as a preparation for nationals," said McDonnell. "A distance runner would get the qualifier early and then not race much other than relays. A jumper might take six steps instead of eight so that they were winning without putting everything into it. You want to have that little extra when you need it."

After Hood led Arkansas to a fifty-five point trouncing of Tennessee at the SEC meet through wins in the mile, 3,000 meter, and distance medley relay, it was fair to wonder whether anyone could beat him in the mile, given his natural speed and aerobic strength. The only problem with that theory was that there were people up in Michigan asking the same questions about Kevin Sullivan of the University of Michigan, who ran an impressive 3:56 early in the season on an oversized track, and Paul McMullen of Eastern Michigan, who put up a nearly equally prolific time of 3:57.54. On March 11, 1995, the stage was set for a titanic showdown between the three milers at the 1995 NCAA Indoor Championships at the RCA Dome in Indianapolis.

Having been competitors since their high-school days in southern Ontario, Hood and Sullivan's rivalry only intensified in college as Sullivan avenged a loss at the 1994 NCAA outdoor meet with a surprising win at the Canadian Championships in Victoria that same summer.

"[Sullivan] and Hood didn't get on too good," admitted McDonnell. "They weren't the best of friends. You know how it is with countrymen sometimes competing with one another."

It was anyone's guess as to which Canadian was going to win the NCAA title this time, but when Paul McMullen sprinted off with six-hundred meters remaining in the slow-paced race, there existed the very real possibility that it might not be either one of them.

Hood passed a fading McMullen before the final bell and still had ten meters on Sullivan, who patiently bided his time before making a strong move past McMullen on the backstretch. By the final curve Sullivan had caught Hood and the two runners ran stride for stride down the final straightaway. With ten meters remaining, Sullivan inched ahead by a margin of 3:55.33 to 3:55.70—a meet-record time made even more impressive by the fact it was negative split off a 2:03 half-mile.

The theatrics were hardly confined to the mile. Nine years following Joe Falcon's dramatic fall in the final straightaway at the NCAA Cross Country Championships, Jason Bunston proved that even the most determined person could overcome such a calamity if it happened early enough in the race. After Jim Svenoy of UTEP tripped and fell in the midst of a dawdling pack bunched together off a slow pace, Bunston crashed into the track on top of him.

"The UTEP guy walked off, but Jason got up and caught the pack and took the lead and won it," remembered McDonnell. "It was all about the team concept and a brilliant performance because that's not easy to do. Usually a toss like that shakes you up a little bit."

Coming as it did following a month of sickness for Bunston and a loss to teammate Graham Hood in the very same event at the SEC Championships two weeks earlier, the win was even more impressive.

In the 5,000 meter, Godfrey Siamusiye handled everything and everyone other than a late surge by Providence's Mark Carroll, who would run 13:05 for 5,000 meters the following summer. With more points in the sprints and jumps, Arkansas won its collegiate-record twelfth indoor national championship in a row.[7]

Tied with Tennessee for second place was a small, suburban Virginia commuter school, George Mason. Only ten years after unleashing Abdi Bile on the collegiate scene, George Mason head coach John Cook had a group of middle-distance stars needing only to overcome the nerves of their first exposure to national-championship contention before they might reasonably be expected to win one of their own.

"I thought we could win a national championship one day if we really put it together," said Cook. "You kind of know when the chemistry comes together, and we had some really good kids."

Part of the chemistry responsible for Arkansas's sustained run of excellence was the readiness of Razorback athletes to step up when others had fallen by the wayside. With Graham Hood nursing an injured Achilles heading into the outdoor conference and national championships, Godfrey Siamusiye took that mantra to heart. When he learned that Tennessee appeared capable of beating Arkansas at the conference championship Siamusiye begged McDonnell to let him triple.

"He tried to talk me out of it," remembered Siamusiye. "It was my idea because I looked around and knew we didn't have the numbers, and other schools were catching up, like Tennessee with their vaulters and Florida with their sprinters. We had a finite amount of people with experience, and we couldn't rely on them, especially in the 800 meter and 1,500 meter. It was too close to call so I talked him into it."

Following a 29:27.76 win over 10,000 meters and an 8:45.58 steeplechase victory, the brutal Alabama heat had taken its toll on the Zambian. With Arkansas still behind Tennessee in the points standings headed into the 5,000 meter, there was never an option in Godfrey's mind as to what needed to be done.

"After the steeplechase I paid for it," said Siamusiye. "I was so dehydrated, but I was okay for the 5,000 meter."

Siamusiye's tactical victory in the 5,000 meter led an Arkansas onslaught that won the meet.[8]

It was only a foreshadowing of Godfrey Siamusiye's equally impressive double at the NCAA Outdoor Championships in Tennessee two weeks later. Against a potent UCLA squad, every point was needed. Siamusiye remarkably doubled back from a 10,000 meter victory to edge Meb Keflezighi of UCLA in the 5,000 meter along with teammate Jason Bunston.[9]

Godfrey's prolific performance became especially important after McDonnell made the decision to hold out Graham Hood in the final after the Canadian aggravated his Achilles in the qualifying rounds.

"I had to pull him," said McDonnell. "[Graham] was crying because he was a senior, but I told him I could never forgive myself if I ended his career. Believe me we would have loved to have him in there, but it wasn't worth the risk. He was still in good shape because it had only recently started hurting him."

Though other milers such as Michael Morin had stepped up to fill the void, McDonnell had sacrificed badly needed points from Hood in the 1,500 meter. As John Godina and the rest of Art Venagas's UCLA throwers racked up point after point, Arkansas responded with Jerome Romain in the triple jump and the first 800-meter national title in school history from Brandon Rock. The meet still hung in the balance.

With a national championship on the line, John's focus turned to the high jump where Ray Doakes was seeking his first national title in his final college season and trying to clear a bar late in the competition.

"He came over to me and said, 'Kid, do you want to be a national champ? You didn't think it was going to be easy did you?' I said, 'I guess not,'" remembered Doakes. "He said if I jumped that height, we would be national champions and win the meet. He turned around and walked back and folded his arms, and I remember thinking to myself, 'There is no way I'm not going to make that height. No way.' I could not do that to John McDonnell or the program. I made it and everybody was happy."

Doakes came through with a clutch clearance of 7 feet, 4½ inches to win his first national title in the high jump and push Arkansas past UCLA for its fourth consecutive NCAA outdoor championship.

John barely had time to digest the victory when he was approached by Jeremy Foley, the athletic director at the University of Florida, regarding the coaching vacancy in Gainesville.

"He was a real nice man and knew a little about my background so he said if you want a cattle ranch we have lots of them down here in Florida," said McDonnell. "I never pursued it seriously. I told him it was an honor, but I'll stay where I am, and he understood that."

When the aggressive Florida athletic director realized his efforts with McDonnell would be fruitless, he focused his attention one notch down the Southeastern Conference food chain.

"[Foley] talked to John first and then he called me next," remembered Doug Brown. "The opportunity to go to Florida and play golf with [football coach] Steve Spurrier was just too much. In all seriousness, I knew Florida had the capability of being a solid program, and after the first year there, we moved up to second and beat Tennessee."

Where Doug Brown was never able to guide the Gators was into first place at either the conference or national championship. Since 1991, all roads had led through Fayetteville, and none of them had been kind to him. The task certainly wasn't about to become any easier in the near future.

Starting with Adam Dailey, a 9:04 two-miler from Austin, Texas, McDonnell continued his string of success with kids from central Texas.

"He was a tough kid and won the state cross-country meet in Texas with those heavy thighs on him," remembered McDonnell. "You'd never think it by looking at him and you wonder how does he do it? He ended up having a fantastic career and senior season here."

From Elora, Ontario, came Matt Kerr, another Canadian athlete with a 3:43 1,500 meter and 8:20 3,000 meter to his name along with a strong cross-country pedigree. Few athletes who ended up as successful as Kerr took as long to mentally and physically adjust to training at Arkansas.

"Kerr didn't like it here at first, and I felt really upset about that," said Jason Bunston. "We tried to close ranks around him because it was a testosterone-heavy program and a success-heavy program, and when you are far from the top of the totem pole, it can be reinforcing until you turn it around."

It would be nearly two years and one major confrontation with Coach McDonnell before the sun came out on Matt Kerr's career in Fayetteville.

For Seneca Lassiter, who roomed with Kerr during their freshman year, success as a Razorback came much earlier. Given Lassiter's East Coast roots in Williamsburg, Virginia, and lack of knowledge of the Arkansas program, he nearly made his mind up about college before even visiting Fayetteville.

"I really liked the facilities at Tennessee, and Coach Brown came down and spoke to my mom," said Lassiter. "I came from a household where I didn't have a father in the home, and he assured me he would take care of me. The next year he ended up at Florida, which was kind of funny."

After being bombarded by coaches from all over the country, Lassiter remembers one call distinctly standing out from the rest.

"Coach McDonnell called me on the phone, and with his accent I could barely understand him, and the phone connection wasn't great," remembers Lassiter. "He said, 'If you want to come to Arkansas, great; if not I wish you the best.' I was kind of like, 'Man, no college coach has told me that.' They were usually saying you need to come here, and you will do this, and you will do that but Coach McDonnell was like, 'We'd love to have you but if not, oh well, I wish you the best.' It wasn't cocky, it was just his personality. I wasn't going to Arkansas at that point anyway."

After Lassiter watched Graham Hood win the Wannamaker Mile before he ran in the high-school mile at the Millrose Games in New York City, he spoke with McDonnell following his own race and put Arkansas back on his list. Though he had agreed to visit Arkansas based on its athletic success, Seneca arrived still carrying the old stereotypes of the state that had been popularized for generations.

"It just goes to show you how little I knew about Arkansas," admitted Lassiter. "When I got here, I wasn't so impressed with Fayetteville and the facilities at the time, but once I got to know Coach McDonnell as a person, everything changed. I got to know about the history of the program, the national championships, the Olympians, all of the All-Americans and sub-four-minute milers, which was my event. Once I learned all of that, it was a no-brainer."

Then came the clincher.

"His wife brought this box, and the next thing she opened this box filled with nothing but rings, and Coach McDonnell said, 'Kid, if you come here, I guarantee you will get some of your own.' I was like where do I sign? He told me he wanted to do it the right way and come to Virginia. Coach McDonnell hates to fly, but he flew to Virginia on the way to Penn Relays and met my mother before I signed my letter of intent."

Coming from a twenty-five mile-per-week background, Lassiter was initially leery of Arkansas because of the negative comments of other coaches about how hard the Razorbacks trained. John assured Seneca he wouldn't run higher than forty-five miles per week during his first year, but it was the cocksure freshman who soon realized he needed a higher training volume to achieve the success he wanted.

"The first day it was so hot, so Coach McDonnell said to run six miles up in the trails. I made it four miles and walked down to the training room. I thought I was going to faint," remembered Lassiter. "So I am in the training room, and Coach McDonnell says, 'You are not going to run cross country.' I was thinking to myself, these guys in cross country, I am eventually going to have to face them in track. So I said, 'I want to be in the top-seven.' Everybody must have thought this kid is cocky. He's an 800-meter runner, and he thinks he can come out and beat us at our distance? That was just the mentality I had."

The next day, Lassiter was back in Coach McDonnell's office.

"He said, 'I want to run more than forty-five miles per week. I can run with those guys,'" remembered McDonnell. "I said, 'Seneca, I don't want you hurt.' He was insistent, and we agreed to move him up gradually to seventy miles, and boy, was he ever dynamite."

The Razorbacks looked like they could use all of the help they could get. With Jason Bunston only having outdoor eligibility, Arkansas was heavily reliant on Godfrey Siamusiye and a group of unproven, untested, underclassmen to carry the load. At the Cowboy Jamboree on September 30, 1995, Godfrey finished a full 1:26 ahead of his nearest teammate and nearly two minutes ahead of Arkansas's fifth runner—a chasm so wide that Oklahoma State was able to come up the middle and beat them.

"Coach wasn't happy about that," remembered Godfrey. "He knew that when we went to nationals, any team could put five runners in between us. He took the time to explain the logic, what we were going to accomplish and how we were going to do it."

Though Ryan Wilson finished only a minute behind Godfrey at the Chile Pepper Cross Country Festival two weeks later, fifth runner Phil Price still found himself two full minutes behind, which was enough for Oklahoma State to edge Arkansas again. The losses were not sitting well.

McDonnell met with his young team to remind them that all was lost without individual and collective pride to carry the day.

"Without pride you have nothing!" he would passionately exhort them in the locker room.

"At the beginning he was hardest on us," remembered Kaley. "He would look at the spread between Godfrey and us and get upset. He would say, 'You guys are running so bad, a high-school team could beat you!'"

What the talks did was elicit a response from his young Razorback team at the SEC Championships, where Godfrey cruised to a victory and was followed seventeen seconds later by Ryan Wilson, and less than a minute later by Sean Kaley, Phillip Price, Adam Dailey, and Matt Kerr to edge Tennessee, 32–58. Though John had prodded his young pack to run closer to Godfrey, restraining his top dog from running away from the rest of them was proving to be a challenge in itself.

"Back then the Teva sandals wrapped around the ankle were just starting to get popular," remembered Danny Green. "One day Godfrey forgot his running shoes and ran a hard eight-miler in thirty-eight minutes on the trails in a pair of sandals. John didn't see it until after and was so mad because Godfrey could have hurt his foot or Achilles, but he had run barefoot plenty of times so it wasn't a big deal."

Aside from controlling Godfrey's training, McDonnell still had to make his leader understand the importance of helping his teammates.

"The way he communicated with us was good," said Godfrey. "At the golf course we were doing mile repeats up the hill, and he wanted us to run no quicker than 4:27, but we did go faster and the group was still there so that was okay. On the next one, Reuben [Reina] and I ran 4:19, and people were dropping, and he wasn't too happy. The next one I didn't want Reuben to beat me, so I ran 4:17, and Coach called me out on the center of the field and wasn't happy. I remember that well."

Realizing he had to do more than simply run fast to be a leader, Godfrey responded to the challenge by mentoring his young teammates in his soft-spoken way.

"I found out later when they all told me that Godfrey would come around during the night and talk to them," remembered McDonnell. "He'd say, 'When I was at Blinn, we never lost a meet, and we're not going to start now because Arkansas doesn't lose either.' He was a leader behind the scenes, and I had no idea he was doing it. He was such a nice guy."

As Seneca Lassiter unexpectedly found himself battling for the seventh spot on the team, the impressionable freshman soaked up everything he could from Godfrey.

"We roomed together at meets, and I learned a lot because I saw his work ethic and saw how he executed a move in races," said Lassiter. "The intensity he brought in practice and the positive attitude he had was a great thing for a young guy like myself. I was the low man on the totem pole, and I got to learn from the best."

Even on easy runs, which were easier for some than others, the cheerful Siamusiye was always quick to offer an encouraging word of praise.

"One time I tried to keep up with Godfrey on a Tuesday in the trails, and he kept talking to me while we were doing 5:10 pace," remembered Kaley. "He would say, 'Come on man, you're doing great!' And I'm thinking, 'No, I'm not!' He was our spiritual leader and captain and had a lot of good advice."

John often alternated between miles or two-mile repeats and anywhere from twelve to twenty 400-meter repeats up and down Razorback hill.

"One of the secrets was we didn't work out much," said Kaley. "We would do two workouts per week but really wouldn't start until late September. Before that we'd tempo and go behind the golf course for ten miles and he'd say, 'Guys, don't go hard,' but John knew we were going to go hard. We would go faster than he wanted, and to his credit, he would be the one holding us back most of the time. He sometimes would stop a workout early. The genius of his program was his motivational ability and competitiveness of all of the athletes in one place."

Bringing a young team short on experience to Iowa State for the 1995 NCAA Cross Country Championships, where Arkansas sought to upend the defending national champions on their home course, McDonnell could use all the help he could get.

"The first mile was downhill and then when you turned around at two miles you started climbing hills, so I said you have to get out," remembered McDonnell. "Alberto Salazar was the guest speaker at the coach's meeting the night before. Someone asked him what he would do if he ran the course. He said, 'I'd go out nice and steady.' So I rubbed my hands together and said, 'Perfect.' Nice and steady was the reverse of how you should run that course. Alberto was a great runner but didn't have much leg turnover, so that's how he probably would have run it. He was someone people really listened to, so that advice helped us."

In the hotel the night before the meet, John reiterated the message to the team.

"It's downhill to start so take advantage of it," remembered McDonnell. "You don't have to exert any energy to get up to the front. Just lift your legs, and they will follow themselves going down the hill."

After the group talk, John came around to each athlete individually. Though Godfrey and Wilson were expected to run at the front, John instructed Kaley to sit in fiftieth and pick people off as he could.

"That made me feel good because he individualized it for each of us," said Kaley. "It was all instinct with John. There was no science behind it. He had better instincts than anyone and would modulate it depending on who it was."

With his pack of Razorbacks in position for the team victory, John knew much would depend on Godfrey Siamusiye, who had to contend with Mark Carroll of Providence College, a 13:05 5,000-meter runner and the presumptive favorite entering the meet.

"Coach looked at me in the eye in the hotel in the morning and said, 'You're going to win, and if you win, we'll win as a team too,'" remembered Godfrey.

After attacking the first mile as McDonnell had instructed, Godfrey threw everything at Carroll to shake him, even setting his watch to beep every two minutes to remind himself to throw in a small surge.

"Godfrey was the best cross-country runner I have ever seen," said Ryan Wilson. "Every turn, corner, hill, and dip he cleared time on you. He had an innate ability to run courses better than anyone else. He killed runners on the country that would beat him on the track."

With Siamusiye and Carroll still running stride for stride at four miles, the Zambian made a devastating move to finish the Irishman off.

"I had spoken to John before, and we reckoned if I took a chance and ran the last two miles quick, maybe at 4:30 to 4:40 for a mile at that point, I would break away," said Godfrey. "So we trained that way. I went as hard as I could for probably four minutes, and I looked back and I had a one-hundred-meter lead, and I realized nobody would catch me. Everyone was getting tired and it was cold too."

Godfrey won his first NCAA cross-country championship by an incredible thirty-six seconds ahead of Carroll. With Ryan Wilson finishing in fifth and the others in the top-fifty, the Razorbacks unexpectedly won their fifth NCAA cross-country championship in six years by edging Ron Mann's Northern Arizona team and their early season nemesis from Oklahoma State by fifty points.[10]

"We had a lot of McDonald's that season but ate at Cracker Barrel after NCAAs!" said Wilson.

The season had been a revelation not just to the entire country after Arkansas won another national championship with a team of mostly underclassmen, but it was an eye-opening lesson for McDonnell twenty-three years and twenty-five national championships into his coaching career.

"Godfrey was running away from guys because we had such a young team and he was head and shoulders above them," said John. "Some of our guys I'd tell them to stay with him for eight miles [on easy days] instead of [running] ten [miles] and, boy, that team won NCAAs despite being so young. I'm thinking, 'Maybe less miles is better,' so it was all experimental."

Although the decision to limit the team's mileage generally to under eighty miles per week was driven by the goal of keeping Godfrey and the young underclassmen healthy after the disaster of the previous fall, keeping the ambitious Godfrey controlled in training over the Christmas holidays was more difficult.

"I wanted to run under 13:30 [5,000 meter] so bad. I had looked on the record books and saw Falcon and O'Mara, and I wanted to get into that group," said Godfrey. "It was my fault. I was doing some hill climbing and took the wrong hill and really inflamed my Achilles. I wasn't in the boot, but it was really sore. I had trouble walking to class. That took a long time. I was in the pool for a while. The week before [indoor] conference was the first time I ran."

It was an ominous sign for the chances of Arkansas extending its fifteen-year conference indoor-championship winning streak. Though Ryan Wilson was in the best shape of his life and Godfrey Siamusiye had returned in time for the SEC meet, the University of Tennessee Volunteers were firing on all cylinders.

Not since 1980 had the Razorbacks been sent home from an indoor conference championship empty-handed but the University of Tennessee Volunteers and new head coach Bill Webb did exactly that, riding pole vaulter Lawrence Johnson, and others to the 1996 SEC Indoor Championships.[11]

"There were a few of them that didn't run well for us, and it was just one of those meets," said McDonnell. "Tennessee was pumped out of their minds. We just didn't do what we needed."

The horizon heading into the 1996 NCAA Indoor Championships looked equally foreboding. Twelve indoor national championships in a row made the idea of anyone other than Arkansas winning the meet unfathomable. After finishing second the previous season, George Mason coach John Cook pulled out all of the stops this time. He took his talented group of middle-distance stars to train at altitude in Albuquerque, New Mexico, for six weeks over the Christmas holidays.[12] By March, Cook brought a team to the NCAA Championships with the physical preparation and now the experience to seal the deal.

"The year before they were supposed to beat us and we had won," remembered McDonnell. "They brought the same guys back and had four of them under 1:47 in the 800 meter."

Yet the Razorbacks were hardly willing to go quietly into the night. Robert Howard won his first national championship in the triple jump, while Ryan Wilson kicked from 500 meters out to beat Adam Goucher of Colorado for the victory in the 3,000 meter.

"The announcer said I had a gap on the field with about two laps to go so I decided to go all out," Wilson told the media after the win in 7:51.66. "I tried to relax but it was difficult, and I tied up a little bit on the last hundred meters."[13]

Arkansas's success ended there. As remarkable as it was that Godfrey Siamusiye was even contending for a national title under the circumstances, he was nonetheless unable to overcome two months of missed training and finished second in the 5,000 meter behind Jason Casiano of Wisconsin.

"Godfrey made a tactical error," said McDonnell. "Even though he hadn't been running more than a few weeks, I told him not to worry about missed training because he was better. Well, that kid jumped him, and Godfrey let him go and then came like crazy at the end and just missed him at the line."

With the meet in the palm of their hands, George Mason nearly began to wilt under the national-championship pressure. Barry Douglas false started in the 60 meter final, while miler Ibrahim Aden fell and did not finish a race that was won by his George Mason teammate, Julius Achon.

"Cook came around to me, and I could tell he was sort of nervous," remembered McDonnell. "He was like, 'How do you do this shit every year?'"

"I think our kids were a little intimidated, and we almost pissed it away quite frankly," said John Cook. "Of all the years I couldn't get a sprinter at George Mason, and the son of a bitch false starts in the final. Then our miler gets knocked off the track. We should have been a little more steadfast, but we weren't used to being an NCAA team. Because Arkansas was Arkansas, I think our kids were a little intimidated and frankly so was our coaching staff, including me."

After scoring big points in the 400 meter, 800 meter, mile, 4 x 400 meter, and distance medley relay, George Mason scored 38 points to edge Nebraska by seven points for its first and only national championship.

"I am so elated. This is the pinnacle of my 27 years in coaching," Cook told the media. "We have a great program and great kids. There is no way I could live through twelve of these. [Arkansas's streak of twelve in a row] will never happen again."[14]

Once George Mason hoisted the NCAA indoor championship trophy for the first time in school history, it finally dawned on Cook the magnitude of the national championship streak his team had ended.

"Right then I almost had compassion for John because I knew that streak would never happen again," remembered Cook. "With another coach it might have been different, but with John he had always been such a gentleman, and it wasn't acrimonious."

As the elation from the win sunk in for Cook, so too did the realization that it would be hard to ever catch lightning in a bottle again at the commuter school in Fairfax, Virginia.

"I kind of got depressed afterwards because I had put so much into it, and I kind of knew this was never going to happen again," said Cook. "I remember the president [of George Mason] was happy but he said, 'Make sure you don't get us into trouble.' You got so good at George Mason that they thought you did something wrong."

Though George Mason also ended Arkansas's five year winning streak in the distance medley relay at Penn Relays and later contended for the NCAA outdoor championship that same spring, Cook was on the verge of retiring from collegiate coaching to work with professional athletes. In the process, he had gained an immense amount of appreciation for the grind McDonnell had gone through year after year, given the toll that even one national championship had taken on him.

"What John did was absolutely unimaginable," said Cook. "I told him I would never want to go through what you must have gone through all of those years. I almost lost my family and I had gotten depressed. It was the hardest damn thing you can imagine. I would have died. What Arkansas had in John was special and it will never happen again."

For his part, McDonnell felt a mixture of disappointment—and relief—that the longest national-championship winning streak in major American collegiate sports history had finally ended.

"It was tough dealing with defeat after so many victories," admitted McDonnell, "but it was also good because I finally started breathing again."

Though McDonnell never welcomed defeat, one of the many factors in his success was his ability to accept and quickly move on from whatever setbacks had beset him or the program. Less than five weeks later, he took Ryan Wilson out to the Mt. San Antonio College (Mt. SAC) Invitational in Walnut, California, where the sophomore beat a field full of Olympians and national champions in the 5,000 meter and in the process set an astounding twenty-five second personal best of 13:28 in front of his friends and family.

"I remember coming off the last turn, and I thought John was going to lose his head, he was jumping up and down," remembered Wilson. "Godfrey, Reuben, and Bunston were behind me, and I just gassed it. Reuben [Reina] passed by me at the bell and then I went by him. At that stage, I was clearing away from everybody. I had confidence issues in whether I could get something done, not whether I could do it, but whether I could complete it. That was a big breakthrough for me."

The year of the Atlanta Olympics, Wilson's time was also a U.S. Olympic Trials qualifier. Rather than allow his athlete's expectations to balloon out of control, McDonnell helped Wilson understand the confluence of factors leading to the massive personal best would be difficult to replicate for some time. Though Wilson did make another improvement two years later, his performance at the same meet the following season could not be defined as anything except disappointing. As always, John managed his young athlete's psyche with tremendous aplomb.

"One of his master cards in coaching was he knew when to get in your face and when to back off," said Wilson. "He had gotten in my face plenty of times after bad races, but when I ran 13:50 the next year at Mt. SAC, he said, "That went so poorly, we're not going to even talk about it." He knew when to do that and how to treat a person. He knew when to do it and with who. I could take a lashing and react to it, but other athletes could not."

That same spring, John got a taste of how the success of the Arkansas program had spread all over the world as athletes from countries he had never even recruited began calling him unsolicited. One day he arrived in his office at the Bud Walton Area at 8:00 a.m. and received an unexpected phone call from an athlete from Melbourne, Australia, of all places.

"This kid with an Australian accent was on the other end," remembered John. "He said, 'Is this Coach McDonnell?' 'Yes,' I said. 'This is Michael Power from Australia.' He started telling me about what attracted him to Arkansas, which believe it or not was the Penn Relays. He said, 'Boy that must be really fun' because he got *Track and Field News*. I said, 'Oh, it is.' So I asked him what times he had run. He said 3:58, and I was like, 'For the mile?' He said, 'Yeah, I was third at World Juniors.' I had to put my hand on the phone and ask Danny [Green] to go look it up. Three or four calls later, and he was coming to Arkansas. There were no ifs, ands, or buts about it."

Though Power was a few years from running at an Olympic level as he took some time to adjust to both the training and the vagaries of the college lifestyle, other distance athletes such as Niall Bruton [Ireland, 1,500 meter] and Godfrey Siamusiye [Zambia, steeplechase] had already been selected for the 1996 Games. For Jason Bunston the process of selection by Canada would prove to be much more arduous.

Though he had run 7:45 for 3,000 meters indoors and had done workouts (such as 5 x 1,000 meters in 2:30–2:32 with 90 seconds recovery) which seemed to indicate he was on track for a 5,000-meter Olympic qualifying time during his final collegiate season, Bunston's training fell behind schedule after he ran for Canada at the World Cross Country Championships at South Africa and contracted salmonella poisoning.

"At Mt. SAC I ran 13:42 [5,000 meter] which was a personal best, but I was so weak," said Bunston. "That was probably my only chance to get the Olympic qualifier [during the college season]. So Athletics Canada knew I had a long season, and my next opportunity to run a fast 5,000 meter was going to be in the summer."

Before that saga could unfold, the Razorbacks had to attend to the collegiate season. They turned the tables on Tennessee at the outdoor SEC Championships—thanks to another triple from the selfless Godfrey Siamusiye in the 10,000 meter, 5,000 meter, and 3,000 meter steeplechase—before travelling to Eugene, Oregon, for the 1996 NCAA Outdoor Championships attempting to do the very same thing to George Mason.

Their efforts hardly got off to a flying start. Four Arkansas underclassmen—Ryan Wilson, Seneca Lassiter, Matt Kerr, and Phil Price—had qualified for the 1,500 meter and not one of them made the final.

"We didn't know what to expect afterwards," remembered Matt Kerr. "[John] came up to us in a nonchalant way and told us to meet him at the track the next morning. He didn't say he was upset. He was pretty sly and had a tiny grin on his face. You didn't know if he was serious or joking and didn't want to find out. We didn't know what to expect."

The next morning all four of them arrived at a local track still unsure of what he had in mind.

"He had us do ten 400s with not much rest, and we averaged about fifty-seven for all of them," said Kerr. "He said, 'We aren't finding anything out we didn't already know. Go enjoy the summer.' It was his way of proving a point to us."

After an abundance of points in the jumps, led by a triple-jump victory from Robert Howard, all eyes were on the 10,000 meter. It seemed to be a very good possibility that Arkansas would score eighteen points in the event with two men, Jason Bunston and Godfrey Siamusiye, both favored to win the event. The suspense over which man would win kept the Hayward Field crowd enraptured for twenty-five laps.

McDonnell wisely hedged his bets. With George Mason breathing down Arkansas's neck, John gave Jason the strategy to beat Godfrey and vice versa. After years of hammering each other on the trails and behind the Razorback Golf Course, Jason Bunston and Godfrey Siamusiye were set for one of the most exciting 10,000 meter races in NCAA championship history in the final track meet of their college careers.

Following McDonnell's instructions not to race each other until they had beaten everyone else, both of them alternated laps until they had dropped James Menon of Wisconsin with less than one mile remaining. When Bunston took off after leading for one lap, the race was suddenly on in full swing.

"They absolutely sprinted the last 500 meters, and it was toe to toe," remembered McDonnell. "Jason almost won it, but Godfrey barely got him coming up the finish."

After just under twenty-nine minutes of back-and-forth racing, only a tenth of a second separated the two men. Godfrey had won in 28:56.39, while Jason finished second in 28:56.50.

"It was one of the greatest races ever," said Phil Price, who was watching from the historic Hayward Field grandstand. "Once they dropped the Wisconsin guy, they just went at it. Jason passed Godfrey, and then Godfrey found another gear from who knows where and inched ahead of him."

"They both wanted to win but were great teammates," said McDonnell. "When they finished, it was such a great race over the last mile that the fans [at Hayward Field] got up and said, 'Get them out onto the track!' At the time nobody was allowed by the NCAA to run the lap of honor, but the Eugene crowd insisted on it. They respected what they had seen and were on their feet the entire time the boys jogged the lap. I said to myself, 'These are real track fans. This is what the rest of America is missing out.'"

While Arkansas was in control of the meet, winning it was far from a foregone conclusion. George Mason was pulling out all of the stops. Four of Cook's runners had qualified for the final of the 800 meter, while Julius Achon and Ibrahim Aden doubled back in the 1,500 meter. That gambit did not work out as Achon and Aden faded to third and ninth in the 1,500 meter, while the four George Mason athletes scored only twelve points in the 800 meter. Once Godfrey Siamusiye and Jason Bunston doubled back to finish behind Alan Culpepper of Colorado in the 5,000 meter, the meet was over.

"We doubled people and probably could have beaten them if we were deeper, but our guys ran their asses off," said John Cook. "Indoors you can win with a few athletes and play some relay games and some distance medley games. Outdoors you have to have a real team."

Having seen his athletes sacrifice themselves to try and pull off the outdoor national championship, Cook was amazed at McDonnell's ability to do it year after year.

"He was really close to his kids," said Cook. "You could tell there was a special relationship there. John was not a rah-rah guy, but his kids would line up for him and go to war. I think they would have jumped off a damn bridge for him if that's what it took to win."

Though McDonnell certainly had reason to enjoy some rest and relaxation after Arkansas won its fifth consecutive NCAA outdoor track-and-field championship, which marked the most undisputed outdoor national championships in a row since Southern California won nine in a row during the 1930s, he had little opportunity to sit back and put his feet up with the Olympics coming to Atlanta that summer.

In the triple jump, the Razorbacks had several current and former athletes with strong prospects of medaling at the Games, which supported the argument that the best jumps group in the world trained in Fayetteville all the more convincing. There was of course the defending Olympic triple-jump champion, Mike Conley, who was still as instrumental as ever in the continued success of the Arkansas jumps program by assisting Dick Booth and continuing to train as a professional athlete in Fayetteville. Along with the indoor and outdoor NCAA champion, Robert Howard, both men represented the United States in the triple jump, while Jerome Romain represented Dominica and Brian Wellman jumped for Bermuda.

With his career winding down, Conley still finished only four centimeters out of another medal by placing fourth in 17.40 meters (57 feet, 1 inch). Wellman was right behind him in sixth in 16.95 meters (55-7) while Romain was twelfth in 16.80 meters (55-1). The youngest athlete of them all, Robert Howard, placed eighth in 16.90 meters (55-5) and appeared to have his best days ahead of him.

Other Razorback jumpers had not been nearly as fortunate. Erick Walder, who had set a collegiate long-jump record during a prolific career that saw him win ten individual NCAA titles and three world-championship medals found himself snake-bitten when it came to qualifying for a U.S. Olympic team. A brilliant career for Walder ended several years later with everything but an Olympic qualification.

"I had never seen such a talented athlete [as Walder] and I trained with Mike [Conley], but he would have said the same thing," said Ray Doakes. "[Erick] was the most talented. The guy had 4.2 [40 meter] speed, a 45-inch vertical. The first two Olympic Trials he was trying to do the triple and long jump which is very difficult to do and that's how he got hurt. In 1996 he hyper-extended his knee in the triple jump and then came back and still jumped 27 feet in the long jump landing on his feet. That's what good shape he was in. The team was made with a 27 feet, 5 inch jump and he did that standing up with a bent knee."

In the high jump, Ray Doakes certainly had every reason to believe he too could contend for medal at the Olympic Games only one year after winning the NCAA high-jump title and occasionally clearing 7 feet, 9 inches in practice. As one who thrived on competition, Doakes usually brought something extra in major meets but a torn bursa sac in the weeks leading into the U.S. Olympic Trials made it hard to do anything.

"I couldn't run full speed [at the trial] so I went from a half approach and was in such condition that I still ended up fourth," said Doakes. "In the United States, it's hard. Other countries take their best athletes to the Games, but in the United States you have to go through the Trials whether it's hot or cold and you're injured or healthy. I still remember [former University of Houston coach] Tom Tellez put out the quote, 'I just saw the best high jumper in the world not make the team because he was hurt.'"

In the 800 meter, Brandon Rock capped two years of remarkable progress since arriving in Fayetteville by making the U.S. Olympic team but nearly collapsed immediately after doing so.

"He almost had a seizure, and when he finished the race, he turned and walked the wrong direction until an official grabbed him," said McDonnell. "He told me later he could hear all of this noise but didn't know where he was. About forty-five minutes later I talked to a doctor, and he told me his blood pressure went up to such a point that he nearly had a stroke. It was a kidney problem. He made the team and ran the Olympics [running 1:48.47 in the preliminaries] but was never the same again."

In the most unbelievable story of all, Calvin Davis won an Olympic bronze medal for the United States in the 400-meter hurdles. Despite having won three NCAA titles in the 400 meter, Calvin Davis was advised by the Arkansas coaches that he lacked the natural leg speed to compete successfully on the international level.

"He had never broken 45 seconds and wasn't that talented but was such a fierce competitor and just knew how to win. [Steve] Silvey and I talked to him and said 'Maybe you should move up to the 800 meter or try the intermediate hurdles,'" said McDonnell. "I'll never forget it he looked at us and said, 'I think I'll run the hurdles because it's only one lap.' I'm not kidding. That was his rationale, and he won a bronze medal. I don't think there was ever a hurdler who won an Olympic medal who practiced a shorter time over the hurdles."

In the distance events, Godfrey Siamusiye finished tenth in the heats of the 3,000-meter steeplechase for Zambia, while Niall Bruton made the semifinals of the 1,500 meter for Ireland. Graham Hood ran for Canada but did not finish the first round of the 1,500 meter.

One man who did not make the team at all despite running the Olympic qualifying time and setting a Canadian record in the 5,000 meter was Jason Bunston. Following the emotion of his effort at the NCAA Outdoor Championships, Bunston reloaded for a few weeks in order to put himself in position to contest the Canadian Olympic Trials, make one final attempt at the Olympic standard in Europe, and presumably have something worthwhile left in the tank for the Olympics if he was selected.

"I tried to run the standard at [Canadian] nationals, so I took the lead and ended up getting beat by Dave Reid and Ian Carswell, but we were all top three," said Bunston. "I ended up going to Europe [on July 6 after the Trials] and ran 13:22.06, which was a Canadian record and Olympic standard."

"He called me up and was so excited," remembered McDonnell. "He said, 'Its past the deadline but we're going to appeal it.' So I wrote a letter and called people at Athletics Canada. I even went in to see [Frank] Broyles and told him the story and asked if we could pay his way and he said, 'Absolutely.' I'll never forget it. I called someone [with Athletics Canada] and he said, 'We have a process,' and I said, 'Yeah, but this is a young kid with a bright future and to get in this year there's no telling what he will do in 2000.'"

That "process" had shown extraordinary flexibility in allowing an equally qualified high-jump athlete named Charles LeFrancois to meet the Olympic selection criteria, which became part of the basis for a successful court injunction by Dave Reid to have his [but not Jason Bunston's] deadline extended to July 5, 1996. No such latitude was coming Bunston's way.

"After he broke the Canadian record, we petitioned and that was the damnedest conference call I ever had in my life," said Paul Poce of the Toronto Olympic Club. "Alex Gardiner was the executive director at the time, and we hadn't gotten two minutes into this conference call on whether they would accept Bunston or not when I realized that they were not going to budge. It was foregone conclusion. I don't know why we spent all of that time and all of that money on lawyers on a conference call. They had not one thought of putting Bunston on that team. I think that soured him."

Despite not having any qualms about sending more officials than athletes to the Olympics over the years,[15] Canada sent zero athletes in the 5,000 meter to an Olympics contested less than nine hundred miles from their border and left the Canadian record-holder sitting at home.

"Policywise all they had to do was send a letter to the Canadian Olympic Committee (COC) saying 'Due to prior commitments this athlete did not make standard until after the Trials,'" said Bunston. "Every time they say these are the guidelines the COC sends us, the reality is that the COC will take the athletes Athletics Canada sends them."

Though Bunston also weighed seeking a court injunction, he ultimately declined to do so in light of the untimely death of former Razorback All-American Dan Gabor on TWA Flight 800.

"That was the week before the Olympics," said Bunston. "He was one of the nicest guys and very well loved and one of the reasons I gave up the fight because perspective came back in."

While McDonnell was equally grieved by the loss of Gabor and attended a funeral ceremony in Fayetteville along with hundreds of others, he wanted to keep fighting.

"That's the one thing I disagreed with Jason about," said McDonnell. "I said, 'You have to fight this thing.' That's what had happened to me [being left off the Irish Olympic team in 1960]. They didn't send me the first time because of lack of funds, and I never got to go again because I was hurt the next time so I said, 'Why put it off?'"

Bunston ran at the international level for several years, but never was selected for an Olympic team.

Despite the fallout from the Olympic Park bombing in Atlanta, the Olympic Games themselves were well run but not as smoothly operated as they had been twelve years earlier in Los Angeles. Transportation within Atlanta became a nightmare and was one of many snafus which led the president of the International Olympic Committee, Juan Antonio Samaranch, to dub the Games "exceptional" rather than "the best ever" as he had done in every Olympiad prior.

Back in Fayetteville, it was a time of transition for the jumps group. Mike Conley retired from the sport to accept a position with United States Track and Field, while Ray Doakes briefly trained in Houston before calling it a career and returning to Fayetteville to work and raise a family.

"My dad was killed by his best friend the week before I was born," said Doakes, "so I said if I ever had kids, I would always be there for them."

Despite the departures of such prominent jumpers within a few years after the Olympiad, the jumps group continued to swell almost until it was ready to burst. Coming in the door was James Ballard, one of the most versatile jumpers in Razorback history (26 feet, 1 inch long jump, 52-8 triple jump, 7-5 high jump) who nonetheless experienced confidence issues working with some of the best jumpers in the world.

"Ballard's self esteem was not where I thought it could be," remembered Booth. "He never really believed in himself. You had all of these guys in there who thought they could win. We trained them to think they should win, and if you aren't winning, then don't stop and suck your thumb about it. Let's find out why not. What I would try and appeal to was the fact that you can only control what you put into it. You cannot stop others from jumping high."

When another 7-5 high jumper from Pine Bluff, Arkansas named Kenny Evans joined the program one season later, it became obvious enough that not everyone could win. Combined with the postcollegiate group that for a period of time included Mike Conley, Edrick Floreal, Gary Johnson, and Brian Wellman, there was a lot of attention to be paid to several high-performance athletes. By now, massaging egos and managing personalities had become one of McDonnell's strong points.

"At one point we had four guys over 7-5 in the high jump," remembered McDonnell. "We had another kid [Kevin Dotson] who jumped 7-4 and it was almost like we didn't need him. He ended up transferring to Missouri Southern and winning a Division II national championship for them."

The distance program certainly had its own abundance of talent that had remained in Fayetteville.

"The first time I showed up for practice, there is Frank O'Mara, Paul Donovan, Joe Falcon, Reuben Reina, Graham Hood, Niall Bruton, Frank Hanley, David Welsh. I could go on and on," said Phil Price. "Then you had guys coming from other programs. Earl Jones [of Eastern Michigan] came to train with John. It was phenomenal the amount of people who came, and they all wanted to know the secret. The key was hard work. Doing the basics and just keep on doing them and doing them."

That same fall, Todd Tressler, a 14:02 5,000-meter runner from Villanova, transferred to Arkansas to use his final season of eligibility and enroll in graduate school. Even with the unique personalities that sometimes found themselves in Fayetteville, McDonnell had certain appearance standards he did uphold.

"I had the Nirvana look my first year with the long hair, and Coach McDonnell came up to me on the first day and said, 'Hey kid, it looks like you need a haircut,'" remembered Price. "I also used to have an earring, but I would always take it out for practice. Well, one day I forgot and as soon as he saw me he said, 'Hey kid, what's that in your ear?' I was like, 'Oh crap!' I took it out and never wore it again."

Though there were always some athletes who lost their way, the discipline from McDonnell combined with the exposure to some of the best distance athletes in the world created an atmosphere and expectation of success for those who might otherwise have taken the wrong path.

"John didn't separate you from those guys," said Price. "He wanted you running with Joe Falcon and Frank O'Mara to see what they are doing. A lot of what his program was about, from Niall O'Shaughnessy all the way up, was kids with leg speed who hadn't necessarily trained at a high level in high school but wanted to work hard."

When the opportunity to sign another Canadian athlete with 1:51 800-meter speed and World Cross Country Championships experience arose, John's interest was piqued. Once he learned that Murray Link had been raised on a dairy farm in Winchester, Ontario, just outside of Ottawa, it became a natural fit.

"Oh, what a dream he was to coach," remembered McDonnell. "They called him the 'Missing Link.' He was just the nicest kid. He had a great career here and was a great team man. When someone wasn't pulling their weight, he'd go over and say something."

Link was also recruited by several major programs, but the opportunity to win a national title, along with his friendship with Sean Kaley of Ottawa and the connection he formed with McDonnell made his decision a no-brainer. The two farm boys had much in common.

"He came off a dairy farm up there, and I said I was raised on one too," said McDonnell. "He was a true gutsy, character all of the way. I remember him coming back after one summer and showed me pictures of all these barns he had painted red. They were big, high barns, and I said, 'Geez, that must have taken you all summer with the roller.' And he said, 'Yeah, it took all summer, but I did it with a brush.' I'm not kidding. His dad made him paint it with a brush, so he would be occupied the whole summer and not running around doing things he shouldn't be. His parents were great and used to come down to races."

Coming in at the same time was Alan Dunleavy from Ireland. The two distance athletes both sometimes struggled to stay at the weight Coach McDonnell thought ideal, but that's where the similarities ended. Each of them simply had different levels of focus for their athletic careers.

"[Dunleavy's] father was a doctor so he walked on here. His first year the sports-information guy called me and said, 'I have an interesting questionnaire from your boy from Ireland,'" remembered McDonnell. "In reply to the question of why he came to

Arkansas, he apparently wrote, 'To live the college life and enjoy what an average stu-dent does at the university.' I asked him, 'Did you write this?' He said, 'Yeah, this is what I want to do.' He did well and was a smart guy, but running was not his first priority."

At nearly sixty years of age, the veteran coach hadn't slowed down a step. Twenty-five years after he began running around every possible point on the course exhorting his athletes to give efforts they didn't know they had in them, John McDonnell remained a significant presence during cross country.

"We'd go to Oklahoma State for the Cowboy Jamboree, and you'd be going up and down these hills, and he'd just pop out of nowhere," said Phil Price, echoing generations of Razorbacks before and after. "He'd be way back there in the bushes by himself way across the course saying, 'Check your instruments, kid,' which meant 'Relax.' Then you'd come up a hill and be hurting, and boom, there he is saying, 'Come on kid, get this kid, get up on him!' He'd be running right next to you with his clipboard almost tapping you with it. And you'd go back down the hill, and a mile later you'd go by some more trees, and you'd hear 'Come on, kid,' and you're wondering where this voice is coming from, and there he is again. He had his running shoes on and got a good workout in running after us."

With Godfrey Siamusiye having won every meet by fifteen seconds or more, the Razorbacks went into the 1996 NCAA Cross Country Championships in Tucson, Arizona, favored to win their second consecutive national championship.

"It was blazing hot," remembered McDonnell. "It was eighty degrees, and it wasn't a cool eighty."

Having won the pre-national meet on the course that same season, a resurgent Stanford program under Vin Lananna was prepared for the first time to challenge Arkansas. Unlike ten years earlier at Dartmouth, Lananna now had athletes with more natural talent and leg speed to handle whatever punishing pace Arkansas set during the first few miles of the race.

"I loved the way his teams ran. It intimidated everyone," admitted Lananna. "We didn't have the talent to run like that at Dartmouth but we did at Stanford. The Hauser [twins, Brad and Brent] had told me their goal was to rebuild Stanford. We had two sen-iors [Greg Jimmerson and Jeremy White] who were part of my first recruiting class, and I told them they would contend for an NCAA championship by their senior year. So I was running out of time."

After running aggressively alongside Arkansas, Stanford exceeded expectations and handled the heat better than anyone else. The Cardinal won its first NCAA cross-coun-try championship over Arkansas, 46–74, despite another individual win by Godfrey Siamusiye in the final race of his collegiate career. Though Godfrey appeared to have a bright future in the sport ahead of him, the Zambian was soon felled by a nasty stomach parasite requiring an operation that essentially ended his career.

"He may be the greatest cross-country runner ever in the NCAA," said Danny Green, "but had nearly a foot of intestines surgically removed after he got sick. You spend a month in a hospital with no insurance and that cannot be cheap."

When Arkansas basketball coach Nolan Richardson learned of the mountain of med-ical costs facing Godfrey, he magnanimously agreed to foot the bill. The two men remained close friends, and Godfrey ultimately began teaching and coaching at Shiloh

Christian High School outside of Fayetteville, while also helping to maintain Richardson's ranch.

The challenge John faced with Godfrey had been preventing him from running himself into the ground. Others needed the opposite treatment. One of John's strengths as a coach was his keen understanding of how to handle each athlete individually. A call to his office could mean different things.

"There were times he'd say, 'Hey kid, come by to see me tomorrow,' and you're thinking, 'Crap,'" said Phil Price. "There were three different ways of knowing whether the meeting was going to go well or if it wasn't. If he said, 'Hey kid, come on in,' and you sit down and start talking then everything was fine. If he said, 'Hey kid, come on in and close the door,' that was trouble. The third way and this only happened to me once, was if he said, 'Hey kid, come on in and close the door,' and then he takes the phone off the hook. Then you knew it was your ass."

That one occasion had occurred during his freshman year when Price had struggled to manage the training and studying, while returning home to Catoosa, Oklahoma, to see his girlfriend every off weekend.

"I was so nervous, there was sweat pouring down the side of my face," remembered Price. "He had a certain standard he wanted, and he wasn't seeing that out of me. So he called me after a bad workout and said, 'This is nonsense. You are better than this and you are going to be better.' So it was basically a message to get my shit together or go somewhere else. And he said we were going to have a time trial on the indoor track, which I ran in 8:13 [3,000 meters]. The light came on for me right then."

Nobody was above being called into the office. Though Ryan Wilson had been an unqualified success on the track and during cross country, McDonnell never hesitated to admonish him if he felt things were not going well academically or otherwise.

"If John didn't think things were going the right way, he would not hesitate to call you into his office," said Wilson. "If that phone got taken off the hook, you knew you were really done for."

"It seemed like he pulled the phone off the hook a lot when I went to see him those first few years," remarked Matt Kerr.

Though McDonnell was irked at losing any national championship the team was favored to win, what irked him more was when he perceived athletes were not meeting their individual potential. Over a year since arriving in Fayetteville, neither Matt Kerr nor Mike Power was meeting that standard.

"The two of them hung around together, joined at the hips, but were floundering, so I decided it was time to lower the boom on them," said McDonnell. "They said they were not happy with how they were doing either. I said it's about making up your minds. You're doing the training, but your heads are not in it. You are party hounds running around town, and everything is more important than track."

Though the results were similarly disappointing with both athletes, McDonnell addressed the symptoms of their problems individually.

"Mike was dating an Irish girl on the team who later became a famous model but he wasn't doing well, and I had to talk with him," said McDonnell. "'Either give up the sport or give her up, or at least ease it up. You are always together and you have no time to yourself. You come to workouts with bloodshot eyes, and you're not getting any rest.'

The next day he came by and said, 'I'm glad we had that talk. It's all over now. When I told her that track is number-one, she threw all of my stuff out into the street.' Everything. And she locked the door. That was the best thing that happened to his career."

Matt Kerr also found himself stuck in neutral—which was as frustrating to him as everyone else.

"It was an issue of mindset versus ability," said teammate Ryan Wilson. "There was a sense that he didn't care. I think he did, but maybe we didn't recognize it. He was a big talent coming in, and running was very easy for him, but he was convinced he didn't have to push himself. It was annoying to see a guy who could cruise a sub-four-minute mile do an eight miler on the trails in forty-six minutes. He was taking over an hour on some runs, nearly walking. John figured out a way to deal with him."

The situation finally came to a head the following fall when Kerr was getting back into shape following a broken foot suffered during the steeplechase the previous season.

"John had me going to the regional [cross-country race], and I said there was no way," remembered Kerr. "I'm not sure if he didn't do that on purpose because I wasn't owning up. I pretty much refused to run it and went in there to tell him not only that but I don't want to be here, and I wanted to transfer. I remember we hashed it out for an hour and were both raising our voices, but by the end of it were shaking hands. He had a pretty good way of turning things around. He asked me what my goals are, and I said to be an All-American indoors and an NCAA champion outdoors. We worked out a plan, and he said if you don't accomplish that [during the 1998 track season], he would release me. I was very hell-bent after that meeting to prove myself, which was exactly what he wanted me to do."

Though success did not happen overnight, the meetings dramatically changed the trajectory of both athletes' careers in Arkansas.

"It was gratifying that they turned it around," said McDonnell, "especially since they were such good high-school kids. It would have been a disaster if they didn't."

It was around that time when Seneca Lassiter also paid a visit to John's office, but on his own volition. Despite being as successful as any athlete during his first eighteen months in the program—with an SEC 800-meter title and All-American certificate from cross country—Lassiter had a burning desire to be the best in the world and a reaction bordering on anger when learning others had beat him to it.

"He came into my office one day his sophomore year and said, 'You know I was reading *Track and Field News* and that Kenyan that set the world record is the same age as me. How come I'm not doing it?'" remembered McDonnell. "I said to him, 'Seneca, the Kenyans are five to six years ahead of us in their development because when you were riding a bus to school every day they were running three or four miles. By the time you are twenty-five you can be as good as that twenty-year-old.' He was a dream to coach though. He ran nice and smooth and wasn't afraid of anyone and was almost cocky."

Lassiter finished second in the mile at the 1997 NCAA Indoor Championships where Sean Kaley had a significant breakthrough of his own by finishing second to Meb Keflezighi of UCLA in the 5,000 meter.[16]

"John and I came up with a race plan to win, and it was always to win because he would say, 'otherwise, why even run the race?'" said Kaley. "He was big on making the big move and forcing people to psychologically decide whether or not they are going to go with you. That race [Meb] got ahead of me, and every time I went to his shoulder, he would accelerate and I couldn't get around him."

Robert Howard won both the long jump and triple jump while James Ballard impressively earned All-American honors in the long jump and high jump despite having to contest both events simultaneously, a contortion that required him to run back and forth between attempts in each event.

By the time Ryan Wilson placed second in the 3,000 meter, Arkansas had reclaimed its NCAA indoor championship by a massive thirty-two-point margin over Auburn.

It was a foretaste of a special outdoor season for the Californian, which would include a victory in the 10,000 meter at the Penn Relays followed two days later by a personal-best anchor split for the winning 4 x 1,500 meter relay team, which won the event once again.

"Penn was the best thing outside of NCAAs," said Wilson. "To get to do that victory lap in front of forty thousand people in the stands and everyone knowing Arkansas and appreciating us being there was special."

During an outdoor season that would feature several heroic performances contributing to SEC and NCAA outdoor championships, it was Shannon Sidney's conference title in the 400-meter hurdles that was the most remarkable, based on the circumstances under which it was accomplished.

"I remember in the prelims he hit two or three hurdles and was in lane nine in the finals," said McDonnell. "[Steve] Silvey told him [Samuel] Matete [of Zambia] had won a world championship out of lane nine. Those two Florida guys were talking trash and [Shannon] ended up winning it."

Also a wide receiver on the 1995 SEC West championship football team, winning the 400 meter hurdles at the 1997 SEC Outdoor Championships remains a memory that will linger forever for him.

"It was amazing that I [even] made the conference final because I had tripped and fallen in the prelims, but got up and managed to get the eighth spot," said Sidney. "I ran like I stole something in the final. I kicked it into another gear. I felt like I had finally pleased Coach McDonnell. I felt I finally accomplished something for him, that of all of his champions, I was finally one of them and not second again. Feeling his hand on your neck when you win, that's not the average, 'Attaboy.'"[17]

The 1997 NCAA Outdoor Championships in Bloomington, Indiana was a more closely contested affair. Despite the retirement of Stan Huntsman a few years earlier, the University of Texas appeared to have a legitimate shot at winning the national championship under new head coach Bubba Thornton.

Nobody was more amped up than jumper Robert Howard. Though McDonnell had maintained his practice of meeting once with the team before championships to review his point expectations for each event, he sensed the team needed a jolt and asked Howard if he could say in a team meeting that he was confident the jumper would score twenty points at the NCAA meet.

"Yes, you say that!" McDonnell remembers Howard almost demanding of him. "Say it!"[18]

When McDonnell told the team he was confident Howard would score twenty points, the rambunctious jumper stood up and began jumping around.

"'Yes! Yes!'" McDonnell remembered Howard yelling. "And he jumped around the middle of the floor. I guarantee you that added fifteen points to our score just on the spirit of it."[19]

Howard had every reason to be confident in his ability to pull out a victory whenever he needed to after capturing the long and triple jump at the SEC meet two weeks earlier with a wrapped hamstring. After Dominich Miller leapt passed him with 26 feet, 3 inches on his final long jump to the shrieks and hollers of the Florida athletes and fans, Howard responded by uncorking an almost unfathomable leap of 27-6 to win the event. Faced with disbelief from the Arkansas coaching staff, Howard shrugged that "He just had to let it out." That was an understatement.

Like many Arkansas athletes, Howard had been prepared to perform his best at the end of the competition when everything was on the line.

"I always had a philosophy, in both our field events and middle distance and distance, that strength is speed," said McDonnell. "The stronger you get, the faster you get. A weak body invites a weak mind. Those last two jumps when everyone was dying, our guys were coming into their own."

Always cool under pressure at meets, Howard walked over to the Florida athlete afterwards.

"He walked over and gave that kid a hug," laughed McDonnell. "That's what he was like. He was a high-strung guy but had a cool head in competition."

Unfortunately, Howard's injury issues were not behind him by the time of the NCAA Outdoor Championships two weeks later. Despite his pledge of twenty points, there were legitimate medical reasons why he nearly didn't participate in the triple jump at all.

"He won the long jump [26-11] but hurt his heel really bad, and we took him to the doctor who said he could give him a shot but it could end his career," said McDonnell. "We figured we could win without him in the triple jump so we tried to talk him out of it. When I talked to him the morning [of the triple jump] he said, 'If it's not okay I won't jump.' So I said, 'We don't need you, and it would be a helluva thing to end your career.' He was limping, and I guess those other guys thought they had him after his first jump was fair, but he came back and got it done. He was a fierce competitor and had a pain threshold like no one else. You know how much that sucker must have hurt in the triple jump."

After Howard sacrificed so much of himself, his teammates had no option other than to do the same. Seneca Lassiter appeared to have the greatest opportunity of adding his name to the pantheon of Arkansas national champions, but to do so, he would first have to contend with Paul McMullen of Eastern Michigan, Bernard Lagat of Washington State, and Kevin Sullivan of Michigan.

"That Kevin Sullivan was a tough sucker," said McDonnell. "The minute the race started, it began raining hard, and there were these puddles on the track. Seneca had a better kick than Sullivan, so the plan was to kick his way to a finish."

Prior to leaving for the track, McDonnell met with Lassiter in the hotel to review the plan.

"Before a championship race, he always comes to our rooms and tells us our race strategy," said Lassiter. "He told me Sullivan was going to make a move and to just cover those moves, so I sat back and keyed off Kevin. After [McMullen] made his move,

Lagat made his move; and so when Kevin came hard around the turn, I knew I had to go with him. You could say I had one still in the chamber, so I started pumping my arms and noticed he was starting to come back. When I caught him, I saw he was broken."

Lassiter won his first national title, but it would not be the final time he and Sullivan would meet at an NCAA Championship. That summer, the Virginia native also followed up with a U.S. title over 1,500 meters.

"It takes a lot to impress Coach McDonnell because he has basically seen it all," said Lassiter, "but I remember [after the U.S. title] that was the most excited I had ever seen him for me. He ran over and picked me up off the ground and said, 'Way to go kid.'"

After finishing third in the NCAA 10,000 meter, Ryan Wilson doubled back in the 5,000 meter and found himself locked with Meb Keflezighi of UCLA and Adam Goucher of Colorado with 800 meters to go.

"I always had a habit of going from further out than John thought I could, but I listened to John that time," said Wilson. "Meb made a move and Goucher matched it but I didn't react, which was a tactical error on my part. I passed Goucher in the final lap but just failed to catch Meb."

It was still enough for Arkansas to win its unprecedented twenty-eighth national championship.

Through all of the triumphs, which required extended periods of time on the road, in the office, or at the track recruiting and coaching, McDonnell remained close with his family, who often joined him at the indoor national championships held at the RCA Dome as well as other meets.

"I remember "Calling the Hogs" a lot in Indianapolis," said his son, Sean McDonnell. "We were always there. I can still smell the track. That indoor track and the rubber had a distinct smell to it. I was very young, but that's something I'll never forget. I loved running around the track after the meet, and it was great to get to know the guys on the team. We went to those meets as much as we could, but when we got to high school, Mom and Dad didn't want us to miss too much class because it became harder to make up missed classes."

Looking back at the season, only a loss to Stanford at the NCAA Cross Country Championships had stood in the way of the Razorbacks capturing their fifth triple crown in program history. Even McDonnell recognized that some things were simply not within his control.

"It was not easy winning all three national titles in one season," said McDonnell. "You had to have great teams and so many things can go wrong in cross country, indoors, and outdoors. One of the things I prided myself on was keeping them healthy and not over-racing them."

As John McDonnell and his athletes continued to produce championships with a mind-numbing consistency, it did not appear as if Arkansas was going away anytime soon. As McDonnell would soon find out to his chagrin, neither were Vin Lananna and the Stanford Cardinal.

Mike Conley tears up at a celebration in McIlroy Plaza in Fayetteville in honor of his Olympic gold medal in 1992. Behind him are Dick Booth, John, and Frank Broyles. *Photo courtesy of John McDonnell.*

John and his family with President Clinton at the White House in 1993 after Arkansas won its tenth consecutive NCAA indoor championship—a Division I record. *Photo courtesy of University of Arkansas Athletics Media Relations.*

John and his children, Heather and Sean, greet the parrots in New Orleans for the NCAA Championships in 1993. *Photo courtesy of John McDonnell.*

Frank Broyles *(left)* with John and Ellen McDonnell in Indianapolis after Arkansas won its tenth consecutive NCAA Indoor Championship in 1993— a Division-I record. *Photo courtesy of John McDonnell.*

Reuben Reina (*left*) and Brian Baker were mainstays on several national championship teams. Reina captured individual national titles in 1990 and 1991, and Baker followed suit in 1994. *Photo courtesy of University of Arkansas Athletics Media Relations.*

Niall Bruton and Graham Hood were teammates and rivals who won twenty All-American certificates and made three Olympic appearances. John managed both within a team that won thirteen NCAA championships during their careers—including their share of Penn Relays distance medley relay wheels. *Photo courtesy of University of Arkansas Athletics Media Relations.*

Eammon Coghlan *(left)* presenting the Penn Relays wheel to Niall Bruton, Calvin Davis, Graham Hood, Brian Baker, and John. *Photo courtesy of John McDonnell.*

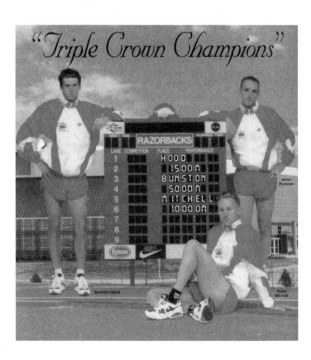

Graham Hood *(top left)*, Jason Bunston *(top right)*, and Teddy Mitchell *(bottom)* after a season in which each of them won NCAA individual titles in the 1500 meter (outdoors), 5000 meter (indoors), and 10,000 meter (outdoors), respectively. *Photo courtesy of University of Arkansas Athletics Media Relations.*

274

Winning never gets old: Ryan Wilson raises his arms after winning the 1996 NCAA indoor 3000 meter. *Photo courtesy of University of Arkansas Athletics Media Relations.*

Brandon Rock showing off a shirt celebrating "National Champions: Back to Back to Back to Back to Back . . ." after the Razorbacks won their unprecedented twelfth indoor national championships in a row in 1995. *Photo courtesy of University of Arkansas Athletics Media Relations.*

John and family in 2002. *Photo courtesy of John McDonnell.*

John and Heather share a father-daughter moment at the Woodland Junior High Spaghetti Dinner. *Photo courtesy of John McDonnell.*

Coaches Steve Silvey, John, and Dick Booth *(front)* lead the team in "Calling the Hogs" after winning back their indoor national title in 1997 with the team decked out in their white warm-ups. Said Vin Lananna of the white warm-ups: "That's when I knew [John] was confident they were going to win." *Photo courtesy of University of Arkansas Athletics Media Relations.*

Matt Hemingway won an SEC title in the high jump, but his greatest triumph came after college with an Olympic silver medal in 2004. *Photo courtesy of University of Arkansas Athletics Media Relations.*

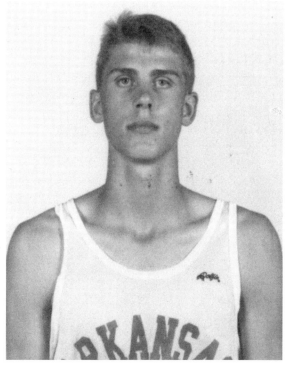

Multiple NCAA 400 meter champion Calvin Davis focused on the 400-meter hurdles after college, which led to an Olympic bronze medal in 1996. *Photo courtesy of University of Arkansas Athletics Media Relations.*

Godfrey Siamusiye was never beaten as a Razorback in cross country. Said Danny Green: "He may be the greatest cross country runner ever in the NCAA." *Photo courtesy of University of Arkansas Athletics Media Relations.*

Godfrey Siamusiye. *Photo courtesy of University of Arkansas Athletics Media Relations.*

Tradition Never Graduates: James Karanu, Mike Power, Seneca Lassiter, and Sharif Karie *(left)* set a Texas Relays 4 x 1500 meter record in 1999 before Power, Karie Lassiter, and Matt Kerr *(right)* duplicated the feat in the 4 x mile at Penn Relays only weeks later. *Photo courtesy of University of Arkansas Athletics Media Relations.*

John never missed his son Sean's motocross when he was in town. *Photo courtesy of John McDonnell.*

Once they dropped James Menon *(middle)* of Wisconsin in the 10,000 meter final of the 1996 NCAA Championships in Oregon, Jason Bunston *(left)* and Godfrey Siamusiye *(right)* had a battle for the ages—with the Oregon crowd standing for the last 800 meters. *Photo courtesy of University of Arkansas Media Relations.*

Robert Howard *(left)* and Melvin Lister *(right)* won a combined fourteen NCAA individual titles in the long or triple jump between 1996 and 2000. *Photo courtesy of University of Arkansas Media Relations.*

Daniel Lincoln went from walk-on to All-American to NCAA champion to Olympian to American record holder within an amazing eight-year odyssey. *Photo courtesy of University of Arkansas Media Relations.*

Daniel Lincoln and Alistair Cragg *(left)* did not allow their rivalry to get in the way of team goals at the 2003 NCAA Championships as they crossed the line together in the 10,000 meter. *Photo by Robert Black.*

12

A Pain in the Neck (1997–2000)

"When John wore his white warm-ups, which I called his medal warm-ups, I was always worried. That's when I knew he was confident they were going to win."
—*Stanford coach Vin Lananna*

When John McDonnell magnanimously congratulated Vin Lananna in a hotel lobby in 1992 on accepting the Stanford job and commented that he was going to be a "pain in my neck," perhaps even John might not have realized how true his words would be less than five years later. After winning an incredible twenty-six out of a possible thirty-eight national championships between January 1984 and June 1996, the Arkansas juggernaut was significantly slowed but not stopped by the revival of the Stanford program. Whether it was during cross-country season, on the track, or in the recruiting wars, the pain in John McDonnell's neck emanating from Palo Alto, California, would only intensify over time.

"Stanford is different than some of the other private schools," said McDonnell. "They have such a name academically, and distance runners have such strong grades that sometimes they can get their school paid for purely academically. I ran up against them all of the time. My gosh, a scholarship to Stanford? If you had a son yourself, and Stanford or Arkansas kept calling and there was a full scholarship at both, you would probably want him to go to Stanford, and I wouldn't blame you. When Vin got there he really pushed that and was supposedly pretty arrogant about it like, 'I'm here to recruit you.' I know of a few kids he said I want to know right now if I offer a scholarship will you come to Stanford and if the answer isn't yes, then our conversation is over. He was apparently that arrogant about it, and I wouldn't doubt it. He had four aces. How could you miss? I'd have done the same thing if I was there."

What Lananna did was bring back a moribund program that hadn't tasted glory since the days of Peyton Jordan. Aside from their common roots in New York City, one other characteristic that McDonnell and Lananna shared was an astonishing work ethic with energy and enthusiasm to burn. Regardless of whether one believed in being good to be lucky or lucky to be good, there was little question that the fortunes of the

Stanford program were changed for the better with the signing of Brent and Brad Hauser that season just as Arkansas's had changed years earlier with Niall O'Shaughnessy and Mike Conley.

"Vin Lananna owes a lot to the Hauser twins," said Ryan Wilson. "They became champions through their will and personality. Stanford was just okay before they got there. The caliber of recruits was good, but they couldn't win until the twins showed up. And they won a lot to John's detriment."

Early in the season Ryan Wilson picked up right where Godfrey had left off by winning every race leading into the NCAA Championships, breaking the tape at the Southern Stampede, Cowboy Jamboree, and the Chile Pepper Festival, which was contested at Fayetteville's Agri Park for the first time.

At the 1997 SEC Cross Country Championships in Columbia, South Carolina, the Razorbacks arrived at the course only to be surprised by the conditions they found.

"We had to go to a military base and most of the course was on sand," remembered assistant coach Steve Silvey. "So John got up at the coach's meeting and suggested seeking an alternative site. He said this course will beat up everyone's athletes and take days or even weeks to recover from. George Watts of Tennessee got up and said something about how [John] shouldn't be so cowardly about running this course, which completely missed the point. So John got back up and said, 'This will not change the result of tomorrow's meet. Let me repeat, it will not change the result.' John was just thinking about the welfare of the SEC distance runners, but some of these short-minded coaches thought it was a chink in his armor."

There were few of those. Twenty seconds after Ryan Wilson crossed the line for the win, Tim Broe of Alabama finished ahead of six Arkansas athletes, the only thing that kept Arkansas from registering a perfect score.

Still, the early season meets were only a preparation for the day of reckoning marked in every Razorback calendar: the NCAA Cross Country Championships on November 27, 1997. After the surprising loss to the Cardinal at the previous season's NCAA meet, the Razorbacks were focused on taking back their national championship trophy at Furman University in South Carolina. It certainly wouldn't be easy. Stanford had registered a perfect score at the Pacific-10 Championships.

"I got the impression talking to John that he didn't think we were very good [in 1996]," said Lananna. "I knew in 1997 there was no chance he was going to get surprised again. When John wore his white warm-ups, which I called his medal warm-ups, I was always worried. That's when I knew he was confident they were going to win."

The morning of the national meet Lananna saw McDonnell decked out in white.

"John loved being at Arkansas and being on top," said Lananna. "He loved that role. He set the bar and went for it every time."

On a fast course, the Razorbacks pushed the pace faster than ever before and dared anyone to go with them.

"Arkansas took that thing out so hard that we were running as fast as we could, and we couldn't catch them," said Lananna. "He had a great team that year. If you asked him the one he was most confident he was going to win, it would have to be that one. I thought he was going to win too."

Standing on a green at the second mile, McDonnell watched as every one of his athletes found themselves in the front pack.

"Seneca was in the top ten and Ryan Wilson was pushing the pace," said McDonnell. "We had a bunch of guys up there and probably got too excited."

That became apparent as the race wore on. Adam Dailey faded to fiftieth while Seneca Lassiter fell back all the way to seventy-eighth. Yet with four runners in the top twenty places, Arkansas still controlled the race with two miles remaining. Of concern was Arkansas's fifth runner, Murray Link, who was running well but beginning to fade while Stanford's fifth runner, Jonathan Riley, was passing runners by the dozen.

"In the last 2,000 meters, the whole face of it changed," said Lananna. "We moved up and they were coming back. Jonathan Riley was in the mid-30s and coming down the hill passing people. John [McDonnell] was there with sweat pouring down his face. He was worried, but so was I. He said to me, 'What do you think?' 'It'll be close,' I said. 'Down to the final straightaway.'"

Ryan Wilson crossed the line in fifth place but was bested by Meb Keflezighi of UCLA to end his perfect season. Sean Kaley and Mike Power finished shortly thereafter in ninth and twelfth respectively.

"We came down the final stretch and I remember Coach was just screaming, 'You gotta keep picking them off!'" said Phil Price. "It was a six-hundred-meter straight shot to the finish, and it came down to the final straightaway. I just remember coming down that hill exhausted, and I saw the Hauser guy in front of me, and Coach was yelling, 'You gotta get him to win the meet!' I don't think I've ever kicked so hard in my life and used so many gears."

By the time Phil Price outkicked Brent Hauser to finish fifteenth, Arkansas had a five-point lead over Stanford through its first four runners. Yet when Stanford's fifth man, freshman Jonathan Riley, passed six runners on the final straightaway to finish a remarkable twenty-third, all eyes turned to Murray Link.

Only a decade after imploring another surprise fifth runner Doug Consiglio to finish strong against a Lananna-coached Dartmouth team at the NCAA Championships, McDonnell was once again relying on a Canadian running over his head to pull the team's chestnuts from the fire.

"I remember with a kilometer to go he's there yelling at me, 'Come on, kid," said Link. "He said I took off like a scalded dog and was picking guys off left and right before dying pretty hard at the end and getting picked off."

ARKANSAS	STANFORD
5 (3) Ryan Wilson	8 (5) Nathan Nutter
9 (6) Sean Kaley	10 (7) Brad Hauser
12 (9) Mike Power	14 (10) Jason Balkman
15 (11) Phil Price	17 (13) Brent Hauser
37 (27) Murray Link	23 (18) Jonathan Riley
56 points	53 points

Though it took some time for the final tally to be announced, Stanford won its second consecutive NCAA cross-country championship by the most razor-thin of margins.

"That was my fault," said McDonnell. "Murray Link was running the race of his life, and with six hundred meters to go, I said you have to get those guys, and he took off like a scalded dog. I remember there was a little dip going down, and he passed about ten guys and then died. He lost those places and then gave some more back. If I had said nothing, he would have held what he had. Gosh, he was devastated, but I said it's not your fault. We had other guys that could have done things."

After one of the most epic finishes to an NCAA Cross Country Championships, McDonnell took the loss as hard as anyone.

"He always took it personally," said Link. "That's just the kind of guy he was."

It was the nature of the sport and its three seasons that profound disappointment could so quickly be followed by redemption. Following a second consecutive SEC indoor championship, this time by an unprecedented 104-point margin (181–77) over Louisiana State in Baton Rouge, Arkansas once again found itself in a battle with Stanford four months later at the 1998 NCAA Indoor Championships in Indianapolis.

On this particular occasion, Arkansas bettered Stanford thanks to individual titles by Robert Howard (triple jump) and Kenny Evans (high jump). In the 3,000 meter, Matt Kerr finished third to earn an All-American certificate and fulfill the first part of his bargain with Coach McDonnell.[1]

Though some rivalries could engender bitter feelings between coaches, it seemed McDonnell and Lananna maintained their friendship amid the heat and passion of intense competition.

"I was good friends with Vin, and there were never any hard feelings," said McDonnell.

Lananna's respect for McDonnell was based in many ways on his astonishment at John's ability to set a high standard and continuously meet it year after year.

"We were good friends and talked to each other as much as possible without giving away our secrets," said Lananna. "He was a heck of a competitor. What I liked about him and where he set the bar was that he wasn't afraid to get in front and say, 'Here I am. I'm really good. If you're going to beat me, you're going to have to work.' When you set yourself up like that, you can piss off a lot of people. He inspired his athletes to believe in the Hogs and that when they put on that jersey it was worth something. That's what I saw with Jumbo Elliott at Villanova, Bill Bowerman and Bill Dellinger at Oregon, and I watched it with John McDonnell at Arkansas."

Less than five months from his sixtieth birthday, John McDonnell had certainly not slowed down his pace. During the academic year and collegiate season, he was in the office early in the morning preparing for practice and often making recruiting calls until late at night. During lunch hour, he and Dick Booth would often run in the trails. He was at every easy run, tempo run, morning run, long run, and workout without fail. When he wasn't coaching or recruiting, or spending time with his family, he was usually working on his ranch in Muskogee. He was a living, breathing perpetual-motion machine, driven as much by a compulsion for collective and individual achievement as he was by the mantra Bridget McDonnell had instilled in him years earlier that "Idle hands makes for the Devil's work."

"He never let a day be wasted at all because he would say it is a gift," said his son Sean McDonnell. "If I come home and see him sitting relaxing on a chair, it's because he's sick. It's just not normal. He just never sits idle. He's always trying to make something better."

Though John had not slowed down his routine any, his body was quietly beginning to rebel against the torrid pace he set at home, at work, and on the ranch.

Only months earlier, McDonnell had been approached by Oregon officials regarding the impending head-coaching vacancy at their program with the anticipated retirement of long-time head coach Bill Dellinger at the conclusion of the 1998 season. Though the opportunity intrigued McDonnell, he requested that they approach him after the season. He already had enough on his plate in Fayetteville.

The indoor-track facility, which had been such a godsend for the program when it was built inside the tennis center in 1981, was never lavish but had served a valuable purpose as a training facility and host for small invitational meets. Eighteen years later, as banked two-hundred-meter tracks and oversized three-hundred-meter tracks began appearing around the country, it could now rightly be considered antiquated.

"I remember an English professor called me up after Frank O'Mara ran his 3:52 mile [in 1986]," remembered McDonnell. "The facility was so small that the athletes ran behind the bleachers, and you couldn't see them. So this professor called me up one day, 'Are you Coach McDonnell?' I said, 'Yeah,' and he said, 'I have something to talk to you about.' He had Frank in one of his classes, so I'm thinking he's going to brag about him, but instead he said, 'I came down to watch Frank O'Mara run a mile, and all I saw was a damn half-mile. I couldn't see the other half of the race.' 'Well,' I said almost defensively, 'I just work here.' So he said, 'Maybe you should work harder.' Oh he gave it to me and chewed me out and then hung up! We did have a Mickey Mouse indoor facility, and I had been asking for years and years to build a new one and [Frank] Broyles kept saying 'We'll do it, we'll do it.'"

The drab metal building once had an endearing and functional practicality to it that helped recruiting in the days when it was the only indoor facility in the Southwest Conference, but it was now outdated for the needs and aspirations of the program.

While some other coaches occasionally fell out with administration over such issues, McDonnell was personally able to maintain a positive relationship with his superiors throughout his career.

"I had a clear path to Coach Broyles office," said John. "If there was anything I needed, I would just go to him. Katie Hill was really my boss and sometimes she'd say, 'Well, you'll have to see Coach about that,' so I went to his office. That's what was so great about Frank. You went in there to talk business, and he was really accessible. Every coach could go in there to talk with him, and he had an open-door policy."

Of the characteristics Steve Silvey admired about McDonnell, foremost was his ability to handle conflict. As Silvey's relationship with Dick Booth began to deteriorate, McDonnell managed the conflict on his coaching staff with the same finesse he had used to iron out so many other wrinkles within the program over the years. McDonnell seemed to have a knack for solving problems.

"He was the master of dealing with people and their conflicts," said Silvey. "He was the most controlled, cool, calm, and collected person ever. If I came in and bitched about this and Dick Booth came in and bitched about that, he would find a way to get it solved without getting upset. He had a way of bringing people together towards a common goal of winning SEC championships and national titles."

"It was usually about who was getting what scholarship and jumpers being on the sprint relay," said Danny Green, who by now was the director of operations. "The thing about Steve or Dick was that whatever John said went, so that kept things civil, but there was no love lost [between Silvey and Booth]."

"They were both big egos," said John. "It had no effect on their coaching or on winning. They were on the same team when it came to that."

The Razorbacks seemed to have more football players contributing during Silvey's six years in Fayetteville than ever before. The hiring of Houston Nutt as head football coach in 1998 had only helped.

"The most football guys we ever had come out were with Houston Nutt, and Silvey worked with football for a bunch of them," remembered McDonnell. "We had a couple of hurdlers as well as Kevin Baker, a 45-second, 400-meter kid from Dallas, who helped anchor our mile relay. We also had an All-American in the triple jump, Richard Smith, who was a football guy. We wouldn't have won the NCAA championship without him."

With few sprint scholarships to work with in a program that had traditionally been distance and jumps centered, Silvey scratched and clawed for talent wherever he could.

"He was fantastic when he went into a person's home, and he had to be because he got those kids for practically nothing," said McDonnell. "I remember he got [Jonathan Leon] from Oklahoma City to walk-on after running 47.9 in high school. His freshman year he ran 45.7 on the relay and ran three years with us before transferring back to Oklahoma for a girl."

That spring, the sprint group was dealt another major blow when Kevin White, who had finished second in the 110-meter hurdles at the previous spring's NCAA Championships, was declared ineligible due to a transcript and enrollment error by the academic staff.

"Someone at Arkansas did a poor job of reading his transcripts, and he ended up being ineligible," said Silvey. "That's the thing about John McDonnell's program. Even when he lost studs in a given year, someone else stepped up every time."

At the Penn Relays in late April, Sean Kaley, Mike Power, and Phil Price did so in the 5000 meter in a major way.

"Coach McDonnell had talked the meet director into letting us run the Olympic Development race rather than the college race," said Phil Price. "Sean ran 13:42, I ran 13:43, and Power ran 13:44. You had the Stanford guys there sitting on the side of the track saying, 'Are you kidding me?'"

Not everything went so swimmingly in Philadelphia that weekend. Despite capturing twelve of the previous fifteen distance medley relays wheels at the Penn Relays, including the previous five, Arkansas and anchor leg Seneca Lassiter were bested by Michigan and Kevin Sullivan.

"I got blasted by Kevin, and he made me look so bad in front of fifty-thousand people," remembered Seneca Lassiter. "He absolutely blew my doors out."

Lassiter would have an opportunity to avenge the humiliation five weeks later at the 1998 NCAA Outdoor Track and Field Championships. After an impressive 800-meter and 1,500-meter double to lead Arkansas to a victory over LSU at the SEC Championships, the junior found himself in the NCAA 1,500-meter final against Sullivan as well as future Olympic champion Bernard Lagat of Washington State.

"Kevin was ready to roll and Bernard was hot after crushing us indoors," said Lassiter. "Lady luck was on my side though. We were running the race when Bernard tripped up on Kevin. I jumped over Kevin and immediately thought to myself, 'Bernard is down and Kevin is down, so that means by the time they get up, I will have twenty meters on them.' So I took off to the front and started pushing the pace, and I was in the lead from 500 meters out. Coming down the home stretch, Gabe Jennings [of Stanford] was eating me up, but I had enough distance that I was able to lean and hit the line first."

Despite having won the 1,500-meter national title only the year before, Lassiter's upset victory was an unexpected bonus at an NCAA meet where every point would be needed against Stanford.

In the 3,000-meter steeplechase, Matt Kerr had a surprise of his own.

"I remember Stanford started the meet by going 1-2-3 in the 10,000 meter, which put us in a hole right away," said Kerr. "We had the intent of winning that championship, so when Coach McDonnell asked me my goals for the race, I told him it was to win it. My main competition was John Mortimer [of Michigan]. He started cranking it in the middle of the race and pushing lap after lap until it got to the point where he couldn't sustain it. It felt really good to win it and was a major monkey off my back. I went in there the fittest I've ever been and had a lot of fun with it."

Not only did the steeplechase victory cement Kerr's name among the list of Arkansas national champions, but also completed the final part of his deal with Coach McDonnell during their heated meeting the previous fall. Coming as it did on a cold day in Buffalo, New York, barely one hundred miles from Kerr's home in Elora, Ontario, Canada, the win was extra special.

"It was a nice stadium [in Buffalo], and they had a good crowd," said McDonnell. "They did a good job hosting but, boy, was it ever cold."

In the jumps, Robert Howard again found himself down by seven inches to Chris Wright of Nebraska before his final long jump on a frigid, forty-degree night. Ever the competitor, Howard stepped-up on his final jump by leaping an entire foot farther to win it. When he also emerged victorious in the triple jump, it was further validation of his ability to perform under pressure and another brilliant performance in the final competition of a storied collegiate career.

"He was a sensational athlete and had a pain threshold like I've never seen," said McDonnell.

Howard's twenty-point performance proved to be pivotal in response to a win by Stanford's Toby Stevenson in the pole vault and the Cardinal onslaught in the distance events. Heading into the 5,000-meter final, Arkansas was only a few points ahead of Stanford, who were expected to score well in the event.

"It was thirty-eight degrees, and we needed Mike Power to come in the top four or five to win the meet," remembered McDonnell. "There were some good guys in there for Stanford, so I told him to take it nice and steady and he finished third. He was always a clutch performer."

Power's finish in the 5,000 meter sealed the national championship for Arkansas.

It was not long after the meet was over when McDonnell was approached once again by Oregon representatives regarding their vacant head-coaching position. Though the Ducks had remained nationally competitive in cross country throughout Bill Dellinger's career, the program had fallen from its once lofty perch. The men's team had not won a national championship on the track since 1984, nor in cross country since

1977, a once unthinkable state of affairs for the program of Harry Jerome, Steve Prefontaine, Mac Wilkins, and Alberto Salazar. By 1998, many alumni and donors, including Salazar and Nike co-founder Phil Knight were prepared to do whatever was necessary to restore the program to what they considered to be its rightful place in the track-and-field universe.

"I was interested for a few weeks and thought seriously about it," admitted McDonnell. "It was mostly Alberto calling. He said everyone on the twelve-person committee wants you."

For several weeks, John and Ellen McDonnell seriously discussed the possibility of transplanting themselves from the community they had called home for over a quarter of a century.

"Just the fact that Nike was up there, and we had friends Ned and Judy Cartwright up in Oregon who told us everyone talked track up there," said Ellen. "They were really into track. Things about it would have been nice but the weather may not have been so nice. It was a lot like Irish weather."

Still, as much as John was intrigued at the possibility of taking over one of the most historic collegiate programs at the cathedral of track and field at Hayward Field, he could not seem to shake a pervasive tiredness that had engulfed his body during the previous year.

"It was a tough decision not to go out there and really take a good look at it," said McDonnell. "It was tempting and I thought about doing it, but I wasn't interested because I couldn't see myself starting over. It was an honor just to be contacted."

With Sean entering Fayetteville High School and Heather set to enroll at the University of Arkansas a year prior to transferring to the University of Texas, the combination of family and business connections along with John's health concerns ended the discussion before it could fully begin. After a few weeks of flirting with the idea of visiting Eugene, McDonnell called Alberto back to let him know he had to pass on the opportunity.

"They would have made it enticing enough that it would have been impossible to turn it down. Alberto told me lots of good things about Phil Knight and what was going to happen. If I wanted an indoor track, I'd have an indoor track, and they were only interested in distance running. [Alberto] and I had been friends for years, and I told him it has nothing to do with money. I just don't feel I can do it. It would have been my dream job, and I would have jumped at the opportunity at a prior stage of my life."

Oregon eventually hired Martin Smith to lead their program back to prominence following Smith's two national championships in cross country at the University of Wisconsin.

The reality was that John and Ellen McDonnell's roots in the Arkansas community had become so deeply embedded that a move elsewhere at that stage in their lives would have been difficult. What also became apparent was that despite the fact that some within the community and university had begun to take John McDonnell and the track program's success for granted, those at the top had not.

"The kind of national publicity that John and his team have brought to the University of Arkansas and to our state is phenomenal. You simply cannot buy that kind of publicity," said Dr. Alan Sugg, president of the University of Arkansas system, to a crowd gathered for the John McDonnell celebration in Little Rock a few years earlier. "As proud as we all are of the national championships that the track and cross-country teams have won, the real winners of the University of Arkansas track program are the athletes who have worked and trained under John McDonnell. Because of his leadership and teaching, they have learned many lessons about how to handle the challenges, the adversities and the joys of life itself. They completely understand what hard work, self-discipline, commitment, and tenacity will achieve. John McDonnell represents the best of what coaching is all about, and we are so proud to have him as our track coach and we hope he is with us for a long time to come. Let's not take him for granted."[2]

On the occasions when United States president Bill Clinton found himself in Fayetteville during previous few years, he sometimes called McDonnell ahead of time to arrange a meeting.

"President Clinton called him to let him know he was going to be at the Arkansas basketball game and wanted to meet the cross-country team," remembered Phil Price. "So the entire security and secret service walked into the Bud Walton Arena, and Bill walked over to Coach McDonnell and shook his hand and gave him a hug. You'd think they knew each other forever. John knew a lot of well-known people with Arkansas roots and was so well liked because he was successful but so down to earth."

The town of Fayetteville and the surrounding communities of northwest Arkansas were thriving in the meantime. Not only had Fayetteville doubled in population to nearly sixty-thousand but nearby Springdale and Bentonville had blossomed to such a degree around the success of Tyson Foods and Walmart that Northwest Arkansas Regional Airport was opened in the fall of 1998 to accommodate heavier traffic.

Despite feeling run-down, John continued to maintain his hectic schedule while remaining focused on securing a new indoor facility. He was hardly alone in that effort. After Frank Broyles finished raising the funds for a massive facility upgrade of the football stadium that would see it increase from 52,000 to 71,000 seats in 2001, the athletic director committed a few million dollars for a new indoor track facility with a banked 200-meter track and seating for 2,500 spectators.

That was when it came to McDonnell's attention that the NCAA would be seeking a new home for the indoor national championships in 2000 after a decade of hosting the event in Indianapolis.

"I went in to Coach Broyles office and told him if we could get it to seat 6,000 spectators, we could probably do the whole NCAA meet, which was what I had always wanted," said John. "He said that would be great. So I decided to go speak with Don Tyson [to raise the difference in cost]."

Having sponsored the outdoor Tyson Invitational in mid-April at John McDonnell Field for over a decade, the head of Tyson Foods was receptive but asked for details. For the meeting, McDonnell had a sketch prepared by a Fort Smith architect of what would be called the Randall Tyson Track Center.

"We were sitting at the coffee table in the middle of his office and he said 'How much?'" remembered John. "Broyles had said if you get one million that would be good. So I asked for three million. It seemed like an hour before [Don Tyson] answered me but it was really only a few seconds. He said 'I'll do it.' I couldn't believe my good fortune. Frank Broyles put some money towards it, and the total was nine million."

The cheapest part of the indoor track facility was the indoor track itself. Originally used for the 1993 World Indoor Championships, which had been held at the SkyDome in Toronto, Ontario, Canada, the boards had been sitting in a storage facility in Canada gathering mold and mildew.

"They didn't know what the hell to do with it," remembered Paul Poce, who had founded the Toronto Olympic Club and served as the head coach for several Canadian Olympic teams, "so Arkansas bought it for one dollar plus shipping charges."

Though the boards needed to be resurfaced, they came at a relative bargain. When the shovel went into the ground the following spring, it would be a mere twelve months until the NCAA Indoor Championships were held at Randall Tyson Track and Field Center in Fayetteville, Arkansas. After winning thirty national championships at other sites and failing in their only opportunity to win the cross-country national championship at home in 1994, the news was exciting not only for the university and the program but for the community of Fayetteville, which would come to embrace the event in the years to come.

"As far as I'm concerned that was when track really came alive in Fayetteville because now we could have a national championship at home," said McDonnell. "People really liked watching it and enjoyed watching us win at home. It made it that much more important."

In the meantime, McDonnell reloaded his distance squad in an effort to win back the cross-country national championship.

From Kentwood, Louisiana, came Ryan Travis, who had run 4:06.9 for the mile in high school. Though not blessed with the natural leg speed of another Cajun miler named Mike Morin, who came to Fayetteville only a few years before him, it did not take long for Travis to dip under 4:00 for the mile.

"He signed here for a half scholarship and was a nice kid but also kind of headstrong," said McDonnell. "I said we are going to run you in unattached at Missouri in the mile. He ran 3:59.8 in his first race and won it. It was amazing he ran that fast because he didn't look like he had much speed but was a tough guy. He ran one 5,000 meter but didn't like it. He just did them at the conference meet for points."

Transferring in from the University of Wisconsin was Andrew Begley, a 14:30 5,000-meter runner, who would eventually marry Amy Yoder, an All-American distance runner on the women's team.

"I had recruited him in high school, but he went to Wisconsin," said McDonnell. "Well, he hadn't gotten along with Martin [Smith], so he contacted me. He was a hard worker and boy was he conscientious. I cannot know for sure but I'd hear that he'd hammer all of the easy runs. He was always suffering from aches and pains and his plantar had to be operated on, which was something he came in with. I had to tell him a few times, 'Andrew, more is not always better. I appreciate you are a tough guy, but slow down.' He never did, and although he ran some good races, he always had some type of nagging injury."

The most ballyhooed signing of all was that of Sharif Karie, a Somalian refugee who had attended high school in Virginia and ran 4:02 for the mile before competing at Lindenwood University in Missouri.

"He ran some good races but never broke through or matched his potential in the 3,000 meter or 5,000 meter," said McDonnell. "He was a talented kid but real frail."

At the first home meet of the fall cross-country season, Karie finished nearly half a minute behind his teammates as they ran the four-mile course in a steady 20:00 pace over four miles. Though Karie ultimately became an eight-time All-American at Arkansas and put forth spectacular performances during his career, there would always be a sense of unfulfilled potential surrounding him.

"He was super talented but I felt like it never came to fruition," said Daniel Lincoln, who was a freshman the same fall. "I think Coach McDonnell struggled to really connect with him and get him to be really disciplined. I don't know if he was inherently lazy, but there always seemed to be a conflict there."

Few would have said the same of Daniel Lincoln after he arrived in Fayetteville as an unknown walk-on from Hot Springs, Arkansas, and left several years later as a four-time NCAA champion, Olympian, and American record holder in the steeplechase.

After being recruited by Baylor and University of Arkansas–Little Rock, Lincoln had run 4:16 for the mile but remained unsigned in June. Though McDonnell knew of Lincoln, he did not recruit him after being told by the high-school coach at the Arkansas School for Math and Science in Hot Springs that he was only interested in Ivy League options. When the high-school senior came by his office during the summer of 1998 to ask for the opportunity to walk on the cross-country team, McDonnell was astonished.

"I'm sitting in my office and was the only person in the [Bud Walton] Arena when I heard a knock at my door and it was Daniel and his mother," remembered McDonnell. "He was really kind of a shy kid and asked if I knew who he was. I said, 'I know who you are, but I thought you were going to an Ivy League school.' Daniel said, 'I'm not going to an Ivy League school.' That is what pissed me off about that coach because he had made it all up. Anyways, he got an academic scholarship here but walked on and didn't receive a dollar of athletic scholarship in four years."

As a raw freshman, there was little possibility Lincoln was going to make the top seven during his first cross-country season but did show glimpses of what was to come later in his Razorback career by running 8:15 for 3,000 meters while competing unattached on the track. Without the expectations of having to perform and contribute immediately, Lincoln soaked up as much as he could from the veteran athletes.

"I remember him being so curious and asking us on this run up the trails what it takes to be good," said Phil Price. "I said, 'Don't get caught up thinking you have to prove yourself every day; don't get injured and you will be fine.' The wisdom was to not get caught up hammering every day because there would always be someone who hammered on any given day."

Heading to the Rim Rock Farm north of Lawrence, Kansas, for the 1998 NCAA Cross Country Championships, Arkansas was the decided underdog against a Stanford team that had won the previous two cross-country national championships. This time it was Stanford who ran more aggressively and assertively early in a race that quickly bottlenecked around a sharp turn one-half mile into the race.

"I'm not sure what [Lananna] told them but the first time up the hill Stanford was pushing it and ended up paying the price," said McDonnell. "They ended up bombing out. It was a tough course at Kansas, and we were used to running hills."

With two miles remaining, Arkansas controlled the race. Sean Kaley was locked in a battle for the lead with Adam Goucher of Colorado and Abdi Abdirahman of Arizona, before Goucher blew everyone's doors off by over twenty seconds.[3] Kaley fell back to fifth, but more concerning was Mike Power, who was unable to finish the race after running in the top twenty.

"Mike was allergic to dust, and it was really dry and hadn't rained for days," said McDonnell. "With all of the guys on the course, it had raised the dust and with a mile to go Mike almost passed out because he was allergic to it. I remember somebody telling me Mike was passing out and I saw him staggering with 200 meters to go but we still had enough to win."

Despite the hiccup late in the race, Arkansas beat Stanford, 97–114, for the national championship.

"It seemed like Stanford changed their strategy, and it backfired on them just as it backfired on us the year before," said McDonnell. "You take chances. They beat us [in 1997] at Furman when they shouldn't have and then [in 1998] they were loaded and we beat them at Kansas. It goes to show you that there is never a sure thing."

Though it hardly seemed possible that the Razorbacks could follow up the cross-country championship by winning the indoor and outdoor crowns for their fifth triple crown in a year when they had lost Robert Howard to graduation, McDonnell and his staff had reloaded with aplomb.

Joining Seneca Lassiter in the middle-distance group was James Karanu, who had run 1:50 for 800 meters at Dodge City Community College in Kansas after growing up in Kenya.

"He and Sharif [Karie] fit in without a problem, and they were just happy to be there," said Murray Link. "I remember James telling stories about the jungle and lions. It wasn't just a story but was real life for him."

In the sprint events, Sam Glover of Pine Bluff, Arkansas, signed with the Razorbacks after a prolific high-school career during which he had run 13.81 (110-meter high hurdles) and 36.80 (300 meter hurdles). In the throws, football player Marcus Clevelle of New Iberia, Louisiana, quickly developed into a force to be reckoned with.

"He was a football player but got his bell rung a couple of times and one time was semiparalyzed for a while," said McDonnell. "He was 6 feet, 8 inches, 335 pounds and not fat. He was the most awesome physical specimen. I told him all you have to do is work hard, and great things will happen."

Clevelle would earn All-American honors after being recruited and coached by Silvey.

"Dick didn't like to spend much time with the other events [other than the jumps]," said Silvey. "So I had to take Marcus to a Last Chance meet to get him qualified because Dick wasn't giving him any love."

Among all of the signings and talent that found itself in Fayetteville that spring, none was bigger than Melvin Lister, who had grown up in Staten Island, New York, before winning everything there was to win at Butler County Community College in Kansas from the 200 meter (20.14), 400 meter (45.67), long jump (26 feet, 5 inches), and triple jump (53-8). Lister could do them all as well as anyone since Mike Conley.

"He was a terrific athlete and could long jump, triple jump, run a leg on the 400-meter relay or the 1,600-meter relay and go 45 in the open 400 meter," said McDonnell. "That's a heck of a combination for someone who could jump 58-something in the triple jump. He had an absolutely terrific career at Arkansas."

Though Lister was recruited by LSU, Arizona State, Ole Miss, and several other programs across the country, he told his coach he wanted a program where he would not be the best jumper on the campus.

"He told me there was only one place to go," said Lister. "I went on a visit to Arkansas and watched practice, and they were so intense."

Even with Mike Conley's retirement from the sport to work with United States Track and Field, Arkansas had a collegiate group of Kenny Evans and Lavar Miller as well as a postcollegiate group that included Robert Howard, Brian Wellman, Jerome Romain, James Ballard, Brandon Craven, and Erick Walder. It did not take long for their collective experience to rub off on the newcomer.

"They showed you how things were done," said Lister. "I remember at my first practice Erick Walder walked to me, walked around me, looked me up and down and said, 'This is the guy who is supposed to save Arkansas?' They had articles and the pressure was getting to me about being the next guy to take over the jumps. I think that pressure got to me and why I didn't qualify (for NCAAs) in the long jump right away."

Though Dick Booth had promised Melvin and his parents during a home visit that he would improve his triple jump by two feet in one year, there were definite growing pains as Lister adjusted to Booth's coaching style and the sheer intensity of his training program.

"Coach Booth pushed us so hard and had a different way of coaching," said Lister. "He would say, 'Just do what I say.' If he told you to move up six inches and not foul it was hard to understand, but you had to trust he knew what he was talking about and do it to the best of your ability."

In the weight room, Lister squatted volumes of weight greater than anything he had attempted before but only a quarter of the way down.

"I didn't understand until later why we would stack so much weight on a bar and do quarter squats," said Lister. "We squatted so much weight that the bar was bending on our back. We felt like superstars and that nobody could lift as much as we could, so the triple jump should be easy. We did a whole lot of box jumping, a whole lot of stadium runs, a whole lot of lifting on the lower body and core. Coach Booth was a mind coach, and if he got into your mind, he could basically get you to do what he wanted. He would get an athlete who was decent and turn them into a maniac."

It took time before Lister's mind was open to what Booth was trying to get him to accomplish. Less than a few months after he arrived in Fayetteville, he had already had enough.

"Melvin came into my office, closed the door and said he wanted to talk with me, and usually that's bad when they close the door," said McDonnell. "He was telling me he can't stand it anymore. Coach Booth is pushing and grinding him into the ground, and he always feels like he's competing against what Mike Conley did. He said, 'Unless you talk to Coach Booth and tell him to ease up on the workouts, I'm out of here.' So he wasn't happy. When he finished talking, I said, 'Let me tell you something, Melvin. Just before you got here, Coach Booth was in my office, and I had to tell him, 'Dick, I'm sick and tired of you telling me how good Melvin Lister is going to be.' He's in here every day telling me the same thing.' I said to Melvin, 'The thing that annoys me and ruins my day is having to listen to Dick two or three times a day telling me how close you are to Mike Conley and how you are going to break every one of his records.'"

Sitting across McDonnell's desk, Lister's demeanor and expression underwent a metamorphosis.

"All of a sudden Melvin said, 'Coach Booth said that about me?'" remembered McDonnell. "I said, 'He sure did. I told him again just this morning to stop coming in to brag about you.' So he said, 'Well, that's different. I didn't know he thought about me like that.' I asked Melvin, 'Do you still want me to ask him to ease up?' 'Oh,' he said, 'there's no doubt he knows what he's doing.' And Melvin had a helluva year after that. Of course, Booth had said those things about him but not nearly to the extent that I exaggerated."

Once Lister adjusted to the pressure of performing at Arkansas and the physical demands of the training, he blossomed as nearly all Arkansas jumpers had before him.

"It was a lot of pressure, but it was something we fed off and actually welcomed because of the way we trained," said Lister. "We didn't perform unless we had that pressure. We fed off each other. It felt like a professional track meet every day in practice. The reporters would ask us at meets if we were nervous, and we would say we compete with the best in the world at practice every day, so collegians don't really scare us."

During workouts, Robert Howard and Melvin Lister challenged each other verbally and physically.

"There were days when Robert would deliberately make Melvin mad and Melvin would turn around and say something to make Robert mad, and then they'd both be mad and have a great workout," said Booth. "Robert would call him out and then go down and beat him or not. At the end of the day, regardless of who had a better workout, they both had a great one. There were other people at the track who must have thought they were about to have a fight because they were badmouthing each other so bad."

Only weeks after losing to Levar Anderson of LSU by nearly three feet in the triple jump at the 1999 SEC Championships, Lister came back with a vengeance at the NCAA Indoor Championships in Indianapolis two weeks later to win the triple jump in a personal best of 55 feet, ¾ inch.[4]

"Coach Booth told me he skipped over Levar Anderson to sign me even though Levar had better stats," said Lister. "We had our share of battles though. He won his share, and I won my share."

Despite Lister's win, the team battle with Stanford was not off to a great start. Sean Kaley finished third behind the Hausers in the 5,000 meter even though he had been in a position to win entering the final lap.

"The Hausers were the bane of my existence," admitted Kaley. "I had beaten them earlier in the season and thought I could blow them out. I talked to John about not making any moves until 800 meters to go. I was pretty fit, but when I went they went with me. I think I ran 1:28 for 600 meters with 800 meters to go. I was pretty tired and both of them just sat on me and went around me. I broke the field, but I also broke myself."

After two consecutive runner-up finishes to Meb Keflezighi and now to the Hausers, Sean Kaley did everything as a Razorback other than win an individual national title.

"He was the best guy that year and I thought he was going to win," said McDonnell.

The following evening Kaley got his revenge on Brad Hauser in the 3,000 meter by placing third amid a seventeen point Arkansas barrage in the event that included a second-place finish from Mike Power and sixth-place finish from Matt Kerr. Though Mike Power would also finish his Razorback career the next year having accomplished everything other than winning an individual national title, few people would have beaten that day's winner, Bernard Lagat of Washington State. Less than twenty-four hours earlier, Lagat also won the mile over Seneca Lassiter.

At the last NCAA Indoor Championships held in Indianapolis, a balanced scoring attack in a variety of events led Arkansas to twenty-three-point victory over Stanford.[5] Still, even in victory McDonnell remained as analytical as ever. He was not happy with Lassiter's performance in the mile.

"I had told him not to take the lead unless it was a potent move," said McDonnell. "Well, he took the lead with 500 meters and did a sprint, and when someone came on, he would sprint again until finally with 200 meters to go, one of them really put it on him and [Seneca] almost jogged it in."

Never one to judge a performance purely by the outcome but rather by the process that had led to that outcome, McDonnell called Seneca Lassiter to his office on Monday to express his disappointment.

"I said, 'Seneca I'd advise you to get your resume ready because you are a senior and will need a job,'" said McDonnell. "And he looked at me, 'What do you mean I need a job?' 'Well,' I said, 'I don't see any future for you in track after getting third running like an idiot. You ran like you didn't give a crap.' He was getting really offended and said, 'Well, I gave it my best. It was just one of those nights. You're hard to please.' I looked at him and said, 'You're telling me you gave it all you had? That's where you and I differ because if you think you gave it your best, then you really need to get a resume together and start looking for a job.' So I had a tape of the race and gave it to him to take home to watch. He wasn't gone an hour when he came back, 'You're right. I ran stupid.' I said, 'You think it looks bad on television. I had to watch it live.'"

As he often did, John had to manage the egos and expectations of several high-performance athletes and the nuances that came along with each of them.

"Seneca hated to lead workouts, and at the time we had [Mike] Power and [Matt] Kerr and James Karanu in the same group," said McDonnell. "For whatever reason Seneca thought James wasn't in his class even though James eventually ran a 3:56 mile and 1:45 800 meter. I remember one time we did 8 x 400 meters in 56.5 with 90 seconds recovery. I went up to Seneca afterwards and said, 'Good job, kid,' and he turned and said, 'How can it be a good workout if he stayed with me' and he pointed back at James. I said, 'Why shouldn't he be? He's not that far behind you.'"

Other issues also arose that threatened the harmony of the training group.

"Then he was saying Power and Kerr don't go fast enough," remembered McDonnell. "I said, 'Seneca, I don't see you leading.' I really got on to him. From now on I said, 'In workouts with those guys, you lead everything up to a 600-meter interval, and I want you leading all of the races.'"

On a cold, thirty-nine-degree day at the Tyson Invitational on April 16, 1999, Lassiter took the message to heart by blasting a 1,500 meter in 3:37.23 for a new personal best.

"He had an awesome senior year and just got better and better as the season went along," said John.

McDonnell took the majority of his mid- and long-distance runners off the track for nearly a month following the indoor national championship meet and onto the golf course to reload before opening up many of them at Texas Relays. Though some athletes over the years struggled during the outdoor season, the process of reloading in March and April often had Arkansas athletes ready for the championship portion of the season following Penn Relays.

"What we were doing up to that point was uphill training on the golf course," said John, "and some downhill running for leg turnover but not on the track."

With James Karanu's newfound strength having translated into even more abundant speed, he certainly didn't look sluggish when he anchored the sprint medley relay to the win at Texas Relays with an 800-meter split of 1:45.9. After years of close calls and disappointments in the 4 x 800 meter at Penn Relays, it appeared this might finally be the year those old Razorback demons were finally exorcised.

Arkansas began its dominating weekend in Philadelphia by winning the distance-medley relay on Friday afternoon over Southern Methodist. The following morning in the 4 x mile relay, the Razorbacks won by an even greater margin—20 seconds over Colorado—and in the process set a meet and collegiate record of 16:07.97.

All that was left was the 4 x 800 meter relay, the one which had gotten away so many times before. Though Seton Hall put up a fight, there was never more than a small doubt the Arkansas quartet of Ryan Stanley, Sharif Karie, James Karanu, and Seneca Lassiter was going to prevail that Saturday afternoon.

"Winning that 4 x 800 meter relay was special because that was the only one Arkansas had never won," said Lassiter. "We finally put it together in my last race as a Razorback at Penn Relays."

With a four-second lead heading into the final straightaway, Lassiter began pumping the baton into the air as he became overcome with the thrill and emotion of the moment.

"I remember him pumping the stick on the turn and Dwight Stones said on television, 'Seneca, don't do that,' like he was hot dogging," remembered McDonnell. "Seneca said, 'Those are all of my fans at the stadium,' and the crowd was going crazy because we had a big lead."

For the first time in Arkansas history, the Razorbacks won the 4 x 800 meter at Penn Relays. It was enough to earn Lassiter the Penn Relays outstanding athlete of the meet award for the second time.

"James Karanu was the one who blew it wide open with a 1:45 leg," said Lassiter. "Those guys did all of the work. I got to run the easy leg."

In the long jump, Melvin Lister joined the illustrious club of Arkansas jumpers with Penn Relays titles to their name by winning the event over Levar Anderson of Louisiana State. It was but one victory in what would prove to be a back and forth rivalry with the LSU star.

After beating Doug Brown's Florida team by nearly fifty points at the SEC Championships, the Razorbacks travelled to the 1999 NCAA Outdoor Championships in Boise, Idaho, to put the finishing touches on their fifth triple crown at the same site where only five years earlier they had won their fourth in such dominant fashion. With Stanford returning Toby Stevenson, the NCAA champion in the pole vault, along with All-American hammer thrower Adam Connolly, and a plethora of distance talent, nobody expected such a runaway win for Arkansas this time around in the thin Idaho air.

"The altitude is only a problem if you tell the guys there is a problem," said McDonnell. "I always told my guys that at 4,500 feet it will affect the guy next to you as much as you, so just compete like you always compete and don't worry about not being able to breathe. When the race is over you will just have a slower time, but winning and losing is the same. It's only when you get above 5,000 feet that you have to be careful not to follow some idiot."

Following another unanswered barrage by Nathan Nutter, Jason Balkman, and Brent Hauser of Stanford in the 10,000 meter, Matt Kerr was not going to be able to fly under the radar this time. In order for Arkansas to defend its national title, he had to defend his steeplechase crown. Unlike two years earlier when he had entered the event on a whim, Kerr was better prepared than ever before.

"John would have us do hurdle walkthroughs, and sometimes he'd put hurdles over the cross-country course because he said you never knew when you were approaching a hurdle," said Kerr. "We used to work on the water jump all of the time. You can shave tenths of seconds on the hurdles, but you can really put someone away on the water jump. I would accelerate on the water jumps and put three or four seconds on them and then wait for them to catch up. So it was almost like a recovery."

McDonnell certainly knew a thing or two about the event. Being the Irish steeplechase champion three-times in his own running career, he did not waste time on frivolous nonessential drills and coached more steeplechase national champions than any other coach during his era.

Once at the NCAA Championships, Kerr surged on Carlos Suarez of UTEP with seven hundred meters remaining in the race.

"I kept putting distance on them on the jumps, and with two laps to go, they ran out of gas," said Kerr. "So the strategy of putting these guys away on the water jumps was something John and I worked on."

In the final collegiate track race of his career, Kerr captured his second consecutive steeplechase national crown along with ten badly needed points for the Razorbacks.

"John was really good at coming up with simple ways of beating people," said Kerr. "He never got too fancy with it, and it always worked. He just brought running to an easy, basic level that anyone could understand. A lot of coaches make it where it is not enjoyable, but John always made running a lot of fun."

Less than twenty months after their blowup in the Bud Walton Arena, Kerr and McDonnell had overcome any differences to form a bond based on mutual trust and respect.

"There were growing pains that everyone went through, but that came with the territory," said Kerr. "You went down there and found you couldn't keep up with your teammates, and it's a shock to the ego, but you just had to restart and rebuild and think about things in a different way. It was still a lot of fun right from the start. Coach McDonnell and I had personality clashes at first, but for me the process of becoming a better runner started when I realized how little time I had spent in his office."

With a well-balanced array of scoring across a variety of event areas, Arkansas won its thirty-third national championship and fifth triple crown with a seven-point win, 59–52, over Stanford. The two schools had now finished either first or second at seven of the previous nine NCAA Championships, turning the meet into a personal chess match between John McDonnell and Vin Lananna. Under such circumstances,

McDonnell used all of the resources at his disposal and never backed off from a title hunt.

"I never redshirted a good guy that was ready to perform," said McDonnell. "You may have seven guys in cross country, and it may seem like enough, but I would have six many times and would need to go back to my seventh man to win. And there were several years on the track when we had someone do something we didn't expect. I always felt if there is a national title on the line, to go for it because the following year there is no guarantee."

For Arkansas, which graduated Seneca Lassiter and Sean Kaley that spring and would see Mike Power and Matt Kerr deplete their eligibility following the fall cross-country season, there was a certain sense of uncertainty amid the turnover. While Kaley remained in Fayetteville to train under McDonnell in the hopes of qualifying for the 2000 Canadian Olympic team, Lassiter also remained in Arkansas for two years before moving to Arizona to train with Bernard Lagat.

It was around that time when the agent, Kim McDonald, who had gotten several Razorbacks into elite meets in Europe, passed away. Though former Razorbacks Frank O'Mara and Reuben Reina continued training with McDonnell in Fayetteville, Graham Hood and Ryan Wilson instead went to Australia to train with Kim Macdonald's group during the summer, which was the same time as the North American winter.

"Kim was managing a group of fifteen or so from all over the world, and I saw that as another step to make it up a level because I knew I would be the worst guy there at the start," said Ryan Wilson. "John didn't say not to go, and he was too classy to say he didn't like the guy, but I think his preference would have been for me to stay in Fayetteville under his guidance, and in hindsight I agree."

Though John appreciated Kim McDonald's connections and management ability, there was a level of frustration when many of his former athletes eventually found themselves pace making, being paid by meet directors to set a fast pace for other runners but not to finish.

"Pacing was a way of making money, and I was deadly against it, but it was something Frank O'Mara and Graham Hood did at the end of their careers," said McDonnell. "I pulled Frank aside once and said, 'What do you think the kids in Ireland think when you've won two world championships, and they go to see you race? Some little kid is sitting there saying, 'Daddy! Daddy! Frank is going to win!' And Frank said, 'I know where you are going. That's a low blow. I get $10,000 for that.' He had three degrees, and I said, 'Why don't you get a job?' Well, he paced for another two or three years but said years later that I was right."

During that summer, John and Ellen moved into a home they had built on three acres just outside Fayetteville while also continuing to operate the ranch in Muskogee, Oklahoma. Amazingly enough for someone who spent nearly four decades of his coaching career at one school, John built, upgraded, bought, sold, or moved into different homes over seven times.

"My dad was always looking for something better," said his daughter Heather. "I think he regretted it sometimes. We had a house on Bridgewater, that he loved but the power lines were there, so we moved for the betterment of the family."

Though John continued to maintain contact with relatives in Ireland, it had been nearly fifteen years since he returned home to the Emerald Isle. Other coaches played golf or vacationed during the summer holidays, but John would unwind by working at the ranch. It was his sanctuary from the world. Those who had difficulty understanding how an activity requiring manual labor could be relaxing didn't understand John. They didn't know he had been raised in an environment where he knew no different and certainly didn't understand the pressure he put on himself throughout the collegiate season.

"He was so dedicated to his athletes," said Ellen. "I used to tell him you need to think of yourself and take a vacation but he said, 'No, this is important.'"

Throughout the season, as McDonnell did everything to insure his athletes succeeded individually and the program succeeded for the university, his stress levels rose considerably, especially before and during races. Though he did not know it yet, that cycle of stress was beginning to take its toll on his body. After only a handful of weeks into the summer, he found himself already preparing for the busy cross-country season ahead.

It was nonetheless one of John's favorite times of the year when the team returned to campus for training camp every August. With a team heavy with upperclassmen, Arkansas entered the 1999 cross-country season as the favorites to win their second consecutive NCAA championship. While most of his runners looked fit and ready to go, not everyone had done what they were supposed to over the summer.

"Daniel Lincoln was a super-smart guy, but at the time he was completely clueless when it came to track," said Danny Green. "He was a tour guide in Colorado that summer where he did a lot of hiking in the mountains, but not much running; so when he got back, he couldn't even finish an eight-mile run that first week and John suspended him until he got into shape."

Halfway through the first week McDonnell called Lincoln into his office and instructed him to close the door behind him.

"I called him in and said, "I thought I told you to do so many miles over the summer,'" said John. "He said, 'Oh, I must have made a terrible mistake. I thought running up and down the mountain was good enough.' At least he was honest. So I said, "Get yourself in shape, but you are not working out with this team. When you think you are ready to workout with us come back.' He said, 'Yes sir, yes sir.' I gave him an idea of what he should do to give him a chance, but I figured I'd never see this kid again."

After a few weeks of working himself back into shape, Lincoln rejoined the team. Though McDonnell could only scratch his head with regards to the decisions Lincoln had made that summer, it was not long before he realized the kid had a pain threshold higher than almost anyone he had ever coached.

"We had a little training room with Band-Aids, but no trainer on Sunday morning, and all of these guys were waiting outside saying, 'Where's Lincoln?'" remembered McDonnell. "I said, 'I think he is putting on his shoes,' so I went inside, and he was on the training table trying to put a bandage on, and I said, 'What's the problem?' He said, 'I have a blister on the bottom of my foot,' and this bandage was so big that I told him that thing isn't going to stay on there. So I said, 'Let me do it for you.' I took it off and on the whole ball of his foot the skin was gone. Completely gone. I'm not kidding you. It wasn't just a blister. So I told him he couldn't run on this. He said, 'Oh yeah, I ran on it yesterday.' He said he'd be all right. So I put some Vaseline on it and wrapped it with gauze, and he ran fourteen miles, and that's when I knew we had a real winner. From there on he was so tough and never complained about anything. He was a jewel."

After Arkansas rolled through the Cowboy Jamboree and Chile Pepper meets, they headed to Nashville, Tennessee, for the SEC Cross Country Championships in the country-music capital of the world.

"I bought a pair of snakeskin boots the day before, and Coach McDonnell saw them and said, 'Hey kid, where did you get those boots?'" remembered Murray Link. "He kept saying, 'I love those boots, kid.' He was just a down to earth country boy. He was more comfortable at his ranch than sitting in his office."

Link's cowboy boots notwithstanding, John was not easily distracted from the task at hand.

"He wanted to win more for you than for him," said Link. "He instilled values and had a simplicity. There were no mind games or special strategy. He stressed to put the work in and be a good person and things will work out."

After Arkansas captured its ninth consecutive SEC cross-country championship and twenty-sixth consecutive cross-country conference title in a row with ease, McDonnell still focused on the small things.[6]

"We were having a premeet breakfast, and John always paid close attention to details for being successful, and he told the team, 'I do not want anyone to eat eggs,'" remembered Silvey. "Well, Sharif [Karie] went ahead and ordered eggs and ran very poorly and afterwards went up to John and said, 'Coach, I cramped, I cramped!' and John said, 'Well, I told you not to eat those g'damn eggs!'"

For the regional meet, John held out Murray Link, James Karanu, Matt Kerr in order to train in Fayetteville. Though it was ostensibly to rest for nationals, what they did was hardly considered rest.

"Those of us who stayed in Fayetteville ran a ten miler in 49:20," said Link. "It was pretty much a race effort, but at least we got to stay in our beds."

Starting at the mailbox at Halsell Road and Oliver Avenue overlooking Donald Reynolds Stadium, the hard ten-miler "behind the golf course" had been the ultimate proving ground of generations of Razorbacks as it wound its way under Interstate 540, around the Razorback Golf Course onto a dirt road back to campus that extended as far as the eye could see.

With several Razorbacks being held out from the regional meet and Daniel Lincoln rounding back into shape, there was still some question as to who would travel.

"I remember Mike Power said, 'You are coming around,' and said you might as well have a word with Coach about it," remembered Lincoln. "So I went into Coach McDonnell's office and asked if I could put my name forward, and he looked at me and said, 'Kid, we have to place first or second at this meet. We can't just put anyone in there.' I felt about two inches tall."

At the 1999 NCAA Cross Country Championships in Bloomington, Indiana, Arkansas placed five runners in the top twenty-five to beat a Wisconsin team led by second-year head coach Jerry Schumacher, 58–185. The margin of victory was the largest by an Arkansas team at a national meet.[7]

"Those were the good days," said McDonnell, rubbing his hands together. "That was the most beautiful race to watch. We had six in the top-twenty when they came by at four miles."

Most amazing of all was James Karanu, who had split 1:45 at the Penn and Texas Relays only seven months earlier. Eight-hundred- meter runners of that caliber often resisted cross country, but Karanu took to it.

"He had the biggest chest and little legs, so he did well in cross country," said Lincoln. "Coach McDonnell took special pride in getting those 800-meter guys to run well in cross country."

Starting with Niall O'Shaughnessy, Espen Borge, Graham Hood, Seneca Lassiter, and now Karanu, few coaches had as many half-milers excel during cross country as well as McDonnell did throughout his career.

"I used to tell James to take it easy in cross country but he wouldn't," said McDonnell. "I'd say those guys are running an eleven-mile loop, so you can do eight, but he'd say, 'Oh coach, they're running slow. I can stay with them no problem!' He was a super team man and when he got tenth that year in Indiana, he started cramping up the final straightaway, and they didn't think he would make it to the line. When he finally crossed the line his entire body went into a cramp, and they had to put him into ice."

With the team championship wrapped up by the last mile, Mike Power continued battling David Kimani of South Alabama for the individual win.

"Power could have beaten him, but Kimani made a move and got away," said McDonnell. "Mike was closing hard at the finish and nearly got him."

With their eligibility finally exhausted, both Matt Kerr and Mike Power graduated from the University of Arkansas that December. It was not long afterwards when Power headed to Melbourne to qualify for the 2000 Australian Olympic team in the 5,000 meter.

"I had trained him solely to make the [Australian] trials and put him on that team," said John. "He left here in January [2000] and two weeks later he ran 13:23 [to qualify]."

Those remaining in Fayetteville saw the program move into the twenty-first century, both literally and figuratively, with the completion of the Randall Tyson Track Center in January 2000. The sparkling facility, with its spacious six-thousand-seat capacity and banked 200-meter track, was a massive upgrade over the barebones indoor facility that the Razorbacks had been calling home for two decades. It was also turned into a great recruiting tool, a place to hang all of those championship banners and demonstrate the commitment to track and field at the university.

Not only was Arkansas hosting the Southeastern Conference Indoor Championships and NCAA Indoor Championships for the first time, but McDonnell moved the mid-April Tyson Invitational to indoors in February and arranged for sponsors and live-television coverage of the professional races.

"Getting that Tyson meet on television gave a whole new lease on life to track," said McDonnell. "It made a big difference when we could advertise that the best in the country were going to be in our backyard. It was a tremendous boost to interest and got a lot of people interested in the sport who would come up to me afterwards and say, 'I never knew track was so interesting.' It was my goal to have nonstop action and get people out there like Penn Relays. The Tyson meet was promoted from outside the university and was always sold out for that reason. Maybe it's sour grapes, but I never felt like our sports information advertised us like we deserved for what we had done and the type of quality athletes coming from other schools and Olympians and future Olympians."

At first, McDonnell was careful how he trained his athletes on the banked track in the new facility.

"We ran on the inside lanes a few times and the guys went on the three-lane flat track outside of it a few times," said McDonnell. "A few of them got on it striding out and said they felt less pressure on the bank than on the flat track. So we did a session of 200s on there and everyone's legs were great, and we did another session of 400s; and it was great, so I began doing long stuff all the way up to 1,600s on it."

After christening the track at a small meet at the end of January, the Randall Tyson Track Center was officially opened for the inaugural indoor Tyson Invitational on February 11, 2000. With an assortment of professionals in every sprint, field, and distance event, the Razorbacks hardly disappointed with seven automatic qualifiers: 60-meter hurdles (Sean Lightfoot), mile (James Karanu), 3,000 meter (Sharif Karie), 5,000 meter (Andrew Begley), triple jump (Melvin Lister), high jump (Kenny Evans), and shot put (Marcus Clevelle). The program was now a first-class operation in every way imaginable.

After winning the triple jump as a professional, former Razorback All-American and Olympian Brian Wellman was positively gushing about the new facility afterwards.

"I was here in 1991 and 1992," Wellman told the media. "I've seen all of the facilities—NCAAs, Indoor Worlds, Nationals. This facility is probably in the top one percent. I don't see any major changes that need to be made."[8]

With so many of the professionals pleased by the meet and the new facility, they continued coming back for years to come.

"This is an awesome facility," said Khadevis Robinson after winning the 800 meter in 1:47.97. "It was great to be on live television, and the whole event turned out to be great as well."[9]

Even collegiate teams such as Oklahoma State and Stanford were wowed by the standard to which the Tyson Invitational had brought indoor track and field.

"It changed indoor track because they had a real good facility to come to and the people in Arkansas bought into it, and it was always sold out," said Oklahoma State coach Dick Weis. "John singlehandedly did more for track and field than anyone. He raised indoor standards. West Coast teams would never come indoors, but now you had Stanford whipping in there, and Oregon came whipping in there, and UCLA; and it changed everything."

Arkansas won its first indoor conference championship on home soil by a healthy margin over Louisiana State thanks to six individual wins.[10] Even Daniel Lincoln, six months after being unable to complete an eight-mile run, finished second in a 5,000-meter personal best and grabbed the last spot to NCAAs.

"I started coming around that winter," said Lincoln. "So in the 5,000 meter, I was just trying to hang on to Begley for as long as I could, and that race I hung on long enough that amazingly I got into nationals."

Before national championships, John held the team meeting and discussed his expectations in each event. It was also an opportunity for him to use psychological leverage based on how he understood particular athletes would respond.

"In the triple jump he said he wanted eight points, and there were three of us in it," said Lister. "So I went to Coach McDonnell and said, 'I'm not used to this. If there are three of us, what are you expecting from each of us?' It kind of made me feel like he didn't expect a ten out of me. He either made a mistake or did it on purpose to make me mad. At that point in my career all you had to do was make me mad. So he looked back to me and said, 'Well, do you think you can do better?'"

Lister did much better—he won the long jump and came back to win triple jump—and was joined by teammates Jason Ward, Kenny Evans, and Lavar Miller for an astounding thirty-seven jumps points.

"At one point we had six scholarships in the field events," said McDonnell. "It was about getting the best possible people. Ted McLaughlin [of SMU] once said, 'I don't care if I win a national championship behind the stands [where the hammer throw was sometimes contested]. I just want to win a national championship.' Well, that was my philosophy too."

The atmosphere in sold-out Tyson Center was as electric as the Razorbacks poured it on with All-American performances in the mile, 3,000 meter, and distance medley relay.[11] After each Hog performance, the decibel level in the indoor field house went up by a few notches.

"WOO . . . PIG . . . SOOIE!!" The crowd thundered.

"That was one of the highlights of being at Arkansas," said Link. "You're at home, and there are six thousand people packed into the building cheering for you. It's one thing to go to Penn with a crowd of fifty-thousand, but these people were cheering for you. To have everybody appreciate you like that was pretty awesome."

Arkansas won the meet going away by a 69–52 margin over Stanford. Sixteen years after "Calling the Hogs" after his first national championship at the cavernous Carrier Dome in Syracuse, New York, in 1984, winning at home in front of passionate Fayetteville fans was a thrill as great as any John had experienced.

"That was like winning our first national championship because we had won them before but they had all been on foreign soil," said McDonnell. "That brought a new level of interest to track in northwest Arkansas because people who had never come to a track meet loved it."

The only worrying trend for McDonnell was being shut out in the 5,000 meter and the plethora of distance points scored by Stanford—which portended poorly for the upcoming outdoor season.

"Our distance runners weren't great at the time," said McDonnell. "Once Power and Kerr were gone, we didn't have as much leadership. It's a big deal for your team having guys that pull the kids together. If you have to tell them it isn't going to happen. You have to have that personal pride. Someone has to step up and say, 'We're going to do something about it fellas.'"

Considering Daniel Lincoln was the last man accepted into the meet, he was positively thrilled to beat anyone—and he did by finishing second to last ahead of Keith Kelly of Providence. Once the outdoor season came around, Lincoln's ascent continued unabated. After another personal best in the 5,000 meter at the Mt. SAC Relays, he soon found himself the test subject in another McDonnell steeplechase experiment.

"I owe Coach McDonnell the whole steeplechase thing," said Lincoln. "He goes through the process with every runner trying to decide whether they will be good in the steeple. I think I went over some barriers and went over the water jump a few times, and then he put me into the fast race at Penn Relays."

On a cold Thursday evening in Philadelphia, Lincoln walked to the starting line without any idea of what to expect and wondering why a disproportionate number of the people still remaining in Franklin Field were huddled around a water jump located in the corner of the uniquely configured track.

"I had no idea what I was getting into, but I got the message right away when both guys on either side of me immediately threw their elbows into my chest," said Lincoln. "So I stayed there, and it seemed like you could take it one barrier at a time and not notice the laps going by because you're distracted. I never got antsy, but I noticed the fans seemed to be enjoying it at the water barrier. I could hear them chanting, 'Fall! Fall! Fall!' I don't even know what place I was. I ran 8:46 but didn't know what that meant. Coach McDonnell and Danny Green seemed excited and said that'll get you to nationals so I was happy."

It was as good a debut as anyone could have expected on a night when Steve Slattery of Colorado took the win in about ten seconds faster. It was also the first pleasant surprise in a weekend when the Razorbacks avenged an upset at the hands of Connecticut in the distance medley relay by unexpectedly winning the 4 x 120 yard shuttle hurdle relay in the second-fastest time in Penn Relays history.

With sprint and intermediate hurdlers ranked in the top five in the country along with a mile relay that appeared capable of contending for a national championship after dominating the competition at the SEC meet, all was going well for Steve Silvey and the sprint group on the track. Off the track things were not running so smoothly as the simmering feud between Silvey and Dick Booth began bubbling to the surface.

"They were both very competitive people and had different views on how to win," remembered McDonnell. "It had everything to do with egos and personalities but didn't affect their coaching. On the track those two were joined at the hip."

Though both men were too professional to allow personality differences to spill over into their coaching, the discord between them became an issue headed into the 2000 NCAA Outdoor Championships where the Stanford Cardinal were expected to field a team as strong as ever.

The major source of disagreement revolved around Melvin Lister. The senior was expected to win the long jump and triple jump. Given the fact that he had run on a mile relay that was in contention to win the national title and a sprint relay that appeared to need all of the help it could get to even qualify for a final, the question naturally became where to enter the five-time All-American.

"Dick brought Melvin in two weeks before national meet and said you cannot run the sprint relay if you want to win the national championship in the long jump," said Silvey. "All year long he had been running the anchor leg of the sprint relay which always served as a great warm-up for the long jump. So when you make an adjustment at the national meet and do things differently, you don't know what the results are going to be. All I wanted to do was have Melvin Lister run the prelims of the 4 x 100 meter to get us to the finals and then in the finals we would have substituted a hurdler in there while he triple jumped. We would have picked up a few points and it would have helped his long jump."

As always, the final call was made by the man whose instincts had so often been correct during the previous thirty-five national championships.

"Silvey wanted him to do it," said McDonnell, "but I didn't. You couldn't kill the goose that laid the golden egg."

On the first day of the 2000 NCAA Outdoor Championships held at Wallace Wade Stadium on the Duke University campus, the favored Razorbacks hardly got off to an auspicious start as their 4 x 100 meter relay without Melvin Lister finished last in the preliminaries. Lister followed that up finishing fourth in the long jump despite having the fourth longest jump in the world that season and having beaten the NCAA champion Savante Stringfellow of Mississippi at the SEC Championships only two weeks earlier.

In the distance events, the early returns were even worse. Both Adam Dailey [10,000 meter] and Daniel Lincoln [3,000-meter steeplechase] fell in their races and finished out of the scoring. Meanwhile Stanford nearly swept the top three spots in the 10,000 meter while their pole vaulter Toby Stevenson finished second. When Marcus Clevelle failed to score for Arkansas in the shot, it was suddenly a full-blown crisis. The Razorbacks ended the second day of a meet they were expected to win down by a 31–5 margin. Though he was concerned, McDonnell did not panic.

"I lost the long jump to a bunch of guys I didn't lose to on my bad days," said Lister. "So Coach McDonnell said, 'What's done is done, but I need you to do something or say something to get this team rallied because it's going downhill right now.' There is a tough side to Coach McDonnell, but there is a side to him that shows how much he cares about you as a person."

On Friday afternoon Melvin Lister began Arkansas's ascent out of the abyss by winning the triple jump, followed up in short order by a fourth-place finish by Sam Glover (400-meter hurdles) and a sixth-place finish by James Karanu (800 meter). Though the Razorbacks pulled even with the Cardinal after Kenny Evans and Lavar Miller went third and fourth in the high jump, the fate of the meet would be decided on the final day.

"Ryan Travis found out a week before the championship that he was hypoglycemic and got a new diet," said McDonnell. "So what did the dietician tell him? Eat two hours before the race. I went by the room [before the 1,500 meter] and he had a pizza, which he told me the dietician had told him to do. So I caught myself and said, 'Oh the dietician told you that? Oh, well she must know.' I knew damn well she didn't know, and he didn't have a good race."

In the same golden summer that the Stanford duo Gabe Jennings and Michael Stember finished first and second at the 2000 U.S. Olympic Trials, they also finished first and second in the NCAA 1,500 meter final—well ahead of Razorbacks Sharif Karie, Ryan Travis, and a fatigued James Karanu.

"We looked good," said Lananna, "but you're never going to count Arkansas out of it."

In the 5,000 meter, Stanford put the meet away with another win by Brad Hauser, who qualified for the Olympics that summer, a fourth-place from Brent Hauser and a sixth-place from Jonathan Riley. Though Murray Link did everything he could to salvage Razorback hopes by placing third, it was for naught.

Drawing little attention nearly one minute later, was an unknown freshman at Southern Methodist named Alistair Cragg, who placed sixteenth.

"The last mile was 4:08," said Link. "I just hung in and did the best I could. Coach was happy even though the meet was over."

The Cardinal had won their first NCAA outdoor championship since 1934.

"I thought we were going to win that meet, but we had a few bad things happen with guys falling and getting tripped in the distance events," reflected McDonnell. "I probably shouldn't have put [James] Karanu in both [the 800 meter and 1,500 meter], but there were a few other events where guys didn't do what they were supposed to. It was just one thing after another, and those Stanford distance guys went wild and did unbelievable stuff we used to do, but this time the shoe was on the other foot."

It was not long after the season ended when Steve Silvey resigned after six years in Fayetteville. Though Silvey's relationship with Booth had deteriorated, and he had other reasons for his move to Dallas before resurfacing at Oregon, his respect for John McDonnell was not diminished to any degree.

"If John had worked at GM or Chrysler he would have been successful," said Silvey. "John could be a fiery SOB and would light you up. I'm not going to lie he would light me up at least once a year, but I liked that fire because it showed me he cared about his sport and his program. So many people hold onto their jobs just for a paycheck way past their prime and cheat the kids and cheat the programs."

Judging by the contingent of Razorbacks qualified for the 2000 Olympic Games held in Sydney, Australia, that summer, it was obvious that the fire was still burning brightly for the program.

Not only was there a plethora of athletes qualified for the Games but in perhaps the most inspiring story of all, former Razorback All-American John Register won a silver medal for the United States in the long jump at the Paralympics after having a leg amputated following a horrific hurdles accident.

In the Olympic high jump, Kenny Evans qualified for the finals but was unable to better his mark of 7 feet, 5½ inches and placed thirteenth. In the long jump, Melvin Lister won the U.S. Trials but a nagging injury kept him from the Olympic final. In the triple jump, Brian Wellman placed twentieth for Bermuda, while Robert Howard made the finals and placed seventh with a leap of 55-11½—the apex of a remarkable career.

Two Razorbacks appeared in the distance events. In the 5,000 meter, Mike Power finished thirteenth for Australia in 13:51.00 in his semifinal heat before the home crowd, a thrill that he would not soon forget. In the 10,000 meter, Sean Kaley ran 28:36.07 to place twelfth for Canada in his semifinal heat after spending the year following graduation continuing to train under McDonnell in Fayetteville.

"It was difficult sometimes because I was not on a college schedule, and I had to get up at 5 a.m. to run because it was so hot," said Kaley, "but I knew I'd make the Olympic team if I didn't change anything."

Six years after arriving in Fayetteville as a scrawny, naïve freshman who had decided upon Arkansas after being promised by McDonnell that it offered him the best opportunity of making the Olympic team, Kaley saw the truth behind such bold words.

"There were definitely people as talented as me or better who went elsewhere and didn't make the Olympic team," said Kaley. "That was a formative experience of my life, being in that pressure cooker and learning to run fast."

Sixty-two years into his life and twenty-nine years into his collegiate coaching career, it was becoming obvious that John McDonnell still had a few tricks up his sleeve. When a resurgent Colorado cross-country team under Mark Wetmore arrived in Ames, Iowa, four months later favored to win their first national title at the 2000 NCAA Cross Country Championships, McDonnell pulled out all of the stops on a brutally cold afternoon where the wind chill dipped to minus nineteen.

"That was the coldest NCAA meet ever," said John. "You'd be out there two or three minutes and your face was ready to crack, so we rented a big bus just for the day. I knew the weather was cold, so the kids went out and jogged and stretched on the bus and did no strides and went right to the starting line. Our kids were warm and everyone else was shaking, so that bus saved us."

For the few minutes the Razorbacks ran outside to warm up, they were also shielded from the cold.

"Danny Green ordered these trench-coat fleece-type outfits, and that's what we wore over our regular suit," said Murray Link. "It was almost like a football jacket it was so big."

Before the race, McDonnell gave his team a plan for victory in the miserable circumstances.

"I told our guys this is a guess, and if I'm wrong change it, but I have a sneaking suspicion nobody will want to lead," said McDonnell. "There'll be a big pack up front so make sure you are at the front of it."

Although Karie and Link both fell early in the race, each of them got back up and trudged to the front. When the leaders came through the three-mile mark in a pedestrian time of 15:15 and McDonnell saw his top five runners with the leaders and the Colorado runners well back, he sensed an upset just might happen.

"[Colorado] started running hard after that, but our guys had leg speed," said McDonnell. "By the time Colorado started cranking up everyone was going so fast."

In a race won by Keith Kelly of Providence College, Arkansas scored 83 points to edge a formidable Colorado squad—which included Jorge and Ed Torres and Steve Slattery—by eleven points.[12]

"That was an upset for sure because Colorado was a much better team," said McDonnell. "There's no doubt in my mind that bus won it for us."

After thirty-six national championships, it seemed nobody could think of simpler ways to beat other people and other teams than John McDonnell. Though an air of invincibility enveloped him and his program, it would not be long before John found out how vulnerable he truly was.

13

A New Lease on Life (2001–2003)

"It was like I hadn't looked in the mirror. I was like, 'My God, where have all of the years gone? I'm an old guy now.'"

—*John McDonnell*

It was a cold morning on January 14, 2001 when John and Ellen McDonnell awoke at 6:00 a.m. to get ready for Sunday mass. As he began preparing himself, John immediately felt something awry.

"My stomach was burning, and I thought it was indigestion, so I took Alka Seltzer, but it made it worse," remembered John. "I was sitting on the end of the bed, and all of a sudden I started feeling cold. The next thing I felt was something running on my face. I was pouring sweat. I told Ellen I need to get to a hospital. She called 911 and put on her jacket and drove me to the emergency room. When we arrived, the medics were ready for us and put me in a wheelchair right away. Then they gave me morphine, and next thing I remembered I was in a hospital bed."

When he awoke two hours later, John learned he had suffered a heart attack.

"I was fortunate because I could have been somewhere on my ranch with nowhere to go to get to a hospital," said John. "I had none of the symptoms that cause a heart attack such as high cholesterol or blood pressure so they said it was caused by stress."

As John lay staring at the ceiling of his hospital room at the Washington Regional Medical Center, he found a new perspective on life had been violently thrust upon him.

"It was a reality check," said McDonnell. "Suddenly all of those national championships didn't mean much. It made me realize there are more important things in life. You could say it was a blessing in disguise."

The stress John felt throughout the process of raising money for the indoor facility was only exacerbated by his already elevated heart rate before meets.

"I was always a type A personality, and before races, I'd be standing there and my heart would start pounding in my chest, and I'd have to take a few deep breaths," said John. "So they gave me a medication to keep calm. I tell you, when you start doing that, it's probably time to get the hell out of coaching."

Though John never gave serious consideration to retirement at that point in time, he did remain in the hospital for three days as the doctors put a stent in his heart. When he was finally released, it was three weeks before he returned, during which time assistant coach Dick Booth took over in his absence.

His daughter, Heather, received a call about the emergency at her sorority house at the University of Texas from her brother, Sean.

"He was like fifteen at the time, and he never called me, so I knew something was wrong," said Heather. "I had just gotten back to Austin four days earlier, and I could tell my father was a little on edge. He wasn't as energetic as usual. I remembered thinking I should have waited."

When she finally reached her father by telephone in his hospital bed, John was in good spirits.

"The first thing he said when he picked up the phone was 'How are you doing' in Gaelic," said Heather. "It was a private joke. He was lying in bed after a heart attack, and he was very light hearted. That was pretty emotional."

Though track and field understandably took a back seat for a few weeks as John recovered from a life-threatening ailment, the scare did not completely squelch his competitive instincts.

"He won a water bottle each week for being the person that did the best in rehab," remembered Ellen. "They wanted to make him watch these movies about heart attacks, which were very depressing. He said, 'No, I know what I have to do.' He was only in rehab for a few weeks."

Upon being discharged from rehab, John began eating differently, even though the heart attack was not related to cholesterol or blood pressure, and took medication to relieve some of the stress he experienced before races.

"He didn't let the pressure get to him as much," said Ellen. "I would see him get worked up but not as much, and I could see he had calmed down."

When John returned to the office one week before the annual Tyson Invitational in mid-February, Dick Booth noticed subtle changes but one overriding similarity.

"I think it may have taken a bit out of his stinger because he was confronted with his own mortality and realized that he wasn't bulletproof," said Dick Booth. "He did slow down a bit, especially after Ellen insisted, but one of John's favorite sayings was that 'a leopard doesn't change his spots.' He remained a committed, hard-driving coach who wouldn't settle for anything less than the best, and I don't think the athletes noticed he was any different."

Though the health scare convinced John and Ellen into making plans for a long-overdue trip to Ireland that following summer for the first time since 1986, there were myriad other issues confronting McDonnell upon his return to his office at the Bud Walton Arena.

Following the departure of Steve Silvey, McDonnell reached back into the past by hiring former Razorback sprints coach Doug Williamson, who had resigned as the head coach at the University of Alabama only a few years earlier. Though the move had all of the makings of a feel-good homecoming for everyone involved, it was not long before McDonnell realized there was no turning back of the clock.

"I knew that Doug was around and was a great coach when I had him [in 1985], so

I decided to call and ask him if he was interested in getting back into it," said John. "He was out in Jackson Hole, Wyoming, running a ski business and had just been divorced so he thought about it and decided to come back."

After a few months it began to dawn on McDonnell that the Doug Williamson he hired was a lifetime removed from the energetic graduate assistant he had hired out of Northwestern University in 1980.

"He was great with everyone, but had just lost it," said John. "He had lost the fire, and it didn't end up working out."

In the distance events, McDonnell had signed another group of athletes from around the country and the world whose careers in Fayetteville would have varying degrees of success. The first was Fernando Cabada from Fresno, California, an 8:59 two-miler who had finished ninth nationally in the event.

"Fernando was a decent talent but not super," said John. "He was tough, but in big races he had problems handling pressure."

Arriving that same fall from Bolton, England, was Chris Mulvaney, a supremely talented athlete with 1:49 (800 meter) and 3:46 (1,500 meter) personal bests in secondary school. After finishing fourteenth at the SEC Cross Country Championships and travelling to the NCAA Cross Country Championships as a reserve that same fall as a true freshman, there seemed to be nothing Mulvaney could not do.

"Oh, he was a tough kid," said John. "He could run 22 seconds for a 200 meter in practice and always wanted to run the last one fast. I told him you're going to pull your hamstring. He could run 12.5 miles to the bridge in 1:04. He could do it all."

Mulvaney had speed to burn and tremendous competitive instincts on the track.

"He would come to my office and sit down and talk and I'd ask, 'What are you thinking about your goals?'" said John. "I remember once I suggested aiming for 3:36 [in the 1,500 meter] after he had run a few races with a dynamite kick in 3:41. He looked at me and said, '3:36? I'm going to run 3:30.' So I said to him, 'You think you are going to drop from 3:41 to 3:30 that quick? Let's get to the 3:36 range first.' He was a nice guy and really coachable with a lot of talent."

With Dirk Heinze, a 1:47 800-meter runner with a cross-country pedigree who had arrived from Germany, the Razorbacks had reloaded once again. Arkansas edged Louisiana State at the 2001 SEC Indoor Championships only weeks after McDonnell's return to the track, but the 108 points they scored were the lowest winning point total since joining the conference.

Two weeks later at the NCAA meet it was Pat Henry's Louisiana State Tigers who turned the tables to capture their first men's indoor national title, despite a second place from Heinze in the 800 meter in a blazing race won by Patrick Nduwimana of Arizona. Though the Razorbacks had been on the periphery of scoring in several events, they were shut out of the sprints entirely.[1]

It was only the second time in eighteen years that Arkansas had failed to win the indoor national championship—as telling a statistic of the Razorback dynasty as any. As much of a change as that may have been for the program, other things had remained the same as a somewhat mellower McDonnell had not altered from the foundational training methods perfected over nearly three decades of coaching.

By this point in his career McDonnell had been giving his distance runners off on Sundays in compliance with NCAA regulations requiring one day off each week. Now on Saturdays during weekends when the Razorbacks were not racing, the long runs generally varied between twelve and fourteen miles.

"They were competitive because you have to imagine five to ten of the top guys in the country," said Link. "You get these attitudes, and sometimes we would hammer those fourteen mile runs in 1:15 and would be rolling."

For about a month during the first part of the cross-country season, the distance runners did mostly mileage runs, which were run on some days with the intensity of tempo runs.

"On the easy days you didn't want to run with Daniel Lincoln or he'd kill you," said All-American Jason Sandfort, who joined the team in 2001. "He'd run fifty-eight minutes for ten miles."

Whether one ran eight miles after McDonnell's "weights and eight" gauntlet on Tuesday and Thursday or ten miles on an easy day, the intensity could catch up to newcomers if they were not careful.

"You could go hard for a little while, but it caught up to you," said All-American Phil Price, who trained with Meb Keflezghi after college. "There were days you ran forty-two minutes for eight miles and some days you ran fifty. The problem was you had freshmen who felt they had to prove themselves because they were the star on their high-school team, and what they failed to realize was so was everyone else on this team."

The basic principles had not changed. Toward the end of September, the distance runners began incorporating workouts on the golf course such as twelve to sixteen 400s alternating uphill and downhill in approximately sixty-two to sixty-five seconds, as well as five or six uphill mile repeats. Every so often McDonnell would throw in wrinkles, such as ten-mile tempos behind the golf course or 2,400-meter to 3,200-meter repeats on a dirt road.

"One way would be a little easier going than the other way, and he would typically want you under nine minutes [for 3,200 meters] on every one so that was really tough," said Sandfort. "We didn't do that workout often, but you wanted him to give you that one because it seemed really hard. When you ran three, two-mile repeats under nine minutes it felt like something special."

Though individual training varied, the average mileage during the fall tended to range between eighty to ninety miles per week, which was slightly less than the Razorbacks had averaged in the 1980s, and much less than some of the large volumes that Arkansas distance runners averaged at the beginning of McDonnell's career. While it took time for many athletes new to the program to adjust to the intensity, the somewhat-moderated volume also represented a significant jump for all but the highest mileage prep athletes.

Once the indoor season was underway, McDonnell began incorporating mile step-downs on the track—starting at 1,600 meters, followed by 1,200 meters, 800 meters, 600 meters, 400 meters, 300 meters, 200 meters—something he believed incorporated every energy system a middle- or long-distance athlete would be exposed to in a race.

"We heard stories about Joe Falcon doing 4:00 miles and how tough he was," said Sean Kaley. "He'd do extra reps when everyone else was out of breath. We'd just start at 4:12 and try to hang on."

Although McDonnell saved particular sessions for particular seasons, the diet of workouts tended not to vary greatly from month to month and year to year.

"He would have this handful of workouts in his repertoire, and I remember talking to the Stanford folks who were our main competition, and they would repeat the workouts maybe once a season and we did the same workouts every two weeks," remembered Kaley. "It drove some people crazy, but I liked it because you could see your progress. It was the same on the trails. We would run on the same runs or trails every day, and it would be impossible not to look at your watch. The key at Arkansas was getting fit to the point where the runs didn't kill you."

Though McDonnell believed in activating fast-twitch fibers at all times of the year, his workouts tended to incorporate longer intervals based on strength-oriented principles.

"I always preached longer intervals," said McDonnell. "I'd say, 'Most people hate this workout, but it's the one that's good for you, and that's why we beat everyone.' Too many people spend too much time doing speed work."

McDonnell remained cautious during the transition into the outdoor season throughout most of his career by training on the grass until after Texas Relays. Though his training regimen typically followed a pattern that he tweaked over the years, few of his athletes could predict that pattern better than Murray Link, a testament to how close their relationship had become over four years.

"Murray and Coach saw eye to eye, and Murray respected him so much and looked up to him that he would do whatever he said," remembered Daniel Lincoln. "Coming from a dairy farm they had a lot in common. Murray also studied Coach and could always predict the workout that was next. Coach would never give us the workout ahead of time. We would show up, and you never knew what you were going to get but Murray was very good at predicting what was next."

Unlike many of his teammates, who had aspirations of qualifying for and winning medals at the World Championships or Olympic Games, Link's goals were a bit more modest and down to earth.

"He planned to go back to the dairy farm in Canada," said Daniel Lincoln, who travelled up to visit Link in Winchester, Ontario. "He'd say, 'I'm going to graduate and move back to Winchester, go to the dairy farm, meet a girl; she's going to come to the farm, and we're going to have lots of kids. So he majored in agricultural and farm management and had no plans to run after college."

With Arkansas out of conference and national championship contention during the 2001 outdoor season, Link went into McDonnell's office early in the spring to suggest trying the 10,000-meter race.

"I had run 3:43 [1,500 meter], but that was pretty much balls out," said Link. "I knew if I ran the 10,000 meter at NCAAs, I could place well because I had decent speed for the event and a lot of guys don't seem to run well because they get their mark early and then shit the bed at NCAAs. Four are going to suck, four will run below average, four will be okay, and four will be awesome. So I was thinking, just be in that four. After I explained my thoughts to John he looked at me and said, 'You know what kid? You can do it.'"

Link's first race over twenty-five laps was at the Mt. SAC Relays in California, where he ran 28:48. At the 2001 NCAA Outdoor Championships seven weeks later, the Canadian senior's family flew out to Eugene, Oregon, for what appeared to be the final race of his Arkansas career—and his career, period.

"We were doing seventy second laps when Ryan Shay [of Notre Dame] took off and I went with him to pull a good 100 meters ahead of everyone else," remembered Link. "With four laps remaining, I was right on his tail and took the lead, which was a mistake, but I was worried about the pack catching us. With two laps remaining he overtook me and slowly pulled away and I finished second [in 29:25]."

It was a special end to a career that ended with finality like few others.

"I don't think he even cooled down after the race," remembered Lincoln.

Within nine months of graduating from Arkansas , Link married and within ten years he and his wife had four children on a farm outside Winchester, Ontario, Canada, with a big red barn and white farmhouse. His dreams had come true.

"He was a little guy who knew exactly what he was going to do," said McDonnell. "He went home the minute he left here and never ran another step. He met a pretty girl, went back to the dairy and got married."

Heading into that same NCAA championship meet in Eugene, McDonnell had an entirely different message for Daniel Lincoln, who was still in the beginning of his Razorback career.

"I had qualified [in the steeplechase], and Dirk Heinze had qualified [in the 800 meter], and Coach McDonnell was on the track talking about the NCAA meet which he didn't do often because he liked to minimize pressure," said Lincoln. "He said to Dirk, 'You should be aiming to win this race,' and then he turned to me and said, 'The same goes for you as well.' I hadn't thought about it before then, but I realized there wasn't anybody leaps and bounds ahead of me setting the track on fire. Steve Slattery [of Colorado] was my age, and we were neck and neck, so that was the first time I thought I could win it. Coach McDonnell planted the seed right then, and I'm sure he did it on purpose."

After Heinze finished third in the 800 meter, Lincoln qualified for the 3,000-meter steeplechase final.

"Coach said to be in position to make a move with five hundred meters to go," said Lincoln. "I didn't want to run in lane three, so with four hundred meters remaining I found myself boxed in, and I remember getting antsy because I could still go but didn't have an out, and I was almost resigned to the fact that someone else was going to win. Then on the water jump the guy in front of me went face first into the pit, and I remember jumping over the barrier and all of a sudden I came down and had this opening. I didn't even have to think about it. I just went and passed a few guys, and it was a sprint finish. I bolted to the front and hit the last barrier and was just hoping the finish line would come early enough."

Lincoln won his first national title in the steeplechase in a time of 8:42.31. It was the culmination of a remarkable transformation for the walk-on from Hot Springs and helped the Razorbacks finish seventh as a team in a national championship won by Bill Webb's Tennessee Volunteers.

That summer, John had another busy summer ahead of him, compounded by the sale of his 2000 acre ranch in Muskogee, Oklahoma, and the purchase of a 2,700-acre ranch in nearby Vinita. Still, while there was never going to be an end of business to attend to at the ranch or at the track office, the events of the past January had finally convinced John, after years of prodding by his wife Ellen, to take some downtime and make the long overdue trip to visit his family in Ireland.

In July 2001, John McDonnell stepped back through the looking glass. What he found startled him. During all of his days spent toiling at the track, office, and ranch—time had indeed marched on.

"Everyone I knew was old," said John. "All of my family, my brother, my sisters, and schoolmates. I realized they were all old. It was like I hadn't looked in the mirror. I was like, 'My God, where have all of the years gone? I'm an old guy now.' That was an eye-opener, and it really shocked me. If I had gone back one year at a time it might have been different."

Though McDonnell had not exactly lost touch with his relatives, many of whom had either come over to visit or, in his brother Michael's case, lived only a few hours away, there were many other friends and acquaintances he had not seen in two decades. Almost all of the five children of his older brother Paddy were now grown. During all of the years that he had won countless NCAA championships and coached hundreds of All-Americans and dozens of Olympians, it hadn't fully sunk into John McDonnell's consciousness until that summer how quickly his life had elapsed before his eyes.

"Sometimes I don't know if it was all worth it," reflected McDonnell. "The thing that made me realize that was going to Ireland after I hadn't gone since 1986. In the end, I don't regret it. I once told [Arkansas governor] Mike Huckabee that I regretted it, and he said to me, 'You shouldn't because everybody's ambition is hoping to do what you did.' It was just such a shock for me at the time."

With the passing of associate athletic director emeritus Wilson Matthews that year as well as the early death of former Razorback All-American Keith Iovine to a pulmonary embolism a few months later, McDonnell remained thankful for the blessings he had in his own life. He returned to Fayetteville in August 2001 refreshed and ready to continue making an impact on the lives and athletic careers of young men.

Despite having won three consecutive cross country national championships, Arkansas returned only one of its top-seven runners (Daniel Lincoln) and entered the cross-country season behind Stanford and Colorado in the Mondo preseason rankings. Still, with Canadian Westley Alkin finally eligible as well as an assortment of other talents arriving in Fayetteville that fall, the Razorbacks were firmly in the hunt.

From just up the road in West Plains, Missouri, came Jason Sandfort, a 9:00 high-school two-miler, who had trained in the West Plains program of Joe Bill Dixon that had won several Missouri high-school state championships and produced former Razorback All-American Chris Zinn eighteen years earlier.

"I had great luck with a few of them," said McDonnell. "Joe Bill Dixon has them run big miles but slow and on grass so there was not much intensity, and he didn't break them. Jason was just a super kid. If you had more of those types you'd have a great team because he was always encouraging to the other guys."

Sandfort heard all about Chris Zinn's exploits as a Razorback and was told by Coach Dixon that he would generate interest from Arkansas if he qualified for the Foot Locker Championships. Sandfort did just that but still had not heard much of anything from Arkansas as the April signing deadline approached.

"I was starting to get really disappointed and began to put Arkansas on the back-burner because I hadn't heard from them in a while," said Sandfort, who was being recruited by Oklahoma State, Missouri, and Illinois State. "Then I got a call from Coach

McDonnell after learning he had been through a heart attack and he said, 'It's been crazy here, but we'd like to have you down here for a visit.' After visiting and meeting the guys and seeing the trophies and speaking to Coach I knew I wanted to go there."

McDonnell rarely made a scholarship offer prior to an official visit, considering it as much of an opportunity for a prospective student athlete to learn about the school as for him to learn about the student athlete and their ability to fit within the framework of the program. He gently poked and prodded.

"Coach did not accept anyone coming in thinking they weren't trying to be an Olympian," said Sandfort. "When I visited, he asked me if I wanted to be an Olympian. I really hadn't thought about it. He raised the bar with expectations for myself because I was able to accomplish a lot, but at the same time, he made me realize there were a lot of other things that trump just being a great runner."

While many true freshmen struggled to adapt to either the volume or intensity of the program, or both, Sandfort already had a massive mileage base underneath him before he arrived.

"Coach Dixon had us regularly run between eighty and ninety miles per week and I had pushed the envelope to one hundred during off seasons," said Sandfort. "It was an unexpectedly smooth transition for me. The only thing different from West Plains was how fast we ran the miles. I wasn't doing as many miles at Arkansas as much as I was doing them faster."

Jason Sandfort had as quick and successful a transition as any runner entering Arkansas. He may have arrived on campus expecting to redshirt, but it was not long before he became one of only a handful of Razorbacks to earn All-American honors during their true freshman cross-country campaign—an exclusive club that included only Joe Falcon, Jason Bunston, and Seneca Lassiter.

"It was a lot of fun," said Sandfort. "Everything was a dream and came along really well."

From Cloud County Community College in Kansas came Silverus Kimeli, a student athlete from Eldoret, Kenya, with excellent range from 800 meters to 5,000 meters, who had just been named the junior-college athlete of the year in 2001. Though Silverus also had a brother, Shadrack, competing at Kansas State, he wrote in the media guide that he had chosen Arkansas for its running reputation.[2]

"He was a really sharp kid and a good student," said McDonnell.

One of the greatest talents in Razorback history also arrived that fall after drifting listlessly through life following a dose of personal tragedy. It was from the abyss that John McDonnell rescued Alistair Cragg, and it was in the autumn of the legendary coach's own career that Cragg in turn carried the Arkansas program back to glory. It turned out to be a match made in Hog Heaven.

Cragg grew up in Johannesburg, South Africa, the son of Ray Cragg, a talented distance runner in his own right, who had encouraged his four boys to run. After distinguishing himself as a junior national champion in his country, Alistair followed his brother Duncan and accepted a scholarship to Southern Methodist University in Dallas, Texas.. Though his freshman season at SMU included impressive performances—8:00 for 3,000 meters and 13:49 for 5,000 meters as a freshman—he had not bonded with the distance coach, Rene Sepulveda, and floundered in the classroom. After qualifying for the NCAA Outdoor Championships in the 5,000 meter, he finished nearly a minute behind the leaders.

When his youngest brother Andrew passed away unexpectedly, it affected Alistair in a profound way. He left SMU after one year to return home with no job, no goals, and no plan to run ever again.

"I was a bum," admitted Alistair. "I was staying at my brother's and had quit running. When I finally decided to get my life back together, I emailed a bunch of schools, and John McDonnell was one of the first to get back to me. When I was at SMU we raced them at the regional, and I couldn't believe that many great athletes were on the same team and that was something I wanted to be part of."

As it happened, fate had also intervened. SMU no longer was able to offer him a scholarship while McDonnell had one available with his team considerably weakened by graduation that spring.

"I saw him at SMU but hadn't paid much attention to him and then of course he went home for a semester and his brother [Duncan] contacted me and told me about what had happened," remembered McDonnell. "I called Alistair and asked him, 'What are your goals?' And he said, 'Whatever you want me to do I will do.' I told him, 'That's easy, but you might regret that!' So it went from there and says a lot about his psychological state at the time with the death of his younger brother. He was a dream to coach and had a fantastic race head. You could ask him to do anything and he would do it."

Cragg arrived in Fayetteville that fall having only run for four weeks total and with only forty miles in his legs during the week prior to training camp.

"He was very raw," said Danny Green. "He was the kind of guy you had to go wake up to get him to practice. Once he got to practice he would bust his butt. He was smart too, but his first semester we struggled to get him to go to class."

It was not long before McDonnell was impressed by how light the South African was on his feet, and how much natural speed he had for a long-distance runner. It also did not take McDonnell very long to realize that the sometimes immature South African lacked self-discipline.

"He kept telling me to take responsibility for everything I do," said Cragg. "My parents brought me up well, but being the third child I thought things were going to just happen. When things bombed in my face at SMU, I was lost. I wondered, 'Why aren't things just happening?' And throughout the time I was failing classes, John would get on me, and if I was not running well, John would get on me. He kept reasserting the need to take control. I became a 900 percent better person than I ever would have been because I had control and took responsibility and stopped expecting people to do things for me."

For a boy who needed a strong hand at a very formative stage of his life, McDonnell provided it. When Alistair's first semester grades came back poor due to his inattention to his studies, McDonnell threatened to kick him off the team just as he had with Malcolm East a quarter of a century earlier.

"He told me he didn't want to put up with this crap and that I was going home [if it didn't change]," said Cragg, who promptly raised his grade-point average to a 3.8 during the following spring.

Though Alistair had come to Arkansas to train with a program and under a coach he both admired and respected, his understanding of and integration into the team structure did not happen overnight.

"Daniel [Lincoln] was the one everyone looked up to, but Alistair showed up and all of sudden he was the man," said Sandfort. "It was always very interesting because Alistair was even more competitive if you were training with him. He was a competitor, and it was almost like he wanted to be in your head and everyone else's head. We were friends but weren't really close during our time together. It was not until after college that he was a lot more cordial."

Though Daniel Lincoln was accepting of Alistair Cragg and what he brought to the team, there was an underlying tension as there had been for generations of Razorbacks battling for supremacy on the team.

"I knew he was good, and I would be the first to yield to another guy, and of course he was better than me," said Lincoln. "I had no problem welcoming him and was not threatened at all. He was coming to the team and held it up in his mind that Arkansas was this powerhouse, and he had to work really hard to make the team. So he came in ready to work hard, and he did work very hard."

"Daniel had won NCAAs out of the blue, so I got this impression that he was a fluke," admitted Cragg. "At first I didn't respect him, and Daniel wanted that respect so there was competitiveness."

When the two of them became roommates the following year, the dynamic of their relationship became even more challenging.

"It was awkward for a while because there was this rivalry, and it was a bit much living together," said Lincoln. "He definitely had my number, and I don't know if he perceived bitterness from me because I wasn't bitter. I was happy to have a good teammate, but there was tension for a while. Our friendship has really developed since we have left college."

On one trip to Stillwater, Oklahoma, for the Cowboy Jamboree during the following season, Cragg and Lincoln began angrily shouting at each other from the back of the fifteen-passenger van.

"It was a heavy argument," remembered Cragg. "Something about one of us leaving crumbs on the counter. We were arguing like two five-year-olds in the back of the van."

It was not long before McDonnell pulled over to the side of the highway and dressed them down.

"He told us what he thought and that we had to be leaders," said Cragg. "Daniel and I had enough respect that we didn't want to push each other's buttons but not enough that we thought one should have any pull over the other."

"There's always going to be egos, but I had the philosophy that you leave your problems at home," said McDonnell. "When you come to practice or races, we are a team and we fight and die together."

Nobody had more experience managing egos and personalities, given the eclectic talents that had come through Fayetteville over the years, and McDonnell had not lost his touch handling them.

"That speaks to Coach McDonnell's success because there was always a healthy rivalry with every generation that came through," said Lincoln. "I think sometimes he encouraged it and stoked the fires. He would let it fester because it gave a guy an edge in workouts or races. He always kept it manageable, but I don't know how he found the balance. I think he reveled in the competition that came up on the team."

At the first cross-country race of his Razorback career during a small home meet at Agri Park on September 8, 2001, Cragg nonetheless felt an immense burden.

"When he gave me the singlet for the first time I never felt so much pressure," said Cragg. "I ran with Daniel and a few others and we just ran easy [19:50 for four miles]."

The gloves came off at the Cowboy Jamboree and Chile Pepper Festival as Lincoln bested Cragg before the South African turned the tables at the SEC Cross Country Championships. Losing only to David Kimani of Alabama, Cragg led the Razorbacks to a 24–85 victory over the Crimson Tide.[3]

"During those first few months at Arkansas I was in bed at 8:00 a.m. every night," said Cragg. "It was very intense. John lets things develop like in an army where you find your corporal and everything falls behind it. You don't want to be at the bottom of the pecking order. Every day you were trying to prove to him and prove to the team who you are. It's your own fault because he didn't put any pressure on you, but you felt like making him smile was one of the best things after a workout. He was a man you did not want to disappoint. He didn't even need to get mad at you, but you went into his office, and you never knew what he was going to say to you. He was good for those of us who needed structure in our lives to be successful."

In a hotel room at Furman, South Carolina, on the night before the 2001 NCAA Cross Country Championships, McDonnell began to discuss his expectations for Cragg during the race.

"John sat on the end of my bed and asked where I think I can finish," remembered Cragg. "I said top fifteen and he said, 'Top three, kid,' and he moved on to the next guy. I thought he was nuts. I never had a person believe in me that much."

The race got off to as hot a start as any in recent memory—the leaders went through the first mile in a staggering 4:17—and the Razorbacks found themselves in the front pack.

"I think Coach thought we could compete for the title," said Jason Sandfort. "He never went to nationals thinking he was not going for the win, and you have to love that. He was the opposite of [Colorado coach Mark] Wetmore because he believes nothing good happens from the back of the pack."

Arkansas finished the day with four All-Americans. Not only had Alistair Cragg finished right where McDonnell predicted in third place, but Silverus Kimeli (13th), Daniel Lincoln (19th), Jason Sandfort (32nd) were not far behind. Ultimately Colorado came from behind late in the race to edge Stanford by one solitary point (90–91) for the national title. With Arkansas's fifth runner Fernando Cabada having faded to seventieth place on the day, the Razorbacks finished third with 118 points.

Cabada got sick when he returned home to California over the Christmas holidays.

"He gained a bit of weight so I said, 'Why don't you take it easy and we'll skip the first few meets and get you ready for the conference meet,'" remembered McDonnell. "It was a good talk and I thought he sort of believed me, but then he said, 'Why don't you let me do step-downs with the guys?' I said, 'Fernando, you cannot do this until you are in shape.' He was one of those stubborn guys, so he got in and couldn't finish the workout and walked off the track and kicked his shoes. I said to him, 'How many times do I have to say you aren't in shape? If I was making you do it I could see you being mad, but you did this, not me.' The next morning I got a call from the coach at Illinois saying he got a call from Cabada last night, and he wanted to transfer. So I called his mother, and she said he is very unhappy. I told her I had given him time to get healthy, but if he wanted to go, then good riddance."

Cabada transferred home to attend Fresno State. When the Bulldogs dropped their program shortly thereafter, Cabada briefly worked in construction before finding success at Virginia Intermont of the NAIA and eventually winning the Fukuoka Marathon.

There was certainly no shortage of eccentric characters on the Razorback roster that season. A full seven months into his Razorback career, Silverus Kimeli still remained a mystery to McDonnell. At 135 pounds he could run with anyone in the country, but at 140 pounds he could barely compete in a local road race. At the Iowa Classic in Ames, Iowa, on February 9, 2002, Kimeli went toe-to-toe with NCAA champion David Kimani of Alabama on the big 300-meter track for eight laps of the invitational 3,000 meter.

"Silverus was on his shoulder and looking great," remembered McDonnell. "With 300 meter to go, Kimani took off and [Silverus] just let him go and started jogging. Kimani ran 7:52 and didn't beat him by much, but I was disappointed because he looked beatable. Kimani didn't have top-end speed. After the race I asked Silverus, 'What happened?' He said, 'I got tired.' I said, 'No shit, didn't you think the other guy was tired?' That was him. He ran until he got tired and slowed down."

It soon became apparent that Kimeli saw another future for himself than as a distance runner.

"He ended up graduating early and asked me to release him to work on his master's degree during his final season at Oklahoma," said McDonnell. "So they gave him a scholarship."

Though John led many African athletes such as Godfrey Siamusiye and later Josphat Boit to greatness, some were less receptive to his message than others.

"Some of them weren't the best team guys," said Danny Green. "Sharif [Karie] bought in but didn't do what John thought he could do. Silverus struggled with his weight. The Kenyans needed to be handled a little differently and patted on the back, which wasn't always John's style all of the time."

With the loss of Dirk Heinze to ineligibility, it was shaping to be an uphill battle at the SEC and NCAA indoor championships. Though the Razorbacks barely edged Tennessee at the conference meet after four underclassmen middle-distance runners (Said Ahmed, James Hatch, Mike Taylor, Chris Mulvaney) won the distance medley relay, the outcome could not have been more different at the national meet in Fayetteville two weeks later.[4]

It was telling of the ultracompetitiveness of the SEC that Arkansas was beaten by not one, not two, but three SEC teams—Louisiana State, Alabama, and Tennessee—with Bill Webb's Volunteers capturing the national championship on the backs of forty points in the 60 meter, 200 meter, 400 meter, and 4 x 400 meter—including two national titles in the short sprints from future Olympic champion Justin Gatlin.[5]

Arkansas freshman Said Ahmed, who had grown up in Boston, Massachusetts, after immigrating to the United States from Somalia, distinguished himself with a third place in the 800 meter. It would be a long and winding road for Ahmed during a career in Fayetteville that rarely had a dull moment.

"He didn't have great speed but ran nice and did a great job in some races," said McDonnell. "His biggest problem was he was a hot head and got into more pushing and shoving and was disqualified several times. He was a good student but was one of those guys that you would tell him exactly what to do before a race, and he wouldn't listen, and then he would say afterwards that he got cut off. I had no time for those types of guys because they always put themselves in a bad position."

Though Arkansas freshman Mike Taylor finished dead last in the 800-meter qualifying rounds, he too continued showing glimmers of greatness. The Portage, Indiana, native would eventually earn two All-American certificates on the track, but left McDonnell continually frustrated by the inability of the talented mid-distance runner to reach what he believed to be his limitless potential.

"He was a total stud, played basketball and still ran 1:50 [800 meter in high school]," said McDonnell. "He had as good a race head as I've ever had and was the perfect specimen for the 1,500 meter. He ran looking terrific, 6 feet, 2 inches, legs up to his ears, light on his feet, and strongly built with lots of power. Gosh almighty, I saw him run a 4:01 mile indoors, and he was lucky if he was 80 percent fit. He wouldn't do the work over Christmas, but once I got him here we'd get him into shape. I had to do everything but drag him out onto the track."

If there was a positive to take from Arkansas's worst finish at the NCAA Indoor Championships since 1981, it would have been nineteen points in the 5,000 meter—including a national title by Alistair Cragg over Jorge Torres of Colorado and All-American performances from Daniel Lincoln and Jason Sandfort.

"Alistair controlled the race because he was just a good racer and in the midst of that Daniel was up there mixing it up with [Dathan Ritzenhein and Jorge Torres of Colorado] before he fell out the back," remembered Sandfort. "I was battling back and forth with Ryan Shay [of Notre Dame] and Tom McArdle [of Dartmouth]. Coach was in his usual spot telling me what to do. I was looking into his eyes and even when I went past him I would look back at him just to get a feel for what he wanted me to do. I think it kind of pissed off Ryan Shay because I would get in front and then slow down."

After launching a kick from 300 meters out, Sandfort edged both runners for fifth. It was one chapter of a storybook freshman year for Sandfort that also saw him win the Penn Relays 10,000 meter seven weeks later.

For Chris Mulvaney, the talent finally seemed to be catching up to the style. After blowing up at the NCAA Cross Country Championships and placing sixth in the mile at the NCAA Indoor Championships, Mulvaney helped Arkansas recapture its 4 x mile relay and distance medley relay titles at Penn. At the 2002 SEC Outdoor Championships, the Englishman truly came into his own.

"[Mulvaney] came in here with all guns blazing," said McDonnell. "He was not short of confidence, let me tell you. The race that made him was against David Kimani [of Alabama in the 1,500 meter]. Kimani liked to go out in 54 seconds and kill everyone. I told Chris to just sit on him, and the moment he slows down go by him. He did and he beat the hell out of him. That race turned him all around."

At the NCAA Championships two weeks later, Mulvaney out-sprinted everyone in the field except Donald Sage of Stanford in a fifty-five-second final lap to finish second.

Though the Razorbacks were not in a position to be "Calling the Hogs" after either the 2002 SEC or NCAA outdoor championships—which were won by Tennessee and Louisiana State respectively—there were more than enough positives to take from the season. Mulvaney's breakthrough as well as an astounding triple by Daniel Lincoln in the 10,000 meter and 5,000 meter and the 3,000-meter steeplechase at the conference meet followed by a win in the NCAA steeplechase two weeks later boded well for the following season.

Still, after failing to win a national championship in any of the three seasons for the first time in nearly twenty years, McDonnell realized changes needed to be made. So high were the standards of the program at the time and so great was McDonnell's distaste for mediocrity that it was inevitable. After the season, he ended the second tenure of Doug Williamson nearly two years after it began.

"He had been out of it for a few years and said he had just lost touch with the kids and couldn't relate to them anymore," said McDonnell. "He was still a great personality and a great coach, but he was just a shadow of his former self. He had lost interest in recruiting. I needed a coach to go out there and beat the bushes, so we decided to part company."

Though McDonnell had always believed it was a mistake to hire friends, he had broken his own rule and soon learned why he had lived by it for so long in the first place.

"I was the one who called Doug [about the position], and he said he'd love it and he probably figured what's to lose," reflected McDonnell. "That's why he took it. He didn't think too much about it, and I didn't think too much about it."

For his next sprint coach, McDonnell needed someone tough, young, hungry, and dynamic—everything Williamson had once been—and also someone who was available.

"You start looking around, and you think there are a lot of guys but this person is settled in here and that person is settled in there," said McDonnell. "We had recruited some good kids out of Barton [County Community College in Kansas] and so I called Lance [Brauman] and brought him down here. He had a recruiting circle, and I liked that he was tough. I knew he could handle the sprinters because it was not as if we weren't going into that area. As it turned out we lucked out into a couple of them."

Brauman was no stranger to winning. A long jumper at Auburn during his collegiate career, he had coached Barton County to ten junior-college national championship teams on the track in five years.

"Lance Brauman has done at Barton what we've done at Arkansas," McDonnell told the media on August 19, 2002. "He knows how to win, and he's very good in sprints and hurdles. Brauman is a good coach and recruiter. He likes to win and he'll fit like a glove here because that's what we like to do."[6]

Throughout his four seasons on the coaching staff, Brauman's recruiting and coaching prowess brought unprecedented success and glory to the Arkansas sprint program on the track, while eventually leading to disaster off of it.

As events in Arkansas and elsewhere proved that spring, McDonnell was finding ways of outlasting not just his own coaching brethren at Arkansas—during the year of basketball coach Nolan Richardson's infamous fallout with the administration—but also his colleagues within the Southeastern Conference. Florida coach Doug Brown may have been waiting for John McDonnell to retire, but it turned out that he was the one who walked off into the sunset first. Despite several top-five finishes at the NCAA Championships, the Florida athletic department and its aggressive athletic director Jeremy Foley parted ways with Brown following the 2002 season.

"There were sixteen head coaches when I got to Florida [in 1995]," remembered Brown. "Seven years later three of them remained. That's just Jeremy Foley. He'd never been a coach and never been an athlete, but he's a good athletic director."

That fall, McDonnell welcomed Seneca Lassiter back into the fold, just as he had welcomed Joe Falcon back a decade earlier following his brief flirtation with other training groups. Not only had McDonnell never charged his postcollegiate athletes a dime, but always extended a welcoming hand based on his mantra that "once a Razorback always a Razorback."

In Lassiter's case, his postcollegiate career had been plagued by fits and starts, injuries, and inconsistency following a brilliant collegiate career. Though he originally signed with the agent Kim McDonald out of college while remaining in Fayetteville to train, McDonald's unexpected passing at forty-seven years of age left Lassiter in a lurch.

"[Future Olympic champion] Bernard Lagat's coach James Li called me and said, 'I hear you wanted to train with the Kenyans,' so I figured I would go down there and do what Kip [Lagat] does," remembered Lassiter. "It made me think everything I had done at Arkansas was wrong because we trained so much harder [at Arkansas] in the intervals and workouts. I thought my legs would be fresher, but that wasn't the case. My body just wasn't responding to Coach Li's training."

Despite winning the 1,500 meter at the 2002 U.S. Championships, Lassiter struggled to maintain the same level of fitness while training with Lagat in Tucson, Arizona.

"Seneca used to call me and say, 'Coach I can't believe the training this guy does," remembered McDonnell. "It was ridiculous stuff; just slow. Seneca would go for an eight-mile run, and all of sudden he'd look back, and Kip would be walking. Seneca would ask, 'What's wrong and [Lagat] would say, 'I'm tired.' I'm not kidding. I finally said, 'Seneca, he must be training at night or in the morning. There's no way he can run those times doing those types of workouts.' One time he ran a 600–500–400–300–200, and they were supposed to start the first one in 1:20 but they were 1:27. Then the 500 meter was supposed to be 70 and it was 73. The 400 meter was way slow, and the 300 was like 42 or 43, and the 200 meter was in 27 seconds. It was just ridiculous for a guy of that caliber. Anyways, Bernard went over that weekend and ran 3:31 [for 1,500 meter] in Europe and when Seneca called me and told me what he had run I said, 'Seneca, there is no doubt in my mind there is something wrong.' I asked him, 'Are you sure he's not doing training on his own?'"

At a World Cup event in 2002, Lassiter, while competing for the United States, ended up pacing for Lagat, who was competing for Kenya, which earned Seneca a suspension and reprimand from the USATF.

"I remember Mike Conley [now with the USATF] called and said, 'John, you're not going to like this, but they thought you were coaching him,'" remembered McDonnell. "I said, 'No, I sure wasn't.' I told them he had switched coaches."

Seneca Lassiter remained publicly supportive of Bernard Lagat the following year when traces of erythropoietin were initially believed to have been found in Lagat's system from a false-positive test that was later cleared by a negative B sample. By that point Lassiter had already made the decision to return to Fayetteville and train once more under Coach McDonnell.

"John would say if the grass is greener on the other side, go smell it," said Lassiter. "Him being the kind of guy he is, he welcomed me back, and I respected him for that."

Ultimately, Lassiter was never able to consistently regain the form he had in college.

"I was trying to push my body to get back," said Lassiter. "I'd have a good workout and then be in the training room for three days. I wasn't consistent, and if you aren't consistent, you aren't going to be good. Having the pride I do, I felt like if I couldn't be number one or number two I wasn't going to do it. For me, running wasn't my first love. It was a God-given talent. My first love was working with youth and at-risk teenagers."

With a master's degree that McDonnell had strenuously encouraged him to attain, Lassiter found a calling outside of athletics and retired shortly thereafter to become a high-school teacher and track coach at nearby Springdale High School.

That fall, the Razorbacks returned a more experienced group full of All-American upperclassmen for the cross-country season. After winning the 2002 SEC Championships with ease, McDonnell rested Chris Mulvaney at the regional meet. Throughout his career, John had coaxed several middle-distance athletes into virtuoso performances at the NCAA Cross Country Championships, but Mulvaney never quite found his form. Even with rested legs, he finished 142nd individually at Terre Haute, Indiana. Given Stanford's dominating victory, it wouldn't have mattered if Mulvaney had even won the race.

With the team race a foregone conclusion, Alistair Cragg battled Jorge Torres of Colorado for the individual title late into the race.[7]

"I'll say until my dying day that Alistair should have beaten him," said McDonnell. "What Alistair did was he went too soon and opened up a gap. He was very confident and went with 2 kilometers to go. I told him to wait for a sprint finish from 400 meters or less. Torres came back on him but had no business beating him."

Cragg finished in second place—less than two seconds behind the individual national champion. On the bus following the meet, the lanky South African walked up to the front.

"I asked Coach his perspective on the day," remembered Cragg. "I thought he was going to say great job but instead he asked me how I was enjoying Arkansas. I said I was and he said, 'Well, I don't want you back next semester. If you don't want to win I don't want you on my team.' He explained to me winning is what gets you a shoe contract [after college]."

"I told him every athlete that finishes ahead of you costs you money," said McDonnell. "You have to be on top. They have no contracts in Ireland, no contracts in England, no contracts in Canada. They can't believe the money that is flowing around the American circuit. You have to be visible and that's what's so great about the American collegiate circuit. It's like a showcase with a huge glass display of athletes."

Though taken aback by the tough message, Alistair Cragg understood the meaning behind it and reacted accordingly. A little over three months later, he defeated Olympic 1,500-meter champion Noah Ngeny of Kenya in the 3,000 meter at the Boston Indoor Games, setting a collegiate record of 7:45.22.

Four weeks later, Cragg put the Razorbacks on his back and carried the team to its first NCAA indoor championship in three seasons with an individual victory over Boaz Cheboiywo of Eastern Michigan in the 5,000 meter (13:28.93), followed by another victory the following afternoon in the 3,000 meter (7:56.68) over Adrian Blincoe of Villanova as well as teammate Daniel Lincoln. Not only had Cragg bested Joe Falcon's 3,000-meter collegiate record but he had now entered the same rarified air Falcon occupied.

Coming as the national championship did before a delirious Fayetteville crowd and by a twenty-four-point margin over Auburn, Cragg was certainly not the only contributor.[8] Triple-jump transfer Jaanus Uudmae led a jumps contingent that scored ten points, while Chris Mulvaney won his first national title in the mile. The fact that Mulvaney had been beaten by one of his own teammates (Alistair Cragg) in that very event at the SEC Championships—only demonstrated the depth of the team. Yet, with so much talent and ego in the same locker room, there was no shortage of banter to go around along with it.

"Chris would run the 800 meter and 1,500 meter at the outdoor conference meet, so he'd tell Alistair before the 1,500 meter that it was a man's race," said McDonnell. "He was challenging him. I'd hear Alistair in the locker room say back, 'I'm going to run the 5,000 meter and 10,000 meter and still kick your ass in the 1,500 meter.' And old Mulvaney would say, 'We'll see about that!'"

It was McDonnell's task as always to manage that dynamic. Since the two of them were in different event groups, Mulvaney and Cragg worked out together only sparingly.

"Chris was probably the best talent I got to train with at Arkansas," said Cragg. "He got under John's skin because he wouldn't listen sometimes and was probably too talented for his own good."

"Mulvaney would do the short stuff with Alistair," recalled McDonnell. "He felt comfortable doing that stuff and Alistair not as comfortable. Alistair had a problem with [Daniel] Lincoln sometimes because he didn't think he pushed some of the workouts hard enough, even though Lincoln was a tough worker and would push the longer intervals."

John managed the trio's training with a great deal of care and the full understanding that between the three of them alone the Razorbacks likely had enough points to capture the outdoor national title.

At the Mt. SAC Relays less than a month later, the Razorbacks validated that opinion by nearly winning every event from 800 meter to 5,000 meter in an ultracompetitive collegiate and postcollegiate field. The trio had another spectacular Penn Relays, rebounding from a loss to Nate Brannen and Nick Willis of Michigan in the distance medley relay to win the 4 x mile relay. On Saturday afternoon, the 4 x 800 meter relay of Mulvaney-Hatch-Stevens-Taylor won the event for only the second time in school history before a frenzied throng of fifty thousand on a cold, wet day in Philadelphia.

Had it not been for the NCAA's implementation of the regional meet during that outdoor season to replace the traditional descending-order list—previously athletes were sent to the national championships based on their best performances throughout the season—McDonnell would have had reason to be positively giddy.

That year, the NCAA added a regional-meet qualifying system for its outdoor national championship. As it was instituted in 2003, teams were sent to the four meets based on geography rather than rankings. No matter how competitive the region, only five athletes advanced automatically. This inevitably led to grossly inequitable regional disparities. Some regions had as many as forty or fifty athletes seeking five automatic spots to advance in a particular event while others had as few as ten—or less. The Mid-East Regional in particular featured Arkansas, Tennessee, and Louisiana State, winners of thirteen of the previous fourteen NCAA outdoor championships, battling for limited spots at the same meet.

"It could never happen [in another sport] because it makes no sense at all," John told the media at the time. "Yet that's what they're doing in our sport."[9]

McDonnell wanted the NCAA to keep the descending-order format as they had indoors, which he believed allowed the best athletes to advance to the NCAA Championships. He viewed the addition of a regional meet outdoors as a step backwards for the sport and was one of many unfortunate decisions he viewed with dismay. Other proposals he had made were ignored.

"Vin [Lananna] and I had been trying to get [the scholarship allotment] passed where five scholarships would be added for cross country, while the other twelve scholarships had to be used exclusively for sprint and field events," remembered McDonnell. "The committee said, 'Great idea John, but I don't think we are ready for five scholarships.' So instead the NCAA voted to enlarge the field at the NCAA Cross Country Championships by adding fifty more bodies."

After competing at the outdoor regional meet during the final six years of his career, during which time the Razorbacks still managed to win the NCAA Championships three times, McDonnell's opinion did not change on the matter.

"This regional thing was a disaster," said McDonnell. "It didn't help the student athlete at all. There are a lot of great people in track and field coaching that wanted the best for the sport, but there was an element of coaches that were some of the most self-serving, narrow-minded, and vindictive people I have ever met in my life. They are like scorpions running around trying to sting everyone. There is no other sport that changes every year like track and field does. Can you imagine what the athletic directors think when they see it takes eleven hours for the javelin [at the regional meet]? They must think these guys are nuts."

Following a win at the 2003 SEC Outdoor Championships by thirty-six points over Tennessee in Knoxville, Tennessee, the Razorbacks cruised through the inaugural Mid-East Regional Meet and won the team title in Columbus, Ohio. The extra racing had come at a cost. All-American senior Robbie Stevens limped through the 800 meter and was doubtful to be able to run the NCAA Outdoor Championships at all.

"He had his Achilles tendon operated on [earlier in the year], and it got butchered," said McDonnell. "I don't know how he ran because he could only work out twice per week and the rest was just jogging. Before the first round he got off the table, and I saw him stumbling but he said, 'Coach, it'll be all right.' I said, 'Robbie, forget it,' and he said, 'Coach, I'm not going to run after this.' So he got off the table limping before each round and then even going into the final."

After running 1:48 in the first round and 1:47 in the semifinal, Stevens heroically went all-out for the national title and finished barely a quarter-second behind winner Sam Burley of Penn in 1:46.85.

"He closed like hell coming up the final straightaway," remembered McDonnell. "If he had stayed a stride closer he would have won it."

With University of Arkansas president Dr. Alan Sugg on hand in Sacramento, California, to take in the festivities, Alistair Cragg and Daniel Lincoln were each favored to win their events in the 5,000 meter and 3,000 meter steeplechase respectively. Yet it was in the 10,000 meter race where both athletes made Alan Sugg and every Razorback fan's trip to California immediately worthwhile.

"Coach asked me if I would do the 10,000 meter at nationals for team points because he thought we could win, so the plan was to finish somewhere between third and sixth," remembered Lincoln. "Boaz [Cheboiywo of Eastern Michigan] was up there with Alistair, and it was his race to win. I was just hanging back and looking up at these guys ahead of me. It was such a long race, and it seemed like it was in slow motion. So I thought, what is the point of me staying back in the pack if I feel so relaxed?"

After running a sixty-five-second lap, Lincoln caught up to the leaders.

"I felt good in that cool dry air in Sacramento," remembered Lincoln. "It was one of those races you always dream about where you feel like you can do anything and everything felt easy. I wish I could reproduce it."

With Boaz Cheboiywo noticeably laboring, Cragg dropped a sixty-second lap to separate himself before Lincoln caught back up to him.

"With 2,000 meters to go, it was just me and Alistair, and we looked around and realized 'Wow, we've got this thing,'" said Lincoln. "That was so rare in such a competitive race to be able to relax, and we were talking and clicking off the laps easy. It was fun."

As the race headed towards its conclusion, it dawned on both athletes that somebody had to win and somebody had to lose.

"With 600 meters to go Daniel asked, 'So how are we going to do this?'" said Cragg. "I said, 'I don't know; I thought we were just going to cross the line.' It was silent for another 100 meters, and I said, 'Daniel, it's yours.' We kept quiet for another 100 meters or so and Daniel said, 'No, we're racing.' I said, 'Daniel, no we aren't racing.' And he said, 'All right, we'll hold hands.' At the time we weren't getting along really well, but everybody thought what great friends we were. I remember the president [Dr. Sugg] was there and a lot of people there were very proud of what happened."

The two athletes ultimately chose to hold hands triumphantly as Daniel Lincoln crossed the line in 28:20.20, less than a tenth of a second before Alistair Cragg. The time broke Pat Vaughn's twenty-year-old school record. It was a great moment in Arkansas Razorback history.

"Then we almost got disqualified for bad sportsmanship [after a coach protested]," said Lincoln.

Though the protest went nowhere, Lincoln and Cragg rebounded to win the 3,000-meter steeplechase and 5,000 meter in successive evenings to help Arkansas win the 2003 NCAA Outdoor Championships by a nine-point margin over Auburn, 59–50.[10]

"The thing that shocked Daniel [Lincoln] was when Alistair slowed up and let him win the 10,000 meter," said McDonnell. "Lincoln kept asking me, 'Why did he do that?' I said, 'Well, he's a good guy. You're a senior and he's a junior and he let you do it.' One of the things Alistair didn't know at the time was that Lincoln had already decided what shoe contract he wanted after college. Alistair thought if he won two events it might help him get a contract after college. Alistair later told me if he knew he had already decided, he might not have done it."

Only five years after sheepishly walking into the Bud Walton Arena on a scorching hot June afternoon and asking McDonnell for the opportunity to run for Arkansas, Lincoln had ended his Razorback career as a four-time NCAA champion and fourteen-time All-American. Within three years of graduation, he would run in the Olympic Games and break an American record in the 3,000-meter steeplechase. By all measures, it was an astonishing and unfathomable success story.

Though he remained training under McDonnell, Lincoln began living most of the year in Little Rock where he enrolled in medical school. It was in Little Rock where his track workouts were timed under the watchful eye of Frank O'Mara, who by that point was steadily rising within Little Rock–based Alltel Wireless, where he would eventually be named chief executive officer.

As well as things were going for Lincoln at the time, McDonnell figures he could have signed an even more lucrative contract had he turned professional under a different set of circumstances.

"The year [Lincoln] got a contract from Nike he still had a cross-country season of eligibility, and I wanted him to run it so he could come out in the spring, which would have made him more marketable, because he would have been the only one and everybody would be thinking track," remembered McDonnell. "Somebody was giving him bad advice that I was just trying to use him for cross country, but I told him our team could only win conference. We couldn't win nationals. He could have come back and finished first, second, and third, and we still wouldn't have won it. So I told him I wasn't doing it for that. I was doing it for his good to get a better deal. If he came out in the spring he wouldn't be competing with anybody, and every [shoe company] would be bidding on him. Well, before NCAAs he came to me and said, 'I think I've made up my mind not to run cross country.' I said let's not worry about it now."

When the two spoke about the subject again after the national championship, Lincoln asked McDonnell if he was aware that Jorge Torres had signed for an amount nearly triple Lincoln's contract.

"I said, 'Yeah, but I tried to get you to wait until the next spring,'" remembered McDonnell. "His face got really red and he said, 'I can't believe it.' So I said, 'Are you happy?' And he said, 'Yes.' So I said, 'If you're happy, I'm happy.' I was tired of trying to convince him of what I was asking him to do."

Throughout his career, Lincoln leaned heavily on McDonnell for advice. Often he took it but sometimes not, such as when he opted for Achilles reattachment surgery against McDonnell's better judgment several years later. The surgery required three follow-up operations before it was fixed, preventing Lincoln from competing at his second Olympics in 2008, and derailing what had been a brilliant career.

"John treated us like men unless we acted like children, and he gave us enough latitude where we might fail," said Lincoln. "He never forced anything, and he respected his athletes enough to let them make mistakes. He doesn't always explain it, but he has really good judgment from his gut. There were a few notable times when I didn't listen to him and made a mistake where he was dead right."

It was that same spring when two bombshells were dropped on the collegiate track-and-field community starting with the death of six-time NCAA champion David Kimani of Alabama. While eating lunch in the university dining hall in Tuscaloosa, Kimani suddenly collapsed and was pronounced dead from cardiac arrest less than an hour later. It was a stunning turn of events for an athlete who had had a healthy rivalry with Razorback athletes for years and seemed to have the world at his feet.

Out in Palo Alto, California, another longtime rival was also on his way out, but on his own volition. After inheriting the Stanford program in shambles in 1992, Vin Lananna had spearheaded a new track facility and won five NCAA championships in just over a decade. With the men's cross-country team all but guaranteed to win another national championship in the fall, Lananna walked away from coaching to accept the position of athletic director at Division III Oberlin College in Ohio.

"I felt like there was nothing left for me to do at Stanford other than maintaining it," said Lananna. "I wanted to have an institutional impact, and at Stanford the track program was never going to have that. It was one of fifty things that were important. I had a great relationship with [athletic director] Ted Leland, who was my boss at both Dartmouth and Stanford. We had a good partnership, we trusted each other, but towards the end I saw he was getting tired, and I thought this was the time to go the administrative route. Oberlin made a fantastic offer to me and so I took the challenge."

With Vin Lananna gone from Stanford, John McDonnell had lost a rival on the track and a kindred spirit off of it. As it turned out, he would not be deprived very long.

14

John McDonnell on Leadership

"In my judgment he is the greatest leader that I've ever known. He epitomizes the very best qualities of leadership because he surrounded himself with very, very talented people in his assistant coaches and athletes while creating an environment of expectations for them."

—Dr. Alan Sugg, University of Arkansas president (1990–2011)

It seemed like my philosophy on leadership was shaped by the people I encountered throughout my life. In coaching, there were three people that really helped me, and one was my coach, Don Appleby, and the others were Larry O'Byrne and Bob Cole, who was my college coach and motivator. Don and Larry were two older guys in the Clonliffe Harriers Track Club in Dublin. The work ethic handed down by the three of them was that nobody gives you anything. You have to earn it. Don't ever make excuses because they can become a habit. Those were the guys I looked up to and gave me the most direction.

After I lost the novice national cross-country championship by a half-mile in 1958, I really wondered if this sport was for me. I thought I was pretty good in the country, but these city guys seemed like they were too good. I rode home in the car with Don and Larry after I got beat, and they said, "Oh no, you'll win it next year. You haven't trained. You'll come back next year." The next year I came back and won it. So that taught me quite a bit about working towards a goal and achieving it.

Ireland was a great country for horse racing, and I remember Vincent O'Brien was someone I admired growing up as the trainer of many of the big horses. The big thing was when the Irish horses would go to England to race. There was a lot of pride on the line, and the rivalry between Ireland and England came to the forefront. So when you're in a small country without much to cheer about, it meant a lot when several of the horses trained by Vincent O'Brien won the English Grand National. He was one of the best.

I had a lot of good leadership influences in my own family. My cousin, Frank Lynn, worked a full-time job at the post office at night, and then during the daytime he had a rental car business. He always seemed to be doing well, and it was because he worked hard at it. He would always go to where the boat came in from England and rent cars to passengers disembarking. That guy could manage conflict better than anybody. He was in a business where people were coming and going and could sometimes be quite demanding, but somehow he managed to keep them all happy. Frank was a decent guy. If somebody had a problem, he'd take care of them.

My father, Michael, and my older brother, Paddy, worked every hour on the clock. Being the oldest boy, Paddy would help my father and I'd tag along with them. Paddy was great when somebody had a problem with a horse because he could train them. They would have me work on the farm, and we would even do jobs for others after we had our own done. My father instilled a work ethic into me, and because of that I never had a problem getting out there and working hard. As my dad used to say: "An honest day's work for an honest day's pay." If you work hard you usually will get on well in life. That's what we did on the farm. We worked hard and long hours. In Ireland it is bright until 10:00 at night and it gets bright at 5:00 in the morning, so those were some awfully long days.

My mother, Bridget, always put her eight kids first. We would be in the hay field or be putting up potatoes when she would call us in for dinner. After everyone was fed, she would sit down to eat. Then as soon as she would finish washing up, she would come back to help us in the field. She was very organized and kept everyone in line.

When I first came to the United States, I wasn't sure if I was going to stay. I came to look around, and when I was there, I found a coach at the New York Athletics Club who asked me if I knew a guy in the club named John Camien. He was a 4:01 miler back then and ran at Emporia State in Kansas, and they said I should take a scholarship there. Of course I didn't know the difference. I thought you just showed up, but I didn't have a scholarship when I got there. So I worked at a restaurant washing dishes and cleaning trash while running and attending school. It was there that I learned that Fran Welch was a great coach. He was a tough guy. He called a spade a spade. You didn't slide around him. I stayed there one semester and then met Malcolm Robinson and eventually went to USL on a track scholarship

My coach at USL was Bob Cole, and he was much different than Fran. One shoe doesn't fit everybody, and if there was anything I learned, it was that there are different styles of leadership. Bob and Fran came from different ends of the spectrum. Bob was a nicer kind of guy, and Fran was tougher. If you did something wrong he let you know about it.

I will never forget we had a practice at Emporia, and it was pouring down rain, and Fran Welch's favorite saying was to "Shake loose and do the tomcat." What he meant was do some stretching. Well, we had this little Italian kid who had walked on from New York, big hairy chest and only 5 feet, 2 and stocky, and he actually started acting like a cat crawling around and meowing. Fran saw that and said to him, "All you guys go home, but you stay here. You're going to run six eight hundreds in the rain." It was a cinder track, and the kid was a sprinter so it was a long way for him. I tell you that guy never opened his mouth again at a meeting.

Arkansas was very fortunate to have great leadership during the last two decades of my career. Dr. Alan Sugg has been wonderful to me personally and has been just a great president for the university. He loved winning and has always been so supportive and understanding of how athletics fits into the big picture.

Frank Broyles, the athletic director, was a great leader because of his foresight and how he handled things. He saw this TV thing and knew that heavily populated areas had more viewers and that was going to be more important than gate receipts in the future. I don't think a lot of people knew it at the time, but Frank had worked for years in television as an analyst and understood the vision of what was going on before the rest of us.

He had a certain managerial style. Frank was not the type of guy for chitchat. He'd see you, and it was strictly business, business, business. Is that it? Out. He was tough. When I was hired I asked, "What do you expect?" He said, "Top half in the SWC and a national championship one out of every fifteen years." When I took over, we didn't have a good team, but I didn't want to cut these kids off scholarship. I just wanted to fade them out as they graduated and he said, "Great idea." But I said when we do start getting better, I need my budget to able to be adjusted. I didn't even know what I could ask for then, but it was probably a quarter of what I was going to get later in my career. Frank thought about it and said, "Be conservative, John. Be conservative, and I think we will work this thing out." That was the budget I had my whole career. I was conservative. We didn't go to a whole bunch of meets and didn't expose our guys to a whole bunch of stressful situations. We weren't always flying to New York and California. I realized you can get a good race in Stillwater, Oklahoma. I didn't need to go to Stanford when I can run right here.

Frank was also very good at managing conflict. Later on when I got better, I could bargain harder, and we had some heated arguments. One time I said, "If you're going to talk like that I'm leaving [the room]." I hadn't even gotten to the door when he said, "Sit down, you're not leaving like that." Then we ironed it out. Another thing he did when we discussed salaries or budget or whatever was to make notes and then after we were done discussing it, he'd say, "Let me get back to you." I honestly believe he had made up his mind talking to me, but he gave himself time to think about it.

We all know about Gov. Bill Clinton, who later became President Clinton. The thing I liked about him was that he wasn't afraid to change his mind. They called him a flip-flopper. I admire people that do that because if you know you made a decision and you realize afterwards that it was the wrong decision, there is no harm eating crow. That's how I coached. If I realized something I did wasn't right I'd change it and do it right instead of being stubborn. That's what I admired about Clinton. He made decisions and talked to people on the other side of the aisle, and if he felt like he needed to, he would modify it. That's the sign of a good leader.

I was influenced by a lot of older coaches such as Ted Banks, Bob Timmons, and Bill Bowerman. I didn't take much from their training necessarily, but I looked at how they organized their teams. I also looked at basketball and football coaches like John Wooden of UCLA and Tom Landry of the Dallas Cowboys. When anything happened disciplinewise they really took care of business and held people responsible. If you let one person away with something, everybody knows about it. If someone went out and did something stupid and I didn't know about it, I guarantee somebody else does. So it erodes your program because a lot of kids think you know. Why shouldn't I know? I remember I cut a kid once after he said something, and it left me with only six or seven kids on the cross-country team. It was a tough decision to make, but I got a taste of it for the simple reason that two of the kids came in and said, "We were wondering when you were going to do that." It wasn't the first time he had done or said something, but sometimes as coaches, we are the last to know.

Managing conflicts is obviously important. A lot of athletes have big egos, but you have to learn how to channel the ego in a positive way. People sometimes wonder because we had so many good kids on the team, "How do you tell each guy how to win when you have more than one in the same race?" I say, "I give each kid the weapon I think he needs to win the race, and the best man will win or the one who makes the least mistakes." I'd tell one kid to kick earlier, and then I'd tell the kicker that I had told the other one to run your feet out from under you. So everyone knew what was coming, but who had the intestinal fortitude to deal with it? It never failed after college that they lived up to what I thought they were all along.

Early in my career it was a bit more difficult getting guys to buy into things. I would say, "Maybe your high-school coach was pretty good, but all I am asking you to do is give me three semesters: cross country, track, and another cross-country season. If you don't click and do what I think you can do, then you come in and tell me what you should do. But I guarantee you if you do what I tell you, things will start happening because you will have a foundation. During your second track season things will happen. I always related it to a house. If you build a good foundation for the house, the floors will not crack, and the walls will not crack, and there will be no cracks in your career. All I want out of you is two good years because with academics and getting away from home and getting used to the system you cannot take shortcuts.

I always made sure these guys realized there was life after track. I don't think I ever met a parent that wasn't interested when you start talking about getting a degree. That's why they want Johnny to go to school: to get a degree. I always pushed education as number one, running as number two, and then a social life is a bad third place. It isn't even in the final straightaway. The parents would laugh at that. Even the kid would say that was about right. I did lose kids during recruiting because of rules about earrings and long hair, and the reason I had those rules was because first impression lasts a lifetime. You're going to leave this college with a degree and need a job. If one person goes in with earrings up and down and on his tongue and then is followed by a clean-cut person who comes in behind with exactly the same qualifications and they are both interviewing with the some old guy sitting behind a desk, I'm telling you who is getting the job. That's the way it is. That's society. So I would say there is no use in coming to Arkansas if you are going that route. You need to sacrifice something. Ryan Wilson sacrificed and got rid of his dreadlocks. I did lose some kids to other schools because of that but it worked out.

It was important to teach people the importance of sacrifice and why making a sacrifice for the team made them a better individual. That sometimes gets lost in our sport because it is so individual. Only if people were capable of doing multiple events at a conference championship would I put them in that situation; otherwise it's like falling between two rocks. One of the reasons it's important to be able to physically handle that is because if you go to the Olympics or World Championships, you usually have to run or jump three personal bests: heats, semifinal, and final. If you haven't already done it and haven't practiced it, it's not going to just happen. Graham [Hood] bought into that but Niall [Bruton] didn't. He always thought we did two or three races at Penn just so we could win all three races.

A lot of kids have problems handling pressure, and when they get to the race, they are like a wet rag because they are so nervous. It didn't matter how much energy they had, but either through physical activity or nerves it was gone. So I found out through the relays that some of the kids—when you put them on the relay—ran out of their flipping minds and looked like a million dollars. I'd ask them afterwards, "How did you run so well?" And they said, "The other guys would be pissed if I ran poorly." So now I could say the next time you run an individual race and you feel nervous, you can relate back to that relay race when you laid it on the line for your teammates. Now you can lay it on the line for yourself. So it helped the team, but it also helped the kids who became great athletes later in their careers but who maybe couldn't handle the individual pressure at first until they got a few relays under their belt.

I'd never run a guy in the same event the weekend after he ran a personal best in that event. If he ran the 800 meter, he'd say, "Coach, I felt great. Put me in next week again. I'm going to break 1:50." I'd say, "No, lets run the mile and then the 3,000 meter and what about getting three personal bests," because every time that kid would want to go back next week. You always feel good when you win, so that's why I'd tell a kid to take a step back and lets come back to it later. It was part of managing expectations for people.

Sometimes we get carried away in this sport with our individual events or event groups. With our coaching staff, I made it all one. That was a strong point in our team concept. The field-event guys would be out there cheering for the track runners and vice versa. If you start making one person or one event more important than another, I think you end up with problems.

There is tremendous mental and physical wear and tear on distance runners. Running thirteen or twenty-five laps, you have to be aware of what's going on around you at all times and use a lot of tactical moves. With jumpers I always made the decision where and when they jumped because of the high risk of injury if they were overused. I'd tell them you are staying out this weekend to rest or maybe just run a relay, but you're not jumping.

I always tried to avoid complacency. A lot of hatred builds up against you when you're at the top, and it even happens in races. Guys from other teams elbowing and you know that didn't come from the athletes. So I always said to our guys, "Don't elbow back because the other guy isn't going to be the one who gets caught." It sort of was handed down, and I didn't have to even talk about it. The athletes knew everyone hated us because we were good, and I'd use some incident that happened to fire them up.

I will never forget the time we set a world record in the distance medley relay at Penn Relays. The Philadelphia newspaper acted as if the race was already over because the other team had an Olympic gold medalist, so I said, "Is this the shit we came up for? To be embarrassed?" There was no way in the world we should have beaten that team, but we did. It's important to find out who your real leaders are on the team, who can take pressure, and they can do a lot of good as well.

I realized very early on that negative motivation is a no-no because you can only use it once. How many times could I send Frank O'Mara home in a rowboat? I learned that in college from a student teacher. He said, "Don't threaten to throw a kid out the window because you can't throw him out the window." Don't make idle threats or something you cannot absolutely carry out.

I do believe in holding people accountable—even when what they have done is great—if it is less than what they are capable of achieving. Some of the athletes would say to me, "You're never happy." I said, "You're not in the final. I don't care about personal bests. You should be in the final." They'd usually prance off, and the next night I'd go around to their room and say, "Look, it's great what you did, but you're selling yourself short. You're way better than you think you are." Boy, everybody likes to hear that. I would tell them, "If you are not performing up to your absolute personal potential, I'm going to get on your ass. I'm not letting you away with it. If you want mediocrity, tell me. I just want to let you know you're way better than that." The kid then starts feeling pretty good about himself and then forgets the negative stuff. Then he starts spilling his guts and telling you where he made a mistake. He might say he should have stayed up on the third lap of the 1,500 meter or whatever. At that point, you can finally rationalize with the kid. I tried not to fall out with anybody. I might chew their ass out, but we'd come back and talk it out.

I really think I put something back into the sport. I raised the bar for coaches' salaries. I had a lot of pride for track and field and had a lot of respect for it. I hate to see people use it as a place to camp and do nothing but bitch and complain about everyone else. There are a lot of those programs out there. Some schools unfortunately don't have the budget, and that's different, but some schools have awfully good budgets and aren't doing squat, but they complain plenty about people beating them. That's something I felt hurts our sport.

Looking back on it, it was fun, and I was lucky to have good athletes, good assistants, and a great wife and family that made it all possible. Any successful leader understands that they cannot achieve much without great people around them.

15

Rising to the Occasion (2003–2006)

"I am his creation."

—Alistair Cragg[1]

If recruiting is the lifeblood of any successful collegiate athletics program, then the Arkansas dynasty appeared to be as healthy as ever entering the fall of 2003.

"You will never see a donkey win the Kentucky Derby," said McDonnell.

There were certainly plenty of thoroughbreds coming to town for that fall cross-country season. McDonnell had signed a group of distance athletes, who on the surface appeared to be as talented a group that had ever come into Fayetteville at one time. It included a 4:03 miler from Florida, Sam Vazquez; a 4:07 miler from Missouri, Adam Perkins; a Footlocker West champion from California, Mike Poe; and a 3:41 1,500-meter runner from Australia, Mark Fountain. With Alistair Cragg in the prime of his career, and McDonnell having regained the bounce in his step after his health scare, the future was looking bright. Still, John had learned in over thirty-plus years of collegiate coaching that not everything is what it first appears to be.

"There were times you'd get a batch of good athletes, and others you'd get a batch of bad athletes," said McDonnell. "They were like a litter of pups. Sometimes you got pure breeds, and sometimes they were all mongrels. It was always an issue of leadership because misery loves company. You only need one guy who is miserable and talks to another and another one talks to another one, and all of a sudden you have a group of guys who are miserable. That happened to me a few times, and it had nothing to do with training."

Though each of the incoming athletes would experience various degrees of success in a Razorback uniform, the end result was collectively less than the sum of their parts, either due to unfortunate circumstances or personal self-destruction. For Mark Fountain and Adam Perkins it was the former.

"[Mark Fountain's] eligibility clock had started so we were not able to get him eligible," said McDonnell. "He had a great personality and in two years was down to 3:33 [1,500 meter]. He ran into problems with his agent not getting him into the right races, but boy did he run aggressive. You had to hold him back or he'd get hurt."

Though Fountain would continue to be coached by McDonnell for nearly six years thereafter, he would never wear the Razorback uniform.

In Adam Perkins's case, his club coach had advised him to forego his final year of high-school competition after he ran a 4:07 mile during his junior year. Although the decision was made ostensibly to seek better competition elsewhere, it ultimately left Perkins unable to find competition anywhere.

"He never checked that he couldn't leave the state of Missouri to run because anyone [in high school] he ran against would be ineligible," said McDonnell. "So he never got to race his senior year."

"Coach McDonnell thought it was the worst decision I made from a competitive standpoint because you need to stay in competition," said Perkins. "I made my commitment to Arkansas, and they weren't too concerned about missing my senior year, but I think it kind of hindered me."

Despite nearly every school offering a full scholarship, Perkins accepted an academic scholarship at Arkansas. After an entire season away from competition, Perkins was literally chomping at the bit during his first year, but like many talented freshmen, the adjustment to training at Arkansas would take time.

"You have high expectations and hopes as one of the top high-school runners in the country going to one of the top programs, so you feel the pressure to perform," said Perkins. "It didn't always feel like it was working out my freshman year, and I struggled."

In the case of Mike Poe and Sam Vazquez, that transition was much smoother—at least initially. Poe finished seventh at the SEC Cross Country Championships and sixty-third at the NCAA Championships, while Vazquez was an All-American in the distance medley relay after running 2:52 for 1,200 meters as a freshman.

"[Vazquez] was a stud and the nicest kid you'd ever meet," said McDonnell. "His freshman year he ran 1:48 [800 meter] and 3:42 [1,500 meter] at the SEC meet. He was gifted and had it all—the head, everything. He just wasn't disciplined in the classroom."

The first sign of trouble occurred midway through his freshman year when Vazquez and Poe were caught sneaking out of the study hall overlooking the football field.

"The study hall was a two-story building, and they'd check in and then go down the fire escape to watch spring football," said McDonnell. "They got caught because one of the monitors in study hall came down and saw them, and he didn't say anything to them but went up as fast as he could, and when they tried to check out, he called them over. I had to suspend them for a couple of months."

When Vazquez's lack of attention to academics threatened his athletic eligibility, he began being pulled in all different directions by those inside and outside the program.

"He didn't pass enough hours and couldn't come back [during his second year]. His dad had a little grocery store [in Florida] and kept telling him if you aren't happy come back home," said McDonnell. "His mother was a great lady and she kept saying, 'He cannot come back here.'"

It was not long before both Vazquez and Poe completely lost their way. While Vazquez became academically ineligible, Poe arrived at cross-country camp his sophomore year tattooed from head to toe.

"The first day he arrived with his legs all tattooed and had shorts on, so I asked him, 'Where did you get those socks?'" remembered McDonnell. "He said, 'They aren't socks, Coach.' So he came up and showed me flames tattooed on both legs. I said to him, 'Are you kidding me?' He looked back and said, 'Coach, I decided over the summer I am going to be my own man, and that's the way it has to be.' I liked the kid, and he had a good freshman year, but I knew if I let him get away with this, I would lose total control. He was challenging me, and the guys were like, 'What are you going to do about it?' Sometimes they put you in a position where you have to make a decision. So I said, 'Mike, I'm not kicking you off the team, but I'd prefer if you quit because you don't fit here anymore. It would be better for both of us. Think about it and let me know.' Two days later he came in and quit and went back to California."

For the upperclassmen on the team seeking their first national championship in cross country, it was frustrating to watch teammates with all of the ability in the world self-destruct. McDonnell's message of prioritizing academics and running above everything else was suddenly falling on deaf ears.

"It was tough because some of those kids didn't end up being able to handle the pressure and wanted the college experience more than running," said Sandfort. "They couldn't balance it all."

With Alistair Cragg nursing a hernia throughout most of the cross-country season, the Razorbacks were dealt a further setback. After losing to SEC rival Georgia at the Cowboy Jamboree on October 4, 2003, for the first time, a national title had become further and further from their reach. Just defending the conference championship appeared to be a task onto itself.

"That was a wakeup call," said McDonnell. "We didn't run Alistair, but we still should have won it."

With Cragg back in the lineup for the 2003 SEC Cross Country Championships in Athens, Georgia, the Razorbacks regained their footing by placing five in the top ten to edge Georgia 33–58 for their thirtieth consecutive conference cross-country championship and thirteenth straight in the SEC.[2]

If the conference meet had been easier to win than expected, the national meet would not be. Stanford scored a mind-boggling twenty-four points to destroy the field on a cold day in Northern Iowa. Though never contending for the win, Arkansas had three runners in the top-twenty—Alistair Cragg, Jason Sandfort, and Chris Mulvaney—and was locked in a tight battle for second.

"Mulvaney was in the top-fifteen at one point," said McDonnell, "but he blew up."

As Mulvaney gradually fell back to fiftieth place during the last mile of the race, the Razorbacks ended up in fifth place behind Wisconsin, Northern Arizona, and Iona College. With Daniel Lincoln having graduated and many things not going according to plan—including Alistair Cragg's hernia that caused him to miss most of the season—the vaunted Arkansas distance depth was no longer able to fill the void.

"I began to put a little more money into the sprinters," said McDonnell. "There were other places putting almost all of their scholarship into distance running. I always tried to put my eggs in more than one basket and put scholarships into points that would win the national meet on the track. If I could get distance runners, I would sign, them but if I couldn't, I'd put it somewhere else. Points are points."

McDonnell had historically invested scholarship dollars more heavily into distance and jumps based on the fact that distance runners have three seasons to compete and jumpers have six opportunities at every meet to get it right. Though the formula of distance and jumps was hardly broken—as evidenced by indoor and outdoor national championships during 2003—McDonnell was ever the opportunist and open-minded to athletes from any event who could score points at the national championship.

Arriving that fall from Barton County Community College were two athletes with talent and potential in the short sprints unlike almost any Arkansas athlete before them—Tyson Gay and Omar Brown. Gay was raised in Kentucky and had run 10.08 (100 meter) and 20.21 (200 meter) during his junior college career, while Brown had run 10.20 (100 meter) and 20.70 (200 meter) and been a member of the Jamaican Olympic team in 2000. While McDonnell invested scholarships in both sprinters, based on his belief in their athletic upside and his confidence in Lance Brauman's ability to maximize it, the two of them nonetheless arrived with a long history of injury issues and could hardly be considered sure things.

"Both were salt-of-the-earth kids," said McDonnell. "They had been hurt, but we took a chance. I'm not patting myself on the back, but we slowed down the competing thing. We didn't compete them every week and got them healthy. I feel if you keep an athlete healthy for a year, the injury won't come back, especially a sprinter who has the cross-country season off. Let them totally recover."

Gay looked at the lack of short-sprint tradition at Arkansas as a challenge rather than a problem.

"[Lance Brauman] was my junior-college coach, and he was there," said Gay. "I also kind of liked that they weren't known for sprinters and wearing body suits. I wanted to go into a new situation and make an impact on a university they haven't had before. With all Coach McDonnell had done, I had the highest respect for him to give me a scholarship. It really meant a lot to me."

Though Brauman worked with Gay and Brown throughout the fall as they returned to health, the other impact sprinter to join the program that season didn't arrive until January and was not even training with the sprinters exclusively when he did.

Wallace Spearmon Jr., was born in Fayetteville after his father, Wallace Sr., starred for the Razorback track team as an All-American twenty years earlier. Spearmon Jr. had grown up with Sean McDonnell, and the two had raced as youngsters, but by the time he graduated from high school, Wallace was as raw a talent as they come. He had played football, basketball, and track at Fayetteville High School, while still managing to sprint 21.3 (200 meter) and long jump (23 feet, 10 inches) during a limited track season.

"When I was younger I didn't really know much about track and just did what I had to win," admitted Spearmon. "I really didn't practice that much."

Though McDonnell had known Spearmon for two decades through the connection with his father and Sean, he did not have a scholarship to offer that first year. Just as former NCAA and Olympic champion Mike Conley had done, Wallace walked on and joined the program in January.

"I could say I thought he would be like his dad, but I didn't," said McDonnell. "I figured he was a nice kid and a talent. You could see it in him. He played football and basketball and fiddled around. He wasn't in here very long when we found out how good he was."

The date was January 24, 2004, to be exact.

"He ran his first race in 20.8 [200 meter] and then 20.5 in his second," remembered McDonnell. "You talk about lighting up a place. He had a brilliant personality, nice kid, and just a dream to coach."

At the 2004 SEC Indoor Championships held at Nutter Fieldhouse in Lexington, Kentucky, the Razorbacks would have to earn points in events different from those they historically had as they sought to defend their seven-year indoor conference championship run against the Florida Gators.

Led with wins by Tyson Gay in the 60 meter and 200 meter, Arkansas scored an all-time high of thirty-eight points in the short sprints to counteract Florida's point haul. As usual, Arkansas scored heavily in the distance events with eighty-two points thanks to wins in the 3,000 meter and 5,000 meter by Alistair Cragg. The outlook in the usually reliable jumping events was much different.

Triple-jumper Jaanus Uudmae had originally accepted a scholarship at Southern Illinois before transferring to Arkansas, as much due to his disenchantment in Carbondale as his attraction to the triple-jump tradition in Fayetteville. Though his father Jaak Uudmae had won an Olympic gold medal for the Soviet Union in the triple jump at the 1980 Olympics in Moscow, the younger Uudmae was not blessed with the same natural speed or talent.

"He was a brilliant young man but wasn't very fast or quick on the runway," recalled McDonnell. "Dick did a good job with him because he was everything that a person could be other than not being very talented. He looked like he might have been a good half-miler."

Uudmae had placed fifth in the triple jump at the previous season's NCAA Championships, but entered the 2004 indoor season injured and unable to compete.

"Jaanus had to have knee surgery," said Booth. "There was no ligament [issues] but he had calcium and cartilage that was bothering him."

Arkansas was nearly shut out of the field events and unable to counteract a fifty-six point barrage by Florida. Any opportunity for the Razorbacks to win the meet in the 4 x 400 meter relay was then taken away when the baton was knocked out of their hands and disappeared amid the athletes cluttered on the infield of Nutter Fieldhouse. Florida was disqualified but Arkansas never retrieved the baton and did not finish either. The Gators held on to win the SEC Championships in a 128–126 upset.

It was again telling of the state of affairs in the ultracompetitive Southeastern Conference that Arkansas had to concern themselves not only with Florida and Auburn in the team battle at the NCAA Championships, but also fourth-place Louisiana State, who were better positioned to score well at the national meet. Entering the meet, there were other subplots at play as well.

Earlier in the season, Nick Willis of Michigan had broken Alistair Cragg's collegiate record in the 3,000 meter by running 7:44.90 on January 31, 2004.

"There were a few things said in the media [by Michigan] after that race, and John was pretty fired up about it," said Cragg. "Nick and I are good friends, and Ron [Michigan coach, Ron Warhurst] is a great guy, but for some reason that indoor season there was a real rivalry between us. John called me into his office on Monday, and I heard every word come out of his mouth. He said we were going to shove it down their throats."

That week, Cragg did the mile step-down workout on the indoor track like many Razorback athletes had done before—but at a speed hardly anyone could have imagined. His first mile was run in 4:00, followed by a 2:57 1,200 meter, an 800 meter, and then a 55 second 400 meter—all of it with three minutes rest.

"Once I got that workout in, John was all pumped up," said Cragg. "When he's like that it's hard not to feed off it."

At the Tyson Invitational less than two weeks later, Cragg retook the 3,000 meter collegiate record by six seconds in an incredible time of 7:38.59.

The stage was thus set for one of the all-time classic showdowns at the 2004 NCAA Indoor Championships. After outkicking Ian Dobson of Stanford, Richard Kiplagat of Iona, and Dathan Ritzenhein of Colorado to win the 5,000 meter in 13:39.63 on the first day, Cragg had twenty-four hours to recover for the 3,000 meter. That same night Willis anchored Michigan's distance medley relay to a win by outkicking Mike Taylor in an equally impressive winning time of 9:27.77. The task ahead of Cragg appeared to be daunting.

The morning of the 3,000 meter, Ron Warhurst sat down for breakfast at a restaurant in Fayetteville and chatted with a gentleman about the race. Unbeknownst to Warhurst it was Ray Cragg.

"Warhurst was talking to him in the restaurant and had no idea it was [Alistair's] dad," said McDonnell. "They began discussing the race and [Warhurst] apparently said Alistair is not in Willis's class at all. The dad asked him, 'Would you like to bet?' He said he didn't want to bet and that's when [Ray Cragg] said to him, 'I bet Alistair Cragg will beat Nick Willis.' [Warhurst] asked him, 'How do you know?' He said, 'I'm his dad.' That's a true story—Warhurst almost dropped when he said that."

Over in the locker room, Alistair and John had slightly less confidence in his ability to beat Willis.

"John asked me, 'What do you think, kid?'" remembered Cragg. "I said, 'I don't know, Coach. I'm stumped.' He said, 'Me too.' I said, 'I've got one plan.' He smiled at me and said, 'I've got one plan too.'"

"Alistair said I'm going to take him right from the gun and try to run his legs off," said McDonnell. "I said, 'Yep, I believe you can do that, but it would be better if you played around for 800 meters because you still have a long way out.' Nobody was going to lead, and Willis had a habit of staying at the back of the pack, so I said after 800 meters take it really casual going down the stretch and then hit him with a 59-second 400 meter. Alistair had a 10-meter jump on him and ran a 59, so Willis must have run a 56 to catch him."

Cragg continued to hammer each 200 meter lap in thirty seconds as Willis remained right on his shoulder. Lap after lap the two athletes pounded away without giving an inch to each other as the noise from the capacity crowd inside the Tyson Center became more and more deafening.

"I could see [John's] eyes get really big when he told me to go at 2,000 meters," said Cragg. "Every time I came around, he kept telling me to go faster and faster. I was running 29-second laps and he kept telling me to go faster and faster."

After spinning his fingers to signal to Cragg to continue putting pressure on Willis by speeding up, McDonnell began to spin both of his hands with 600 meters remaining.

"I told Alistair if I thought he was ready to go, I would use my entire hand," said McDonnell. "I could see Willis's legs beginning to buckle, but with 300 meters to go he was still there. Alistair put it down and beat him."

After a slow first 800 meters, both athletes had nearly run a 4:00 mile to the finish—Cragg crossed the line in 7:55.29 followed by Willis in 7:56.44. The win electrified the capacity crowd jammed into the Randall Tyson Track Center

"WOO! . . . PIG! . . . SOOIE!" the crowd thundered for several minutes

After the race, both Cragg and McDonnell embraced amidst the euphoria.

"That was probably my favorite running experience ever," said Cragg. "You had people on the team like Wallace Spearmon and Tyson Gay and alumni like Frank O'Mara in the stands. You look in the record books, and it's nice to see those kinds of people are backing you up."

Thirty-two seasons into his career, John McDonnell realized he had not seen everything.

"That was one of the best collegiate races I ever saw," said McDonnell. "It was a classic. Afterwards, Alistair told me, 'When you [told me to go faster with 600 meters remaining], I was going flat out at the time, and I was thinking what the hell do you think I was doing?' I said to him, 'Believe it or not, you picked it up,' even though he didn't feel like he was. I told Alistair I would watch [Willis's] face and body language, which he wouldn't be able to see. I never had someone as ballsy as [Alistair] was."

"I asked Coach after the race, 'Wasn't I going fast enough?'" said Cragg. "He said, 'Yes, but I wanted you to bury him.' When he gets really excited, it's like he's in the race. That's why I enjoyed running for him because I never felt like I was alone out there because he would pretty much feel everything you feel."

As much excitement as there was in the building after Alistair Cragg's thrilling victory, Chris Mulvaney quickly discovered that competing in the NCAA Championships at home can be a double-edged sword. Despite twelve sprint points from Tyson Gay and Wallace Spearmon, Arkansas found itself behind LSU after the Tigers exploded for twenty-four unanswered points in the triple jump. Only a year after he won the national title in the mile, Chris Mulvaney finished a disappointing ninth and failed to score. In a national meet in which Arkansas was edged by LSU 44–38, it was the difference.

"We were in a team battle, and [Mulvaney] bombed and the [Arkansas] papers just roasted him," remembered Danny Green. "It was a good thing having [the NCAA Championships] here but there was also a lot of pressure put on [the athletes], which wouldn't have happened in Indianapolis."

When the Razorbacks travelled to Mt. SAC Relays the following month, it was no longer the distance runners grabbing all of the attention. The 4 x 100 meter relay won the event, while Wallace Spearmon Jr. continued a remarkable freshman campaign with a personal best 200 meter of 20.35—into a headwind.

"When I was in college I was cocky and arrogant," admitted Spearmon. "One of my friends Maurice Bridges said, 'It was so hard to like you because you were so arrogant. You didn't know anything about times and were doing things you weren't supposed to be doing.' I remember one time before a race I took a knee and said, 'Dear Lord, please just let whatever I do today be wind legal.' Maurice looked at me weird and said, 'What did you just say?' I said, 'I asked for this to be wind legal.'"

When Spearmon dipped below twenty seconds for 200 meter shortly thereafter, both he and Tyson Gay were emerging as national title contenders in their respective events. Never before had a Razorback won the 100 meter or 200 meter at the NCAA Championships. Now it looked like two of them might accomplish it at the same time. Though Spearmon was focused more on the 200 meter and longer sprints while Gay was trained for the 200 meter and shorter sprints, neither gave an inch to the other in workouts or races.

"It was pretty competitive," said Gay. "You have to understand when you are a young sprinter coming in, you always look at the older people as if you want to beat them. That's just how it is and that's how it honestly was with Wallace and I."

"Tyson was a lot more reserved than I was," said Spearmon. "He was a little cocky, but people didn't see it because he didn't talk as much. He appears humble but . . . you just have to know Tyson."

Along with Omar Brown and Terry Gatson, sprints coach Lance Brauman had the cadre of Razorback sprinters firing on all cylinders heading into the Penn Relays.

Gatson's 45.9 400-meter split on the distance medley relay was the fastest on the day and gave the Razorbacks a big lead before Alistair Cragg held off a late charge by Chris Lukezic of Georgetown. The quarter-miler's work was hardly done that warm afternoon—Gatson was called upon to run the 400-meter leg on the sprint medley relay less than three hours later, with Spearmon and Brown leading off the 200 meter legs. The trio handed the baton to anchor leg James Hatch a few steps behind Tennessee before the Arkansas junior abused Marc Sylvester with a 1:47.6 leg to break the tape.

"The Penn Relays are special," McDonnell told the media. "This is the meet that I look forward to. I don't have to worry about motivation. If you can't get motivated here, you should get out of track."[3]

On a typically rainy Saturday afternoon, the Razorbacks handed Alistair Cragg another twenty-meter lead in the 4 x mile relay, which he carried to the win to cap a successful weekend.

After donning ball caps with Jason Sandfort during his 10,000 meter win at the SEC Outdoor Championships amid a torrential downpour in Oxford, Mississippi, Cragg backed up his bold locker-room words by edging Chris Mulvaney again in the 1,500 meter and then coming back to win the 5,000 meter as well. As well as things were going, the racing had taken its toll on Cragg.

Nursing an Achilles injury as he entered the NCAA Outdoor Regional meet, Cragg only needed to finish in the top-five spots in the 5,000 meter at the regional or jog the race distance to be granted one of the four at-large qualifying spots to the NCAA Championships since he was the number-one seed in the country.

"I hurt my calf [earlier in the season], and we went to Penn and did everything you have to do as a Razorback," said Cragg. "When we got to regionals, the rules say you have to give an honest effort. Matt Tegenkamp [of Wisconsin] was hurt too, and I remember speaking to him and his coach and I was like, 'I don't think I can run this. I can probably jog around in 15:00.'"

Seeking clarification on their options, McDonnell spoke with the meet referee.

"We talked to John Chaplin, and he said, 'Look, he's got the leading time in this event. This is just a prelim. I'll tell them he's injured and he goes on.'" remembered McDonnell.

"I asked, 'Should we get a doctor?' He said 'You can if you want.' So we got the LSU doctor, and he saw a lump on his Achilles. We still went back to Chaplin and said, 'If all he has to do is jog, he can go out and run in his flats.' I'll always remember Chaplin said, 'Nonsense! Nonsense! Why would a world-class athlete like you have to go out and jog! What purpose is that?' So we thought, 'No problem.'"

When the automatic qualifiers were announced the following week, including Alistair Cragg's automatic qualifying time in the 10,000 meter [which was not contested at the regional meet], Cragg's name was excluded from the 5,000 meter list despite having the fastest time in the country at 13:16.98. The NCAA committees ruled that Chaplin had exceeded his authority[4]—disqualifying Lady Razorback sprinter Veronica Campbell and Tennessee sprinter Sean Lambert under similar circumstances.

"We got a call Monday that he was out of the 5,000 meter," said McDonnell. "The NCAA is a bunch of renegades as far as I am concerned. How often is the meet referee overruled? Only when it's Arkansas. When you are on the top they don't like you. I had a lot of enemies who never did a damn thing in their lives and tried to get other people in trouble. I felt bad for Alistair."

If he was not going to be permitted to contest the 5,000 meter at the NCAA Championships, Cragg could at least take solace in the fact that his time had already qualified him for the Olympic Games.

"It was just bad advice," Cragg said of the decision to skip the 5,000 meter at the regional meet. "We still won the [national championship], and John was pumped about that, but he was more concerned about me going into an Olympic year."

As he often did amidst adversity, McDonnell radiated a calm confidence to his team in meetings.

"He gave people a lot of confidence when it came time to win a championship," remembered Tyson Gay. "Some coaches give you a pep talk, and it goes in one ear and out the other. Coach McDonnell gave us confidence. I saw how he carried himself, and that's how I wanted to carry myself. In my eyes he carried himself like a man, but he knew when it was time to get down to business. People couldn't rattle him out of his game plan. He'd say, 'If you go out and do your job, Tyson you do your job, Alistair Cragg do your job, Lance [Brauman] have your 4 x 100 meter ready, I'll have my guys ready, and we're going to win a championship.' There was just a lot of confidence. I can't describe it but it wasn't arrogance."

Despite the fact that the 10,000 meter at the 2004 NCAA Outdoor Championships was moved to Friday following a torrential downpour in Austin, Texas, Cragg got things started on the right note by edging Robert Cheseret of Arizona for the win in his final collegiate race.

In the 1,500 meter, Chris Mulvaney also won his third national title after holding off Nathan Robison of Brigham Young, which was sweet redemption after the disappointment indoors.

"After indoors, nobody worked harder than me," said Mulvaney. "I wasn't going to throw away all of that hard work. It's nice to finally get that first place. If I had lost by half a second, I would have been pretty gutted."[5]

The Razorbacks also received eleven unexpected points in field events that were now tutored by volunteer coaches. Jeremy Scott, who had been coached by volunteer coach

Greg Culp, placed third in the pole vault, while javelin thrower Eric Brown, who had been coached by volunteer coach Andrew McDonough, placed fourth. Brown's performance was extraordinary considering he was not ranked in the top ten entering the meet.

"Lo and behold the day of reckoning came and [Eric] stepped forward," said McDonnell of the All-American javelin thrower. "That tells me something about the kid. When a guy can come out and perform at that level in a national championship, he has a special gift to get up for a big meet."[6]

Still, what undoubtedly won the meet for Arkansas occurred in the 100 meter and 200 meter. Never before had the Razorbacks won a sprint event under 400 meters at the NCAA Championships.

"I had some good competition—Brandon Christianson from Texas, Demi Omole from Wisconsin, and Michael Frater [of TCU], who was the silver medalist at the 2003 worlds," remembered Gay. "A lot of it was instinct. I felt a little bit of pressure because I had lost the indoor race so I wanted to redeem myself."

Tyson Gay did more than redeem himself. He won his first national title in 10.06.

"I remember that very vividly," said Gay. "I had a lot of self-motivation going into that. It meant a lot to win my first title and the first Arkansas title [in the 100 meter]."

"That was big for Tyson," McDonnell told the media afterwards. "He's a competitor and a real team man. I'm so happy for him because indoors he didn't have a real good meet, and Tyson takes stuff like that personally. He felt he let people down. Boy, he paid them back tonight."[7]

After running the first straightaway on a 4 x 100 meter relay that placed fifth overall that same afternoon, Gay came back to finish fourth in the 200 meter. The event was won in 20.12 by Wallace Spearmon Jr., who capped off a remarkable six months with both his and the Razorbacks' first national title in the 200 meter.

Arkansas won its thirty-ninth NCAA championship by a 65–49 margin over Florida thanks to a variety of contributions across the board—including sixteen relay and individual points from Tyson Gay—a number that would become even more relevant only a few years later when the NCAA recalculated the tally.

"As a team effort it was fantastic," McDonnell told the media. "I don't know of one guy who didn't lay it on the line."[8]

After a remarkable season on the track, neither Gay nor Spearmon qualified for the Olympic team but nonetheless attracted attention from shoe companies with an eye to the future. Their time would come.

"I didn't think about going professional," Spearmon said after his freshman year. "I didn't make the final of the Trials, and Tyson got hurt, so the Nike guys talked to us and just said, 'We are watching you.'"

Although admittedly not short of confidence after winning a national title, Wallace nonetheless resisted the temptation to gloat to his All-American father.

"I'm not going to tell him [he's been one-upped]," Spearmon said. " He is old but he's still a little bigger than me."[9]

It also did not take long for the younger Spearmon to be put back in his place by those who had won national titles a handful of times themselves.

"If you went to Arkansas, you knew what you were there for," said Spearmon "If you didn't get it done, the coaches and athletes were probably going to rag on you.

Former Razorbacks Melvin Lister and Robert Howard kept it positive, but they would try and break me down. They'd give me crap, 'Oh, you're not going to make the practice squad.' Even when I won a national title they said, 'Good job, but that was still weak!'"

Both men had earned the right to candidly express their opinion to anyone. That summer Lister won the triple jump at the Olympic Trials with a world-leading mark of 58 feet, 4 inches and though his performance in Athens was not as proficient (he failed to make the final), he became the first athlete in American history to win both the triple jump and long jump at the U.S. Olympic Trials.

In the high jump, Matt Hemmingway, who had moved to Manhattan, Kansas, to train with Cliff Rovelto, did even better. He became the latest Razorback to win an Olympic medal with a leap of 2.34 meters to earn silver. It was the culmination of a long journey for the high jumper from Colorado, who had come out of retirement to capture the medal.

Amidst the brutal Athens heat—several projects essential to the Games were not completed, among other oversights by the Games organizers—Daniel Lincoln and Alistair Cragg both overcame the conditions to make the finals of the 3,000 meter steeplechase and 5,000 meter. Lincoln placed eleventh with a time of 8:16.66 while Cragg finished twelfth in 13:43.06—nearly twenty seconds slower than the preliminaries.

"I made the final but didn't run great," said Cragg. "I kind of freaked out."

The South African wasn't running against collegians anymore—and as it turned out he was not running for South Africa either. With misgivings about the state of affairs at Athletics South Africa and fortunate enough to have Irish ancestry in his background, Cragg had changed nationalities two years earlier and competed for Ireland. Now finished as a collegian, Cragg remained in Fayetteville training under the man who had "created him".[10]

"He went with [agent] Mark Wetmore," said McDonnell. "I said to Mark, 'What do you think he's worth?' He was comparing him to the Torres twins and stated a figure. I said to him, 'You must be kidding me. He's worth more than that.' He said, 'Yeah, I know but he's not American.' I said, 'Yeah, but Alistair is worth it.' He kind of hemmed and hawed and said, 'Gee, I really like Alistair.' So he came down and talked to him and visited him and Adidas gave him what I asked for."

Despite Nike's connection with McDonnell and Arkansas, their offer fell short. As he had done throughout his career, McDonnell never charged a coaching fee for Cragg or any of the professionals he trained. John had asked a lot physically and mentally from his athletes over the years, and they had given it to him. His investment in them was now purely an emotional one. He cherished their successes and felt the agony of their failures.

There were times McDonnell felt powerless to control impulsive decisions of student athletes whose greatness on the track was matched by their imprudence off of it. After four seasons of competition as a Razorback and three individual NCAA titles to his name in the mile or 1,500 meter, Chris Mulvaney needed another year to complete his degree and graduate from the University of Arkansas. Instead he returned to England. While he once had a future as bright as any miler in the world, Mulvaney soon left the sport entirely to pursue a career in male modeling.

"It was sad [he didn't graduate] because I respected the guy for what he did," said McDonnell.

Though Adam Perkins had gotten off to the slowest start of any of the incoming Razorbacks the previous fall, he was now thriving in the classroom (including a lab course he took with Sean McDonnell) and set for the best season of his career on the track now that the training no longer seemed impossible.

"The workouts felt almost like races, so the races became the easy part," said Perkins. "I learned about that and about pushing my limits and divorcing myself from thinking too much, not overanalyzing the situation, and letting running speak for itself."

While some of those who arrived in Fayetteville had become less receptive to remaining focused on school and academics, McDonnell became no less adept at delivering that message while managing a group of athletes from diverse backgrounds towards a common goal.

"I think that's what Coach McDonnell was best at," said Perkins. "He could get guys that didn't have much in common and bring all of these mentalities towards a common goal."

McDonnell could also still attract underdeveloped foot soldiers who wanted to attend Arkansas for the right reasons. After breaking the Louisiana high-school state cross-country course record in the 5,000 meter, Tyler Hill was one such athlete.

"He turned down LSU, even though they wanted to give him a scholarship," said McDonnell. "He wanted to run at Arkansas. I knew I had the right kid because he was sacrificing something."

Another was Seth Summerside, a former soccer player who held the small-school Missouri state records in the 800 meter through 3,200 meter, but sought a greater challenge for himself after two years at University of Missouri-Kansas City (UMKC). On his visit to Fayetteville, Summerside remembers being mesmerized by McDonnell's message.

"He told me there is no magic in this program," said Summerside. "It's about having the desire to be a champion and wanting to be the best. He said this program is about pride. I knew after talking to him that I was coming here."

Though Summerside's aerobic base was so deficient that he struggled to even run seven-minute mile pace for runs—a far cry from the tempo paces of his new teammates—he was able to hang in on the intervals and McDonnell brought him along slowly.

"He had a knack for maximizing your ability," remembered Summerside. "He was a master at finding where your potential was and exploiting it. He had this knack of being aggressive but conservative at the same time. If you are coaching yourself, it can be difficult to find that balance because you are biased. Coach had this way of pushing you right up to the edge. He could tell just by looking at you if that was enough or if you needed to do another. He had a certain balance to him and it just worked."

As he watched Summerside blossom from a runner who couldn't break 26:00 for 8,000 meters into one who set the fastest ever American debut at the time in the 10,000 meter in 28:02, McDonnell was equally impressed. Had Summerside not been felled by the misfortune of multiple staph infections shortly after his collegiate career ended, an Olympic bid would not have been out of the realm of possibility.

"Seth had a real storybook career," recalled McDonnell. "He went to a little private school with twenty kids or so and ran 1:56 for the 800 meter and then went to UMKC. He kept calling me and talking about coming down and I said, 'Well, you can walk on,' and I was thinking, 'What's this kid going to do,' but he turned out great. He was not only a great athlete but a great kid."

There was certainly something special in the environment McDonnell had created in Fayetteville.

"Having guys like Mark Fountain around was such a valuable resource," said Summerside. "We would meet off campus and do training runs together. They were so smart and raised the mentality and expectations of the group. Mark was top in the world, and if you could come close to doing a workout like him, that really lifted you up. That was huge having those people around."

It was from the far corners of the world that McDonnell signed the remainder of his class—Shawn Forrest, Marc Rodrigues, and Josphat Boit. Like fellow Australian Olympian Michael Power before him, Forrest came to Arkansas from Melbourne with impeccable prep credentials—3:45 for 1,500 meters and 8:04 for 3,000 meters—and a determination to train with and be like the best. While that would come in time, just getting to Fayetteville in August 2004 was proving to be the biggest challenge of all.

After the international office at the university misdated his student visa, Forrest was denied entry into the country. Homeland Security had changed since McDonnell came to the United States forty years earlier, and the attacks on September 11, 2001, hadn't helped matters. An attempt to enter from Canada with newly issued documentation was also denied and Forrest was sent back to Australia.

"The guy at the American embassy up in Canada was a real jerk and yelled at him, 'Out of here! Out of here! Next! Young boy, head back to Australia!'" remembered McDonnell. "Shawn called me from Canada crying on the phone because they wouldn't let him into the country. He had to fly back to Australia and get an updated I-20 form."

Forrest had been recommended to John by Mark Fountain with one small caveat.

"Mark told me, 'The thing about Shawn is he's different . . . but I can't explain it,'" laughed McDonnell. "So I said, 'You're lots of help!' Shawn was a great guy and ended up running really well."

That same fall, McDonnell signed Marc Rodrigues, from Johannesburg, South Africa, who had run at Cloud County Community College in Kansas. Rodrigues had range from 1:50 (800 meter) all the way to 30:02 (10,000 meter) and could seemingly do anything he wanted.

"He was a tough guy who ran pretty well," said McDonnell, "but he was a bit of a playboy and never really committed to running."

Josphat Boit certainly had a circuitous route of his own to Fayetteville. Originally from Eldoret, Kenya, Boit first came to Central Methodist College in Missouri for one year. When that school ran out of money and was no longer able to honor his scholarship, Boit was forced to transfer to Cowley County, a junior college in Arkansas City, Kansas. It was an eye-opening experience for him.

"Whenever I came to the United States the first time I thought all of the schools were the same," said Boit, "but after the first school didn't have enough money I thought, 'Whoa, maybe something is different.' So the next time I wanted to go to a school with a great tradition of running and pick a good coach."

Boit was being recruited by Division I programs all over the country—including Tennessee, Alabama, and Oklahoma. Though he was first exposed to the dominance of the Arkansas distance runners at the Chile Pepper Festival in 2002, it was not until he was personally recruited by John McDonnell that Boit became truly sold on the idea of coming to Fayetteville.

"It was really special meeting him," remembered Boit. "When I was at Cowley, a lot of coaches came to recruit me. Coach McDonnell came, and he drove a pickup truck and I thought, 'Oh my, he looks so old, and he came all the way from Arkansas to see me.' The other coaches told me if I go to Arkansas, they will burn me out but Coach McDonnell was straight. He said, 'If you want to be great, this is the school you want to come to, but if you just want to get your degree and move on with your life then this isn't the place for you.' I thought that was interesting, and of course the results spoke for themselves. They were the best in the nation."

After McDonnell lost out on Simon Ngata, when the junior-college national champion signed with SEC rival Georgia, he had concerns about Boit despite the phenomenal times he had been purported to have run in Kenya. John had no way of verifying them. When he watched Boit and Rodrigues fail to break 32:00 in the 10,000 meter at the Texas Relays—albeit in brutal heat—those worries were hardly allayed.

"You talk about being dicey about giving a scholarship out," said McDonnell. "I asked JB, 'Did you run 13-anything [5,000 meter] overseas?' He said, 'Yeah, 13:17.' I don't know if he, did but I said, 'G'damn.' He said, 'Coach, I know what you are going to say. It's awfully cold up here [in Kansas], and I just do what I have to do. Really, coach, you won't be disappointed.' So he came and was a really nice guy and genuine."

Once in Fayetteville, Boit adapted well and took to McDonnell's training like a fish to water.

"It worked well for me," said Boit. "It was a little different than I was used to. Everything was really structured, and they didn't do any pace work until after the first two meets, just runs. Even that was different because normally when I did four hundreds it was five or six but here it was sixteen of them."

After never beating Simon Ngata during their junior-college careers, Boit generally got the better of Ngata once he became an Arkansas Razorback. The first such meeting between the two took place at the 2004 SEC Cross Country Championships at Agri Park in Fayetteville, Arkansas.

"We raced a lot in junior college, so it was a big deal for me," said Boit. "We met at SEC, and Simon said I looked a lot skinnier than he thought."

Boit beat Ngata, winning the individual title, and freshman Shawn Forrest did as well to help the Razorbacks win their thirty-first consecutive conference cross-country championship.

Ranked second behind Wisconsin in the final Mondo Division I national poll of the season, the Razorbacks arrived at the national meet in Terre Haute, Indiana, with one thing on their minds: winning.

"Before the race [Coach McDonnell] said this will be a real test for you," remembered Boit.

Josphat spent much of the race battling with Matt Gonzales of New Mexico and Simon Bairu of Wisconsin for the lead before Bairu edged both of them to win the individual race by three seconds.

"For some reason I thought I had both of them," said Boit, "but it didn't work out."

Although Sandfort and Rodrigues had both placed in the top twenty-five, neither Forrest (92) nor Matt Gunn (136) were able to hang with the leaders, and the Razorbacks placed third overall with 202 points.

In spite of Simon Bairu's individual victory for the Badgers, heavily favored Wisconsin was nipped by Colorado for the national championship, 90–94. After years of being lambasted for their come-from-behind strategy, Colorado had timed things perfectly to win a tight race once again.

It was also one of a few close calls for Jerry Schumacher's Wisconsin cross-country team during that decade. After running for Martin Smith during his own collegiate career in Madison, the young coach had ascended to the head position and quickly put his own stamp on the already tradition-rich program by finishing second place on four occasions during his first six seasons.

"I remember telling [Jerry], 'You're the future,'" said McDonnell. "He did a great job there. I personally think they could have won more national titles, but that's the thing about those big meets. On paper they had some great teams that didn't win, but nobody really knows what happens behind the scenes. Guys can get sick or have off days."

Though McDonnell's philosophy on training and many other things largely jibed with the young Wisconsin coach, his thoughts on roster management sometimes differed.

"Schumacher worked hard to get some good talent at Wisconsin, but there were times he redshirted guys and might have lost a title because of it," remembered McDonnell. "I always felt if there was a national title on the line to go for it because the following year there is no guarantee."

With true freshman Matt Withrow redshirting for the Badgers only months before he qualified for the 2005 World Cross Country Championships in France (where he was the top finisher for the United States in the senior race) it is a matter of speculation as to whether the outcome of the 2004 NCAA Cross Championships might have been changed by his inclusion on the starting line for Wisconsin.

"If I could go back I'd probably put [Withrow] on the line," admitted Schumacher. "His training from September to November was never indicative of [running as well as he did in March], but from December to February we had a whole different athlete. If I saw the Matt of January back in October, he would have been on the line. I did look back upon that, and maybe he could have pulled it out because he was talented and tough. It was a lesson learned for sure."

Heading into the track season, McDonnell remained a model of consistency. He was at every practice, and his distance runners performed many of the same workouts [with small variations) as they had for decades. It did not take long for many of the newcomers to buy into the Hog training mentality.

"[Shawn] Forrest ran harder than anyone," said Sandfort. "He did [14½ mile runs] in 1:14."

McDonnell continued to keep as close an eye on the weight of his athletes as he ever had and still went to great lengths to explain how thin the line truly was for peak performance.

"He knew when you gained weight just by looking at your face and would use the analogy of the horse who had been handicapped five pounds," remembered Perkins.

"Coach used to say if you go home and your mom thinks you're sick, that means you are in shape," said Razorback All-American Phil Price, who later became a television weatherman in Tulsa. "When you're truly fit, you are on that line of getting sick or injured, and that's the line people have trouble managing."

McDonnell continued to preach the need for consistency, hard work, and focus in one's life if an athlete hoped to attain academic and athletic success. He also set a tone for discipline that penetrated every event group on the team—no exceptions. Only a few years earlier he had left eight-time NCAA champion Robert Howard at home when he was a few minutes late for the bus to Nebraska (Howard ended up driving his own car and meeting the team at a gas station outside Kansas City), and he held everyone to the same standard.

"I don't think he let anyone off the hook," said Sandfort. "He didn't treat anyone special and would go out of his way to congratulate someone who ran tough or had a good workout for them. He would praise an individual when they needed it, or to someone else he would not let them think they were too hot in their head. When someone sacrificed for the betterment of the team, he made them aware he appreciated it and that was the key to being a winner."

McDonnell was able to make demands of his athletes, and they continued to respond to those demands because they felt like he cared not only about their athletic careers but the rest of their lives. It didn't matter if they were distance runners, jumpers, sprinters, vaulters, or throwers. Every Razorback understood he demanded excellence, and they did everything humanly possible—in some cases even what seemed to be impossible—to satisfy him.

"As great as John is as a coach, he is ten times the man, and a lot of times he would became almost like a father figure to some of us," said Phil Price. "Nobody wants to disappoint their father. You wanted to do well and you wanted to perform well, but he also had in his mind what you were capable of doing, and when you didn't perform to what he thought you were capable of, he would let you know. You may have run a time that you were happy with, but he would pull you off to the side and say, 'Great performance,' and then he'd tell you where you can get better. It was this thing where you keep pushing to get better and better."

Others recalled how easy John made it to achieve the seemingly hardest things in the sport.

"If you believe in something or believe in somebody and that person is a good person and humble and knows what he's talking about, then it's very easy to be successful if you listen to him," said Seneca Lassiter. "Coach McDonnell has the ability to make a young man believe like it's nobody's business. Even though he had this aura about him, he would crack jokes with you and talk to you and relate to you like he was on your level even though he is forty years older. If I went elsewhere, the outcome would not have been the same. I believed in him. If he told me I could run through a brick wall, I'd say which one."

Having competed in the pole vault for Arkansas half a century earlier, Dr. Alan Sugg observed McDonnell at various NCAA championship and home meets for decades during his time as president of the University of Arkansas and very succinctly summed up his observations.

"In my judgment he is the greatest leader that I've ever known," said Sugg. "He epitomizes the very best qualities of leadership because he surrounded himself with very, very talented people in his assistant coaches and athletes while creating an environment of expectations for them. He is so genuine, humble, knowledgeable, and kind but tough. In being a leader you have to be a kind, long-suffering, gentle, understanding son of a bitch. And he was a son of a bitch at the end of it all. It was going to work because even though his athletes had tremendous self-discipline, they respected him and would do anything to honor their coach. If he said run a little bit faster or jump higher, they did it. In the process, they learned a whole lot in terms of understanding how to be successful through hard work and doing things the right way."

The Razorbacks burst into the 2005 indoor season as the number-one ranked team in the country even before they were augmented by the addition of Peter Kosgei, who had transferred from Division II Harding University that January. The valedictorian of his high-school graduating class at Chepkongony Christian Secondary School in Kapsabet, Kenya, the distance runner had been recruited to Harding by missionaries but was immediately attracted by the Arkansas program. Despite making the move for athletic reasons, Kosgei was adamant about not transferring until he was accepted into his academic program.

"I came here because they had a very good [athletics] program, but my main concern was to go to business school," said Kosgei. "I came from Kenya to go to school, so if I wasn't going to study what I wanted, there was no reason. Running helped get me my education, not the other way around. I could have gone to Europe to run professionally. I came to school, and my main goal was to have my degree first."

Kosgei had been a Division II All-American during three semesters at Harding but soon reached a new level in Fayetteville. He quickly bonded with Josphat Boit and ran personal bests in the 3,000 meter and 5,000 meter within three months—including winning each event at the 2005 SEC Indoor Championships to help Arkansas win a sixty point blowout and avenge its loss to Florida during the previous season.[11]

As satisfying as retaking the conference championship was to those wearing the Red and White, everyone had their eyes on avenging an equally disappointing loss at the previous season's national championship. Heading into the week of the 2005 NCAA Indoor Championships, there was certainly plenty of optimism the Razorbacks were on the verge of winning their fortieth national championship in program history.

Jaanus Uudmae had rebounded from an injury plagued year to capture the SEC title in the triple jump, while Arkansas had several qualifiers in the distance events and continued to be a force to be reckoned with in the sprint events, with a plethora of qualifiers in the short sprints and relays.

All of that momentum would soon come to a screeching halt before the national championships even started. For one thing, Gay had been felled by hamstring issues since his sparkling 6.55 sprint in the 60-meter dash at the Tyson Invitational, and the chances of him competing lessened with each passing day.

The most devastating blow nearly came only days before the national championship. After LaShawn Merritt of East Carolina turned professional during the middle of the collegiate indoor season and signed a lucrative contract with Nike, it appeared the shoe company had its sights set on convincing Wallace Spearmon Jr. to do the same and was not wasting any time in that effort.

Late in the afternoon of Wednesday March 2, 2005, less than ten days before the NCAA Indoor Championships, McDonnell received a call from Nina Mullinga, Wallace's mother.

"She thought I knew, so she said, 'Coach, I'll see you at the meeting tonight,'" remembered McDonnell. "I said, 'Hold on, what meeting?' She told me the whole story. I said, 'What! I don't mind him going, but by gosh we have a season to finish.'"

A few minutes later, McDonnell had another unexpected visit in his office.

"Tyson [Gay] came in and asked, 'Do you know about this?'" remembered McDonnell. "If Wallace had signed, it would have hurt their 4 x 100 meter relay outdoors."

"I remember that very vividly," said Gay. "[Wallace] had run fast indoors, and some shoe companies were interested in him so he thought about turning pro. It affected us because there were rumors circulating, and other guys like me wanted to win a title. You have to also understand him being a young kid, and you have this many people in his ear pulling him this way, and other people pulling him another way."

Ultimately McDonnell was able to convince Wallace and his mother to wait until the academic year was over before signing any contract. It would turn out to be a fortuitous decision for all involved.

By the first day of the 2005 NCAA Indoor Championships the following week, Spearmon proved his value was only going up. After setting a collegiate and American indoor record in the 200-meter preliminaries with a time of 20.21 on Friday afternoon, the Fayetteville native outdid himself later that evening by winning the final and lowering his mark further to 20.10—over a quarter-second ahead of second-place Walter Dix of Florida State. The Tyson Center exploded with a deafening roar followed by a cacophony of local fans delirious with excitement "Calling the Hogs."

"*WOO! . . . PIG! . . . SOOIE!*"

As Spearmon rounded the track for his victory lap, there was no sign of letup in the building.

"*WOO! . . . PIG! . . . SOOIE!*"

While the decibel level in the field house would reach similarly high levels the following day when Kerron Clement of Florida broke Michael Johnson's indoor world record in the 400-meter dash with a time of 44.57, the pandemonium following Spearmon's run had the added thrill of a local boy and Razorback earning his place amongst the pantheon of American sprinting legends—and on his hometown track.

"Wallace was just phenomenal," said McDonnell. "He was always good in practice, but raised it to another level in competition. He had a great head. He was cool, calm, and collected."

The excitement in the building had hardly subsided as Josphat Boit and Peter Kosgei swapped the lead with one another during the early stages of the 5,000 meter.

"Coach's strategy was to make it a race and not to lose with a lot left in you," said Boit. "So we went and swapped leads, but it didn't work out well."

"I was in good shape, no question," admitted Kosgei, "but I didn't know very much about running, and I had no idea about tactics. The guy from Stanford [Ian Dobson], Robert Cheseret from Arizona, [Chris] Solinsky, and [Matt] Tegenkamp—I didn't know any of those guys."

Both Razorbacks were unable to respond as those four runners, plus Matt Gonzales of New Mexico, came flying by them during the last 1,000 meters of the race. Boit still finished sixth and was followed by Kosgei in seventh, but the real damage happened shortly thereafter in the distance medley relay.

After Adam Perkins (1,200 meter), Terry Gatson (400 meter), Harun Iman (800 meter) handed off to anchor Said Ahmed, the miler held a small lead on Nate Brannen of Michigan, who began closing hard and made up significant ground with every stride. Into the final straightaway, Brannen's momentum seemed to be driving him inexorably past Ahmed, who was in lane two and on the edge of lane three before falling across the line just ahead. The Razorbacks scored ten badly needed points—but it would be a short-lived victory.

"The finish judge said there was no contact," said McDonnell. "Our guy moved out a bit, but it wasn't like he pushed him. All of a sudden a coach from the Big 12 runs over and tells [Ron] Warhurst [of Michigan] to protest it because that kid moved out, and they ended up in lane three. It was the first time I saw a team disqualified without a foul or interference being called by an official."

The ten points were subtracted from Arkansas, who ended the day in a precarious position. Like few other times in his career, McDonnell was seething with anger. The following morning he called a team meeting in the locker room to regroup after such a devastating setback to their national title hopes.

"Coach was really pissed about that," said Adam Perkins. "He gave us a pep talk about how they took a national title from us, so let's shove it down their throats."

"It was a hellfire and brimstone speech about how they screwed us, and everybody was against us," remembered Danny Green. "They came out of that meeting fired up and ready to go."

If John's intention was to light a fire under his team, all he did was fan a flame that was already burning brightly. It was a highly charged atmosphere in the Tyson Center for the start of the second day. Some of the Arkansas athletes not competing that weekend held up a banner that read 'MCDONNELL 39, WARHURST 0,' in reference to the national championships won by each coach. An almost equally large Michigan contingent cheered wildly after Nick Willis began the day with a victory in the mile.

Once the meet got underway, the old Hog mentality had taken hold. One Arkansas athlete after another stepped up with personal-best performances under the most adverse of circumstances.

After barely even being accepted into the meet as the final qualifier in the 800 meter, James Hatch finished second with a personal best of 1:47.40. In the 400 meter, Terry Gatson shaved a full second off his personal best to finish second in 45.29—this coming after he hadn't even medaled at the SEC meet and entered the NCAA meet ranked seventh. Jaanus Uudmae put forth his highest finish to that point in the triple jump at the NCAA meet by placing fourth.

After one personal best after another, Arkansas entered the 3,000 meter with an eight-point lead over Florida, who had the top-ranked 4 x 400 meter set to finish the meet.

"Coach told me and Adam [Perkins] if we scored three points, it was a done deal," said Kosgei. "He told me to stick in ninth or tenth and then as the race goes on to move up. So I did that and felt strong and kept kicking and kicking and closed the gap on Tegenkamp but couldn't catch Solisnky."

Kosgei finished second in 7:54.45—followed by Adam Perkins in sixth. The meet was over.

"*WOO!* . . . *PIG!* . . . *SOOIE!*" The crowd chanted.

In the 4 x 400 meter, Florida won the event as expected with Kerron Clement anchoring their side but not before Wallace Spearmon (who had run 46.16 earlier in the season) put the Razorbacks briefly into the lead in their heat with a blazing opening lap. His adrenaline ran out around 300 meters.

"It was a crazy atmosphere," said Spearmon. "I went out so hard, and I'm glad [the meet wasn't on the line] because I died a horrible death."

More than ever, McDonnell cherished accepting the program's fortieth national championship trophy at home after the most inspiring and complete team victory in recent memory.

"That was great because we shoved it down their throats after they disqualified us, and we still found a way to win," said McDonnell. "It was a fantastic atmosphere. People were going wild. The kids ran out of their minds. Even coaches that never said much to me would say, 'Coach, that has to be the best performance you had because they were all personal bests, and just one great performance after the other.'"

Though it can be difficult to compare memories over time, Danny Green had been present at Franklin Field when Joe Falcon outkicked Sammy Cheruiyot to win the distance medley at Penn Relays in 1989, he had competed as an All-American on teams that had won NCAA triple crowns, and been the director of operations to witness titanic battles such as Alistair Cragg's race against Nick Willis a year earlier.

"That was the greatest meet I have ever been a part of," said Green unequivocally of the 2005 NCAA Indoor Championships. "Guys just did things over and beyond."

There were multiple times during the meet and even throughout the season when it could have gone another direction. At an age when most coaches are retired or past their prime, John McDonnell still had a knack for pushing the right buttons at the right time —whether it involved contriving strategy during the day of a race or helping an athlete reset their mentality ahead of time. It was no coincidence that James Hatch finished fourteen places higher than he was ranked only six days after he was called to Coach McDonnell's office and asked to close the door following what had been an underwhelming season.[12]

Thirty years after he had retired from coaching football, Arkansas athletic director Frank Broyles watched with amazement as the drama unfolded before him.

"I used to always wonder how he could get such peak performances," said Broyles. "He took what he could get and made them into champions through commitment, hard work, and preparation. He had a knack for motivating them and preparing them to perform their best at the national championship. That's the knack few coaches have, and he was the best at it."

The NCAA meet also demonstrated once again how tight-knit the Razorback program was across and within event groups. In a few short months, Josphat Boit and Peter

Kosgei quickly became kindred spirits. The two later decided to room together and keyed off one another as training partners. Only a few weeks after the NCAA Indoor Championships, both athletes entered the 10,000 meter at the Stanford Invitational having done nothing but easy runs on the grass following the conclusion of the indoor season.

"They were in great shape speed-wise, so all we did was run distance for a few weeks and strides," said McDonnell. "I said, 'We are not getting ready for it because if we keep going, we'll have no time off.'"

Amidst typically perfect California weather, both Boit and Kosgei broke the Arkansas school record in the 10,000 meter with runs of 28:07.27 and 28:08.97 respectively. Coming as early as it did during the outdoor season, the times were as much of a surprise to the athletes as it was to their competition.

"Going outdoors I was expecting something good, but I didn't know we were going to run that," admitted Kosgei. "We just hung in there and it turned out to be a good race."

Though Boit was sidetracked with an Achllles problem shortly thereafter until the conference championship, the prodigious early season performance further cemented his faith in McDonnell.

"When he talks, you feel like everything will be good," said Boit. "So you do whatever he tells you."

Assistant coach Lance Brauman returned every member of the 4 x 100 meter relay team that finished fifth at the previous NCAA championship and was now rightfully considered a favorite to capture the first national title in the event in Arkansas history. While Tyson Gay was still on the mend, Wallace Spearmon Jr. continued his all-out assault on the 200-meter record book by breaking 20 seconds for the first time with a 19.97 wind-legal school-record performance at Mt. SAC Relays.

Still, there was reason to wonder whether a 4 x 100 meter relay that seemed unbeatable on paper would ever be able to put it together on the track. Both Spearmon and Gay were beaten straight-up by LSU freshman sensation Xavier Carter (the X-Man) in the 200 meter at the SEC meet, while the Arkansas 4 x 100 meter relay of Gay, Spearmon, Omar Brown, and Michael Grant finished sixth, running out of the slow heat.

"I used to read the chat boards, and they would talk about LSU and Florida because people always think tradition carries on. I thought we had the best team, period," said Gay. "We had won [the slow heat at SEC], but didn't run fast so [SEC 400-meter champ] Kelly Willie [of LSU] said, 'You guys just have a bunch of fast names, but you never run anything fast.' We were running slow, but were just running according to our competition because, honestly, nobody could beat us. So I told [Willie], 'Man, when the time comes, we're going to kill you.' And he said, 'Okay Tyson, all you're doing is talking and talking.'"

Two weeks later at the Mid-East Regional in Bloomington, Indiana, Arkansas edged LSU in the 4 x 100 meter by the slimmest of margins, 38.75 to 38.77, to break a school record and back Gay's bold words.

"I said to [Willie], 'I told you we run to our competition!'" remembered Gay. "There was a lot of trash talking."

After blowing out Florida at the SEC Outdoor Championships by fifty points, the NCAA meet was expected to be much tighter—especially after Tyson Gay false started in the 100 meter at the regional meet and failed to qualify in the event. That the Razorbacks were still able to pull off another national championship victory, the forty-first in school history, was testament to contributions from a variety of event areas.[13]

As had been the case the previous season, the sprinters came through in a big way starting with a national title by the 4 x 100 meter relay in a school-record time of 38.49. Running the anchor leg, Omar Brown brought the baton home for the Razorbacks.

"Omar was the type of guy who runs his best when he is out in the open," said Gay, "so Coach Brauman thought it would be best to have someone who can run tall and open on the anchor leg."

In the 200-meter dash, Wallace Spearmon Jr. elevated his game when it mattered most by beating Xavier Carter of LSU in an NCAA final for the ages with a personal best and world-leading time of 19.91. Gay was third in 20.16 only a day after running a then–world-leading time of 19.93 in the preliminaries.

"The only thing better is if they both ran 19.91 together," said an ecstatic Brauman. "It's been a great year. What can I say?"[14]

Arkansas edged Florida 60–49 for its forty-first NCAA championship, and it was not lost on keen observers of the sport that for the first time in Razorback history the 200 meter put the national meet out of reach rather than the 5,000 meter.[15]

"People say, 'Oh you've changed the philosophy of your team," McDonnell told the media afterwards. "Whatever scores points, that's what we're going to have."[16]

The means had shifted, but the end result was the same for the forty-first time since March 1984—the Arkansas Razorbacks were national champions. While losing to Arkansas was getting old for their rivals at the SEC and NCAA championships (Florida coach Mike Holloway told the media "we've got what we call the Arkansas problem"[17]) Dr. Alan Sugg took no less joy from personally witnessing each victory.

The president of the university picked up a copy of the *Sacramento Bee* during the meet and read an article entitled "Dynastic Arkansas Becomes a Target," which he felt perfectly encapsulated the Arkansas Razorbacks place in the sport of track and field:

> Hey, every sport needs a Yankees. Every sport needs a team to hate, a team to respect, a team of which to be jealous—somebody to hunt and chase and occasionally cuss at. The Yankees of college track and field reside in Fayetteville, Ark., and they train and run and jump and win under John McDonnell. McDonnell is a 66-year-old Irish native with a strong constitution and the capability of saying many bad words in a lilting brogue when things don't go his way, which isn't often. He's also the gentlemanly face of track at the NCAA Championships this weekend at Sacramento State. He knows everybody in the place, and they all shake his hand and wish him well, and then as soon as he leaves they start plotting his program's downfall. Or, as Southeastern Conference rival coach Mike Holloway of Florida put it, "We've got what we call 'the Arkansas problem.'" Best get used to it. There is Arkansas, and then there is the field. You won't get John McDonnell to say that, of course. He's well aware of the major players on the national track scene, schools that are tough as nails, schools that find a way to compete at a consistently high level. But

when people in this sport speak of the college game, they speak first and foremost of Arkansas, the team to beat. There's no better feeling in track than to take down the Razorbacks, if only because it's so damned hard. Now, the game is to try to poke holes in the Arkansas program. You can't do it, of course. McDonnell still recruits young men who win regardless of the conditions, who understand what it means to pull on the Razorback uniform, and to be wearing a target on their backs.[18]

Shortly after the season ended, both Tyson Gay and Wallace Spearmon turned professional. Gay signed a contract with agent Mark Wetmore.

"That may have been the first sprinter Wetmore ever had," said McDonnell. "Tyson was very conservative. That's why I was so proud of him. Even when he signed that contract and got all of that money, he didn't buy a new car but fixed his old one."

Both athletes also remained training with Lance Brauman, who was coaching Olympic champion Veronica Campbell of the Lady Razorbacks. At the World Championships that summer in Helsinki, Spearmon placed second, and Gay was fourth in the 200 meter behind Olympic champion Justin Gatlin.

Following the incident with the Nike representatives in March, McDonnell made the decision to switch his entire team to Adidas the following season. Spearmon stayed with Nike initially and commanded an even greater contract than Gay—validating McDonnell's advice from the previous March that his value was only going up.

"They were both hot that year," remembered McDonnell. "After the NCAA outdoor meet, I got them in touch with their respective agents. Both of them went with different people. They already had a sprint coach so it didn't matter."

Things were also going well for the postcollegiate distance athletes John McDonnell continued to coach during their fledgling professional careers.

Only a year removed from making the Olympic 5,000-meter final, Alistair Cragg continued his meteoric rise to the top of the distance running world. Back in February at the Boston Indoor Games, Cragg had defeated his second Olympic champion in three years when he held off a late charge by the 10,000-meter and 5,000-meter world-record holder Kenenisa Bekele of Ethiopia to win in a time of 7:39.89.

"I don't know what to think when a guy like that comes around you," Cragg told the media afterwards. "You don't know how strong he is or how strong you are, it's a matter of just sticking to the plan and following what Coach told me to do. He's never failed me. I had thought I'd just follow what Coach McDonnell said, and take off.[19] Ninety-nine times out of a hundred he would have beaten me. I just had to make sure I was there in case the wheels came off, or he made a mistake. "That's what Coach said, 'Make sure you're there. Once you're there, you'll forget about who he is, how you're feeling, and where you are. Your racing instincts will kick in, no matter who's around you.' And it did, it happened."

Cragg also captured the gold medal in the 3,000 meter at the European Indoor Championships the same year, but the grind of the professional circuit began to gradually wear on him. After running with leader Eliud Kipchoge at the 2004 Rome Golden Gala 5,000 meter, which was won in 12:46.53, Cragg faded badly to 13:37.35 and admitted publicly afterwards he contemplated not even finishing.[20]

"When Alistair was in college, he was totally focused and wasn't afraid of anybody," said McDonnell. "All of a sudden when you leave college and race in Europe, everyone is a stud around you. He told me once when he finished a 5,000 meter in 13:07 and placed eighth that he walked off the track and nobody knew who he was. That stuff started bothering him. I said, 'Alistair, that's a personal best. What's wrong with that?' He said, 'It's just tough.'"

Daniel Lincoln was only a year away from breaking the American record in the 3,000-meter steeplechase with a time of 8:08.82 and being ranked eighth in the world. When Lincoln's contact with Nike came up for renewal in 2006 after he set that American record, McDonnell learned he could have earned a contract with Adidas that would have also retroactively covered his medical school.

"Daniel called me and said, 'Nike won't release me,'" remembered McDonnell. "I said, 'Your contract is up.' He said, 'Yeah, but when I was talking to the agent, we had a cup of coffee, and he said this is what we'll ask for. He wrote it on a paper napkin and said just to make sure there is no misunderstanding you sign it, and I'll sign it.'" I told him, 'You just signed a flipping contract, buddy.'"

McDonnell remembers Lincoln becoming flustered at the news.

"He said, 'It was just a paper napkin. The lawyer said it won't stand up,'" remembered McDonnell. "I said, 'You've signed a contract. You can get a lawyer to try and beat it, but I don't think you will.' And he didn't. Nike held him to it."

Despite some of the unfortunate circumstances surrounding his contract, Lincoln's running career continued to blossom as he made progress toward a medical degree.

Months after Martin Smith left Oregon following the legendary coach's well-documented falling out with Nike co-founder and Oregon booster, Phil Knight,[21] another coach found himself subject to a similar recruiting campaign as McDonnell had been six years earlier. Only two years after leaving Stanford to accept an athletic director's position at Oberlin College, where he hoped to make an institutional impact, Vin Lananna accepted the Oregon head-coaching position to accomplish much the same thing.

"Track has an institutional impact at Oregon," said Lananna. "They wanted to take Oregon track to the next level, to host meets, operate the facility, win titles, get great crowds, and have a postcollegiate club."

While Smith had been successful leading the Ducks to national prominence in track and field, the once plentiful crowds at Hayward Field were dwindling and the cross-country program failed to qualify for the NCAA Cross Country Championships—an unacceptable state of affairs for the Oregon powerbrokers who valued distance-running success. Once again, Lananna had his work cut out for him.

By the time August 2005 rolled around—it seemed to arrive sooner for McDonnell each year—the veteran coach welcomed another bumper crop of new athletes for his thirty-fourth cross-country campaign.

From Massachusetts came Chris Barnicle, an 8:50 two-miler, who was sixth at the Foot Locker Cross Country Championships, while signee Kenny Cormier of Arizona had won the Foot Locker national meet—the first incoming Razorback to have done so since Reuben Reina in 1985. McDonnell also signed the runner right behind Cormier at Foot Locker, Scott Macpherson of Plano, Texas. Having been heavily recruited by schools all over the country, Macpherson remembered McDonnell's track record and patience on the phone impressing him.

Arkansas had as strong a lineup as ever entering the fall of 2005. Combined with the athletes returning to Fayetteville that fall, they began the season ranked ahead of Wisconsin in early season polls.

If the Badgers had taken a low-key strategy by not racing hard until Big Tens, the Razorbacks had done the opposite. Arkansas began by dismantling eventual fourth-ranked Iona at the Meet of Champions in New York on September 24, 2005, followed by a massive win over eighth-ranked Oklahoma State on a sloppy day in Stillwater the following weekend, then a win over fifteenth-ranked UTEP at the Chile Pepper Festival in mid-October, followed by another SEC championship over twentieth-ranked Alabama, and a regional win against seventh-ranked Texas in Waco, Texas, in mid-November. Arkansas had run the gauntlet—beating five top-twenty-ranked programs in the space of seven weeks—and looked no worse for it.

Throughout the season, McDonnell continued to closely monitor the pulse of his team.

"Coach was always the one pulling back the reins on us," remembered Seth Summerside. "I remember he came up to the trails specifically because we were running too fast and that happened several different times. We were extremely competitive. You had all of these athletes from around the country in a very competitive atmosphere. Coach was amazing at fanning that flame of competiveness between the athletes, but before the big meets, he would knock the competitiveness off between us, and it was a team atmosphere, and he would do a good job communicating what we needed to do."

Although the outcome of the SEC Championships was never in doubt, there was concern when officials sent the leaders through a tangent on the course, which could have led to their disqualification—and thus possibly changed the outcome of the race and the thirty-two year conference-winning streak.

"I was worried at first when they started talking about disqualifying people," McDonnell said. "We figured out that we still would have won, even if our top three finishers didn't count. It would have been a real shame for the guys if anything would have happened, because it was such a classy race."[22]

The Razorbacks had other things to be concerned about. A nearly flawless performance by Wisconsin at the 2005 Big Ten Championships had put the Badgers back atop the rankings. On November 21, 2005, there was an element of the immovable object meeting the unstoppable force.

"What I loved about John was that even though he was at the top, and I was a young coach trying to overthrow the empire, he always took the time to talk to me," said Wisconsin coach Jerry Schumacher. "He set the standard, and you knew whenever you were facing Arkansas, you had to bring your A game because it was going to be serious. I know he always wanted to keep beating us."

Though McDonnell had complimented Schumacher privately that he was "the future" of distance coaching, he certainly was not ready to concede the present on that particular Monday afternoon.

"Coach said we were going for the win," remembered Josphat Boit. "We knew Wisconsin was good, but he analyzed that if everyone took care of business, we were going to be champions after the race."

It had been over two decades since McDonnell had wondered if his team would ever win a national championship after several close calls. Schumacher found himself in a similar predicament.

"You want to get the monkey off your back," admitted Schumacher of the second-place finishes in 1999, 2002, 2003, and 2004. "From the public's perspective, they are looking at the second-places finishes and wondering, 'When are they going to win?' I didn't feel that way [since only the 2004 meet had been close], but you also don't want national titles to slip away because you never know what's going to happen."

After the heartbreak of previous season, Schumacher sensed something different before the race.

"It was a different feeling," said Schumacher. "You just knew something great was going to happen because you felt it from the team. There was no nervousness, just excitement to get to the line and show what we were capable of doing. If anybody was going to beat us, they were going to have to be really good."

The Badgers dominated from the gun. Though Boit and Kosgei both stuck with the leaders and competed well for Arkansas, by the time freshman Kenny Cormier crossed the finish line in twenty-second place, six Wisconsin runners already had done so, led by individual winner Simon Bairu of Canada and third-place finisher Chris Solinsky. Wisconsin ran away with the national title—beating Arkansas 37–105. Though "the future" had finally arrived, Schumacher still retained his reverence for McDonnell.

"You see him at meets and pick up these little nuggets from him," said Schumacher. "You sense this teacher and competitor all wrapped up into one. It just solidified the whole idea of coaching for me. If there was ever a complete coach, it was John McDonnell. He was it."

Over thirty-four years since he had begun coaching collegiately and twenty-eight since becoming head coach, McDonnell proved along with his assistant coaches—if it still needed to be proven—that they were still at the top of their game. For what would be the final time during his career in Fayetteville, the veteran coach pulled another rabbit out of his hat at the 2006 NCAA Indoor Championships.

Only weeks after losing to Richard Kiplagat of Iona at the Tyson Invitational despite running a personal best of 13:40.63 over 5,000 meter, Josphat Boit was at a loss as to what he could possibly do differently. McDonnell had promised him he would be an individual national champion if he came to Arkansas, but after losing to Kiplagat in cross country and lacking his natural speed, Boit was running out of opportunities.

"After Kiplagat outkicked me at Tyson, I went to Coach's office on Monday," said Boit. "He said, 'Okay kid, I know you are getting worried about Kiplagat.' He told me I did really well and showed me the mistake I made. He said, 'Kiplagat kicked ahead of you, and that's why he won.' He said he would have a plan for me at nationals and not to worry about it until then. So I said, 'Okay, Coach has a plan."

During the early afternoon of the national meet, McDonnell gave Boit his instructions.

"He said to sit on Kiplagat and wait and then make sure when they are ringing that bell [with one lap to go] that you are in front," said Boit. "He said when you make that last move, make it count."

After following his coach's instructions precisely, Boit electrified the crowd at the Tyson Center by unleashing a devastating kick past Kiplagat on the homestretch with just over one lap remaining. Though the Iona runner fought back valiantly, Boit crossed ahead of him to win his first national title.

"Josphat ran a brilliant tactical race," McDonnell told the media afterwards. "He moved at the right time. I've never seen anyone put ten or eleven yards on a guy, and then he just exploded. He had to do that with the caliber of runners he was dealing with. Josphat has good speed. He has never really used it, but he used it really well tonight."[23]

A few minutes later, Said Ahmed found redemption by anchoring Arkansas to victory in the distance medley relay. This time, Ahmed heeded McDonnell's advice to not be overly aggressive.

"All I could think about was last year," Ahmed said afterwards. "I thought about it every lap. Arkansas hadn't won a distance medley relay title since 1994. I was really surprised to hear that. I wanted to win one before I left. You have to give credit to all the legs. Brian Roe really opened it up for us. I have to thank them because this is how I wanted to take my jersey off at Arkansas."[24]

As Ahmed circled the track to delirious chants from the Fayetteville crowd, the demons of last season were finally exorcised.

"WOO! . . . PIG! . . . SOOIE!"

The win had been possible because of the selflessness of Adam Perkins, who ran the 1,200 meter just an hour after the mile, and Brian Roe, who agreed to forego the individual 800 meter for the good of the team.

The next day, Jaanus Uudmae overcame knee injuries and a lack of natural speed to capture his first national title in the triple jump—twenty-four hours after finishing a career-best sixth in the long jump.

"That was a big win for him because he had jumped great for not being a naturally gifted athlete," said McDonnell.

Arkansas won the national championship by a 53–45 margin over LSU. As they had many times before, the individual and team victories electrified the capacity Tyson Center throng, who could always be counted to launch into a rendition of "Calling the Hogs" after each victory. For the forty-second time in his career McDonnell accepted a national championship trophy with the same grace and humility as always, amid a home crowd that appreciated winning.

Yet if it appeared that winning was becoming a foregone conclusion, that was anything but the case. Every national championship was a challenge, and each year McDonnell was forced to battle the same demons of complacency that threatened to engulf any program defending a championship. That season had been no different and with the team not running up to the standard he set for them during the middle of the winter, McDonnell took the opportunity to set them straight when he handed out the previous year's rings.

"After the last ring was handed out he said, 'You better enjoy it because this could be your last one for a long time,'" remembered Summerside. "Everything got quiet. At the time we weren't training well or racing well, and he said, 'Have some g'damn pride.' It's not about you but the athletes that came before you and made Arkansas what it is today."

As gratifying as the season turned out to be for John, in the back of his mind he had already begun mulling over retirement, and it appeared he might have the opportunity to leave the sport on top. With Sean set to graduate from university that year with an engineering degree and Heather teaching in Austin, Texas, the thought of spending more time with Ellen and his children and at the ranch appealed to him after years of slogging it out at track meets or in the office. It would not be long before events would intercede that would put off those plans indefinitely.

John Tyson and John McDonnell in 2007. The Tyson family's generosity led to the indoor facility and the televised Tyson Invitational. *Photo courtesy of University of Arkansas Media Relations.*

John with the check for $3 million from Don Tyson that led to the construction of the Tyson Center in 2000. *Photo courtesy of University of Arkansas Media Relations.*

Tyson Gay *(top left)* and Wallace
Spearmon Jr. *(right)* added a new dimension to the Arkansas sprint program,
including an unprecedented national title
in the 4 x 100m relay *(top right)* in 2004.
*Photo courtesy of University of Arkansas
Athletics Media Relations.*

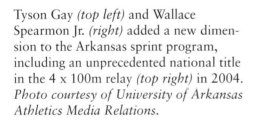

"Come on, kid!"

"Check your instruments . . ."

"You gotta get that sucker!"

"Faster . . . Faster!"

John exhorting his runners from his usual spot behind the first curve at the Tyson Center. *Photos courtesy of University of Arkansas Media Relations.*

Alistair Cragg's career was resurrected by John, and in turn, Cragg led the Arkansas program back to glory. *Photo courtesy of University of Arkansas Media Relations.*

Yep, he's still there: It took nearly a 4:00 last mile for Alistair Cragg *(left)* to beat future Olympic silver medalist Nick Willis of Michigan *(right)* in the 3000 meter at the 2004 NCAA Indoor Championships. *Photo courtesy of University of Arkansas Media Relations.*

Chris Mulvaney winning the 1500 meter national title outdoors in 2004. *Photo courtesy of University of Arkansas Media Relations.*

Woo! Pig! Sooie! John *(right)* waves to the hometown crowd after the 2005 NCAA Indoor Championship after Wallace Spearmon Jr. *(left)* lit up the Tyson Center. It was the most gratifying national title of his career. *Photo courtesy of University of Arkansas Media Relations.*

John and Dick Booth, assistant coach for field events, circa 2006. John and Dick worked together for twenty-six years. *Photo courtesy of John McDonnell.*

John inducted into the USATF Hall of Fame in 2005 with Wes Santee. *Photo courtesy of John McDonnell.*

Dr. Alan Sugg *(left)* joined John after the USATF Hall of Fame induction to celebrate the honor. *Photo courtesy of John McDonnell.*

McDonnell with his final staff in 2008: *(from left)* director of operations Danny Green, Dick Booth, John, and Kyle White. *Photo courtesy of University of Arkansas Athletics Media Relations.*

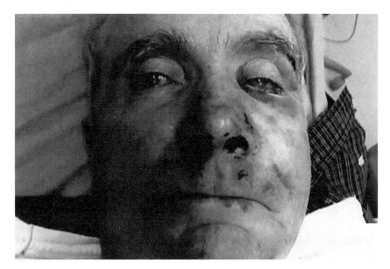

Despite a close encounter with a bull in 2007 *(top)*, John continued working at the ranch in Vinita in retirement with his favorite New Holland tractor *(bottom)*. *Photo courtesy of John McDonnell.*

2006 SEC Championships at John McDonnell Fiel[d]

From having no facility on campus in 1973, Arkansas boasted the finest indoor (*top*, Tyson Center) and outdoor (*bottom*, John McDonnell Field) facilities in the country before John retired in 2008. *Photo courtesy of University of Arkansas Athletics Media Relations.*

Fayetteville was a different place in 2001 than it was when John arrived in 1972—a fact attested to by the highway signs entering town. By 2008, Arkansas had won forty-two NCAA track and field championships. *Photo courtesy of John McDonnell.*

John speaks with new head coach Chris Bucknam *(left)* at the 2009 Chile Pepper Festival. *Photo courtesy of University of Arkansas Athletics Media Relations.*

John was honored along with his family at halftime of the football game against Alabama in September 2008 for his thirty-six years of service to the University of Arkansas and excellence in the sport. *Photo courtesy of John McDonnell.*

Retirement offered John the chance to spend more time with Sean, Heather, and Ellen.
Photo courtesy of John McDonnell.

John with Enda Kenny, prime minister
(Taoiseach) of Ireland, in July 2012.
Photo courtesy of John McDonnell.

16

The Final Years (2006–2008)

"The hatred for Arkansas is overshadowing one of track and field's better coaching jobs ever seen. McDonnell shifted kids here and there, the kids reacted with heart seldom seen in today's sporting events. The early burial of the Razorbacks was cast aside by runners who believe in their coach and his system. [This] may be one of McDonnell's finest titles."

—*Letsrun.com after the 2006 SEC Outdoor Championships*

The first hint of serious trouble at Barton County Community College started on a relatively small scale in 2003 as the NCAA began investigating allegations of falsified transcripts involving basketball players at the junior college in Great Bend, Kansas. When the school's own internal investigation subsequently uncovered widespread improprieties involving the misappropriation of federal work-study funds and Pell Grants involving payment of student athletes for jobs they did not perform, it wasn't long before other dominoes began to fall in other sports in the athletic department. A former basketball coach was indicted in United States District Court in February 2004 for his role in the scheme and the president of the college was eventually dismissed. Soon enough federal investigators began asking former Barton track-and-field coach and current Arkansas assistant Lance Brauman what he knew and when he knew it.

"Lance told them he didn't know anything about it because he just sent them to work study," said McDonnell.

It was not long before Brauman himself was indicted on three counts in December 2005 and on six additional counts in March 2006. As the latter charges involved possible NCAA violations, they spurred an investigation into the connection between Tyson Gay and possible violations at the University of Arkansas.[1]

"[The NCAA] were interested because of the fraud at the junior college and wondered if Tyson had anything to do with it," said McDonnell. "Our compliance people went up there with an attorney representing the university and interviewed Lance to see if anything happened. Lance asked me what he should tell them and I said, 'The truth.' I asked him, 'Did you do anything wrong?' He said, 'No.'"

After thirty-four seasons and forty-two national championships, neither McDonnell nor his program had been implicated in any major rules violation. While there had been accusations from certain opposing coaches over the years regarding alleged rules violations, McDonnell's program had a clean record, and he wanted to keep it that way.

Part of the standard procedure at the University of Arkansas when a new student athlete arrived on campus for the first time was that the incoming student be educated by the compliance office regarding NCAA regulations as they pertain to just about everything.

"Lance knew the rules that if we have a guy on campus that's ineligible he cannot get a ride. If he gets a tutor, it has to be on his dime. He cannot get anything for free," remembered McDonnell. "We were in the office on Monday morning having a meeting when Danny Green said, 'Coach, Tyson Gay arrived on campus.' So I lifted the phone and dialed the compliance guy [Derrick Gragg] and said, 'This is Coach Mac, Tyson arrived yesterday, and I wanted to let you know.' So he asked for his phone number, and I gave it to him, and he said he'd take care of meeting with Gay. It was his job to tell a guy you cannot stay with a former athlete and cannot do this and cannot do that."

It was not long after that during that summer of 2003 when Tyson Gay was in fact involved in a series of minor violations committed by Brauman in his capacity as assistant coach at Arkansas—among them were facilitating unpaid tutoring by Brauman's sister-in-law for a correspondence course, providing free transportation through his wife for the approximately four-hundred-mile drive to and from the junior college in Great Bend, Kansas, as well as arranging free lodging for two weeks through another athlete.[2] In later arriving at the conclusion Gay had received free lodging for two weeks, the NCAA ignored the fact that Gay and the athlete in question had arrived at a private agreement where Tyson would pay for the food of the apartment in lieu of rent for the short time he resided there.

Nonetheless, the total benefit Tyson Gay received was calculated to be $361.40. None of the violations were recruiting-related since they took place after Gay had already decided upon and arrived at Arkansas and the NCAA later admitted the violations were "not egregious" and of a "secondary"[3] nature that would not have prevented Gay's prompt reinstatement had they been reported upon before Gay ever competed for Arkansas.[4]

The major issue facing Arkansas was that with two previous major violations cases involving the basketball and football programs within the previous ten years, any additional charges threatened to put the university at risk of being a "repeat violator," which would cause it to incur additional NCAA sanctions. As the possibility of additional violations came to light as a result of the federal investigation of Lance Brauman at Barton County Community College, the university conducted its own internal investigation of the activities of the track program.

Upon discovering the violations involving Gay through its own internal investigation and interview with Brauman, the University of Arkansas reported them to the NCAA. The university subsequently imposed penalties on the track program involving the loss of three scholarships for three years as well as a prohibition on recruiting junior-college athletes during that same time period.[5] The penalties were significant because nineteen junior-college athletes had been signed over three decades, and it left the program with 9.6 scholarships instead of the maximum of 12.6.

"When [the university] suggested penalizing ourselves three scholarships I said, 'Are you kidding me?' It should have been a slap on the wrist and something where the compliance person was fired for not doing his job," said McDonnell. "As it turned out, it killed us because there were junior-college athletes we could have signed later that would have helped us win national championships."

While the penalties imposed by the university took effect immediately, which hampered the program's competitiveness for the next few years, the final decision of the NCAA Committee on Infractions would not be forthcoming for some time. With deep misgivings about the quality of defense the university was prepared to present at any hearing before the committee and the belief that he could not leave in the midst of the uncertainty, McDonnell put off his retirement plans indefinitely.

"I was ready to retire in 2006 before any of that happened," said McDonnell, "but I didn't want to leave in the middle of the investigation and with everything unsettled. I wasn't going to run away from something. Even though I had nothing to do with it, I was still the head coach."

Though McDonnell and his program had been a target for allegations of rules violations for years and various disqualifications at major meets, it was during the fallout from the Tyson Gay investigation that McDonnell learned a great deal about his friends and his enemies.

"It was what I always knew," said McDonnell. "It was just like all of the disqualifications over the years. When you are at the top, it's lonely because everyone is out to get you, and nobody can give you credit that you did it right. It's always the guys that play golf on Saturday afternoon and don't do their job that have a hard time realizing that, 'Maybe this guy is outcoaching me.' [The investigation] was a real sore point at the end of my career, especially after all of the times we got turned into the NCAA for nothing. If we turned left on a street, they would turn us in for not turning right."

That spring, McDonnell and his team competed for the first time in the newly renovated John McDonnell Field, which included a brand new Mondo track, elaborate press boxes, scoreboard, coaching offices, locker areas, and seating for up to ten thousand spectators. The total cost of the facility was $9 million, and while the original concept envisioned bowl seating, only the east and west grandstands were ultimately constructed due to time and budget constraints.

The team itself faced an array of health woes during the 2006 outdoor campaign. Freshman distance runners Chris Barnicle and Kenny Cormier were both felled by mononucleosis in the spring after their symptoms were initially overlooked.

"Chris was a great little athlete, but he got mono and was misdiagnosed," remembered McDonnell. "Three times he was tested while he ran cross country, indoors, outdoors and was misdiagnosed. That hurt his career because he had to drop out of races because he was so weak. The same thing happened to Kenny. It was just absolutely incompetent people in positions they shouldn't be in and was a shame. Chris and Kenny were great guys."

Only months earlier, McDonnell had welcomed another prodigious talent to campus from Dublin, Ireland—Colin Costello, the European Junior Champion over 1,500 meters, who had run 1:49 for 800 meters and held the Irish junior record for the mile in 4:01.35.

"A lot of people were after him, but Alistair [Cragg] was the key," said McDonnell. "He had talked to Alistair and said he wanted to come to Arkansas. I had some great talents come in here, and he was one of them. He was a nice individual, but my goodness he had no drive. I met his father and mother, and they were great people, but said he had never been away from home. Well, when he got to Arkansas he found out there were girls in this world and, my gosh, that was his downfall."

Though Costello scored at the conference meet in the 1,500 meter, he got off to a slow start that spring and never truly got on track at Arkansas.

The sprint events, already decimated by the graduation of Tyson Gay and Omar Brown as well as the loss of Wallace Spearmon Jr. to the professional ranks, were further weakened by Lance Brauman's preoccupation with his federal trial in Wichita, Kansas, as well as some of the aches and pains that slowed the junior national 100 meter champion, J-Mee Samuels, during his freshman campaign.

Even on their newly refurbished home track, Arkansas's chances against Tennessee at the 2006 SEC Outdoor Championships appeared bleak. Amid all of the adversity that seemed to have engulfed the program on and off the track, the premeet rankings indicated that it would be difficult for the Razorbacks to win. What the numbers and raw data were unable to quantify however was the savvy of a veteran coach who had demonstrated seventy-eight times previously that he knew how to physically, mentally, and emotionally prepare and motivate his athletes to win a conference title.

Thirty-two points in the 10,000 meter got the Razorbacks off to a better-than-expected start before Eric Brown, who was coached by Andrew McDonough, unleashed a throw over 251 feet to win the javelin. In the triple jump, freshman Nkosinza Balumbu—the Californian whose name literally meant "lion of the world"[6]—won with a personal best of 53 feet, 4 inches.

"[Balumbu] didn't have a lot of speed but was a really, really great kid," said McDonnell. "He looked like a Kenyan distance runner. He was a little toothpick. You thought he was going to break his leg."

Entering the 5,000 meter, the Razorbacks still found themselves trailing badly. Some of the Tennessee athletes even took the liberty of celebrating a championship that had not yet been won.

"A Tennessee athlete walked in front of Coach McDonnell and Coach Booth on the south end of the stadium and said, 'It looks like there is a crack in the foundation of the program. You just built this stadium and are going to lose your first SEC Championships here,'" recalled Summerside. "Well, we came back in that 5k and ended up winning the meet. Coach said beforehand that this is it, and we were geared up and knew what was at stake."

The Razorbacks answered the challenge. Josphat Boit courageously came back after winning the 10,000 meter to also capture the 5,000 meter and rallied four other teammates to score twenty-seven points in the event. It was a stunning performance attributable to Arkansas's superiority in the distance events. Once again the winning formula was evident for all to see: a head coach whose athletes were prepared and motivated to lay everything on the line for him.

In summarizing another epic conference-championship victory, this time by a 137–128 margin over Tennessee, the headline on LetsRun.com the following morning included the following observations:[7]

The hatred for Arkansas is overshadowing one of track and field's better coaching jobs ever seen. McDonnell shifted kids here and there, the kids reacted with heart seldom seen in today's sporting events. The early burial of the Razorbacks was cast aside by runners who believe in their coach and his system. The 2006 SEC outdoor title may be one of McDonnell's finest titles. That 5k was a jewel.

The enmity some of the programs in the SEC had for Arkansas only made the win sweeter.

"In most conferences the coaches were friendly with one another, but in the SEC there was some bad blood," recalled Kyle White. "[The other coaches] respected John but were jealous. It probably started in the 1990s when they realized he was going to win for a long time."

What McDonnell proved over and over again was that he was more adept than almost anyone at helping his own athletes find the finish line before everyone else. Josphat Boit followed up his conference triple by winning the 10,000-meter title at the 2006 NCAA Outdoor Championships, once again executing a strategy perfectly laid out for him by his coach.

"I was feeling really good, and he just told me to take it hard for the last two miles," said Boit. "So I made a move with two miles, and nobody responded, so I just kept going and it was a steady win for me."

Though others also captured All-American honors at the NCAA championship meet in Sacramento, ultimately Arkansas did not have the numbers to capture a national title won for the first time by Florida State.[8]

It was not long after the season ended when some unwelcome news arrived. It had been no secret to McDonnell that Brauman's federal trial had been going abysmally. On July 12, 2006, Lance Brauman was convicted by a federal jury on five counts of embezzlement, theft, and mail fraud during his coaching tenure at Barton County.[9]

"He was a young coach and went along with what all the coaches at Barton were doing," remembered McDonnell. "We had to dismiss him at Arkansas as soon as the verdict came down in Wichita. Coach Broyles called me and asked, 'Did you hear about Lance?' So I said, 'Yes, I already asked him to resign.'"

It was a stunning turn of events for Lance Brauman. Only a year after his unprecedented success coaching the sprinters at Arkansas had made him the most ballyhooed assistant coach in the country—with the gravitas, toughness, intelligence, and youth to potentially ascend to a head-coaching role at some point in time—Brauman was out, and McDonnell was now looking for a new sprint coach.

As he began that process, John was looking for many of the same things he had wanted back in 2002: a young, energetic coach who had experienced success at a smaller program. Kyle White fit both criteria. Not only had White had success coaching the sprinters at University of Texas-Arlington, but was an Arkansas graduate who had sprinted and jumped for the Razorbacks two decades earlier.

"John was looking for someone he could trust," said White. "He had gone through a lot of crap. He knew I could take care of business on the track, but more importantly he knew me."

White also owed a debt of gratitude to McDonnell for helping motivate him twenty years earlier when all could have been lost for him as an undergraduate student.

"I pretty much flunked out of school. I went to John about it, and he explained some life lessons and said that flunking out was the best thing that could happen to me because I would find out what life was really like," remembered White. "It was the best thing he could have told me because I ended up coming back. I was among the 1 percent of students who flunked out and returned. John wasn't just a coach who won championships. It was a passion, and he would do what was best for you."

After a few conversations, it took McDonnell only a few weeks to decide Kyle White was the man to lead the Razorback sprinters moving forward.

"Kyle had done a tremendous job at Texas-Arlington with the sprinters and the hurdlers, and that is an area we want to continue to strengthen," McDonnell told the media on July 28, 2006. "He is a former Razorback high jumper and hurdler and is from Texas originally. He is familiar with our system and will be a huge asset to our program."[10]

While Josphat Boit had graduated that same summer, he opted to continue training under McDonnell with Alistair Cragg.

"The NCAA didn't want to mix pro guys with college guys, so we had to run later or earlier than the college guys," said Boit. "That happened right when I got out of college, but Coach was still there. It seems like people that know nothing about running make the rules."

With the loss of scholarships from the Brauman violations, McDonnell was left with very little in the way of scholarship money to replace Boit on the cross-country roster. He thus made no major additions other than accepting the transfer of Mickey Cobrin, a 3:49 1,500-meter runner from UCLA.

"Mickey would rub some guys wrong on the team, but he was a good guy," said McDonnell. "He did great for me, ran a 3:58 mile right behind Alistair, and loved training with the top guys."

With Shawn Forrest recovering from illness, the Razorbacks were upset by UTEP on their home course but recovered in time to decimate Florida and Alabama at the 2006 SEC Cross Country Championships. By the time they travelled to Terre Haute, Indiana, in November, they once again had the look and expectations of a team prepared to win a national championship.[11] It was an aspiration shared by Colorado, Stanford, Iona, and the defending champions from Wisconsin, who had graduated individual winner Simon Bairu from the previous season's national-championship team and needed to fire on all cylinders to win what was expected to be a much closer meet.

"The previous year we had Josphat but also a lot of younger guys on the team," said Peter Kosgei. "In 2006, it was an open race, and you could not predict the winner. I think we should have won it."

As always, McDonnell gave his team a plan for victory.

"The thing with Coach Mac was if he tells you to run a specific race and strategy, and you lose he takes the blame," said Kosgei. "If he gives you instructions, and you do your own thing, you take the blame."

For most of the race, which was run in tremendously sloppy conditions, Kosgei keyed off Chris Solinsky of Wisconsin, who entered the race as one of the favorites to win the individual title.

"The day before, Solinsky said he was going to put the hammer down with 3,000 meters to go, and I knew he had the potential to do it," said Kosgei. "So I said as soon as he takes off, I'm going to go with him, and even if I don't beat him, I will have a good race. At the 6k mark I was sitting on Solinsky and let the other guys go but by the time we got to 8k I said, 'Man, this guy isn't moving.' He was crumbling, and by that time the lead group was ahead, so I was in no-man's land. I took off but the other group was already gone."

As Solinsky drifted back to seventy-third place, taking Wisconsin's national title hopes with him, Kosgei shot up to finish eighth but was unable to catch the leaders. Seth Summerside and Scott Macpherson each captured All-American certificates, but the rest of the team was unable to keep up. The Razorbacks finished tied for fifth place with resurgent Oregon at 196 points.

"We could have won it," said Kosgei. "We had a solid group but just didn't put it together. If we had one more guy in the 20s and another in the 50s we could have won. It was a wide open race."

Despite no finishers in the top ten and only two in the top twenty-five, Colorado executed its late-race strategy to perfection to win the 2006 NCAA Cross Country Championships. Sensing an opportunity had slipped away, McDonnell was hardest on himself.

"After the race he told us it was his fault we hadn't won," remembered Scott Macpherson. "We really felt like we had let him down."

Although Arkansas was able to capture the indoor conference meet a few months later, the scholarship limitations meant their margin of error for winning the 2007 NCAA Indoor Championships was slim. By the time Colin Costello was disqualified in the mile, it was none.

"Colin took the lead with a quarter to go from [Leonel] Manzano," remembered McDonnell. "Unintentionally Manzano clipped him with his knee and hit his trail leg coming up and [Colin] fell flat on the track. Manzano didn't do it on purpose, but Colin was put in the final [by the official]. Then Bubba [Thornton of Texas] protested that one. [The committee] ended up taking the kid who finished last in the race and wasn't even interfered with and put him in and Costello was thrown out. "

After the official on the track, who originally threw the yellow flag to indicate Costello had been interfered with, did not change his decision, the matter was referred to the NCAA Games Committee, which reviewed the film and decided that Costello would not advance since he had not been impeded.[12] The next morning, McDonnell sharply criticized the NCAA in the newspaper.

"[The NCAA] sent me a letter of reprimand, but it didn't make a difference to me," said McDonnell. "Oh, I blasted them and called ESPN and asked them to send a copy of the tape. It was as clear as day that [Manzano] tripped him. I sent [the tape] to [the NCAA Committee] and never heard a word back. They were the worst. It was a certain group that just hated me."

Amazingly enough, the man whose astonishing rise in the coaching world actually posed the greatest threat to Arkansas hegemony maintained a warm relationship with McDonnell. Now in his eighth season as the head cross-country coach at Wisconsin, Jerry Schumacher's teams had beaten Arkansas five years in a row during the fall—including the 2005 NCAA Cross Country Championships. The young coach had brought another cadre of distance runners to Fayetteville, along with head track coach

Ed Nuttycombe's sprint and multievent athletes, as Wisconsin sought its first indoor national title.

"Obviously it's hard to go into Arkansas and try to win anything," said Schumacher. "I studied the success that a lot of coaches had and a big person you have to study is John McDonnell with all of the titles he has won. He's super competitive, he's very sharp, and as an aspiring young coach, I had a look at what he was doing and how he was doing it and realized that he was winning these national titles with distance runners and sprinkling in other areas. Ed Nuttycombe saw that as well with distance running as the backbone of the program, and it was a similar model to what John did in his earlier years."

After scoring twenty-eight points in the distance events, eighteen from Chris Solinsky in the 3,000 meter and 5,000 meter, as well as eight more points from Demi Omole (60 meter), and four from Joe Detmer (heptathlon), Wisconsin captured its first NCAA indoor championship.

The Razorbacks eleventh-place NCAA finish indoors was their worst since 1981 but only emblematic of other problems. Colin Costello's fall in the preliminary round of the mile was hardly the only thing that had gone wrong since he arrived in Fayetteville.

"He was a nice guy, but academics were not very high on his agenda," said McDonnell. "He didn't go to class. I remember one time he left my office and was going to take a test. He had ten minutes to be there and instead he went back to bed. So it was just impossible. I asked him why he had done that, and he had some lame excuse."

Meeting after meeting, McDonnell was unable to get through to the young Irishman. Soon Costello became academically ineligible and never finished his degree at Arkansas.

Weighing heavily on McDonnell was the fact that the NCAA seemed to be in no hurry to arrive at a decision regarding the violations involving Tyson Gay, which remained a black cloud over the program.

"They kept postponing the hearing," remembered McDonnell. "One time a doctor couldn't be there, and then they scheduled another meeting on the day of the NCAA Outdoor Championships so that pushed it back another six months."

The latter was another example of the lack of communication between those hired by the University of Arkansas to defend its track program and those they were hired to defend—particularly when that defense team agreed to a hearing date without asking McDonnell whether or not it conflicted with a national championship in his sport.

As this was unfolding, it became increasingly apparent that athletic director Frank Broyles was on the verge of retirement. For fifty years, Broyles had set a standard of excellence as both a football coach and then athletic director. He had been well served in both roles by Wilson Matthews, Lon Farrell, Orville (Butch) Henry III, and Terry Don Phillips among others. At eighty-three years of age, time was inevitably going to catch up to the seemingly ageless Broyles. On February 18, 2007, Broyles formally announced to the board that he would retire at the conclusion of that year—his fiftieth at the University of Arkansas.

Broyles was eventually replaced by Jeff Long from the University of Pittsburgh. Although retiring along with Broyles did enter his mind, it was not an option McDonnell seriously contemplated with the neverending violation saga still unresolved and a program to steer through the turbulence.

At the SEC Outdoor Championships, Arkansas finished third with 100 points—a very respectable finish that nonetheless represented their worst performance since entering the conference. No longer was there a Randy Stephens, Frank O'Mara, Joe Falcon, Godfrey Siamusiye, or Alistair Cragg to put the team on his back and lead it to victory. The trend of complacency was hardly confined to one person or event group, and McDonnell continued to remind his athletes that no program was immune to it.

"Most teams self-destruct from the inside, so I always told them that they could not just put on the jersey and run out there and collect trophies," said McDonnell. "The last few years I'd point out one of the kids who hadn't won a team title and say we had to do this for him. When you put on the red and white, you are a target. The respect that we've earned we're not going to lose. So if we're going to get beat, we're going to get beat by a better team."

That summer, McDonnell agreed to appear before the Committee on Infractions on August 11, 2007, not to defend himself personally against any allegations (he was not named or cited by the NCAA at any point), but to fight for his program. Accompanied by an outside attorney hired by the university, McDonnell did not have a great deal of confidence that everyone was as committed to the defense as he was. Despite the fact the attorney had approximately two decades of experience with the NCAA, McDonnell remembers him being caught off-guard on several occasions throughout the proceedings.

"I knew it wasn't good when he got that big folder out and started flipping through pages and had nothing on the tip of his tongue," said McDonnell. "If he worked at the NCAA for twenty years, you would figure he knew them. He wasn't prepared at all. They even sent a memo of what they were going to discuss beforehand, and he still wasn't prepared."

It would be several months before the committee issued its final report. Despite the uncertainty surrounding the program and murmurings of McDonnell's possible retirement, there were still athletes drawn to the legendary coach. After winning a national championship at Colorado the previous fall before running 14:10 for 5,000 meters on the track, James Strang wrote to McDonnell seeking a transfer.

"If he had shown up here the year before we probably would have won NCAAs instead of Colorado," remembered McDonnell. "At Colorado, it was a personality thing, and he wanted more scholarship than he was getting. I didn't have a scholarship to give but he had two great years here."

The McClary twins, Alex and Andy, were in a similar predicament. Originally from Texarkana, they had moved to Washington and posted impressive prep credentials in the middle-distance events. After enrolling at the University of California, they had grown unhappy and showed up at McDonnell's office one day to announce they were transferring to Arkansas. McDonnell was unable to offer the transfers athletic aid and redshirted all of them throughout the cross-country season.

Out of high school came Lane Boyer of Kansas, a 9:03 3,200-meter runner and class valedictorian from Kansas, as well as Duncan Phillips, the Texas state cross-country champion, who had 1:50 800 meter speed.

"Lane was a tough little guy," remembered McDonnell. "Duncan was a rare talent."

Throughout his career McDonnell had rarely raced true freshmen during their first collegiate cross-country season, preferring to redshirt them as they got their academics sorted and adjusted to the elevated volume and intensity of the program. That Boyer and

Phillips would race immediately was a function of necessity more than anything else. With two of his All-Americans from the previous season (Kosgei and Summerside) having graduated and Colin Costello ineligible, McDonnell fielded a team during the fall of 2007 that was as undermanned as any he had coached in decades.

The fifth-ranked Razorbacks were beaten by ninth-ranked Oklahoma State and Division II champions Abilene Christian by four points at the Cowboy Jamboree at the end of September.

"It was alright, not a great race for us," McDonnell told the media afterwards. "We should have won. We were winning with a quarter of a mile left in the race. We usually hold on if we are winning that far into the race. We let a lot of guys pass us and that's inexcusable."[13]

Arkansas was better prepared for the competition at the 2007 SEC Cross Country Championships. On a cold and wet day in Lexington, Kentucky, the Razorbacks beat Florida and eventual number-six national finisher Alabama by nearly fifty points each to win their thirty-fourth consecutive conference cross-country championship and seventeenth straight in the SEC. Neither streak may ever be broken.

"It is one of my greatest achievements," McDonnell beamed afterwards. "I take great pride in it because so many things can happen, good and bad. It's unpredictable. To have enough depth is really the key. To win something like this for thirty-four years straight is pretty special."[14]

Yet the achievement was attained only two days after the NCAA Committee on Infractions finally released its long-awaited report in the Tyson Gay saga—ending an emotional roller coaster of a week.

"That was the worst moment of my career," McDonnell said ruefully of the decision. "I felt we had run a good, clean program, and I thought I knew everything that went on around my guys. Maybe I stayed too long. You trust people, and I had great people working for me, and for that to happen right at the end of my career hurt. I believe a lot of it had to do with a compliance officer who never bothered speaking with Tyson about what he could and couldn't do. He dropped the ball."

Contained within the report was a public reprimand, censure, and a three-year probationary period for the institution, in addition to show-cause hiring restrictions and other penalties levied against Lance Brauman personally. Interestingly, the report began by stating that the self-imposed reductions in scholarships for three years were not necessary and the scholarships could be restored immediately[15]—which would have been good news if two years had not already elapsed. The ruling validated McDonnell's contention that the university's penalties were unnecessary and ultimately unhelpful. It could be argued that the reduction in scholarships and inability to recruit junior-college athletes cost the Razorbacks one or more national championships after 2006. Still, it was on paragraph six of the penalties that the committee imposed its harshest penalty of all and took away two NCAA titles.

> The institution will vacate all NCAA, school and conference individual records as well as all individual meet results attained by the prospect (then a student-athlete) during the time he attended the institution and competed on the track team. Further, all team results from any competitions in which the aforementioned student-athlete participated during the same time frame, as well

as the record of the head coach, will be reconfigured to reflect the vacated records/results. This includes the 2004 and 2005 NCAA Division I Outdoor Track and Field Championships won by the institution.[16]

Thus, the NCAA arrived at a decision that deprived sixty-seven uninvolved student athletes of a national championship (in some cases two national championships) based on violations totaling $361.40, which it admitted were of a "secondary nature" and "not egregious." That it was able to make this decision in the same era when it selectively enforced far bigger alleged violations in the sport of football at other institutions[17] is a galling example of a rather twisted logic and double standard at play.

"It was just outrageous," said McDonnell. "The thing that bothered me was what did I have to do with [repeat violations by] basketball and football? We were the perfect sport to go after. We're visible, we had won several national championships, and there is not huge money [in track]."

McDonnell was also upset at the manner in which Tyson Gay's name was sullied.

"Tyson Gay was a class act," said McDonnell. "For his name to be dragged through mud was outrageous."

Though Gay expected a penalty, he did not feel the one handed down was proportionate.

"If you bend the rules, you have to deal with the consequences," said Gay, "but at the same time when you beat people on the track fair and square, it's kind of hard to take that away."

As one of the other sixty-seven uninvolved student-athletes whose two national championships were taken away, Adam Perkins remembers being very surprised at the extent of the punishment.

"Coach Mac didn't share it with us unless you asked, but I didn't think it was that big of a deal," said Perkins. "I didn't think we would have national championships taken away over a couple hundred dollars of gas. I may be kind of biased but it seemed ridiculous."

Additionally, since the individual points accrued by Tyson Gay alone at both the 2004 and 2005 NCAA Outdoor Championships were not greater than the margin of victory, Arkansas argued in its appeal that if the relay points were divided by four for the purpose of counting individual points (as is done for points calculation purposes at every college championship meet) that Tyson Gay's points contribution was not greater than the margin of victory. The appeals committee refused to consider that argument.[18]

"That by itself would have dismissed the whole thing," remembered McDonnell. "It was something they just didn't understand. They were professors and lawyers. They might have understood some things, but it sure wasn't track."

McDonnell had to regroup quickly. With the team heading to Terre Haute, Indiana, for the 2007 NCAA Cross Country Championships, the Razorbacks found themselves in the precarious position of running two true freshmen—Lane Boyer and Duncan Phillips—while relying on a front five lacking much national-championship experience. The margin for error was not great and neither were the results. Arkansas finished twenty-third overall with 470 points—its lowest finish since 1974.[19]

Less than two years after arriving in Eugene, Oregon, Vin Lananna had turned around his second Pac-10 cross-country program in a decade by leading Oregon to its first national championship in thirty years through the efforts of local wunderkind Galen Rupp. Just as he had done at Stanford, Lananna continued to attract and sign many of the best high-school athletes in the country.

That was proving to be increasingly difficult with McDonnell's hands tied by the scholarship limitations during his final few seasons. Three scholarships represented nearly a quarter of the team's entire scholarship budget, which could mean missing out on quite a few athletes based on McDonnell's practice of splitting the scholarships up.

As if enough things weren't already going wrong, McDonnell had a brush with death the next week at the stockyards in Joplin, Missouri.

"I was making dinner for Thanksgiving when I got this call," remembered Ellen McDonnell. "John was selling cattle at the stockyards in Missouri. When they were unloading the cattle at the stockyards, a worker left the gate open and a two-thousand pound bull came into the parking lot and charged John. Later we heard John had rode the bull's head for about twenty feet before the bull knocked him down and started at him with its head until a cowboy roped the bull and someone dragged John away."

McDonnell's sternum was broken in two places, and he was hospitalized in Joplin, Missouri, for eight days.

"It took me an hour to get to the hospital, and they wouldn't let me see him because they said he wasn't stable yet," said Ellen. "I was really worried when they finally let me in because I didn't recognize him. The doctors couldn't believe he didn't have concussions or a cracked head."

Just a few weeks later, the sixty-nine-year-old McDonnell was back at practice as fiery and energetic as ever and still physically setting the pace he expected of his athletes.

"We're like, 'Man, Coach just got hit by a bull, and he's training in front of us,'" said Scott MacPherson. "If a bull can't take him out, nothing is going to take him out."[20]

If McDonnell was able to escape the bull, he would not be able to outrun time. He was asked by nearly every incoming recruit about the possibility of him retiring, and opposing coaches had an advantage in recruiting because McDonnell's retirement was very likely just around the corner. Girma Mecheso, a Foot Locker finalist who had immigrated to Georgia from Ethiopia, signed with Arkansas but later requested a released when McDonnell made his retirement official.

With the prohibition on recruiting junior-college athletes still in effect, McDonnell also had to turn down two eventual All-American athletes that wanted to sign at Arkansas but ended up enrolling at and competing for SEC rivals in January 2008.

"To penalize ourselves like that didn't make any sense," said McDonnell.

While it is speculation as to whether either or both student athletes could have helped Arkansas win an indoor national championship the following March—adding two All-Americans certainly would not have hurt. Even without them, Arkansas won the SEC Indoor Championships and placed sixth at the 2008 NCAA Indoor Championships, but not before a stern tongue lashing from McDonnell after what he considered a lackluster performance at the Tyson Invitational in mid-February.

"We just don't have enough guys going out there laying it on the line. Nobody's doing anything exceptional," McDonnell told the media. "They're just status quo, just going out there and going through the motions. You can't win with mediocre performances."[21]

The team lacked a leader but typically it was not the final result that irked McDonnell, but the sense some were not fulfilling their potential. Still, with the investigation completed a few months earlier and the program's future cleared up, McDonnell sensed it was finally time to step away from the program.

A few weeks later, on April 22, 2008, he called a press conference to announce his retirement from collegiate coaching.

"I want to thank Frank Broyles, the man that hired me 36 years ago. He took a chance on a guy that never really proved himself but I guess he saw something in me that I didn't think I had in myself. It worked out really well," said McDonnell before a room of friends, family, coaches, athletes, administrators, and media. "I'd also like to thank the President of the University, Dr. Alan Sugg. He has been a great supporter of track and field and every one of our current track athletes knows who he is. The other people I want to thank that made this all possible are my assistant coaches. The first has been with me twenty-five years, Dick Booth. He is without a doubt the greatest field event coach, not in America, but in the world. He has had more high, long and triple jumpers ranked in the world than any other coach. Kyle White has been our sprint coach for the last two years. He was a high jumper here. He is now coaching the No. 3 sprinter in the world (J-Mee Samuels) under his wings here at the University of Arkansas. He also coaches and works with world champion Wallace Spearmon, Jr."[22]

"The faculty and staff at the university, for 36 years," continued McDonnell. I don't how you guys put up with me. They are absolutely super. They have never turned down any request I made. So many things go into success. It's not just the head coach. It's the whole administration. That's what I had behind me. When I asked for help, I got it. When I asked for assistants, I got them. The faculty and staff were absolutely superb. Track and field would not be where it is today without the Tyson Family. They gave us the money to build our indoor track which put track on the map for us, the country and the world."[23]

"It's just time," McDonnell later said at the same press conference. "My health is good but you don't know what's in store for you, so you want to spend time with your wife. Ellen has been a track widow for thirty-six years. She raised the kids and every time something happened, I was out of town. I wish I could have spent more time with the kids when they were growing up. There was always a meet. Heather, my daughter, played tennis and won two state championships and I never saw her do it. Sean my son, was racing motorcycles and doing well and I didn't see him doing it enough. Sean graduated with an undergraduate degree in mechanical engineering and Heather received her Masters in Education Administration and I never was able to attend their graduation ceremonies because we had the SEC Championships those weekends. I regret missing them but I don't know what I could have done differently. I haven't lost the fire to coach but it's time for me to get away from the pressure. It's the pressure I put on myself. It's been a terrific ride and I've been very fortunate."[24]

"I don't know how many years I've got left," continued McDonnell, "but I want to make the best of them. I want to spend some time with my family while they're still around and I'm still around."[25]

After operating at such a high intensity for so many years, McDonnell no longer wished to sustain the punishing pace he had set throughout his singularly successful career.

"My wife has sacrificed a lot for the sake of track and field," said McDonnell. "She's raised our kids and did a great job and now it's time for us to do some things together. I've flown over every state and been to a lot of them, but you just fly in, live in a hotel and don't see anything but where we are having the meet. I want to see the things I've been missing."[26]

Now the athletic director emeritus, Frank Broyles, was effusive in his praise of his longtime coach.

"I have been very proud of John and appreciative of everything that you have done," said Broyles. "I'm proud to have been your friend. I'm proud you were part of our program all these years. He has coached with dignity and integrity and he always kept his humility. That's exactly what you want in a coach, plus the fact that his students excel in the classroom. I've been so proud to see that our track team has led the nation in grades while winning national championships. Through John's leadership, we did that. John took a sport that most people thought was an individual sport and made it into a team sport which inspired the athletes. They weren't just running for themselves, they were running for the team. We saw this year after year and we continued to win. People always say the toughest thing in coaching is to repeat. Not for John McDonnell."[27]

Two of the men most responsible for setting the Arkansas dynasty in motion were Niall O'Shaughnessy and Mike Conley. As surprised as Mike was when the day finally arrived, Conley supported the decision.

"I never thought it would happen because John has been retiring for about ten years," said Conley. "I thought they'd have to come in with a tow truck and drag him out of the office. I think it's good for him. John always talked to us about life after track and now he'll get to enjoy other things in life."[28]

Others present in the room that day were equally surprised at the finality of the announcement.

"We heard word about it, and there were rumors going around that he was going to do it, but nobody actually believed it," said Wallace Spearmon Jr. "Even when I got a phone call saying come to the meeting room, I was like, 'Yeah, all right.' I still didn't believe it until it came out of his mouth."

Sean McDonnell had been urging his father for years to retire, and though Heather McDonnell was as tearful as anyone in the room during press conference, she was not caught off-guard by the news.

"He's a hard worker, but when I moved to Austin and Sean graduated, he learned how to relax," said Heather. "It was nothing to do with us, his runners, or his cattle; he just learned how to relax. He was always very chilled, but I think he internalized things. He said to me that when you start winning, you have to keep winning, and it gets kind of stressful. When he retired, he finally wanted to relax."

John McDonnell had finally escaped from the wind tunnel. Though he had originally planned to retire two years earlier—before the NCAA investigation—and strongly considered retirement when Frank Broyles announced his own during the spring of 2007, John had again considered stepping down in December 2007 after the report on the NCAA investigation was finally released.

"I almost stepped down right before Christmas," admitted McDonnell, "but I didn't think it would be fair to the athletes at that point."

Though many things had changed in the athletic department in a short period of time, what hadn't changed was that McDonnell continued to do everything he could to ensure that current Arkansas student athletes were focused on academics and athletics as he had done for years.

That spring, McDonnell brought his team to Auburn, Alabama, for the 2008 SEC Outdoor Championships, an event that would mark the final conference meet of his career. The Razorbacks chances of winning the meet did not appear very good against strongly favored LSU.

"Auburn and Alabama were really cutting into the distance points we used to mop up on," said Danny Green. "On paper, scoring it out, we didn't look like we had the points to win."

LSU scored heavily in the short sprints, while Arkansas countered with wins by Nkoszina Balumbu (triple jump) and Alain Bailey (long jump). With the meet deadlocked heading into the final day, McDonnell's decision to pull the redshirt off freshman javelin thrower Luke Laird proved fateful. The freshman, who was coached by Andrew McDonough, was not expected to contribute much.

"We thought [Laird] might get a point," admitted Danny Green.

Not only did Laird score a point—he won the event with a lifetime personal best toss of 228 feet—beating NCAA champion Chris Hill of Georgia, who had fouled out.

Then something even more unexpected happened. Only two days after finishing second and third in the 10,000 meter, Shawn Forrest and James Strang rallied with the meet on the line in the 5,000 meter.

"James and Shawn were just starting to come into their own," remembered Green, "but we didn't think they could beat Tyson David [of Alabama]. We figured twelve points at most."

Strang outkicked the favored David by a half-second to win the event and the Razorbacks scored seventeen points to put the meet away by a 131.5–122 margin.

"That was a heck of a performance," McDonnell remembered of the upset victory.

New athletic director Jeff Long was in attendance to witness what Frank Broyles had long grown accustomed to seeing—athletes mentally and physically prepared exactly when they needed to be. Amidst the euphoria of the conference championship, the Razorbacks gave the new athletic director his first Gatorade shower on the track. It was a moment that meant a lot to everyone.

Only a month earlier, at McDonnell's retirement press conference, Long had gushed about involving McDonnell in the hiring process for his successor.

"I would not be a very bright man if I didn't call upon the greatest there has ever been in NCAA track to advise me," Long told the media. "He will have an important role."[29]

When the time came to identify candidates throughout the spring, Long travelled to the SEC and NCAA Outdoor Championships to solicit opinions from certain coaches and observe others. He also relied upon associate athletic director and former women's track-and-field/cross-country coach Bev Lewis.

"I gave them names of people I recommended, and some of them were interviewed and some were not," said McDonnell. "They ended up getting a good man."

At the 2008 NCAA Outdoor Championships in Des Moines, Iowa, Arkansas placed seventeenth and was never in contention to win, as much as McDonnell's athletes would have loved to send him out with a national title.[30] After the meet was finally over, McDonnell spoke to the media calmly about his plans to spend more time at home with Ellen as well as visiting his children. He discussed his plans for the ranch and how he planned to remain in Fayetteville for the remainder of his life. Never a fan of flying, he then got into his SUV with Ellen and drove home to Arkansas.

17

Retirement

"He is a friend who became the most successful coach in the history of intercollegiate athletics. You don't have that kind of success that many times over that many years without caring for the well-being of your athletes."

—Former United States president Bill Clinton

Throughout his career, McDonnell had offered suggestions for the betterment of the sport on various committees and implemented some of those ideas at events such as the Tyson Invitational, which had been televised every February since 2000. He was approached about a coaching position for the 2000 Olympics in Sydney, Australia, but ultimately didn't consider it because the opportunity conflicted with the fall cross-country season. He was able to serve as a distance coach for the United States at the 2003 World Championships in Paris, which did not conflict since it was in the middle of the summer.

When the USATF honored McDonnell at the end of his career by naming him as the middle-distance coach for the United States Olympic team for the 2008 Olympic Games, he happily accepted the appointment.

"I knew I was retiring, so when I was asked to do it in 2008, I accepted," said McDonnell.

It was as much a well-deserved tribute to McDonnell's prolific career as it was an acknowledgement of his expertise in the event area.

Unfortunately, the head track coach for the U.S. Olympic team, Bubba Thornton of Texas, informed McDonnell there was a conflict since he coached individual athletes competing for other countries. Despite the fact that the rule had never been enforced and U.S. medal hopefuls Tyson Gay and Wallace Spearmon Jr. were both Razorback athletes who continued to train in Fayetteville, the conflict existed because McDonnell coached Alistair Cragg, who competed for Ireland. John resigned.

"[Bubba] said some of the other coaching staff members contacted him about it," remembered McDonnell. "I spoke to some of the others on the coaching staff, and they said they knew nothing about it."

Now a detective for the Bentonville Police Department, Joe Falcon observed how McDonnell publicly handled the situation with the same grace and humility he had long since come to admire.

"That is what he instilled in me," observed Falcon. "He always led by example in a humble way. John never tooted his own horn."

For his part, Thornton publicly expressed disappointment about the decision.[1] Heading into the 2008 Beijing Olympics, which were being held in China for the first time amid protests from humanitarian group, the Texas coach nonetheless appeared confident of the U.S. team's chances.

"This is the dream team," Thornton thundered to the *Sunday Times*. "I want people to hear our anthem so much that they're humming it when they come out of the stadium."[2]

After two dropped batons in the relays and a Jamaican sweep in the 100 meter and 200 meter, it turned out to be what many considered to be the worst American sprint performance in the history of the Olympics. In reality, nothing was going to stop Usain Bolt at an Olympiad where he broke the world record in the 100 meter (9.69) as well as the 200 meter (19.30)—into a slight headwind. Though Wallace Spearmon Jr. placed third in the 200 meter, he and former UTEP sprinter Charundy Martina (who finished second for Netherlands Antilles) were disqualified for stepping out of their lanes. Only a year after winning the World Championships, Tyson Gay did not make the final after sustaining a hamstring injury earlier in the season.

In the 5,000 meter, Alistair Cragg qualified for the final after running 13:38.57 in the prelims, but did not finish the race.

For a time, Cragg remained training under McDonnell along with Mark Fountain and Josphat Boit, but by 2008 he had become disenchanted with the resources available to him as a professional athlete in Fayetteville. Not long afterwards Cragg made the decision to move to California to train at altitude—although his training was still ostensibly directed by McDonnell for another year.

"It wasn't John, it was the atmosphere," said Cragg. "I didn't think the right people were coming to Fayetteville, and nobody was feeding off each other anymore. I think John knew he was retiring and didn't want to take anyone that he didn't want to disappoint. When he retired it also kind of took my structure away and [Josphat] Boit's structure away. The new people didn't know us, and there were these NCAA laws, and we couldn't use things at certain times, couldn't use the weight room, couldn't use the training center. As a track athlete in Fayetteville there was not a lot at your fingertips, and I'd get hurt. I knew leaving him that my track career was coming to an end, but I had to do it for my own mental state."

On the first few occasions Cragg did not finish races, he attributed it to a variety of minor injuries that had not been adequately addressed by the sports-medicine staff at his disposal in Fayetteville.

"He had problems with his lower back and aches and pains that caused him to drop out of races," remembered McDonnell. "He said, 'The doctors here are no good,' and asked if I minded if he went to California and continued sending him workouts. So he went out there and started off with a 3:37 [1,500 meter] and 13:17 [5,000 meter], and he looked great doing it right after some hard, grinding workouts. Then he went to Europe [in 2009], and I told him I would join him there but he dropped out of a few races. So I said, 'I'm not going over there if you are dropping out of races.'"

When Alistair returned to North America following his European tour, McDonnell discussed their relationship as coach and athlete.

"He was a super athlete and person, but it was time for me to get out of it if I wasn't helping him," said McDonnell. "We parted company, and he had tears in his eyes."

John simply felt that with Alistair in California, coaching him over long distance was not going to work, especially given the hands-on approach he felt was best. Though their professional relationship came to an end, the two remained good personal friends.

Simultaneously, Daniel Lincoln began having serious problems with his Achilles tendon. He had nursed the issue even during the 2006 season when he broke the American record in the 3,000 meter steeplechase, but the problem had degenerated by 2008. Against McDonnell's advice, Lincoln opted to surgically repair the tendon—a procedure which required three additional operations after the initial one did not go well. It derailed his 2008 Olympic aspirations and ended his career prematurely.

"Daniel told me that Nike wasn't going to pay his medical expenses unless he moved to Portland," said McDonnell.

So Lincoln moved up to Portland shortly afterwards to attempt to train with the Oregon Project under Jerry Schumacher, whom Nike had lured away from the University of Wisconsin in 2008 to coach one of their professional groups. While Schumacher's departure from Wisconsin left a void that needed to be filled at one of the elite distance programs in the country, there was no question that Arkansas was the elephant in the room among collegiate head-coaching positions during the summer of 2008.

After a lengthy process that reached its conclusion weeks after the NCAA Outdoor Championships, Jeff Long announced his decision regarding the next Arkansas head coach on June 27, 2008.

"Chris Bucknam is an outstanding coach and the right person to lead our men's cross country and track and field program," Long told the media. "He enjoyed remarkable success at Northern Iowa despite working with fewer available resources than other top-15 national programs."[3]

Bucknam's team at Northern Iowa finished eleventh at the 2008 NCAA Outdoor Championships and won thirty-five Missouri Valley Conference Championships during a twenty-five year span.

"Chris is an outstanding coach and real go-getter," McDonnell said to the media. "He has been very successful and his teams have captured numerous championships in cross country, indoor and outdoor track and field. He has achieved success at a national level without the benefit of the resources of other top national programs."[4]

Though some alumni of the program and members of the local media had publicly lobbied for Dick Booth to be hired as the head coach, others had difficulty accepting the fact that anyone other than John McDonnell would be coaching the Razorbacks. During their final semesters in Fayetteville, James Strang and Shawn Forrest both asked to have their training guided by McDonnell.

"I didn't want to be in that predicament to be honest with you, but I understood they didn't want to change coaches during their last semester," said McDonnell. "I told Chris [Bucknam], 'It's up to you.' He said it was okay."

At the 2009 NCAA Outdoor Championships, which were held at John McDonnell Field in Fayetteville for the first time, Forrest found himself the heavy underdog in a three-way battle late in the 10,000 meter race with NCAA champions Galen Rupp of Oregon and Samuel Chelanga of Liberty. As he had done countless times before, Forrest looked over into the corner at McDonnell for guidance.

"He was feeling good at the time, and with 800 meters left, I told him to go," said McDonnell, who came to watch the event. "He was such a good kid that he went too fast. I figured he might beat one if he split them and that would be a success."

Forrest caught the pair off-guard with a strong move in the last kilometer before Rupp ended up catching him and winning the event. A stunned Chelanga did not catch him. Even in retirement, McDonnell was as adept at finding different ways to beat people.

That one example notwithstanding, McDonnell has remained uninvolved in the coaching of the Arkansas athletes aside from listening and consulting when the new head coach needs a sounding board for whatever issues arise during a particular week.

"Chris likes to walk up in the trails, and it's kind of funny to hear him bitch and complain about things going on," said McDonnell. "I laugh because I'm glad it's not me anymore. Chris has a type A personality like me, and I have to say sometimes, 'Chris, it's only track.'"

Such perspective comes easier to McDonnell in retirement than it did throughout his career. Though he still cares deeply about the program and the university he put so much time and energy into throughout his life, McDonnell has tried to stay out of the new head coach's business.

"John comes by and talks but doesn't come to practice much," said Danny Green, who has remained as a director of operations with the program. "It would be hard for Chris to get much done with John around and that's not John's nature."

Upon Bucknam's hiring, Dick Booth was retained for the first season after McDonnell's retirement—a decision meant to provide stability during a season when the Razorbacks captured the indoor and outdoor SEC championships. On July 8, 2009, the long-time field-event coach was fired and replaced shortly thereafter by Travis Geopfert of Northern Iowa.

"I don't think there is anything wrong with Chris getting his own people," said McDonnell. "The kid they brought in is a good coach. The only thing I wish they would have done was tell Dick after the conference meet. By July 8 almost all of the jobs were gone."

Nearing retirement and initially fearful he might not be working at all during the 2009–10 season, Booth placed a call to long-time rival Mike Holloway of the University of Florida about their coaching vacancy that summer. Six days later Booth was on his way to Gainesville.

"He had a great head coach in John McDonnell," Holloway told the media. "When they were there, they were a great partnership. When we talked about him coming here, that was part of the talk. I wanted to have that kind of partnership with him also."[5]

As time would eventually bear out, the unique relationship Booth had with McDonnell would be difficult to replicate anywhere else. Never before had two coaches who were so singularly successful in their own respective event areas worked together under the same roof of one program for so long—another testament to their compatibility and the tremendous people-management skills of McDonnell.

Amid all of the transitions, McDonnell took a step back from the action. He was initially approached to coach the professional Oregon Project in Eugene, but desired to remain in Arkansas and spend his last few years with his family and at the ranch.

Though McDonnell was leaving behind the life of a coach, he had not lost his sense of humility. Whether you attribute it to the separation of John's ranching career from his coaching career or to his self-effacing nature, or both, it was not until a film crew came for a documentary at the ranch that John's ranch foreman, Steve Rhoades, even became aware of the extent of McDonnell's coaching accolades.

"John will hardly talk about it," said Rhoades. "I asked him once about a year ago to show me just one of those rings and he never has. I've heard they're like a big ol' rock. That's just like him though."[6]

"He said, 'Jesus, why didn't you tell me what you did?'" remembered McDonnell. "I didn't like to talk about it when I come over [to the ranch]. I like to talk to the guys about something else."

The ranch in Vinita has remained a going concern—keeping the rambunctious McDonnell occupied and relaxed. Now that he is taking a bigger role in the operations, it is also keeping him humble.

"I always had planned to have something to do and was a busybody who could not sit down," said McDonnell. "So I have taken a more active role in managing the ranch. It's like therapy. I'm glad I kept it. It's a lot better than your 401k. We sold out our cattle we had kept in the winter and will only have cattle from April to August from now on. We are keeping the ranch if Sean and Heather want it someday."

After switching from mama cows to stockers cattle, which are raised from March to August, the ranching operation slows down considerably throughout the winter, giving both John and Ellen McDonnell more time to spend with their grown children.

"It's been busy, and we can't seem to find time to do what we want to do, but we definitely see our son and daughter more now," said Ellen. "We keep saying we're going to do some more travelling but don't always have the time."

After not travelling to Ireland between 1986 and 2001, John and Ellen have returned to the isle on multiple occasions in the decade that followed and since his retirement. On more frequent occasions, they find themselves in Austin, Texas, visiting their daughter, Heather.

"Last Christmas I bought dad a Texas shirt that he actually wore," said Heather. "Mom reckoned he shouldn't wear it out because it might look bad."

From the hundreds of student athletes he coached over the years, whom he spent more time with than his own family, McDonnell still receives letters of thanks decades after he coached some of them.

"I love getting a call or card from the kids," admitted McDonnell. "Even the kids I really didn't think I did a lot for say, 'You have no idea what you meant to me and the hard work and ethic you instilled in me.' That makes me feel good because, let's face it, there is life after track, and you want the kids to walk away with something. You can win a gold medal but you cannot eat it."

The numbers objectively demonstrating McDonnell's unprecedented coaching success are certainly staggering enough—40 NCAA championships, 84 conference championships, 116 NCAA individual champions, 652 All-American certificates, 30 national coach of the year Awards, 23 Olympians (including gold, silver, and bronze medals), and inclusion in several halls of fame, including the National Track and Field Hall of Fame, the United States Track and Field and Cross Country Coaches Association Hall of Fame, the USATF Hall of Fame, the Arkansas Sports Hall of Fame, the University of Arkansas Hall of Honor, the University of Louisiana-Lafayette Sports Hall of Fame, the Penn Relays Wall of Fame, and the Mayo Sports Hall of Fame in Ireland, as well as specific honors such as the Outstanding Alumni Award from the University of Louisiana-Lafayette, Honorary Alumni as well Faculty Distinguished Alumni Achievement Award at the University of Arkansas, and the Wes Gordon Golden Deeds Award from the Fayetteville Chamber of Commerce, among several others. The list goes on but as one of the assistants who helped McDonnell achieve a significant portion of those accolades would attest, the journey was as much of a thrill as the destination.

"As I get older and more reflective, the championships mean less and less and the experience in total means more," said Dick Booth. "I just think how blessed I've been to think John McDonnell took a chance on a high-school coach who had never coached or recruited at the college level. It was fun and a blessing to both of us. I'm sure when we are a couple of old codgers sitting on the porch, we will ask how in the world did a couple of guys from a remote farm in Ireland and a tiny 1A town in eastern Kansas get together to do this. It's mind boggling and interesting at the same time."

For McDonnell, winning was an important and worthwhile goal. While some coaches are content to settle for mediocrity and convince themselves they are focused on giving their athletes a worthwhile experience, McDonnell believed the truly valuable experience came through seeking excellence and maximizing one's talents to the utmost both in the classroom and on the track. He never stopped emphasizing that an education came first, running came second, and an active social life was a distant third. It was never losing that disappointed him most but rather the failure of individual student athletes to reach their potential in the sport and in life. While there were some who did lose their way in spite of his best efforts to steer them on the straight road, those were far outnumbered by the others touched by the man who taught them the simplest and most important lessons in life.

Boys became men, mediocrities became champions, and walk-ons became Olympians. Fatherless athletes came to Fayetteville and soon saw John as their father. They in turn became the fathers for their own families. Seemingly uncoachable athletes learned from the most successful coach in American collegiate sports history, and some later became successful coaches themselves at the high-school or collegiate level. If Frank Broyles had a coaching tree that extended further than any other collegiate football coach, the same could be said of John McDonnell in track and field.

In northwest Arkansas, several of McDonnell's former athletes have successfully led high-school programs—starting with Carlton Efurd (Rogers), Mike Power (Bentonville), Seneca Lassiter (Springdale), and Godfrey Siamusiye (Shiloh Christian); while Randy Stephens (Mountain Brook High School in Alabama) and others continue to lead high-school programs throughout the country. At the college level, that tree extends even further: Edrick Floreal (Kentucky), Stanley Redwine (Kansas), Matt Kerr (Boston College), Jerome Romain (Tennessee), Kyle White (Stanford), Dave Barney (Paradise Valley Community College), Steve Baker (Oklahoma, Texas, McNeese State), and Tom Aspel

(Arkansas Tech) among others. Many continue to call McDonnell for his advice on any number of topics, which he would graciously provide based on his belief that "once a Razorback, always a Razorback."

Throughout the University of Arkansas community, there were several visible symbols of McDonnell's impact—the Wall of Honor in Bud Walton Arena, the beautiful John McDonnell Field, as well as the Randal Tyson Track Center and the forty national-championship banners hanging from its rafters.

Only a few decades after McDonnell first arrived at a sleepy town in the northwest corner of Arkansas, signs now adorn Highways 16 and 45 entering Fayetteville welcoming visitors to the "Track Capital of the World." Though he would sometimes lament the lack of coverage the sport received in the media, nowhere was that coverage more deserved than at the various national championships and international-level invitational meets that saw the world's best come to Fayetteville to compete. McDonnell raised the standard at Arkansas and around the country.

He prepared his athletes to face anything that was thrown at them on the track or in life. Only two years after the seemingly unbeatable Usain Bolt rewrote every world record at the Beijing Olympics, Tyson Gay returned to beat him at the 2010 World Championships. Though Lance Brauman continued to guide Gay's training, it was the exposure to such high-level competition during his collegiate career at Arkansas that originally prepared him for anything.

"Coach McDonnell matured us at a very early age by having the Tyson Invitational," said Gay. "When we were in college, we were racing against professional athletes. So we ran some of the faster times in the world and had to deal with media interviews and signing autographs. You could say we were superstars for the University of Arkansas. So I matured fast, but it also kept me hungry for more success."

When All-American distance runner Mark Anderson found himself struggling in medical school, his former teammate and fellow medical student Harold Smith had two words for him.

"Razorback Hill," remembered Anderson.

For those who had summoned the will to surmount the fifth uphill mile interval through a sea of sweat and lactic acid on a weekly basis, other challenges did not seem so great. They understood better than anyone what the human will could achieve after doing the very things they once thought to be impossible.

McDonnell had a certain cocksure humility that permeated his athletes and made them believe in him and themselves. Part of it was his grounded and decent nature that engendered his athletes respect and made them crave his respect. Yet there was also an aggressive conservatism to his style that gave his athletes a trust in whatever he planned and a willingness to make sacrifices for the program and themselves. That style also struck fear deep into the hearts of other teams. Just as other athletes knew the Razorbacks were likely not to slow down after whatever blistering pace they had set through the first mile of a cross-country race, other coaches also began to understand that there would be no easy or painless victories to be had in Fayettenam, a place where tradition never seemed to graduate.

As his remarkable career reached its zenith, McDonnell exuded an air of infallibility. He rarely seemed to go wrong and hardly ever seemed to lose. Whatever doubts he had about himself and his plan for any particular workout, race, or meet—and he did have those doubts as any human naturally would—he kept hidden from almost everyone, except his wife, Ellen.

"Never let them see you sweat," John would say with his subtle smile, which includes the unspoken rejoinder to never fail to learn from your mistakes.

His success and the success he helped hundreds of athletes achieve is remarkable not only for spectacular nature of those performances but also the consistency with which they were delivered. Month after month, year after year, national championship after national championship, McDonnell continued to give of himself, making the extraordinary seem ordinary. His ability to inspire greatness and guide others past the pitfalls of complacency was a challenge he managed to surmount with mind-numbing frequency for thirty-six years.

Though not all of his athletes arrived in Fayetteville with strong academic pedigrees, McDonnell insisted they meet certain academic standards—a fact borne out by the multiple occasions his teams posted the highest grade-point average in the country the same year they won the NCAA Championships. One particular athlete, Matt Gunn, an all-conference distance runner and national qualifier in cross country, won the prestigious Walter Byers Scholarship in 2005, which is the most prestigious postgraduate scholarship awarded based on academic excellence by a student athlete.

At a lavish gala held by the Arkansas athletics department in the Randal Tyson Center during the fall of 2008, hundreds of former athletes, family members, coaches, and luminaries were on hand to commemorate McDonnell's brilliant career. Former president Bill Clinton thought it worthwhile to offer his congratulations in a taped video address while SEC commissioner Mike Slive commented on John's successes in multiple areas of his life. Longtime Arkansas athletic director Frank Broyles also offered his thoughts on John's unique ability to lead young men to peak performances.

"How do you have a peak performance?" Broyles asked the crowd rhetorically. "You get [athletes] mentally and emotionally ready. Any coach can get them physically ready but the great coaches get them mentally and emotionally ready. John was better than anyone at doing just that."[7]

University of Arkansas president Dr. Alan Sugg, who was a regular observer of Razorback performances at the Penn Relays or NCAA Championships, recalled walking around with McDonnell after meets and the reaction of several people who stopped simply to shake his hand.

"It was really like walking around with God," said Sugg. "I can happily say John McDonnell is the most productive and successful leader I have ever known. I am so proud to be a friend of his."[8]

On a night when new athletic director Jeff Long announced the commissioning of a statue of John McDonnell to be erected at the outdoor track, Sam Seemes of the United States Track and Field and Cross Country Coaches Association announced the establishment of the John McDonnell Program of the Year Award to be awarded to the men's Division I program that demonstrates the most success among all three seasons—cross country, indoor track, and outdoor track.

"John McDonnell's program established a bar of success at the height of infinity in every sport he coached," said Seemes.[9] "Not only should the coaching legacy of John

McDonnell be honored on an annual basis but also the total program philosophy of John be honored as well."

Before the dinner was complete, McDonnell handed a baton off to his athletes, who handed it around the hall amid Irish music before the baton was placed into the hands of Chris Bucknam. He was inheriting a prodigious tradition along with the enormous burden of expectations that came with it.

Once everyone was seated, McDonnell thanked those who had contributed to his success.

"I would not be here tonight but for the athletes and great assistant coaches I had," said McDonnell. "If you surround yourself with great people you will be successful."[10]

At a dinner in his honor, McDonnell remained as self-effacing and humble as ever about the success he had inspired others to individually and collectively achieve.

"He was so dedicated and self-motivated and humble," remembered Ellen. "He always just wanted people to do well."

In a room filled with doctors, lawyers, engineers, executives, teachers, managers, coaches, and fathers, many of whom had come to Fayetteville with seemingly impossible hopes and dreams only to see those aspirations become reality, it was obvious that John McDonnell had helped many of them do just that.

Appendix I

John McDonnell's All-Time Head Coaching Record

Year	Conference Cross Country	NCAA Cross Country	Conference Indoors	NCAA Indoors	Conference Outdoors	NCAA Outdoors
1972–1973	4	26	—	—	—	—
1973–1974	2	—	—	—	—	—
1974–1975	1	27	—	—	—	—
1975–1976	1	13	—	—	—	—
1976–1977	1	10	—	—	—	—
1977–1978	1	21	3	17	7	—
1978–1979	1	10	1	31	6	—
1979–1980	1	10	2	37	4	50
1980–1981	1	2	1	11	2	22
1981–1982	1	3	1	2	1	24
1982–1983	1	3	1	3	1	7
1983–1984	1	5	1	1	1	3
1984–1985	**1**	**1**	**1**	**1**	**1**	**1**
1985–1986	1	2	1	1	2	4
1986–1987	1	1	1	1	2	4
1987–1988	1	1	1	1	1	3
1988–1989	1	10	1	1	1	9
1989–1990	1	5	1	1	1	2
1990–1991	1	1	1	1	1	7
MOVE FROM SOUTHWEST CONFERENCE TO SOUTHEASTERN CONFERENCE						
1991–1992	**1**	**1**	**1**	**1**	**1**	**1**
1992–1993	**1**	**1**	**1**	**1**	**1**	**1**
1993–1994	**1**	**1**	**1**	**1**	**1**	**1**
1994–1995	1	10	1	1	1	1
1995–1996	1	1	2	3	1	1
1996–1997	1	2	1	1	1	1
1997–1998	1	2	1	1	1	1
1998–1999	**1**	**1**	**1**	**1**	**1**	**1**
1999–2000	1	1	1	1	1	2
2000–2001	1	1	1	3	3	7
2001–2002	1	3	1	4	2	7
2002–2003	1	6	1	1	1	1
2003–2004	1	5	2	2	1	1 (**X**)
2004–2005	1	3	1	1	1	1 (**X**)
2005–2006	1	2	1	1	1	5
2006–2007	1	5	1	7	3	63
2007–2008	1	23	1	6	1	17

Bold finishes indicates **NCAA Triple Crown**

(**X**) indicates **vacated title**

Cross Country Conference and NCAA Championship Record

Year	Conference Champion (Points)	Conference Runner-up (Points)	Location (Distance) and Arkansas Finishers (Place, Time)	NCAA Team Champion (Points) and Individual Champion (Time)	NCAA Team Runner-up (Points)	Location (Team Points, Team Finish) and Arkansas Finishers (Place, Time)
1972	Texas (29)	Rice (72)	C. Station, TX (4 mile) S. Houk (12, 20:22) K. Wisner (17, 20:46) J. Smith (23, 21:07) L. Bauldree (26, 21:13) R. Hendee (27, 21:14) T. Smith (44, 22:23)	Tennessee (134) Neil Cusack, E. Tennessee (28:23)	E. Tennessee (143)	Houston, TX (640, 26) R. Hendee (114, 30:37) S. Houk (164, 30:57) K. Wisner (195, 33:25) L. Bauldree (216, 33:52) D. O'Connor (238, 34:21)
1973	Texas (40)	Arkansas (50)	Austin, TX (4 mile) S. Houk (2, 19:22) R. Melancon (9, 19:42) R. Hendee (11, 19:45) N. O'Shaughnessy (12, 19:46) S. Barr (16, 19:57) D. Reilly (17, 20:00) T. Aspel (22, 20:14)	Oregon (89) Steve Prefontaine, Oregon (28:14)	UTEP (157)	Spokane, WA None
1974	Arkansas (30)	Rice (61)	Houston, TX (4 mile) R. Nance (2, 19:26) R. Melancon (5, 19:29) N. O'Shaughnessy (6, 19:30) S. Baker (8, 19:36) T. Aspel (9, 19:37) D. Reilly (11, 19:45) S. Penn (12, 19:49)	Oregon (77) Nick Rose, W. Kentucky (29:22)	W. Kentucky (110)	Bloomington, IN (661, 27) S. Baker (66, 31:14) T. Aspel (191, 32:29) S. Penn (213, 32:57) R. Nance (220, 33:07) D. Reilly (235, 33:31) N. O'Shaughnessy (244, 33:53)
1975	Arkansas (36)	Texas (74)	Houston, TX (4 mile) R. Melancon (1, 18:50) N. O'Shaughnessy (3, 19.09) S. Baker (8, 19:28) D. Carroll (11, 19:36) S. Houk (13, 19:38) T. Aspel (15, 19:41) S. Penn (22, 19:56)	UTEP (88) Craig Virgin, Illinois (23:23)	Washington State (92)	State College, PA (350, 13) N. O'Shaughnessy (30, 29:30) S. Penn (96, 30:15) T. Aspel (99, 30:18) S. Baker (132, 30:35) S. Houk (147, 30:42) D. Carroll (189, 31:01) R. Melancon (266, 33:31)
1976	Arkansas (29)	Texas (71)	Lubbock, TX (5 mile) N. O'Shaughnessy (1, 24:44) S. Baker (5, 25:24) M. East (6, 25:26) S. Penn (7, 25:27) M. Clark (10, 25:42) T. Aspel (24, 26:33) L. Archer (31, 27:01)	UTEP (66) Henry Rono, Washington State (28:06)	Oregon (117)	Denton, TX (373, 10) N. O'Shaughnessy (7, 28:43) S. Penn (119, 30:11) S. Baker (127, 30:14) M. Clark (128, 30:15) T. Aspel (179, 30:49) R. Archer (203, 32:34)
1977	Arkansas (59)	Rice (63)	Waco, TX (6 mile) M. Clark (2, 30:13) S. Baker (5, 30:24) A. Conroy (13, 31:19) P. Vaughn (17, 31:54) T. Camien (22, 32:21) M. Lawther (24, 32:31) M. Anderson (30, 32:58)	Oregon (100) Henry Rono, Washington State (28:33)	UTEP (105)	Spokane, WA (482, 21) M. Anderson (80, 30:22) M. Clark (101, 30:46) S. Baker (112, 30:52) A. Conroy (181, 31:44) T. Camien (199, 31:53) P. Vaughn (202, 31:56) M. Lawther (250, 33:07)

Year	Conference Champion (Points)	Conference Runner-up (Points)	Location (Distance) and Arkansas Finishers (Place, Time)	NCAA Team Champion (Points) and Individual Champion (Time)	NCAA Team Runner-up (Points)	Location (Team Points, Team Finish) and Arkansas Finishers (Place, Time)
1978	Arkansas (29)	Rice (62)	**Fayetteville, AR (6 mile)** M. Anderson (1, 30:08) M. Muggleton (3, 30:27) A. Conroy (6, 30:44) P. Vaughn (7, 30:58) T. Camien (12, 31:20) D. Taylor (21, 32:06) F. O'Mara (32, 33:04)	UTEP (56) Alberto Salazar, Oregon (29:29)	Oregon (72)	**Madison, WI (301, 10)** **M. Muggleton (18, 30:02)** D. Taylor (62, 30:43) P. Vaughn (106, 31:03) A. Conroy (104, 31:06) M. Anderson (134, 31:29) T. Camien (156, 31:41) R. Stephens (166, 32:41)
1979	Arkansas (36)	Rice (66)	**Willis, TX (6 mile)** A. Conroy (4, 31:53) M. Muggleton (6, 32:07) D. Taylor (7, 32:12) P. Vaughn (8, 32:15) S. Delano (11, 32:25) F. O'Mara (14, 33:01) M. Anderson (21, 33:51)	UTEP (86) Henry Rono, Washington State (28:13)	Oregon (93)	**Bethlehem, PA (291, 10)** **D. Taylor (31, 29:56)** **A. Conroy (46, 30:15)** P. Vaughn (96, 30:56) M. Muggleton (99, 30:59) F. O'Mara (127, 31:19) S. Delano (169, 31:47) M. Anderson (229, 34:10)
1980	Arkansas (23)	Texas (71)	**Dallas, TX (6 mile)** M. Anderson (1, 30:28) D. Barney (4, 30:48) T. Conroy (5, 30:53) D. Taylor (6, 31:05) P. Vaughn (7, 31:10) F. O'Mara (12, 32:17) Ra. Reina (17, 32:40)	UTEP (58) Suleiman Nyambui, UTEP (29:10)	Arkansas (152)	**Wichita, KS (152, 2)** **M. Anderson (8, 29:27)** **D. Taylor (10, 29:32)** A. Conroy (43, 30:18) F. O'Mara (70, 30:39) Ra. Reina (84, 30:46) D. Barney (100, 30:53) P. Vaughn (145, 31:25)
1981	Arkansas (32)	Texas (67)	**C. Station, TX (6 mile)** D. Barney (1, 29:58) D. Taylor (3, 30:05) S. Jones (8, 30:54) T. Moloney (9, 31:10) R. Carroll (11, 31:26) F. O'Mara (12, 31:29) A. Leonard (20, 30:06)	UTEP (17) M. Motshwarateu, UTEP (28:45)	Providence (109)	**Wichita, KS (175, 3)** **D. Taylor (9, 29:35)** **F. O'Mara (29, 30:35)** **D. Barney (34, 30:09)** R. Carroll (79, 30:35) Ra. Reina (91, 30:58) T. Moloney (111, 31:15) A. Leonard (125, 31:28)
1982	Arkansas (21)	Texas (70)	**Georgetown, TX (6 mile)** T. Leonard (2, 30:15) Ro. Reina (3, 30:25) Ra. Reina (4, 30:37) P. Donovan (5, 30:41) D. Swain (7, 30:52) R. Carroll (12, 31:25) T. Moloney (20, 31:54)	Wisconsin (59) Mark Scrutton, Colorado (30:12)	Providence (138)	**Bloomington, IN (142, 3)** **P. Donovan (20, 30:54)** **R. Carroll (28, 30:56)** **A. Leonard (29, 30:57)** Ro. Reina (52, 31:28) Ra. Reina (66, 31:36) D. Swain (73, 31:52) T. Moloney (83, 31:56)
1983	Arkansas (29)	Texas (42)	**Houston, TX (5 mile)** T. Moloney (1, 24:36) P. Donovan (3, 24:55) D. Swain (5, 25:09) Ro. Reina (9, 25:21) I. Cherry (11, 25:30) G. Taylor (13, 25:35) H. Smith (14, 25:40)	UTEP (108) (X) Zakaria Barie, UTEP (29:22)	Wisconsin (164)	**Bethlehem, PA (206, 5)** **P. Donovan (10, 30:13)** **Ro. Reina (49, 31:00)** T. Moloney (63, 31:08) H. Smith (64, 31:09) D. Swain (73, 31:15) I. Cherry (76, 31:16) G. Taylor (140, 32:22)

Year	Conference Champion (Points)	Conference Runner-up (Points)	Location (Distance) and Arkansas Finishers (Place, Time)	NCAA Team Champion (Points) and Individual Champion (Time)	NCAA Team Runner-up (Points)	Location (Team Points, Team Finish) and Arkansas Finishers (Place, Time)
1984	Arkansas (35)	Texas (88)	**Lubbock, TX (5 mile)** D. Swain (1, 24:41) E. Borge (4, 25:18) J. Falcon (7, 25:35) G. Taylor (11, 25:44) Ro. Reina (12, 25:44) I. Cherry (16, 26:05) D. Consiglio (21, 26:23)	**Arkansas (101)** Ed Eyestone, Brigham Young (29:28)	Arizona (111)	**State College, PA (101, 1)** **D. Swain (14, 30:09)** **P. Donovan (23, 30:21)** **J. Falcon (24, 30:21)** E. Borge (37, 30:36) G. Taylor (56, 30:53) I. Cherry (128, 31:55) Ro. Reina (174, 33:35)
1985	Arkansas (26)	Texas (60)	**Georgetown, TX (5 mile)** J. Falcon (3, 24:22) I. Cherry (4, 24:22) C. Zinn (5, 24:26) E. Borge (6, 24:35) K. Iovine (8, 24:43) D. Consiglio (10, 24:59) M. Byrd (14, 25:15)	Wisconsin (67) Timothy Hacker, Wisconsin (29:17)	Arkansas (104)	**Milwaukee, WI (104, 2)** **J. Falcon (5, 30:01)** **C. Zinn (17, 30:18)** I. Cherry (42, 30:45) E. Borge (44, 30:47) R. Cooper (51, 30:56) K. Iovine (54, 31:02) D. Consiglio (78, 31:23)
1986	Arkansas (21)	Texas (47)	**Waco, TX (5 mile)** J. Falcon (1, 23:41) C. Zinn (3, 23:59) Ru. Reina (4, 23:59) R. Cooper (6, 24:27) I. Cherry (7, 24:27) G. Taylor (9, 24:42) D. Consiglio (32, 26:16)	**Arkansas (69)** Aaron Ramirez, Arizona (30:27)	Dartmouth (141)	**Tucson, AZ (69, 1)** **J. Falcon (2, 30:32)** **R. Cooper (18, 31:26)** **Ru. Reina (21, 31:28)** **I. Cherry (28, 31:35)** C. Zinn (37, 31:48) G. Taylor (38, 31:48) K. Iovine (143, 33:41)
1987	Arkansas (38)	Rice (67)	**Fayetteville, AR (5 mile)** Ru. Reina (3, 24:06) C. Zinn (7, 24:29) A. Hallock (8, 24:30) M. Taylor (9, 24:32) R. Cooper (11, 24:38) D. Consiglio (23, 25:24) J. Falcon (33, 26:01)	**Arkansas (87)** Joe Falcon, Arkansas (29:14)	Dartmouth (119)	**Charlottesville, VA (87, 1)** **J. Falcon (1, 29:14)** **C. Zinn (7, 29:28)** **Ru. Reina (18, 29:52)** A. Hallock (47, 30:17) D. Consiglio (52, 30:26) M. Taylor (100, 31:06) R. Cooper (105, 31:13)
1988	Arkansas (24)	Texas (48)	**Willis, TX (5 mile)** Ru. Reina (1, 24:14) C. Zinn (2, 24:14) J. Meyers (6, 24:59) R. Cooper (7, 25:10) E. Henry (8, 25:11) A. Hallock (14, 25:45) P. Thomas (18, 25:53)	Wisconsin (105) Bob Kennedy, Indiana (29:20)	N. Arizona (160)	**Madison, WI (265, 10)** **C. Zinn (5, 29:31)** J. Myers (54, 30:33) E. Henry (57, 30:34) R. Cooper (101, 31:14) A. Hallock (129, 31:36) Ru. Reina (143, 31:59) P. Thomas (152, 32:09)
1989	Arkansas (27)	Texas (53)	**Dallas, TX (5 mile)** E. Henry (2, 24:38) B. Baker (4, 24:41) A. Hallock (6, 24:56) Ru. Reina (7, 25:00) D. Welsh (8, 25:01) F. Hanley (18, 25:48) G. Contreras (22, 26:04)	Iowa State (54) John Nuttall, Iowa State (29:30)	Oregon (72)	**Annapolis, MD (235, 5)** **E. Henry (22, 30:27)** D. Welsh (66, 31:15) F. Hanley (75, 31:21) B. Baker (84, 31:29) A. Hallock (89, 31:31) Ru. Reina (102, 31:41) J. Boakes (109, 31:51)

Year	Conference Champion (Points)	Conference Runner-up (Points)	Location (Distance) and Arkansas Finishers (Place, Time)	NCAA Team Champion (Points) and Individual Champion (Time)	NCAA Team Runner-up (Points)	Location (Team Points, Team Finish) and Arkansas Finishers (Place, Time)
1990	Arkansas (15)*	Texas (51)	C. Station, TX (5 mile) B. Baker (1, 24:11) J. Boakes (2, 24:21) N. Bruton (3, 24:21) E. Henry (4, 24:21) F. Hanley (5, 24:21) G. Contreras (7, 24:43) D. Green (19, 25:30)	Arkansas (68) Jonah Koech, Iowa State (29:05)	Iowa State (96)	Knoxville, TN (68, 1) E. Henry (5, 29:31) J. Boakes (14, 29:49) B. Baker (21, 29:58) F. Hanley (27, 30:04) N. Bruton (44, 30:24) M. Skinner (108, 31:18) I. Alsen (124, 31:27)
			MOVE FROM SOUTHWEST CONFERENCE TO SOUTHEASTERN CONFERENCE			
1991	Arkansas (15)*	Tennessee (88)	Athens, GA (5 mile) B. Baker (1, 24:17) G. Hood (2, 24:36) N. Bruton (3, 24:36) E. Henry (4, 24:44) F. Hanley (5, 24:45) D. Welsh (6, 24:51) D. Miner (9, 25:10)	Arkansas (52) Sean Dollman, Western Kentucky (30:17)	Iowa State (114)	Tucson, AZ (52, 1) N. Bruton (2, 30:35) B. Baker (3, 30:36) G. Hood (7, 30:44) D. Welsh (16, 30:58) E. Henry (48, 31:49) F. Hanley (54, 31:56) G. Contreras (107, 32:40)
1992	Arkansas (23)	Tennessee (96)	Lexington, KY (5 mile)	Arkansas (46) Bob Kennedy, Indiana (30:15)	Wisconsin (87)	Bloomington, IN (46, 1) D. Welsh (5, 31:09) M. Morin (11, 31:18) F. Hanley (13, 31:21) J. Bunston (15, 31:27) N. Bruton (25, 31:40) J. Schiefer (56, 32:17) A. Dressel (94, 32:51)
1993	Arkansas (18)	Tennessee (75)	Baton Rouge, LA (5 mile) N. Bruton (2, 25:04) D. Welsh (3, 25:04) F. Hanley (5, 25:08) J. Bunston (6, 25:13) M. Morin (7, 25:20) A. Dressell (12, 25:50) D. Munz (13, 25:51)	Arkansas (31) Josephat Kapkory, Washington State (29:32)	Brigham Young (153)	Bethlehem, PA (31, 1) J. Bunston (2, 29:40) N. Bruton (3, 29:43) T. Mitchell (8, 29:51) B. Baker (16, 30:08) M. Morin (25, 30:28) D. Gurry (43, 30:45) J. Schiefer (166, 33:14)
1994	Arkansas (38)	Tennessee (42)	Prairie Grove, AR (5 mile) J. Bunston (1, 23:50) R. Wilson (4, 24:31) G. Hood (5, 24:39) C. Paradello (13, 25:11) G. Sidari (15, 25:15) P. Price (17, 25:18) M. Morin (18, 25:20) B. McGuire (28, 25:47)	Iowa State (65) Martin Keino, Arizona (30:08)	Colorado (88)	Prairie Grove, AR (266, 10) J. Bunston (10, 30:39) M. Morin (54, 31:41) R. Wilson (69, 31:58) G. Hood (89, 32:11) P. Price (118, 32:31) C. Paradello (130, 32:45)
1995	Arkansas (32)	Tennessee (58)	Starkville, MS (5 mile) G. Siamusiye (1, 23:47) R. Wilson (4, 24:04) S. Kaley (8, 24:36) P. Price (9, 24:43) A. Dailey (10, 24:45) M. Kerr (11, 24:53) C. Paradello (13, 24:58) S. Lassiter (16, 25:17)	Arkansas (100) Godfrey Siamusiye, Arkansas (30:09)	N. Arizona (142)	Ames, IA (100, 1) G. Siamusiye (1, 30:09) R. Wilson (5, 30:57) S. Kaley (38, 31:49) P. Price (43, 31:53) M. Kerr (50, 32:01) A. Dailey (65, 32:21) S. Lassiter (86, 32:39)

Year	Conference Champion (Points)	Conference Runner-up (Points)	Location (Distance) and Arkansas Finishers (Place, Time)	NCAA Team Champion (Points) and Individual Champion (Time)	NCAA Team Runner-up (Points)	Location (Team Points, Team Finish) and Arkansas Finishers (Place, Time)
1996	Arkansas (15)*	Alabama (64)	**Oxford, MS (5 mile)** G. Siamusiye (1, 23:39) R. Wilson (2, 24:01) S. Kaley (3, 24:12) M. Power (4, 24:16) M. Kerr (5, 24:23) S. Lassiter (8, 24:37) P. Price (11, 24:49) T. Tressler (12, 24:51)	Stanford (46) Godfrey Siamusiye, Arkansas (29:49)	Arkansas (74)	**Tucson, AZ (74, 2)** **G. Siamusiye (1, 29:49)** **S. Kaley (7, 30:47)** **R. Wilson (8, 30:47)** **S. Lassiter (28, 31:37)** P. Price (41, 31:52) M. Power (48, 32:01) M. Kerr (112, 33:13)
1997	Arkansas (19)	Alabama (66)	**Columbia, SC (5 mile)** R. Wilson (1, 23:46) M. Power (3, 24:08) P. Price (4, 24:17) S. Lassiter (5, 24:26) S. Kaley (6, 24:27) A. Dailey (7, 24:32) M. Link (8, 24:47) A. Dunleavy (13, 25:09)	Stanford (53) Meb Keflezighi, UCLA (28:54)	Arkansas (56)	**Furman, SC (56, 2)** **R. Wilson (5, 29:13)** **S. Kaley (9, 29:39)** **M. Power (12, 29:45)** **P. Price (15, 29:57)** M. Link (37, 30:21) A. Dailey (50, 30:38) S. Lassiter (78, 31:06)
1998	Arkansas (19)	Tennessee (63)	**Knoxville, TN (5 mile)** M. Power (1, 23:55) S. Kaley (3, 24:17) M. Kerr (4, 24:24) S. Lassiter (5, 24:32) A. Begley (6, 24:46) A. Dailey (7, 25:00) M. Link (13, 25:36)	**Arkansas (97)** Adam Goucher, Colorado (29:26)	Stanford (114)	**Lawrence, KS (97, 1)** **S. Kaley (5, 30:12)** **A. Begley (16, 30:46)** **M. Kerr (19, 30:54)** **S. Lassiter (28, 31:01)** A. Dailey (49, 31:24) E. Zack (131, 32:29)
1999	Arkansas (17)	Tennessee (59)	**Nashville, TN (5 mile)** M. Power (1, 24:10) A. Begley (2, 24:25) J. Karanu (3, 24:28) M. Kerr (5, 24:45) M. Link (6, 24:48) S. Karie (9, 25:16) A. Dailey (13, 25:31)	**Arkansas (58)** D. Kimani, South Alabama (30:09)	Wisconsin (185)	**Bloomington, IN (58, 1)** **M. Power (2, 30:09)** **A. Begley (7, 30:40)** **J. Karanu (10, 30:44)** **M. Link (22, 31:03)** **M. Kerr (24, 31:04)** A. Dailey (39, 31:18) S. Karie (73, 31:49)
2000	Arkansas (27)	Alabama (43)	**Tuscaloosa, AL (5 mile)** J. Karanu (2, 24:23) M. Link (3, 24:30) D. Lincoln (4, 24:35) M. Thompson (8, 25:18) F. Schimper (10, 25:29) R. Travis (11, 25:34) S. Karie (13, 25:41) C. Mulvaney (14, 25:51)	**Arkansas (83)** Keith Kelly, Providence (30:14)	Colorado (94)	**Ames, IA (83, 1)** **J. Karanu (11, 30:42)** **S. Karie (13, 30:45)** **M. Link (16, 30:47)** **D. Lincoln (24, 30:56)** **R. Travis (34, 31:02)** M. Thompson (110, 31:49) Fras Schimper (172, 32:20
2001	Arkansas (24)	Alabama (85)	**Auburn, AL (5 mile)** A. Cragg (2, 23:48) D. Lincoln (3, 24:07) S. Kimeli (4, 24:18) D. Heinze (8, 24:41) F. Cabada (11, 24:47) W. Alkin (20, 25:19) C. Mulvaney (38, 25:53)	Colorado (90) Boaz Cheboiywo, Eastern Michigan (28:47)	Stanford (91)	**Furman, SC (118, 3)** **A. Cragg (3, 29:10)** **S. Kimeli (13, 29:40)** **D. Lincoln (19, 29:51)** **J. Sandfort (32, 30:04)** F. Cabada (70, 30:37) C. Mulvaney (157, 31:33)

Year	Conference Champion (Points)	Conference Runner-up (Points)	Location (Distance) and Arkansas Finishers (Place, Time)	NCAA Team Champion (Points) and Individual Champion (Time)	NCAA Team Runner-up (Points)	Location (Team Points, Team Finish) and Arkansas Finishers (Place, Time)
2002	Arkansas (31)	Alabama (52)	**Gainesville, FL (5 mile)** A. Cragg (2, 24:20) D. Lincoln (3, 24:30) S. Kimeli (5, 25:03) J. Sandfort (6, 25:12) L. Bordes (15, 25:44) W. Alkin (24, 26:15) S. Ahmed (60, 28:46)	Stanford (47) Jorge Torres, Colorado (29:04)	Wisconsin (107)	**Terre Haute, IN (214, 6)** **A. Cragg (2, 29:06)** **D. Lincoln (14, 29:59)** **J. Sandfort (31, 30:29)** S. Kimeli (78, 30:57) C. Mulvaney (143, 31:32) W. Alkin (202, 32:17) L. Bordes (235, 33:11)
2003	Arkansas (33)	Georgia (58)	**Athens, GA (5 mile)** A. Cragg (3, 25:08) J. Sandfort (4, 25:09) M. Poe (7, 25:31) C. Mulvaney (9, 25:35) J. Harper (10, 25:35) M. Gunn (11, 25:35) S. Vazquez (15, 25:50)	Stanford (24) D. Ritzenhein, Colorado (29:14)	Wisconsin (174)	**Waterloo, IA (215, 5)** **A. Cragg (8, 29:33)** **J. Sandfort (24, 30:06)** C. Mulvaney (63, 30:33) M. Poe (80, 30:43) M. Gunn (95, 30:50) J. Harper (116, 31:00) S. Vazquez (167, 31:26)
2004	Arkansas (23)	Florida (72)	**Fayetteville, AR (5 mile)** J. Boit (1, 23:09) S. Forrest (2, 23:20) M. Rodrigues (23:33) J. Sandfort (7, 23:44) M. Gunn (9, 23:57) S. Ahmed (12, 24:04) L. Bordes (14, 24:08)	Colorado (90) Simon Bairu, Wisconsin (30:37)	Wisconsin (94)	**Terre Haute, IN (202, 3)** **J. Boit (3, 30:41)** **J. Sandfort (20, 31:26)** **M. Rodrigues (25, 31:33)** S. Forrest (92, 32:29) M. Gunn (136, 32:58) A. Perkins (187, 33:28)
2005	Arkansas (23)	Alabama (73)	**Columbia, SC (4.95 mile)** J. Boit (1, 22:59) S. Forrest (3, 23:03) K. Cormier (4, 23:11) M. Rodrigues (7, 23:27) P. Kosgei (8, 23:31) A. Perkins (13, 23:46) S. Summerside (15, 23:51)	Wisconsin (37) Simon Bairu, Wisconsin (29:15)	Arkansas (105)	**Terre Haute, IN (105, 2)** **J. Boit (7, 29:49)** **P. Kosgei (12, 29:53)** **K. Cormier (28, 30:10)** M. Rodrigues (40, 30:21) S. Forrest (51, 30:30) S. Summerside (137, 31:20) A. Perkins (144, 31:23)
2006	Arkansas (21)	Florida (73)	**Baton Rouge, LA (5 mile)** S. Summerside (2, 23:56) P. Kosgei (3, 23:57) S. Forrest (4, 23:58) S. Macpherson (5, 24:06) K. Cormier (7, 24:16) A. Perkins (19, 24:56) J. Norris (21, 25:00) C. Costello (26, 25:15)	Colorado (94) Josh Rohatinsky, Brigham Young (30:44)	Wisconsin (142)	**Terre Haute, IN (196, 5)** **P. Kosgei (8, 31:04)** **S. Summerside (44, 31:48)** **S. Macpherson (48, 31:56)** K. Cormier (74, 32:15) S. Forrest (117, 32:44) A. Perkins (192, 33:39) T. Hill (226, 34:15)
2007	Arkansas (36)	Florida (74)	**Lexington, KY (5 mile)** S. Forrest (3, 23:57) T. Hill (5, 24:10) C. Barnicle (8, 24:19) S. Macpherson (9, 24:22) M. Munoz (11, 24:32) L. Boyer (25, 25:07) D. Phillips (26, 25:10)	Oregon (85) Josh McDougal, Liberty (29:22)	Iona (113)	**Terre Haute, IN (470, 23)** S. Forrest (52, 30:42) M. Munoz (64, 30:49) C. Barnicle (108, 31:10) T. Hill (174, 31:42) S. Macpherson (183, 31:48) L. Boyer (215, 32:27) D. Phillips (248, 34:35)

* indicates perfect score
(X) indicates vacated championships (ie. UTEP, 1983)

Arkansas National Championships and **All-American** performances in **Bold**

Indoor Conference and NCAA Championship Record

Year	Conference Champion (Points)	Conference Runner-up (Points)	Location and Individual Champions (Event, Performance)	NCAA Champion (Points)	NCAA Runner-Up (Points)	Location and All-Americans (Event, Place, Performance)
1973			Fort Worth, TX None			Detroit, MI None
1974			Fort Worth, TX N. O'Shaughnessy (880y, 1:56.8)			Detroit, MI N. O'Shaughnessy (880y, 6)
1975			Fort Worth, TX L. Adams (660y, 1:12.8) N. O'Shaughnessy (880y, 1:51.7) R. Melancon (2-Mile, 8:58.9) R. Melancon (DMR, 10:05.2) D. Reilly (DMR, 10:052) M. Stephens (DMR, 10:05.2) S. Baker (DMR, 10:05.2)			Detroit, MI N. O'Shaughnessy (1000y, 5, 2:12.3)
1976			Fort Worth, TX R. Melancon (2-Mile, 8:56.75)			Detroit, MI None
1977			Fort Worth, TX N. O'Shaughnessy (1000y, 2:06.75) S. Baker (2-Mile, 9:04.61)			Detroit, MI N. O'Shaughnessy (Mile, 2nd, 4:01.1)
1978	Houston (93)	Baylor (87)	Fort Worth, TX (3) T. Camien (4x800m, 7:42.20) T. Camien (DMR, 10:07.2) M. Clark (Mile, 4:05.91) M. Clark (DMR, 10:07.2) R. Gaynor (4x800m, 7:42.20) D. Long (4x800m, 7:42.20) P. Mitchell (440y, 49.24) P. Mitchell (DMR, 10:07.2) N. O'Shaughnessy (1000y, 2:08.69) N. O'Shaughnessy (DMR, 10:07.2)	UTEP (44)	Auburn (38)	Detroit, MI (17) M. Anderson (DMR, 4, 9:53.74) T. Camien (DMR, 4, 9:53.74) M. Clark (DMR, 4, 9:53.74) P. Mitchell (DMR, 4, 9:53.74) N. O'Shaughnessy (Mile, 2, 4:06.99)
1979	Arkansas (92)	Houston (71)	Fort Worth, TX (1) M. Anderson (DMR, 9:59.77) T. Camien (4x800m, 7:39.6) M. Clark (Mile, 4:08.25) M. Clark (4x800m, 7:39.6) M. Clark (DMR, 9:59.77) R. Gaynor (4x800m, 7:39.6) T. Kastl (H. Jump, 7'2) P. Mitchell (440y, 49.24) M. Muggleton (3-Mile, 13:45.34) M. Muggleton (DMR, 9:59.77) F. O'Mara (4x800m, 7:39.60) K. Perron (DMR, 9:59.77) R. Stephens (880y, 1:52.69)	Villanova (52)	UTEP (51)	Detroit, MI (31) M. Muggleton (2-Mile, 3, 8:41.3)
1980	Texas A&M (103)	Arkansas (95)	Fort Worth, TX (2) M. Muggleton (3-Mile, 13:32.8) S. Redwine (600y, 1:10.52) R. Stephens (880y, 1:51.51)	UTEP (76)	Villanova (42)	Detroit, MI (37) P. Mitchell (DMR, 4, 9:47.6) F. O'Mara (DMR, 4, 9:47.6) R. Stephens (DMR, 4, 9:47.6) D. Taylor (DMR, 4, 9:47.6)

Year	Conference Champion (Points)	Conference Runner-up (Points)	Location and Individual Champions (Event, Performance)	NCAA Champion (Points)	NCAA Runner-Up (Points)	Location and All-Americans (Event, Place, Performance)
1981	Arkansas (96)	Houston (81)	**Fort Worth, TX (1)** S. Redwine (600y, 1:09.97) P. Vaughn, (3-Mile, 13:47.14)	UTEP (76)	SMU (51)	**Detroit, MI (11)** P. Mitchell (DMR, 5, 9:50) T. Moloney (DMR, 5, 9:50) F. O'Mara (DMR, 5, 9:50) R. Stephens (DMR, 5, 9:50) S. Redwine (600y, 2, 1:10.5) P. Vaughn (3-Mile, 6, 13:38.7)
1982	Arkansas (129)	Texas (87)	**Fort Worth, TX (1)** R. Carroll (DMR, 9:59.85) M. Conley (L. Jump, 25'1.5) B. DuPont (DMR, 9:59.85) J. Parrietti (DMR, 9:59.85) R. Stephens (1000y, 2:07.25) R. Stephens (DMR, 9:59.85) D. Taylor (Mile, 4:06.88) P. Vaughn (3-Mile, 13:33.40)	UTEP (67)	Arkansas (30)	**Detroit, MI (2)** M. Conley (T. Jump, 4, 53'8.5) P. Donovan (DMR, 4, 9:53.6) P. Jones (DMR, 4, 9:53.6) T. Moloney (DMR, 4, 9:53.6) E. Williams (DMR, 4, 9:53.6) S. Redwine (600y, 4, 2:07.37) **R. Stephens (1000y, 1, 2:07.37)** D. Taylor (2-Mile, 8:47.3) P. Vaughn (3-Mile, 13:10.9)
1983	Arkansas (147)	Houston (63)	**Fort Worth, TX (1)** R. Carroll (3-Mile, 13:57.41) F. Cleary (Mile Relay, 3:14.69) M. Conley (L. Jump, 25'9.75) P. Donovan (DMR, 9:51.53) S. Lofquist (Shot, 66'6.5) F. O'Mara (Mile, 4:08.88) F. O'Mara (DMR, 9:51.53) J. Pyle (DMR, 9:51.53) S. Redwine (880y, 1:50.96) S. Redwine (Mile Relay, 3:14.69) P. Robinson (Mile Relay, 3:14.69) P. Robinson (DMR, 9:51.53) E. Williams (Mile Relay, 3:14.69)	SMU (43)	Villanova (32)	**Detroit, MI (3)** M. Conley (L. Jump, 6, 24'6.75) **M. Conley (T. Jump, 1, 56'6.25)** P. Donovan (4x800m, 4, 7:26.4) T. Moloney (4x800m, 4, 7:26.4) D. Swain (4x800m, 4, 7:26.4) E. Williams (4x800m, 4, 7:26.4) S. Lofquist (Shot, 3, 65'9) S. Redwine (880y, 2, 1:51.3)
1984	Arkansas (118)	Baylor (82)	**Fort Worth, TX (1)** Ma. Conley (DMR, 10:05.33) M. Conley (L. Jump, 25'8) M. Conley (T. Jump, 54'5.5) K. Iovine (DMR, 10:05.33) B. Jasinski (H. Jump, 7'4.25) Ro. Reina (2-Mile, 8:58.70) G. Taylor (DMR, 10:05.33) D. Wehmeyer (DMR, 100:05.33)	**Arkansas (38)**	Iowa State (36)	**Syracuse, NY (1)** **M. Conley (L. Jump, 1, 25'8)** **M. Conley (T. Jump, 1, 55'8)** B. Dupont (DMR, 3, 9:41.13) L. Looney (DMR, 3, 9:41.13) D. Swain (DMR, 3, 9:41.13) G. Taylor (DMR, 3, 9:41.13) M. Kobza (Shot, 4, 63'6) T. Moloney (1500m, 2, 3:52.99)
1985	Arkansas (156)	Baylor (60)	**Fort Worth, TX (1)** E. Borge (DMR, 10:03.39) M. Conley (DMR, 10:03.39) M. Conley (L. Jump, 26'1.75) M. Conley (T. Jump, 54'1) D. Consiglio (1000y, 2:10.35) P. Donovan (Mile, 4:02.23) P. Donovan (2-Mile, 8:43.75) R. Haley (440y, 47.38) B. Jasinski (H. Jump, 7'5.25) W. Spearmon (DMR, 10:03.39) M. Taylor (DMR, 10:03.39)	**Arkansas (70)**	Tennessee (29)	**Syracuse, NY (1)** E. Borge (DMR, 2, 9:39.7) F. Cleary (4x400m, 2, 3:08.7) **M. Conley (L. Jump, 1, 25'10.25)** **M. Conley (T. Jump, 1, 55'11.75)** D. Consiglio (DMR, 2, 9:39.7) **P. Donovan (1500m, 1st, 3:43.48)** B. DuPont (4x400m, 2, 3:08.7) R. Haley (4x400m, 2, 3:08.7) B. Jasinski (H. Jump, 2, 7'4) M. Kobza (Shot, 4, 64'9) L. Looney (DMR, 2, 9:39.7) C. Moss (4x400m, 2, 3:08.7) W. Spearmon (DMR, 2, 9:39.7) D. Swain (3000m, 4, 7:54.6) J. Wells (L. Jump, 2, 25'3)

Year	Conference Champion (Points)	Conference Runner-up (Points)	Location and Individual Champions (Event, Performance)	NCAA Champion (Points)	NCAA Runner-Up (Points)	Location and All-Americans (Event, Place, Performance)
1986	Arkansas (92)	Texas A&M (61)	Fort Worth, TX (1) R. Bradley (4x800m, 7:40.80) P. Donovan (Mile, 4:05.75) P. Donovan (2-Mile, 8:47.00) C. Efurd (4x800m, 7:40.80) J. Falcon (4x800m, 7:40.80) B. Jasinski (H. Jump, 7'0.75) M. Taylor (4x800m, 7:40.80)	Arkansas (49)	Villanova (22)	Oklahoma City, OK (1) J. Falcon (3000m, 7, 8:16.51) D. Consiglio (1000m, 2, 2:19.3) P. Donovan (3000m, 1, 7:54.6) P. Donovan (4x800m, 1, 7:20.52) R. Haley (500m, 1, 59.82) K. Iovine (4x800m, 1, 7:20.52) B. Jasinski (H. Jump, 4, 7'2.5) M. Kobza (Shot, 5, 64'11.25) L. Looney (4x800m, 1, 7:20.52) W. Moncrieffe (4x800m, 1, 7:20.52) G. Taylor (Mile, 3, 4:03.1) M. Taylor (4x800m, 1, 7:20.52) J. Wells (L. Jump, 8, 25'2.5)
1987	Arkansas (93)	Texas (59)	Fort Worth, TX (1) J. Falcon (Mile, 4:09.67), J. Falcon (2-Mile, 8:50.51) R. Haley (600y, 1:08.26) G. Taylor (1000y, 2:09.75)	Arkansas (39)	SMU (31)	Oklahoma City, OK (1) L. Brown (4x400m, 2, 3:08.3) L. Brown (4x800m, 1, 7:18.67) M. Clemmons (4x400m, 2, 3:08.3) J. Falcon (3000m, 1, 7:56.79) R. Haley (500m, 1, 59.90) R. Haley (4x400m, 2, 3:08.3) L. Looney (4x800m, 1, 7:18.67) W. Moncriefe (4x800m, 1, 7:18.67) J. Register (4x400m, 2, 3:08.3) Ru. Reina (Mile, 6, 4:05.8) M. Taylor (4x800m, 1, 7:18.67)
1988	Arkansas (143.5)	Houston (89)	Fort Worth, TX (1) L. Brown (800m, 1:49.15) J. Falcon (Mile, 4:02.14) J. Falcon (3000m, 8:03.45) T. Jefferson (L. Jump, 25'10) J. Register (55mHH, 7.32)	Arkansas (34)	Illinois (29)	Oklahoma City, OK (1) J. Falcon (Mile, 1, 3:59.78) J. Falcon (3000m, 1, 7:55.8) T. Jefferson (L. Jump, 2, 26'3) M. Taylor (Mile, 3, 4:00.5)
1989	Arkansas (130)	Baylor (70)	Fort Worth, TX (1) L. Brown (800m, 1:49.79) A. Conroy (4x800m, 7:34.12) R. Cooper (4x800m, 7:34.12) J. Falcon (Mile, 3:58.67) J. Falcon (3000m, 8:11.31) K. Gaston (4x800m, 7:34.12) A. Hallock (4x800m, 7:34.12)	Arkansas (34)	Florida (31)	Indianapolis, IN (1) E. Floreal (L. Jump, 2, 26'2.25) E. Floreal (T. Jump, 1, 56'2.75) J. Falcon (Mile, 1, 3:58.06) Ru. Reina (5000m, 3, 14:19.4)
1990	Arkansas (145.6)	Baylor (83.5)	Fort Worth, TX (1) M. Boykins (4x800m, 7:37.63) S. Cramier (4x800m, 7:37.63) E. Floreal (L. Jump, 25'6) E. Floreal (T. Jump, 53'7.5) K. Gaston (4x800m, 7:37.63) A. Hallock (4x800m, 7:37.63) Ru. Reina (Mile, 4:02.87) Ru. Reina (3000m, 8:01.35)	Arkansas (44)	Florida (29)	Indianapolis, IN (1) J. Boakes (Mile, 5, 4:00.5) R. Bradley (4x800m, 2, 7:20.5) E. Floreal (L. Jump, 2, NA) E. Floreal (T. Jump, 1, 54'10.75) G. Contreras (4x800m, 2, 7:20.5) D. Gabor (4x800m, 2, 7:20.5) E. Henry (Mile, 2, 3:59.1) E. Henry (4x800m, 2, 7:20.5) G. Johnson (T. Jump, 3, 53'8.25) M. McGahee (P. Vault, 7, NA) Ru. Reina (3000m, 1, 7:56.62)

Year	Conference Champion (Points)	Conference Runner-up (Points)	Location and Individual Champions (Event, Performance)	NCAA Champion (Points)	NCAA Runner-Up (Points)	Location and All-Americans (Event, Place, Performance)
1991	Arkansas (151)	Baylor (93)	**Fort Worth, TX (1)** J. French (200m, 21.55) E. Henry (5000m, 14:12.2) G. Hood (800m, 1:49.18) G. Johnson (T. Jump, 52'10) Ru. Reina (Mile, 4:05.63) Ru. Reina (3000m, 7:50.85)	**Arkansas (34)**	Georgetown (27)	**Indianapolis, IN (1)** N. Bruton (4x800m, 2, 7:20.1) G. Contreras (4x800m, 2, 7:20.1) J. French (200m, 2, 20.79) E. Henry (Mile, 7, 4:03.75) E. Henry (4x800m, 2, 7:20.1) G. Hood (800m, 4, 1:48.1) G. Hood (4x800m, 2, 7:20.1) G. Johnson (T. Jump, 4, 52'8) **Ru. Reina (3000m, 1, 7:50.99)**
			MOVE FROM SOUTHWEST CONFERENCE TO SOUTHEASTERN CONFERENCE			
1992	Arkansas (146)	Florida (123)	**Gainesville, FL (1)** N. Bruton (Mile, 4:08.95) J. French (200m, 20.77) F. Hanley (5000m, 14:01.1) C. Phillips (55mHH, 7.32) E. Walder (L. Jump, 26'0) B. Wellman (T. Jump, 54'10.75)	**Arkansas (53)**	Clemson (46)	**Indianapolis, IN (1)** B. Baker (5000m, 10, 14:37.41) M. Boykins (4x800m, 3, 7:20.7) N. Bruton (3000m, 5, 8:05.4) G. Contreras (4x800m, 3, 7:20.7) J. French (200m, 6, 21.00) D. Gabor (4x800m, 3, 7:20.7) F. Hanley (5000m, 5, 13:48.7) G. Hood (Mile, 2, 4:03.8) G. Hood (4x800m, 3, 7:20.7) G. Johnson (T. Jump, 4, 54'2) M. Morin (3000m, 10, 8:15.84) J. Schiefer (Mile, 4, 4:04) **E. Walder (L. Jump, 1, 26'3.5)** **E. Walder (T. Jump, 1, 55'4.75)** B. Wellman (T. Jump, 3, 54'4.5)
1993	Arkansas (156)	Tennessee (81)	**Baton Rouge, LA (1)** J. Bunston (3000m, 8:05.31) C. Davis (400m, 47.07) R. Doakes (H. Jump, 7'2.25) M. Mitchell (Mile, 4:04.13) E. Walder (L. Jump, 26'9.25) E. Walder (T. Jump, 55'2.75)	**Arkansas (66)**	Clemson (30)	**Indianapolis, IN (1)** **N. Bruton (Mile, 1, 4:00.05)** C. Davis (400m, 2, 46.16) C. Davis (4x400m, 5, 3:07.7) J. French (4x400m, 5, 3:07.7) F. Hanley (5000m, 2, 13:57.2) V. Henderson (200m, 3, 21.12) V. Henderson (4x400m, 5, 3:07.7) M. Mitchell (Mile, 8, 4:07.81) D. Miner (3000m, 9, 8:17.16) M. Morin (Mile, 3, 4:00.7) C. Phillips (55mHH, 3, 7.41) C. Phillips (4x400m, 5, 3:07.7) J. Schiefer (Mile, 10, 4:17.69) **E. Walder (L. Jump, 1, 27'4)** **E. Walder (T. Jump, 1, 55'3.75)**

Year	Conference Champion (Points)	Conference Runner-up (Points)	Location and Individual Champions (Event, Performance)	NCAA Champion (Points)	NCAA Runner-Up (Points)	Location and All-Americans (Event, Place, Performance)
1994	Arkansas (157.3)	Tennessee (87)	**Gainesville, FL (1)** B. Baker (DMR, 9:44.32) N. Bruton (DMR, 9:44.32) J. Bunston (3000m, 7:56.7) C. Davis (400m, 46.75) R. Doakes (H. Jump, 7'7.25) F. Hanley (5000m, 13:59.6) G. Hood (DMR, 9:44.32) D. Thompson (DMR, 9:44.32) E. Walder (L. Jump, 25'10.75) E. Walder (T. Jump, 56'2) C. Phillips (55mHH, 7.24)	**Arkansas (94)**	Tennessee (40)	**Indianapolis, IN (1)** **B. Baker (DMR, 1st, 9:30.07)** **N. Bruton (Mile, 1, 3:59.34)** **N. Bruton (DMR, 1, 9:30.07)** **J. Bunston (5000m, 1, 13:48.07)** **C. Davis (400m, 1, 46.18)** **C. Davis (DMR, 1, 9:30.07)** R. Doakes (H. Jump, 2, 7'6) F. Hanley (5000m, 6, 13:57.3) **G. Hood (DMR, 1, 9:30.07)** C. Phillips (55mHH, 7, 7.41) J. Romain (L. Jump, 5, 25'7.5) J. Romain (T. Jump, 2, 55'2.25) D. Thompson (200m, 6, 21.08) **E. Walder (L. Jump, 1, 27'8)** **E. Walder (T. Jump, 1, 56'6.75)** D. Welsh (5000m, 3, 13:51.2)
1995	Arkansas (143)	Tennessee (88)	**Baton Rouge, LA (1)** R. Doakes (H. Jump, 7'4.5) M. Hemmingway (H. Jump, 7'4.5) G. Hood (Mile, 4:06.25) G. Hood (3000m, 8:06.09) G. Hood (DMR, 9:46.25) C. McIntyre (DMR, 9:46.25) B. Rock (800m, 1:49.43) B. Rock (DMR, 9:46.25) J. Romain (T. Jump, 53'11) G. Siamusiye (5000m, 14:00.55) C. Wilson (DMR, 9:46.25)	**Arkansas (59)**	George Mason/ Tennessee (26)	**Indianapolis, IN (1)** **J. Bunston (3000m, 1, 8:06.81)** R. Doakes (H. Jump, 2, 7'4.25) M. Hemmingway (H. Jump, 3, 7'3) G. Hood (Mile, 2, 3:55.7) C. McIntyre (DMR, 6, 9:37.3) B. Rock (800m, 5, 1:49.9) B. Rock (DMR, 6, 9:37.3) J. Romain (T. Jump, 6, 53'7.5) G. Siamusiye (5000m, 2, 13:58.9) D. Thompson (200m, 2, 20.86) C. Wilson (3000m, 13, NA) C. Wilson (DMR, 6, 9:37.3) R. Wilson (DMR, 6, 9:37.3)
1990	Tennessee (102)	Arkansas (93.5)	**Lexington, KY (2)** G. Siamusiye (5000m, 14:11.18) R. Wilson (Mile, 4:01.99) R. Wilson (3000m, 8:10.23)	George Mason (39)	Nebraska (31)	**Indianapolis, IN (3)** **R. Howard (T. Jump, 1, 54'10.75)** S. King (H. Jump, 8, 7'1.5) P. Price (Mile, 11, NA) G. Siamusiye (5000m, 2, 13:58.9) **R. Wilson (3000m, 1, 7:51.66)**
1997	Arkansas (147.5)	Florida (101)	**Gainesville, FL (1)** R. Howard (L. Jump, 26.6.25) R. Howard (T. Jump, 55'2) J. Huffman (DMR, 9:51.63) S. Kaley (5000m, 14:06.77) S. Lassiter (DMR, 9:51.63) D. Levy (DMR, 9:51.63) H. Loudermilk (DMR, 9:51.63) R. Wilson (3000m, 7:59.16)	**Arkansas (59)**	Auburn (27)	**Indianapolis, IN(1)** J. Ballard (H. Jump, 3, 7'5) J. Ballard (L. Jump, 6, 25'1.75) B. Craven (T. Jump, 9, 51'9) A. Howard (T. Jump, 6, 52'11.5) **R. Howard (L. Jump, 1, 26'9)** **R. Howard (T. Jump, 1, 55'11)** S. Kaley (5000m, 2, 14:02.01) S. Lassiter (Mile, 2, 4:01.3) S. Lassiter (DMR, 6, 9:41.3) J. Leon (DMR, 6, 9:41.3) M. Power (DMR, 6, 9:41.3) P. Price (DMR, 6, 9:41.3) T. Tressler (5000m, 9, 14:28.99) R. Wilson (3000m, 2, 7:54.7)

Year	Conference Champion (Points)	Conference Runner-up (Points)	Location and Individual Champions (Event, Performance)	NCAA Champion (Points)	NCAA Runner-Up (Points)	Location and All-Americans (Event, Place, Performance)
1998	Arkansas (181)	LSU (77)	**Baton Rouge, LA (1)** D. Brown (DMR, 10:01.77) K. Evans (H. Jump, 7'3.25) R. Howard (L. Jump, 26'4.25) S. Kaley (5000m, 14:08.50) M. Kerr (Mile, 4:03.21) M. Kerr (DMR, 10:01.77) S. Lassiter (800m, 1:50.19) S. Lassiter (DMR, 10:01.77) J. Huffman (DMR, 10:01.77) R. Wilson (3000m, 7:59.16)	**Arkansas (56)**	Stanford (36.5)	**Indianapolis, IN (1)** J. Ballard (L. Jump, 10, 23'7.25) A. Dailey (5000m, 13, 14:23.7) K. Dotson (H. Jump, 14, 7'1.5) **K. Evans (H. Jump, 1, 7'6)** R. Howard (L. Jump, 4, 25'0.75) **R. Howard (T. Jump, 1, 54'1.25)** J. Huffman (DMR, 2, 9:30.45) S. Kaley (5000m, 2, 13:58.87) M. Kerr (3000m, 3, 7:53.89) S. Lassiter (Mile, 3, 4:03.6) S. Lassiter (DMR, 2, 9:30.45) J. Leon (400m, 10, 47.31) M. Power (3000m, 8, 8:01.6) M. Power (DMR, 2, 9:30.45) P. Price (Mile, 7, 4:07) R. Stanley (DMR, 2, 9:30.45) R. Wilson (3000m, 13, NA)
1999	Arkansas (152)	S. Carolina (81)	**Gainesville, FL (1)** K. Evans (H. Jump, 7'4.5) S. Glover (DMR, 9:40.23) S. Kaley (5000m, 14:03.23) J. Karanu (DMR, 9:40.23) S. Lassiter (800m, 1:47.69) S. Lassiter (DMR, 9:40.23) M. Power (Mile, 4:01.80) M. Power (3000m, 7:56.06) R. Travis (DMR, 9:40.23)	**Arkansas (65)**	Stanford (42.5)	**Indianapolis, IN (1)** M. Clavelle (Shot, 5, 62.7.25) K. Evans (H. Jump, 2, 7'6) S. Kaley (3000m, 3, 7:56.3) S. Kaley (5000m, 3, 13:58.7) J. Karanu (800m, 8, 1:47.73) J. Karanu (DMR, 3, 9:35.13) S. Karie (DMR, 3, 9:35.13) M. Kerr (3000m, 6, 7:58.43) S. Lassiter (Mile, 3, 3:57.2) M. Link (DMR, 3, 9:35.13) **M. Lister (T. Jump, 1 55'0.75)** L. Miller (H. Jump, 5, 7'3.75) M. Power (3000m, 2, 7:55.36) R. Stanley (DMR, 3, 9:35.13) R. Travis (Mlle, 6, 3:59.51)
2000	Arkansas (168)	LSU (84.5)	**Fayetteville, AR (1)** A. Beasley (DMR, 9:42.74) M. Clavelle (Shot, 64'1) K. Evans (H. Jump, 7'5) J. Karanu (800m, 1:48.37) J. Karanu (DMR, 9:42.74) A. Begley (5000m, 13:56.74) J. Landreth (DMR, 9:42.74) M. Lister (T. Jump, 54'4.25) R. Travis (DMR, 9:42.74)	**Arkansas (69.5)**	Stanford (52)	**Fayetteville, AR (1)** M. Clavelle (Shot, 3, 63'6.75) K. Evans (H. Jump, 2, 7'7) J. Karanu (3000m, 5, 8:02.1) J. Karanu (DMR, 3, 9:33.31) S. Karie (3000m, 3, 8:01.1) S. Karie (DMR, 3, 9:33.31) J. Landreth (DMR, 3, 9:33.31) M. Link (Mile, 7, 4:03.34) **M. Lister (L. Jump, 1, 26'8.25)** **M. Lister (T. Jump, 1, 54'7.5)** L. Miller (H. Jump, 4, 7'3.75) R. Travis (1500m, 8, 3:42.3)

Year	Conference Champion (Points)	Conference Runner-up (Points)	Location and Individual Champions (Event, Performance)	NCAA Champion (Points)	NCAA Runner-Up (Points)	Location and All-Americans (Event, Place, Performance)
2001	Arkansas (108)	LSU (81)	**Lexington, KY (1)** K. Baker (DMR, 9:47.74) K. Evans (H. Jump, 7'1.75) D. Heinze (DMR, 9:47.74) S. Karie (DMR, 9:47.74) M. Link (5000m, 14:07.29) C. Mulvaney (DMR, 9:47.74)	LSU (34)	TCU (33)	**Fayetteville, AR (3)** K. Evans (H. Jump, 3, 7'5) S. Glover (DMR, 2, 9:34.51) D. Heinze (800m, 2, 1:45.95) D. Heinze (DMR, 2, 9:34.51) S. Karie (DMR, 2, 9:34.51) D. Lincoln (3000m, 7, 8:09.41) D. Lincoln (5000m, 7, 13:58.98) M. Link (5000m, 5, 13:52.31) C. Mulvaney (DMR, 2, 9:34.51) R. Travis (Mile, 9, 4:00.64) J. Ward (T. Jump, 7, 52'9.5)
2002	Arkansas (137)	Tennessee (130)	**Fayetteville, AR (1)** S. Ahmed (DMR, 9:44.86) J. Hatch (DMR, 9:44.86) D. Lincoln (5000m, 14:04.14) C. Mulvaney (DMR, 9:44.86) M. Taylor (DMR, 9:44.86)	Tennessee (62.5)	Alabama (47)	**Fayetteville, AR (4)** S. Ahmed (800m, 3, 1:47.80) A. Cragg (3000m, 5, 8:03.48) **A. Cragg (5000m, 1, 13:49.8)** D. Lincoln (3000m, 8, 8:05.61) D. Lincoln (5000m, 4, 13:57.71) C. Mulvaney (Mile, 6, 4:03.31) M. Robinson (T. Jump, 5, 52'7.5) J. Sandfort (5000m, 5, 14:00.65) M. Thomas (60mHH, 7, 7.80)
2003	Arkansas (120)	Florida (90.5)	**Gainesville, FL (1)** A. Cragg (Mile, 3:59.14) A. Cragg (3000m, 7:56.99) D. Lincoln (5000m, 13:49.42)	**Arkansas (54)**	Auburn (30)	**Fayetteville, AR (1)** **A. Cragg (3000m, 1, 7:55.68)** **A. Cragg (5000m, , 13:28.93)** D. Lincoln (3000m, 3, 7:57.43) D. Lincoln (5000m, 6, 13:49.94) **C. Mulvaney (Mile, 1, 4:05.7)** J. Sandfort (5000m, 13, 14:22.4) R. Smith (L. Jump, 7, 25'2.5) R. Smith (T. Jump, 7, 53'0.75) R. Stevens (800m, 8, 1:49.9) M. Thomas (60mHH, 4, 7.64) J. Uudmae (T. Jump, 5, 53'8.25) R. Washington (L. Jump, 8, 25'0.75)
2004	Florida (128)	Arkansas (106)	**Lexington, KY (1)** R. Botha (DMR, 9:41.80) A. Cragg (3000m, 7:59.25) A. Cragg (5000m, 13:42.95) C. Mulvaney (DMR, 9:41.80) M. Taylor (DMR, 9:41.80) S. Vazquez (DMR, 9:41.80)	LSU (44)	Arkansas (38)	**Fayetteville, AR (2)** **A. Cragg (3000m, 1, 7:55.29)** **A. Cragg (5000m, 1, 13:39.63)** T. Gatson (DMR, 2, 9:32.12) J. Hatch (DMR, 2, 9:32.12) W. Spearmon Jr. (200m, 8, 20.93) M. Taylor (DMR, 2, 9:32.12) S. Vazquez (DMR, 2, 9:32.12)

Year	Conference Champion (Points)	Conference Runner-up (Points)	Location and Individual Champions (Event, Performance)	NCAA Champion (Points)	NCAA Runner-Up (Points)	Location and All-Americans (Event, Place, Performance)
2005	Arkansas (155)	Florida (92)	**Fayetteville, AR (1)** S. Ahmed (Mile, 4:01.05) S. Ahmed (DMR, 9:46.91) M. Grant (DMR, 9:46.91) H. Iman (DMR, 9:46.91) P. Kosgei (3000m, 7:56.00) P. Kosgei (5000m, 13:53.85) B. Roe (DMR, 9:46.91) W. Spearmon Jr. (200m, 20.35) J. Uudmae (T. Jump, 52'11)	**Arkansas (56)**	Florida (46)	**Fayetteville, AR (1)** S. Ahmed (Mile, 6, 4:03.96) J. Boit (5000m, 6, 13:47.99) O. Brown (200m, 5, 20.72) O. Brown (4x400m, 7, 3:06.16) T. Gatson (400m, 2, 45.29) T. Gatson (4x400m, 7, 3:06.16) J. Hatch (800m, 2, 1:47.40) P. Kosgei (3000m, 2, 7:54.45) P. Kosgei (5000m, 7, 13:48.26) A. Perkins (3000m, 6, 8:03.43) **W. Spearmon Jr. (200m, 1, 20.10)** W. Spearmon Jr. (4x400m, 7, 3:06) J. Uudmae (T. Jump, 4, 53'6.5) D.Wittenmyer (4x400m, 7, 3:06.16)
2006	Arkansas (141)	Tennessee (106)	**Gainesville, FL (1)** S. Ahmed (Mile, 4:01.15) J. Boit (3000m, 8:02.23) P. Kosgei (5000m, 13:58.19) J. Uudmae (T. Jump, 53'8.5)	**Arkansas (53)**	LSU (45)	**Fayetteville, AR (1)** S. Ahmed (Mile., 3, 4:13.23) **S. Ahmed (DMR, 1, 9:37.02)** N. Balumbu (T. Jump, 5, 53'2.5) J. Boit (3000m, 3, 8:04.28) **J. Boit (5000m, 1, 13:49.93)** **J. Dodson (DMR, 1, 9:37.02)** P. Kosgei (3000m, 8, 8:10.53) P. Kosgei (5000m, 8, 14:11.4) A. Perkins (Mile, 12, 4:03.72) **A. Perkins (DMR, 1, 9:37.12)** M. Rodrigues (3000m, 7, 8:08.02) **B. Roe (DMR, 1, 9:37.02)** J. Uudmae (L. Jump, 6, 25'10) **J. Uudmae (T. Jump, 1, 54'4.5)**
2007	Arkansas (126)	Tennessee (115.5)	**Lexington, KY (1)** N. Balumbu (T. Jump, 52'2)	Wisconsin (40)	Florida St. (34)	**Fayetteville, AR (7)** A. Bailey (L. Jump, 3, 25'6.75) N. Balumbu (T. Jump, 3, 53'1.5) P. Kosgei (3000m, 8, 8:03.02) P. Kosgei (5000m, 2, 13:39.88) M. Stewart (L. Jump, 8, 25'0)
2008	Arkansas (130)	Florida (102)	**Fayetteville, AR (1)** A. Bailey (L. Jump, 25'6.25) N. Balumbu (T. Jump, 53'5.5) C. Bilbrew (DMR, 9:45.71) M. Cobrin (DMR, 9:45.71) D. LaCava (DMR, 9:45.71) Al. McClary (DMR, 9:45.71)	Arizona St. (44)	Florida St. (41)	**Fayetteville, AR (6)** A. Bailey (L. Jump, 7, 25'10.25) **N. Balumbu (T. Jump, 1, 54'3.25)** M. Cobrin (Mile, 8, 4:05.99) T. Hill (5000m, 8, 14:06.22) An. McClary (Mile, 9, 4:06.46) J. Samuels (60m, 5, 6.64) J. Samuels (200m, 3, 20.67)

Arkansas National Championships Teams and **Individuals** are in **Bold**

Outdoor Conference and NCAA Championship Record

Year	Conference Champion (Points)	Conference Runner-up (Points)	Location and Individual Champions (Event, Performance)	NCAA Champion (Points)	NCAA Runner-Up (Points)	Location and All-Americans (Event, Place, Performance)
1973			Austin, TX None			Baton Rouge, LA None
1974			Austin, TX None			Austin, TX None
1975			Lubbock, TX N. O'Shaughnessy (880y, 1:48.8)			Provo, UT None
1976			Waco, TX R. Melancon (3-Mile, 13:44.9) N. O'Shaughnessy (Mile, 4:02.8)			Philadelphia, PA R. Melancon (5000m, 6, 14:05.1
1977			Austin, TX N. O'Shaughnessy (Mile, 3:59.47)			Champaign, IL N. O'Shaughnessy (1500m, 3, 3:41.5)
1978	Texas A&M (126)	Baylor (82)	Austin, TX (7) None	UTEP/UCLA (50)	Oregon	Eugene, OR (did not score) None
1979	Texas (110)	Texas A&M (96)	Austin, TX (6) M. Muggleton (5000m, 13:58.07)	UTEP (64)	Villanova (48)	Champaign, IL (did not score) None
1980	Texas A&M (138)	Houston (107)	Austin, TX (4) M. Anderson (10,000m, 31:42.66) C. Freeman (4x400m, 3.05.02) P. Mitchell (4x400m, 3:05.02) F. O'Mara (3000mSC, 8:53.33)* *run without water jump S. Redwine (4x400m, 3:05.02) K. Washington (4x400m, 3:05.02)	UTEP (69)	UCLA (46)	Austin, TX (50) S. Lofquist (Shot, 5, 62'5.25) P. Vaughn (10,000m, 8, 30:49.5)
1981	Texas A&M (121)	Arkansas (98)	Dallas, TX (2) S. Lofquist (Discus, 193'8) F. O'Mara (3000mSC, 9:02.45)	UTEP (70)	SMU (57)	Baton Rouge, LA (22) S. Lofquist (Discus, 5, 197'8) R. Stephens (800m, 3, 1:47.8)
1982	Arkansas (134)	Houston (115)	Houston, TX (1) R. Carroll (5000m, 14:06.81) M. Conley (L. Jump, 26'7.25) R. Stephens (800m, 1:48.06) R. Stephens (1500m, 3:44.10) P. Vaughn (10,000m, 29:26.10)	UTEP (105)	Tennessee (94)	Provo, UT (24) M. Conley (L. Jump, 2, 26'10.25) P. Vaughn (10,000m, 10, 29:59.3)
1983	Arkansas (133)	Texas (111)	Fort Worth, TX (1) M. Conley (L. Jump, 25'10.75) F. O'Mara (1500m, 3:42.81) F. O'Mara (5000m, 14:12.38) S. Redwine (800m, 1:50.15) Ra. Reina (10,000m, 30:33.17)	SMU (104)	Tennessee (102)	Houston, TX (7th) M. Conley (L. Jump, 2, 27'2) M. Conley (T. Jump, 3, 55'5) **F. O'Mara (1500m, 1st, 3:40.51)** S. Redwine (800m, 3, 1:46.1)

Year	Conference Champion (Points)	Conference Runner-up (Points)	Location and Individual Champions (Event, Performance)	NCAA Champion (Points)	NCAA Runner-Up (Points)	Location and All-Americans (Event, Place, Performance)
1984	Arkansas (142)	Texas (90)	**Austin, TX (1)** M. Conley (L. Jump, 26'11) M. Conley (T. Jump, 55'5) P. Donovan (1500m, 3:43.53) P. Donovan (5000m, 14:20.4) B. Jasinski (H. Jump, 7'5)	Oregon (113)	Washington St. (94.5)	**Eugene, OR (3)** F. Cleary (4x100m, 6, 39.61) **M. Conley (L. Jump, 1, 27'0.25)** **M. Conley (T. Jump, 1, 56'11.75)** M. Conley (4x100m, 5, 39.61) M. Davis (L. Jump, 3, 26'7.75) M. Davis (4x100m, 5, 39.61) W. Spearmon (4x100m, 5, 39.61) P. Donovan (1500m, 4, 3:38.31) M. Klee (P. Vault, 5, 17'8.5) M. Kobza (Shot, 5, 64'2.5) T. Moloney (1500m, 2, 3:52.99)
1985	Arkansas (167)	Texas (80)	**Fayetteville, AR (1)** F. Cleary (4x100m, 38.81) M. Conley (L. Jump, 27'4) M. Conley (T. Jump, 56'3.25) M. Conley (4x100m, 38.81) P. Donovan (1500m, 3:40.31) R. Haley (400m, 44.67) R. Haley (4x100m, 38.81) B. Jasinski (H. Jump, 7'5.5) M. Kobza (Shot, 66'9.5) W. Spearmon (4x100m, 38.81)	Arkansas (61)	Washington St. (46)	**Austin, TX (1)** F. Cleary (4x100m, 6, 39.48) M. Conley (200m, 2, 20.21) **M. Conley (L. Jump, 1, 27'2)** **M. Conley (T. Jump, 1, 58'1.75w)** M. Conley (4x100m, 6, 39.48) M. Davis (4x100m, 6, 39.48) P. Donovan (1500m, 3, 3:42.8) **R. Haley (400m, 1, 44.70)** R. Haley (4x100m, 6, 39.48) B. Jasinski (H. Jump, 3, 7'6) M. Kobza (Shot, 4, 65'8.25) J. Register (L. Jump, 6, 25'11)
1986	Texas (115)	Arkansas (110)	**Houston, TX (2)** M. Davis (L. Jump, 27'3.25) R. Haley (400m, 44.48) J. Falcon (5000m, 14:13.75) G. Taylor (1500m, 3:45.52)	SMU (53)	Washington St. (52)	**Indianapolis, IN (4)** F. Abejidi (T. Jump, 8, 52'7.5) E. Borge (1500m, 3, 3:42.5) D. Consiglio (1500m, 6, 3:44.3) M. Davis (L. Jump, 4, 25'11.5) R. Haley (400m, 2, 45.01) M. Kobza (Shot, 7, 64'2.5) **J. Pascoe (P. Vault, 1, 18'0.5)**
1987	Texas (145)	Arkansas (113)	**Lubbock, TX (2)** L. Brown (800m, 1:46.95) R. Cooper (3000mSC, 9:02.02) J. Falcon (5000m, 14:32.59) J. Falcon (10,000m, 30:14.72) R. Haley (400m, 44.96) G. Taylor (1500m, 3:44.73)	UCLA (81)	Texas (28)	**Baton Rouge, LA (4)** L. Brown (4x400m, 4, 3:02.2) M. Clemmons (4x400m, 4, 3:02.2) R. Cooper (3000mSC, 4, 8:39.3) **J. Falcon (10,000m, 1, 29:10.66)** R. Haley (400m, 3, 44.82) R. Haley (4x400m, 4, 3:02.2) J. Register (4x400m, 4, 3:02.2)
1988	Arkansas (155)	Texas (149)	**Austin, TX (1)** R. Cooper (3000mSC, 8:49.7) J. Falcon (5000m, 14:06.54) J. Falcon (10,000m, 30:27.36) E. Floreal (T. Jump, 56'3.25) T. Jefferson (L. Jump, 26'7.25) M. Taylor (1500m, 3:44.68)	UCLA (82)	Texas (41)	**Eugene, OR (3rd)** R. Cooper (3000mSC, 3, 8:39.3) **J. Falcon (1500m, 1, 3:38.91)** **E. Floreal (T. Jump, 1, 56'4.75)** T. Jefferson (L. Jump, 8, 26'3.75) Ru. Reina (5000m, 5, 13:58.1) C. Zinn (10,000m, 8, 29:02)
1989	Arkansas (163)	Texas A&M (156.5)	**Waco, TX (1)** R. Cooper (10,000m, 30:43.61) R. Cooper (3000mSC, 8:39.9) J. Falcon (1500m, 3:43.9) J. Falcon (5000m, 14:10.34) E. Floreal (L. Jump, 25'10.25) E. Floreal (T. Jump, 55'4.25)	LSU (53)	Texas A&M (41)	**Provo, UT (9)** R. Cooper (3000mSC, 2, 8:45.34) E. Floreal (L. Jump, 7, 25'10.75) **E. Floreal (T. Jump, 1, 56'4.75)** G. Johnson (T. Jump, 6, 53'8.25)

Year	Conference Champion (Points)	Conference Runner-up (Points)	Location and Individual Champions (Event, Performance)	NCAA Champion (Points)	NCAA Runner-Up (Points)	Location and All-Americans (Event, Place, Performance)
1990	Arkansas (162)	Texas (131)	**C. Station, TX (1)** J. Boakes (1500m, 3:58.29) R. Bradley (800m, 1:48.75) E. Floreal (T. Jump, 53'2.75) Ru. Reina (5000m, 14:35.38) Ru. Reina (10,000m, 29:54.63)	LSU (44)	Arkansas (36)	**Durham, NC (2)** J. Boakes (1500m, 3, 3:40.7) R. Bradley (800m, 6, 1:47.9) E. Floreal (L. Jump, 2, 26'4) **E. Floreal (T. Jump, 1, 56'6.5)** G. Johnson (T. Jump, 8, 52'1) E. Kaminski (Javelin, 7, 229'3) Ru. Reina (5000m, 3, 14:10.9)
1991	Arkansas (218)	Texas (132)	**Houston, TX (1)** B. Baker (5000m, 14:10.19) J. Boakes (800m, 1:48.76) J. Boakes (1500m, 3:44.93) J. French (200m, 20.23) E. Henry (10,000m, 30:28.5) C. Phillips (400mH, 50.83) B. Wellman (T. Jump, 57'1.5)	Tennessee (51)	Washington St. (42)	**Eugene, OR (7)** J. Boakes (1500m, 8, 3:43.6) J. French (200m, 3, 20.15) A. Hallock (3000mSC, 4, 8:34.8) C. Phillips (100mHH, 9, 13.79) H. Smith (5000m, 7, 14:09) E. Walder (T. Jump, 14, 47'11.75) **B. Wellman (L. Jump, 1, 56'10.25)**

MOVE FROM SOUTHWEST CONFERENCE TO SOUTHEASTERN CONFERENCE

Year	Conference Champion (Points)	Conference Runner-up (Points)	Location and Individual Champions (Event, Performance)	NCAA Champion (Points)	NCAA Runner-Up (Points)	Location and All-Americans (Event, Place, Performance)
1992	Arkansas (176)	Tennessee (149)	**Starkville, MS (1)** F. Hanley (10,000m, 29:56.4) M. Morin (1500m, 3:43.04) C. Phillips (110mHH, 13.98) E. Walder (L. Jump, 28'1w)	**Arkansas (60)**	Tennessee (46.5)	**Austin, TX (1)** B. Baker (5000m, 5, 14:05.4) N. Bruton (1500m, 8, 3:41) R. Doakes (H. Jump, 4, 7'4.25) A. Dressell (10,000m, 12, 31:02.4) F. Hanley (10,000m, 2, 30:03.1) V. Henderson (110mHH, 9, NA) G. Hood (800m, 5, 1:46.8) G. Johnson (T. Jump, 2, 56'4.75) M. Morin (1500m, 5, 3:39.8) **E. Walder (L. Jump, 1st, 27'9.5)** E. Walder (T. Jump, 10, 52'4.5) **B. Wellman (T. Jump, 1, 56'9.25)** D. Welsh (10,000m, 3, 30:03.1)
1993	Arkansas (163)	LSU (138)	**Knoxville, TN (1)** N. Bruton (1500m, 3:44.20) N. Bruton (5000m, 14:00.96) R. Doakes (H. Jump, 7'4.25) F. Hanley (10,000m, 30:13.75) E. Walder (L. Jump, 27'6)	**Arkansas (69)**	LSU/Ohio St. (45)	**New Orleans, LA (1)** M. Boykins (4x400m, 5, 3:07.7) N. Bruton (1500m, 4, 3:45.6) **C. Davis (400m, 1, 45.04)** C. Davis (4x400m, 5, 3:07.7) R. Doakes (H. Jump, 2, 7'5.75) J. French (4x100m, 7, 39.37) J. French (4x400m, 5, 3:07.7) D. Green (5000m, 13, NA) F. Hanley (5000m, 3, 13:59.9) F. Hanley (10,000m, 3, 29:14.1) M. Hemmingway (H. Jump, 8, 7'2) V. Henderson (4x100m, 7, 39.79) V. Henderson (4x400m, 7, 3:03.6) C. Phillips (4x100m, 7, 39.79) J. Schiefer (1500m, 11, 3:45.68) D. Thompson (4x100m, 7, 39.79) **E. Walder (L. Jump, 1, 28'0)** E. Walder (T. Jump, 3, 55'4.25) D. Welsh (5000m, 2, 13:59.2) D. Welsh (10,000m, 6, 29:46)

Year	Conference Champion (Points)	Conference Runner-up (Points)	Location and Individual Champions (Event, Performance)	NCAA Champion (Points)	NCAA Runner-Up (Points)	Location and All-Americans (Event, Place, Performance)
1994	Arkansas (223)	Tennessee (145)	Fayetteville, AR (1) J. Bunston (5000m, 14:00.75) C. Davis (4x400m, 3:05.44) R. Doakes (H. Jump, 7'5.75) J. French (4x400m, 3:05.44) V. Henderson (4x400m, 3:05.44) G. Hood (1500m, 3:48.38) M. Hughes (4x400m, 3:05.44) T. Mitchell (10,000m, 30:23.63) C. Phillips (110mHH, 13.62) C. Phillips (400mHH, 51.40) J. Romain (T. Jump, 54'8.75) E. Walder (L. Jump, 27'4.75)	Arkansas (83)	UTEP (45) Boise, ID (1)	**B. Baker (5000m, 1, 14:22.09)** N. Bruton (1500m, 5, 3:45.6) J. Bunston (5000m, 2, 14:25.3) R. Doakes (H. Jump, 4, 7'5.75) J. French (4x100m, 5, 39.37) V. Henderson (4x100m, 5, 39.37) **G. Hood (1500m, 1, 3:42.1)** T. Mitchell (5000m, 11, 15:11.1) **T. Mitchell (10,000m, 1, 29:39.54)** C. Phillips (110mHH, 5, 13.84) C. Phillips (4x100m, 5, 39.37) J. Romain (T. Jump, 2, 55'1) D. Thompson (4x100m, 5, 39.37) **E. Walder (L. Jump, 1, 27'4.5)** **E. Walder (T. Jump, 1, 55'5.75)**
1995	Arkansas (171)	Tennessee (155.5)	Tuscaloosa, AL (1) R. Doakes (H. Jump, 7'4.5) B. Rock (800m, 1:46.2) J. Romain (T. Jump, 56'0.5) G. Siamusiye (3000mSC, 8:42.7) G. Siamusiye (5000m, 13:56.94) G. Siamusiye (10,000m, 29:27.63) D. Thompson (200m, 20.31)	Arkansas (61.5)	UCLA (55)	Knoxville, TN (1) J. Bunston (5000m, 4, 14:39.5) **R. Doakes (H. Jump, 1, 7'4.5)** M. Hemmingway (H. Jump, 3, 7'2) M. Morin (1500m, 5, 3:40.8) **B. Rock (800m, 1, 1:46.37)** J. Romain (T. Jump, 2, 55'2) **G. Siamusiye (10,000m, 1, 28:59.6)** D. Thompson (200m, 7, 20.68) C. Wilson (10,000m, 10, NA) R. Wilson (5000m, 8, 14:43.2)
1996	Arkansas (170)	Tennessee (141)	Lexington, KY (1) R. Howard (T. Jump, 55'1) H. Jones (110mHH, 13.82) S. Lassiter (800m, 1:49.66) G. Siamusiye (3000mSC, 8:45.58) G. Siamusiye (5000m, 14:13.57) G. Siamusiye (10,000m, 29:30.76) R. Wilson (1500m, 3:44.12)	Arkansas (55)	George Mason (40)	Eugene, OR (1) J. Bunston (5000m, 3, 14:39.5) J. Bunston (10,000m, 2, 28:56.5) M. Hemmingway (H. Jump, 2, 7'2) R. Howard (L. Jump, 4, 25'6) **R. Howard (T. Jump, 1, 56'1.75)** S. Lassiter (1500m, 14, NA) G. Siamusiye (5000m, 2, 14:38.7) **G. Siamusiye (10,000m, 1, 28:56.39)** R. Wilson (1500m, 13, NA)
1997	Arkansas (188)	Tennessee (115)	Auburn, AL (1) R. Howard (L. Jump, 27'6.75) R. Howard (T. Jump, 55'6.25) S. Kaley (5000m, 14:06.33) M. Kerr (3000mSC, 3:52.97) S. Lassiter (1500m, 3:44.4) S. Sidney (400mH, 51.12) K. White (110mHH, 13.41) R. Wilson (10,000m, 29:45.8)	Arkansas (55)	Texas (42.5)	Bloomington, IN (1) A. Dailey (5000m, 10, 14:17.3) **R. Howard (L. Jump, 1, 26'11.25)** **R. Howard (T. Jump, 1, 55'6.5)** **S. Lassiter (1500m, 1, 3:40.22)** P. Price (1500m, 6, 3:42.4) K. White (110mHH, 2, 13.43) R. Wilson (5000m, 2, 13:46.2) R. Wilson (10,000m, 3, 29:06.8)
1998	Arkansas (183)	LSU (135.5)	Gainesville, FL (1) K. Evans (H. Jump, 7'4.5) R. Howard (L. Jump, 25'1.75) R. Howard (T. Jump, 54'11.5) S. Kaley (10,000m, 29:26.87) M. Kerr (3000mSC, 8:40.30) S. Lassiter (800m, 1:46.56) S. Lassiter (1500m, 3:43.38) M. Power (5000m, 14:02.37)	Arkansas (58.5) .	Stanford (51)	Buffalo, NY (1) K. Evans (H. Jump, 4, 7'3.25) **R. Howard (L. Jump, 1, 27'5.5)** **R. Howard (T. Jump, 1, 55'8.25)** J. Huffman (1500m, 5, 3:45.5) S. Kaley (10,000m, 8, 29:03.31) **M. Kerr (3000mSC, 1, 8:36.95)** **S. Lassiter (1500m, 1, 3:42.34)** M. Power (5000m, 3, 13:41.6) T. Rush (200m, 6, 20.92)

Year	Conference Champion (Points)	Conference Runner-up (Points)	Location and Individual Champions (Event, Performance)	NCAA Champion (Points)	NCAA Runner-Up (Points)	Location and All-Americans (Event, Place, Performance)
1999	Arkansas (147.5)	Florida (100.67)	**Athens, GA (1)** A. Dailcy (10,000m, 29:51.73) M. Kerr (3000mSC, 8:44.08) S. Lassiter (800m, 1:46.99) S. Lassiter (1500m, 3:37.29) M. Lister (T. Jump, 53'11.25)	**Arkansas (59)**	Stanford (52)	**Boise, ID (1)** M. Clavelle (Shot, 5, 63'2) K. Evans (H. Jump, 3, 7'5.5) S. Glover (400mH, 5, 50.39) J. Karanu (800m, 5, 1:47.9) S. Karie (1500m, 5, 3:50.1) **M. Kerr (3000mSC, 1, 8:44.29)** S. Lassiter (1500m, 2, 3:47.6) **M. Lister (L. Jump, 1, 26'10)** M. Lister (T. Jump, 5, 53'9.25) M. Power (5000m, 4, 14:06.9)
2000	Arkansas (171)	LSU (134)	**Baton Rouge, LA (1)** K. Baker (4x400m, 3:03.32) M. Clavelle (Shot, 63'11) A. Dailey (10,000m, 30:14.63) S. Glover (400mH, 49.76) S. Glover (4x400m, 3:03.32) J. Karanu (800m, 1:47.42) J. Karanu (1500m, 3:41.40) M. Lister (L. Jump, 27'10.25) M. Lister (4x400m, 3:03.32) R. Stanley (4x400m, 3:03.32)	Stanford (72)	Arkansas (59)	**Durham, NC (2)** K. Baker (4x400m, 2, 3:02.02) D. Brown (110mHH, 5th, 13.78) A. Dailey (10,000m, 10, 28:34.41) K. Evans (H. Jump, 3, 7'4.5) S. Glover (400mH, 4, 49.08) S. Glover (4x400m, 2, 3:02.02) E. Jackson (100mHH, 14, 13.99) J. Karanu (800m, 6, 1:46.46) J. Karanu (1500m, 7, 3:42.02) S. Karie (1500m, 5, 3:41.1) M. Link (5000m, 3, 13:50.89) M. Lister (L. Jump, 4, 26'0) **M. Lister (T. Jump, 1, 54'7.5)** M. Lister (4x400m, 2nd, 3:02.02) L. Miller (H. Jump, 4th, 7'3.75) R. Stanley (4x400m, 2, 3:02.02) R. Travis (1500m, 8, 3:42.3)
2001	Tennessee (153)	Florida (107.5)	**Columbia, SC (3)** K. Evans (H. Jump, 7'4.5) D. Lincoln (3000mSC, 8:44.94)	Tennessee (50)	TCU (49)	**Eugene, OR (7)** K. Evans (H. Jump, 3, 7'4.25) D. Heinze (800m, 3, 1:47.35) S. Karie (10,000m, 12, 30:11.8) **D. Lincoln (3000mSC, 1, 8:42.31)** M. Link (10,000m, 2, 29:25.7)
2002	Tennessee (147)	Arkansas (133)	**Starkville, MS (2)** D. Lincoln (3000mSC, 8:44.07) D. Lincoln (5000m, 14:07.64) D. Lincoln (10,000m, 29:24.55) C. Mulvaney (1500m, 3:42.91)	LSU (64)	Tennessee (57)	**Baton Rouge, LA (7)** A. Cragg (5000m, 5, 14:01.72) **D. Lincoln (3000mSC, 1, 8:22.34)** D. Lincoln (5000m, 3, 14:00.01) C. Mulvaney (1500m, 2, 3:43.03)
2003	Arkansas (149)	Tennessee (111.5)	**Knoxville, TX (1)** A. Cragg (5000m, 13:41.04) A. Cragg (10,000m, 28:42.73) D. Lincoln (3000mSC, 8:32.85) C. Mulvaney (1500m, 3:42.31)	**Arkansas (59)**	Auburn (50)	**Sacramento, CA (1)** S. Ahmed (1500m, 5, 3:42.83) A. Carroll (100m, 7, 10.46) A. Carroll (200m, 8, 21.48) **A. Cragg (5000m, 1, 13:47.87)** A. Cragg (10,000m, 2, 28:20.29) **D. Lincoln (3000mSC, 1, 8:26.55)** **D. Lincoln (10,000m, 1, 28:20.20)** C. Mulvaney (1500m, 2, 3:40.44) R. Stevens (800m, 3, 1:46.85) M. Taylor (1500m, 11, 3:50.01)

Year	Conference Champion (Points)	Conference Runner-up (Points)	Location and Individual Champions (Event, Performance)	NCAA Champion (Points)	NCAA Runner-Up (Points)	Location and All-Americans (Event, Place, Performance)
2004	Arkansas (153)	Florida (120)	**Oxford, MS (1)** A. Cragg (1500m, 3:40.18) A. Cragg (5000m, 14:08.77) A. Cragg (10,000m, 28:46.64) J. Scott (P. Vault, 18'0.5)	**Arkansas (65.5)(X)**	Florida (49)	**Austin, TX (1)(X)** S. Ahmed (1500m, , 3:45.66) M. Bridges (400mH, 9, 50.99) E. Brown (Javelin, 3, 246'03) **A. Cragg (10,000m, 1, 29:22.43)** J. Hatch (800m, 8, 1:47.78) **C. Mulvaney (1500m, 1, 3:44.72)** J. Sandfort (10,000m, 12, 30:28.8) J. Scott (P. Vault, 4, 18'0.5) **W. Spearmon Jr. (200m, 1, 20.12)** M. Thomas (110mHH, 8, 13.55)
2005	Arkansas (152)	Florida (116)	**Nashville, TN (1)** J. Boit (10,000m, 29:39.58) J. Hatch (800m, 1:47.35) P. Kosgei (3000mSC, 8:36.73) P. Kosgei (5000m, 13:56.12) J. Uudmae (T. Jump, 53'4.25)	**Arkansas (60)(X)**	Florida (49)	**Sacramento, CA (1)(X)** J. Boit (10,000m, 6, 28:52.69) E. Brown (Javelin, 4, 232'2) O. Brown (200m, 8, 20.38) T. Gatson (400m, 7, 45.68) P. Kosgei (3000mSC, 2, 8:29.13) P. Kosgei (10,000m, 3, 28:39.29) A. Perkins (1500m, 4, 3:38.54) **W. Spearmon Jr. (200m, 1, 19.91)** J. Uudmae (T. Jump, 5, 53'2.25)
2006	Arkansas (137.5)	Tennessee (126.5)	**Fayetteville, AR (1)** N. Balumbu (T. Jump, 53'4.5) J. Boit (5000m, 13:52.17) J. Boit (10,000m, 29:01.83) E. Brown (Javelin, 251'9)	Florida St. (67)	LSU (51)	**Sacramento, CA (5)** J. Boit (5000m, 2, 14:13.81) **J. Boit (10,000m, 1, 28:37.64)** E. Brown (Javelin, 2, 238'8) A. Perkins (1500m, 6, 3:45.67) M. Rodrigues (10,000m, 5, 28:49.23) S. Summerside (5000m, 16, 14:35.2)
2007	Tennessee (129.5)	LSU (122)	**Tuscaloosa, AL (3)** N. Balumbu (T. Jump, 52'10.75)	Florida St. (54)(X)	LSU (48)	**Sacramento, CA (63)** N. Balumbu (T. Jump, 6, 52'5.5) J. Samuels (100m, 9, 10.28)
2008	Arkansas (141)	Florida (129)	**Gainesville, FL (1)** A. Bailey (L. Jump, 26'0.75) N. Balumbu (T. Jump, 53'1.5) L. Laird (Javelin, 228'4) J. Strang (5000m, 13:44.18)	Texas A&M (48)	Florida/Florida St./LSU (44)	**Des Moines, IA (17)** N. Balumbu (T. Jump, 3, 54'4) S. Forrest (10,000m, 2, 28:47.08) P. Kosgei (3000mSC, 5, 8:37.61) J. Strang (10,000m, 9, 29:10.73)

X) indicates vacated championships

Arkansas National Championships Teams and **Individuals** are in **Bold**

Olympians

Year	Location	Athlete (Country) (Event) (Place, Performance)
1976	Montreal, CANADA	Niall O'Shaughnessy (Ireland)(1500m)(4h1, 3:40.12)
1980	Moscow, U.S.S.R.	None
1984	Los Angeles, U.S.A.	**Mike Conley (United States)(T. Jump)(Bronze Medal, 17.18m)** Paul Donovan (Ireland)(1500m)(4h2, 3:45.70) Frank O'Mara (Ireland)(1500m)(4h4, 3:41.76)
1988	Seoul, KOREA	Doug Consiglio (Canada)(1500m)(Did not advance) Edrick Floreal (Canada)(Triple Jump)(11fB, 16.11m) Frank O'Mara (Ireland)(5000m)(Did not advance)
1992	Barcelona, SPAIN	**Mike Conley (United States)(T. Jump)(Gold Medal, 18.17m)** Paul Donovan (Ireland)(5000m)(10h3, 14:03.79) Edrick Floreal (Canada)(L. Jump)(16fB, 7.62m) Graham Hood (Canada)(1500m)(9, 3:42.55) Frank O'Mara (Ireland)(5000m)(4h2, 13:38.79) Reuben Reina (United States)(5000m)(5h2, 13:40.50) Brian Wellman (Bermuda)(Triple Jump)(5, 17.24m)
1996	Atlanta, U.S.A.	Mike Conley (United States)(T. Jump)(4, 17.40m) **Calvin Davis (United States)(400mH)(Bronze Medal, 47.96)** Graham Hood (Canada)(1500m)(DNF) Robert Howard (United States)(T. Jump)(8, 16.90m) Brandon Rock (United States)(800m)(Did not advance, 1:48.47) Jerome Romain (United States)(T. Jump)(12, 16.80m) Godfrey Siamusiye (Zambia)(3000m SC)(10h1, 8:37.41) Brian Wellman (Bermuda)(T. Jump)(6, 16.95m)
2000	Sydney, AUSTRALIA	Kenny Evans (United States)(H. Jump)(13, 2.20m) Robert Howard (United States)(T. Jump)(7th, 17.05m) Sean Kaley (Canada)(10 000m)(12h1, 28:36.07) Melvin Lister (United States)(L. Jump)(12fA, 7.73m) Michael Power (Australia)(5000m)(13h1, 13:51.00) Brian Wellman (Bermuda)(T. Jump)(11fA, 16.47m)
2000	Sydney, AUSTRALIA	**John Register (United States)(L. Jump)(Paralympics Silver Medal)**
2004	Athens, GREECE	Alistair Cragg (Ireland)(5000m)(12, 13:43.06) **Matt Hemmingway (United States)(H. Jump)(Silver medal, 2.34m)** Daniel Lincoln (United States)(3000m SC)(11, 8:16.86) Melvin Lister (United States)(T. Jump)(9fB, 16.64m)
2008	Beijing, CHINA	Alistair Cragg (Ireland)(5000m)(6h1, 13:38.57)(DNF, final) Tyson Gay (United States)(100m)(5SFH2, 10.05) Tyson Gay (United States)(4x100m)(DNF) Wallace Spearmon Jr. (United States)(200m)(3rd, 19.95 disqualified)

Appendix II

Arkansas National Champions as of John McDonnell's Retirement

Said Ahmed
1 Individual

Brian Baker
2 Individual

Josphat Boit
2 Individual

Lorenzo Brown
1 Relay

Omar Brown
1 Relay

Niall Bruton
2 Individual
1 Relay

Jason Bunston
2 Individual

Mike Conley
9 Individual
1 Olympic Gold
1 Olympic Silver
2 World Titles
World Cups

Alistair Cragg
7 Individual

Calvin Davis
2 Individual
1 Relay
1 Olympic Bronze

Ray Doakes
1 Individual

Jeremy Dodson
1 Relay

Paul Donovan
2 Individual
1 Relay
1 World Indoor
Silver

Kenny Evans
1 Individual

Joe Falcon
7 Individual

Edrick Floreal
5 Individual

Tyson Gay
1 Individual
1 Relay

Michael Grant
1 Relay

Roddie Haley
3 Individual

Graham Hood
1 Individual
1 Relay

Robert Howard
9 Individual

Keith Iovine
1 Relay

Matt Kerr
2 Individual

Seneca Lassiter
2 Individual

Daniel Lincoln
4 Individual

Melvin Lister
5 Individual

William Looney
2 Relay

Teddy Mitchell
1 Individual

**Wayne
Moncrieffe**
2 Relay

Chris Mulvaney
2 Individual

Frank O'Mara
1 Individual
2 World Indoor
Titles

Jeff Pascoe
1 Individual

Adam Perkins
1 Relay

Reuben Reina
2 Individual

Brandon Rock
1 Individual

Brian Roe
1 Relay

**Godfrey
Siamusiye**
4 Individual

**Wallace
Spearmon Jr.**
3 Individual
1 Relay

Randy Stephens
1 Individual

Matt Taylor
2 Relay

Jaanus Uudmae
1 Individual

Erick Walder
10 Individual

Brian Wellman
2 Individual

Ryan Wilson
1 Individual

Clyde Scott
1 Individual
1 Olympic Silver
(Before McDonnell)

All photos courtesy of University of Arkansas Athletics Media Relations.

Notes

Chapter 1: Growing Up in Ireland (1938–1963)

1. County Mayo: An Outline History. Bernard O'Hara and Nollaig O'Muraile, February 12, 2002, http://www.mayohistory.com/HPreHist.htm.
2. County Mayo.
3. County Mayo.

Chapter 2: Early Experiences in America (1963–1972)

1. Andrew White, "New York in the 1960's," *The American Prospect.* October 21, 2001.
2. Bob Holt, "McDonnell's Career Almost Pre-Empted," *Arkansas Democrat-Gazette,* August 30, 1998.
3. Bobby Ampezzan, "Track Record," *Arkansas Democrat-Gazette*, June 14, 2009.
4. "Track Record."

Chapter 3: Starting Out at Arkansas (1972–1978)

1. Orville Henry and Jim Bailey, *The Razorbacks: A Story of Arkansas Football* (Fayetteville: The University of Arkansas Press. 1996), 5.
2. *The Razorbacks*, 290.
3. *The Razorbacks*, 290.
4. *The Razorbacks*, 272.
5. Nate Allen, *Tales from Hog Heaven* (Champaign, IL: Sports Publishing, 2002), 179 .
6. *The Razorbacks*, 287.
7. Nate Allen, *More Tales from Hog Heaven* (Champaign, IL : Sports Publishing, 2004), 186.
8. For results, see appendix, page 404.
9. For results, see appendix, page 404.
10. *More Tales from Hog Heaven*, 188.
11. *Tales From Hog Heaven*, 141.
12. *The Razorbacks*, 291.
13. For results, see appendix, page 404.
14. For results, see appendix, page 410.
15. *More Tales from Hog Heaven*, 192.
16. *Arkansas Track and Field/Cross Country Media 'Guide*, University of Arkansas Athletics Media Relations, 1977–78.
17. For results, see appendix, page 410.

Chapter 4: Climbing the Mountain (1978–1981)

1. *More Tales from Hog Heaven*, 207.
2. *More Tales from Hog Heaven*, 207.
3. "Proposal to Host NCAA Championships," University of Arkansas Athletics Department, fall 1978.
4. For results, see appendix, page 410.
5. "Razorback Cross Country Roundup," University of Arkansas Athletics Media Relations October 3, 1979.
6. "Razorback Cross Country Roundup," University of Arkansas Athletics Media Relations November 7, 1979.

7. For results, see appendix, page 405.

8. "Razorback Cross Country Roundup No. 5.," University of Arkansas Athletics Media Relations, October 20, 1980.

9. "Razorback Cross Country Roundup No. 8.," University of Arkansas Athletics Media Relations. Nov. 17, 1980.

10. For results, see appendix, page 405.

11. For results, see appendix, page 405.

12. For results, see appendix, page 405.

13. For results, see appendix, page 411.

Chapter 5: Reaching the Pinnacle (1981–1984)

1. *Tales from Hog Heaven*, 107.

2. For results, see appendix, page 411.

3. *More Tales From Hog Heaven*, 191.

4. "Hogs Finish Second at NCAA Indoor Meet," *Arkansas Democrat-Gazette,* March 14, 1982.

5. "News from the Penn Relays," University of Arkansas Athletics Media Relations, April 24, 1982.

6. "Southwest Conference Notes," Southwest Conference, May 14, 1982.

7. *John McDonnell: The Greatest Coach Ever*, DVD, University Arkansas Media Relations, 2009.

8. For results, see appendix, page 418.

9. For results, see appendix, page 418.

10. *John McDonnell: The Greatest Coach Ever.*

11. *More Tales from Hog Heaven*, 215.

12. *More Tales from Hog Heaven*, 215.

13. *More Tales from Hog Heaven*, 215.

14. Bob Holt, "30 NCAA Titles and Counting," *Arkansas Democrat-Gazette* August 30, 1998.

15. For results, see appendix, page 411.

16. For results, see appendix, page 411.

17. *University of Arkansas Track and Field Media Guide*, University of Arkansas Athletics Media Relations, 1983–84, 2.

18. "NCAA Cross Country Championships," University of Arkansas Athletics Media Relations, November 23, 1983.

19. "Arkansas Quadrangular," University of Arkansas Sports Information, January 20, 1984.

20. For results, see appendix, page 411.

21. "Razorbacks win NCAA Indoor Track Championship," University of Arkansas Athletics Media Relations, March 10, 1984.

Chapter 7: On Top of the World (1984–1986)

1. For results, see appendix, page 419.

2. *More Tales from Hog Heaven*, 192.

3. *More Tales from Hog Heaven*, 216.

4. *More Tales from Hog Heaven*, 216.

5. For results, see appendix, page 411.

6. *More Tales from Hog Heaven*, 194.

7. For results, see appendix, page 419.

8. *The Razorbacks*, 343.

9. *The Razorbacks*, 354.

10. "University of Arkansas Cross Country Prospectus," University of Arkansas Athletics Media Relations, 1985.

11. "Razorback Cross Country Update," University of Arkansas Athletics Media Relations, October 21, 1985.

12. For results, see appendix, page 406.

13. "Razorback Pentangular Roundup," University of Arkansas Athletics Media Relations, January 17, 1986.

14. "Arkansas Invitational Roundup," University of Arkansas Athletics Media Relations, January 25, 1986.

15. For results, see appendix, page 411.

16. For results, see appendix, page 419.

17. "Southwest Conference Roundup," University of Arkansas Athletics Media Relations, May 17, 1986.

18. "Southwest Conference Roundup," University of Arkansas Athletics Media Relations, May 17, 1986.

Chapter 8: Fayettenam (1986–1988)

1. "South Carolina's Frye Comments on McDonnell Retiring," University of South Carolina Athletics Media Relations, April 22, 2008.

2. "Southwest Conference Cross Country," University of Arkansas Athletics Media Relations, November 3, 1986.

3. "Southwest Conference Quotes." University of Arkansas Athletics Media Relations, November 2, 1987.

4. "Penn Relays Quotes," University of Pennsylvania Athletics Media Relations, April 30, 1987.

5. For results, see appendix, page 419.

6. "Southwest Conference Quotes," Southwest Conference, May 15, 1988.

7. For results, see appendix, page 419.

Chapter 9: Closing Out the Decade (1988–1991)

1. *The Razorbacks*, 355–66.

2. *The Razorbacks*, 355–66.

3. "Razorback Cross Country Prospectus," University of Arkansas Athletics Media Relations, 1988.

4. "NCAA Indoor National Championships Quotes," NCAA, March 11, 1989.

5. Ted Silary, "Prediction Inspires Arkansas," *Philadelphia Daily News*, April 29, 1989.

6. "Prediction Inspires Arkansas."

7. "NCAA Championship Quotes," NCAA, June 3, 1989.

8. "Razorback Invitational Roundup," University of Arkansas Athletics Media Relations, September 23, 1989.

9. For results, see appendix, page 412.

10. "Southwest Conference Roundup," Southwest Conference, February 17, 1990.

11. "Southwest Conference Roundup," Southwest Conference, May 19, 1990.

12. "Penn Relays Distance Medley Championship Quotes," University of Pennsylvania Athletics Media Relations, April 27, 1990.

13. "Penn Relays Distance Medley Championship Quotes."

14. "Penn Relays Distance Medley Championship Quotes."

15. "Southwest Conference Preview," University of Arkansas Athletics Media Relations, October 22, 1990.

16. "Perfect Score Gives Razorbacks 17th Straight Cross Country Title," University of Arkansas Athletics Media Relations, October 29, 1990.

17. For results, see appendix, page 407.

18. "Hogs Hold Off Iowa State to Win NCAA Title," University of Arkansas Athletics Media Relations, November 19, 1990.

19. For results, see appendix, page 413.

20. "NCAA Indoor National Quotes," NCAA, March 9, 1991.

21. Mike Kern, "Hogs Get Lean to Nip Hoyas," *Philadelphia Daily News*, April 27, 1991.

22. For results, see appendix, page 420.

23. "Southwest Conference Quotes," Southwest Conference, May 19, 1991.

24. For results, see appendix, page 420.

Chapter 10: The Triple Crown of Triple Crowns (1991–1994)

1. "Arkansas Wins First SEC Championship," University of Arkansas Athletics Media Relations, November 4, 1991.

2. "Arkansas Wins First SEC Championship."

3. "Hog Harriers begin Season," University of Arkansas Athletics Media Relations, September 3, 1991.

4. For results, see appendix, page 413.

5. "NCAA Indoor National Championship Quotes," NCAA. March 14, 1992.

6. "NCAA Indoor National Championship Quotes," NCAA. March 14, 1992.

7. Mike Vaccaro, "French Finds Strength beyond the Pain." *Northwest Arkansas Times,* April 1, 1992.

8. "Penn Relays Quotes," University of Pennsylvania Athletics Media Relations, April 24, 1992.

9. Mike Kern, "Nova Men Fall," *Philadelphia Daily News,* April 24, 1993.

10. For results, see appendix, page 420.

11. "Hogs Defend SEC Cross Country Title," University of Arkansas Athletics Media Relations, November 2, 1992.

12. For results, see appendix, page 407.

13. "Cross Country Wins National Championship," University of Arkansas Athletics Media Relations, November 23, 1992.

14. "Cross Country Wins National Championship."

15. For results, see appendix, page 413.

16. "NCAA Quotes," NCAA, March 13, 1993.

17. "Hogs Keep Appointment with Sports Fan Clinton," *The Morning News,* April 27, 1993.

18. "Hogs Keep Appointment with Sports Fan Clinton."

19. "Hogs Keep Appointment with Sports Fan Clinton."

20. For results, see appendix, page 420.

21. "Hogs Beaten at Home for First Time Since 1970," University of Arkansas Athletics Media Relations, October 16, 1993.

22. "Hogs Beaten at Home for First Time Since 1970."

23. For results, see appendix, page 407.

24. For results, see appendix, page 414.

25. "NCAA Division-I Indoor Championships Mile Recap," NCAA, March 12, 1994.

26. "NCAA Division-I Indoor Championships Quotes," NCAA, March 12, 1994.

27. "NCAA Division-I Indoor Championships Quotes," NCAA, March 12, 1994.

28. Bob Holt, "30 NCAA Titles and Counting," *Arkansas Democrat-Gazette,* August 30, 1998.

29. Kenny Moore, *Bowerman and the Men of Oregon* (New York: Rodale Press, 1996), 403–4.

30. For results, see appendix, page 421.

31. "NCAA Championship Quotes," NCAA, June 3, 1994.

32. "NCAA Championship Quotes," NCAA, June 3, 1994.

Chapter 11: A New Generation (1994–1997)

1. "Arkansas Picked Number One," College Sports, September 8, 1994.
2. "Hogs Number One in Cross Country Poll," University of Arkansas Athletics Media Relations, September 8, 1994.
3. "Hogs win 21st Straight Championship," University of Arkansas Athletics Media Relations, October 29, 1994.
4. "Hogs Look to Win Fifth Straight NCAA Title," University of Arkansas Athletics Media Relations, November 20, 1994.
5. Hogs Look to Win Fifth Straight NCAA Title."
6. "NCAA Post Race Quotes," NCAA. November 21, 1994.
7. For results, see appendix, page 414.
8. For results, see appendix, page 414.
9. For results, see appendix, page 421.
10. For results, see appendix, page 407.
11. For results, see appendix, page 414.
12. Chris Lear, *Sub 4:00: Alan Webb and The Quest for the Fastest Mile,* (New York: Rodale Press, 2002), 180.
13. "NCAA Indoor Championship Quotes," NCAA, March 9, 1996.
14. "NCAA Indoor Championship Quotes."
15. James Christie, "Faster, Higher, Defiant," *Globe and Mail,* July 10, 2004.
16. For results, see appendix, page 414.
17. *More Tales from Hog Heaven.*
18. Bobby Ampezzan, "Track Record," *Arkansas Democrat Gazette,* June 14, 2009.
19. "Track Record.

Chapter 12: A Pain in the Neck (1997–2000)

1. For results, see appendix, page 415.
2. Speech at John McDonnell Celebration, Dr. Alan Sugg, Little Rock. August 29, 1994.
3. Chris Lear, *Running with the Buffaloes*, (Guilford, CT: Lyons Press, 1999), 244.
4. For results, see appendix, page 415.
5. For results, see appendix, page 415.
6. For results, see appendix, page 408.
7. For results, see appendix, page 408.
8. "Tyson Invitational Quotes," University of Arkansas Athletics Media Relations. February 12, 2000.
9. "Tyson Invitational Quotes."
10. For results, see appendix, page 415.
11. For results, see appendix, page 415.
12. For results, see appendix, page 408.

Chapter 13: A New Lease on Life (2001–2003)

1. For results, see appendix, page 416.
2. *Arkansas Track and Field Media Guide*. University of Arkansas Athletics Media Relations, 2001–2.
3. For results, see appendix, page 408.
4. For results, see appendix, page 416.
5. For results, see appendix, page 416.
6. *Arkansas Track and Field Media Guide*. University of Arkansas Athletics Media Relations, 2002–3, 25.
7. For results, see appendix, page 409.

8. For results, see appendix, page 416.

9. Bob Holt, "New Regional Format Has Track Coaches Fuming," *Arkansas Democrat-Gazette*, May 20, 2003.

10. For results, see appendix, page 422.

Chapter 15: Rising to the Occasion (2003–2006)

1. Frank Litsky, "Arkansas Coach Says It's Time to Retire," *New York Times,* April 26, 2008.

2. For results, see appendix, page 409.

3. "Penn Relays Quotes," University of Pennsylvania Athletics Media Relations, April 23. 2004.

4. *More Tales from Hog Heaven*, 217.

5. *More Tales from Hog Heaven*, 219.

6. Andrew Jensen, "Hogs Put on a Show in Austin," *Hawgs Illustrated*, July 2004, 22

7. "Hogs Put on a Show in Austin, 22."

8. "Hogs Put on a Show in Austin, 22."

9. *More Tales from Hog Heaven*, 218.

10. "Arkansas Coach Says It's Time to Retire."

11. For results, see appendix, page 417.

12. Andrew Jensen, "Mad Hogs Triumph," *Hawgs Illustrated*, 42.

13. For results, see appendix, page 423.

14. Andrew Jensen, "Among the Greatest," *Hawgs Illustrated*, July 2005, 26

15. "Among the Greatest," 26.

16. John Schumacher, "Master Motivator," *Sacramento Bee,* June 5, 2005.

17. John McDonnell Retirement Speech, Dr. Alan Sugg, September, 18, 2008.

18. Mark Kreidler, "Dynastic Arkansas Becomes Target," *Sacramento Bee,* June 11, 2005.

19. "Cragg—Ninety-nine times out of a hundred Bekele would have beaten me." IAAF.org. Feb 1, 2005, http://www.iaaf.org/news/printer,newsid=29355.htmx, http://www.iaaf.org/news/Kind=2/newsId=28384.html.

20. "Cragg takes long winding road to success." IAAF.org. May 12, 2005.

21. Ken Goe, "Life Has Worked Out for Martin Smith and for the Ducks," *The Oregonian*, June 5, 2010.

22. "Arkansas Captures SEC Championships Despite Bizarre Finish," University of Arkansas Athletics Media Relations, October 29, 2005.

23. "Razorback Seniors Lead Way," University of Arkansas Athletics Media Relations, March 10, 2006.

24. "Razorback Seniors Lead Way."

Chapter 16: The Final Years (2006–2008)

1. "University of Arkansas, Fayetteville Public Infractions Report," NCAA, October 25, 2007, 13

2. "University of Arkansas, Fayetteville Public Infractions Report," 1.

3. "University of Arkansas, Fayetteville Public Infractions Report," 7.

4. "University of Arkansas, Fayetteville, Public Infractions Report," 10.

5. "Report 276 of the NCAA Infractions Appeals Committee," NCAA, September 22, 2008, 5.

6. Alex Abrams, "Big-Time Leader," *Hawgs Illustrated,* July 2008.

7. LetsRun.com. May 15, 2006, http://www.letsrun.com/2006/homepage0515.php.

8. For results, see appendix, page 423.

9. United States Attorney Eric Melgren. Kansas, "Former Barton Coach Convicted on 5 Counts." July 12, 2006, http://blogs.kansascity.com/crime_scene/files/former_barton_county_coach_convicted.pdf.

10. "Kyle White Added to Arkansas Track and Field Staff," University of Arkansas Athletics Media Relations, July 28, 1996.

11. For results, see appendix, page 409.

12. "Tumultuous Night at NCAA Track Leads to Four All-American Honors," University of Arkansas Athletics Media Relations, March 9, 2007.

13. "Hogs Third at Cowboy Jamboree." University of Arkansas Athletics Media Relations, September 29, 2007.

14. "Hogs Win SEC Cross Country Championships," University of Arkansas Athletics Media Relations, October 27, 2007.

15. NCAA Committee on Infractions, October 25, 2007, 9.

16. "University of Arkansas, Fayetteville, Public Infractions Report," 9.

17. Tayler Branch, "The Shame of College Sports," *The Atlantic,* October 2011.

18. "The Shame of College Sports."

19. For results, see appendix, page 409.

20. Sean Keeler, "Legendary Coach Ends career This Weekend," *Des Moines Register,* June 13, 2008.

21. Alex Abrams, "Big Time Leader," *Hawgs Illustrated,* July 2008, 23.

22. "John McDonnell Press Conference Transcript," University of Arkansas Media Relations, April 22, 2008.

23. "John McDonnell Press Conference Transcript."

24. "Arkansas Coach Says It's Time to Retire."

25. Nate Allen, "The Finish Line: McDonnell Set to Retire after Outdoor Track Season." Northwest Arkansas Times, April 22. 2008.

26. Bob Holt, "Architect of Track Dynasty to Retire," *Arkansas Democrat-Gazette,* April 22, 2008.

27. "John McDonnell Press Conference Transcript."

28. "John McDonnell Press Conference Transcript."

29. "McDonnell Set to Retire after Outdoor Track Season.".

30. For results, see appendix, page 423.

Chapter 17: Retirement

1. "Mann Named to US Olympic Team Coaching Staff." USATF. Mar. 19, 2008.

2. Rick Broadbent, "Michael Johnson Backs Usain Bolt to Win Sprint Duel," *The Sunday Times,* August 14, 2008.

3. "Bucknam Named Cross Country, Track and Field Head Coach," University of Arkansas Athletics Media Relations, June 27, 2008.

4. Bucknam Named Cross Country, Track and Field Head Coach."

5. "In His Fifth Decade of Coaching, Dick Booth Has Seen a Bit of Everything," Gatorzone.com. February 11, 2011, http://www.gatorzone.com/story.php?id=19795.

6. Bobby Ampezzian, "Track Record," *Arkansas Democrat-Gazette,* June 14, 2009.

7. *John McDonnell: The Greatest Coach Ever.*

8. *John McDonnell: The Greatest Coach Ever.*

9. *John McDonnell: The Greatest Coach Ever.*

10. *John McDonnell: The Greatest Coach Ever.*

Index

Andrew Maloney competed for Canada in the 800 meter and coached track and field and cross country for six years at the University of Tulsa before spending the past two years coaching at the University of Guelph. He publishes *Athletics Illustrated* and previously published a baseball novel, *End of a Dynasty*. He now works as an ice hockey agent for Maloney & Thompson Sports Management in Guleph, Ontario.

John McDonnell was the head coach of the Arkansas Razorback track-and-field teams from 1978 until his retirement in 2008, during which time he won an unprecedented forty national championships. He currently spends his time in Fayetteville and on his ranch.